SELECTED ESSAYS ON BOOKS AND PRINTING

A. F. JOHNSON

SELECTED ESSAYS
ON BOOKS AND PRINTING

edited by Percy H. Muir

1970
AMSTERDAM: VAN GENDT & CO
LONDON: ROUTLEDGE & KEGAN PAUL
NEW YORK: ABNER SCHRAM

© 1970 A. L. VAN GENDT & CO NV AMSTERDAM

This book or parts thereof should not be reproduced in any form by print, photoprint, micro-
film, or any other means without previous permission in writing from the publishers.

ISBN 90-6300-016-2

Commonwealth of Nations
ROUTLEDGE & KEGAN PAUL LTD LONDON
7100-6468-3

North America
ABNER SCHRAM (SCHRAM ENTERPRISES LTD) NEW YORK
8390-0016-2

German Language Area
DR ERNST HAUSWEDELL & CO HAMBURG

Library of Congress Catalog Card Number 69-20319
SET AND PRINTED AT THE STAMPERIA VALDONEGA
VERONA · ITALY

ACKNOWLEDGEMENTS

The editor and the publishers wish to express their indebtedness to many persons and institutions for permission to reprint material included in the present collection, viz., the Bibliographical Society and the Editor of *The Library*, London; Mrs. Helen Macy and the George Macy Companies, New York, on behalf of the Limited Editions Club; the Cambridge University Press and the Trustees of the Estate of the late Stanley Morison; Dr. Alois Ruppel and the Gutenberg Gesellschaft, Mainz; the Editor and Publishers of *Print Magazine*, New York; Mr. John Ryder and the Bodley Head, London; the late James Shand and the Shenval Press, London; the Edinburgh Bibliographical Society; Messrs. Percy Lund, Humphries & Co, London and Bradford; the Monotype Corporation Ltd., London.

Valuable co-operation and most welcome advice was received from Mr. Harry Carter, Oxford; Mr. John Dreyfus, London; Mr. Sem Hartz, Haarlem; Dr. H. D. L. Vervliet, Antwerp.

Mr. James Mosley and the St Bride Foundation, London, M. Jacques Guignard of the Bibliothèque de l'Arsenal and Mlle Brin of the Bibliothèque Nationale, Paris, and Dr. Dennis E. Rhodes of the British Museum have been most helpful in supplying certain photographs, thus considerably relieving the ungrateful task of Mr. Colin Clair, who has been collecting the illustrations.

The 'Selected Handlist of Typographic and Calligraphic Writings of A. F. Johnson' compiled by Sheila Jones (*Signature*, New Series, No 13) has proved extremely useful in composing this volume.

Mr. Laurie E. Deval read the proofs with great care and contributed many valuable suggestions.

CONTENTS

INTRODUCTION

Alfred Forbes Johnson spent all his working life in the Department of Printed Books at the British Museum. Although perhaps not part of his duties, a man with a vocation finding himself in such surroundings will almost inevitably consider it a duty, albeit a pleasant one, to add to the stock of human knowledge. In point of fact Johnson's initiation to this insidious pleasure arose directly from his official activities.

A. W. Pollard who, as Keeper of the Printed Books, was Johnson's chief was also the Honorary Secretary of the Bibliographical Society. In 1922, three years after Johnson had joined the Department, Pollard virtually assigned him the job of reading a paper to the Society on some aspect of his work on the sixteenth-century French books that he was then cataloguing. The result was the paper on 'Books Printed at Lyons in the Sixteenth Century' which is reprinted at pp. 123-145 in the present volume. It is a remarkable paper for a novice to have produced and, although some of the argument may no longer be accepted as valid, the main impression on the reader is of the assurance and technical facility with which the findings are presented. Equally striking is the fact that he lighted at once on a method of presentation that would serve him well in the years to come. Thirty-five years after venturing on the nursery slopes Johnson found himself President of the Society that had witnessed his novitiate. For his Presidential Address he chose a similar subject, and treated it in an exactly similar way. Then, in 1957, he discussed 'Italian Sixteenth-Century Books' (pp. 110-122). His opening words are an exact parallel of those he used in 1922 and analysis and synthesis pursue parallel paths in both papers.

It will be noticed that the period is also the same in both papers – the sixteenth century. It was a period in which Johnson found himself increasingly at home and in which most of his pioneer work was done. This is summed up in 'Printing in the Sixteenth Century', 1938, a contribution to a *History of the Printed Book* published by The Dolphin in New York (see pp. 41-82).

Two years elapsed between his initial essay in 1922 and his next appearance in print in which he joined Stanley Morison in an erudite historical and technical analysis of 'The Chancery Types of Italy and France' (see pp. 83-109). This was first printed in No. 3 of *The Fleuron*. In a way it was a sequel to Morison's article in No. 2 on 'The Ideal Type'.

Morison himself has indicated Johnson's share of the work.[1] Confessing his own weakness in 'enumerative bibliography' Morison was introduced by A. W. Pollard to Johnson who undertook to 'list the typographical italics based on the chancery cursive', whereby 'S. M's output has been materially corrected and increased'.

'Enumerative bibliography' is typical Morisonian terminology. It expresses very neatly what was certainly Johnson's strong point, as shown in his first paper and clearly appreciated by Pollard.

---

1. In a note to entry 22 in J. Carter, *A Handlist of the Writing of Stanley Morison*, 1950.

His collaboration with Morison had a notable influence on the subjects and methods of Johnson's future bibliographical investigations. His association with this essay drew his attention to the close and important connexion between calligraphy and type design, the major outcome of which was the pioneer 'Catalogue of Italian Writing-Books of the Sixteenth Century' (see pp. 18-40) published in 1950 but begun twenty years earlier. Indeed, in 1930, when Johnson began to make notes for his 'Catalogue' his rising interest in the subject emerges very clearly in much of his work at this time.

It is already evident in 'The Classification of Gothic Types', 1929 (pp. 1-17), and recurs constantly in his later writings on the significance for the bibliographer of the history of type faces.

This is another example of the profound influence on Johnson of his early collaboration with Morison. It emerges, perhaps, most clearly in 'The Supply of Types in the Sixteenth Century', 1943 (pp. 146-160), where he undertook the daunting task of examining and comparing the originals of entries in Proctor's *Early Printed Books in the British Museum* – in which the compiler had suggested the use of 140 different type faces – and came up with the surprising conclusion that there existed, in fact, only 'one set of capitals, with one copy, and twenty-eight body types'. His Appendix to this essay, analysing the types used by the Wittenberg Printers between 1521 and 1540 is no less remarkable. Clearing the ground of so much misunderstanding, replacing utter confusion by organized information, this was a major performance, the result of long, patient, hard slogging which must often have been tedious.

Johnson was ideally placed for investigations of this kind. Not only was the source material ready to hand, but, like most of his work, it was explicitly based on the resources of the British Museum. Also like much of his work it was published in *The Library*, the organ of the Bibliographical Society.

His preoccupation with type faces led naturally to investigation of type-founding which culminated in two interrelated works, his revised edition of Talbot Baines Reed's *History of the Old English Letter Foundries*, 1952, and the joint publication with Mr. W. Turner Berry of the Catalogue of *Specimens of Printing Types by English and Scottish Printers and Founders*, 1935, the latter with an introduction by Morison which was the subject of some controversy in *The Library*, where it had been somewhat caustically reviewed by Mr. David Thomas. The recension of Reed was in itself an effective rejoinder to Mr. Thomas's opinion that it 'would be a task of immense labour – and little profit'; and the 'Catalogue' had already replaced the lists of type-founders in the original edition of Reed.

In 1946 Johnson published a short paper 'On Re-Reading Updike' (pp. 281-287) which is a reminder that several of his papers are in the nature of glosses on the seminal work of the great American historian of typography.

If, generally speaking, he is less at ease when he steps outside the sixteenth century his edition of Reed alone showed that he had something novel and valuable to contribute to later periods; and his collaboration with Mr. W. Turner Berry and Mr. W. P. Jaspert in compiling an *Encyclopaedia of Type Faces* (1958) has greatly increased the range of his benefactions.

A. F. Johnson, in short, was an early recruit to the company of Updike, Morison, and others who took the initiative in exploring the history of printing in a new way, by looking at type faces as well as at the printers who used them. Their studies in the origin and distribution of particular types has also had its part in the modern renaissance of good printing, though here Johnson's part has been of lesser importance. Unlike most of his companions in the field he had no practical experience as a printer, which makes not less remarkable his scholarly contributions to the technique of a fascinating subject.

He shares a fate common to all pioneers in that later investigation has modified some of his conclusions. His paper on 'The Goût Hollandois' (pp. 365-377) is a case in point. The mystery of the so-called Janson types has been elucidated by Harry Carter and G. Buday (see footnote page 377), but Johnson's pioneer essay cleared the ground of much accumulated misunderstanding and thus helped to pave the way to a solution. Indeed one can hardly stress too greatly this pioneer aspect of much of Johnson's work and the debt due to him on that score. The collection of his papers in the present volume goes some way towards repayment of that debt.

P. H. Muir

SELECTED ESSAYS ON BOOKS AND PRINTING

THE CLASSIFICATION OF
GOTHIC TYPES

IF a subject is worth discussing at all, it will be agreed that an exact and adequate terminology is needed. Many readers must have felt that writers on typography are handicapped by the lack of such a terminology; this is especially so in the case of the large family of types known to us as Gothic. Considering the great variety of these types one must confess that the vocabulary in our language by which they can be distinguished is singularly poor. The three old French terms, *lettre de forme*, *lettre de somme*, and *lettre bâtarde* are familiar, but there are no English equivalents in general use, nor do they cover the whole ground, especially when we turn to German founts of the fifteenth century. Although the types of German incunables are of extraordinary variety, they are not independent creations unrelated to one another, and therefore it should be possible to classify them in a number of groups with accepted names, so that when a book is described as printed in a certain class of type, the description would call up a definite impression. Something more is needed than the initials G. L. (for Gothic Letter) if we wish to express ourselves with any precision. Incidentally it may be remarked that the word gothic itself is objectionable, apart from its vagueness; it has in our sense nothing to do with the Goths and was a term of derision used by Italians of the Renaissance, e. g. Vasari. However, the word is so well embedded in the language that it may well seem useless to attack it. When we read that the Wittenberg German Psalter of 1524 or Dürer's *Underweysung der Messung*, 1525, is printed in Fraktur, we know with more or less exactness what is intended; but when we are told that the *Catholicon* of 1460 is printed in a semi-gothic type the term is too vague to be of much help to us. The M forms of Dr. Haebler have their uses as a method of referring to or indexing incunable types, but they do not meet the need we have in mind. Even for one who could memorize the 101 forms they do not represent or pretend to represent a scientific classification.

The Germans, however, have not stopped at the M forms and of recent years have attempted to tackle this problem of nomenclature. They have introduced some new terms, which have not been translated into English nor used in the original by English writers; hence the obscurity of some passages in *Printing: a short history of the art*, edited by R. A. Peddie, 1927; the section on German printing in this work was written by Dr. Ernst Crous, and his account on p. 12 of the types used in the fifteenth century, and again on p. 23 in the sixteenth century, will need interpretation for most English readers. Dr. Crous has explained his terms elsewhere and it was no doubt lack of space which forbade explanation in the English volume. It is proposed here to give some account of this new classification and to compare it with what English writers have had to say on the point, with the object of seeing whether an English vocabulary has been or can be formed.

The starting-point in our investigation must be the article by Dr. Alfred Hessel, of

Göttingen University, entitled 'Von der Schrift zum Druck' in the *Zeitschrift des Deutschen Vereins für Buchwesen*, 1923, p. 89, seq. Dr. Hessel's terms were adopted and the subject further illustrated in *Die gotischen Schriftarten* by E. Crous and J. Kirchner, Leipzig, 1928. Kirchner deals with the manuscript hands and Crous with the printed books; the 135 illustrations enable us to follow exactly their system of grouping and the meaning of the new terms. Dr. Hessel's article and the very nature of Crous and Kirchner's book emphasize afresh the fact, that as far as letter-form is concerned there is no break between the hand-written and the printed book. Dr. Hessel's terms are applied equally to both; for the most part they were first used by calligraphers or by writers on palaeography. A classification of types must be based ultimately on differences in penmanship. The earliest types and the hands on which they are based fall into three principal groups, corresponding to three main divisions of subject matter. These are: (*a*) the most formal letter used for liturgical and biblical texts; (*b*) a less formal and smaller letter used for legal and classical texts and the like, and (*c*) a still less formal and more cursive letter used for books in the vernacular.

(*a*) The most formal gothic letter is narrow and tall and characterized by an almost complete absence of curves. It may be described as drawn rather than written. A scribe who makes a formal gothic h follows a very different process from one writing a current h, and uses a different kind of pen. The various grades of hands are arrived at by entirely dissimilar methods of penmanship. It is unnecessary to describe at greater length this letter, which is familiar in the type of the 42-line Bible and of the Mainz Psalter to most probably under the name 'lettre de forme'. This old French term was used, and the letter illustrated, by Geofroy Tory in his *Champ fleury*, 1529, but that is by no means its earliest use. It is found in inventories of the library of Charles V of France between 1411 and 1424 and of John, Duke of Berry, of 1416.[1] The term which the Germans usually employ is Textur, or Textura, meaning 'woven', from the resemblance of a page in this letter to a woven pattern. Abb. 30 in Crous and Kirchner is a much reduced reproduction of an advertisement by a calligrapher, one Johann vander Hagen of Bodenwerder on the Weser. This sheet had already been described in Wattenbach's *Das Schriftwesen im Mittelalter*, 1871 (and [3rd ed.] 1896, pp. 489, 490), and was further described, accompanied by a slightly reduced reproduction, by Hessel in *Archiv für Urkundenforschung*, ix. 164, 1925. They assign the sheet to the first half of the fifteenth century. I introduce it here on account of the headings which the calligrapher gives to his letters. Besides six hands used for documents he shows six book hands, among them a Textus[2] quadratus, a Textus semiquadratus, that is, a shorter and squarer Textur, and a Textus sine pedibus, without the pointed or diamond-shaped feet usual in Textur. The Germans have called the letter also Missalschrift, Mönchschrift, and Quadrat. (Fig. 1.)

(*b*) In printed books the less formal hands or first standard types (I wish to avoid the words 'text type' for a reason which will appear later) begin with Schöffer's *Du-*

1. See L. Delisle, *Recherches sur la librairie de Charles V.* 1907.
2. For earlier uses of the word, see Wattenbach, op. cit.

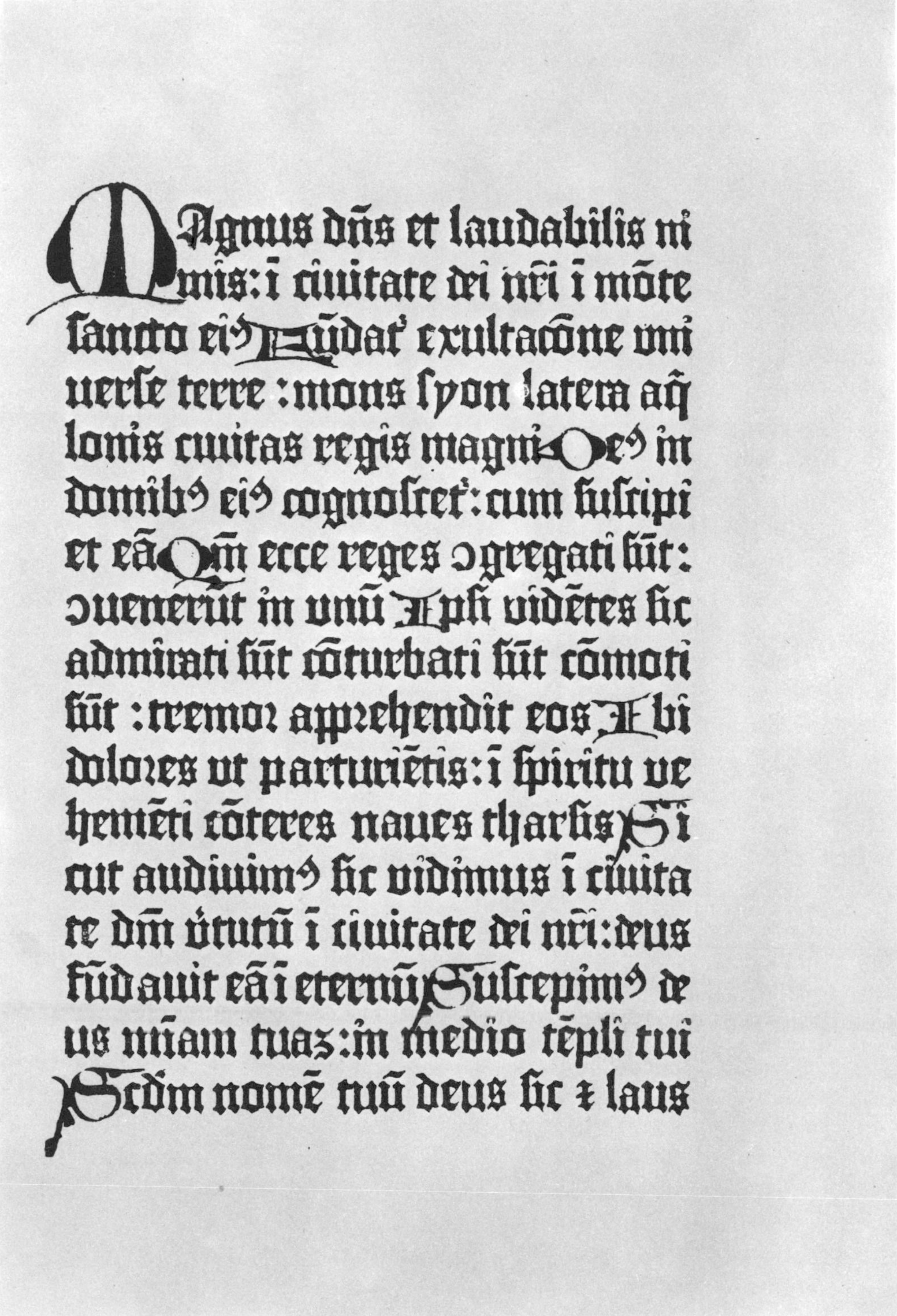
Magnus dñs et laudabilis ni
mis: ĩ ciuitate dei nr̃i ĩ mõte
sancto ei⁹ Fundat' exultacõne uni
uerse terre : mons syon latera aq̃
lonis ciuitas regis magni Deus in
domib⁹ ei⁹ cognoscet': cum suscipi
et eã Qm̃ ecce reges ↄgregati sũt:
ↄuenerũt in unũ Ipsi uidẽtes sic
admirati sũt cõturbati sũt cõmoti
sũt : tremor apprehendit eos Ibi
dolores ut parturiẽtis: ĩ spiritu ve
hemẽti cõteres naues tharsis Si
cut audiuim⁹ sic vidimus ĩ ciuita
te dñ̃ ṽtutũ ĩ ciuitate dei nr̃i: deus
fũdauit eã ĩ eternũ Suscepim⁹ de
us mĩam tuaz: in medio tẽpli tui
Scd̃m nomẽ tuũ deus sic ⁊ laus

FIG. 1. Text. From *Psalterium*. Friedrich Creussner, Nuremberg, 1480 (?).

randus type of 1459. Dr. Hessel calls the group to which this type belongs Gotico-antiqua. The manuscript letter on which it is based goes back to the fourteenth century and was used by the earlier Italian humanists. It represents an attempt to revert to the Carolingian minuscules and its name appears therefore to be justified, Antiqua being the usual German name for our roman. It is a gothic hand with considerable roman tendencies. Abb. 17 in Crous and Kirchner shows that Petrarch's formal book hand was in this style, and the letter has even been called Petrarcaschrift. Its characteristics are its roundness, the appearance of descenders like roman but with no serifs and even without feet; long s and f end on the line; the a is open as in roman and the g has the shape of a figure 8. The d is purely gothic (tough there is often a second d), as are the ligatures of the round forms such as b and d with e and o. The effect of the increased height of the ascenders and length of the descenders is of course to add to the amount of white on the page and to impart a lighter appearance when compared with Textur. It is a renaissance letter in its openness; medieval calligraphy preferred the close-set page with as little white as possible. We have departed so far from this medieval standard that we now criticize William Morris, whose Troy and Chaucer types are Gotico-antiquas, for using a letter which in 1460 was chosen as a standard type because of its openness and legibility. The term Gotico-antiqua is new in typography, and even, I believe, in palaeography. Not only that, but it represents an entirely new grouping of types, amongst which are the type of the *Catholicon*, and several standard types of Schöffer, of Günther Zainer of Augsburg and his school, and of the first printers at Basle. Whether the classification is of any value as applied to manuscript books is for the palaeographers to decide. Even if they should reject it, it may prove to be a valid and useful grouping in typography. Whatever objections may be taken to the name, the grouping is an important contribution to our subject. If we are told that the *Sachsenspiegel* printed by Bartholomaeus von Unckel at Cologne in 1480 is set in a Gotico-antiqua we carry away a fairly definite idea of that type, much more definite than is conveyed by a vague term such as 'halb-gotisch'. There are distinctions among Gotico-antiquas. The type of Zainer's Advertisement of 1471 differs considerably, for instance, from that of the *Catholicon*, but the differences will be found to be in size and colour rather than in design. Again all types which might be classed in this group do not show all the characteristics mentioned; some have the closed a as in Textur (Zainer's, for instance), some an a usual in our next group; others tend still more towards the the roman, for example, in the design of the d and g. (Fig. 2 and 3.)

(*c*) The vernacular hands called Bastarda. For an early, certainly not the earliest, use of the name we may again refer to the sheet of Johann vander Hagen. A bastard script is current or cursive, written quickly and without the deliberation of (*a*) or even of (*b*). It is further characterized by a one-storied (einstöckiges) a, familiar to us in italic, by descenders running down to points, including long s and f; the ascenders are often looped, though by no means in all Bastardas. The earliest founts of this group are the smaller types of the Mainz Indulgences, one of them being more throughly bastarda than the other; the 30-line Indulgence has s and f with pointed descenders, the 31-line not. Fifteenth-century Bastardas are of great variety and differ much in respect of roundness

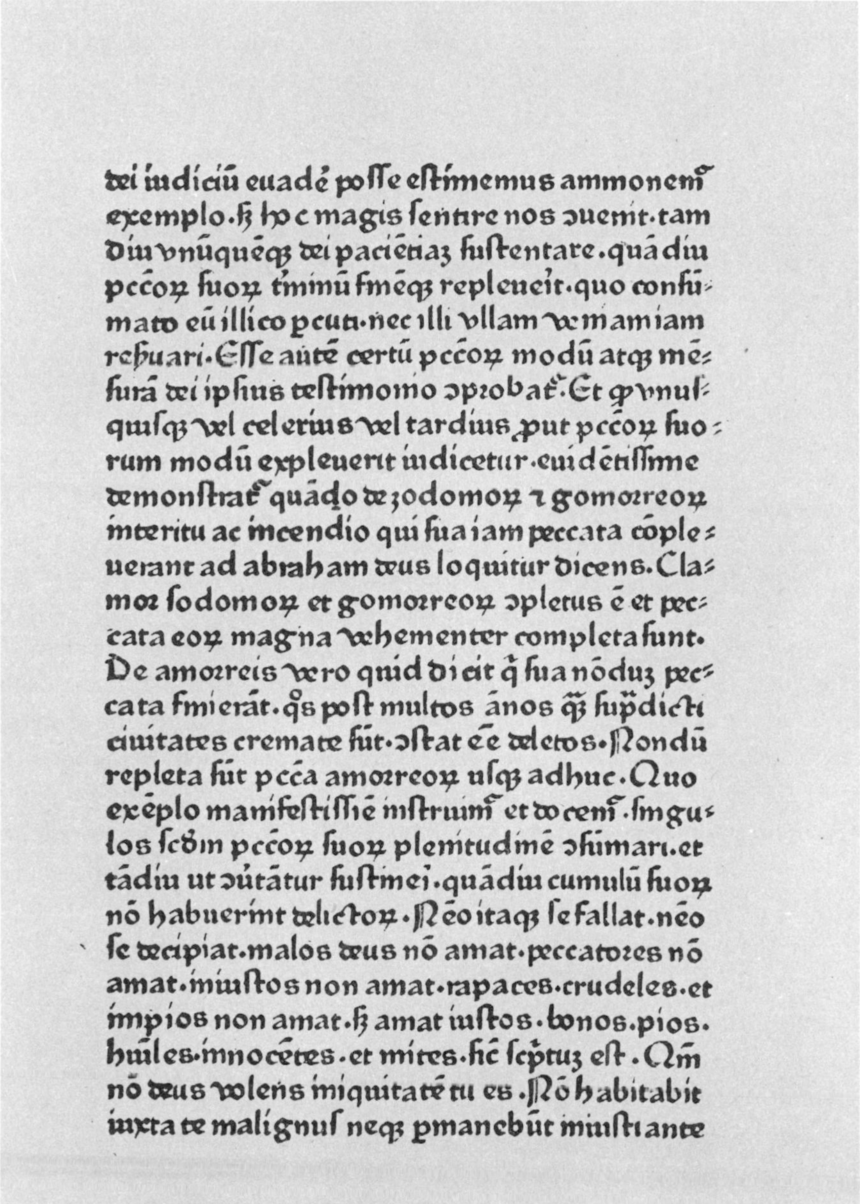

dei iudiciũ euadẽ posse estimemus ammonem̄
exemplo. ꝫ hoc magis sentire nos cõuenit. tam
diu vnũquẽq; dei paciẽciaꝫ sustentare. quã diu
peccoꝝ suoꝝ t'minũ finẽq; repleuerit. quo cõsũ-
mato eũ illico pcuti. nec illi vllam veniam iam
reseruari. Esse autẽ certũ peccoꝝ modũ atq; mẽ-
surã dei ipsius testimonio cõprobat'. Et q vnus-
quisq; vel celerius vel tardius put peccoꝝ suorum modũ expleuerit iudicetur. euidẽtissime
demonstrat' quãdo de sodomoꝝ et gomorreoꝝ
interitu ac incendio qui sua iam peccata cõple-
uerant ad abraham deus loquitur dicens. Clamor sodomoꝝ et gomorreoꝝ cõpletus ẽ et peccata eoꝝ magna vehementer completa sunt.
De amorreis vero quid dicit q̃ sua nõduꝫ peccata finierãt. q̃s post multos ãnos q̃ꝫ supdicte
ciuitates cremate sũt. cõstat ẽe deletos. Nondũ
repleta sũt pccã amorreoꝝ usq; adhuc. Quo
exẽplo manifestissĩe instruim' et docem'. singu-
los scdm peccoꝝ suoꝝ plenitudinẽ cõsumari. et
tãdiu ut cõtãtur sustinei. quãdiu cumulũ suoꝝ
nõ habuerint delictoꝝ. Neo itaq; se fallat. neo
se decipiat. malos deus nõ amat. peccatores nõ
amat. iniustos non amat. rapaces. crudeles. et
impios non amat. ꝫ amat iustos. bonos. pios.
huiles. innocẽtes. et mites. sic sc'ptuꝫ est. Qm̃
nõ deus volens iniquitatẽ tu es. Nõ habitabit
iuxta te malignus neq; pmanebũt iniusti ante

FIG. 2. Fere-humanistica. From Saint Augustine, *De vita Christiana*. Fust & Schöffer, Mainz, 1465(?).

and colour. I fancy that it may be possible to form further subgroups here. Among later Bastardas the Germans distinguish four sub-groups:

(1) Schwabacher, of which the first fount has been found with Friedrich Creussner at Nuremberg from 1485. This of course is not a new grouping; although in English I know of no clear description of the letter, all German histories of printing describe it. The name was certainly in use by printers as early as 1576.[1] Recent German books do not appear to have given any further explanation as to why the little town of Schwabach in Bavaria should have given its name to this type. Plates of the letters are given in Hessel, Crous and Kirchner, and in Kautzsch's *Die Entstehung der Frakturschrift*, Mainz, 1922, by the side of Fraktur. By the end of the fifteenth century its design has become fixed in upper-case as well as lower-case. The typographic characteristics so far laid down have been among minuscules only, for in all the earlier German founts the variations among majuscules defy classification. The upper-case was a separate fount often revealing little attempt at harmony with the lower-case. In the Gotico-antiquas, for example, the capitals range down to pure roman. But with these later Bastardas we can begin to include the upper-case. The H and M (Haebler's M 81) of Schwabacher can be conveniently used for the purpose of reference.

(2) The Upper-Rhine type (M 44) is a Bastarda with looped or blunt ascenders, at least in its early days. The earliest founts date from about the same year as Schwabacher, with Grüninger of Strasburg and Schöffer of Mainz in 1485. The Breydenbach type is perhaps the best known representative. J. Wegener, in *Die deutsche oberrheinische Type*, 1909, has traced this group down to 1550, taking as his basis M 44. It appears to me that this is a misuse of the M forms, for in the later stages the lower-case of these Upper-Rhine types is identical with Schwabacher. It is unsound to separate two series of types because of differences in some few capitals. The later group might perhaps be called Upper-Rhine Schwabacher. (Fig. 4.)

(3) The Wittenberg letter with M 48 is first found in the hands of Lotter at Leipzig in 1558 (cf. the illustration in Proctor's *Index*, Pt. II, Lotter's type 11), but was most popular with the printers of Wittenberg. The letter is a rather large and somewhat squarer Schwabacher. (Fig. 5.)

(4) Fraktur, the last and historically most important of the Bastardas, is so well known that I need say little of it here.[2] There are one or two points which may be mentioned. As to the name, in typography it can be traced back to the origin of the type. It was used by the calligrapher Johann Neudörffer, for instance, who designed some of the first Frakturs. But it is much older than that and occurs on the sheet of Johann vander Hagen.[3] As used by Vander Hagen it appears to be closer to its original meaning of 'broken' than with the printers. In type it is characterized by its restlessness; the feet run up to points and the loose ends of the capitals have been aptly compared to elephants' trunks. I find this comparison useful; if you are looking for Frakturs, look for elephants' trunks. The letter is narrower and therefore more economical in use than Schwabacher,

1. See *Archiv für Gesch. des deutschen Buch-handels*, X. 142.
2. See further, p. 39.
3. See also Wattenbach, *op. cit.*, for earlier occurrences.

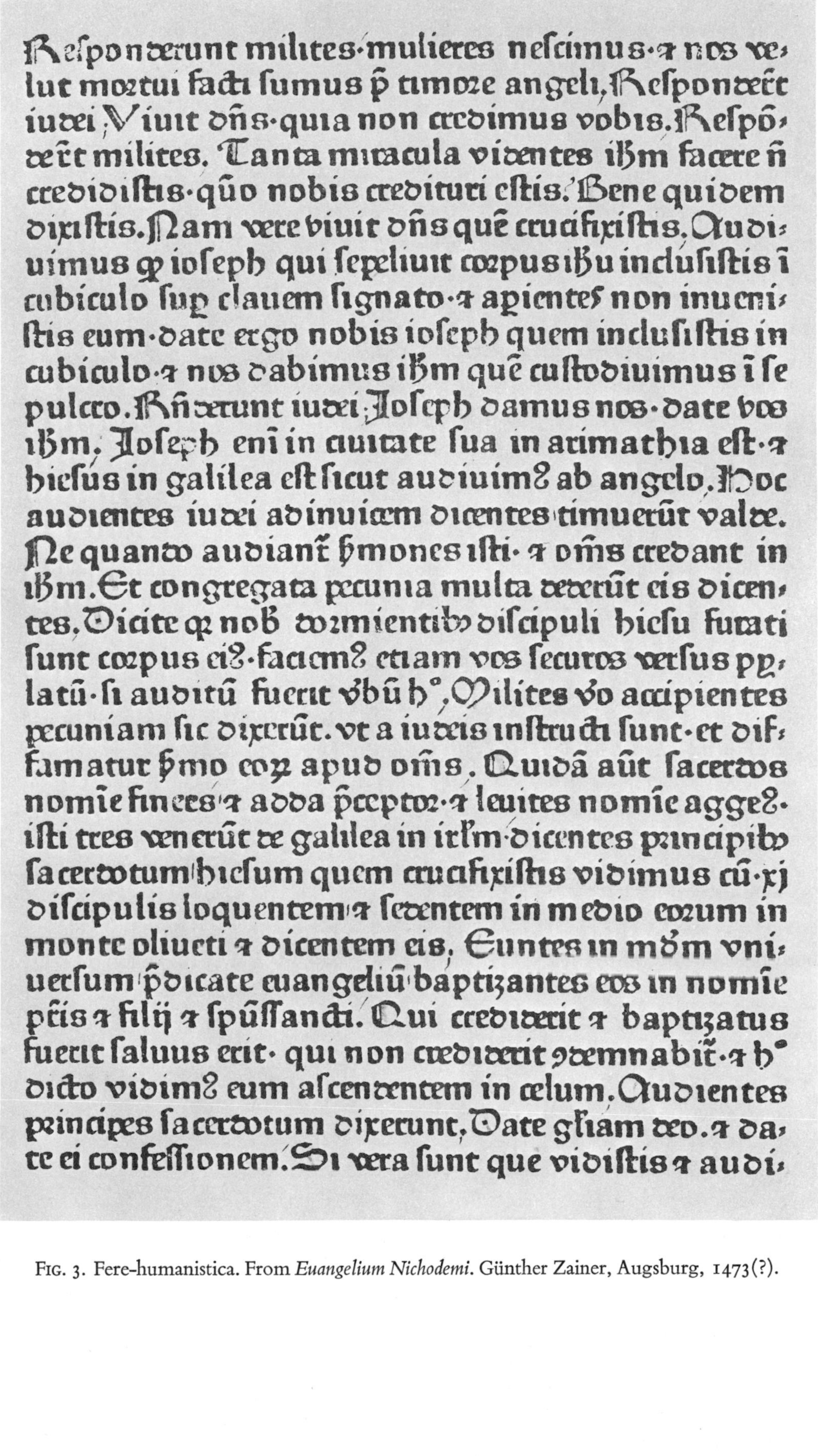

Responderunt milites·mulieres nescimus·ꝗ nos ve-
lut mortui facti sumus p̄ timore angeli,Responꝺet
iudei;Viuit dn̄s·quia non credimus vobis.Respō-
ꝺet milites. Tanta miracula videntes iḣm facere n̄
credidistis·quo nobis credituri estis.Bene quidem
dixistis.Nam vere biuit dn̄s quē crucifixistis.Audi-
uimus ꝙ ioseph qui sepeliuit corpus iḣu inclusistis ī
cubiculo sup clauem signato·ꝗ apientes non inueni-
stis eum·date ergo nobis ioseph quem inclusistis in
cubiculo·ꝗ nos dabimus iḣm quē custodiuimus ī se
pulcro.Rn̄derunt iudei;Ioseph damus nos·date vos
iḣm. Ioseph eni in ciuitate sua in arimathia est·ꝗ
hiesus in galilea est sicut audiuim̄ ab angelo.Hoc
audientes iudei adinuicem dicentes·timuerūt valde.
Ne quando audiant h̄mones isti·ꝗ om̄s credant in
iḣm.Et congregata pecunia multa dederūt eis dicen-
tes.Dicite ꝗ nob dormientib discipuli hiesu furati
sunt corpus ei̇̈·faciem̄ etiam vos securos versus pp-
latū·si auditū fuerit v̄bū h°,Milites v̄o accipientes
pecuniam sic dixerūt·vt a iudeis instructi sunt·et dif-
famatur h̄mo cor apud om̄s. Quidā aūt sacerdos
nomie finees·ꝗ adda p̄ceptor·ꝗ leuites nomie aggė̈·
isti tres venerūt de galilea in irl̄m·dicentes principib
sacerdotum·hiesum quem crucifixistis vidimus cū·xj
discipulis loquentem·ꝗ sedentem in medio eorum in
monte oliueti ꝗ dicentem eis. Euntes in mōm vni-
uersum p̄dicate euangeliū baptizantes eos in nomie
p̄tis ꝗ filij ꝗ spūssancti. Qui crediderit ꝗ baptizatus
fuerit saluus erit·qui non crediderit condemnabit·ꝗ h°
dicto vidim̄ eum ascendentem in celum.Audientes
principes sacerdotum dixerunt,Date gl̄iam deo·ꝗ date ei confessionem.Si vera sunt que vidistis ꝗ audi-

FIG. 3. Fere-humanistica. From *Euangelium Nichodemi*. Günther Zainer, Augsburg, 1473(?).

which may explain its survival. The only other explanation which would account for the ultimate victory of Fraktur is that its fussiness appealed to the taste of German printers after 1550. Between the years 1514 and 1525 at least eight versions of the letter were cut, for the details of which Crous or Kautzsch's *Die Entstehung der Frakturschrift* may be consulted. (Fig. 6.)

We still have to deal with one more letter, one of great importance towards the end of the fifteenth century. This is the rounded gothic of the Italians, sometimes called by palaeographers the Bolognese letter, from its use at the University of Bologna. In typography the Germans call it Rotunda (cf. the heading on Vander Hagen's sheet). This is not a new group, but it has hitherto lacked an accepted name. German printers of the fifteenth century, e. g. the Brothers of the Common Life at Rostock, used the phrase 'Litterae Venetae' of the gothic founts brought or copied from Italy, that is, our Rotundas. From the British Museum *Catalogue of Fifteenth-century Books* we find that Eucharius Silber at Rome described a small Rotunda, which he appears to have acquired from Adam Rotweil of Venice, as 'littera Veneta'. Venetian to a modern printer means a roman in the style of Jenson, but in fifteenth-century typography Jenson's Rotundas had a much wider vogue than his roman. The name used by the Italian writing masters of the sixteenth century was 'littera moderna', modern possibly as opposed to the roman Antiqua; but it may be that the name was in use at an earlier date, and that the ancient letter suggested was the pointed or formal Textura, which has a history longer by several centuries than that of the Rotunda. In contrast with Textur, Rotunda is full of curves, e. g. the b, c, e, h, o, etc. The feet of Textur have in part disappeared; cf. the m, only the third limb of which has a foot. In contrast with Gotico-antiqua it is without the tendency to roman, the a is closed, and the ascenders and descenders are shorter. In the g the bowl often takes on the shape of a trapezium. It is familiar to us in the gothics of Jenson and Ratdolt; Ratdolt's specimen sheet, so often reproduced, is convenient for reference. In Germany Rotunda makes an isolated appearance with Koelhoff at Cologne in 1472 but becomes common only in the eighties. Towards the end of the century its larger sizes vied with Textur for use as heading types and in liturgical works, while the smaller sizes took the place of the Gotico-antiquas and finally became the stock type in Europe for theological, legal, and scholastic texts. Though round, Rotunda was not so broad as Gotico-antiqua and was thus more economical. There are many fine books printed in Rotunda, but it suffered degradation by the end of the century and the usual stock type in this style used throughout Europe, *c.* 1500, is surely the most uninteresting of all early types. (Fig. 7.)

Such is the scheme of Dr. Hessel and if put to a practical test I think it will be found to work. Consider, for example, the reproductions in Voulliéme's *Die deutschen Drucker des fünfzehnten Jahrhunderts*, Berlin, 1922, a book which shows a large variety of types and therefore offers a very severe test; you will certainly find letters characteristic of one group appearing in types of another group. You will find Gotico-antiquas with Rotunda elements or vice versa. During the period when Rotundas were driving out Gotico-antiquas there is considerable confusion between the two groups. The type of the Calendar of Regiomontanus on p. 125 and the similar Calendar printed by Rat-

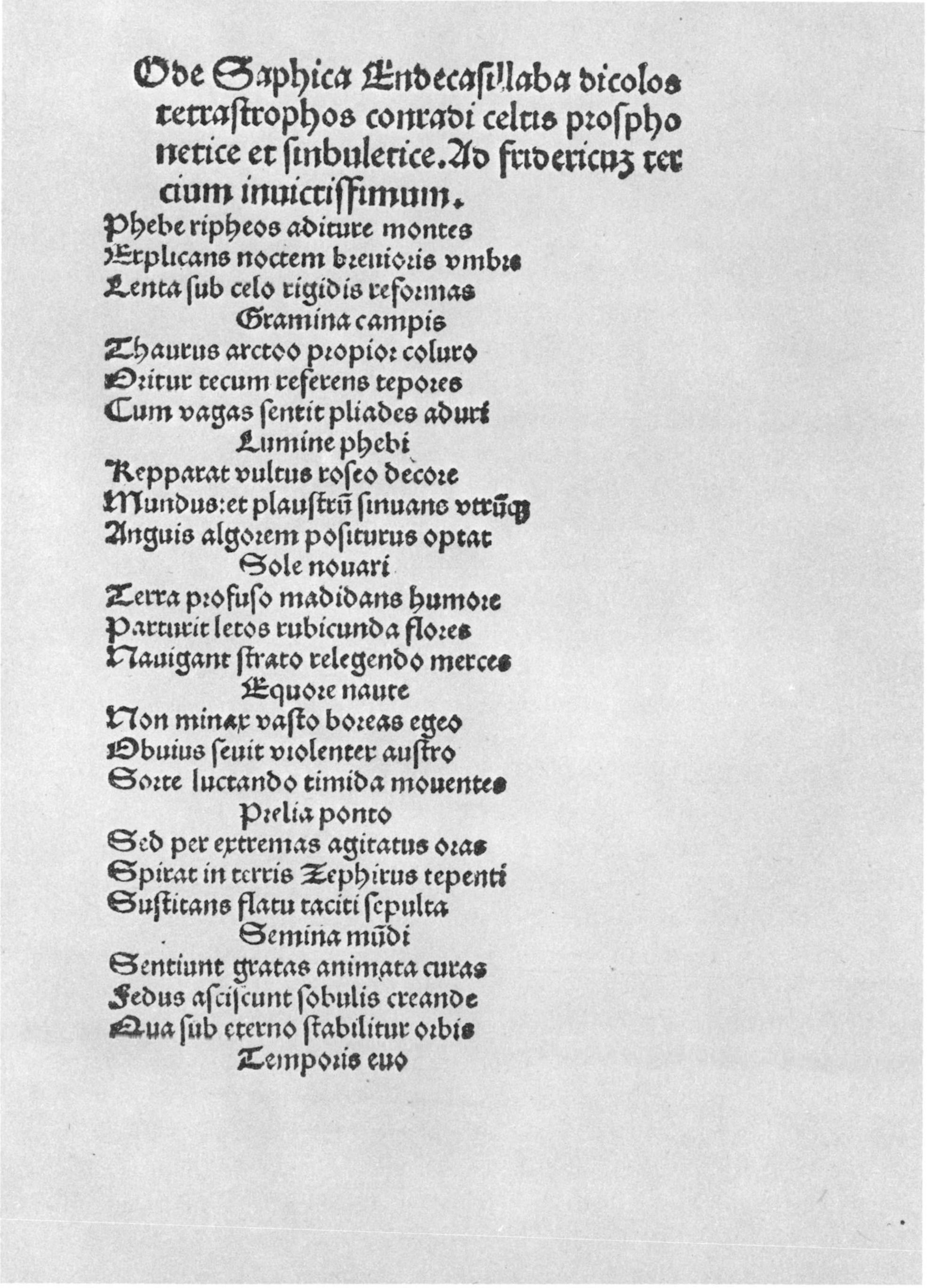

Ode Saphica Endecasillaba dicolos
tetrastrophos conradi celtis prospho
netice et sinbuletice. Ad fridericuz ter
cium inuictissimum.
Phebe ripheos aditure montes
Explicans noctem breuioris vmbre
Lenta sub celo rigidis reformas
          Gramina campis
Thaurus arctoo propior coluro
Oritur tecum referens tepores
Cum vagas sentit pliades aduri
          Lumine phebi
Repparat vultus roseo decore
Mundus:et plaustru sinuans vtrug
Anguis algorem positurus optat
          Sole nouari
Terra profuso madidans humore
Parturit letos rubicunda flores
Nauigant strato relegendo merces
          Equore naute
Non minax vasto boreas eges
Obuius seuit violenter austro
Sorte luctando timida mouentes
          Prelia ponto
Sed per extremas agitatus oras
Spirat in terris Zephirus tepenti
Sustitans flatu taciti sepulta
          Semina mudi
Sentiunt gratas animata curas
Fedus asciscunt sobulis creande
Qua sub eterno stabilitur orbis
          Temporis euo

FIG. 4. Schwabacher. From Conradus Celtes, *Proseuticum ad divum Fridericum III pro laurea Apollinari*. Friedrich Creussner, Nuremberg, [1487].

dolt shown on Pl. 1 you will perhaps give up in despair. But on the whole the majority of the types shown will fit in with the scheme outlined. It is a German scheme primarily intended for the classification of German types, but it can of course be applied to the typography of other countries. All the main groups, for example, are represented among English types, though some of them appear in isolated cases. The only early representative of the Gotico-antiquas is the first type of Theodoric Rood at Oxford which came from Cologne. Lettou's type, of Roman origin (cf. Duff, Plate XXII) is a Rotunda, while Pynson followed by De Worde used small Rotundas for notes to accompany the usual black letter. That typical English gothic letter is a small Textur, squarer because of its size but not rounded. Our Bastardas are either Flemish (Caxton's) or French, introduced by Pynson from Rouen.

Turning to English bibliographers I find that one writer has attempted a classification of German types over a short period, namely, Proctor in the second part of his *Index*, German books from 1501 to 1520. In the Type Index of that volume the gothic types are grouped as follows: (*a*) Square Church Types = Textur; (*b*) Rounded Church and Heading Types = Rotunda; (*c*) Latin Text Types = small Rotundas, and (*d*) Vernacular German Types = Bastardas. Proctor's third division is really the same as the second, classified according to the manner of using; also the term Latin Text Type does not seem to be well chosen; it suggests roman. In the first part of his *Index* Proctor had already used the term Church type, but that appears to be the only term of precision there used. Nor do I find any further exact terminology in the British Museum *Catalogue of Fifteenth-century Books*. Incunabulists are naturally concerned first to establish the differences among types, not their resemblances. Among the reasons which led Dr. Haebler to choose the capital M for the basis of his Repertorium was the fact that it appeared in so many different varieties. Earlier English writers on typography often use the three French terms[1] but with no corresponding translations. Perhaps the only English term used with any consistency of a definite group is black-letter (also called English) of the small Textur of De Worde and his successors. We can at least say that we have a name for the commonest English gothic letter. But the name is not a good one, as the type is not distinguished by its colour from other gothics or even some romans. Unfortunately also the initials B. L. in catalogues are used indiscriminately of all gothics used in England. The word Secretary has been used to indicate any English bastard type, and this use is at least as old as Rowe Mores. But the Secretary hand is a late Tudor hand, which Mr. Jenkinson says was first fully developed by about 1550. It was not translated into type until the end of the century, and that type is a script corresponding to the French 'lettre de civilité'. It would be more correct to confine the term in typography to that letter. The use may arise from a heading in the first English writing book, John Baildon's *A Book containing divers sorts of hands*, 1571, where a letter called Bastard Secretary is shown. This heading does not of course imply that bastard = secretary, but that the particular secretary shown is more cursive than another.

---

1. i. e. *lettre de somme*, *lettre bâtarde*, and *lettre de forme*.

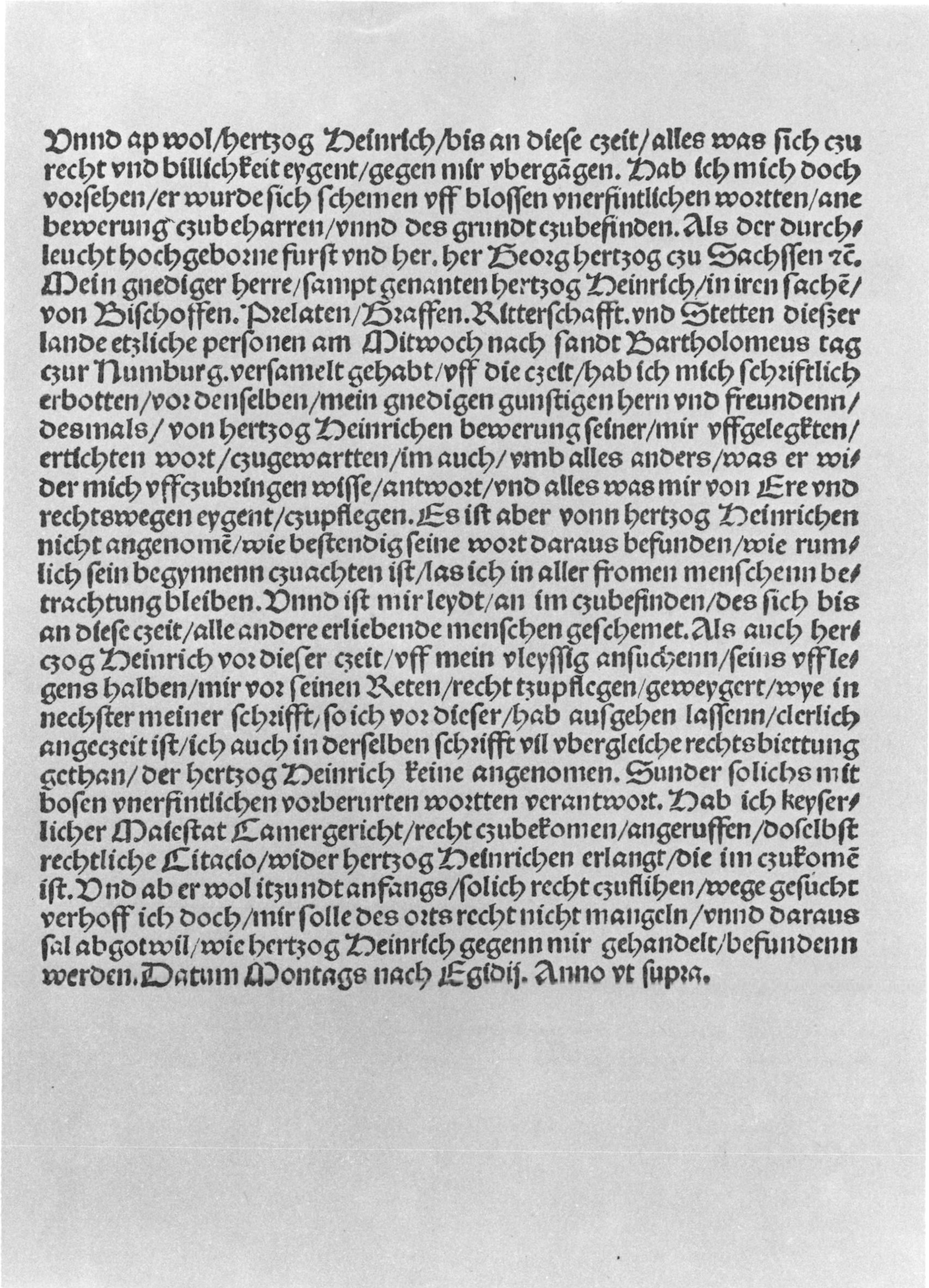

Vnnd ap wol/hertzog Heinrich/bis an diese czeit/alles was sich czu
recht vnd billichkeit eygent/gegen mir vbergägen. Hab ich mich doch
vorsehen/er wurde sich schemen vff blossen vnerfintlichen worttē/ane
bewerung czubeharren/vnnd des grundt czubefinden. Als der durch/
leucht hochgeborne furst vnd her. her Georg hertzog czu Sachssen rc.
Mein gnediger herre/sampt genanten hertzog Heinrich/in iren sachē/
von Bischoffen. Prelaten/Graffen. Ritterschafft. vnd Stetten dieszer
lande etzliche personen am Mitwoch nach sandt Bartholomeus tag
czur Numburg. versamelt gehabt/vff die czelt/hab ich mich schrifftlich
erbotten/vor denselben/mein gnedigen gunstigen hern vnd freundenn/
desmals/ von hertzog Heinrichen bewerung seiner/mir vffgelegkten/
ertichten wort/czugewartten/im auch/vmb alles anders/was er wi/
der mich vffczubringen wisse/antwort/vnd alles was mir von Ere vnd
rechtswegen eygent/czupflegen. Es ist aber vonn hertzog Heinrichen
nicht angenomē/wie bestendig seine wort daraus befunden/wie rum/
lich sein begynnenn czuachten ist/las ich in aller fromen menschenn be/
trachtung bleiben. Vnnd ist mir leydt/an im czubefinden/des sich bis
an diese czeit/alle andere erliebende menschen geschemet. Als auch her/
czog Heinrich vor dieser czeit/vff mein vleyssig ansuchenn/seins vffle/
gens halben/mir vor seinen Reten/recht tzupflegen/geweygert/wye in
nechster meiner schrifft/so ich vor dieser/hab ausgehen lassenn/clerlich
angeczeit ist/ich auch in derselben schrifft vil vbergleiche rechtsbiettung
gethan/der hertzog Heinrich keine angenomen. Sunder solichs mit
bosen vnerfintlichen vorberurten wortten verantwort. Hab ich keyser/
licher Maiestat Camergericht/recht czubekomen/angeruffen/doselbst
rechtliche Citacio/wider hertzog Heinrichen erlangt/die im czukomē
ist. Vnd ab er wol itzundt anfangs/solich recht czuflihen/wege gesücht
verhoff ich doch/mir solle des orts recht nicht mangeln/vnnd daraus
sal abgotwil/wie hertzog Heinrich gegenn mir gehandelt/befundenn
werden. Datum Montags nach Egidij. Anno vt supra.

FIG. 5. Wittenberg Letter. From Heinrich von Schleinitz, (*A letter concerning his dispute
with Henry, Duke of Saxony*). Michael Lotter, Leipzig, 1510.

In Updike's *Printing Types* the three French terms are used supplemented by descriptions of varying length. He has a reproduction from the *Catholicon* [fig. 17] and calls the type 'a round gothic' and again 'a lettre de somme'. Is then 'lettre de somme' French for Gotico-antiqua? Another plate entitled 'lettre de somme' [fig. 9] printed from actual type presumably of French origin reveals the fact that this type is not a Gotico-antiqua but a small Rotunda. A similar letter in Fournier's *Manuel typographique* seems to prove that the letter traditionally known in French printing offices as 'lettre de somme' was a small Rotunda. But Fournier himself, followed by Auguste Bernard and other French writers, uses the term of the earlier standard types of Schöffer. Updike then has some excuse. I have failed to trace the term farther back than Tory, who gives no explanation.[1] The suggested derivation from the fact that the type was used for an edition of the *Summa* of St. Thomas Aquinas or some other *Summa* is possibly correct, if, as seems likely, the term was purely typographic. Whatever its original meaning, it has been used by French writers, followed by English writers, indiscriminately of all early standard types, including Bastardas.

To return to Updike, of a Rotunda of Koberger's [Fig. 16], he says 'a type less pointed than the first gothic types'; again a Gotico-antiqua according to Hessel with bastarda elements of Mentelin of Strasbourg [Fig. 21] is described as 'semi-gothic'. Ulrich Gering's first gothic [Fig. 33], another Gotica-antiqua, is 'a gothic fount of transitional character'. Of De Worde's Rotunda [Fig. 66] Updike says 'the smaller has a round quality which is a little like the Italian gothic types of the time'. Lettou's Rotunda [Fig. 68] is 'like the transitional gothic type'; Gordon Duff called this fount 'a small Italian gothic'. Of a Rotunda of Berthelet's [Fig. 281] Updike writes 'midway between bâtarde and lettre de forme'. In Reed's *Old English Letter Foundries* the same type is described as 'a curious semi-gothic'; the only thing curious about it is its appearance in England. Of course in all these cases the reader is assisted by the reproduction, without which he would be hopelessly lost. It will be admitted that Updike has made a gallant effort to convey his meaning without an accepted vocabulary to work with.

As far as my researches go I find very few English terms, and these either wrongly used, like Secretary, or unsatisfactory, like black-letter, because derived from an unessential property. The best of them, like Proctor's Church type and Latin text type, are derived from the use which the particular type generally serves. None of them describes the design of the letter, and the design is the important characteristic which the name ought in some way to suggest. Of the three French terms, one only, the 'lettre de forme', has a precise meaning for English typography. 'Lettre bâtarde' is made to do duty for all varieties of bastard hands, instead of being confined to the particular version used in France. 'Lettre de somme' is applied to Gotico-antiquas, and also to some Bastardas, such as the Indulgence types, and even then both uses may be wrong, if we are to trust Fournier's specimen. The confusion arises from the fact that the hand-

---

1. The note in Wattenbach, p. 297, 1896 edition, seems to be a mistake; the term is not used in the inventory of the Library of the Duke of Berry, 1416.

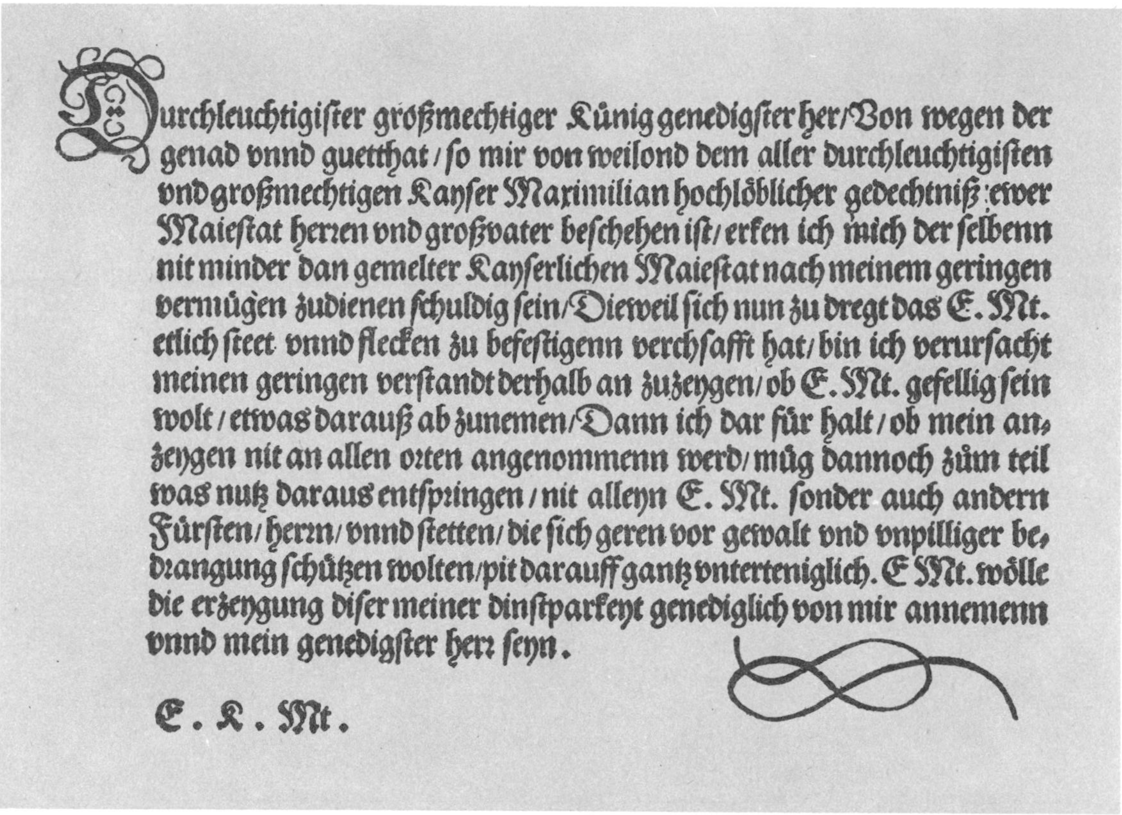

Durchleuchtigifter großmechtiger Künig genedigfter her/Von wegen der
genad vnnd guetthat/so mir von weilond dem aller durchleuchtigisten
vnd großmechtigen Kayser Maximilian hochlöblicher gedechtniß:ewer
Maiestat herren vnd großvater beschehen ist/erken ich mich der selbenn
nit minder dan gemelter Kayserlichen Maiestat nach meinem geringen
vermügen zudienen schuldig sein/Dieweil sich nun zu dregt das E.Mt.
etlich steet vnnd flecken zu befestigenn verchsafft hat/bin ich verursacht
meinen geringen verstandt derhalb an zuzeygen/ob E.Mt. gefellig sein
wolt/etwas darauß ab zunemen/Dann ich dar für halt/ob mein an=
zeygen nit an allen orten angenommenn werd/müg dannoch zum teil
was nutz daraus entspringen/nit alleyn E.Mt. sonder auch andern
Fürsten/herrn/vnnd stetten/die sich geren vor gewalt vnd vnpilliger be=
drangung schützen wolten/pit darauff gantz vnterteniglich. E Mt.wölle
die erzeygung diser meiner dinstparkeyt genediglich von mir annemenn
vnnd mein genedigster herr seyn.

E . K . Mt.

Fig. 6. Early Fraktur. From Albrecht Dürer, *Etliche underricht zu befestigung der Stett.*
Heinrich Andreae Formschneider, Nuremberg, 1527.

written letters and the types based on them have been studied apart and by different people, and further from the fact that neither French nor English writers have attempted to define exactly what they mean by such terms as they use.

Last of all there is a book which is very much to the point in our search, Stanley Morison's *German Incunabula in the British Museum*, London, 1928. The detailed examination of some of the types displayed in this handsome volume from the point of view of a typographical expert and lover of good lettering is most illuminating and, as far as I am aware, something new in this field. The high esteem with which the author regards the type-designing and type-setting of such men as Sensenschmidt of Nuremberg and Georg Reyser of Würzburg will probably surprise those, like myself, whose knowledge of fifteenth-century printing is acquired rather from the literature on the subject than at first hand. However, it is not my task to review this work, but to examine the terminology employed in the interesting introduction and notes, and call attention to his classification. The author was not primarily concerned with the grouping of types, but he was faced with the problem of arranging his plates. Naturally a chronological or topographical arrangement did not answer his purpose, but an arrangement by styles of letter, in accordance with the method of penmanship employed by the scribe. This is exactly what makes the book so important for our purpose. His grouping agrees fairly closely with that of Hessel and Crous, a striking testimony to the validity of their classification, especially as it was arrived at quite independently.

His five type groups are: 1. Formal Pointed-Text = Textura. 2. Round-Text = Rotunda. 3. Fere-humanistica = Gotico-antiqua. 4. Bastard. 5. Mixed.

(1) Pointed-Text is no doubt used to emphasize the distinction from Round-Text, but in the introduction the author uses the single word Text of this letter. His authority for the use of Text as the English equivalent of Textur is of the best. Jenkinson, who uses the word in *The later Court Hands in England*, says that it was well established in the fourteenth and fifteenth centuries. It was the name used by John Baildon, in the writing book of 1571. It was not merely a technical term but is found in the literary language. In *Love's Labour's Lost*, v. ii. 42, we read 'Fair as a text B in a copy-book'. On that passage Dover Wilson's glossary says 'the text hand was one of the more elaborate and formal of the various Elizabethan scripts'. The only objection to the revival of the term is the possibility of confusion owing to our use of text-type in the sense of body or standard type. We must either always capitalize Text = Textur, or abandon *text*-type. Small Text would be a correct name for English black-letter. It is rather remarkable that small Texts do not occur at a very early date in German printing. The first body types were either Bastardas or Gotico-antiquas. It would no doubt be very difficult to cut legible Text of a really small size.

(2) Round-Text follows very naturally from Text. The *O.E.D.* gives examples of its use, under Text, but, of course, one cannot say what letter exactly was meant. On p. 19 Morison implies that the Bolognese letter differed slightly from Round-Text.

(3) Fere-humanistica is a term taken from Ehrle and Libaert's *Specimina Codicum Latinorum Vaticanorum*, 1912, where it is applied to Petrarch's hand. It is perhaps a rather better term than Gotico-antiqua, as it avoids the objectional word gothic and more

I

Vorrede in das Bairisch lantrechtbůch.

Jr Ludwig von gottes genaden·Mar/
graue tzů brandenburg·Wir Stephan.
Wir Ludwig·Wir Wilhalme von gottes
genadé Pfaltzgrafé bey rein vñ Hertz/
og in bayren ic·Habé angesehen deli gé/
presté den wir gehabt haben in vnserem
lande tzů bayren an dem rechten·Vnnd
dauon sey wir zů rat wordé mit vnserm herré vñ vätterlein
kaiser Ludwigé vó rom·Añ setzen vñ bestättigé alles das
hernach geschriben steet nach seiné gebot vñ haissen vnse
rem land zů bairn zů füderůg vñ zů sunderé genaden·Das
ist geschehé do man zalt vó cristi gepurt dreüzehenhůdert
vnd in dem sechsund viertzigsten jar des nächsten samf/
tags nach dem obersten ic.

Wie man dz recht behalté sol.

Oa von gepieten wir bey vnseren hulden allen vn/
seren Richtern vnd Amptleüten in vnserem lande
tzů bayren überal jn stetten vnd merckten vnnd auff dem
land·Das sy die selben recht also behalten bey iren ayden
die sy vns od vnserm vieztumb darumb schweren inůssen
Vnd das sy darnach von wort zů wort·von stuck zů stucke
armen vnd reichen vngeuerlich richtensóllen.

Das ist das rechtbůch also gancz vnd alt gepesseret.
vnd auch neü artickel gesamlet·auß allen gerichten stetté
vnd merckten nach des Kaisers haissen.

a j

Fig. 7. Round Text. From *Das Bayrisch lantssrechtpuch*. Erhardt Ratdolt, Augsburg, 1945.

exactly defines the letter. But it is not English, nor has the author suggested an English equivalent. If this interesting group of types is to be recognized a good designation is needed. An English term can perhaps be dispensed with, as the group has but one representative among English types and that one of German origin.

It will be noticed that the new terms coined by German writers are Latin. Possibly this was done deliberately with a view to their international use. In the case then of Rotunda and of Fere-humanistica, if that word be accepted, it may be unnecessary and even undesirable for the English to enlarge the vocabulary. But there are also types which are definitely national. Just as the Germans have their Schwabacher and Fraktur, so it would seem desirable that the particular variety of small Text used by English printers should have an English name. As the French have their Civilité, so we should have our Secretary.

(4) Bastard. There is no reason why we should continue to use bâtarde, when there is a good English word available. Sir Hilary Jenkinson finds it in use about 1530 and it is Baildon's word. In Morison's Introduction he speaks of Bastard Text, Bastard Round-Text, and their small varieties, but he does not follow this up in detail in the notes on Bastard, although the examples of Bastard are arranged according to their degree of pointedness or roundness. Schwabacher of course is not a translatable term and in any case is purely a German letter. There are, however, one or two interesting English books printed abroad in Schwabacher, Tyndale's New Testament, 1526, for example, and Coverdale's Bible printed at Zürich in 1535. The heading type of the Zürich edition is in Fraktur, a term which also requires no translation.

(5) Of Morison's mixed types it may be pointed out that several will, as far as the lower-case is concerned, fall into the previous groups. What the author has to say in the Introduction of the development of capitals bears out the claim that types cannot be classified by the upper-case. Every fount of type is really two founts, which are only remotely related.

The suggested vocabulary then and classification of gothic types, as far as we have carried it, is as follows:

I. Text instead of Lettre de Forme or Church type – with small Text for the familiar English black-letter.

II. We have to choose between Gotico-antiqua and Fere-humanistica or devise a better term.

III. Rotunda or Round-Text and Small Round-Text instead of Italian gothic and Proctor's Latin text types.

IV. Bastard, our English bastards being Flemish and French, and last of all (except for some Law hands), Bastard Secretary.

Chance seems generally to decide in what sense any particular word shall be used or whether it shall survive at all. But in the case of technical terms the members of the Bibliographical Society, if they agreed on a terminology and consistently used it, could no doubt influence the issue.

JOHANN VANDER HAGHEN'S ADVERTISEMENT

The headings of the sections in this reduced facsimile of the specimens and advertisement of Johann vander Haghen, of Bodenwerder on the Weser, of the first half of the fifteenth century, read as follows:

Textus Quadratus.	Textus prescisus vel sine pedibus.
Nottula Simplex.	Notula actua.
Semiquadratus.	Textus Rotundus.
Nottula fracturarum.	Argentum.[1]
Bastardus.	Nottula Conclauata.
Separatus.	Argentum extra pennam.[2]

1. Not a description of the letter below it, which is a Rotunda.
2. The letter is a Bastarda.

The name and advertisement of the calligrapher are given in the last entry on the right:

Volentes informari in diversis modis scribendi Magistraliter et artificialiter prout nunc scribitur in curiis dominorum scilicet in diversis textibus et nottulis necnon cum auro et argento similiter tum omni metallo extra pennam venient ad me Johannem vand haghen et informabuntur in brevi temporis spacio secundum diligenciam discipulorum pro precio competenti etcetera.

[1929]

A CATALOGUE OF ITALIAN WRITING-BOOKS
OF THE SIXTEENTH CENTURY

INTRODUCTION

This catalogue in its original form was compiled about twenty years ago, and has been laid aside and taken up again on several occasions. One result of the long delay is that the list is more nearly complete, or less incomplete, than it would have been if published as originally planned. That it is still very imperfect I am well aware. The more copies one sees bearing the same date, the more variants one finds. Moreover, although this is a catalogue of Italian printed books, no particular search in Italian libraries has been possible. Italian libraries must be rich in their early writing-books, but they are not rich in published catalogues. A further result of the deferred publication is that some of the references have become out of date. For instance, the firm of Birrell & Garnett no longer survives, but a manuscript catalogue of their writing-books has been deposited in the British Museum. The collection of the late G. W. Jones was sold at auction shortly before the 1939-45 war.[1] Only in some cases have I been able to trace the present owners of their books. Books on the geometrical formation of letters, such as the works of Pacioli, Fanti, and Verini, are not included in this catalogue.

As to the method adopted in making the individual entries, in the case of the first editions an attempt is made to reproduce, typographically, titles which are set in type, but not titles which are cut on wood or engraved. The word 'woodcut' is used only of the process of cutting in relief and the word 'engraved' only of the process *en creux*, engraving on copper. Where, however, the information has been supplied by others, consistency is difficult. The titles of later editions are not repeated unless the wording has been changed. No measurements of the usual quartos have been given; Italian books of the sixteenth century in quarto are very consistent in size. Each entry ends with a reference to the library of individual owner from whose copy the description has been made. A second copy is mentioned when it is known to vary in some particular, or in some cases where the book appears to be very scarce. Many of these books are certainly very rare, at any rate north of the Alps. The Ruano, Rome, 1554, for instance, I have never seen mentioned in a bookseller's catalogue, and I know of only one copy in this country. The first editions of Cresci seem to be equally scarce.

I have received helpful notes from many collectors and librarians, so many in fact that it is impossible to name and thank them all here. In some cases I regret to say I have no longer a record of the source of a particular piece of information. But there are three specialists on the subject of calligraphic models to whom I owe special thanks: first of all to Stanley Morison, who originally urged me to take on this task. He has provided many notes and has quite recently[2] compared my descriptions with copies in American collections. Morison has reproduced many early writing-books. Mr. Graham

1. Sir Ambrose Heal's collection was disposed in about 1944.
2. Shortly before original publication. See also p. 40.

Pollard, at the time when he was connected with Birrell & Garnett, was a great stand-by. I owe much, too, to James Wardrop, whose work on Italian calligraphers is well known. He has been of special help with the biographies of the writing-masters.

THE CATALOGUE

LUDOVICO DEGLI ARRIGHI DA VICENZA

The earliest critical account of Ludovico degli Arrighi da Vicenza as a calligrapher is contained in G. Manzoni, *Studii di bibliografia analitica*, Bologna, 1881, and for his work as a printer there appears to be little earlier than A. F. Johnson and S. Morison, 'The Chancery Types of Italy and France' in *The Fleuron*, No. 3, 1923.[1] In 1926 a facsimile of the two parts of Arrighi's writing book was published by the Officina Bodoni with an introduction by Stanley Morison. In *The Fleuron*, No. 7, 1930, Morison contributed a note on a book published by Arrighi at Rome in 1510, the earliest record of his name so far discovered. The fullest account of what is known of his life is to be found in James Wardrop, 'Arrighi Revived', *Signature*, No. 12, 1939.

Wardrop has traced three manuscripts written by Arrighi, one dated Rome 1517. Since Arrighi was already a bookseller in Rome in 1510, was employed as a writer of briefs at the Camera Apostolica and signed a manuscript from Rome in 1517, it seems likely that all his working life was spent in that city, and that the earlier story that he was first a writing master in Venice is unreliable. His last known book appeared in May 1527, the month in which the sack of Rome began. Not improbably his life ended in that catastrophe.

★

LA OPERI || NA || di Ludouico Vicentino, da || imparare di || scriue- || re || littera Can- || cellares- || cha ||

[A 1 v°] IL MODO || & || Regola de scriuere littera || corsiua || ouer Cancellarescha || nouamente composto per || LVDOVICO || VICENTI- || NO. || Scrittore de breui || alci || in Roma nel Anno di nra || salute || MDXXII ||

[D 4 v°] Finisce || la || ARTE || di || scriuere littera Corsiua || ouer Cancellares- || cha || Stampata in Roma per inuentione || di Ludouico Vicentino || scrittore || CVM GRATIA & PRIVILEGIO [*white on black*] ||

16 leaves, in quarto, sig. A–D in fours; the whole printed from blocks. C 3 v°, C 4 r° & v°, D 1 v°, D 3 r° and v°, and D 4 r° are signed by Vicentino. Describes 'Chancery' letter only.   (*Brit. Mus.*)

Il modo de temperare le || Penne || Con le uarie Sorti de littere || ordinato per Ludouico Vicentino, In || Roma nel anno MDXXIII || con gratia e Priuilegio [*white on black*] ||

[d 3 v°] Sta'pata in Ventia || PER || Ludouico Vicentino Scrittore || & || Eustachio Celebrino Intagliat- || tore ||

16 leaves, in quarto, sig. a–d in fours. Sig. a treats of the pen, sig. b 1 & 2 show the 'lettera mercantesca', b 3 r° 'littera per notari', b 3 v° and b 4 r° 'lettera da bolle', b 4 v° 'littera da brevi', c 1 r° roman letters; c 1 v° – d 1 r° initials; d 1 v° 'littera formata', d 2 r° italic and roman types; d 2 v° a plate of initials; d 3 r° roman and italic used in the book; d 3 v° the colophon; d 4 r° roman capitals; d 4 v° blank; a 1 v°, a 2 r° and v°, a 3 v°, a 4 r°, d 1 v°, d 2 r°, and d 3 r° are printed from type, an italic. The preface refers to Arrighi's book on the Chancery letter of the previous year. Arrighi signs the plates on b 1 v°, b 2 v°, b 3 r°, b 4 r° and v°, c 2 r°.   (*Brit. Mus.*)

30 leaves imposed and printed as one book with *Il Modo de temperare le Penne* (see above); quarto; signed (A I omitted) A II to A XV, unsigned from v° of XV to the end; woodcut colophon occupying whole of final page: Ludo. Vicentinus Rome in Parhione || scribebat || ANN MDXXIII || Deo, & virtuti omnia debent.   (*Chicago, Newberry Library*)

Essling (No. 2181) describes a copy of the two parts in 30 leaves, sig. A–C, a–d in fours, except c in six.

LA OPERI || NA || di Ludouico Vicentino, da || imparare di || scriue- || Re || littera Can || cel- || lares- || cha || Con molte altre noue littere agiunte, et una bellissima || Ragione di Abbacho molto necessario, à chi || impara à scriuere, & fare conto || vgo Scr. || [i. e. Ugo da Carpi scrisse]

20 leaves, in quarto, sig. A–D in fours and four leaves unsigned. On A 3 r° in place of the address to the reader there is a privilege in favour of Ugo da Carpi from Pope Clement VII, dated 3 May 1525, which contains the words: 'Dilectus filius Vgo de Carpi ad communem omnium utilitatem nouas litterarum notas, et characteres impressurus, quibus Adulescentuli ad scribendi Artem percipiendam facile diriguntur, Et si alias per Ludouicum Vicen-

[1]. See pp. 83–109.

tinum fuit impeditus, ut is, hos nouos characteres in lucem dare, ac uendere non posset: Nos tamen communem hominum et utilitatem, et iusticiam attendentes, et praecipue quia is (ut constat) ab eodem fuit defraudatus, uolumus, ac de integro concedimus, ut ipse Vgo possit ipsos characteres imprimere, libellosque formare quos, et quoties uoluerit, eosque dare uaenum. Minimeque eidem, et emptoribus obstare litteras, ac breue per ipsum Ludouicum contra eundem impetratum et reliqua, ut in nostris litteris latius apparet.' In the colophon on D 4 v° the words: Finisce || la || ARTE || di scrivere littera Corsiva || ouer Cancellares-||cha || Stampata in Roma per inventione || No, [sic] Ludouico Vicentino. 'RESURREXIT VGO DA CARPI' are added, and instead of the concluding words Con gratia & privilegio is the word SE-PVLCH|RVM [cut in white on a black cartouche].

(Leipzig, Börsenverein; Chicago, Newberry Library)

This edition is copied from the blocks of the first part of Arrighi. The original blocks remained in their unaltered state; as may be seen in the editions of 1533 and 1539. Giacomo Manzoni (Studii di bibliografia analitica, 1881, Studio secondo, p. 34, seq.), from whom the title has been copied, says that Ugo da Carpi, who may have cut the original blocks, and who evidently thought he had some claim against Arrighi, recovered these blocks and printed this edition of 1525 from them. The additional four leaves of the 'Abbaco' of Angelus Mutinensis reappear in the Thesauro de Scrittori of 1535. (See below.) B IV v° and C I differ in text and arrangement from Arrighi's edition.

REGOLA || DA IMPARARE SCRIVERE || VARII CARATTERI DE || LITTERE CON LI || SVOI COMPASSI || ET MISVRE. || ET IL MODO DI TEMPERA || re le penne secundo le sorte di lettere che uorrai || scriuere, ordinato per Ludovico Vicentino || con una recetta da far inchiostro || fino nuouamete stampato. || MDXXXII. ||

Colophon: Stampato in Vinegia per Nicolo d'A- ||ristotile detto Zoppino. Nel anno || de nostra salute MDXXXII. || del mese d'Agosto. || [Device of St. Nicholas]

30 leaves in quarto, sig. A I-XV (one gathering). Text in italic. The title-page, printed from type, is surrounded by a woodcut border in four parts and contains a device of a hand holding a pen. Printed from the blocks of the edition of 1522 and the second part of 1523. The 'recetta' mentioned on the title-page does not appear.

(ESSLING, Livres à figures Vénitiens, No. 2186; BIRRELL & GARNETT)

[Another edition]
Colophon: Stampato in Venetia per Nicolo d'A-ristotile || detto Zoppino. MDXXXIII. ||

30 leaves in quarto, sig. A. A reissue of the edition of 1532; on the last leaf is the 'recetta', in italic, and the imprint, also in italic.   (Brit. Mus.)

La Operina di Ludovico Vicentino da imparare di scriuere littera cancellerescha.

Valerio d'Orico & Luigi frat. Brisciani, Roma, 1538.

28 leaves, in quarto.

(VOYNICH, a manuscript catalogue)

LA OPERI || NA || di Ludouico Vicentino, da || imparare di || scriue- || re || littera can- || cellares- || cha. ||

[A 28 r°] STAMPATA || IN ROMA, IN || CAMPO DI FIORE, || PER VALERIO D'ORI- || CO, ET LVIGI, || FRATELLI, || BRISCIANI. || ANNO || MDXXXIX. ||

28 leaves, in quarto, sig. A I-XIIII. A reprint from the blocks of the two parts of Arrighi's book, with new signatures, and with the omission of the pages printed from type in the second part of the book.
(Brit. Mus.)

LA OPERI || NA || di Ludouico Vicentino, da || imparare di || scriue- || re || littera can- || cel-lares- || cha. ||

EXCVDEBAT IOANNES LOE || ANNO M.D.LXIII. ||

28 leaves, in quarto, sig. A-G in fours. A copy of the two parts of Arrighi's book, printed at Antwerp.
(Bibl. Nat.)

[Another edition] . . .
EXCVDEBAT IOANNES LOEVS || ANNO M.D.XLV. ||

28 leaves, in quarto, sig. A-G in fours. (Bibl. Nat.)

[Another edition] . . .
EXCVDEBAT ANTVERPIAE IOAN || NES LOE, ANNO MDXLVI ||

28 leaves, in quarto, sig. A-G in fours. (Brit. Mus.)

L'Operina di Ludovico Vicentino . . .
Roma per M. Valerio Dorico et Louisi fratelli Brixiani, 1548. In quarto.

(MANZONI, p. 46)

ESSEMPLARIO || DE SCRITTORI IL QVALE || INSEGNA A SCRIVERE || diuerse sorti di lettere. || Col modo di temperare le penne secondo le lettere, & cono- || scer la bontà di quelle, e carte, e far Inchiostro, Verzino, || Cenaprio, & Vernice, con molti altri secreti || pertinenti alli Scrittori, come per te || medesimo leggendo || imparerai. || Con una ragione d'Abbaco breue, || & utilissima. || [Device of the Dorici] In Roma per Valerio, & Luigi Dorici fratelli. 1557.

36 leaves, in quarto, the first half of the gathering numbered 1-18. Title in type; text woodcut in chancery; Arrighi's address 'Al benigno lettore' followed by his woodcut title La Operina and signed Ugo Scr. Apparently reprinted in part from the blocks

of Ugo da Carpi's edition of 1525. (See above.) On 17 r° is the 'Sepulcrum' plate bearing his name, on 24 r° is a new Hebrew alphabet, on 30 v° 'Lettera formata', 31 and 32 gothic entrelac initials, 33-6 the 'Abbaco'. The pages are surrounded by short rules. (*Brit. Mus.*)

[Another edition] 36 leaves, in quarto. The pages from type have been reset, and the rules surrounding the pages are different.

(DAVIS & ORIOLI, *Cat.* XLIV, No. 453, *a copy wanting the first and last leaves.*)

J. D. F. Sotzmann, in the *Archiv für die zeichnende Künste*, 1856, pp. 275-303, mentions an edition published at Venice in 1632.

GIOVANANTONIO TAGLIENTE

In a note on Tagliente in *Signature* No. 8, N. S. James Wardrop has given some details of his life, reproducing a document of 1491, a petition to the Doge and Council of Venice. From his Writing Book of 1524 we already knew that he was then advanced in years. He assisted a relative, Geronimo Tagliente, in the preparation of an arithmetic book, entitled *Libro di abaco*, of which the first edition was printed at Venice in 1515. The book was many times reprinted. Later editions often appear in catalogues under the names of subsequent editors, Giovanni Roccha and L. A. Uberti. G. A. Tagliente also published a pattern book at Venice in 1531. The best account of his publications is in P. Riccardi, *Bibliotheca matematica*. See also G. Manzoni, op. cit.

*

Lo presente libro Insegna La Vera arte delo Excellē || te scriuere de diuerse varie sorti de litere Lequali se || fano ꝑ' geometrica Ragione, & Con La P'esente || opera ognuno Le Potra Imparare impochi giorni ꝑ || Lo amaistramento, || || ragione, || & || Essempli, come qui seguente || vederai. || Opera del tagliente nouamente || composta cum gratia nel anno di ñra salute || MDXXIIII ||

24 leaves in quarto, sig. A-F in fours (B is not numbered). The dedication to M. Hieronymo Dedo (A ii) and the last eight leaves are printed from type, a calligraphic italic. Without imprint, but probably printed at Venice. On the verso of the title-page is a woodcut of a writer's implements. The book contains examples of the 'Lettera cancellaresca', 'mercantesca', 'francesca', 'antiqua tonda', 'fiorentina', 'bollatica', 'imperiale', and Hebrew, Persian and Chaldee alphabets. (See Fig. 1.) (*Brit. Mus.*)

[Another edition] . . . MDXXIIII.
44 leaves, in quarto, sig. A-F (G and H not signed), i-l in fours. This edition has two additional alphabets in eleven leaves (E 4 v° to H 3 r°) showing the geometrical construction of Rotunda, resembling the plates after Sigismondo Fanti in the *Thesauro dei Scrittori*. (ESSLING, No. 2183)

Another copy, in the possession of Stanley Morison, has some variants. The title is on A 1 v°, and on the recto is the title 'Opera di Giouanne Antonio Taiente che insegna a scriuere di molte qualita di lettere intitulata Lucidario'.

[Another edition] . . . MDXXV.
24 leaves, in quarto, sig. A-F in fours. Reprinted from the blocks of the first edition, with the alteration of the date on the title. The plates are in a different order and six are new, on B 4 v° a mercantile hand, D 1 v° and 2 r° roman capitals white on black, D 2 v° roman white on black, D 4 r° Textura, white on black, and E 1 r° 'lettera formata', i. e. Rotunda. Six of the original plates (those on B 1 v°, C 1 r°, C 4 v°, Chancery, D 2 v° and 3 r°, Hebrew, white on black, and D 4 v°, Chaldee) are omitted. The pages in type have been reset. On F 4 r° are the words 'Intagliato per Eustachio Cellebrino da Vdene', white on black. (*Brit. Mus.*)

[Another edition] . . . MDXXV.
28 leaves, in quarto, sig. A-G in fours. The extra sheet, G, consists of text in italic; sig. F has been reset and is without the reference to Celebrino.
(BIRRELL & GARNETT)

[Another edition] . . . MDXXV.
40 leaves, in quarto, sig. A-K in fours. On the recto of the last leaf is the device of Antonio Blado, of Rome; the verso is blank. (ESSLING, No. 2184)

Opera di Giouanniantonio Tagliente che insegna a || scriuere de diuerse qualita de lettere intitulata || Esemplario. || Con gratia et priuilegio. || MDXXV. ||

Oblong (101 × 152 mm). 16 leaves; title; verso, copies of the two woodcuts from Celebrino's book; preface 'Al benigno lettore: Considerando &c . . .' 1 leaf; 6 pp. cursive Chancery; 8 pp. of Mercantile etc.; ABC in 9 pp. of blocks white on black; 5 pp. instructions & colophon: Hauendo io Giouanniantonio Tagliente prouisionato dal Serenissimo Dominio Venetiano, con ogni debita cura dimostrato a fare de diuerse qualita di lettere in questa picola operina et forzatomi di narrare quāto e stato bisogno circa allo amaestramento di lo imparare, Ormai io fare fine rendendo della presente opera gloria et honore al summo dispensator delle diuine gratie et che longamente ui conserui tutti in questa uitta et ne laltra ui doni felice beatitudine &c. Some of the blocks of the original edition are printed half at a time; the title is set in italic and has a woodcut border of knotted work (reproduced in *Eustachio Celebrino*, Pegasus Press, 1929).

(*Chicago, Newberry Library*)

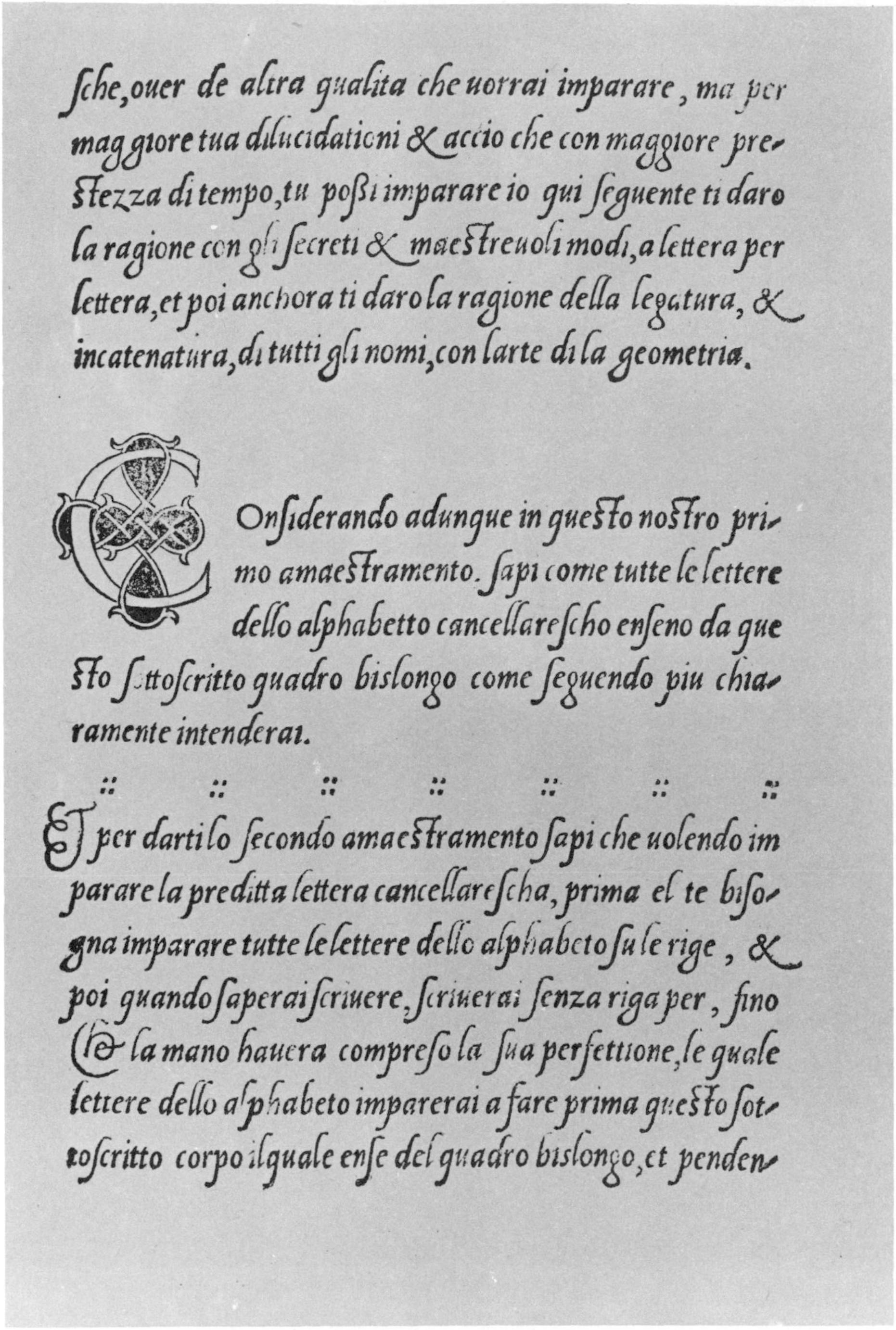

sche, ouer de altra qualita che uorrai imparare, ma per
maggiore tua dilucidationi & accio che con maggiore pre-
stezza di tempo, tu possi imparare io qui seguente ti daro
la ragione con gli secreti & maestreuoli modi, a lettera per
lettera, et poi anchora ti daro la ragione della legatura, &
incatenatura, di tutti gli nomi, con larte di la geometria.

Onsiderando adunque in questo nostro primo amaestramento. sapi come tutte le lettere
dello alphabetto cancellaresco enseno da que
sto sottoscritto quadro bislongo come seguendo piu chiaramente intenderai.

⁝   ⁝   ⁝   ⁝   ⁝   ⁝   ⁝

Et per darti lo secondo amaestramento sapi che uolendo im
parare la preditta lettera cancellarescha, prima el te bisogna imparare tutte le lettere dello alphabeto su le rige , &
poi quando saperai scriuere, scriuerai senza riga per , fino
che la mano hauera compreso la sua perfettione, le quale
lettere dello alphabeto imparerai a fare prima questo sottoscritto corpo ilquale ense del quadro bislongo, et penden-

FIG. 1. Tagliente, 1524.

Lo presente libro Insegna . . . MDXXV.

Colophon: Stampata in Vineggia per Giou-anniantonio & fradelli da Sabbio. MDXXVII.

28 leaves, in quarto, sig. A–G in fours.

(ESSLING, No. 2185)

[Another edition]
Stampato in Vinegia, per Giouanni Antonio de Nicolini da Sabio, MDXXIX.

In quarto.   (YEMENIZ CAT. 1867, No. 637)

[Another edition] Venice, 1530.   (Brunet)

[Another edition] . . . MDXXXI.

Colophon [f. 26 r°]: Stampato in Vinegia per Giouanniantonio & i Fratelli da || Sabbio, del mese di Nouēbrio, MDXXXI. ||

26 leaves, in quarto, sig. A–N (one gathering). A reissue from the blocks of the 1525 edition in a slightly different order, with one new alphabet on f. 14 v° and f. 15 r° of decorated initials copied from pt. 2 of Arrighi's book. The woodcut of implements occurs on f. 20 r°. The pages printed from type have been reset, but are still in the same italic.

(Brit. Mus.)

A copy in the Newberry Library is dated 1530 in the colophon.

[Another edition] . . . MDXXXII.

Colophon: Stampato in Vinegia per Giouanni-antonio di Nicolini da || Sabio, & i Fratelli, MDXXXII del mese di Nouēbrio. ||

28 leaves, in quarto, sig. A–O (one gathering). Verso of last leaf blank.   (New York, Metr. Mus. of Art)

[Another edition] . . . MDXXXII.

Colophon: Stampato in Vineggia per maestro Stephano da Sabio || MDXXXIII nel mese di Nouembre. ||

32 leaves, in quarto, sig. A–O, with four extra leaves inserted in the centre (one gathering). Ff. 15 v° to 18 v° contain an alphabet of 'lettere moder-ne' taken from Sigismondo Fanti's book Theorica et pratica. Otherwise the plates in this edition are the same as that of 1531. On the verso of the last leaf is a woodcut of a city.

(Vict. & Albert Mus.)

[Another edition] . . . MDXXXIIII.

Colophon: Stampato in Vineggia per maestro Stephano da Sabio.

28 leaves, in quarto.   (Berlin Kunstgewerbemuseum)

[Another edition] . . . MDXXXIIII.

Colophon: Stampato in Vinegia per Giouan-tonio de Nicolini da Sabio MDXXXIIII, nel mese di Settembre.

28 leaves, in quarto, sig. A–O, one gathering.

(BIRRELL & GARNETT)

[Another edition] . . . MDXXXVI.

Stampato in Venegia per Pietro di Nicolini da Sab||bio, del mese di Nouembrio || M.D.XXXVI ||

32 leaves, in quarto, sig. A–O, with four extra leaves inserted in the centre.

(M. SANDER, Le Livre à figures italien, Milan, 1942, 7172; Leighton's Cat., 1916, No. 1285)

[Another edition] Venice, 1537.
(Noted by C. L. RICKETTS)

[Another edition] . . . MDXXXIX.

Stampato in Venegia per Giouanniantonio de Nicoli- || ni de Sabio, M.D.XXXIX. ||

28 leaves, in quarto, sig. A–O. On the recto of the last leaf is a woodcut of an astronomer taking an observation.   (Bibl. Nat.)

[Another edition] . . . MDXXXX.

Colophon: Stampato in Vinegia per Pietro de Nicolini da Sabbio.

27 leaves, in quarto.   (Berlin, Kunstgewerbemuseum)

[Another edition] . . . MDXXXXII.

Colophon: In Vinegia per Giouanni Antonio, e Pietro fratelli de Nicolini da Sabio. Nel anno del Signore MDXXXXII.

28 leaves, in quarto, sig. b–o.
(RICCARDI, Bibl. Matematica)

[Another edition] Venice, 1544
(Noted by C. L. RICKETTS)

[Another edition]
Colophon: Excudebat Antverpiae || Ioannes Loëus. Anno MDXLV. ||

28 leaves, in quarto, sig. A–G in fours. The blocks of the Venice editions are copied.   (Brit. Mus.)

The Duc d'Estrées Catalogue, 1740, No. 8899, mentions an Antwerp edition of 1546.

[Another edition] Venice, Rampazetto, 1545. In quarto.   (Graesse)

Graesse mentions also editions by Rampazetto of 1546 and 1550.

[Another edition] . . . MDXXXXVI.

Colophon [f. 28 r°]: In Vinegia per Giouann' Antonio, e Pietro fratelli de Nicolini da Sabio || Nel anno de nr̃o Signore. MDXLVI. ||

28 leaves, in quarto, sig. A–O. The plates on ff. 18–21 (devices and a gothic alphabet – Textura) are new and on the verso of the last leaf is the cut of a man using an astronomical instrument. The pages printed from type are reset.   (Brit. Mus.)

[Another edition] . . . MDXXXXX.

Colophon: In Vinegia per Pietro di Nicolini da || Sabio, M.D.L. ||

28 leaves, in quarto, sig. A–O. A reissue of the edition of 1546 with a resetting of the pages printed from type. (*Brit. Mus.*)

[Another edition]
Colophon: Antuerpiae ex Officina || Joannis Loei, Anno M.D.L. ||

28 leaves, in quarto, sig. A–G in fours. A copy of the Venice edition. (*Bibl. Nat.*)

[Another edition]
Venice, per Pietro di Nicolini da Sabio, 1551. In quarto. (Noted by C. L. RICKETTS)

[Another edition] . . . MDXXXXXIII.
Colophon: In Vinegia per Francesco Rampazetto. || L'Anno MDLIII. ||

28 leaves, in quarto, sig. A–O. A reissue of the edition of 1550, with resetting of the pages printed from type. (*Brit. Mus.*)

[Another edition] . . . MDXXXXXIIII.
F. Rampazetto, Venice. 26 leaves, in quarto. (RICCARDI, *Bibl. Matematica*)

[Another edition] . . . MDXXXXXIIIII.
Colophon: In Vinegia, per Francesco Rampazetto. || L'Anno MDLVI. ||

28 leaves, in quarto, sig. A–O.
(BIRRELL & GARNETT)

[Another edition] . . . MDXXXXXX.
Colophon: In Venetia per Francesco Rampazetto. || MDLX. ||

26 leaves in quarto. (*Chicago, Newberry Library*)

[Another edition] s. l. 1561. In quarto.
(RICCARDI, *Bibl. Matematica*)

[Another edition] . . . MDXXXXXXII.
Colophon: In Venetia per Francesco Rampazetto || M.D.LXII. ||

28 leaves, in quarto, sig. A–O. (Maggs Cat. 509)

[Another edition]
Venice, Rampazetto, 1563. In quarto.
(Noted by C. L. RICKETTS)

[Another edition] . . . MDLXV.
Colophon; In Venitia, appresso Francesco Rampazetto. || M.DLXV. ||

26 leaves, in quarto, sig. A–O. (*Bibl. Nat.*)

[Another edition] Venice, 1568.
(Noted by C. L. RICKETTS)

UGO DA CARPI

Ugo da Carpi was a block-maker and not a calligrapher. His work as the perfector of the method of producing coloured woodcuts, known as chiaroscuro, has earned him a place in all the dictionaries of artists. Much more is known about him than about the contemporary writing masters. L. Servidori of recent years has published several articles about his life and work. Ugo da Carpi was born in 1479 or 1480 and died in 1533, as has been shown by Servidori in his article in the *Gutenberg Jahrbuch* for 1937. Formerly it was thought that he was dead by July 1523, which made it difficult to understand his share in the *Thesauro dei scrittori* and other writing books. It appears that he cut the blocks for the first part of Arrighi's book. In 1525 he obtained from the Pope a copyright in this book, but did not recover the blocks. As to this point there is some uncertainty, as no one has been able to compare the first editions. But since a later edition of Carpi's version, Rome, 1535, certainly does not contain the original blocks, the uncertainty is slight. The *Thesauro dei scrittori* is then a copy of portions of Arrighi, Tagliente, and Sigismondo Fanti.

*

THESAVRO DE SCRIT || TORI || *Opera artificiosa laquale con grandissima arte si per pratica* || *come per geometria insegna a Scriuere diuerse sorte littere:* || *cioè Cancellarescha: merchantescha: formata: Cursiua: Antiqua: mo-* || *derna: et bastarda de piu sorte: cum uarij, e, bellissimi exempli &* || *altre sorte littere de uarie lingue: cioè Grecha: hebraicha: Caldea* || *& Arabicha: Tutte extratte da diuersi et probatissimi Auttori: &* || *massimamente dalo preclarissimo* SIGISMVNDO || *fanto nobile ferrarese: mathematico: et Architettore eru-* || *ditissimo: dele mesure, e, ragione de littere primo* || *inuentore: Intagliata per Vgo da* || *Carpi: Cum gratia: et Pri-* || *uilegio* || CON VNA RAGIONE DABBACO || *Anchora insegna de atemperare le Penne secundo diuerse sorte-* || *littere, e cognoscere la bontade de quelle, e, carte: e fare inchiostro* || *et, Verzino. Cenaprio e Vernice: cum multi alti secreti per-* || *tinenti alo Polito: et Eccellente Scrittore: come per se medesi-* || *mo legendo impararai. Ne lanno di nostra salute.* || M.D.XXV. ||

46 leaves, in quarto, sig. A–K, and GG after G, in fours, except sig. A in six. A 1 r° woodcut title; A 1 v°, a cut of a writer's utensils, copied from Tagliente's book; A ii r°, the address to the reader, printed from type; A ii v°, a new plate of Greek minuscules; A iii – E iv plates copied from Tagliente and the second part of Arrighi's book: F & G consist of an alphabet described by Fanti in book 2 of his *Theorica et Pratica*, 1514; GG contains the four leaves of the 'Ragione dabbaco' by Angelus Mutinensis; H–K instructions. Before the words 'Con una ragione dabbaco' is a cut of two hands, the right holding a pen and drawing an S, the left holding an A with

a pair of compasses. Without imprint, but printed by Blado at Rome, whose device occurs on the recto of the last leaf.

(MANZONI, p. 51, seq.; *Plimpton Coll., Columbia, N. Y.,* a copy which is 'Ex Libris Iac. Manzoni'.)

[Another edition] . . . MDXXX [ ]
48 leaves, in quarto, sig. A-A24. A reissue from the blocks of the 1525 edition. The 'Epistola alli lettori', set in an Aldine italic, is on A 1 v°; the copy of the plate from Tagliente representing the utensils is on A 2 r°. On A 3 r° is the title of Tagliente's book with the date altered to MDXXXII. The words 'Con una Ragione dabbaco' on the title-page have been removed. One of the plates, f. 31, is a repeat. The title-page is cropped. Possibly the 1532 edition.

(*Chicago, Newberry Library*)

What appears to be a copy of the edition of 1530 is recorded in Maggs' Cat. 509, No. 1528.

[Another edition] . . . MDXXXV.
48 leaves, in quarto, sig. A-A24. A reissue of the 1525 edition with a different arrangement of the plates. The words 'Con una Ragione dabbaco' on the title-page have been removed. The cut of utensils is on A 1 v°, and the 'Epistola alli lettori' in roman on A 2 3°. On A 3 r° is the title of Tagliente's work with the date altered to MDXXXII. No device of Blado.   (*Brit.Mus.; Chicago, Newberry Library*)

Another issue of 1535 has the 'Epistola alli lettori' printed in italic and other slight variants in the text.

(*Brit. Mus.*)

[Another edition] . . . MDXXXV.
48 leaves, in quarto, sig. A-A24. A reissue of the 1535 edition. The part printed from type has been reset, the 'Epistola' being in roman. From the woodcut initials used the book must have been printed about 1545. They are the initials copied by Blado from those of Giolito of Venice.

(G. W. JONES)

Essling mentions in the footnote to No. 2188 editions by the Nicolini at Venice of 1539, 1545, 1547 and 1550.

EUSTACHIO CELEBRINO

Celebrino's little book on the mercantile hand, of which only three copies are known, was reproduced in facsimile by the Pegasus Press in 1929, edited by Stanley Morison, whose introduction collects the available information about Celebrino's work as a calligrapher, wood-engraver and writer for the Venetian press. Morison describes also the uses and users of the mercantile hand. Celebrino's early work appeared at Perugia in 1511; from 1522, to about 1535, he was working in Venice, where he produced a number of woodcut illustrations for Venetian printers, published some verse and other books of no literary merit. We have noted already that he cut the blocks for the second part of Arrighi's writing book and some at least of the blocks for Tagliente's book.

Il modo d'Imparare di scriuere || lettera Merchantescha || Et ectiam, à far lo Inchiostro, et cognoscer || la Carta. || Con el modo temperare la || penna. || Composto et fatto per lo Ingenioso Maistro || Eustachio Cellebrino da || vdene: || lo año santo M.D.XXV. ||

Four woodcut leaves, in octavo, unnumbered and without signatures. With a small cut of a hand holding a pen on the title-page, and on the verso of the last leaf a cut of the writer's implements. Reproduced by the Pegasus Press, 1929. (*Plimpton Coll., Columbia,*

(*N. Y.; Berlin, Kunstgewerbemuseum*)

GIOVAMBATTISTA PALATINO

Giovambattista Palatino was a native of Rossano in Calabria, who afterwards acquired Roman citizenship. Little is so far known of his life, beyond what is to be inferred from his works. He was one of the most deservedly popular and (despite the strictures of G. F. Cresci, *q. v.*) one of the most accomplished and versatile of Renaissance scribes. He was prominent in the intellectual circles of his time, and appears to have been on terms of friendship with Claudio Tolomei, Dionisio Atanagi, and Girolamo Ruscelli. He was Secretary of the Accademia dei Sdegnati, founded during the pontificate of Paul III by Tolomei and others. According to a document cited by A. Bertolotti (*Artisti subalpini in Roma,* p. 42) Palatino was associated with G. B. Romano in cutting the inscription which adorns the Porta del Popolo in Rome. Two engraved maps in A. Marlianus,

Romae Topographia, 1544, are signed by Palatino; but it is not certain that he is to be credited with the cutting of the blocks. Besides the engraved 'copy books', two manuscript specimen books by Palatino are known. The first, discovered in the Bodleian Library two years ago (Cod. Canon. Ital. 196), has examples dated 1538 and 1541. The second, formerly in the Kunstgewerbemuseum, Berlin (No. 5280), bears the dates 1543, 1546, 1549, and 1574.   J. W.

*

LIBRO NVOVO || D'IMPARARE A SCRIVERE TV- || TE SORTE LETTERE ANTICHE ET MO- || DERNE DI TVTTE NATIONI, || CON NVOVE REGOLE || MISVRE ET ES- || SEMPI || Con vn breue & vtile trattato de le Cifere, Composto per || Giouambattista Palatino

Cittadino Romano. || [Woodcut portrait of the author.] CON GRATIE ET PRIVILEGI. ||

Colophon: Stampata in Roma appresso Campo di Fiore nelle || Case di M. Benedetto Gionta, per Baldassare di || Francesco Cartolari || Perugino, a di 12. || d'Agosto, MDXL. ||

52 leaves, in quarto, sig. A-N in fours. Title in type; A 1 v° blank; A 2 r° privilege from Paul III, dated 16 August 1540, in italic type; A 2 v° verses by Tommaso Spica in woodcut chancery letter; A 3, 4, dedicatory address to Cardinal di Lenoncorte, in roman type, dated from Rome, August 1540. Sig. B-D and E 1 r° examples of 'lettere cancellaresche'; the rest of sig. E 'lettera mercantile'; sig. F 1 r° 'lettera di bolle', v° 'lettera di brevi'; sig. F 2 and F 3 r° 'Cancellaresca formata'; sig. F 3 v° 'Lettera Napolitana'; sig. F 4 'Lettera Francese'; sig. G 1 r° 'Lettera Spagnola'; v° 'Lettera Longobarda'; sig. G 2 r° 'Lettera Tedesca', v° 'Lettera Francese'; sig. G 3 - M. 2 various alphabets, including Greek, Roman, Hebrew, Arabic, etc.; sig. M 3 r° 'Lettera formata', v° woodcut of implements similar to Tagliente's cut, but independent in design; M 4 - N 2 r° text 'Degl Instrumenti' in roman; N 3 r° – N 4 r° 'modo et ordine che deveria tener' in small type; N 4 v° a device of a moth and lighted candle with the motto: 'Et so ben ch'io vo dietro a quel che m'arde'.

The pages printed from type are in roman, except the privilege. In the dedicatory address Palatino assigns the invention of printing to Gutenberg in 1452 and mentions Jenson as the perfector of the art.
(*Brit. Mus.*)

The copy in the Newberry Library has some difference in the setting of the title and has the date 'il di XII Agosto MDXXXX'.

[Another edition]
Antonio Blado, Rome, 1540.

52 leaves, in quarto, sig. A-G in eights, except G in four. The illustrations are printed from the same blocks as the previous edition, but the letterpress is reset in roman type throughout, with different, and poor, decorated initial letters.
(*New York, Metropolitan Museum of Art. Copy on blue paper wanting the title-page and the last leaf*)

[Another edition]
Colophon: In Roma nella contrada del Pellegrino per || Madonna Girolama de Cartolari || Perugina. Il Mese di Maggio. M.D.XLIII. ||

52 leaves, in quarto, sig. A-G in eights, except G in four. (MANZONI, p. 161; TREGASKIS CAT. 973, No. 286)

[Another edition] Rome, 1544, In quarto.
(Noted by C. L. RICKETTS)

[Another edition] LIBRO DI M. GIOVANBATTISTA || PALATINO Cittadino Romano, Nel qual || s'insegna à Scriuere ogni sorte Lette||ra . . . Riueduto nuoua-

mente, & corretto dal proprio Autore, || CON LA GIVNTA DI QVINDICI TAVO- || LE BELLISSIME. || [The Portrait of Palatino.] CON GRATIE, ET PRIVILEGI ||

Colophon: In Roma in Campo di Fiore, per Antonio || Blado Asolano il mese d'Ottobre, || M.D.XLV. ||

64 leaves, in quarto, sig. A-H, in eights. On the verso of the last leaf but one is the moth and candle device; the last leaf is blank. The letterpress is printed in italic, except the dedication to Cardinal Ridolfo Pio da Carpi, dated October 1545, in roman (A III and A IIII). With the woodcut initials which Blado copied from Giolito. The new plates, referred to in the title, are dated 1545. They include 'lettera rognosa', 'tagliata', 'notaresca', 'Fiammenga', and 'moderna'. The first enlarged edition.
(MANZONI, p. 161; BIRRELL & GARNETT)

An edition of 1546 is mentioned in the Duc d'Estrées' Catalogue of 1740, No. 8902.

[Another edition]
Colophon: In Roma in Campo di Fiore, per Antonio || Blado Asolano, il mese di Genaro. || MDXLVII. ||

64 leaves, in quarto, sig. A-H in eights.
(*Vict. & Albert Mus.*)

[Another edition]
Colophon: Il mese di Luglio, || MDXLVIII. ||

64 leaves, in quarto, sig. A-H. A reissue of the edition of 1547 with a simple alteration of date.
(*Brit. Mus.*)

[Another edition]
Colophon: Il mese di Agosto || M.D.L. ||

64 leaves, in quarto, sig. A-H. The pages printed from type have been reset. A reissue of the 1548 edition. (*Brit. Mus.*)

According to Manzoni, there were two editions in 1550.

[Another edition]
Colophon: Il mese di Settembre. || MDLIII. ||

64 leaves, in quarto, sig. A-H. In this reissue the letterpress from E 4 is in roman type. (*Brit. Mus.*)

[Another edition]
Colophon: In Roma dirimpetto à santo Hieronimo, per || Antonio Mario Guidotto Mātouano. || & Duodecimo Viotto Parmesano socio, alli XVI. de No- ||uēbre, MDLVI. ||

64 leaves, in quarto, sig. A-H. Palatino's device is here on the recto of H 8. Letterpress in roman; no change in the plates. A copy on blue paper is recorded (*see Cat. della Libreria Capponi*, Rome, 1747, p. 281). (*Brit. Mus.*)

[Another edition]
Colophon: In Roma per Valerio Dorico alla ||

FIG. 2. Amphiareo, 1555.

Chiauica de Santa Lucia. || Ad instantia de m. Giouan della Gatta. || L'Anno MDLXI. ||

64 leaves, in quarto, sig. A-H. Preface in italic, remaining letterpress roman.   (*Brit. Mus.*)

COMPENDIO || DEL GRAN VOLVME DE L'ARTE DEL BENE ET || LEGGIARDRAMENTE SCRIVERE || TUTTE LE SORTI DI LETTERE || ET CARATTERI, || Con le lor Regole misure, & Essempi, || DI M. GIOAN-BATTISTA PALATINO || CITTADINO ROMANO. || . . . *Et con l'aggionta d'alcune Tauole, & altri particu-lari* . . . IN ROMA *alla Chiauica di S. Lucia, per li Heredi di Valerio* || & *Luigi Dorici Fratelli Bresciani l'Anno* 1566. ||

Colophon: In Roma per gli Heredi di Valerio, & Aloigi || Dorici Fratelli, Nel mese di Giugno || L'Anno MDLXVI. ||

64 leaves, in quarto, sig. A-H in eights. A I r° title in type; A I v° the portrait of Palatino; A 2 r° privilege of Paul III, A 2 v° verses by Tommaso Spica, in roman. A III – A v a new preface by Palatino, in italic; A VI is a woodcut title-page; Il Modo d'im-parare à Scriuere la lettera || Cancellaresca Romana, || nella forma che' è detta || corrente. || Con le sue proprie Regole, et misure proportionate, || Ritrouato, et Composto || da M. Giovanbattista Palatino, Citta-

dino || ROMANO || & da lui stesso di nuouo corretto, || L'Anno di nostra || Salute, || MDLXVI. || Con Gratie & Privileggi. || A VI v° - C III new plates headed 'Cancellaresca Romana' i. e. testegiatta; the text being identical with that of *Libro*, bearing dates, 1540, 1564, 1565 and 1566; C IIII to the end the blocks of the earlier editions, with the moth and candle device on H VIII v°; letterpress in roman.
(*Brit. Mus.*)

[Another edition] 1575.
(Noted by C. L. RICKETTS)

[Another edition] . . . [Sessa's device]
IN VENETIA, || *Appresso gli Heredi di Marchio Sessa.* 1578. ||

62 leaves, in quarto, sig. A-H in eights, except H in six. Preface in italic, remaining letterpress in roman. A reissue of the edition of 1566.   (*Brit. Mus.*)

[Another edition] . . . [Sessa's device]
In Venetia, MDLXXXVIII. || Appresso Aluise Sessa. ||

Colophon: In Venetia, || per Gio. Antonio Rampazetto. || MDLXXXVIII. ||

62 leaves, in quarto, sig. A-H in eights, except H in six. The moth and candle device occurs on the recto of the last leaf.   (*Brit. Mus.*)

DOMENICO MANZONI

Domenico Manzoni of Oderzo, near Venice, pub-lished his *Quaderno doppio*, a work on book-keeping, at Venice in 1540. There were a number of editions, including that of 1564, entitled *Libro mercantile*, which contains some examples of writing. Beyond his school book of 1546 nothing further seems to be known of him. See Riccardi's *Bibl. Matem.*

★

LIBRETTO || MOLTO VTILE || *per impara a leg-* || *gere, scriuere* || & *abaco.* || CON ALCVNI FONDA- || MENTI DELLA || dottrina christiana. || [A fleuron] CON GRATIA ET PRIVILEGIO, || *In Vinegia per Comin de* || *Trino* Lanno, MDXLVI. ||

24 leaves, in octavo. The title printed in red and black is in a woodcut border bearing the initials D M, copied from a Holbein border done for Adam Petri at Basle. The author's name, Domenico Man-zoni, is given in the printer's address to the readers on f. I v° printed in 'Basle' italic. ff. 2-4 r° in Ro-tunda, ff. 4 v° - 6 r° roman, f. 6 v° and f. 7 r° Aldine italic; ff. 7 v° - 9 r° 'littera cancellaresca', 'merchan-tesca', 'bastarda' and again Chancery. The remainder

of the book is in Aldine italic, except on the recto of the last leaf, where there are a few lines in a type based on the 'lettera mercantile'. A school book containing prayers and an arithmetic.
(*Brit. Mus.*)

LIBRO MERCANTILE || ORDINATO CON SUO || Gior-nale & Alfabeto, per tener conti doppi || al modo di Venetia, et potrà seruir || in ogn'altro luogo, || AGIUNTOVI ALCVNE || COSE NECESSARIE, et || vtili à maggior intelligenza di || ciascune. || CON ALCVNE SORTI DI LITTERE || cancellaresche, mercantesche, et bastarde || ET DVE ALFABETI || di miniature bellissimi || DI DOMINICO MANZONI || DA VDERZO. IN VENETIA || MDL.VIIII. ||

In quarto. The calligraphic part occupies the last eight leaves.   (RICCARDI, *Bibl. Matematica*)

Earlier editions of this work – the first appeared in 1540, with the title 'Doppio quaderno' – did not contain the specimens of letters. Riccardi notes later editions in 1565, 1573 and 1574.

VESPASIANO AMPHIAREO

Vespasiano, a Franciscan, was born at Ferrara in 1501, died 1563. In the dedication to his 1554 edition he says that he had been teaching writing for thirty years. According to Sbaralea's *Scriptores Trium Or-*

dinum S. Francisci he belonged to the family of Albertacci. He is not recorded as publishing any other work.

★

VNO NOVO MODO D'INSEGNAR A SCRIVERE ET FOR-
MAR LETTERE DI PIV SORTE || CHE DA ALTRI NON
PRIMA C'HORA VSATE: || NOVAMENTE DA FRATE
VESPASIANO MINORITANO || TROVATO, E DA LVI PVR
HORA DATO IN LUCE. || CON IL SVO PRIVILEGIO. ||
[Device of Troiano]

48 leaves, oblong octavo (140 × 220 mm), sig. * in
four, A-E in eights, F in four. Title, imprint on
verso: In Vinegia, per Curtio Troiano d'i Nauo. ||
MDXLVIII; 2 pp. of dedication to the Doge, Francesco Donato, 4 pp. of text, 85 pp. of woodcut
alphabets, etc., 2 pp. of text, verso of last leaf blank.
Each leaf mounted, but not necessarily a made-up
copy. *(Chicago, Newberry Library)*

OPERA DI FRATE VESPA || SIANO AMPHIAREO DA
FERRARA DEL || L'ORDINE MINORE CONVENTVALE,
NELLA QVALE || SI INSEGNA A SCRIVERE VARIE
SORTI DI LETTERE, ET MASSIME || VNA LETTERA
BASTARDA DA LVI NOVAMENTE CON SVA || IN-
DVSTRIA RITROVATA, LAQVAL SERVE AL || CAN-
CELLARESCO ET MERCANTESCO. || POI INSEGNA A
FAR L'INCHIOSTRO NEGRISSIMO CON TANTA || *fa-
cilità, che ciascuno per semplice che sia, lo saprà far
da se. Ancorha a macinar l'oro et scriuere con || esso
come si farà con l'inchiostro parimente a scriuere con
l'azuro, & col Cinaprio || opera utilissima e molto
necessaria all'uso humano.* || CON PRIVILEGIO. ||
[Device of Giolito]

IN VINEGIA APPRESSO GABRIEL GIOLITO DE ||
FERRARI ET FRATELLI MDLIIII. ||

48 leaves, oblong (144 × 200 mm), sig. * in four,
A-E, in eights, F in four. Title in type, verso blank;
preliminary leaves, including the dedication to the
Doge, Francesco Donato, in italic; sig. A-F 3 r°
printed from blocks; F 3 v° and F 4 r° in italic type;
F 4 v° blank. Illustrations of the manner of constructing Rotunda and roman capitals by geometrical
means are given, D 6 - F 3 r°. *(Brit. Mus.)*

Two other variants of this edition are known. They
have printers' flowers on the title-page in place of
Giolito's device, and have no printer's name. There
are slight variations in the setting of the title and
dedication. One variant has a different woodcut A
at the beginning of the dedication. This A occurs in
the edition of 1556. (BIRRELL & GARNETT)

[Another edition] . . . [Cut of hands holding pen
and compass]
IN VENETIA, MDLV.

48 leaves, oblong, sig. * in four, A-E in eights, F in
four. A reissue of the 1554 edition, with the letterpress reset. No printer's name, but from the woodcut initials used it appears to have been printed by
Geronimo Scotto. (See Fig. 2.)   *(Brit. Mus.)*

[Another edition] . . . [Device of Comin da Trino]

IN VINEGIA PER COMIN DA TRINO DI MONFERRATO,
|| L'ANNO M.D.LVI. ||

48 leaves, oblong sig. * in four, A-E in eights, F in
four. Differs from the two preceding editions in the
setting of the letterpress only.   *(Brit. Mus.)*

[Another edition] Venice, 1557.
(Noted by C. L. RICKETTS)

[Another edition] Venice, 1558.
(Noted by C. L. RICKETTS)

[Another edition] . . .
IN VENETIA. MDLVIIII,

48 leaves, oblong, sig. * in four, A-E in eights, F in
four. No printer's name. The types and woodcut
initials are different from the editions of 1554, 1555,
and 1556.   *(Brit. Mus.)*

[Another edition] Venice, 1564.
(Noted by C. L. RICKETTS)

[Another edition] . . .
IN VENETIA, MDLXV.

48 leaves, oblong. A reissue of the edition of 1559.
(G. W. JONES)

[Another edition] . . . Venice, 1566.
48 leaves; 4 preliminary leaves, A-E in eights, F in
four.   (M. HERTZBERGER, Amsterdam)

[Another edition] . . . AGGIVNTOVI DI NVOVO DUE
BELLISSIMI ALPHABETI . . . di Maiuscole . . .[cut of
hand holding pen]
IN VENETIA, MDLXXII.

56 leaves, oblong, sig. * in four, A-F in eights, and
G in four. No printer's name. In this edition the
instructions at the end are printed on one page.
(BONFI, *Annali di Giolito*; Brit. Mus.)

Birrell & Garnett had a fragment of another edition,
containing the additional 'Maiuscole' and with the
instructions occupying two pages. This is perhaps an
edition between the 1565 and the 1572.

[Another edition] Venice, 1575.
(Noted by C. L. RICKETTS)

[Another edition] Alessandro Gardano, Venice, 1580.
(Plimpton Coll., Columbia, N.Y.)

[Another edition] Cavalcalupo, Venice, 1583.
(BONGI)

[Another edition] . . .
IN VENETIA, APPRESSO GIO. ANTONIO RAMPAZETTO,
1588.

56 leaves, oblong, sig. *A* in four, A-F in eights,
and G in four. The title-page is followed by three
leaves of text and 51 plates (? the last leaf blank).
(Vict. & Albert Mus.)

[Another edition] 1589. No printer's name (BONGI)

[Another edition] 1596. (Noted by C. L. RICKETTS)

Another edition appeared in 1620.

FERDINANDO RUANO

Ruano was a Spaniard, a native of Badajoz, who was employed at the Vatican Library as a 'Scrittore latino' from 1541 till his death in 1560. In the Vatican Library are a number of manuscripts copied by him. The *Sette Alphabeti* seems to have been his only published book. The 'C. Paceñ.' on the title-page is in full 'Clericus Pacensis' i. e. of the Diocese of Badajoz. See G. Levi della Vida, *Ricerche sulla formazione del più antico fondo dei manoscritti orientali della Biblioteca Vaticana* (No. 92 of *Studi e Testi*), and R. Bertieri, *Gutenberg Jahrbuch*, Mainz, 1940, and especially James Wardrop's 'The Vatican Scriptors' in *Signature* No. 5. N. S.

*

SETTE || ALPHABETI || DI VARIE LET- || TERE. || FOR-MATI CON RAGION GEOMETRICA || Da Ferdinando Ruano. c. Paceñ. || scrittor della biblioteca ||

Vaticana. || Nouamente posti in luce. || IN ROMA per Valerio Dorico & Luigi fratelli || Bressani, nel M.D.LIIII. ||

44 leaves, in folio (270 × 203 mm), sig. A-E in eights and F in four. Title in type, verso the dedication; A 2 - B 6 treat of the method of forming the roman alphabet, capitals and lower-case, with woodcut illustrations; B 8 - D 5 r° of the 'lettera moderna'; D 5 v° - E 2 'lettera cancellaresca formata'; E 3-5 'lettera maiuscola bollatica'; E 6 - F 4 'lettera maiuscola thedesca'.

On the title-page are the arms of Cardinal Marcello Cervino to whom the book is dedicated. On the verso of the last leaf is the device of the Dorici. The text is in italic. (See Fig. 3.)

(*Vict. & Albert Mus.; Vatican Lib.*)

GIOVANNI FRANCESCO CRESCI

Cresci, a son of Bartolomeo Cresci of Pistoia, was brought up in Milan, proceeded to Rome in 1552 and in 1556 became a Scriptor in the Vatican Library. He worked at the papal court under the Popes Pius IV and Pius V as calligrapher of the 'Capella pontificia'. According to F. de Boni, *Biografia degli artisti*, his writing book was copied in 1566 under another name, the blocks being cut by Cesare Moreggio. This seems to refer to Palatino's *Compendio*, in which the new plates owe something to Cresci and in which the help of Moreggio is mentioned. After the death of Pius V in 1572, Cresci returned to Milan and lived on into the seventeenth century. His son Gianfrancesco was also a calligrapher. In 1622, after the father's death, the son published *L'Idea con le circonstanze naturali che a quella si ricercano, per voler legittimamente posseder l'arte maggiore e minore dello scrivere*, a work by the elder Cresci, which is an attack on Palatino (copy in the Bibl. Nat.). See Pouget, *Dictionnaire de Chifres*, Paris 1767. The account there given of the relations of Cresci and Palatino, written by Paillasson, does not altogether agree with the account in Boni. As late as 1638 G. B. Bidelli published at Milan specimens of Cresci's hands, along with the *Regole* of Marcello Scalino. See Wardrop's 'The Vatican Scriptors' in *Signature* No. 5. N. S.

*

ESSEMPLARE || DI PIV SORTI LETTERE DI M. Gio. || Francesco Cresci Milanese, Scrittore della || Libraria Apostolica. || [A Fleuron] DOVE SI DIMO-STRA LA VERA ET NVOVA FORMA DELLO || *Scriuere Cancellaresco Corsiuo, da lui ritrouata, & da molti hora communemente posta in vso.* || *Con vn breue trattato sopra le Maiuscole antiche Romane, per il qual s'intende la vera* || *regola di formarle secondo*

l'arte, e 'l giuditio de gli antichi. Si descrivue ancora la || *prattica, che con la penna al buon Scrittore s'appartiene hauere in dette* || *Maiuscole, & altri sorti di lettere, nouamente dal detto* || *Autore composto, & à commune vtilità* || *dato in luce.* || IN RO-MA, PER ANTONIO BLADO AD INSTANZA || DEL AVTORE, MDLX. || [A Fleuron] *Con priuilegio per Anni X.* ||

Oblong. 14 leaves and LVI numbered woodcut plates. The title-page, within a woodcut border, is followed by a privilege for ten years granted by Pope Pius IV and dated 5 July 1560. Then comes the author's dedication to Cardinal Borromeo, dated 7 September 1560, then an address to the readers, and an index. In the preliminary matter is a statement that the plates were cut by Giovan Francesco Aureri da Crema, intagliatore in Roma, after Cresci's designs. Pls. I-XXXI Chancery hand, pl. XXXII and XXXIII 'lettera bollatica', pls. XXXIIII-XXXVII 'mercantile', pls. XXXVIII-XXXI Chancery, XXXXII and XXXXIII roman, XXXXIIII-LV an alphabet of large roman capitals, printed white on black. Each page is surrounded by woodcut borders.

> L'ART ANCIEN, *Lugano, copy on vellum, in a binding of Count Giulio Cesare Borromeo; Vienna, Österreich, Mus. f. Kunst; Rome, Bibl. Vittorio Emanuele II; Chicago, Newberry Library.*

[Another edition] . . .
Roma, A. Blado, 1563. Oblong 4°.
    (A. van der Willigen Cat., Amsterdam, 1875)

[Another edition] . . .
In Roma Per Antonio Blado Ad Instanza di Giovan Dalla Gatta. 1566.

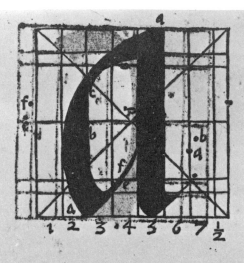

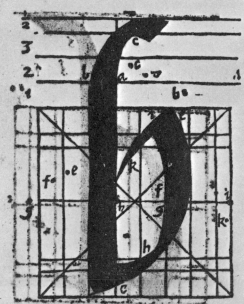

LA lettera .A. si forma nel suo quadro il qual
tu partirai come io t'ho detto: & per far il suo
caso metterai il compasso nel punto del .a. che sta
nella 7. linea sotto il diametro, & risponda sopra
la .6. linea doue ti segna un'altra .a. & farai me
zo circolo che fornisca alla .3. linea doue trouarai
un'altra .a. Il suo ouato, ouer cauo si forma in tre
mezi circoli, cioè mettendo il compasso nel punto
del .b. che trouarai alla .7. linea sotto il diametro,
& risponda alla .3. linea, & cominciarai dal detto
diametro doue ti segna l'altro .b. & uenirà al me
zo della terza testa: il secondo sarà il punto del .c.
il qual trouarai nella linea che serra il quadro à
mano manca sopra il diametro, & risponderà il
compasso alla .3. linea cominciando dal detto diametro, et andarà di sopra fin alla linea angolare:
il terzo sarà il punto del .d. il qual trouarai nella
.5. linea sopra il diametro, & risponda di sopra
la medesima linea, & alla prima linea sotto quella
del quadro, & uenirà fin alla angolare, che si lie
ghe con quella del .c. La sua tondezza di sotto si
forma mettendo il compasso nel punto del e, & ri
sponda sotto la .3. linea, & farai mezo circolo che
arriui alla .5. linea sotto il diametro, farai unaltro
mezo circolo sopra questo, & discosto un quinto
mettendo il compasso nel punto del .f. liquali due
punti .e, & .f. trouarai a man dritta di fuora al
quadro, & sarà formato il caso. La sua gamba
uuole esser dritta, et discosta dal detto caso due te
ste. In loco di base farai una testina sguinza con-
forme a i punti che trouarai. E te bisogna auuer
tire che come hai fatto questa .a. farai il b.c.d.e.
g.h.o.p.q.x. con quelli medesimi punti, et circoli. Et questo ti basti hauendo l'essemplare inanzi.

LA lettera .B. si forma come l'a, saluo chel suo astillo esce fuora del quadro tre teste, & meza,
& della prima testa sopra il quadro farai la sua tondezza con un poco di testina anchora in ton
do: & per farla seguirai l'ordine de i punti come nell'a. & questo astillo ti seruirà per d.f.h.l.

FIG. 3. Ruano, 1554. (Reduced.)

Oblong. 14 leaves of text with LVI woodcut plates. The privilege is dated 1560. A reissue of the edition of 1560.   (*Berlin, Kunstgewerbemuseum*)

[Another edition] . . .
Heredi di Antonio Blado, Roma. 1568.

Oblong. 16 leaves of text and 56 plates.
                              (*Leipzig, Börsenverein*)

[Another edition] . . .
In Venetia appresso Francesco Rampazzetto, ad instantia di Gio. Antonio degli Antonij. 1575. Oblong 4°. 44 leaves.
                    (LIBRERIA VINCIANA, MILAN, 1947)

ESSEMPLARE || DI PIV SORTI LETTERE, || *Di M. Gio. Francesco Cresci Milanese, Scrittore in Roma.* || *DOVE SI DIMOSTRA LA VERA ET NOVA FORMA DELLO Scriuere Cancellaresco Corsiuo, da lui ritrouata, & da molti hora comunemente posta in vso.* || *Con un breue Trattato sopra le Maiuscole antiche Romane, per il qual s'intende la* || *vera regola di formarle secondo l'arte, e 'l giudicio de gli antichi* || *Si descriue ancora la pratica, che con la penna al buon Scrittore s'appartiene hauere in dette* || *Maiuscole, & altre sorti di lettere, nouamente dal detto Autor e composto,* || *& à commune vtilità dato in luce.* ||

In Venetia Appresso gli Heredi di Francesco Rampazetto, Ad instantia || *di Gio. Antonio de gli Antonij.* M.D.LXXVIII. ||

[Decoration of printer's flowers.]

Oblong (156 × 210 mm), sig. ★, ★★, ★★★, A-H, in fours. 16 leaves and LVI plates numbered on both sides.   (*Brit. Mus.*)

A variant of the 1578 edition has different flowers on the title-page and a different order of the woodcut borders. The preface also has been reset and some lines added which were omitted in the first issue at the top of the second page.
                              (BIRRELL & GARNETT)

[Another edition] . . .
In Vinegia, Presso Altobello Salicato, MDLXXXIII. || *Alla Libraria della Fortezza.* ||

Oblong. 16 leaves and LVI numbered plates. A re-issue of the edition of 1578.   (G. W. JONES)

[Another edition] . . .
IN VINEGIA, Presso Altobello Salicato, MDC.

Oblong, sig. †, ††, †††, A-H in fours. 16 leaves and LVI numbered plates. A reissue of the edition of 1578.   (*Brit. Mus.*)

IL PERFETTO SCRITTORE || *Di M. Gio. Francesco Cresci Cittadino Melanese.* || *Doue si veggono i veri Caratteri, & le natural* || *forme di tutte quelle sorti di lettere, che* || *à vero scrittor si*

appartengono. || *Con alcun' altre da lui nuouamente ritrouate.* || *Et i modi, che deue tenere il mastro* || *per ben insegnare.* ||

Colophon: STAMPATO IN ROMA || in casa del proprio autore & intaglia- || to per l'Eccellente intagliator || M. Francesco Aure-||ri da Crema. ||

Oblong (153 × 235 mm). 51 leaves. Title, in an engraved border, containing a portrait of Cresci, one leaf; privilege from Pope Pius V, dated 'Septimo idus Martij, anno sexto', i. e. 1571, verso blank, one leaf; four further leaves of preliminaries including a preface dated 1 November 1570, followed by 45 leaves of plates, sig. A-M in fours, except I, which is a single leaf. The plates are surrounded by woodcut borders. A 1 - G 3 r° treat of 'cancellaresca' and 'antica tonda', G 4 - M 4 'ecclesiastica', 'bollatica', 'mercantile' and 'francese'. A different work from the 'Essemplare'.
          (*Berlin, Kunstgewerbemuseum; Chicago, Newberry Library; Vict. & Albert Mus.; Vatican Lib.*)

Mr. A. L. VAN GENDT, Amsterdam, had a copy with the words 'Parte prima' at the end of the title. The title itself is the same in wording, but differs in the setting.

IL PERFETTO SCRITTORE || DI M. GIO. FRANCESCO CRESCI || CITTADINO MELANESE || Doue si contengono le vere forme delle Maiuscole || antiche Romane, necessarie all'arte || del perfetto scriuere. || Co 'l suo discorso. || *Con un vaghissimo capriccio di molti groppi accommodati* || *sopra la forma d'vn Alfabeto Maiuscolo cancellaresco,* || *da lui ritrouato,* || *Et insieme l'auiso di quello, che deue osseruare lo scrittore* || *nel far capricci alle sorti di lettere.* || *Opera nuouamente, à commune vtilita data in luce.* || Parte seconda. ||

Oblong (153 × 235 mm). 40 leaves. 4 preliminary leaves, including the title-page with a copper-engraved border and a dedication dated 1 November 1570, followed by intaglio alphabets of initials in 36 leaves. The plates of the first set of roman initials are surrounded by letterpress arabesque borders and printed white on black, woodcut; the second set is also roman, white on black, woodcut; the third set is one of 'maiuscole cancellaresche', i. e. entrelacs, and is engraved, some plates bearing the monogram of Andrea Marelli.
                    (*Berlin, Kunstgewerbemuseum*)

A copy in the Met. Mus. of Art, N. Y., has the third set of initials first, and the first set third. The plates measure 152 × 214 mm.

IL PERFETTO SCRITTORE || *di M. Gio. Francesco Cresci Cittadino Milanese.* || *Doue si si veggono i veri Caratteri, & le natural* || *forme di tutte quelle sorti di lettere, che* || *à vero scrittor si appartengono,* || *Con alcun'altre da lui nuouamente ritrouate.* || *Et i modi, che deue tenere il mastro* || *per ben insegnare.* ||

Colophon: IN VENETIA, || Nella Stamparia de i Rampazetti. || Ad instantia di Gio. Antonio de gli Antonij. ||

Oblong (178 × 240 mm). 48 leaves, sig. A-F in eights. The title-page has an engraved border. Each page is surrounded by a woodcut border. Another edition of the first part printed at Rome in 1570. (*Brit. Mus.*)

In the Catalogue of the Libreria Vinciana, Milan, 1947, an imperfect copy of an edition of *Il Perfetto Scrittore* is entered, which, according to the Catalogue, is probably not that of Rome, 1570, nor the Venice edition.

IL PERFETTO CANCELLARESCO CORSIVO || DI GIO-VAN FRANCESCO CRESCI || GENTILHVOMO MILANESE || COPIOSO D'OGNI MANIERA DI LETTERE APPARTE-NENTI || à Secretarij, adornato di bellissime, & vaghe Inuentioni di Caratteri; & col- || legamenti, nuouamente posti in vso dallo stesso Autore. || Con vn'breue discorso circa l'honore, & vtile, che apparta al Secretario lo scriuer' bene. || Et con vtili dechiarationi quando s'hanno ad vsare dette diuerse Forme di Lettere, & perche. || LIBRO TERZO || [Printers' flowers] CON

LICENTIA DE' SVPERIORI. || IN ROMA, Appresso Pietro Spada ad instantia dell'Autore, & di || M. Pietro Pauolo Palombo Libraro. M.D. LXXIX. ||

Oblong (128 × 190 mm). The first line of the title is in a border of printers' flowers. 6 preliminary leaves and 52 numbered and engraved plates, printed on one side of the leaf only. Fol. 2 is occupied by a dedicatory address from the author to Hippolito Agostini, f. 3 by verses addressed to Cresci, and ff. 4-6 by an address to the readers. (*Brit. Mus.*)

IL QVARTO LIBRO || DI LETTERE FORMATELLE || & Cancellaresche corsiue. || DEL S. GIOAN FRANCE-SCO CRESCI || Gentil'huomo Milanese. || *Nuouamente posto in luce per Siluio Valesi Parmeggiano.* || Con vn Alphabetto di lettere maiuscole a groppi, & vno di lettere Ecclesiastice || del R. P. D. Fulgentio Valesi Monaco Cisterciense. || [four flower units] IN ROMA, per Pietro Spada. || Ad instantia di detto Siluio. Lanno 1596. || *Con licentia delli Signori Superiori.* ||

Oblong (130 × 190 mm). 33 leaves; title, 2 pp. of text and 31 metal (?) cuts of Chancery hands and alphabets; many dated 1579, 1580, without titles of the hands; cancellarescha corsiva; cancellarescha formata for use in Latin text; moderna; gothic entrelac initials. (*Chicago, Newberry Library*)

AUGUSTINO DA SIENA

OPERA DEL REVERENDO || PADRE DON AVGVSTINO DA || SCIENA MONACHO CERTOSINO; NELLA || quale si insegna à scriuere varie sorte de littere, tan- || to cancellaresche, quanto mercantesche, || CON VARIE SORTI DE LITTERE TODES- || CHE, ET CON DIVERSE SORTI DE ALPHABETI BELLIS- || simi, & con alcune dechiarationi del temperar del- ||la penna, & vna recetta per far l'inchiostro || negrissimo con tanta facilità, che ciasche || duno per semplice che sia lo farà. || OPERA NVOVA NON PIV DATA IN LUCE. || [A fleuron and printer's device] IN VENETIA per Francesco de Tomaso di Salo || e compagni in Frezzaria, al segno della Fede. ||

40 leaves, in quarto, sig. A-E in eights. Each plate is surrounded by a woodcut border, of which there are four varieties. Some of the plates are dated 1565. The second and the last leaf are printed in roman type. (*Berlin, Kunstgewerbemuseum*)

[Another edition] . . .
IN VENETIA per Francesco di Tomaso di Salò || e compagni . . . MDLXVIII. ||

40 leaves, in quarto, sig. A-E in eights. (*Brit. Mus.*)

[Another edition] . . .
In Venetia; Per Francesco de Tomaso di Salò, e compagni || . . .MDLXXIII ||

40 leaves, in quarto, sig. A-E. (*Bibl. Nat.*)

GIULIANTONIO HERCOLANI

Hercolani appears in G. Fantuzzi, *Notizie degli Scrittori Bolognesi*, 1783, tom. 3, p. 274, under the form Ercolani. His father was Giovanni Francesco. He was a Doctor of Law and also Prior of the Church of La Maddalena in Bologna. He had his tomb prepared and composed his own epitaph dated 1567, and according to Fantuzzi lived for many years

beyond that date. In 1577 he published his *Secretario breve*, a manual on the writing of letters.

★

ESSEMPLARE VTILE || Di tutte le sorti di l're cancellaresche correntissime, et altre vsate, cosi nella Corte de N. S^re come in quella della ||

Maestà Cesarea, et di i SS^{ri} e Principi Italiani: Fatto da me Giuliantonio Hercolani Bolognese || A GLORIA DE IDDIO || & A || Riuerentia de || L'Illmo e R^{mo} Mons^{gre} Card^{le} Paleotti Vescouo E Prencipe & Sor Mio Col^{mo}. || Sotto l' || Ombra della cui eccel^{te} virtù intendo che riposi questa mia fatica à giouamento di tutti quegli che sensa spesa d' || alcun'altro Maestro uorrano presto imparare et sapere is- || criuere tutte le mie l're. ||

Oblong. The engraved title-page is followed by 33 other engraved and numbered plates printed on one side only, many bearing the date 1571. The first plate after the title is a highly involved gothic L (Lettori); plates 2-4 are devoted to instruction; with plate 5 begins the series of writing specimens.

(*Chicago, Newberry Library*)

L° SCRITTOR' VTILE || et brieue Segreta-rio || Da me Giuliantonio Hercolani fatt'in testi-monio || della mia diuotissima seruitù || All'Illmo

& R^{mo} Mons^{re} il Sor Card^{al} Sansisto & Mio S^{or} || & Padrone Col^{mo} || p giouare à tutti quegli, alli quali piacerà. || l'anno 1574. ||

Oblong (190 × 255 mm, page measurement). An engraved title-page with a border, followed by 33 numbered plates (the plates of the 1571 edition), most of them signed and with the date altered to 1574. Printed on one side of the leaf only. Pl. 1 gothic L; pls. 2-12, 14-18, 20-2 Chancery letter; pl. 13 gothic G; pl. 19 gothic M; pls. 23-6 'lettera moderna'; pls. 27-30 grotesque initials; pls. 31-3 roman capitals. Followed by four additional leaves with the title 'Giunta . . . doue si insegna à ciascuno di fare Vernice bianca, Inchiostro, . . . In Bologna, Per Alessandro Bernacci'. Printed in italic. A copy in the Newberry Library has a dedication plate following the title addressed to Cardinal Gustavillani and Cardinal di Vercello, dated 1574. A copy in the Metropolitan Museum of Art, New York, has a dedication following the title addressed to Cardinal Paleotti and at the end six further plates in the place of the four leaves. (See Fig. 4.)

(*Vict. & Albert Mus.*)

CONRETTO DA MONTE REGALE

Conretto describes himself on the title-page of his book as 'scrittore, arithmetico e geom.'. In Riccardi, *Bibl. Matem.*, there is entered a work entitled *Invention Nouvelle pour faire toute sorte de compte*, by Monte Regale, Piemontese, 1585. The copy was in the Libri collection and was described in the Libri catalogue, 1859, as unique. The title-page is re-produced in D. E. Smith, *Rara Arithmetica*, 1908 (? the Libri copy, in the Plimpton collection, Co-lumbia), from which it appears that the author was Professor of Mathematics at Paris. He may be identified with Conretto, whose writing book, in both editions, is almost as rare.

*

VN NOVO ET FACIL || MODO D'IMPARAR' A SCRI-VERE || varie sorti di lettere con le sue dichiara-tioni, & diuerse maniere || d'Alfabeti di Maiu-scole moderne, Con altre regole per || scriuere con Oro, Argento & altri colori; || *La vera ricetta di far Inchiostro perfetissimo in tre maniere; & gl'auertimenti che si deue* || *hauere nel temprar le penne,* || *Nuouamente descritto dal* CONRETTO *da monte Regale di Piemonte,* || *Scrittore, Arithmetico e Geom.* || Con priuilegio della sereniss. Signoria di Venetia, & d'altri Prencipi. || [a rule].

IN VENETIA, MDLXXVI. || *Per Pietro Dehuchino ad instantia del proprio Autore.* ||

Oblong (140 × 190 mm). 40 leaves, sig. A-K in fours. Title in type (within woodcut border in four pieces), verso blank; dedication to Vincentio Gon-zaga of Mantua, dated Venice 20 February 1576, A 2 - A 3 r° in italic. A 3 v° - A 4 v° a 'trattato' on the most famous Italian scribes, in which are men-tioned Vespasiano, Palatino and Cresci, and a num-ber of others who do not appear to have published their work. Among these are Vicenzo Busdrago, the printer of Lucca and Francesco Moro [Poliviani] of Padua, whose manuscript specimen book is now in the Victoria and Albert Museum. B-C 3 r° further introductory text, printed partly in italic, partly in roman; each page is surrounded by borders of prin-ters' flowers. The plates, surrounded by woodcut borders, deal with the Chancery letter (C 3 v° - F 3 r°); 'mercantile' (F 3 v° - G 2 r°); initials of 'bollatica moderna' (G 2 v°); 'moderna formata' (G 3, 4); roman (H 1-4 r°), and plates of Gothic and roman initials.   (*Vict. & Albert Mus.*)

[Another edition] . . .

In Venetia, appresso Bartolomeo Carampello. MDLXXXIII.

Obl. quarto. 40 leaves surrounded by woodcut borders. Sig. A-K in fours.

(*Berlin, Kunstgewerbemuseum, an imperfect copy*)

SALVADORE GAGLIARDELLI

The notice of Gagliardelli given in Pouget, *Diction-naire des Chifres*, adds nothing to what can be gather-ed from his writing book. In the preface Gagliardelli acknowledges his debt to Cresci, F. de Monterchi

and Cesare Moreggio. The two latter do not appear to have printed specimens of their hands. Destailleur, according to the *Catalogue des livres rares*, 1891, had both Gagliardelli's printed book and also some spec-

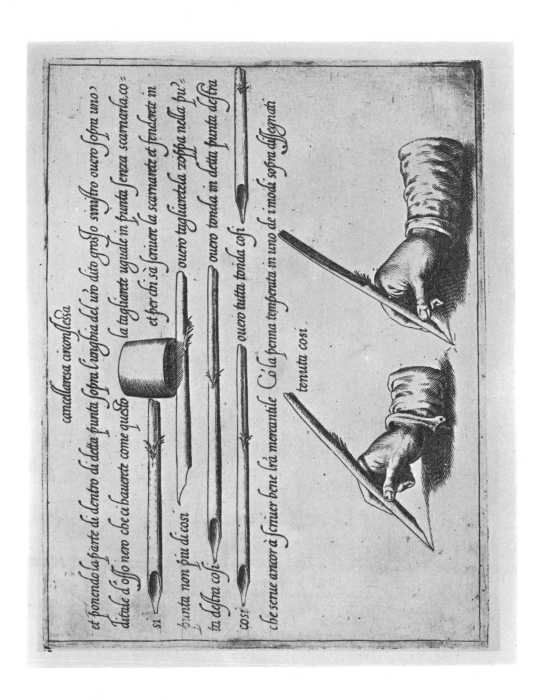

FIG. 4. Hercolani, 1574. (Reduced.)

imens of his hands in manuscript. The manuscript, showing the chancery hand only, is now in the Victoria and Albert Museum. Bradley (*Dict.* II., p. 8) records a Horae, now at Parma, written by Gagliardelli at Florence in 1591.

*

SOPRASCRITTE || DI LETTERE || IN FORMA CANCEL-LERESCA, CORSIVA, || Appartenenti ad ogni grado di persona; || DI SALVADORE GAGLIARDELLI SCRIT-TORE || in Fiorenza. || Date in luce in tal carattero per commune vtilità de gli studiosi della buona forma || dello scriuere, Per esercitarsi nelle acco-madate Abbreuiature, Ne' tratti || diuersi, Nelle variate Maiuscole, che in esso sono, cosi nello scritto, || come anco nel modo del dire di esse Soprascritte. || Con la Tauola per ordine, alla quale ciascuno ricorrerà; Perche in essa si di-chiarano || particolarmente le Soprascritte, che si contengono || in questo Libro. || Con l'Ag-giunta di questa [   ] Stampa, come à piè della Tauola si dice. || Stampato in Firenze, Per l'Au-tore detto di sopra. || Con Priuilegio del Sere-nissimo GRAN DVCA di Toscana || Per anni Dieci. || CON LICENZA DE' SVPERIORI. ||

Oblong (190 × 260 mm). 84 leaves. Title within woodcut border, verso blank; fol. 2 dedication to the Salviati dated 12 January 1583, verso blank; ten further leaves of preliminaries, including the Table, printed in roman and with borders of printers' flowers; the 72 plates, unnumbered, have woodcut borders. This edition is described at the end of the preliminaries as 'la seconda stampa'.

(Entry made from a copy in the Brit.Mus. now lost. The copy in the Vict. & Albert Mus. differs in the preliminary leaves. Vienna, Österreich. Mus. f. Kunst)

Davis & Orioli, Cat. 136, No. 25, records an earlier edition, without the words 'la seconda stampa. The title is in a typographic border and there are only eight preliminary leaves.

MARCELLO SCALZINI

There is an article on Scalzini or Scalino by C. Pasero in *La Bibliofilia*, 1933, pp. 430-9. According to the portrait by Giacomo Franco in 1581 he was twenty-five years old, and at that time he had been twelve years in Rome. He tells us that his first instructor was Scipione Cristiani, another master who is only a name to us. He makes extravagant claims for his system, chiefly on account of his 'velocità'. His book seems to have been a success and in spite of his two privileges, from the Pope and the City of Venice, there were a number of pirated editions. After leaving Rome he appears to have had a school at Venice. In 1608 he was in the service of the Grand Duke of Tuscany. We have seen that in 1638 his *Regole* were republished along with some Cresci specimens. Among his pupils he mentions his broth-er Lucantonio, P. Nicola Bruni da San Severino and his brother Antonio Bruni, and Cristofero Lavizzano of Modena. The work of the last mentioned only is now known.

*

IL SECRETARIO || DI MARCELLO SCALZINI || DETTO IL CAMERINO || della Città di Camerino, Citta-dino Romano, || Inuentore, Scrittore in Roma. || Nelquale si vedono le varie & diuerse sorti, & vere forme di lettere Cancellaresche corsi- || ue Romane nuoue da Secretario al presente vsi-tate, da lui con molto studio ritrouate, || prima introdotte; & poi da altri Scrittori in Roma, in Venetia, & in altre Città d'Italia. || Con tutte quelle Regole; & Auertimenti, che bisognano per bene & perfettamente impararle || à scriuere con velocità, & in brieue tempo senza la pre-senza del Maestro. || Con Motu proprio di N. S. PAPA GREGORIA XIII. Che nessuno, per anni diece, possa stampare || quest'Opera, né inta-gliare, né far intagliare, ò stampare in qual si voglia, modo à similitudine, & imita- || tione di qual si voglia delle forme, & sicurezze di mano contenute in essa. || Con priuilegio della SERE-NISSIMA SIGNORIA DI VENETIA, che nessuno pos-sa || stampare, ò intagliare, né far' intagliare à similitudine & imitatione come di sopra, per anni XX. || [a fleuron]

IN VENETIA, Appresso Domenico Nicolini, Ad in-stantia del proprio autore, 1581.

Obl. quarto. Title-page, two leaves of preliminaries, an engraved portrait of Scalzini signed: Giacomo francho fecit, and 50 other engraved plates, num-bered 6-55 and printed on one side of the leaf, followed by *Regole*, etc., pp. 55-82. The dedication to Cardinal Sirleto is dated from Venice, 6 May 1581, and the privilege from Gregory XIII, 5 January 1580. The plates show Chancery letter only. Several have the decoration known as 'command of hand'. Some plates are signed with the monogram Æ attributed by Nagler (*Monogrammisten*, I, 522) to Giacomo Franco; but the identification is not accepted in Thieme & Becker.

(Berlin, Kunstgewerbemuseum)

Il Secretario dell' Camerino Inventore. Delli ca-ratteri cancellareschi corsivi romani nuovi, che al presente per tutta l'Europa si costumans . . . Venetia, ad instanti adell'Autore.

Oblong quarto. 26 leaves.

(A. L. VAN GENDT, AMSTERDAM)

[Another edition] . . .

Ad instantia di M. Helena Moresini, 1585.

(*Nuremberg, German. Museum*)

[Another edition] . . .

In Venetia, MDLXXXVII. Appresso Domenico Nicolini. || Ad instantia del Commissario di M. Helena Moresini. ||

Oblong (170 × 225 mm). A reissue of the edition of 1581.   (*Vict. & Albert Mus.*)

IL SECRETARIO || DI MARCELLO || SCALINO DA CA-MERINO || CITTADINO ROMANO, || GENTILHVOMO DEL SERENISSIMO, || ET CATHOLICO CARLO EMA-NVELLE || Duca di Sauoia, &c. || Oue si contiene la scelta de' caratteri cancellareschi Corsiui, ||

CON LA NVOVA AGGIVNTA DI MOLTI VTILISSIMI || ESSEMPI, AL PRESENTE FATTAVI DA LVI || IN TV-RINO. ||

Oblong. 29 leaves. Title-page, one leaf; dedication to Carlo Emanuele, Duca di Savoia, dated Turin, 20 December 1589, one leaf; pl. 1 the portrait; pl. 2 an engraved title with the words 'IN VENETIA || ad instantia dell'autore' at the foot; pls. 3-26 the examples; pl. 27 an engraved border and a dedication to Count Francesco Brembati filled in in manuscript. The copper plates are printed in sanguine.

(*New York, Metropolitan Museum of Art*)

Another issue, with the plates printed in black, has no portrait; the second title is numbered '1' and the last plate is lacking. (BIRRELL & GARNETT) The 'Regole nuove' of Scalino, published at Brescia in 1591, contains text and an engraved portrait only. [Another edition] Venice, 1599. Oblong, 8 leaves of text and 54 plates.   (*Leipzig, Börsenverein*)

SIMONE VEROVIO

Verovio is known chiefly as a publisher of music at Rome in the years 1586 to 1608. See Eitner, *Quellen-Lexikon der Musiker*.

★

Il primo libro delli || Essempi di Simone || Verovio || In Parione all'insegna del Martello || Romae 1587 || Martin van buyten sculpsit. ||

Oblong (158 × 203 mm). Engraved title-page and 38 leaves of Chancery handwriting, the majority signed: Simone Verovio, 1587.   (BIRRELL & GARNETT)

Essemplare di XIIII lingue principalissime.

An engraved broadside within a narrow border (368 × 461 mm); of the fifteen compartments one is signed by Verovio, one, the dedication to the Cardinal of Verona (Agostino Valiero), by Nicolo van Aelst (? the publisher), and dated 31 May 1587. The engraver, Martin van Buyten, has put his name

on the border. Presumably Verovio is responsible for the specimens.   (*Brit. Mus.*)

Esemplare || Di lettere Cancellaresche cor || sive di Simone Verovio. || Stampato in Roma in parione all'insegna del martello. || Con licentia de Sup. ||

Obl. octavo; 20 numbered, engraved plates. The dedication on pl. 2 is dated 30 November 1593. A different work from that of 1587.

(*Berlin, Kunstgewerbemuseum*)

The copy of Verovio, 1593, recorded in the Catalogue of V. S. Moretti, Rome, 1929, has, apparently, a different title-page.

[An engraved broadside (340 × 460 mm plate measurement), divided into fifteen compartments, showing the Chancery hand. Five of the specimens are signed by Verovio. The last compartment bears a colophon: 'Rome, L for 1598'.]? Giosef Longhi.

(*Brit. Mus.*)

LODOVICO CURIONE

Curione was a Bolognese but worked in Rome, where he died on 28 April 1617. A. Bertolotti, *Artisti Bolognesi, Ferraresi ed altri a Roma*, 1886, reproduces a document, dated 8 October 1593, according to which Martinus Vambutier, i. e. Van Buyten, promises to retouch ('retoccare') book 2 'Lanatomia'. There may then have been a second edition of this book.

★

Del modo di scrivere le Cancellaresche Corsive, Libro primo. In Roma, appresso Iacomo Tornieri, 1590.

Oblong 4°. 42 unnumbered leaves. Title-page, two

leaves of introduction, one leaf blank, and 38 examples, within borders.

(LIBRERIA VINCIANA, MILAN, 1947)

Lanotomia || delle Cancellaresche corsiue & altre || maniere di Lettere || di Lodovico Cvrione || Con la quale senza la presenza del Maestro si può || peruenire a una uera intelligenza di quest'arte || Libro secondo || Imparione alla insegna del martello, ||

Martins van buyten sculpsit hoc opus Romae 1588. Con priuilegio di N. S.

Oblong (192 × 260 mm, plate 148 × 207 mm). An engraved title-page and 45 numbered and two unnumbered engraved plates printed on one side only, within borders; pls. 1-45 chancery, 46 and 47 roman. (*Brit. Mus.*)

A copy in the Metr. Mus., N. Y., has 3 plates unnumbered. It also lacks the eighth line of the title. An edition of Book 1 is recorded in 1605 (*Börsenverein, Leipzig*), and Servidori in his *Reflexiones sobra la verdadera arte de escribir*, Madrid, 1789, p. 29, says it appeared in 1590.

Il Teatro || Delle Cancellaresche corsiue per Secretari || et altre maniere di lettere. || Di Lodovico Cvrione || Libro Terzo. ||

Imprione alla insegna del martello. ||

Oblong (192 × 260 mm). The title-page is engraved and bears the inscription: 'Martin' van buyten Hollandus sculpsit anno Dni 1593'. Followed by an engraved portrait of Curione, three leaves of text, and 42 other plates printed on one side; pls. 1-33 Chancery; pls. 34-8 mixed alphabets; pls. 39-42 roman; some of the plates are surrounded by, command of hand'. (*Brit. Mus.*)

A copy in the Metr. Mus., N. Y., is without the last line of the title.

IL CANCELLIERE || DI LODOVICO CVRIONE || ORNATO DI LETTERE || Corsiue et d'altre maniere di caratteri || vsati a scriuersi in Italia. || Libro quarto. || Roma, 1582. ||

Obl. quarto, 42 leaves, with an engraved title-page and borders. The title-page is signed: Dom^{ci} Falcini formis senis. (*Berlin, Kunstgewerbemuseum*)

An edition of 1605 bears the name of the engraver 'Francesco Villamena'. In 1619 G. G. Rossi, Rome, published an edition of the four books.

IACOMO ROMANO

IL PRIMO LIBRO DI SCRIVERE || DI IACOMO ROMANO || DOVE S'INSEGNA LA VERA MANIERA || DELLE CANCELLARESCHE CORSIVE, || E DI TUTTE QVELLE SORTI DI LETTERE || CHE A VN BVON SCRITTORE Si appartengono di Sapere, & che al presente sono in vso. || Con li avertimenti et regole, sopra ciascuna || sorte di Lettera, con le quali ogni mediocre ingegno potrà facilmente da se stesso || imparare: con il modo di temperar le penne per dette sorti di lettere, || & come si deuono tenere in mano, per scriuer bene. || STAMPATO IN ROMA, || per Pietro Spada appresso il proprio Autore, con licenza de Superiori, || Et Priuilegio di Nostro Signore. || MDLXXXVIIII. ||

Oblong (162 × 227 mm), sig. A-Y in fours? 84 leaves printed on one side of the leaf, each surrounded by a woodcut border. Facing the title-page is a woodcut portrait of Romano. Sig. O to the end contains roman alphabets and initials printed white on black. (G. W. JONES, *an imperfect copy*)

STEFANO GHEBELINO BRESCIANO

Tesoro essemplare per imparar a scrivere le piv occorrenti sorti di lettere che vsano a presenti tempi. Co'l secreto di far buon inchiostro, & temperar ben la penna. Aggiontovi il modo di tener conto de libri ordinariamente; & altre cose vtili e necessarie ad ogn'vno che trafichi, o habbia maneggio di casa. Per Stef. Ghe. Brescia no. In Brescia per Vincenzo Gabbio, 1591.

Oblong octavo. The book illustrates the Chancery hand, the Lettera commune mercantile, roman, etc. (*Mitteilungen des German. Mus., Nuremberg*, 1886, p. 81)

ALBERTO MURETI

La prima parte della teorica, e pratica di bene scrivere, formar Tiri diuersi e Groppi doppi, sciolti e collegati di nuouo, intagliata da Iacomo Granthuōme Fiammengo. Silvester Marchetti, Siena, 1594.

Oblong folio. Two portraits, 8 pages of text, and 37 plates. (*Leipzig, Börsenverein*)

GIACOMO FRANCO

Franco was an engraver, designer, and dealer in prints. A full account of his work is given by C. Pasero in an article in *La Bibliofilia*, 1935, pp. 332, seq. The natural son of the engraver Giovanni Battista Franco, he was born at Venice in 1550 and died there in 1620.

★

Il Franco modo di scriver Cancellaresco moderno, raccolto da gli essemplari di più famosi scrittori de' nostri tempi, intagliato et publicato da Giacomo Franco. Venetia, 1595.

Oblong quarto. An engraved title-page, two leaves of text, one plate of arms, and 40 plates.

(*Leipzig, Börsenverein*)

Del Franco Modo || Di Scrivere || Cancelleresco moderno || Libro Secondo. || Raccolte da gli Essemplari di piu famosi Scrittori || de nostri tempi, Intagliato et Publicato da || Giacomo Franco. || In Venetia || con Priuilegio 1596.

Oblong (171 × 234 mm). 45 leaves; title, emblematic view of Venice, 2 pp. of dedication, 1 leaf of foreword, and 41 engraved plates (pl. 36 is misnumbered 20). Engraved by Franco from examples by Scalzini, Cortese, Cresci, Curione, Sopranini, Tosta of Naples, and Franco himself. Cortese, Tosta and Sopranini are otherwise unknown.

(*Chicago, Newberry Library*)

SCIPIONE LEONE

[Twelve engraved plates, 130 × 200 mm, signed by Scipione Leone and the first dated 1598] Examples of the Chancery hand, except f. 10, roman, and f. 12, 'Lettera moderna'. (*Brit. Mus.*)

Qvaranta || Mostre cancelleresche || di Scipione Leoni Bolognese || Giosef Longhi Forma al insegna di S. Paolo ||

Oblong octavo. 40 numbered plates, undated. Apparently different from the preceding.

(*Berlin, Kunstgewerbemuseum*)

He published his pocket preceptor of 24 copper plates *Il Libro Primo di Cancellaresche Corsiue* in Rome 1601 with a dedication d. Rome 1596.

CESARE PICCHI (PICCHIO)

In Bertolotti, *Artisti Bolognesi*, there is a notice of payment made to one Cesare Picchi, 'vasaio', a potter, for work at the Palazzo Apostolico in Rome in the years 1583-5. Some specimens of Picchi appear in the selection from Curione, published in 1613.

★

[An engraved broadside (371 × 484 mm, plate measurement) within a narrow border, divided into fifteen compartments. The first compartment is a dedication to Fabio Spinosa, is dated 1593, and is signed: Gio. Antonio de Pauli (? the publisher). It bears the engraver's name: 'Christofero blanco fece'. Compartment 2 shows roman capitals and the rest the Chancery hand of which ten are signed by Picchio. The last compartment bears a colophon: 'Cesare Capranica for. Romae 1597'.] (*Brit. Mus.*)

[An engraved broadside (362 × 470 mm, plate measurement) divided into seventeen compartments, showing the Chancery hand and one specimen of roman. Most of the examples are signed by Picchi. The last compartment has a colophon: 'L fo 1598'.] ?Giosef Longhi. (*Brit. Mus.*)

Cancellaresche corsive per Secretarij. Libro I. Martinus van Buyten sculpsit. Roma.

Oblong quarto. An engraved title-page and 38 plates, dated 1598. (*Leipzig, Börsenverein*)

A broadside (Birrell & Garnett), with examples of writing by Picchi of which one compartment is dated 1593, bears the names of the engravers Giovanni Battista Rossi and Cristoforo Blanco.

MARCO ANTONIO DE ROSSI (RUBEIS)

GIARDINO DE SCRITTORI || DI Marc' Antonio Rossi Romano. || ALL'ILL^MO ET R^MO SIG^RE IL S^R CARD. ALDOBRANDINO || Nel quale si vede il vero modo di scriuer facilissimamente tutte || le sorte di lettere, che al presente sono in vso, et che sono || necessarie ad ogni qualità di Persona. || Con vn' Alfabeto di Maiuscole Antiche Rom. || fatte per ragion' di Geometria e || Stampato in Roma appresso il proprio Autore. || Con Priuilegio di N. Sig.^RE & Licenza de superiori. || M.D.IIC. ||

Oblong. 132 engraved and numbered leaves (165 × 234 mm, plate measurement) mostly within borders. Preceded by the title-page, a leaf containing a portrait of Aldobrandino signed 'Temp in.' 'Phls Thoms sculp.' i. e. engraved by Philippe Thomassin after Antonio Tempesta, and a leaf bearing the Cardinal's arms. The title-page and the portrait of Rossi, at the age of twenty-one, on f. 1 are signed by Camillo Spalucci and the engraver Thomassin. The last twelve leaves, the geometrical alphabet, are not numbered in some copies. Fol. 120 is apparently a title-page for this alphabet, reading 'Il Quarto libro del Giardino de' Scrittori . . .'

(*Vienna, Österreich. Mus. f. Kunst; Brit. Mus.; Harvard Univ. Lib., a copy in a silverworked binding. All imperfect.*)

The Breslauer copy has 32 plates printed in red. A copy described in Destailleur's *Cat. de Livres rares* and now in the Newberry Library has 23 preliminary leaves containing dedicatory verses occupying sig.

A-D followed by six blank leaves; then plates of chancery cursive beginning with pl. 7. The book is much fuller than any preceding specimen book, and although strongly influenced by Cresci's chancery cursive and his formal chancery and other hands, is independent in its initials and in other directions.

IL QVARTO LIBRO || DEL GIARDINO DE SCRITTORE || DI MARCANTONIO ROSSI ROMANO. || Nel quale si vede il vero modo di scriuere facilisimmamente || per ragione Geometria le Maiuscole || Antiche Romane, || con priuilegio di N. S. || Et licenza de Superiori, 1598.

Title-page in letterpress; twelve leaves of capital letters A-Z in copperplate; extracts from Rossi's *Giardino di Scrittori* of the previous year.

(*Chicago, Newberry Library*)

FRANCESCO PEDARRA

[An engraved broadside (354 × 484 mm, plate measurement) divided into fifteen compartments and showing the Chancery hand. Six of the compartments are signed by Francesco Pedarra. The compartment at the foot of the second column bears the publisher's monogram: 'L f. 1598'.] ? Giosef Longhi.

I have found no mention of a calligrapher Pedarra (but see the next entry). The examples take the form of addresses to his patrons. Among them is Curione and here he refers to 'Martino fiamengo nostro intagliatore', i. e. Martin van Buyten. The last example ends: 'Scrisse in Napoli'.

(*Brit. Mus.*)

MARTIN VAN BUYTEN

Corona di varii caratteri per imparare a scrivere . . . Raccolti di tutti le piu eccellente Scrittori . . . di nostri tempi. Napoli, 1600.

Oblong 4°. 38 engraved leaves. Title-page, two pages in type and 36 engraved examples 'del Verovio, Curione, Picchi, Garsia, Luca da Jarre, Pedarra, Bernaudi, Marc. Ant. Rossi', etc. Engraved by Van Buyten. Dedicated to Gio. A. Spinola.

(A. VAN DER WILLIGEN CAT., AMSTERDAM, 1875)

[This list was originally published in 1950 and was then a pioneer study of great importance which has inspired further investigation, notably by Mr. Nicolas Barker who hopes to publish his conclusions shortly.

The locations given in brackets at the end of each entry include copies then in the possession of booksellers, e. g. Birrell & Garnett and A. L. van Gendt. It will be appreciated that in most instances such locations are unlikely to be extant. In general the locations that are no longer operative are given in roman, others in italics. The locations are in any case for convenience and do not pretend to be exhaustive.]

[1950]

A SHORT HISTORY OF PRINTING
IN THE SIXTEENTH CENTURY

THE history of the printing press in the sixteenth century is full of interest and variety. It was an age of many master printers, who maintained a high standard of workmanship – the Aldine family in Italy, the Estiennes and Simon de Colines at Paris, Jean de Tournes at Lyons, and Christophe Plantin at Antwerp. It is a period especially important for the evolution of type forms, many of which are still influencing the typography of our generation. Not only are many types used today based on designs of the sixteenth century, but the form of the book, as we know it, is in most of its details the form evolved by the printers of that age. A book printed by Jean de Tournes was built up in much the same way as a book published in New York or London in the twentieth century.

Italy

The great Venetian printer Aldus Manutius had already made some reputation by printing a number of the Greek classical authors. With the publication of his Virgil in 1501, printed in a new letter known as italic, he started a project which was in two respects to prove of considerable importance in the history of the press. In the first place italic, throughout the sixteenth century, in Italy and in France became almost as popular as roman, and in the second place the Virgil, a small octavo in format, established the vogue of the small book. Aldus's intention was to publish a series of handy volumes for readers and for that purpose he employed a type which was more condensed than roman and would therefore permit the printing of a long text in a volume much less bulky than had been usual in earlier days of printing. The type was based on a cursive variety of roman which had been used for many years at the Papal Chancery for the inditing of briefs. It was called by Aldus *cancelleresco* or *corsivo*; our name italic is derived from the French and is open to the objection that it is not more particularly an 'Italian letter' than the roman.[1]

There are two persistent errors relating to the origin of italic, which have been many times exposed, but which are still repeated. One is that the new letter was based on the handwriting of Petrarch. This is due to a misreading of a passage in the Aldine Petrarch of 1501, where it is stated that the text, not the type, was based on the manuscript in Petrarch's own hand. The second error is the identification of Aldus's type-cutter, Francesco da Bologna, with the painter Francesco Raibolini. This identification was shown to be impossible by Giacomo Manzoni in his *Studii di bibliografia analitica*, 1881, and further in 1883 Adamo Rossi published a document from which it appears that the type-cutter's surname was Griffo.[2] It is known that Griffo was the designer not only

---

1. The whole question of chancery types is treated at greater length on pp. 83 sqq.
2. See his article in the *Atti della r. deput. di storia patria per le provincie di Romagna*, 1883, p. 412.

of the first italic, but also of the Greek and roman types of Aldus, and consequently he takes his place in typographical history in the ranks of the leading designers. It is well known that the cursive Greek types of Aldus are the source of almost all succeeding Greek types: of the importance of the Aldine roman we shall have to speak further in connection with the Garamond roman. Our knowledge of Griffo is derived mainly from three contemporary books. First of all, Aldus himself gives him due credit in the preliminaries of the Virgil of 1501. Geronimo Soncino, a member of a well-known family of Hebrew printers, used a second italic, cut by Griffo, at Fano in 1503. In the dedication of Soncino's Petrarch, the fact is recorded and Aldus's obligations to Griffo are emphasized. Lastly, Griffo himself, in another Petrarch, printed at Bologna in 1516 in another of his italics, again tells the story.[1] His career ended in disaster in 1518, in which year he killed his son-in-law in a quarrel and henceforth disappears from history.[2]

Aldus's italic and his pocket series were soon copied. The Giunta at Florence, for example, had a similar italic by 1503, and there were also anonymous copies in Italy. Two printers of Lyons, Balthazar da Gabiano and Barthélemy Trot, copied not only the italic, but also the series of books issued by Aldus in the new letter, and the Venetian printer's privilege and protests availed him nothing. An obscure printer at Erfurt, Sebald Striblitza, was the first to introduce the new letter into Germany, in 1510, and about the same time we find italics at Paris at the press of Guillaume Lerouge. Johann Froben at Basle used italic first in 1519, but it was not until 1528 that it reached England, imported from the Netherlands by Wynkyn de Worde.

The Aldine italic was not a handsome letter, and if there had been no further development one can hardly imagine that the new type would have had such a lasting history. It was a more formal variety of the chancery hand which was to ensure its success. This later version was cut for a writing master at Rome, Lodovico degli Arrighi of Vicenza, himself a writer of briefs at the Papal Chancery. In 1522 he published a specimen book of his hands, the first writing master's manual,[3] and in 1524 began to print at Rome in a new cursive type based on his own script. Unlike Aldus, Arrighi did not require a condensed type, since his intention was to print verse and short tracts in an elegant format. In his type there were few ligatures, each letter being carefully formed; ascending letters were bent over at the top and not finished off with serifs; ascenders were tall and descenders long. The result was something very unlike the niggardly Aldine italic, in spite of the fact that both were derived from the same script. Arrighi printed about a score of small books in this cursive in 1524 and 1525, in partnership with Lautizio de Bartolomeo dei Rotelli, an engraver and possibly the actual punch-cutter of the firm. After 1525 the fount appears to have been sold to the well-known author Gian Giorgio Trissino, or to his printer Tolomeo Janicolo of Brescia. In 1529 Janicolo reprinted Trissino's works at Vicenza in Arrighi's cursive, and it is in these handsome folios embellished with a device of Jason's Golden Fleece, that Arrighi's cursive is most familiar to book collectors of today (Fig. 1).

1. The relevant passages are given in full in Johnson's *Type Designs*, pp. 124-126.
2. See E. Orioli in the *Atti della r. deput. di storia patria per le provincie di Romagna*, 1899, pp. 162, *seq.*
3. See p. 19.

ƐPISTOLA DEL TRÍSSINO
DE LE LETTERE
N℧ωVAMENTE AGGIVNTE
NE LA LING℧A
ITALIANA.

Con Grazia ε Proḣibizione del Sommo Pontefice, ε del Senato
Veneto, che nessuno possa ʃtampare queʃta ωpera.

FIG. 1. Dante Alighieri, *De la volgare eloquenzia*. (Tr. G. G. Trissino.) Tolomeo Janicolo,
Venice, 1529. (Margins reduced.)

Arrighi continued printing at Rome with a second cursive type of somewhat similar design; the chief difference in the new type is in the ascending letters, which now have the more usual serif terminals. The last book printed by Arrighi was an edition of the Latin poems of Hieronymus Vida, which appeared in May, 1527, the very month of the sack of Rome. As Arrighi's name appears on no later document, it may be that he was one of the many victims of the invading army. His italic types, more particularly the second version, had great influence on subsequent cursive typography both in Italy and abroad, and he therefore deserves a prominent place in any account of sixteenth-century printing.

Arrighi was the only printer of distinction who practiced the art at Rome in the first quarter of the century. Marcellus Silber, whose career began in the incunable period, has to his credit the first book printed in Ethiopic, Johann Potken's Psalter, 1513. Jacopo Mazzocchi (at work from 1506 to 1527) was perhaps the best printer among Arrighi's contemporaries. His work also was ended by the sack of Rome in May, 1527, although he himself survived and issued at least one book at Zurich, the *Libri de re rustica*, 1528. Zacharias Kallierges, a well-known printer of Greek at Venice, was at work in Rome from 1513 to 1523. The official printer to the Papal Court, Antonio Blado of Asolo (1490-1567), began printing as early as 1516, but produced little of note before 1530. He is credited with some 430 books, many of which, however, were bulls, encyclicals, and so forth, of little bulk. He acquired Arrighi's second italic, and it is to the books set in this italic that he mainly owes his reputation as a typographer. The earliest appears to have been the *Sonetti* of Jacopo Sannazaro, 1530, a book which in its absence of decoration follows the simple style of Arrighi. Blado's books in roman are chiefly his work as the papal official printer and are of little interest typographically. His editions of the various works of Machiavelli, printed in 1531 and 1532, are set in an italic of the Aldine school and are perhaps as good examples of book production with such types as are to be found. He was also a considerable printer of Greek, at first for the Vatican and afterwards on his own account. In 1539 he was chosen by Pope Paul III and Cardinal Cervini to print Greek manuscripts in the Vatican Library. The type used was cut by Giovanni Onorio Magliese da Lecce for Cardinal Cervini, and, as one would expect, was similar to the *grecs du roi*, the famous Greek which was being cut at Paris for the printing of the manuscripts in the royal library. Both these types were cursive letters, full of ligatures, descended from the Aldine Greek. The first book which Blado printed in the new Greek was Eustathius's commentary on Homer, four volumes, which appeared between 1542 and 1550. The Greek with which Blado printed at a later date on his own account was of a similar design.

Among Blado's contemporaries were Francesco Prisciano, the Dorici brothers from Brescia, and Vincenzo Lucchino, all more or less imitators of Blado. In the second half of the century there is little to record except the efforts of the Papal Court to found a press and type-foundry of its own. In 1560 Paulus Manutius, son of Aldus, was invited to Rome to help in this work, and in 1562 the first book appeared, a work of Cardinal Pole's, with a preface by Manutius. Manutius returned to Venice in 1570 and the venture came to an end. In 1587 a new start was made and the Stamperia Vaticana was established under another Venetian printer, Domenico Basa; with him was associated for a time the younger Aldus, son of Paulus Manutius. The Stamperia Vaticana was also equipped with a foundry for which the distinguished French type designer, Robert Granjon, worked in the last few years of his life. Among other founts he cut some Arabic for the new press and the Arabic edition of the Gospels printed by them in 1590 in Granjon's type is a particularly handsome volume.

Venice, with all its wealth, was a far more important centre of printing than Rome or any other Italian city. The best work produced at Paris and Lyons in this century was certainly above anything to be seen at Venice, but in quantity Venetian books were second to none. Aldus Manutius continued the task, begun in the previous century, of printing the Greek classics. He and his successors, his father-in-law Andrea d'Asolo, and later Paulus Manutius (*b*.1513), carried on the italic series which began with the Virgil of 1501. An occasional book in roman from this press, like the edition of Baldassare Castiglione's *Il Cortegiano* of 1528, was worthy to be compared with the *Hypnerotomachia Poliphili* of 1499. The Venetian branch of the Giunta continued the publication of liturgical works of considerable interest, while in the printing of Hebrew Venice led the rest of the world with Daniel Bomberg and, later, Giustiniani. Bomberg came from Antwerp and was at work in Venice from 1515 to 1550. Giustiniani, a Venetian nobleman, began printing in 1545. Among the writing masters of Venice, one, Giovan Antonio Tagliente, like Arrighi at Rome, made some typographical experiments. The firm which most nearly corresponded in style with the Roman printer Blado was that of the brothers Nicolini da Sabbio. The majority of their books were printed in an italic very like the fount which Blado acquired from Arrighi; the restraint and simplicity of their style were again similar. They were also printers of a number of books in Greek, some of which appeared at Verona. Other contemporaries were the Sessa family, whose cat device was well known at Venice for many years, Nicolò Zoppino of Ferrara, working at Venice from 1508 to 1544, Francesco Bindoni, and Maffeo Pasini. Paganino de Paganini was the printer of a famous book on the proportions of letters, the *Divina Proportione* of Luca Pacioli. He and his son Alessandro, who later moved to Toscolano, possessed some curious types, which were a mixture of roman and italic.

Among the smaller houses the best printer at Venice in the first half of the century was Francesco Marcolini of Forlì, who was settled in Venice by 1534 and produced about 100 books between 1535 and 1559. He was typical of his generation in that he printed almost entirely in italic. The fount which he seems to have preferred was very similar to the Blado italic. *Il Petrarca spirituale*, 1536, is the best example of his books in this type and in the restraint of its style is reminiscent of the men who originated these more formal chancery letters. Marcolini was an intimate friend of Pietro Aretino and printed many editions of his books, some in the italic of *Il Petrarca spirituale*. His edition of a volume of letters addressed to Aretino, which appeared in 1551, is printed in a smaller type of the same school. Others of his books are set in Aldine italic, notably his Dante of 1544, a volume in which the text is surrounded by the notes, set in a smaller italic. The Dante also contains some interesting woodcuts. His editions of Vitruvius and of the architect Serlio (Fig. 2), and his own book *Il Giardino dei pensieri*, all con-

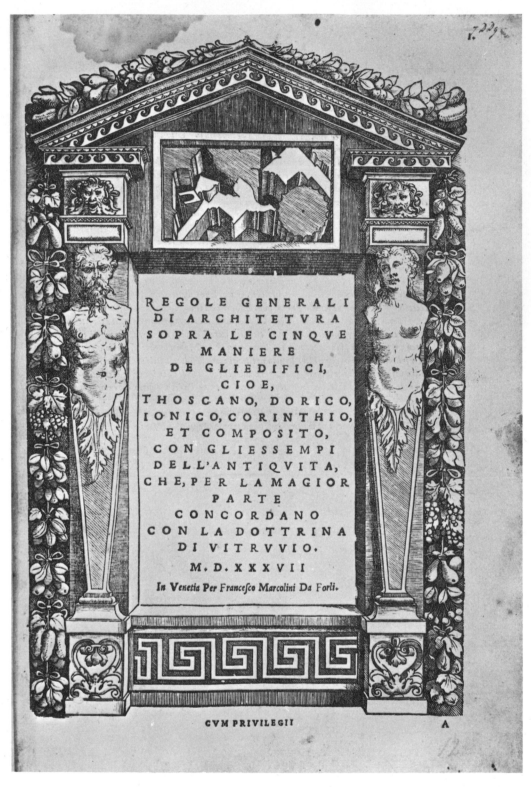

FIG. 2. Sebastiano Serlio, *Regole generali di architettura*. Francesco Marcolini, Venice, 1537. (Reduced.)

tain many woodcut illustrations. There are in his books a number of woodcut portraits of considerable merit. In his later period he came under the influence of Giolito and began to use the initials of the late Renaissance style derived from that printer. He is at his best, however, in the simplicity of his earlier volumes, set off by one of the most beautiful of printers' devices, a figure of Truth attacked by Calumny and upheld by Time.

Gabriel Giolito de' Ferrari was the most prolific printer of his generation at Venice, and a man who had considerable influence on his contemporaries in the matter of book decoration. The house was established by the father, Giovanni, of Trino, in 1539. According to S. Bongi's *Annali di Gabriel Giolito*, between 1539 and Gabriel's death in 1578 about 850 books were printed. In the first half of his career Giolito printed mainly editions of Italian classics and the works of contemporary men of letters. He issued twenty-eight editions of the *Orlando Furioso*, twenty-two of Petrarch's Sonnets, and nine editions of the *Decameron*. After 1560 he printed a large number of devotional works, therein reflecting the change which came over Italian life with the Counter Reformation.

Giolito's typography is of no special interest, but in the decoration of his books he introduced new fashions in woodcut initials, title-borders, and illustrations. His illustrations to the *Orlando*, the *Decameron*, Ovid, and many other volumes belong definitely to the late Renaissance and are sharply contrasted with earlier Venetian work. They may be compared with the work of contemporary artists in France. Giolito's artists, who have remained anonymous, produced dark backgrounds by cross-hatching much more freely than had hitherto been the custom in Italy. The woodcut initials of Giolito's books were similar in technique; each initial represented a scene in itself, and the subject of the picture was connected with the initial; a G, for instance, is illustrated by the story of Ganymede, L for Laocoön, P for Persephone, and so on. The idea was not new, but Giolito had several complete series of such initials cut, series based on Greek mythology, on ancient history, and others on games and sports. One may prefer the purely decorative initials of earlier periods, but at least Giolito made a hit with his new style and was widely copied in Italy. Among others, Blado at Rome, the Giunta at Florence and even the Aldine firm imitated him.

Giolito's title-borders are also of the late Renaissance style, forerunners of the engraved title-pages with their over-elaborate decorations. He had six different woodcut title-borders, two for octavos and four for quartos, most of them architectural and mythological in style. He had also one engraved title-page cut by or after Enea Vico for Lodovico Dolce's *Vita di Carlo Quinto*, 1567. This plate and some of the woodcut borders are remarkably similar in their architectural basis and symbolical figures to hundreds of other plates which were to be engraved in the next century in all the chief centres of printing.

During the period in which Giolito was at work the Venetian press was pouring out books in profusion. Among Giolito's contemporaries, most of whom were much influenced by him in the matter of book decoration, were Comin da Trino, Giovanni Griffio, related to the Lyons Gryphius, Michel Tramezzino, who printed Italian versions of the popular French romances such as *Amadis de Gaula*, the brothers Spinelli, who had an unusual italic and some good decorative material (Fig. 3), and Vincenzo Valgrisi, who rivalled Giolito in his illustrated editions of the *Orlando*.

At Florence the charming woodcuts which decorate the *Rappresentazioni*, the Savonarola sermons, and some popular poems, began about 1490 and were at their best in the years before 1500. They continued into the sixteenth century; Piero Pacini, for instance, one of the chief printers of the school, was at work until 1514, and his son until 1523; Francesco di Giovanni Benvenuto printed from 1511 to 1546. Blocks belonging to these and other printers of the best period were occasionally used throughout the century, often in a very worn state. Apart from this group, whose books survive mainly on account of their woodcuts, the only printers of importance at Florence were the Giunta family. Filippo di Giunta (*d.* 1517), the brother of Lucantonio, who was at work in Venice, and his son Bernardo, who printed till 1551, throve to some extent by plagiarizing Aldus. Filippo was one of the first to copy the italic and he and his son produced many volumes of the Greek and Latin classics in the Aldine style. However much they owed to Aldus the house produced some excellent volumes, for example the *Decameron* of 1527 and a Dioscorides of 1547. Bernardo came later under the Giolito influence; like most of his contemporaries he copied the Giolito initials and provided himself with a new device in the late Renaissance style (see Firenzuolo's play *Trinutia*, 1548). Bernardo's successors in 1568 printed an edition of Vasari's *Vite de' più eccellenti pittori*, well known for its series of woodcut portraits. The chief printer at Florence in the late Renaissance style was Lorenzo Torrentino, a Dutchman invited to Florence in 1547 by Cosimo I. He was a follower of Giolito in the style of his initials and ornate title-borders, but most of his types were French. We shall refer again to the importation of French types into Italy. We know that Torrentino had a canon roman cut by Guillaume Le Bé, who was at that time at work in Venice, cutting Hebrew type for Giustiniani. Most of the italic types, in which Torrentino's smaller books are set, are the same as those being used by Jean de Tournes at Lyons and were probably cut by Robert Granjon.

Italy in the Middle Ages had been a country of city-states and was still in the sixteenth century divided up into a number of independent realms. Hence it is that the art of printing was established and flourished in a large number of towns besides the three most important cities, Rome, Venice, and Florence. Books of considerable interest were produced at Bologna, Ferrara, Milan, Naples, Parma, and a number of other smaller cities. At Bologna the work of Anselmo Giaccarello in the middle years of the century shows the influence of French typography. His fine device of Hercules and the Hydra is another example of the many excellent and little-known printers' marks to be found in Italian books. The work done by Silvestre in the cataloguing and reproduction of French printers' devices has unfortunately no companion volume for Italy. Ferrara was the home of Ariosto and can boast of the first edition of the *Orlando*, printed by Giovanni Mazzocchi in 1516. To the wealth and variety of italic types cut in sixteenth-century Italy Ferrara too made its contribution. The cursives of Francesco Rossi (1521-1573) and of the partners Giovanni di Buglhat and Antonio Hucher are examples. At Milan also we find some unusual and attractive italics. Minuzio Calvo,

FIG. 3. Aelianus Tacitus, Περὶ στρατηγικῶν τάξεων ἑλληνικῶν. Andrea & Jacopo Spinelli, Venice, 1552. (Reduced.)

who printed first at Rome, produced several books at Milan set in Arrighi's earlier type, the one used by Trissino at Vicenza. (Cf. O. Lupano's *Torricella*, 1541.) At the same period G. A. Castiglione was using a cursive of the same style, which is perfectly upright. A fine instance of it is found in B. Castiglione's *Gallorum Insubrum antiquae sedes*, 1541 (Fig. 4). This excellent design reminds us that the inclination of italic letters was not originally an essential characteristic. Printing at Naples was in the main a pale reflection of the work of Blado at Rome. At Parma the house of Viotto did good work for several generations. Erasmo Viotto was the printer of the first edition of Tasso's *Gerusalemme liberata* in 1581.

It was not until the second half of the sixteenth century that the art of engraving began to be applied with any frequency to book illustration, and then chiefly in Italy and the Netherlands. The earliest engraved title-page is that of the *Purifica della conscientia* of Thomas Aquinas, Florence, 1512. In 1517 an engraved vignette is found at Rome on the title-page of Amadeo Berruti's *Dialogus de amicitia vera*. The real popularizer of engraving as applied to the book was Enea Vico of Parma, a medallist and antiquary, a number of whose books of plates were printed at Venice, the earliest with an engraved title-page being of 1548. Four of the earliest engraved title-pages appeared at Lucca, at the press of Vincenzo Busdraghi, the first in 1551, in a book on Genoa by Paolo Interiano and the other three in the three volumes of Busdraghi's edition of Matteo Bandello's *Novelle*, 1554. These are all anonymous. In contrast with woodcut title-borders, the engraved title was generally signed and was cut for a particular book. The woodcut title-border was used indiscriminately for any book, the design often having no relation to the contents of the volume.

One of the finest examples we have of the early architectural title plates was printed at Rome by Blado for Antonio Labacco's *Libro appartenente a l'architettura*, 1552. The plate and the engraved illustrations of the book were cut by the author's son, Mario Labacco. The plate was copied in a well-known French atlas, Bougereau's *Théâtre français*, Tours, 1594. Another book printed by Blado, Camillo Agrippa's *Trattato di scientia d'arme*, 1553, is illustrated with fine engravings representing duelling. With Antoine Lafrery, a Frenchman settled in Rome, we meet an established dealer in prints. Between 1544 and 1553 forty-two plates bearing his imprint are known, some of them being engraved title-pages. In the later years of the century numerous examples of the engraved title-page are to be found throughout Italy. Paulus Manutius, who began to print for the Academia Veneta in 1558, used an engraved device, a figure of Fame, on the title-pages of the Academy's books. Even an engraved initial is found in Aldus Manutius's *Vita di Cosimo de Medici*, 1586, but such initials are a form of decoration belonging to the next century. The difficulty of the two printings necessitated by the combination of the plate and the formes of type and the difficulty of printing on the back of the paper which had received the impression of the plate added to the expense of such decoration.

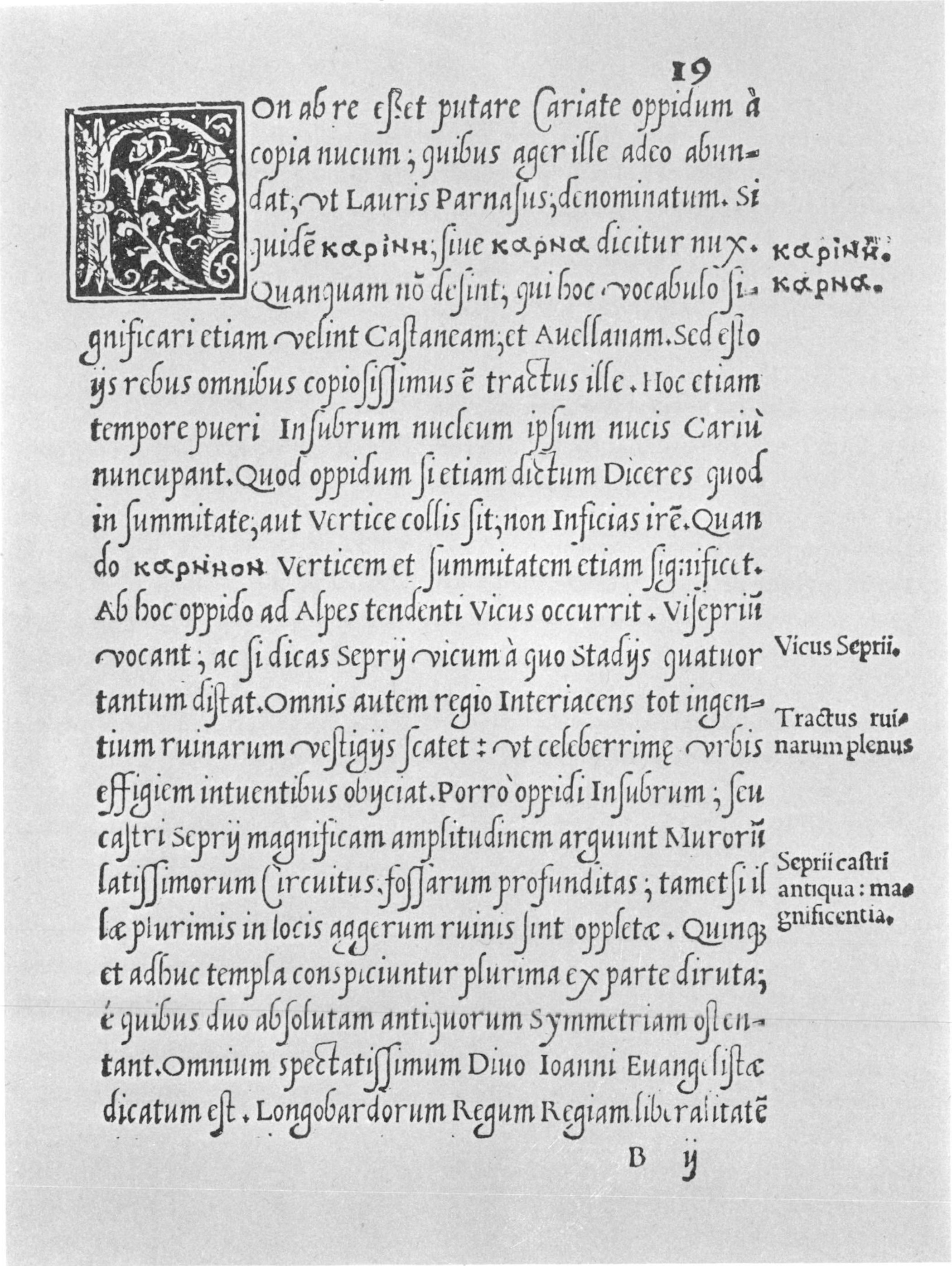

19

N on ab re eßet putare Cariate oppidum à copia nucum; quibus ager ille adeo abundat, vt Lauris Parnasus; denominatum. Si quidē καρiΝΗ; siue καρΝα dicitur nux. Quanquam nō desint; qui hoc vocabulo significari etiam velint Castaneam; et Auellanam. Sed esto ijs rebus omnibus copiosissimus ē tractus ille. Hoc etiam tempore pueri Insubrum nucleum ipsum nucis Cariù nuncupant. Quod oppidum si etiam dictum Diceres quod in summitate; aut Vertice collis sit; non Inficias irē. Quando καρΝΗοΝ Verticem et summitatem etiam significet. Ab hoc oppido ad Alpes tendenti Vicus occurrit. Visepriù vocant; ac si dicas Seprij vicum à quo Stadijs quatuor tantum distat. Omnis autem regio Interiacens tot ingentium ruinarum vestigijs scatet : vt celeberrimę vrbis effigiem intuentibus obyciat. Porrò oppidi Insubrum; seu castri Seprij magnificam amplitudinem arguunt Murorū latissimorum Circuitus; fossarum profunditas; tametsi illæ plurimis in locis aggerum ruinis sint oppletæ. Quinq; et adhuc templa conspiciuntur plurima ex parte diruta; è quibus duo absolutam antiquorum Symmetriam ostentant. Omnium spectatissimum Diuo Ioanni Euangelistæ dicatum est. Longobardorum Regum Regiam liberalitatē

B ij

Margin notes: καρiΝΗ. καρΝα. | Vicus Seprij. | Tractus ruinarum plenus | Seprii castri antiqua: magnificentia.

FIG. 4. Baldassare Castiglione, *Gallorum insubrum antiquae sedes*, Giovanni Antonio Castiglione, Milan, 1541.

Germany and German-speaking Switzerland

There are two matters of special interest in the history of German printing in the period of the Reformation. In the first place, German books were enriched by a wealth of woodcut illustrations, title-borders, and initials, and secondly, there were developments in the evolution of gothic types which were to influence German typography down to the present day. The particular variety of *bastarda* known as Fraktur, which was to prove the national German type, now first appeared. Germany more or less cut herself off from the rest of Europe by refusing to adopt, at any rate for books in the vernacular, the new types of the Renaissance, roman and italic.

In Germany, as in Italy, sixteenth-century books were in general of a smaller size than before 1500. The small Aldine classics had their direct influence in Germany, but the popular size was the small quarto. The short pamphlets of a controversial character, called forth in enormous numbers by the crisis of the Reformation, almost invariably appeared in this format, the small quarto. This output of Reformation tracts, of translations of the Bible, and of the works of the reformers meant a large increase in the work of the printing press and led to the introduction of printing into towns where the art had not hitherto been practiced. The chief cities which had been of importance in the early days of printing – Mainz, Cologne, Strasbourg, Augsburg, and Nuremberg – were still active centres, at least in the first half of the century. To these were now added Wittenberg, which, owing to the residence of Luther there, became the chief disseminator of Protestant literature. Two German-speaking Swiss cities, Basle and Zürich, also became important, Basle throughout the century, Zürich because of one press only, that of Christoph Froschauer, the printer of Ulrich Zwingli. Last of all, Frankfurt in the second half of the century took the lead as the most important German city in the sphere of book production, largely owing to the activity of the publisher Sigmund Feyerabend.

Between the decoration of German incunables and the books of the Reformation period there is a complete break in style, the earlier being gothic and the later Renaissance, that is to say, under the influence of Italian art. In some cases Italian work was directly copied; for example, Holbein copied a border from an Italian Bible of 1493, and Urs Graf a border used by Jacopo Mazzocchi at Rome. But on the whole there was little direct imitation. During a comparatively short period, down to about 1535, the German printers procured for the decoration of their books an astonishing mass of woodcut illustrations, title-borders, and initials. The number of title-borders is especially remarkable, amounting if we include the work of Holbein and Urs Graf, to something like a thousand blocks, produced within a quarter of a century. The principal artists who worked for the Strassburg printers, Johann Schott, Johann Knoblouch, and the others, were Hans Schäuffelein, Hans Baldung Grien, and Johann Wechtlin. There was also the mysterious unknown artist who designed some unusual borders for the printer Grüninger (cf. the title-page of J. Geiler's *Die Brösamlin*, 1517). At Augsburg we have Daniel Hopfer, who designed some fine borders of heavy Renaissance ornament for Silvanus Otmar, and Hans Weiditz, later at Strasbourg. This artist, whose work seems to have been confined to book illustration (Fig. 5) and decoration, is credited with some forty borders and a vast number of illustrations, many of which appeared in books printed by Heinrich Steyner at Augsburg years after they were cut, (cf. Petrarch's *Von der Artzney bayder Glück*, 1532). Weiditz at first designed title-borders for Johann Miller, and for Grim and Wirsung at Augsburg, and later for Schott and Wolfgang Köpfel at Strasbourg. At Nuremberg we find Hans Springinklee and Erhard Schön working for Friedrich Peypus, and for the Kobergers the publishers, much of whose work was printed at Lyons. Most of these artists worked for the three great collections of woodcuts produced for the Emperor Maximilian, the *Theuerdank*, the *Weisskunig*, and the *Triumphzug*. At Cologne we have the work of Anton Woensam, who seems to have supplied all the woodcut material used by the little group of printers of that city. The artist who worked for Johann Schoeffer of Mainz remains anonymous. Some of Schoeffer's blocks have, however, recently been attributed to Conrad Faber von Creuznach and others to Gabriel Zehender.[1] Lastly in Saxony we have the Cranachs and the most prolific of this group, Georg Lemberger, who worked for the presses directly connected with Luther; the presses of J. Grüninger, Melchior Lotter, and Hans Lufft. At no other time in the history of printing was such care devoted to the decoration of four-page tracts, which many of these books were. The fact that there was so often no connection between the design of the title-border and the subject matter of the tract was nothing unusual in that age.

At the beginning of the sixteenth century German typography was mainly gothic, and was to remain so, at least for books in German. The fact that Germany alone resisted the invasion of the Renaissance types of Italy was probably due to nationalist pride. The German printers, who were conscious that their predecessors had invented the art, would be less influenced by the prestige of Italian culture than their French and English contemporaries. There were but few roman types in Germany of 1500 and even Latin texts were commonly set in *rotunda*, the round form of gothic borrowed from Italy, which had become the stock European type and had superseded the old *textura*. *Textura* was still used as a heading type and for service books. As to italic, apart from the type of Striblitza of Erfurt, mentioned above, there were no German italics before 1519, and no great use of them after that date. For books in German the usual type was Schwabacher, or its offshoot, the Upper Rhine type. In the Wittenberg neighbourhood there is found a different design of *bastarda* (with M 48) which has received the name of the Wittenberg letter. It is found first at the press of Melchior Lotter of Leipzig in 1508. With this exception Schwabacher remained the traditional type for books in German down to the second half of the century. Schwabacher is a round letter of good design and heavy face, with an upper case in harmony with the lower. Fraktur has in contrast narrow and pointed letters, and a calligraphic upper case, far removed from earlier gothic capital.

---

1. See F. Thormählen, 'Die Holzschnittmeister der Mainzer Livius-Illustrationen,' in the *Gutenberg Jahrbuch*, 1934.

By 1550 the letter which was to dethrone Schwabacher was becoming more and more popular. The origin of this type, Fraktur, is historically a matter of importance in German typography. The writing master Johann Neudörffer, in his *Nachrichten* of 1547, says that one of the first Frakturs, the type in which the *Theuerdank*, Schönsperger, 1517, was printed (the Theuerdankschrift), was designed by Vincenz Rockner and cut by Hieronymus Andreae (*Formschneider*) of Nuremberg. More recent research has shown that this type and the earlier Gebetbuch type were based on the hands of Leonhard Wagner of Augsburg, as they appear in his manuscript writing book compiled between 1507 and 1510.[1] Between 1513 and 1524 eight varieties of Fraktur were cut. The first three were cut for the Emperor Maximilian's printer, Hans Schönsperger of Augsburg. The first was the Gebetbuch type, used in the *Liber horarum ad vsum Ordinis Sancti Georgii*, 1513. The second, the Theuerdankschrift, dates from 1517, and the third, the Gilgengartschrift, from the same year. The Gebetbuch type and the Theuerdankschrift were widely used as heading types, but the third, the smallest, seldom appeared. The next in date was the curious type (in two sizes) used by Grim and Wirsung at Augsburg from 1520 (Fig. 5). In 1522 appeared the first Fraktur in what was to prove the traditional design, the type cut by Johann Neudörffer for Hieronymus Andreae. This was the type used by Dürer for the printing of his three books, *Underweysung der Messung*, 1525, *Etliche Underricht zu Befestigung der Stett*, 1527, and the *Vier Bücher von menschlicher Proportion*, 1528. Dürer was clearly interested in the new design, but there is no evidence that he was himself responsible for it. In 1524 there were three copies, that of Cranach and Döring at Wittenberg, of Wolfgang Köpfel at Strasbourg, and of Johann Petri at Nuremberg. On Petri's specimen sheet issued in 1525 three sizes of Fraktur were shown, of which the largest was used for the main text of *Der Psalter teutsch*, 1525, one of the most remarkable books set in the early Frakturs.

In spite of these eight early designs it was quite a generation before Fraktur became a serious rival of Schwabacher as a text type. Fraktur was the narrower letter and more economical of space, but it was certainly the inferior design. Froschauer of Zürich printed the German Bible in Fraktur in 1548, and with the generation of Feyerabend, Schwabacher was doomed, to survive as a secondary letter only.

Of the two German-speaking Swiss towns where printing was practiced, Zürich had but one press of importance, that of Christoph Froschauer, printer for Zwingli and the printer of some English Bibles. Froschauer had some woodcut material, borders and initials, designed by Hans Holbein. The city of Basle was much wealthier in printers, and in any account of sixteenth-century printing deserves further treatment. Basle was fortunately situated on the road from northern Europe to Italy, and has been called the gateway by which the new learning entered Germany. Already by 1500 the press of Johann Amerbach was well known for its scholarly work. Throughout the sixteenth century many editions of the classics appeared at Basle and a much larger proportion of books was set in roman and italic types.

The first artist of the Renaissance who worked for the Basle printers was Urs Graf

---

1. See K. F. Bauer's 'Leonhard Wagner der Schöpfer der Fraktur,' in *Zeitsch. f. Bücherfreunde*, 1936, Hft. 1.

Argument der dritten Wirckung.

Sempronio nach dem er Celestinam auff der strass er-
raicht het/strafft er sy vmb jr langksamkait mit ainan-
der disputierrnd wast fügs sy auff die angefangen ma
teri brauch wolte/auff das lest gieng Celestina zů dem
haust Pleberij vnd Parmeno belib in dem haust Cele
stina bey seinem bůlen Elicia.

Sempronio/ Celestina/ Elicia.

Chaw wol get die bartet alt so lancksam/
ire füst hetten minder rů zů kumen/nitt
on vrsach sagt man behalter knecht thůt
selten recht/ hoya Celestina wie gemach
gestu Cele. Wast zů thon bistu kumen
mein sun Sempro. Diser vnser krancker waist nitt

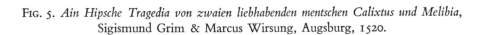

FIG. 5. *Ain Hipsche Tragedia von zwaien liebhabenden mentschen Calixtus und Melibia*,
Sigismund Grim & Marcus Wirsung, Augsburg, 1520.

of Solothurn, who settled in Basle in 1509. The woodcut border which he designed for Adam Petri in 1512, containing medallions of a king and queen, and the 'Humanitas' border, designed for Johann Froben's edition of Erasmus's *Adagia*, 1513, were the earliest architectural borders to appear at Basle. It was this edition of the *Adagia* which attracted Erasmus himself to Basle. Not only had Erasmus's books a very large sale, but the editorial work which Erasmus did for Froben's books brought further distinction to the press. The settling of the first man of letters of Europe in Basle, together with the arrival of Hans Holbein, brought that city into the very first rank as a typographical center. Holbein came to Basle in 1515 and between that year and his first departure for England in 1526 provided an astonishing amount of material, Biblical illustrations, headpieces, initials, and title-borders, for Johann Froben, Adam Petri, Thomas Wolff, Andreas Cratander, and Valentinus Curio. Much of this work was cut on metal. The sharp impressions obtained from these metal cuts are characteristic of the decoration of Basle books of the Holbein period.

This period was very brief. The Reformation itself, in the person of Œcolampadius, brought in various restrictions and a diminished market. However, for many years Basle remained the chief centre in the German-speaking countries for editions of the classics; witness the many volumes printed by Johann Oporinus down to 1568. Peter Perna (1522-1582), a Protestant exiled from Lucca, was another good printer of the late Renaissance. Basle seems also for a period to have been an important centre of type production. It is known that much of the Greek type used at Paris before 1540 came from Basle, and there is record of the purchase of italic from that city by a Paris printer, Chrestien Wechel. The characteristic Basle roman is found throughout Europe and new romans of distinction appeared there as late as 1550 (Fig. 6). The printers of Lyons, Sebastian Gryphius and his contemporaries, were largely supplied from Basle. There is one italic in particular of some interest in the development of type forms which originated in Basle and was marketed throughout Europe. In 1538 a large edition of the works of Galen, in Greek, was brought out by a group of Basle printers, Cratander, Bebel, M. Isingrin, Hervagius, and J. E. Froben. The long preface of thirteen folio pages of the editor Gemusaeus is set in a new italic, a sprawling letter with inclined capitals. All the early italics, whether derived from Aldus or Arrighi, had used an upright, roman, upper case. The first printer who experimented with an inclined upper case appears to have been Johann Singrenius of Vienna, about 1524. The Basle type won enormous popularity and for a score of years could be found wherever the printing press was at work. Its importance historically rests in its sloping capitals, which were copied by Robert Granjon and all subsequent designers of italic.

In most of the countries of Europe there was a marked decline in the quality of book production in the later years of the century, and in none was it more marked than in Germany. The Catholic reaction led to severe restrictions on the liberty of the press, and the economic consequences of a continued state of war had a disastrous effect. The use of cheaper paper and of old and worn woodcuts became general. However, the presses of Cologne, Strasbourg, and Leipzig continued to bebusy, and some Catholic centres, for instance Ingolstadt, increased their output, owing to the activities of the Jesuits.

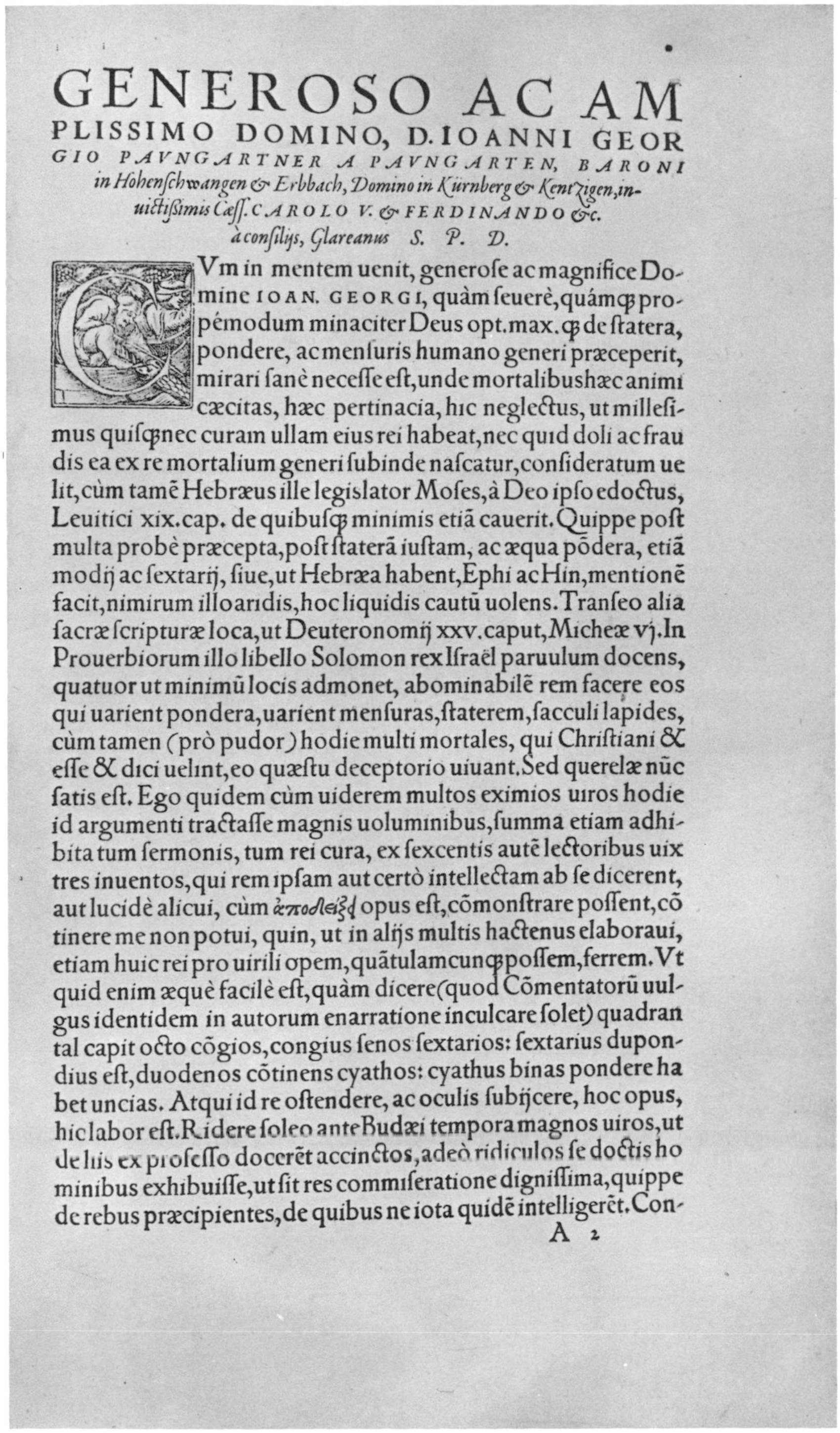

GENEROSO AC AM

PLISSIMO DOMINO, D.IOANNI GEOR
*GIO PAVNGARTNER A PAVNGARTEN, BARONI
in Hohenschwangen & Erbbach, Domino in Kürnberg & Kentzigen,in-
uictissimis Cæss. CAROLO V. & FERDINANDO &c.
à consilijs, Glareanus S. P. D.*

Vm in mentem uenit, generose ac magnifice Domine IOAN. GEORGI, quàm seuerè,quámcꝫ pro-
pémodum minaciter Deus opt.max.cꝫ de statera,
pondere, ac mensuris humano generi præceperit,
mirari sanè necesse est,unde mortalibushæc animi
cæcitas, hæc pertinacia, hic neglectus, ut millesi-
mus quiscꝺnec curam ullam eius rei habeat,nec quid doli ac frau
dis ea ex re mortalium generi subinde nascatur,consideratum ue
lit,cùm tamē Hebræus ille legislator Moses,à Deo ipso edoctus,
Leuitici xix.cap. de quibuscꝺ minimis etiā cauerit.Quippe post
multa probè præcepta,post staterā iustam, ac æqua pōdera, etiā
modij ac sextarij, siue,ut Hebræa habent,Ephi ac Hin,mentionē
facit,nimirum illo aridis,hoc liquidis cautū uolens.Transeo alia
sacræ scripturæ loca,ut Deuteronomij xxv.caput,Micheæ vj.In
Prouerbiorum illo libello Solomon rex Israël paruulum docens,
quatuor ut minimū locis admonet, abominabilē rem facere eos
qui uarient pondera,uarient mensuras,staterem,sacculi lapides,
cùm tamen (prò pudor) hodie multi mortales, qui Christiani &
esse & dici uelint,eo quæstu deceptorio uiuant.Sed querelæ nūc
satis est. Ego quidem cùm uiderem multos eximios uiros hodie
id argumenti tractasse magnis uoluminibus,summa etiam adhi-
bita tum sermonis, tum rei cura, ex sexcentis autē lectoribus uix
tres inuentos,qui rem ipsam aut certò intellectam ab se dicerent,
aut lucidè alicui, cùm ἀποδείξͅ opus est,cōmonstrare possent,cō
tinere me non potui, quin, ut in alijs multis hactenus elaboraui,
etiam huic rei pro uirili opem,quātulamcuncꝺpossem,ferrem.Vt
quid enim æquè facilè est, quàm dicere(quod Cōmentatorū uul-
gus identidem in autorum enarratione inculcare solet) quadran
tal capit octo cōgios,congius senos sextarios: sextarius dupon-
dius est,duodenos cōtinens cyathos: cyathus binas pondere ha
bet uncias. Atqui id re ostendere, ac oculis subijcere, hoc opus,
hic labor est.Ridere soleo ante Budæi tempora magnos uiros,ut
de hiis ex professo docerēt accinctos,adeò ridiculos se doctis ho
minibus exhibuisse,ut sit res commiseratione dignissima,quippe
de rebus præcipientes,de quibus ne iota quidē intelligerēt.Con-

A 2

FIG. 6. Henricus Loritus, *Liber de asse & partibus eius*. Michael Isingrin,
Basle, 1550. (Reduced.)

As early as 1540 Ingolstadt has to its credit Peter Apian's *Astronomicum Caesareum*, a book decorated with a fine alphabet of woodcut initials, and a good example of the treatment of early scientific works.

One city only deserves a longer treatment – Frankfurt on the Main. In the business side of the book trade the Frankfurt fairs had played an important part from the early days of printing, and it is therefore somewhat strange that no printer should have settled there until well into the sixteenth century. The first printer of note was Christian Egenolff, who moved from Strasbourg to Frankfurt in 1530. He and his heirs continued printing there throughout the century, but it was as typefounders that the house was to become really important. The foundry started by Conrad Berner and continued by the Luther family played a great part in the typographical history of the seventeenth century, and even before 1600 the roman and italic types displayed in their first specimen sheet of 1592 can be traced in many towns of Germany. The well-known series of travel books edited by the De Brys at Frankfurt may be cited as an example. How these French types, romans of Claude Garamond and italics of Robert Granjon, were first acquired is not clear, possibly through Jacques Sabon, a Lyonese who came to Frankfurt after a period of work at Antwerp for Christophe Plantin, or through André Wechel, who moved his press from Paris to Frankfurt after the massacre of St. Bartholomew.

Even more important for the history of the book in Frankfurt was the career of the great publisher Sigmund Feyerabend (1560-1590). Feyerabend employed most of the Frankfurt printers and decorated his books by the help of the leading German artists of his generation. His earlier books contain the woodcuts of the Nuremberg artist Virgil Solis (*d.* 1562), his Biblical illustrations and Ovid cuts, for instance. But from 1564 the artist especially associated with Feyerabend was Jost Amman. Amman was born in Zürich in 1539, became a pupil of Virgil Solis, and lived most of his life in Nuremberg. His first work to be published at Frankfurt was a series of Biblical woodcuts, and perhaps the best known were the cuts illustrating the *Eygentliche Beschreibung aller Stände*, 1568. He designed many devices both for Feyerabend and for the men who printed for that publisher. The woodcut title-borders, with a few engraved frontispieces, which he provided for Feyerabend's books, are most typical of the association of this artist and publisher. Amman's borders are in the style of the day, but he outdoes all his contemporaries in the piling up of ornament. A whole series of such title-pages may be seen in Heitz's *Frankfurter Druckerzeichen*, most of them bearing the initials I. A. Feyerabend's books were generally folios in the German language, frequently historical works, and almost invariably set in Fraktur. Sometimes the title-pages were type-set and in those cases of inordinate length. Even the fussiness of Fraktur capitals did not satisfy the publisher and lettering reproduced from a wood block would be added. Feyerabend's work is interesting, the most imposing in the German book trade, and at the same time characteristic of the deterioration of taste in that generation.

France

At the beginning of the sixteenth century French book production was still medieval both in typography and decoration. The *livres d'heures* were being produced after the original style and the leading publisher of Paris, Antoine Vérard, was still bringing out editions of popular literature set in the traditional *lettres bâtardes*. The next generation was to bring a complete change from the gothic of the fifteenth century to the types and modes of decoration of the Italian Renaissance. In certain classes of books the tradition of gothic types persisted for many years, more particularly in the provinces. As late as 1550 the great law books produced at Lyons were still set in *rotunda*, and the popular romances were printed by Oliver Arnoullet in *lettres bâtardes*. But in Paris one can say that by 1530 the leading printers had definitely adopted roman and italic types and a style of decoration inspired by Italian art. There was, however, no direct copying of Italian book production. On the contrary there was evolved a distinctly French Renaissance style, and with such success that Paris rapidly became the leading city in Europe in all the arts of the book.

The revolution begins with the work of scholar printers who were themselves interested in the new learning, men like Jodocus Badius and Henri Estienne. Badius came from the Low Countries. After studying in Italy he became a press-reader for the house of Johann Trechsel in Lyons, before setting up as a printer in Paris. The books which he produced were mostly folios, set in *rotunda* or in a somewhat heavy roman. The Italian influence is to be found in his decorative material, woodcut initials copied from Venice, but on a *criblé* background in the French style. His well-known woodcut title-border, representing a Renaissance arch hung with trophies, was taken directly from a Venetian border used in an Italian version of Livy, 1493. Henri Estienne, the founder of one of the most distinguished families of printers, used initials similar to those of Badius, and had also some excellent and original woodcut borders in the light style of the Renaissance. One may be seen in his *Quincuplex Psalterium* of 1509. Guillaume Lerouge, whose predecessors were noted for their woodcut illustrations of the gothic school, was the first Paris printer to use italic, about 1510. His italics were of three sizes, almost upright, and with the largest an upper case of gothic initials was used. Gilles de Gourmont was the first Paris printer to acquire a fount of Greek, in 1507, another indication of the spread of the new learning.

Henri Estienne's successors, his manager, Simon de Colines, who married his widow, and his son Robert Estienne, may be called the first French Renaissance printers. These two men, together with Geofroy Tory the book decorator and Claude Garamond the engraver of types, transformed the French book. They copied the small format from Aldus, published the Latin and Greek classics at prices suitable for students, popularized italic types and produced a reformed roman which was to be the standard European type for two centuries. Colines was printing from 1520, the year of Henri Estienne's death, till 1546. At first he controlled the Estienne press, but from 1527, when Robert Estienne was of an age to succeed to his father's business, Colines printed on his own account. Philippe Renouard's catalogue of his work credits him with 734 books. To the decoration and illustrations of his books we shall refer again (Fig. 7). Besides Aldine italics Colines had two cursives clearly derived from Arrighi. One, first appearing in 1528, has the ascenders with calligraphic terminals and other features connecting it with the type of the Roman printer. The second is a larger type closely resembling the italic of Arrighi's last years. It was used for the main text of the *Raison d'architecture antique*, a translation of Vitruvius, 1539, among other books. To Colines also belonged the earliest of the new romans of the Garamond school. It has been called the Terentianus fount, because of its use in a book by Terentianus Maurus, printed by Colines in 1531. It had in fact already been used in two tracts by Guillaume Bochetel printed for Geofroy Tory in March and May of the same year.

Robert Estienne had a considerable reputation in his day as a Latin scholar. The Latin dictionary which he both compiled and printed in 1538 remained a standard work for many years. He started printing with a definite programme intended to promote the study of Latin. He first produced a number of grammatical works and followed these by a series of classical texts. Many of his texts were set in Aldine italic, while one notable book belongs to the school of Arrighi, an edition of Luigi Alamanni's *La Coltivazione*, 1546. This handsome volume is set in a formal chancery type and is printed without decoration, with the simplicity of Arrighi's books. Estienne's 'Garamond' roman dates from 1532, being first used in a grammatical work by Jacques Dubois. An edition of Virgil and a magnificent folio Latin Bible appeared in the same year in the new type, a design to which we shall return (Fig. 8). Estienne's interest in Biblical texts and Protestant tendencies made him suspect in the eyes of the Sorbonne and after the death of his patron Francis I, who had made him king's printer for Greek, he decided, in 1551, to withdraw to Geneva. He had printed some 450 books at Paris, and was to produce another sixty at Geneva before his death in 1557. The Geneva house was continued by his son Henri II, even more famous as a scholar and editor of Greek texts, while another son, Robert II, remained in Paris and carried on the excellent standard of printing of his father. Two brothers of Robert I, François and Charles, had also printed at Paris a number of books worthy of the family tradition.

Claude Garamond was certainly the most important designer of types of the sixteenth century, since his models of both roman and Greek typefaces were to remain in vogue for two centuries. In his later years he became also a publisher of books; and a Latin preface which he wrote in 1545 for one of his publications is an important source of our knowledge of his career. The book is the *Pia et religiosa meditatio* of David Chambellan, and Garamond states in the preface that after cutting types for others all his life he has now decided to design something for himself. He says that he had cut the small italic in which the book is printed after the Aldine model and had also cut a larger size. At the same period he was engaged in cutting the *grecs du roi*, the famous Greek types intended for the printing of the Greek manuscripts in the royal library. There is a record of payment being made to Garamond in 1541 in this connection. The three sizes of the Greek design were based on cursive models like the Aldine and included a very large number of tied letters. They are generally accepted as being the finest designs of

FIG. 7. Joannes Ruellius, *De natura stirpium*. Simon de Colines, Paris, 1536. (Reduced.)

5

PAVLI IOVII NOVOCOMEN-
fis in Vitas duodecim Vicecomitum Mediolani
Principum Præfatio.

ETVSTATEM nobi-
liſſimæ Vicecomitum fami-
liæ qui ambitioſius à præalta
Romanorū Cæſarum origi-
ne, Longobardíſq; regibus
deducto ſtemmate, repete-
re contédunt, fabuloſis pe-
nè initiis inuoluere viden-
tur. Nos autem recentiora
illuſtrioráque, vti ab omnibus recepta, ſequemur: có-
tentíque erimus inſigni memoria Heriprandi & Gal-
uanii nepotis, qui eximia cum laude rei militaris, ci-
uilífque prudentiæ, Mediolani principem locum te-
nuerunt. Incidit Galuanius·in id tempus quo Medio-
lanum à Federico AEnobarbo deletū eſt, vir ſumma
rerum geſtarum gloria, & quod in fatis fuit, inſigni
calamitate memorabilis. Captus enim, & ad trium-
phum in Germaniam ductus fuiſſe traditur: ſed non
multo póſt carceris catenas fregit, ingentíque animi
virtute non ſemel cæſis Barbaris, vltus iniurias, patriā
reſtituit. Fuit hic(vt Annales ferunt) Othonis nepos,
eius qui ab inſigni pietate magnitudinéque animi, ca
nente illo pernobili claſſico excitus, ad ſacrū bellum
in Syriam contendit, communicatis ſcilicet conſiliis
atque opibus cū Guliermo Montiſſerrati regulo, qui
à proceritate corporis, Longa ſpatha vocabatur. Vo-
luntariorum enim equitum ac peditum delectæ no-

A.iii.

FIG. 8. Paolo Giovio, *Vitae duodecim vicecomitum Mediolani*. Robert Estienne,
Paris, 1549. (Reduced.)

their class, and they certainly imposed themselves on subsequent Greek typographers for many generations.

The King's printer for Greek at this period was Robert Estienne, and the capitals used at first with the *grecs du roi*, such of them as were roman, were the capitals of the new roman of 1532 already mentioned. Later on these capitals were revised and we get an upper case identical with that of the Garamond romans displayed on the specimen sheet of the Frankfurt foundry of Conrad Berner, afterwards the Luther foundry, issued in 1592. That valuable sheet shows seven sizes of *romains de Garamond*. The lower case also of Estienne's type of 1532 is identical with the lower case of the Frankfurt types. It seems to follow then that it was Garamond who cut Robert Estienne's new roman. In the same year, 1532, two other new romans of the same style appeared at Paris, one at the press of Antoine Augereau, and the other at the press of Chrestien Wechel. According to La Caille, Augereau was an engraver of types, but his career was a short one, for in 1534 he was burned as a Protestant and printer of suspected books.

Earlier histories of printing state that Garamond cut his new romans on the model of the Venetian printer Jenson and that he cut them about 1540 for the King's foundry. There was no King's foundry in the sixteenth century, and the confusion has probably arisen from the fact that the so-called *Caractères de l'Université* of the Imprimerie Royale founded by Cardinal Richelieu in 1640 were thought to have been handed down from Garamond. It has been shown by Beatrice Warde (Paul Beaujon) in her article on Garamond in *The Fleuron*, No. 5, that these types were cut by Jean Jannon of Sedan about 1620. As to the Jenson model that story has likewise been disproved. Stanley Morison[1] has pointed out the striking resemblances between Estienne's roman and the first roman used by Aldus in the *De Aetna* of Pietro Bembo, 1496. Apart from the general similarity of design, the modest height of the capitals, and the comparative narrowness of these two romans in contrast with Jenson, some small peculiarities of serif formation in the type of Griffo, repeated in Garamond, are a convincing proof of Morison's thesis.

Before considering the career of Geofroy Tory, who is of the first importance in the development of French book illustration, it would be well to notice certain other influences affecting the Paris printers. The decoration of the books of hours was undergoing a change at the hands of artists of the Renaissance. A few cuts copied from Albrecht Dürer are found about 1515 in the Hours of Simon Vostre, but on the whole the change was decidedly one of deterioration. A comparison of the Hours printed by Thielman Kerver with the earlier editions of Philippe Pigouchet is sufficient evidence of this decadence. The book illustrators of Basle also had considerable influence, and at one time it almost seemed that the woodcuts and metal cuts of Urs Graf and Hans Holbein and their imitators might become as much the vogue at Paris as they were at Basle. The man who was largely responsible for the introduction of the Basle style was Conrad Resch, a citizen of Basle, who was publishing in Paris from 1516 to 1526. His shop in the Rue St. Jacques, formerly known as the *Corne de Cerf* was renamed the

---

1. 'The Type of the Hypnerotomachia Poliphili,' in the *Gutenberg Festschrift*, 1925, pp. 254-258.

Decameron de Bocace. 1.nouuelle.　　　Fucil.117

ꝺ Chimon deuint ſaige par eſtre

AMOVREVX: ET CONQVESTA PAR
*force ſamye Ephigene ſur la mer: dont il fut mis en priſon à Rhoddes: & ung nŏ-
mé Liſimaque len tira hors: auec lequel il print de rechef Ephigene & Caſſandre
au meillieu de leurs nopces : & ſen fuirent auecques elles en Candie doud apres
les auoir eſpouzées ilz furent rappellez en leurs maiſons.*

Nouuelle premiere.

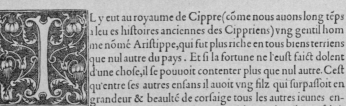

L y eut au royaume de Cippre (cŏme nous auons long téps
1 leu es hiſtoires anciennes des Cippriens) vng gentil hom
me nŏmé Ariſtippe, qui fut plus riche en tous biens terriens
que nul autre du pays . Et ſi la fortune ne l'euſt faiĉt dolent
d'une choſe, il ſe pouuoit contenter plus que nul autre. Ceſt
qu'entre ſes autres enfans il auoit vng filz qui ſurpaſſoit en
grandeur & beaulté de corſaige tous les autres ieunes en-
fans qu'on euſt ſceu veoir : mais il eſtoit preſque tout fol, & tel qu'il nen ſaloit
rien eſperer de bon. Le nom duquel eſtoit Gallois : toutesfois pource que iamais
pour aucun trauail de precepteur , ne pour flaterie ou batterie que luy feiſt ſon
pere, ou par induſtrie d'autruy, on ne luy auoit peu mettre en la teſte lettres , ne
aucune ciuilité , ains auecques vne voix groſſe & difforme, auoit les geſtes & fa-
cons de faire beaucop plus cŏuenables à beſte brutte que à homme. Il eſtoit appellé d'ung chaſcun cŏme par mocquerie Chymon, qui vault autát à dire en leur
langue, cŏme il faiĉt auſi en la noſtre, groſſe beſte. La perdition de la vie duquel
le pere ſupportoit auec grát ennuy: & deſia ayant du tout perdu leſperáce qu'on
pouuoit

FIG. 9. Giovanni Boccaccio, *Le decameron*. Etienne Roffet, Paris, 1545. (Reduced.)

Écu de Basle. In 1519 and 1520 he had three title-borders, which were the work of Urs Graf, all signed with Graf's monogram. Other border-strips by Graf and some copied from him are found in Paris books. Copies of Graf's initials are found as late as 1545 in a book well known for its delicate woodcuts, a French version of Boccaccio's *Decameron*, printed by Étienne Roffet (Fig. 9). Conrad Resch had a device designed by Holbein, and the printer Pierre Vidoue, whose books are full of Basle influence, had another Holbein device (Silvestre 65). Chrestien Wechel, who had been manager for Resch and followed him at the *Écu de Basle* from 1526, had one original Holbein border and also a copy of his Cleopatra border. Wechel, too, had a number of Holbein initials, some original and some copies. As late as 1550 and 1551 they are found in books which Wechel printed for the spelling reformer Louis Meigret. Copies of Holbein's Old Testament illustrations, originally printed at Lyons in 1538, are found at Paris in the middle years of the century. Another German artist, Hans Weiditz, is represented at Paris and at Lyons by copies of his well-known set of initials cut on wood by Jobst Vercer.

Another Paris book illustrator of the Renaissance school was Oronce Finé (1494-1555), a professor of mathematics. A collected edition of his works entitled *Protomathesis*, printed by Gerhard Morrhé in 1532, contains a statement that the illustrations are by the author himself. Among the decorative material of the book is an alphabet of large initials of which the O bears the initials O. F. and a portrait of Finé in the centre. These initials were afterwards used by Michel de Vascosan down to 1554. Finé came from the Dauphiné and adopted the dolphin as a decorative motive. His book illustration can be traced back to 1515; in that year a cut of a celestial globe signed with his monogram occurs in G. Peurbachius's *Theorice nove planetarum*. Simon de Colines had at least three title-borders, used in mathematical works, which can safely be attributed to Finé. The total amount of his work of this class was considerable.

Geofroy Tory of Bourges (*c.* 1480-1533) was the artist to whom is mainly due the French Renaissance style of book decoration. He drew his inspiration from Italy and especially from the Aldine *Hypnerotomachia Poliphili*. His style bears no resemblance to that of contemporary German artists; as a draughtsman he was very much their inferior, but he introduced a style of book decoration which was more in harmony with the new typography of Colines and Garamond. In early life Tory was a schoolmaster and the earliest mention of his name is as an editor of school texts (the first was an edition of Pomponius Mela, 1508). In February, 1523, after a prolonged visit to Italy, he rented a shop in the Rue St. Jacques, to which he gave as a sign his device of the *pot cassé*. Here he did business as a publisher, book decorator, and finally printer. His important publications were a number of Books of Hours and the philological work to which he gave the title *Champfleury*, 1529. We have direct evidence for attributing the decorations and illustrations of these books to Tory himself and from them we can form an idea of his style. Whether Tory was also a woodcutter, as claimed by his biographer Auguste Bernard, is still a matter of doubt. Many of the Tory illustrations are marked with the Lorraine cross. At that particular period in Paris this cross appears to have been used by a firm of woodcutters and it is possible that Tory established the firm. The dates of the first appearance of the mark at Paris fit in well with what is known of Tory's career, but on the other hand he is not known to have had any connections with Lorraine.

As a printer Tory's influence was slight. In fact as a typographer he was a reactionary. The absence of italic and of any of the new romans from the books which he himself printed completely disposes of the claims which Bernard makes for him as a cutter of types. Of that extraordinary book *Champfleury* this is not the place for a full account. The fantastic allegories in which the author indulges make the book almost unreadable today. Nevertheless, besides autobiographical material, it contains matter of importance in the history of the French language and played its part in popularizing the use of the roman letter in France.

The middle years of the century at Paris were a period of great activity for the printing press, remarkable both for the number of books produced and for the high standard of workmanship. Many famous books appeared, such as the French version of the *Polifilo*, published by Jacques Kerver in 1546; Paolo Giovio's *Vitae . . . Mediolani principum*, R. Estienne, 1549; and Jean Cousin's *Livre de perspective*, J. Le Royer, 1560. Denys Janot, who became King's printer for French in 1544, produced many popular books with woodcut illustrations of the Tory school. He and his successors were responsible for the remarkable series of folio volumes of the French *Amadis de Gaula*. Michel de Vascosan, a son-in-law of Badius, favoured a style of simplicity and his imposing volumes are admirable specimens of the use of Garamond romans. There were many printers of Greek texts, like Guillaume Morel and the scholar Adrien Turnèbe. The books of Ronsard and the other members of the Pleiad were excellently produced. It is, in fact, hardly possible to open a Paris book of the period which is not of first-rate quality.

French provincial printing was, with one exception, comparatively unimportant. Printing at Rouen had its influence on English and Scottish printing; there was good work produced at Poitiers and in some other towns, but space precludes their treatment here. The exception is of course the city of Lyons, whose printers for one generation rivalled even those of Paris. In the early years of the century Lyonese printers were active in plagiarizing the Aldine classics in italic, and book decoration was in general much influenced by Italian work. At Lyons there was a great school of printers of law books, who produced ponderous tomes in which gothic types still persisted. The influence of Basle came in with the scholar printer Sebastian Gryphius, who in his earlier years used mainly Basle types and ornaments. The typographical work of the unfortunate Étienne Dolet was very much in the Basle style. The two famous series and the Old Testament illustrations, were printed at Lyons.

But the finest Lyonese printer and in his generation perhaps the best printer in Europe was Jean de Tournes (at work 1542-64). He was trained in the office of Gryphius, but as a printer he was related to the Paris press rather than to that of Lyons. His roman text types were of the Garamond school and his italics were most probably cut by another famous Paris punch-cutter, Robert Granjon. Tournes was interested in Italian literature and one of the earliest of the Italian books which he printed was an edition of Petrarch, 1545, for which the printer himself wrote an interesting preface. From this we learn that it was his intention to print the poets and that he had procured new types to this end.

Among the French poets printed by Tournes were François Habert, Pernette du Guillet, Louize Labé, Margaret of Navarre, Clément Marot, and Pontus de Tyard, all beautiful editions set in italic. His historical works in folio, the books of Claude and Guillaume Paradin, of Jean Le Maire, Comines, and Froissart, are splendid displays of his roman types. All his books were freely decorated with arabesque initials, headpieces, and fleurons; in fact the arabesque is the distinguishing mark of a Tournes book. Many of his books were illustrated with woodcuts after the designs of Bernard Salomon, who seems to have worked almost entirely for Tournes. This Lyons printer evolved a charming style of his own which he owed to no one, either at Paris or elsewhere (Fig. 10).

Robert Granjon, who designed the excellent series of italics used by Tournes, influenced sixteenth-century typography almost as much as Garamond. His father, Jean Granjon, was a Paris publisher, and he himself printed a few books at Paris from 1549 in partnership with Michel Fezendat. From a document of 1546 we know that he was in the habit of visiting Lyons every year, and from another document of August, 1547, that he had already supplied types to Gryphius and Tournes at Lyons. The italics shown on the Egenolff-Berner specimen sheet, Frankfurt, 1592, are definitely ascribed to Granjon. From these various sources we can form a conspectus of his italic designs and can trace his types in many centres of printing, even outside France, in the books of Oporinus of Basle, of L. Torrentino at Florence, of Plantin at Antwerp, in Germany, and in London. The Elzevirs were using his italics throughout the seventeenth century. By 1557 Granjon had settled in Lyons and was married to the daughter of Bernard Salomon. He there printed some twenty volumes in the type which he called *lettres françaises*, a script type based on contemporary French handwriting. His design was very soon copied and owes its name civilité to the fact that Erasmus's *La Civilité puérile* was one of the earliest books printed in a type based on Granjon's.

Granjon experimented also with the building up of printers' flowers into headpieces and borders of arabesques; it is to him we owe this method of book decoration which became so popular in the last quarter of the century, more particularly at Antwerp and London. Granjon spent the last few years of his life at Rome working for the Vatican Press, mainly on Oriental types.

The period which has just been outlined was one of great prosperity for French printers, but it was a period by no means free from troubles, due both to the censorship of the press and to labour disputes. The authorities of Church and State from the beginning recognized the importance of the printing press in the dissemination of new and possibly dangerous ideas, and took steps to control its output. At Paris, even before the appearance of printed books, the Faculty of Theology of the University had acquired the right to license copiers of manuscripts; no manuscript and later no printed book could be sold without their permit. This right was affirmed by a decree of June, 1521, and by a later decree of 1547. In the latter decree, however, theological works only were specified. The Faculty published lists of prohibited books, lists which are among the earliest of the numerous *Indices librorum prohibitorum*. For infringement of

Lapocalypſe
figuree,

Par maiſtre Iehan Duuet, iadis Orfevre des Rois,
François premier de ce nom, &
Henry deuxieme.

A LYON,
Auec priuilege du Roy pour douze ans.
M. D. LXI.

FIG. 10. Jean Duvet, *L'apocalypse figuree*. Jean de Tournes, Lyons, 1561. (Reduced.)

these restrictions the death penalty could be inflicted. That this was no dead letter is witnessed by the fate of many French printers with inclinations toward the New Religion. Antoine Augereau, printer and punch-cutter, was hanged and burned at Paris in 1534, for printing a poem of Margaret of Navarre. Étienne Dolet, the turbulent printer of Lyons, after escaping the clutches of the law on at least two occasions, was finally captured at Troyes in 1544, and after a prolonged trial and imprisonment of two years was hanged and burned at Paris in 1546. He was convicted of blasphemy, sedition, and the selling of prohibited books. Robert Estienne, in spite of the fact that he was king's printer for Greek and had been protected by the King against the University, found it advisable in the end to withdraw to Geneva. This was a route taken by many another French printer, so much so that in the second half of the century Geneva became an important centre of French book production. Labour troubles reached a crisis in 1539, when there was a strike at Paris and an even more serious strike at Lyons. The conditions under which the journeymen worked were extremely bad and the hours of labour incredibly long, some fourteen hours a day, even after a settlement was reached. The journeymen's chief demands were for an improvement in wages and a limitation of the number of apprentices. The state of affairs was so serious at Lyons that some master printers withdrew to the neighbouring town of Vienne. The civil authorities at Lyons had to appeal to the King and a royal decree of December, 1541, settled matters for the time being. But the journeymen were by no means satisfied, and troubles continued until a more reasonable settlement of the differences was arrived at by a decree of September, 1572.

But it was neither the censorhip of the press nor labour troubles which was responsible for the great falling off in both the quality and the quantity of books printed in France toward the close of the century. The chief cause was the Wars of Religion which began in 1562 and resulted in the general impoverishment of France. After the occupation of Lyons by the 'Ligue' in 1563 many Protestant printers began to emigrate to Geneva. We find also that even a publisher like Guillaume Rouille, a Catholic whose books were not of a controversial nature, had to reduce his business to a very restricted output by reason of the economic conditions. The number of books published at Paris very much decreased and cheaper methods of production were resorted to. The printing of pamphlets reporting events connected with the Wars provided some work for the press. The murder of the Duke and the Cardinal de Guise in 1589 and the final struggle between Henry III and Henry of Navarre called forth a stream of tracts. But such work was for the most part slight and done as economically as possible.

Even at the worst, however, there were a few good printers left in Paris. Men like Frédéric Morel, Jamet Mettayer, and Abel l'Angelier still maintained something of the old standards. Some of the small volumes in duodecimo, printed in the 1590's, generally set in italics, were very pleasing and as good books as were being produced anywhere in Europe. Some of them had engraved title-pages, although that method of book decoration was comparatively rare in France before 1600. There were perhaps not more than twenty issued at Paris.

The Netherlands

Between the years 1500 and 1540 there were over 2,800 books produced in the Low Countries, more than half of them printed at Antwerp, according to Nijhoff and Kronenberg's *Nederlandsche Bibliographie*. In the early years of the century the important printers were Hendrik Eckert van Homberch, Michel Hillen van Hoochstraten, Willem Vorsterman, Martin de Keyser, Simon Cock, and Thierry Martens. The printing of these men and their successors was naturally much influenced by the foreign presses, at first by German and Basle printers, and afterwards by the French. Basle types were much used and the woodcut borders and initials of the Holbein school were freely copied. Another source of Netherlands ornaments was Cologne; imitations of the designs of Anton Woensam are often seen.

Nevertheless the Netherlands printers were by no means solely dependent on other countries. Woodcuts after the designs of Jan van Swart and Lucas van Leyden offer examples of good native work, and there was no lack of punch-cutters at any time in the century. The national type was a variety of *textura* and books in the Dutch language continued to be printed in such types even after 1600 (Fig. 11). The so-called Lettersnijder type was a local *textura* characterized by a particular set of capitals and received its name from Hendrik Lettersnijder, who was working at Antwerp at the end of the fifteenth century. At Ghent the printer Joos Lamprecht (1536-56) styled himself *tailleur de lettres*, and we know of at least one roman type cut by him. Henrick van der Keere was another type designer who came from Ghent. In 1547 the University of Louvain published a Latin Bible, printed by Bartholomaeus Gravius, which was recognized as the standard Vulgate down to the publication of the Vatican Bible of 1590. For this Louvain Bible several new types were cut by a native designer or possibly by a Frenchman working in the Netherlands, François Guyot. The records of the Plantin-Moretus Museum at Antwerp give many details of Plantin's relations with local letter-founders.

From the plates in Nijhoff's *L'Art typographique dans les Pays-Bas*, we find little evidence of French influence before 1540. But soon after that date the style of book production becomes definitely more French, and this, be it noted, some years before Plantin set up his press in Antwerp. Books such as Peter Cock's editions in French of the architectural work of Sebastiano Serlio, the fourth book in 1545 and the third in 1550, and C. Cantiunculas's *Paraphrases in libros institutionum Iustiniani*, printed by S. Sassenus at Louvain in 1549, a book in which a Granjon italic was used, illustrate this development.

Christophe Plantin, who was printing at Antwerp from 1555 to 1589, was a Frenchman born in the neighbourhood of Tours. There is no printer of that century of whom we know more. The records of his firm and much of his typographic material have survived and are preserved in the Plantin-Moretus Museum at Antwerp. The work of Max Rooses based on these records enables us to follow the career of a great master printer in all its details. He himself published a specimen of his types, the *Index characte-*

Fo.ij.

Den eersten boeck der Architecturen
van Sebastiaen Serlius / tracterende van Geometrien.

Dat eerste Capittele.

HOe nootelijck dat die alder sekerste conste van Geometrien eenē iegelijcken Constenare ende werckman is / mogen betuigen alle die ghene die eenen tijtlanck sonder de selue gestudeert ende gewrocht hebben: die selue dan naderhant tot eenigher kennissen vander voerseyder const gecomē zijnde / en sullen niet alleenlijck hemseluen verlachen / maer inder waerheyt moeten bekennē dat alle tgene dat welcke van hemlieden te voren geordineert ende gemaect es / niet besiens weert en was. Midts dat dan die leeringe van Architecturē veel edele consten beuangende es / zoe sal ten eersten van noode zijn dat die Architect / ten alderminsten (nach hijs niet meer hebben) zoe vele daer af wete / dat hy die beghinselen van Geometrien verstae / op dat hy in dat getal vande steenbederuers niet en zy / de welcke den naem van eenē Architect voeren / eñ en souden nauwelijck weten te andwoordene / wat een punct / een linie / een pleine / oft een corpus ware / Ja noch veel min souden zij weten te seggene / wat correspondentie oft harmonie ware: maer volgende duer haer goetduncken andere blinde voergangers / die sonder redene gewrocht hebben / zo maken zijt noch ergere: dat welcke een oorsake is van vele onbesnedene wercken / diemen in diuersche plaetsen siet. Waeromme dat die Geometrie den eersten graet es van allen goeden consten / vande welcke dat ick den Architect zoe vele te kennen geuen wille / dat hy met goeden redenen zijn werck sal mogen verandwoorden: Aengaende den speculatien van Euclides / ende andere auctoren die van Geometrien gescreuen hebben / die sal ick voerby gaen / nemende alleenlijck sommige bloemkens wt haren hof / om daer mede duer den cortsten wech / die my mogelijck zijn sal / te tracterene van diuersche duersnijdinge van linien / met sommigen demonstratien / ende meyne oock die selue zoe opentlijck in scrifte ende in figuren te stellene / datse een ieghelijck sal connen begrijpen ende verstaen: aduerterende den lesere dat hy aende tweedde figure niet en gae / voer dat hy deerste wel verstaen heeft / ende altijts zoe voorts gaende / sal hy tot zijnder meyningen mogen comen.

A.ij.

FIG. 11. Sebastiano Serlio, *Den eersten boeck der architecturen.* Widow of Pieter Coecke van Aelst, Antwerp, 1553. (Reduced.)

IVSTI LIPSI
A D
ANNALES
COR. TACITI
LIBER
COMMENTARIVS.

ANTVERPIÆ,
Apud Chriſtophorum Plantinum.
cIɔ. Iɔ. Lxxxv.

FIG. 12. Iustus Lipsius, *Ad Annales Cor. Taciti liber commentarius*. Christophe Plantin,
Antwerp, 1585. (Reduced.)

rum, 1567, and in Rooses's books we are given a mass of information as to his dealings with type-founders, artists, woodcutters, and engravers, and as to the economic side of his business. Plantin received valuable privileges for the printing of liturgical works in the Spanish Netherlands, and these privileges enabled him to support the costly undertaking of his Polyglot Bible and to leave to his heirs a prosperous business.

Plantin's early books are very much in the French style, although many of his types were supplied by designers in the Netherlands. His own characteristic style is heavier and perhaps a little over-ornamented. He published many illustrated books, and employed most of the distinguished woodcutters and engravers of his adopted country, especially Peter van der Borcht, Abraham De Bruyn, and the brothers Wierix. Throughout his career his typography and presswork were always excellent (Fig. 12). Many of his roman types came from Claude Garamond. From Robert Granjon he acquired many italics, Greek types, and civilités. Civilité became more popular in the Netherlands than in the country of its origin, and Plantin had also types of this class from native designers. When his work is compared with that of a printer like Jean de Tournes one realizes that he just missed being of the first class. Nevertheless his is one of the great names in the history of printing.

In the second half of the century there were distinguished schools of engraving in the Netherlands, rivalling even those of Italy, and even surpassing Italy in the production of engraved maps. The *Theatrum orbis terrarum* of Abraham Ortelius, printed by Plantin, is a famous book and there were a number of other atlases of distinction. Hubert Goltzius of Bruges was one of the earliest printers of engraved title-pages. His *Vivae omnium fere Imperatorum imagines*, 1557, contains engraved plates in the chiaroscuro method. Hieronymus Cock and Philippe Galle, besides being themselves engravers, were established as publishers of engraved work and carried on a similar business to that of Antoine Lafrery at Rome.

Spain and Latin America

It is commonly said of printing in Spain that the incunable period lasted longer there than in other countries. Down to about 1530 the book was built up in much the same way as before 1500 and the standard of production was equally high. Many splendid volumes were printed in this period, volumes set in the rounded gothic or *rotunda* and decorated in the characteristic Spanish style. On the title page was a large woodcut, often heraldic, or in the case of the romances of chivalry, a woodcut of a knight or the like. The title too was often cut on wood, and, as in the incunable, the imprint appeared in the colophon. Roman types came in very gradually and became popular only when a decline in the quality of the work of the printers was already in evidence.

Printing in Spain was widely distributed over a number of cities and not centred at the capital as in France and England. The reason for this is partly geographical and partly due to the fact that there was no fixed capital until 1560. Printing did not begin in that capital, Madrid, until 1566. The other important centres were Seville, Alcalá de Henares,

Salamanca, Saragossa, Valencia, Barcelona, Toledo, Valladolid, Burgos, and Medina. The total output of all the Spanish presses throughout the century has been estimated by Dr. H. Thomas as about 10,000 books. For purposes of comparison it may be noted that the output of the city of Lyons alone for the same period has been estimated as about 13,000 books.

The books printed by the Crombergers at Seville, by George Coci at Saragossa, and by Arnald Guillen de Brocar at Alcalá, offer good examples of the Spanish style. The Crombergers, who were Germans, printed many editions of Spanish romances. The *Amadis de Gaula*, 1535, is set in the usual *rotunda* and has on the title-page a large woodcut of a mounted knight. The Crombergers decorated their books with woodcut initials of great beauty. The letters are left in white on a black ground with arabesque tracery. Many similar alphabets are found in early Spanish books. George Coci, another German, was the printer of the first edition of books I-IV of *Amadis de Gaula*. The edition of Livy which he produced in 1520 is very Spanish, in spite of the fact that it contains woodcuts which had appeared originally in a Livy printed at Mainz by J. Schoeffer in 1505. Arnald Guillen de Brocar, again a foreigner, from the south of France, printed some ninety books between 1489 and 1523, at various towns, at Pampeluna, Logroño, Alcalá, Toledo, and Valladolid. His edition of the *Rhetorica* of George of Trebizond, Alcalá, 1511, has an heraldic cut on the title page, a characteristically Spanish initial, and the title in *rotunda* (Fig. 13). His edition of Petrarch's *Trionfi*, 1512, is a similar volume, with a large cut of the royal arms on the title-page. The *Cronica del rey Don Juan* of Pérez de Guzmán, printed by Brocar in 1517, is an equally fine volume.

In the same year Brocar completed the printing of his great Polyglot Bible in six volumes, known as the Complutensian Polyglot (*Complutum* is the Latin name for Alcalá). The first volume completed was the New Testament and bears the date of January 10, 1514. The work was not published until 1522. Six hundred copies were printed, at a cost, we are told, of 50,000 gold ducats. The Old Testament is set in three columns, the versions being Hebrew, Latin, and Greek, with the Chaldaic text for the Pentateuch at the foot. The New Testament is set in two columns, Greek and Latin. The six volumes are almost a complete display of all Brocar's materials, his types, initials, decorative border-pieces, and three varieties of his device. The most interesting of the types is the Greek used in the New Testament, which is not a cursive letter in the Aldine style, like that used for the Septuagint, but a more formal, upright letter. When used in mass it makes a most imposing page and convinces one that the prestige of Aldus has stood in the way of the sound development of Greek typography. Several attempts have been made in recent years to revive the style of Greek lettering of Brocar's type. Robert Proctor's 'Otter' type was based on the Complutensian and Dr. Victor Scholderer's 'New Hellenic' belongs to the same school.

In spite of the fact that so many of the printers at work in Spain were foreigners, their books are not likely to be confused with those produced in other countries. Foreign influences can be traced, but where copies of German or Basle borders were used, the books do not lose their national quality, at least not until the typography began to change, mainly owing to the influence of the great French type designers. Down to

FIG. 13. George of Trebizond, *Opus rhetoricum*. Arnaldo Guillen de Brocar, Alcalá, 1511. (Reduced.)

1540 only a handful of books were set in roman, and those are generally connected with the work of humanistic scholars like Antonio de Lebrija. The appearance of a book in the Spanish language, *Las Obras de Boscan*, Barcelona, 1543, set in roman, is significant of the coming change. Yciar's *Arithmetica*, Saragossa, 1549, is an example of the mixture of the two styles; it has a woodcut border in the late Renaissance manner, not unlike contemporary work at Lyons, but the text is set in *rotunda*. Some Basle types reached Spain. Updike (Figure 229) reproduces a page from a book printed at Granada by Sancho de Nebrija in 1545, a Latin translation of Pulgar's *Chronica de los reyes catholicos*. The page is set in Basle roman and, as Mr. Updike says, might be from one of Froben's books. A still more striking example is a Spanish translation of the *Odyssey*, printed at Salamanca in 1550 by A. de Portonaris. The printer came of an Italian family, well known as Lyonese book producers. The text of the *Odyssey* is entirely set in the Basle italic, and there is nothing at all Spanish about the book.

In the last half of the century books in roman and italic became more frequent, although the *rotunda* was by no means entirely abandoned. The influence is now mainly French, but unfortunately the Spanish printers for the most part failed to make good use of the new material. It is hard to find a really satisfactory Spanish book set in roman during the reign of Philip the Second. However, a book printed by Andres de Angulo at Alcalá in 1569, a life of Cardinal Ximenez by Alvar Gomez de Castro (see Updike, Figure 230) is one of the few exceptions and a fine piece of work. The decline in the quality of book production, so general toward the end of the sixteenth century, began in Spain almost as early as in Germany, a fact for which it is difficult to account. It is probably not unconnected with the discovery of America and the economic consequences of that event.

The first printer in the New World, in the city of Mexico, was Juan Pablos, an Italian (Paoli) from Brescia and a servant of Juan Cromberger of Seville. The contract signed by Cromberger and Pablos has been preserved. It is dated June 12, 1539, and gives many interesting details of the business arrangements. Pablos reached Mexico in September of that year and immediately printed a *Breve y mas compendiosa doctrina Christiana*, in Spanish and Mexican. No copy of this book has survived, and only a fragment of Pablos's second work, a *Manual de adultos*, 1540. Before his death in 1560 he had printed thirty-seven books, mostly religious works. The bibliography of Mexican books of J. T. Medina records 204 books printed in Mexico by 1600. Another important document relating to the Mexican press is a contract dated September, 1550, between Pablos and Antonio Espinosa, a typefounder of Seville. Espinosa undertakes to proceed to Mexico and to cut and cast for Pablos. The result of his work appears in the books printed after 1553. The earlier books were set in rotunda, but now roman types and an interesting italic appear. The *Dialectica* of Aristotle of 1554 shows the romans. The volume is of a remarkably high standard of workmanship, and has on the title page a woodcut border which is a close copy of a border used by Whitchurch in London.[1] This is surely one of the most curious cases known of the interrelations of

1. See L. E. Osborne in *The Library*, 1928, pp. 301-311.

widely remote presses. The *Speculum coniugiorum* of Alonso de la Veracruz, 1556, and the same author's *Phisica speculatio*, 1557, are printed in Espinosa's rather unusual italic – there is little doubt that the type, as well as the romans used by Pablos, was cut by him. From 1559 Espinosa was printing for his own account, and the parent press was carried on by Pedro Ocharte, a Frenchman who had married a daughter of Pablos. Espinosa's *Missale Romanum*, 1561, is a splendid example of a number of notable service books which came from the Mexican press.

The only other American city where there was a printing press before 1600 was Lima in Peru. One of the Mexican printers was Antonio Ricardo of Turin, who arrived in Mexico in 1570 and appears to have been at first associated with Ocharte. From 1577 to 1579 he was printing in Mexico and then decided to try his fortunes in Lima. He arrived there at the end of 1580, but found that many difficulties had to be overcome before he was allowed to print. Finally in 1584 Ricardo set up the *Doctrina christiana y catecismo para instruccion de los Indios*. There is reason to believe that work on this book was interrupted for a more urgent task, the printing of the King's *Pragmatica sobre los diez dias del ano*. This decree of four pages probably appeared in July, 1584, and the Catechism in August. Medina records twelve books printed by Ricardo before 1600.

Great Britain and Ireland

The output of the printing press in England between 1500 and 1600 was fairly high, but the standard, it must be admitted, was below that of Continental printers. A large proportion of the printers were of foreign birth, for example, Wynkyn de Worde, Pynson, John Rastell, Reyner Wolfe, Thomas Vautrollier, and many others. Many books too were printed abroad for the English market, at Antwerp, Paris, and Rouen, especially liturgical works for English dioceses. The Coverdale Bible of 1535, formerly thought to have been printed at Zürich, has been shown to have been printed at Cologne or Marburg.[1] The Great Bible of 1539 was printed at Paris by F. Regnault, though finished in London by Richard Grafton. At a later period many English books were printed abroad for reasons of religion, by Protestants in Queen Mary's reign, and by Catholics in the reign of Queen Elizabeth I.

The decoration of books by means of woodcut title-borders and initials was characteristic of the century and was as popular in England as elsewhere. Many of the borders were copies of Continental work and in a few cases actual blocks were imported. The original designs were not good and the technique of the block-cutting was poor. A few engraved title-pages appeared, of which the earliest, that of Thomas Geminus, 1545, is the best known. Perhaps the best English title-pages before 1600 were those decorated with printers' flowers; e. g., William Lambarde's *A Perambulation of Kent*, printed by E. Bollifant, 1596, and Tasso's *Godfrey of Bulloigne*, A. Hatfield, 1600.

Wynkyn de Worde (*d.* 1535) and Richard Pynson (*d.* 1530) were the leading printers of the early years. De Worde printed about 800 books in his career. The books which

1. See L. Shepherd in *The Library*, December, 1935.

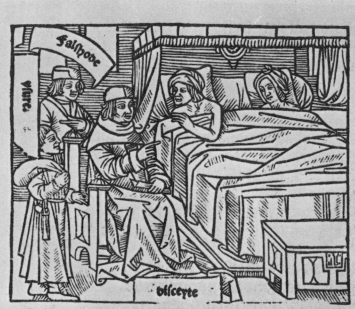

FIG. 14. Pierre Gringore, *The Castell of Laboure*. (Tr. Alexander Barclay.)
Richard Pynson, London, [1505?].

he and Pynson issued, set in black letter or *textura*, were the best productions of that generation (Fig. 14). Thomas Berthelet (at work 1525-55) who succeeded Pynson as King's printer, Richard Grafton (at work 1539-53), King's printer to Edward VI, Reyner Wolfe, an importer of Basle types, Richard Jugge (at work 1541-77), and Richard Tottel (at work 1550-94) were all important printers. John Day (at work 1546-84) is generally admitted to be the best English typographer of the century. His success was largely due to the support given to him by Archbishop Parker. Certainly such books as William Cunningham's *Cosmographicall Glasse*, 1559 (Fig. 15), and the *Ælfredi Regis res gestae*, 1574, approach the best Continental standards. Day's types were acquired for the most part in the Netherlands.

Printing in Scotland began in 1508 with the press of Chapman and Myllar at Edinburgh. Both this press and others at Edinburgh appear to have acquired material at Rouen. Humphrey Powell, a London printer, moved to Dublin in 1550 and was the first printer in Ireland. Of English provincial presses the most interesting was that of Jan Siberch at Cambridge, who came from the neighbourhood of Cologne. In 1520 and 1521 he printed nine books in a roman type. The second Oxford press (the first belongs to the incunable period) was set up in 1517 by John Scolar, with materials acquired from De Worde. From 1519 to 1585 there was a gap in Oxford printing; in the latter year Joseph Barnes set up his press, the first of an unbroken series of Oxford printers.

The usual body type of English printers of the generation of De Worde was a *textura*, the most formal of gothic types, and a type still obtainable in England. This remained the standard type for certain classes of books, liturgical works, Bibles, and legal texts, for long after 1600. The authorized version of the *Bible*, 1611, was set in *textura*. The first roman type – or white letter, as some of our printers called it – was introduced by Pynson in 1509, probably at the persuasion of Petrus Gryphus of Pisa, who came to England in February, 1509, as papal collector. His *Oratio*, intended to be delivered before Henry VII, but never spoken owing to the King's death, was printed by Pynson in a roman type procured from Paris. Two other books of the same year, Alexander Barclay's *Ship of Fools* and a tract by Savonarola were partly set in the new roman. De Worde's two romans also came from Paris, and his italic from Antwerp. Berthelet had a better italic, which is found first at Cologne, then at Strasbourg, at Paris, and in the Netherlands. A little later we find that the italic of Johann Froben of Basle, the characteristic Basle roman and the Basle italic mentioned above were all widely used in London. In the later years of the century Garamond romans and Granjon italics were in most offices. The well-known double pica roman of John Day (Updike, Figure 256), is first found in the Louvain Vulgate of 1547, and his double pica italic (Updike, Figure 257) was a popular Antwerp type. Practically all the romans and italics and many of the gothic types of English sixteenth-century printers have been traced to Continental sources. It is just possible that Thomas Berthelet cut some of his own types, but there seem to have been no professional punch-cutters at work in England before 1600. From the Register of Aliens we know of a typefounder named Paul Rotteforde, who in 1571 had been fourteen years in England, and of a Dutchman, Gabriel Guyett or Guyot, who was living in Day's house in 1576. The latter was probably a relative of François

✿ THE PRÆFACE OF THE
Author, setting out the dignitie, and Ample vse of Cosmographie.

I FEVER THERE wer Art for all mēs vse inuented, Science set forth wherein consisteth Sapience, or Treasure worthy to be had in estimation: no doughte (louynge Reader) either Cosmographie is the same, or els it is not to be founde vppon th'Earth. For if we do well consider with oure selues what her office is, there is no man I suppose, so meane witted, but will confesse her ample vse, nor yet so simply learned but must acknowledge her manifold benefites. And if I shall begin with the defence of our Coūtry, which ought to be more præcious, thē Parentes wife Children or Consanguinitie, Cosmographie herein do so much profite, that without it both valeaunt Corage, Policy and Puissaunce oftentimes can take no place. For by her we are taught whiche way to conduct most safely our ooste, where to pitch oure tentes, where to winter: yea, and where most aptlye to encounter with them in the fielde. VVhich thing Alexander the mighty Conqueroure vnderstanding, accustomed to haue the Mappe and Carte of the Country, by his Cosmographers set out, with which he would warre. Commaunding it also to be hanged in open markets for all men to behold, wherby the Capitaines did forsee, and seke out where was the easiest places to arriue, and the Souldiors allured with the commodities of the Countries, were made the willinger to the thinge. This was it which gat him so many victories, and made him so great à Cōqueror. This was it which obteined the Romanes their fame, more then ther force and strength. This hathe bene to all men profitable, and iniurious to no man. On the contrarye parte, what domage, yea vtter subuertion hathe folowed to moste noble Princes, and valeaunte Capitaines throughe Ignorance of this Art, histories full well can testify.

A.iiij.   And

FIG. 15. William Cunningham, *The Cosmographicall Glasse.* John Day, London, 1559. (Reduced.)

Guyot, who cut types for Plantin. Benjamin Simpson is the first Englishman referred to as a typefounder, in 1597. A founder, of course, was not necessarily a punch-cutter. Day at least had someone in his office capable of cutting the special letters needed for his Anglo-Saxon type. The Secretary type, the English form of civilité, which was in the office of the Barkers, where it is first found in 1576, has not been found abroad.

English printers were subjected to censorship in much the same way as their contemporaries on the Continent. The State attempted to check the spread of heresy through printed books by a system of licensing. For the greater part of the century there were in England two extremes of heresy in the eyes of the authorities, the Puritans on the one hand and the Catholics on the other. Legislation concerning the press was at first directed to the question of foreigners at work in England and imported books. As an indication of the state of affairs we find, according to Gordon Duff, that no classical texts were printed in England before 1535, and we have already mentioned the number of printers bearing foreign names. In 1523 it was decreed that apprentices were to be of English birth, and that not more than two foreign journeymen were to be employed in one house. An act of 25 December, 1534, put an end to the dealing in foreign unbound books. At that date, of course, books were normally imported in sheets.

The proclamations in the reign of Henry VIII against the sale of Lutheran books were many. By a proclamation of November 16, 1538, censorhip was definitely established. In 1557 the Stationers' Company was given a charter and made use of for the purpose of controlling the trade. Printing was restricted to a known circle and it was therefore easier to trace the material of the secret presses. By an injunction of Elizabeth of 1559 all books were to be licensed and books already printed could be prohibited. A Star Chamber decree of 1566 reaffirmed these regulations and obliged printers to enter into recognizances that they would obey the rulings of the Stationers' Company. A Star Chamber decree of 1586 actually restricted all printing to London and to one press each at Oxford and Cambridge. The number and activity of the secret presses suggest that all these regulations cannot have been strictly enforced. However, after the seizure of the Marprelate Press in 1589 control seems to have been more complete.

Apart altogether from religious questions the book trade was restricted in another way, by the granting of privileges for classes of books to particular printers. Grafton and Whitchurch received a privilege for the printing of service books, Tottell for law books, Thomas Marshe for school Latin texts, and Richard Jugge, in the first part of Elizabeth's reign, for Bibles. When Christopher Barker from the year 1577 was privileged to be the sole printer of Bibles, service books, and all official publications, matters reached a crisis. It was one thing to secure a printer's copyright in a particular book, but these wholesale restrictions aroused much opposition. John Wolf, who took the lead in the struggle against these monopolies, was imprisoned for a time in 1582. Ultimately he appears to have been bought off, and matters remained much as before.

Other Countries

Printing in other countries, although of local interest, was of no importance in the general development of book production. A few references only will be given here.

There were presses at work in three Scandinavian countries, Denmark, Sweden, and Iceland, and all were in the main an extension of German printing. In L. M. Nielsen's *Dansk typografisk Atlas*, 1934, a very good picture of Danish printing is presented. The typography was German and the book decoration German or Netherlandish. The Antwerp printer Johan Hoochstraten for a time managed a press at Malmö. Lorentz Benedicht at Copenhagen was perhaps the best and most original printer in Denmark in the second half of the century. He was himself also a woodcutter. The private press of the astronomer Tycho Brahé at his castle Uranienborg, 1584-97, is also of interest. In Sweden Paul Grijs, the first printer of Swedish birth, had a press at Uppsala from 1510 to 1519. There was printing also at Söderköping, and at Stockholm. Jürgen Richolff of Lübeck printed Gustaf Vasa's Swedish Bible at Uppsala in 1541. Amund Laurentsson, who succeeded Richolff at the Royal Press, by that time moved to Stockholm, had printed nearly a hundred books by 1575. He was the first to use roman type in Sweden, in 1559. In Iceland, printing was begun at Hólar in 1534, by Jón Matthiason under the patronage of the last Icelandic Catholic bishop, Jón Arason. Jón Jonsson printed the Icelandic Bible in 1584, also at Hólar.

For printing in eastern Europe and the Slavonic countries the reader may be referred to the chapter by L. C. Wharton in *Printing*, edited by R. A. Peddie, 1927. The distinguished Viennese printer, Hieronymus Vietor, moved to Cracow about 1515 and made that city an important centre of printing. The reproductions in S. Lam's *Le Livre polonais*, 1923, show that there was some original book decoration produced in Poland. In Bohemia there were important presses at Prague. At Moscow there were two presses before 1600, the earlier being set up in 1553, and one at Riga dating from 1588. Early in the century Hebrew presses were at work at Constantinople and Salonika, at the former from 1504 and at Salonika from 1512. Gershon Soncino, who had printed many Hebrew books in northern Italy, later worked at Salonika and at Constantinople.

★

Book production in the sixteenth century attracts us by its high standard of workmanship in the leading cities and by its remarkably varied character. The style of book decoration of each country was peculiar to itself, and in the course of the century was in more than one instance entirely transformed. In Paris, even in one generation, the book was revolutionized, from the gothic productions of Antoine Vérard to the delicate Renaissance work of Geofroy Tory. In typography we find gothic designs of the fifteenth century still surviving, new roman types, some of which are in use to this day, and a surprising variety of italic types cut by Italian and French designers. We have reached the period of the specialized typecutter, a professional who sold his types or matrices to printers all over Europe.

[1938]

For References see pp. 447-448.

THE CHANCERY TYPES OF ITALY AND FRANCE*

In the article entitled 'Towards an Ideal Type,' which appeared in the second number of *The Fleuron*, the briefest incidental reference was made to certain sloping varieties of the neo-caroline script which developed during the early decades of the fifteenth century. It was explained that this hand was adopted during the pontificate of Nicholas V (1447-51) for the exclusive use of that department of the Vatican chancery which was concerned with the engrossing of papal briefs.

Upon the model of this papal script, or as it became known throughout Italy, the *cancelleresca* or *chancery*, a number of printing types were cut; and it is proposed in this article to offer some account of these and of the printers who used them.

Analysis of the chancery type yields a number of interesting characteristics. First: the upper case is upright as becomes a rigid and somewhat static form. Secondly, the more dynamic lower case, though it generally slopes as becomes a cursive character, is also found upright.[1] The terminations to the lower case ascenders and descenders vary. They occur as either round kerns (A) or pointed serifs (B).

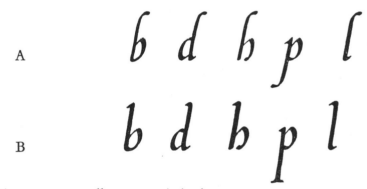

A

B

There are generally two varieties in

There can be little doubt that for all its beauty the chancery letter, originally at least, was accounted as the poor relation in the family of letters. As script it was used for correspondence and for documents of lesser importance; and as type it was first used for the cheapest class of classical text, and that at the lapse of thirty or more years after the introduction of printing into Italy.

Its debut in typography cannot be rated higher than as a partial success. It is much

---

* Jointly with Stanley Morison.
1. This is important when it is realized that in England and U.S.A. the tendency is to regard *italic* as essentially a sloping character.

less elegant than serviceable, and its utility is seriously compromised by the presence of an enormous number of ligatures – Updike has counted no fewer than sixty-five tied letters in the Aldine *Virgil*, 1501, and *Dante*, 1502.

But when the author of *Printing Types* proceeds: 'This Aldine character became the model for all subsequent italic types' (Vol. I, p. 129), we think we detect room for qualification. More exactly, perhaps, the Aldine type may be claimed to have suggested or to have made possible the general use of the chancery type in typography. It is the fact, of course, that more or less close reproductions of Aldus's chancery type were made immediately by many printers in various centres; but it remains the case that the passage of a few years witnessed the development of another chancery series – founded quite independently of the Aldine design. This second school of chancery types (we will not at the moment call them italics, since at least one of them is not inclined) is intimately connected with the city of Rome, with the Vatican chancery and in particular with the work of the scribe Lodovico degli Arrighi of Vicenza, whose typography has been passed over in silence, although he not only produced some of the most beautiful books printed in this, or indeed in any, period, but was also a source of inspiration to other better-known printers. In the second number of *The Fleuron* it was pointed out that Blado's larger italic is practically the same as Arrighi's, and reproductions were given from two pages of his books. In Fumagalli's Dictionary there is a mere reference to Arrighi in connection with Janicolo at Vicenza, while under the heading *Rome* there is no mention of him at all. The only considerable account of him is in Giacomo Manzoni's *Studi di Bibliografia Analitica* (Studio secondo, 1882), where, however, he is considered as the author of the earliest writing book and little is said of his career as a printer. Arrighi's writing book was probably engraved by Ugo da Carpi (the well-known woodcutter who later issued an edition of the book with a privilege granted to himself and not to Arrighi) and printed at Rome in 1522. In this book Arrighi describes himself as 'scrittore de' brevi apostolici' – an interesting fact, since all cursive types were based on the chancery hand of these 'scrittori de' brevi', and here we find one of them actually turning printer. In this writing book will be found many of the characteristics of Arrighi's types, and although as the book is printed from blocks, flourishes are possible with which printing from cast type could not compete. Apart from this calligraphic book and its continuation, *Il modo di temperare le penne*, also engraved and printed at Venice in 1523, no books appear to have been printed or written by Arrighi before 1524. The earliest book in that year bearing the date of a month is the *Coryciana*, a collection of Latin poems in honour of Janus Corycius and edited by Blosius Palladius, one of the Papal secretaries. The colophon reads 'Impressum Rome apud Ludovicum Vicentinum et Lautitium Perusinum, Mense Julio MDXXIIII.' As to this second printer, Lautitius Perusinus, whose name appears with Arrighi's on many of the books printed in 1524 and 1525, and not afterwards, he is in one imprint styled 'intagliatore,' and therefore Manzoni conjectures that he was the actual engraver of the new types. Probably he may be identified with the medallist, whose full name appears to have been Lautizio de Bartolomeo dei Rotelli. He has the distinction of being referred to by Benvenuto Cellini, who praises him for his work

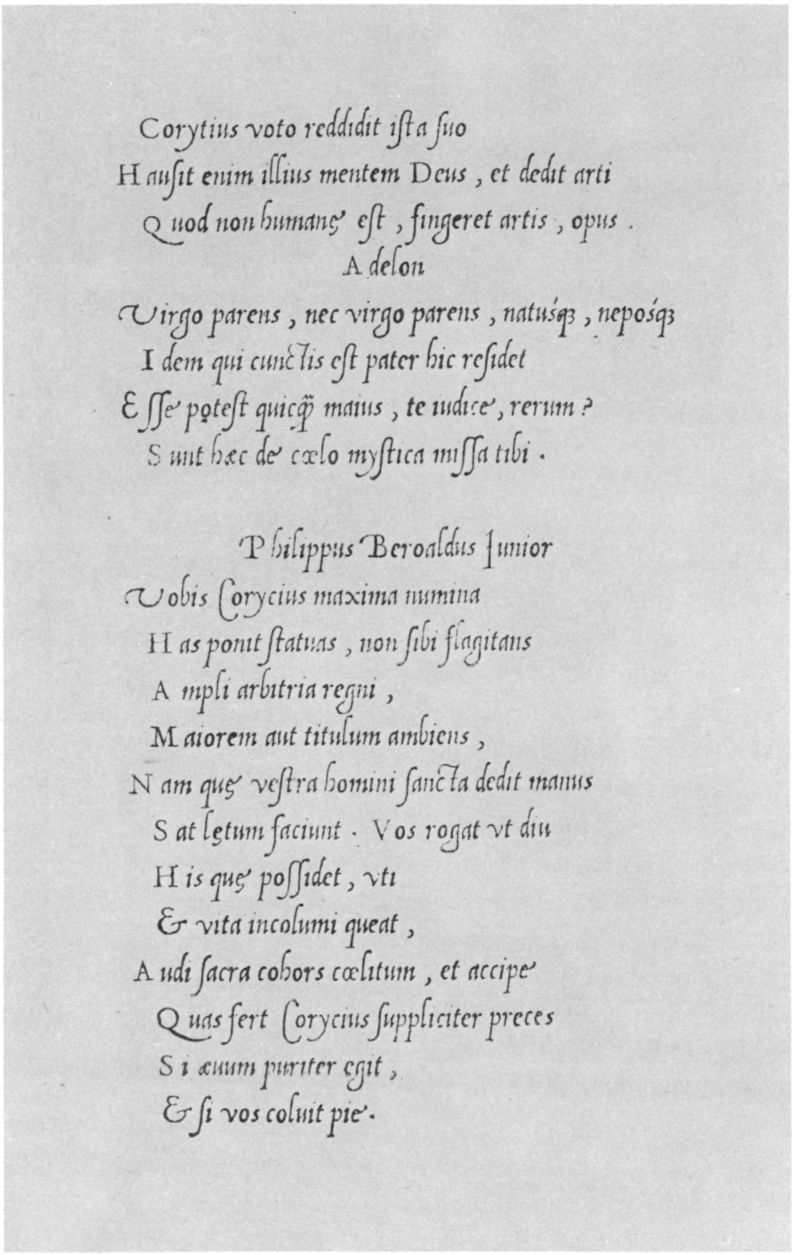

Corytius voto reddidit ista suo
Hausit enim illius mentem Deus , et dedit arti
Quod non humanæ est , fingeret artis , opus .
            Adeson
Virgo parens , nec virgo parens , natusq3 , neposq3
Idem qui cunctis est pater hic residet
Esse potest quicq̃ maius , te iudice , rerum ?
Sunt hæc de cœlo mystica missa tibi .

            Philippus Beroaldus Iunior
Vobis Corycius maxima numina
Has ponit statuas , non sibi flagitans
Ampli arbitria regni ,
Maiorem aut titulum ambiens ,
Nam quæ vestra homini sancta dedit manus
Sat lętum faciunt . Vos rogat vt diu
His quæ possidet , vti
& vita incolumi queat ,
Audi sacra cohors cœlitum , et accipe
Quas fert Corycius suppliciter preces
Si æuum puriter egit ,
& si vos coluit pie .

FIG. 1. Arrighi's first italic. From Blodius Palladius, *Coryciana*. Ludovico Arrighi & Lautizio Perugino, Rome, 1524. This is the printers' first book.

as an engraver of seals. The *Coryciana* is a quarto, like all Arrighi's books, and printed throughout in one size of a most beautiful cursive.

The aim which Aldus set before himself of producing cheap editions of the classics was not shared by Arrighi. His object was the fine book, and he certainly achieved his end. Most of his works were editions of contemporary Latin and Italian poems, where he was under no necessity to restrict himself as to space. His first fount is interesting because of its similarity to the writing books and the chancery hand, and also because, in addition to the upright capitals, we find for the first time what are known to the printer as 'swash' capitals. Such capitals add distinction to the cursive type of Francesco Marcolini produced at Venice some ten years later, but here they are found at Rome some time before Marcolini began to print.

Also in 1524, but with no date of month, appeared *Baptistae Casalii in legem agrariam . . . oratio*; and a book with the imprint *Romae* but without name of printer, *G. Sauromanus . . . de religione ac communi concordia*, the work of a German lawyer who studied in Rome and became a Roman citizen. Both books are in the same fount as the *Coryciana*. They are both prose works and show that the type was almost as suitable for a speech as for a poem. But Arrighi's best known work during this year was the printing of several of the books of Gian Giorgio Trissino, author of the tragedy *Sophonisba* and of the unreadable epic *Italia liberata dai Goti*. Trissino, a wealthy nobleman from Arrighi's native town Vicenza, had recently come to Rome. The first work of his printed by Arrighi appeared in the spring of this year, according to Morsolin's biography of Trissino (p. 123), and was a *Canzone* addressed to the Pope, Clement VII. The poem bears no imprint, but is printed in Arrighi's cursive, with the addition of the Greek letters devised by Trissino for the improvement of Italian spelling. Trissino's scheme was to distinguish the two sounds of the Italian *o, e,* and *z* by using the corresponding Greek letters for one of the sounds, to differentiate the vowel and consonant *i* and *u,* by using *j* and *v,* with other minor reforms. Although some of Trissino's suggestions have been generally adopted and others have been forgotten, from the point of view of the typographer it may be said that the introduction of the Greek letters in no way spoilt the effect of the italic. The letters harmonized quite well. In this Trissino was more fortunate than some other spelling reformers.

The *Canzone* was followed in July by the first edition of Trissino's tragedy, *Sophonisba,* which had been completed some ten years before. There appear to have been two editions of the tragedy since some copies have the date September in the colophon. In October appeared two other books by Trissino, the *Oratione . . . al serenissimo Principe di Venetia* and the *Ritratti;* also, still in 1524, the *Epistola de la vita che dee tenere una donna vedova,* and finally the *Epistola de le lettere nuovamente aggiunte ne la lingua italiana,* without imprint. In this letter, addressed to Clement VII Trissino pays a handsome tribute to Arrighi.

After expounding his theories on spelling reform he continues: 'Now these new letters have been made (*messe in opera*) here in Rome by Lodovico Vicentino, who, as in calligraphy he has surpassed all other men of our age, so, having recently invented this most beautiful method of doing in print all that was formerly done with the pen,

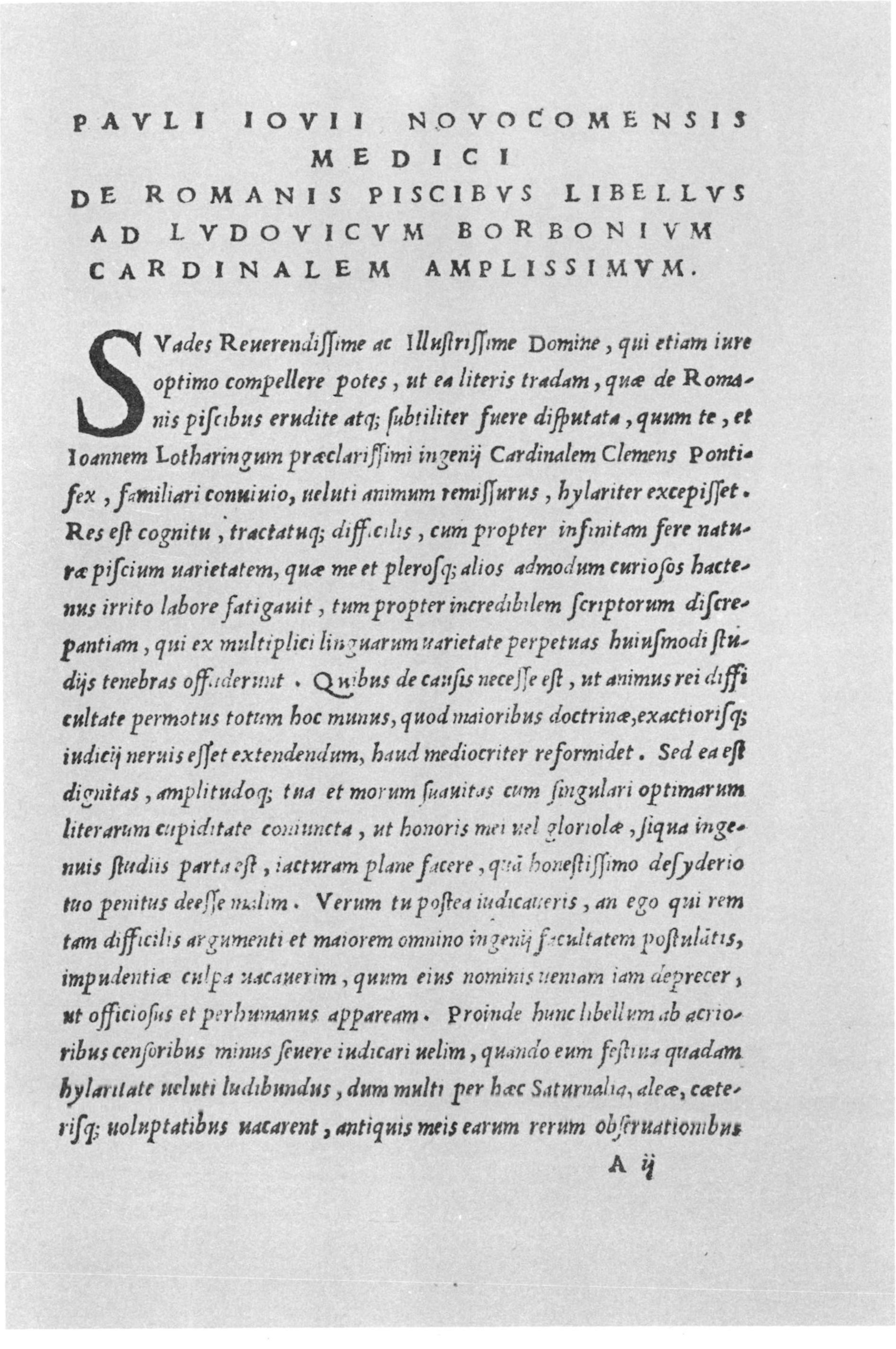

PAVLI IOVII NOVOCOMENSIS
MEDICI
DE ROMANIS PISCIBVS LIBELLVS
AD LVDOVICVM BORBONIVM
CARDINALEM AMPLISSIMVM.

SVadeſ Reuerendiſſime ac Illuſtriſſime Domine , qui etiam iure
optimo compellere potes , ut ea literis tradam , quæ de Romanis piſcibus erudite atq; ſubtiliter fuere diſputata , quum te , et
Ioannem Lotharingum præclariſſimi ingenij Cardinalem Clemens Pontifex , familiari conuiuio , ueluti animum remiſſurus , hylariter excepiſſet .
Res eſt cognitu , tractatuq; diſſicilis , cum propter infinitam fere naturæ piſcium uarietatem , quæ me et pleroſq; alios admodum curioſos hactenus irrito labore fatigauit , tum propter incredibilem ſcriptorum diſcre-
pantiam , qui ex multiplici linguarum uarietate perpetuas huiuſmodi ſtu-
dijs tenebras offuderunt . Quibus de cauſis neceſſe eſt , ut animus rei diffi
cultate permotus totum hoc munus , quod maioribus doctrinæ , exactioriſq;
iudicij neruis eſſet extendendum , haud mediocriter reformidet . Sed ea eſt
dignitas , amplitudoq; tua et morum ſuauitas cum ſingulari optimarum
literarum cupiditate coniuncta , ut honoris mei uel gloriolæ , ſiqua inge-
nuis ſtudiis parta eſt , iacturam plane facere , quâ honeſtiſſimo deſyderio
tuo penitus deeſſe malim . Verum tu poſtea iudicaueris , an ego qui rem
tam difficilis argumenti et maiorem omnino ingenij facultatem poſtulatis ,
impudentiæ culpa uacauerim , quum eius nominis ueniam iam deprecer ,
ut officioſus et perhumanus appaream . Proinde hunc libellum ab acrio-
ribus cenſoribus minus ſeuere iudicari uelim , quando eum feſtiua quadam
hylaritate ueluti ludibundus , dum multi per hæc Saturnalia , aleæ , cæte-
riſq; uoluptatibus uacarent , antiquis meis earum rerum obſeruationibus

A ij

FIG. 2. Early use of leading. From Paolo Giovio, *De romanis piscibus.*
Minutius Calvus, Rome, 1527.

in his beautiful types he has gone beyond all other printers.' This is, perhaps, a little un-fair to Aldus and Francesco Griffo, as Arrighi was not the first to cast italic types, but it is surely true that his italics surpass all others in beauty of form. In our view, Arrighi produced the finest italic of his day and, at any rate at Rome, was unrivalled as a printer. Minitius Calvus was by this time printing with italic types of the Aldine school, but his books are only remarkable for the fact that his pages are well leaded. As to the other Roman printers they, including Blado, were so far content with uninteresting roman types. Trissino certainly found the right man for his purpose, and we may fairly concur that the compliment to his printer is thoroughly deserved.

Soon afterwards Trissino left Rome and in 1529 he reprinted these and others of his works in his native town of Vicenza at the press of Tolomeo Janicolo of Brescia. Fumagalli gives some account of Janicolo, and that printer has elsewhere received considerable praise for these beautiful editions of Trissino's works; and not unde-servedly, but for the fact that it is not mentioned that they are a fairly close copy of Arrighi's editions. A few letters of Janicolo's type are different and more of the Greek letters are introduced, but otherwise everything is a repetition of Arrighi's work.

The first book which Janicolo issued in these types, in January 1529, was Trissino's Italian translation of Dante's *De vulgari eloquentia*. The fact that this was the first appear-ance in print of any version of this famous book has especially directed attention to Janicolo. Some of these books printed in this year are in folio, whereas Arrighi's were in quarto. Also Janicolo adopted a handsome printer's device, using it sometimes, on the title-page and sometimes in the colophon. Although the device bears Janicolo's initials – T. JA. – and although he used it on books other than those of Trissino, e. g. in the colophon of the *Praeservator sanitatis*, a Latin poem by Franciscus Bernardinus – it was actually Trissino's device. It represents Jason's Golden Fleece guarded by the dragon surrounded by a Greek quotation from Sophocles' *Oedipus Tyrannus* – τὸ ζητούμενον ἁλωτόν 'what is sought can be caught.' Janicolo used another variety of the device when he later moved to Venice; there, in 1548, he printed Trissino's comedy *I Simillimi*, with the Greek letters, but in another and less interesting italic. Also he issued the continuation of the *Italia liberata*, of which the first part had been printed at Rome in 1547 by the Dorici.

Trissino's spelling reforms led to much controversy, and a number of pamphlets on both sides were published, of which at least two were printed by Arrighi. These are: *Discacciamento de le nuoue lettere inutilmente aggiunte ne la lingua toscana* by Agnolo Firenzuola, dated December 1524 in the colophon, and *De le lettere nouamente aggiunte, Libro di Acriano Franci intitolato . . . il Polito*, undated, but belonging to the same period. Adriano Franci is a pseudonym of Claudio Tolomei. Both these books are printed in the same italic as the Trissinos, but naturally without the Greek letters or even the distinction of *u* and *v*.

Presumably also of the year 1524 is the one example we have seen of a papal bull printed by Arrighi; though there is no date in the colophon the bull is dated 'pri. Idib. Junii 1524,' and is a proclamation 'contra homocidas.' It is singular that the great majority of papal bulls, briefs, and edicts should continue to be printed in the somewhat

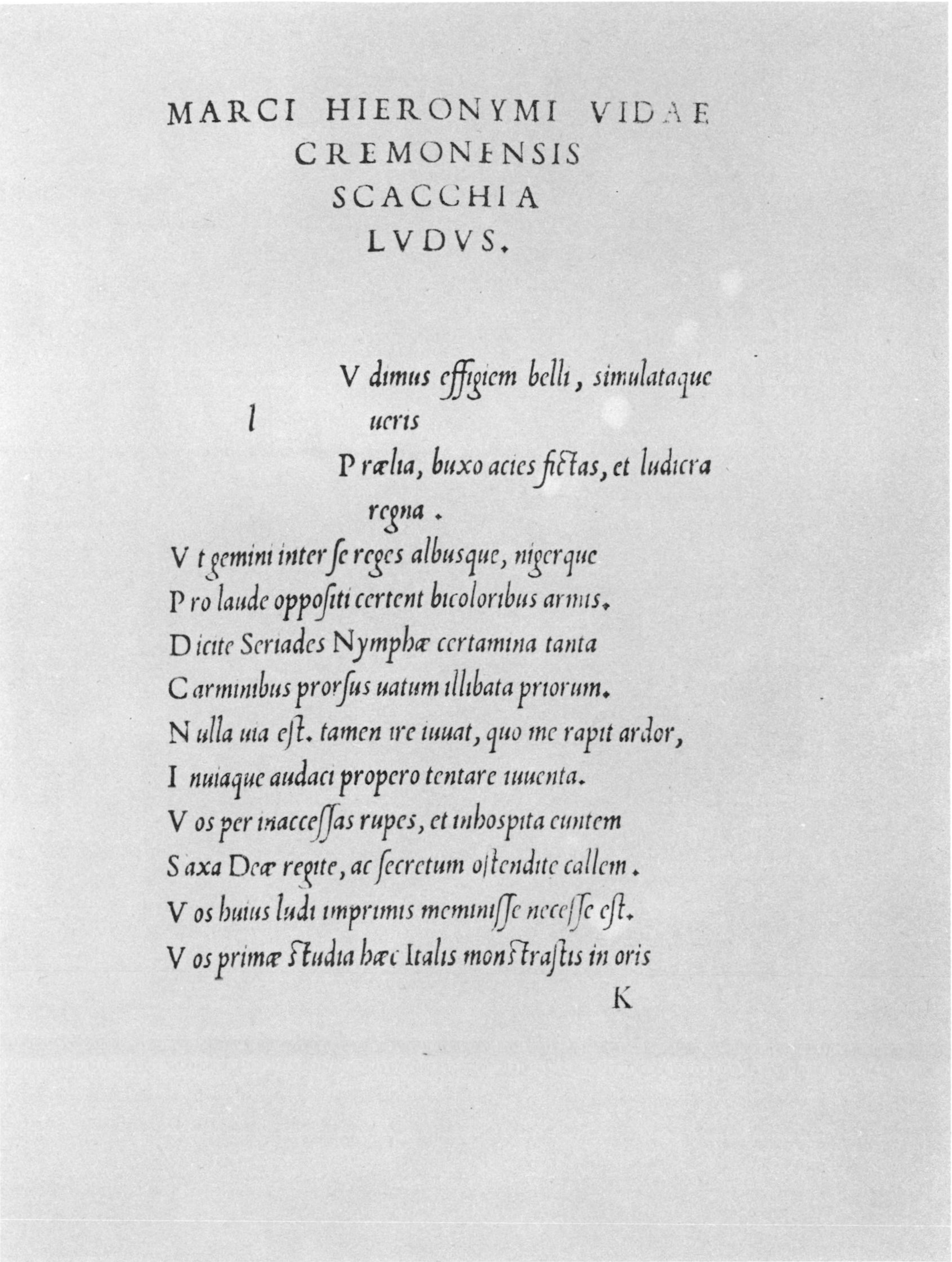

MARCI HIERONYMI VIDAE
CREMONENSIS
SCACCHIA
LVDVS.

l

V dimus effigiem belli, simulataque
ueris
Prælia, buxo acies fictas, et ludicra
regna.
Vt gemini inter se reges albusque, nigerque
Pro laude oppositi certent bicoloribus armis.
Dicite Seriades Nymphæ certamina tanta
Carminibus prorsus uatum illibata priorum.
Nulla uia est. tamen ire iuuat, quo me rapit ardor,
Iniaque audaci propero tentare iuuenta.
Vos per inaccessas rupes, et inhospita euntem
Saxa Deæ regite, ac secretum ostendite callem.
Vos huius ludi imprimis meminisse necesse est.
Vos primæ studia hæc Italis monstrastis in oris

K

FIG. 3. Arrighi's second italic. From Marcus Hieronymus Vida, *Scacchia ludus*.
Ludovico Arrighi, Rome, 1527.

DELLE FICHE.   59

re à quelli Homaccioni la necessità di quella guerra; la potenza, &
la infideltà d' Cartaginesi; e'l pericolo della Republica Romana.
Laqual sua oppenione, hauendo qualche controuersia.

(Però che Scipiaua Consiglione
Che si douesse cartar Conseruagine)

imaginateui, che subito, che egli scoperse il Fico uenuto da quelle
parti in poche hore, per mostrar loro la uicinità de'nimici; per la
bontà, & per la dignità di quel frutto, s'accendessero quelli Sci-
ptoni, quei Fabii, quei Marcelli, & tutti quei Barbassori al conqui-
sto delle Fiche Africane, come gia i Franciosi delle Fiche d'Italia : &
che unitamente acconsentissero al parere del Vecchio Catone. La qual
diliberatione fu la securezza, la gloria, & la grandezza della Cit-
tà di Roma . & se fu lo sterminio di Cartagine; douete sapere;
che io truouo nelle Storie di Iuba: che fra le Fiche, e i Cartaginesi erano occulte nimicitie . & che'l Fico di Catone era uenuto
per mare in poste Imbasciadore de gli altri Fichi à far Lega co
i Romani . La qual Lega trouo; che durò poi fino al tempo di Sca-
tinio : il quale fece la lege contra à quelli, che cominciauano à tener pratica con le Mele . & però il Fico in questo caso s'ha da scu-
sare, se fu cagione della rouina di Cartagine : la quale gli era piu to-
sto nimica, che Patria . & dall'altro canto si dee lodare: che fa-
cesse quell'opera: & fosse collegato alla Monarchia dell' Imperio
Romano.

Troppo faccenda haurei, & troppi affanni,
    A narrar cio, ch'io n'ho trouato altroue.
Nessun di quel ch'io passo mi condanni.
Ch'io saprei dirui mille cose nuoue:
    Ma perche penso, che sia detto assai;
    Sarà ben, ch'l parlar modo ritro e.
Io non credetti quando dentro entrai,
    Che douesse l'Istoria esser si lunga:
    Onde senza biscotto m'imbarcai.

Fig. 4. The italics of Blado. From Agresto da Ficaruolo, *Commento sopra la prima ficata del padre Siceo*. Antonio Blado, Rome, 1539.

uninteresting roman type of the period used by the Roman printers, when chancery types actually based on the chancery hand were available, the authorities having, in addition, this beautiful example from Arrighi's press to serve as a model. The only other bull printed in cursive at about this period which we have seen was printed by Minitius Calvus and is hardly to be compared with Arrighi's. Roman types appear to have become traditional for this class of printing, and even Blado, when he became 'Tipografo Cameral,' still issued many edicts in roman type.

After this very busy year we find only three books of Arrighi's dated 1525. They are: 1. *Zachariae Ferrerii . . . Hymni novi ecclesiastici*, dated 'Kal. Feb. 1525,' a very good example of his work except for the crowding of capitals on the title-page (or half-title; none of Arrighi's books has a fully-developed title-page). Bishop Ferrerius, it may be recorded, was another native of Vicenza. 2. *Petri Cursii poema de civitate Castellana faliscorum*, dated 29 March, 1525, another volume of renaissance Latin poetry. 3. *C. Mar-(celli) . . . in Psalmum usque quo Domine oblivisceris me*, dated 12 April 1525, a commentary on Psalm 12 by Christopher Marcellus, Archbishop of Corfu. This is the last book we have discovered printed in the small italic and the last also to contain the name of Lautitio Perugino.

The four books which appeared in 1526, together with a fifth undated, are printed in a new and larger fount (Fig. 3); this type is less exuberant, more sober than the earlier one; the swash capitals and exaggerated ascenders and descenders have gone. While the first italic was eminently suitable for a volume of lyrics, perhaps the new type is better adapted for everyday printing. The five books are: 1. *Specchio di Esopo*, a dialogue of Pandolfo Collenuccio edited by his son. So far all Arrighi's books have been printed throughout in one fount of type; but in this book the imprint is in a smaller Aldine italic. 2. Further dialogues of Collenuccio entitled *Apologi IIII*. 3. *Panegirico di Francesco (Cattani) de Diacceto*. 4. *Ioannis Mariae Archiepiscopi* (Pope Julius II) . . . *Oratio de pace*. In this book there is actually a preface in an Aldine cursive with a woodcut initial in the contemporary Roman style, and another small initial at the beginning of the text. These are the only two initials we have met in the books printed by Arrighi. The undated book is the *Itinerarium Philippi Bellucii*, a Latin poem.

The cursive in which these five books are printed is especially interesting because it appears to be the model on which Blado based his larger type. Several of the letters in Blado's type differ in detail, but the two are so nearly akin that it is impossible that they should be independent. From the dates it appears to be certain that Blado copied Arrighi and not vice versa. There is a Blado of 1526, a work by Jacobus Silvester, printed in a smaller italic not unlike the type cut by Francesco Griffo for Soncino. But this larger italic was not used much before 1530 (a good example may be seen in the edition of Sannazaro's *Sonetti* of 1530). Neither Blado nor any other printer at Rome appears to have copied Arrighi's smaller italic. The italic type in which the first editions of Machiavelli were printed is again different and more Aldine in cut.

The second book on calligraphy was issued at Venice in 1524 by Giovanni Antonio Tagliente. The calligraphic part of the book, like Arrighi's, was engraved, but there is a certain amount of text printed in a fount not unlike Arrighi's larger type. The same was used on the title-page and in the colophon of another book of Tagliente's: *Luminario di arithmetica*, issued in 1525. Both these books, therefore, are contemporary with Arrighi's experiments with this style of type, and one can hardly imagine that they were not known to Arrighi, who must have been keenly interested in Tagliente as a calligrapher.

There is still an earlier example of a similar style of type in Arrighi's own book, *Il modo di temperare le penne* (Fig. 5), which was engraved by Eustachio Celebrino and printed at Venice in 1523. Part of the book is printed from type, an italic of the school of Arrighi's second italic (Fig. 3), but which resembles Tagliente's type more closely than Arrighi's in some details; for instance, the kerns of the *d*, *h*, and *l* are inclined to the right, whereas in Arrighi's type these letters have a serif to the left, although in his first face he had used ascenders turning over to the right.

But at Venice the most distinguished printer whose books are almost all in italic was Francesco Marcolini da Forlì. Some of his types were in the Aldine tradition, and what excellent results he could obtain with them may be seen in his folio edition of the Letters of Pietro Aretino (1528) or the Dante (1544). Aretino speaks with great approbation of Marcolini as a printer, and, whatever else he was, Aretino was at any rate an artist. A larger italic used by Marcolini belongs definitely to the same family as those of Arrighi, Blado and Tagliente. In this type was printed one of his most beautiful books, *Il Petrarcha spirituale* of 1536, in quarto. On the title-page is a woodcut portrait of Petrarch and on the verso of the title-page another fine woodcut attributed to Niccolò Boldrini. Again we have an abundance of swash capitals, which Marcolini also used at times with his Aldine italics (see Fig. 6). Many of Marcolini's books are well known both for their woodcuts and for the beauty of their typography. Until he came, towards the end of his career, under the influence of Giolito and fell a victim to the fashion for woodcut initials he was a model of restraint and allowed his types to speak for themselves. A reproduction of a page of one of his books was given in Stanley Morison's article (*Fleuron*, No. 2). The beautiful italic there shown (*Fleurom* No. 2, p. 65, fig. 12) appears to be of the Aldine school, though it is so much less condensed that at first sight it seems to be of a different class. The exuberant capitals also are a contrast to the monotonous sobriety of those of Aldus.

According to Brunet Arrighi was printing until 1528, but he does not say what books he printed in that year. We know of only one book printed in 1527, in May, and nothing later. The mercenary armies who sacked Rome so thoroughly in 1527 entered the city on the 6th of May, and it seems likely that Arrighi was one of the many who either perished or was ruined in that catastrophe. The book, printed in May 1527, was an edition of the Latin poems of Hieronymus Vida and is in the larger italic (Fig. 3). The copy in the British Museum is on vellum, and on the first page of the text an illuminated initial and border have been added. With the exception of the one book referred to above Arrighi used no woodcut initials, but, in the fifteenth-century fashion, left blanks, with a lower-case guide letter, to be filled up by the illuminator. Actually very few copies can have been so illuminated but the practice of leaving the blank persisted for many years, as, for example, in the books from the Aldine Press. For the

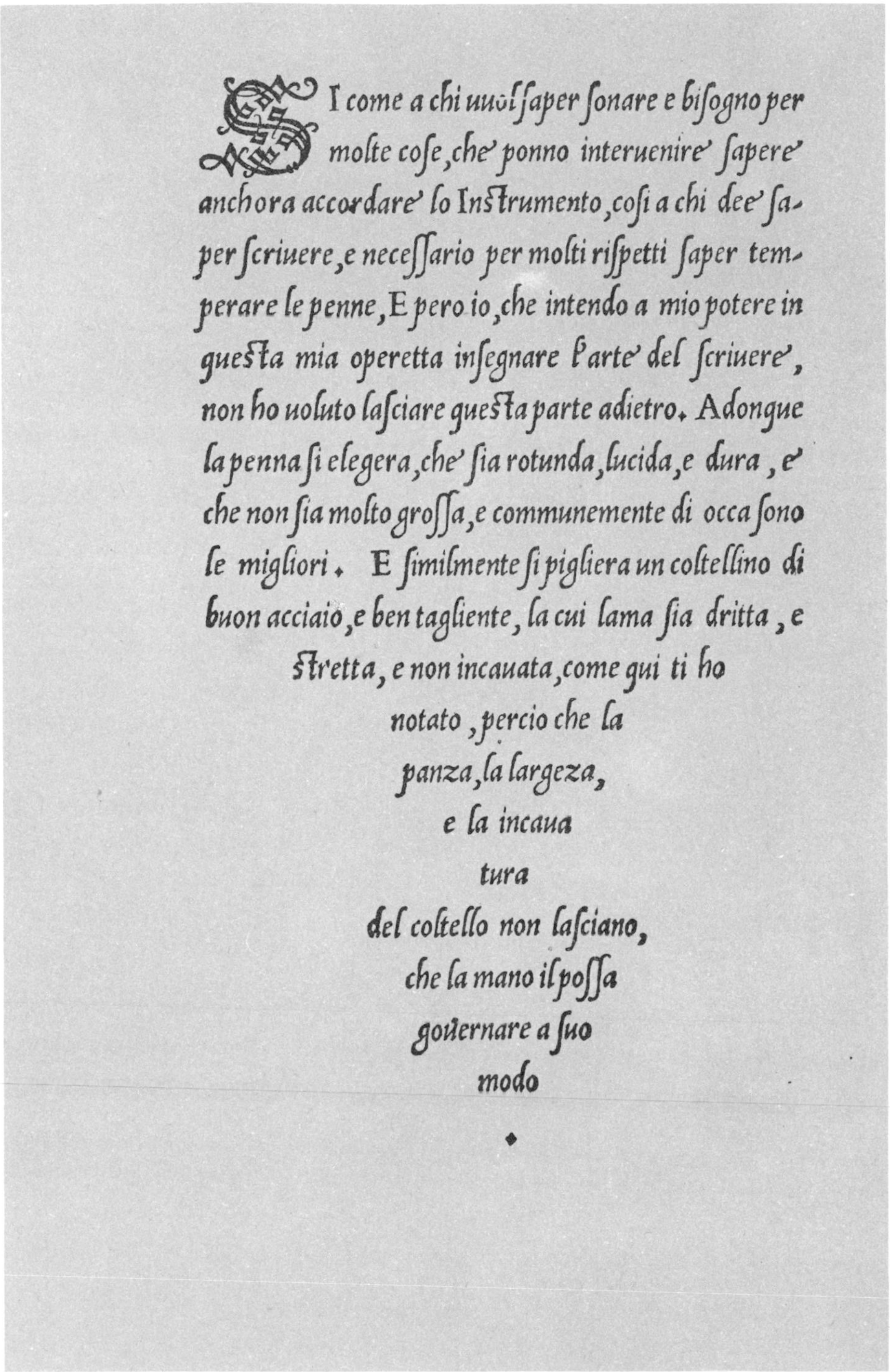

SI come a chi uuôl faper fonare e bifogno per molte cofe, che ponno interuenire fapere anchora accordare lo Inftrumento, cofi a chi dee faper fcriuere, e neceffario per molti rifpetti faper temperare le penne, E pero io, che intendo a mio potere in quefta mia operetta infegnare l'arte del fcriuere, non ho uoluto lafciare quefta parte adietro. Adonque la penna fi elegera, che fia rotunda, lucida, e dura, e che non fia molto groffa, e communemente di occa fono le migliori. E fimilmente fi pigliera un coltellino di buon acciaio, e ben tagliente, la cui lama fia dritta, e ftretta, e non incauata, come qui ti ho notato, percio che la panza, la largeza, e la incaua tura del coltello non lafciano, che la mano il poffa gouernare a fuo modo

FIG. 5. Arrighi's italic engraved by Eustachio Celebrino. From Ludovico Arrighi, *Il modo di temperare le penne*. Ludovico Vicentino & Eustachio Celebrino, Venice, 1523.

SONETTI ET CANZONI
DI MESSER FRANCESCO
PETRARCHA DIVENVTO
THEOLOGO ET SPIRI⁊
TVALÉ PER GRATIA DI
DIO ET STVDIO DI FRATE
HIERONIMO MARIPETRO
MINORITANO⹁

SONETTO PRIMO⹁

Oi,ch'afcoltate in rime fparfe il fuono
De miei noui fofpir; ch'efcon dal core
V   *Per la memoria di quel cieco errore ;*
Che mi fe in parte altr'huom da quel,
Poi che del uario ftil piu non ragiono,   *(ch'i fono;*
Ma piango il fallo mio pien di dolore,
Il uan defir , e'l fuggitiuo amore,
Pieta, prego ui moua a mio perdono⹁
Conofco ben, fi come al popol tutto
Materia fui d'error ⁊ onde fouente
Di me medefmo meco mi uergogno⹁
Hora, drizzato al ciel , ff ero far jrutto
Di uero ben ; ch'io ueggio chiaramente,
Che quanto piace al Mondo è breue fogno⹁
        C

FIG. 6. Marcolini's italic with swash capitals. From *Il Petrarca spirituale (di H. Maripetro)*. Francesco Marcolini, Venice, 1536.

most part Arrighi's books are severely undecorated and so good was his typography that he could well dispense with other decoration.

It is difficult indeed to understand why this remarkable printer should not be better known and why his earlier italic should have been unable to compete with the Aldine cursive types and with types derived from France. An increased interest in Arrighi will probably bring to light many more books than the twenty-one here enumerated.

His first italic found one imitator other than Janicolo at Vicenza; the printer, F. Minitius Calvus, whom we have already mentioned as working at Rome. He was printing in that city certainly in 1531, but by 1540 he is found at Milan. In that year appeared a book entitled *Torricella, Dialogo di Otho Lupano*, In Milano, dal Caluo. MDXXXX (Fig. 7). The title is surrounded by a woodcut border which had already appeared at Rome, while the text of the speech is printed in an italic which is a close copy of Arrighi's first italic. Swash capitals are numerous and are used in the headings with roman type also. In 1541 appeared a speech entitled *Antonii Comitis pro decreto illustrissimi principis Alphonsi Avali . . . in aleatores oratio*. There is no printer's name, but the preface, printed in an Aldine italic, is by F. Minitius Calvus, the same woodcut border is used on the title-page and the text is again in Arrighi's italic. Other books printed by Calvus in this same italic are: in 1540, *De sacris diebus Carmelitae opus aureum*, a Latin poem by Baptista Spagnuoli (in 8vo); in 1541, *Institutioni di Mario Equicola* (in 4to), with another woodcut border on the title-page which also had been used at Rome. In 1542 he appears to have been succeeded by Andrea Calvo, presumably a son, and in that year was issued an edition of Boiardo's *Orlando Innamorato*, with the imprint 'stampato in Milano nelle case di Andrea Caluo.' The text of the poem is printed in double columns in Aldine italic like that of scores of other editions of Boiardo, Ariosto and their imitators published in the sixteenth century, The preface of our edition is in the Arrighi cursive, while the imprint on the title-page and some preliminary verses are in a curious upright chancery. This type, by several of its characteristics, belongs to the series of types we have been considering and seems to have been derived from another Milanese printer, Giovanni Antonio Castiglione.

In the annals of printing at Milan the name of Castiglione or Castellione occurs several times. There was a Pier Antonio Castellione in the fifteenth century and a Giovanni Castellione early in the sixteenth century. Giovanni Antonio was printing from about 1535. In 1546 he issued a fine folio volume in gothic letter, and in Spanish the *Cronica* of Alvaro de Luna. He was also a printer of liturgical works, in some of which for the preliminary matter he employed the upright chancery to which we have referred, e. g. in the *Sacramentarium Patriarchale secundum morem Comensis ecclesiœ*, a quarto of 1557. Of books printed throughout in the upright chancery are the *Gallorum Insubrum antiquae sedes* 1541 (4to) by Bonaventura Castillioneus, presumably a relative of the printer (Fig. 8), and *Manifesti del signor Don Rodrigo di Benavides*, undated, but about 1558 (4to). Again we find the swash capitals and other characteristics which connect this type with Arrighi's, but the peculiarity consists in the uprightness of the letter. Until this type had been seen one might have been inclined to say that an essential feature of a cursive type is that it should slope, but Castiglione's finally settles that ques-

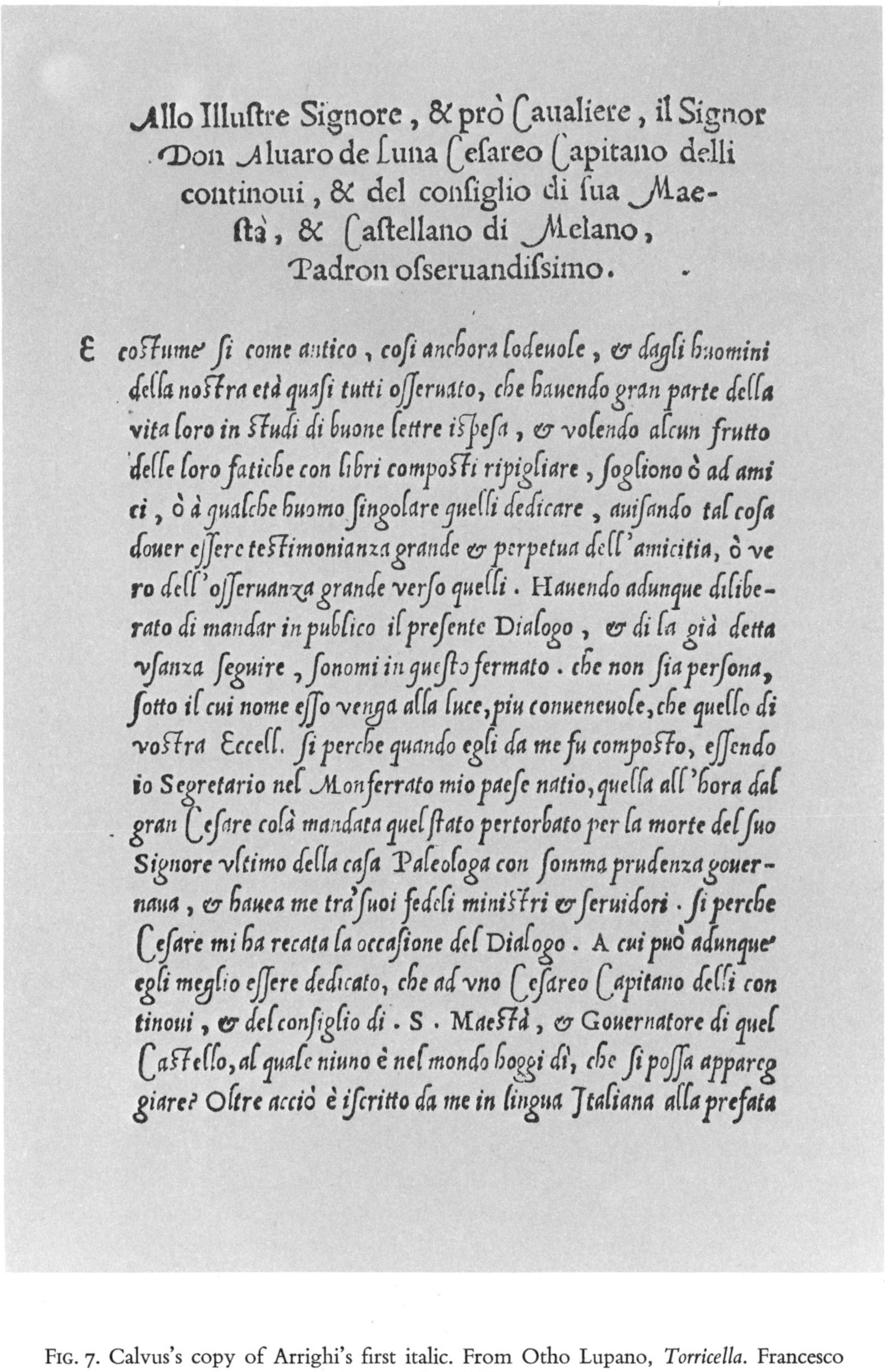

Allo Illustre Signore, & prò Caualiere, il Signor
Don Aluaro de Luna Cesareo Capitano delli
continoui, & del consiglio di sua Maestà, & Castellano di Melano,
Padron osseruandissimo.

E costume si come antico, cosi anchora lodeuole, & dagli huomini
della nostra età quasi tutti osseruato, che hauendo gran parte della
vita loro in studi di buone lettre ispesa, & volendo alcun frutto
delle loro fatiche con libri composti ripigliare, sogliono ò ad ami
ci, ò à qualche huomo singolare quelli dedicare, auisando tal cosa
douer essere testimonianza grande & perpetua dell'amicitia, ò ve
ro dell'osseruanza grande verso quelli. Hauendo adunque dilibe-
rato di mandar in publico il presente Dialogo, & di la già detta
vsanza seguire, sonomi in questo fermato. che non sia persona,
sotto il cui nome esso venga alla luce, piu conueneuole, che quello di
vostra Eccell. si perche quando egli da me fu composto, essendo
io Segretario nel Monferrato mio paese natio, quella all'hora dal
gran Cesare colà mandata quel stato pertorbato per la morte del suo
Signore vltimo della casa Paleologa con somma prudenza gouer-
naua, & hauea me trà suoi fedeli ministri & seruidori. si perche
Cesare mi ha recata la occasione del Dialogo. A cui può adunque
egli meglio essere dedicato, che ad vno Cesareo Capitano delli con
tinoui, & del consiglio di . S . Maestà, & Gouernatore di quel
Castello, al quale niuno è nel mondo hoggi dì, che si possa appareg
giare? Oltre acciò è iscritto da me in lingua Italiana alla prefata

FIG. 7. Calvus's copy of Arrighi's first italic. From Otho Lupano, *Torricella*. Francesco
Minizio Calvo, Milan 1540.

tion. It must definitely be classed with chancery types. This brings out the fact that while their common characteristic is their cursive nature, it does not follow that a slope is essential. It is worthy of note that Castiglione uses very small upper case cursive with this type in 1541 – and that in the later book of 1558 he had introduced capitals all but as high as the ascenders.

On page 47 of Fumagalli's Dictionary will be seen another example of upright cursive, again with very small capitals, used in a book by Gaudentius Merula, printed at Borgo Lavezzaro, near Novara, 1543. This is the earliest book printed at that place and the type must have been derived from Castiglione. It may be noted that Bonaventura's book of 1541 contains some verses by Merula, and they were both humanists interested in the Gallic history of Lombardy.

In addition to this upright chancery, Castiglione had another cursive of the school of Blado, of which we give an example from an undated book showing his device (Fig. 9). In this book Castiglione makes the mistake of employing larger capitals. A similar letter, used by another printer of Milan, Giovanni Antonio Borgia, of the same period, will be seen in the sonnets of Antonfrancesco Rainerio, printed in 1553 (Fig. 10).

Probably the majority of Italian books of the sixteenth century were printed in cursive, and of those again the majority in types which are descended from those cut by Francesco Griffo. But the examples we have given in this article will show that there were other kinds of italic, and among them some of the most successful experiments in typography.

The story of the supersession of the chancery types of the Aldus and Arrighi categories and their derivatives by the cursives of Garamond, Le Bé and Granjon is not material to the present article. It may be stated, however, that by 1550 Italy was to a great extent employing French romans and cursives. These cursives were descended from a branch of the family of types of which Arrighi's was the head. When Simon de Colines (Paris, 1529-46) elected to provide his office with cursive founts, he based his designs upon the existing Italian models. These, as we have seen, were in two series and, as we should expect, both were copied by Colines. He produced three italics between the years 1528 and 1536. Of these A (Fig. 11; used first in such books as the *Martial* of 1533) recalls the Aldine; B (Fig. 12) and C (Fig. 13) derive immediately from the letters of Arrighi. Fount A approaches the Aldine prototype so nearly as to deserve little description here. It differs from the 1501 letter only in that it makes comparatively sparing use of ligatures and includes *v* in addition to *u*; and it may be pointed out that this variety does not appear to have been used by Colines before 1533. No swash capitals are included in this fount.

Fount B, while resembling the general colour of the Aldine italic, makes several notable departures from it. First in importance is the change in the lower case ascenders from a bracketed serif to a rounded kern. The most obvious difference in the lower case will be found in the *g*. An important new factor in the upper case is the presence of the swash letters *V N*. This fount was first used in 1528 for the *De Virginitate* of Paulus Cerratus.

All these characteristics are to be found in the *Coryciana* (Fig. 1), printed and published

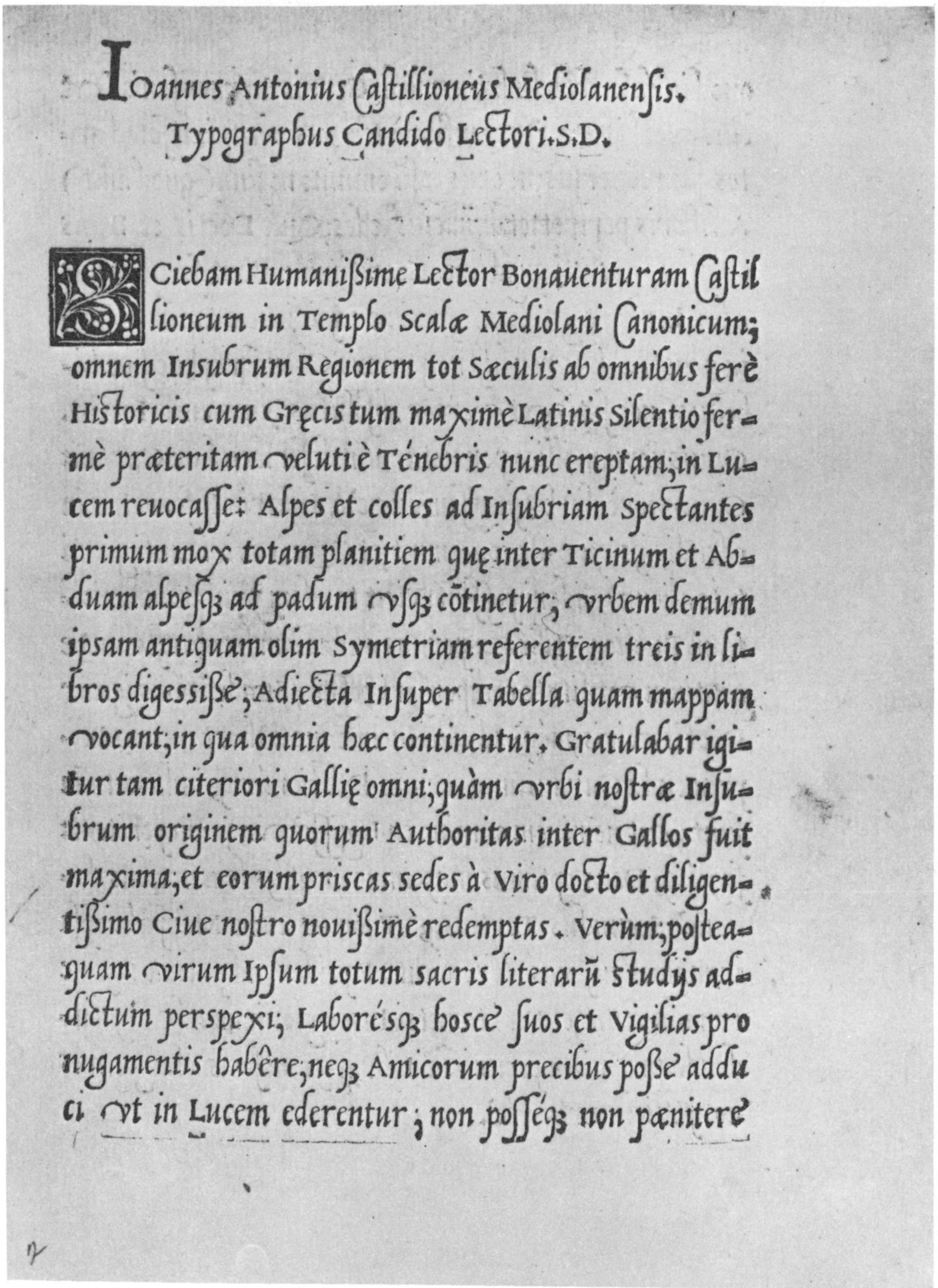

Ioannes Antonius Castillioneus Mediolanensis.
Typographus Candido Lectori, S.D.

Ciebam Humanißime Lector Bonauenturam Castil
lioneum in Templo Scalæ Mediolani Canonicum;
omnem Insubrum Regionem tot Sæculis ab omnibus ferè
Historicis cum Græcis tum maximè Latinis Silentio fer=
mè præteritam veluti è Ténebris nunc ereptam, in Lu=
cem reuocaße: Alpes et colles ad Insubriam Spectantes
primum mox totam planitiem quæ inter Ticinum et Ab=
duam alpesq ad padum vsq cõtinetur, vrbem demum
ipsam antiquam olim Symetriam referentem treis in li=
bros digessiße, Adiecta Insuper Tabella quam mappam
vocant, in qua omnia hæc continentur. Gratulabar igi=
tur tam citeriori Galliæ omni, quàm vrbi nostræ Insu=
brum originem quorum Authoritas inter Gallos fuit
maxima, et eorum priscas sedes à Viro docto et diligen=
tißimo Ciue nostro nouißimè redemptas. Verùm, postea
quam virum Ipsum totum sacris literaru studijs ad=
dictum perspexi; Labores que hosce suos et Vigilias pro
nugamentis habêre, neq Amicorum precibus poße addu
ci vt in Lucem ederentur; non poßeq non pænitere

Fig. 8. Castiglione's nearly upright italic in Arrighi's style. From Bonaventura Castiglione, *Gallorum insubrum antiquae sedes*, Giovanni Antonio Castiglione, Milan, 1541.

by Arrighi in 1524. If, in addition, attention is directed to the fact that the conspicuous Aldine circular ampersand *&* followed by Colines is deserted in Fount B for the severer *&* shape, one cannot resist the deduction that the cutter of Colines B had before him one of Arrighi's books. The case is even stronger in respect to Fount C which Colines was employing *circa* 1536. Here we have a letter which has no relation in colour, set, or line with the Aldine. Fig. 13 is a reproduction from the *Raison darchitecture antique extraicte de Vitruve*, 1539, and should be looked at with fig. 3. Comparison will suggest, if indeed it does not demonstrate, the relation of Colines C to Arrighi's second italic. It is interesting to observe that while Arrighi A and Colines B are identical in their possession of the kerned ascender, Arrighi II and Colines C have each returned to the bracketed serif. The *h* remains constant. The *g* has reverted to the Aldine form, the *v* form is employed to begin all such words as *vt, vsus, vtilitas,* and the upper case is still upright. This last remained the characteristic of italic founts in Italy until about 1550, and in France until the advent of the later types of Garamond and Granjon.

Tradition has it that these two were master and pupil respectively. There is 'hearsay' (but not evidence) to the effect that Garamond was associated with Colines and Tory, and it is known that in 1530 the trade of type-founding was separated from that of printing and organized as an independent guild. Garamond therefore may well have had a hand in the Colines italics B and C, the first of which appeared in 1528. The A fount, which is more exclusively Aldine in cut, dates from 1533, and may or may not be from the hand of Garamond. It may well be pointed out here that ascriptions of type to the latter should be received with caution.

Lottin says that Garamond was active as early as 1510. M. Dumoulin[1] says, with more definition than seems advisable, that Garamond 'grava aussi de la gothique; puis enthousiasmé par les types de Nicolas Jenson, il les reproduisit vers l'année 1515, sans toutefois dépasser les mérites de son modèle.' Of course, there is nothing intrinsically improbable in either of the dates mentioned. In 1510 Garamond might be thirty years of age, and in the one piece of irrefragable evidence which we possess, he claims to have been interested in typefounding from his youth. This passage occurs in the preface addressed 'Reverendo in Christo patri ac dominoMathaeo de Longejoue Suessionensis Episcopo, *Claudius Garamondus* typographus salutem,' which forms part of the preliminary matter of the *Pia et religiosa meditatio* of D. Cambellanus, 1545.[2] He proceeds: 'Tum vero foeliciter me rem aggressurum si quam proxime fieri posset, Italicam Aldi Manutii literam, novis exprimerem caracteribus . . . Italicarum itaque proxime ad Aldinos literarum typos sculpo, quam foeliciter alii judicabunt.' This book, therefore, is printed in a neo-aldine italic, but which possesses sloping capitals and swash variants. These at least can be proved to be cut by Garamond (Fig. 14). There are others of similar but not identical cut, perhaps cut by him or his pupils. Fig. 15 shows a couple of pages from an edition of *Valerius Maximus* printed by François Gryphius at Paris in 1545.

Monsieur Dumoulin (p. 102, etc.) gives specimens of the series known as *caractères*

1. Joseph Dumoulin: *Vie . . . de Fédéric Morel*, 1901, p. 100.
2. A translation of the preface is given below, p. 106 sqq.

COMPENDIOLO
DI MOLTI DVBBI, SEGRETI
ET SENTENZE INTORNO AL CANTO
FERMO, ET FIGVRATO, DA MOLTI ECCELLENTI

& consumati Musici dichiarate, Raccolte dallo Eccellente
& scienzato Autore frate Pietro Aron
del ordine de Crosachieri
& della Inclita Citta
di Firenze.

In memoria eterna erit Aron, Et nomen eius nunquam destruetur.

In Milano per Io, Antonio da Castelliono stampatore.

FIG. 9. Castiglione's italic with larger capitals. From Pietro Aron, *Compendiolo di molti dubbi intorno al canto fermo et figurato*. Giovanni Antonio Castiglione, Milan, [1550?].

de l'université used by the Imprimerie Royale, 1640, and usually stated to have been cut in 1540. He includes in addition, reproductions of another series: *Gros Texte* (14-point), *Saint Augustin* (12- or 14-point), *Philosophie* (10-point), *petit romain* (9-point), *Gaillarde* (8-point), and *nonpareille* (6-point), all roman and cursive. It is outside our present scope to discuss these romans, highly interesting as they are; but with the 1592 Egenolff-Sabon-Berner specimen before us and its definite ascriptions, we can at least say that all were most probably cut by Garamond. In the case of the Sabon cursive series a similar statement can hardly be made.

First, they are easily distinguishable from the cursives *de l'Université*. In comparison the latter appear less disciplined, contain far fewer swashes and ligatures, and yield a much less restful effect in composition, due to the fact that the designer of the Sabon series more agreeably and homogeneously inclined his upper and lower case. Garamond, indeed, as is natural perhaps in a pioneer, appears a little nervous in his handling of inclined capitals. The designer of the second series was perhaps a pupil, and, it would seem, certainly a little bolder. The Egenolff sheet[1] already referred to is of considerable service to us at this point. The specimen displays nine romans, seven ascribed to Garamond, two to Granjon. Of the italics, *Gros Texte* and *Cicero* are credited to Granjon, the *Augustin* is mutilated, but may be presumed to be Granjon's. The text to the size next below *Cicero* reads: *Curs. Garamond ou Immortel de Granjon*, and the smallest sizes are cryptically described as *Curs. Petit Text de G.* and *Curs. Non parel.* They pair with two fellow romans described respectively as *Rom. Gailliard de Granjon* and *Rom. Non parel.*

The cursives just mentioned, which appear to be Granjon's, differ from another series which appeared in Lyons, where Granjon had long had connexions (from a document referred to by Baudrier, *Art. Granjon*, vol. 2, p. 53, he appears to have supplied types to Gryphius and De Tournes before August, 1547), and whither he transferred himself in 1557. According to Updike, the cursive types used in Jean de Tournes's 16mo Bible, 1558, and in the *Metamorphose figurée* of 1557, are 'very exquisite' and 'no doubt Granjon's.' Updike adds that from 1570 almost all Lyons printers used this kind of italic type. It has inclined capitals. In the *A* of some sizes the curved stroke sweeps across the top of the main stroke exactly in the fashion of a cursive of Gryphius (Fig. 16), to which reference must now be made. The patient reader will discover the influence of this last in two or three Lyonese founts. We show (Figs. 16 & 17) cursives used by Rouillé, which, in our opinion, cannot but be related to the Gryphius italic.

Fig. 16 represents the earliest use of a cursive with inclined capitals which we have encountered. It occurs in the fine folio *Dolet*, printed by Sebastian Gryphius at Lyons in 1538. While this type (104 in Updike) presents a notable departure from the Aldine italic, it is none the less independent of the Arrighi letter and its derivatives. We cannot throw much light upon the origins of this interesting face. M. Marius Audin[2] claims that Gryphius used it in 1527-8, and states, without giving a reference, that it was secured from Froben of Basle, who was employing it as early as 1518. Whether or not it is of Basle provenance, the letter certainly exerted very considerable influence. It may be

1. Described in *Fleuron* No. 1, p. 32 foot p. 66. See also pp. 272-280 in the present volume.
2. *Le Livre*, Paris, Crès, 1924, p. 44 foot p. 67.

Le caste Muse in vn bel cerchio vnite,
C'honoran' l'amenissimo Helicona;
Et Apollo, ch'à Voi tanto simiglia,
Di sua man tutte vn'immortal corona
Tesson' per Voi, sol ch'à veder le gite:
Et verso il Vaticano alzan le ciglia:
Quinci; dou'elle vn tempo à merauiglia
Regnaro. Hor chi le'nuita, ò le raccoglie?
Chi non le volge adietro & le respinge?
Voi solo, il crin di cui porpora cinge,
Ne i ricchi fregi; & ne l'aurate spoglie
L'impresse vostre voglie
Mostrate: & per Voi solo anco si vede
Il Pegaso vn bel fonte aprir co'l piede.

Et quindi é, che'n humil sommesso canto
Già le più pellegrine Alme discerno
Sotto voce tentar le vostre lodi;
Come vaghi Augelletti, allhor che'l Verno
Parte; & veste la Terra vn più bel manto,
Prouan se stessi in bassi & dolci modi:
Poi, quando vien, ch'à verde Olmo s'annodi
Frondosa Vite; & che fann'arco i rami,
Empion' di suon le Selue, empion' i Campi.
Et Voi Signor, con luminosi lampi;
Acciò ch'ogni altra età, v'ammiri, & brami,
Questa più sempre v'ami;

FIG. 10. Castiglione's italic in Blado's style. From Antonio Francesco Rainerio, *Cento sonetti*. Giovanni Antonio da Borgo, Milan, 1553.

found in Venice, Rome, Padua, and in other towns of Italy. Some of its characteristics may be traced in later designs used in Paris, and above all in Lyons.

The admission of inclined capital letters to the cursive forms a highly important departure from the general spirit of the old chancery type. These founts acquire henceforth a momentum of their own, ligatures and flourishes being gradually reduced in number until at the present time customers are even impatient of the ct and st, which alone remain to us. Another important and perhaps more significant indication of secured independence is to be found in the lower case cursive *h*. This character, so long as it was a written one, had naturally and inevitably a curved body. From the time of its earliest beginnings when the h was no more than a half-uncial, it preserved its straight stem and round body throughout the caroline, gothic, semi-gothic periods; and during the early and late renaissance periods the finest scribes, however much they modified, retained these characteristics. As any practised writer knows it is the only way in which to make a fine h. Whether or not Jenson assisted the Da Spiras to cut their

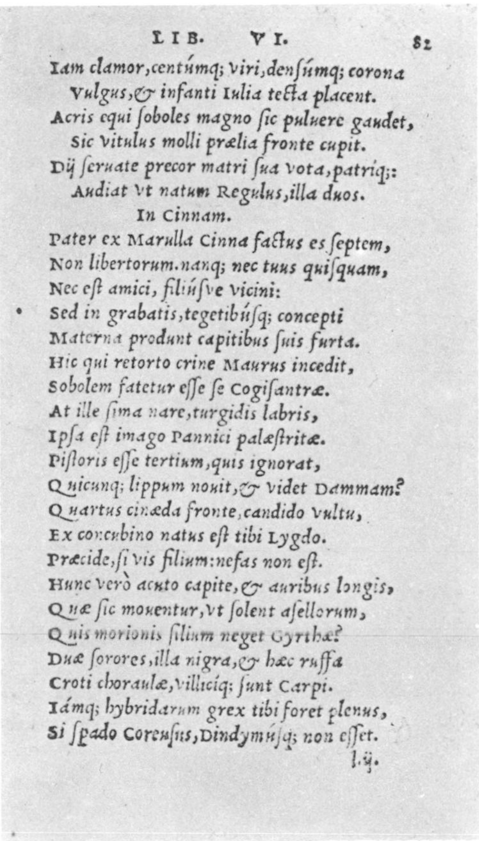
LIB. VI. 82

Iam clamor, centúmq; viri, denſúmq; corona
Vulgus, & infanti Iulia tecta placent.
Acris equi ſoboles magno ſic puluere gaudet,
Sic vitulus molli prælia fronte cupit.
Dij ſeruate precor matri ſua vota, patriq;:
Audiat vt natum Regulus, illa duos.
In Cinnam.
Pater ex Marulla Cinna factus es ſeptem,
Non libertorum. nanq; nec tuus quiſquam,
Nec eſt amici, filiúſve vicini:
Sed in grabatis, tegetibúſq; concepti
Materna produnt capitibus ſuis furta.
Hic qui retorto crine Maurus incedit,
Sobolem fatetur eſſe ſe Cogiſantræ.
At ille ſima nare, turgidis labris,
Ipſa eſt imago Pannici palæſtritæ.
Piſtoris eſſe tertium, quis ignorat,
Quicunq; lippum nouit, & videt Dammam?
Quartus cinæda fronte, candido vultu,
Ex concubino natus eſt tibi Lygdo.
Præcide, ſi vis filium: nefas non eſt.
Hunc verò acuto capite, & auribus longis,
Quæ ſic mouentur, vt ſolent aſellorum,
Quis morionis filium neget Gyrthæ?
Duæ ſorores, illa nigra, & hæc ruffa
Croti choraulæ, villicíq; ſunt Carpi.
Iámq; hybridarum grex tibi foret plenus,
Si ſpado Coreuſus, Dindymúſq; non eſſet.
l.ij.

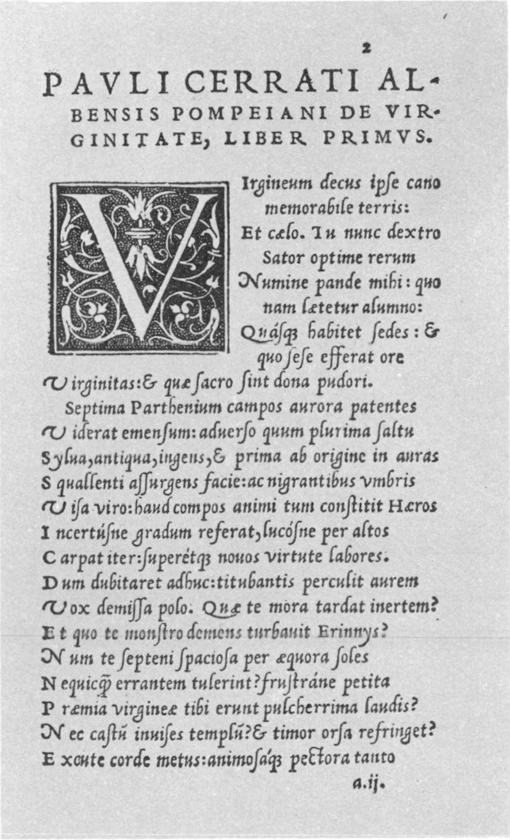
2

PAVLI CERRATI ALBENSIS POMPEIANI DE VIRGINITATE, LIBER PRIMVS.

Virgineum decus ipſe cano
memorabile terris:
Et cælo. Tu nunc dextro
Sator optime rerum
Numine pande mihi: quo
nam lætetur alumno:
Quáſq; habitet ſedes: &
quo ſeſe efferat ore
Virginitas: & quæ ſacro ſint dona pudori.
Septima Parthenium campos aurora patentes
Viderat emenſum: aduerſo quum plurima ſaltu
Sylua, antiqua, ingens, & prima ab origine in auras
Squallenti aſſurgens facie: ac nigrantibus vmbris
Viſa viro: haud compos animi tum conſtitit Heros
Incertúſne gradum referat, lucóſne per altos
Carpat iter: ſuperétq; nouos virtute labores.
Dum dubitaret adhuc: titubantis perculit aurem
Vox demiſſa polo. Quæ te mora tardat inertem?
Et quo te monſtro demens turbauit Erinnys?
Num te ſepteni ſpacioſa per æquora ſoles
Nequicquam errantem tulerint? fruſtráne petita
Præmia virgineæ tibi erunt pulcherrima laudis?
Nec caſtū inuiſes templū? & timor orſa refringet?
Excute corde metus: animoſáq; pectora tanto
a.ij.

FIG. 11. Colines's italic 'A'. From Marcus Valerius Martialis, *Epigrammaton libri XIIII.* Simon de Colines, Paris, 1533.

FIG. 12. Colines's italic 'B'. From Paulus Cerratus, *De virginitate libri III.* Simon de Colines, Paris, 1528. (Slightly reduced.)

roman of 1479 is not known. The h in this fount preserves a full bow made according to the wholesome doctrine of the humanist scribes to the same proportions as the lower case b. When in the next year Jenson came to cut his type, he equipped it with a particularly poor lower case h, whose line is altogether disagreeable; first because the body of the letter is too full for the ascender, and worst of all because it is no longer curved. A mischievous influence on typography, we submit, is to be traced to this innovation. In face of the applause which the technical excellence of Jenson's letter occasioned in his day and ours, few printers had the courage to preserve the bowed *h*. Among these Ratdolt's name occurs immediately to our memory; also, Griffo's design for the Aldine *Polifilo*, 1499, though there is undoubtedly to be noticed a certain re-

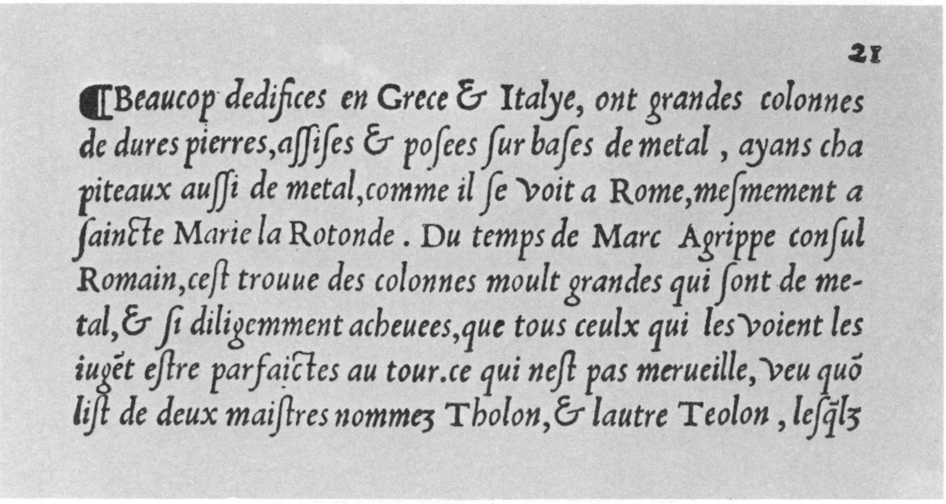

21

Beaucop dedifices en Grece & Italye, ont grandes colonnes
de dures pierres,aſſiſes & poſees ſur baſes de metal , ayans cha
piteaux auſſi de metal,comme il ſe voit a Rome,meſmement a
ſainćte Marie la Rotonde . Du temps de Marc Agrippe conſul
Romain,ceſt trouue des colonnes moult grandes qui ſont de metal,& ſi diligemment acheuees,que tous ceulx qui les voient les
iugēt eſtre parfaićtes au tour.ce qui neſt pas merueille,veu quō
liſt de deux maiſtres nommez Tholon,& lautre Teolon , leſq̄lz

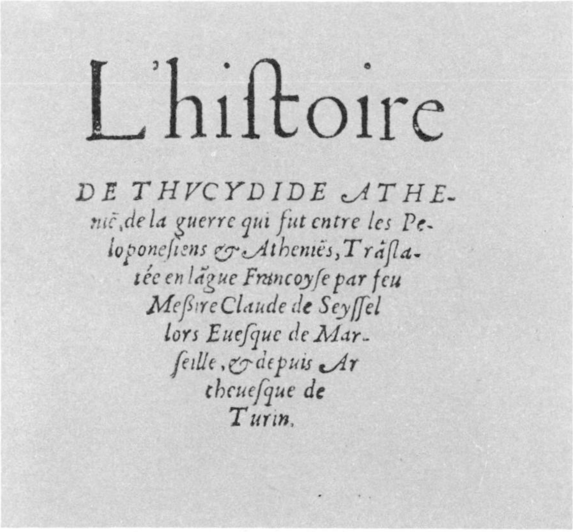

L'hiſtoire

DE THVCYDIDE ATHE-
niē,de la guerre qui fut entre les Pe-
loponeſiens & Atheniēs,Trāſla-
tée en lāgue Francoyſe par feu
Meſſire Claude de Seyſſel
lors Eueſque de Mar-
ſeille,& depuis Ar
cheueſque de
Turin.

FIG. 13. Colines's italic 'C'. From *Raison d'architecture antique extraicte de Vitruve*. Simon de Colines, Paris, 1539.

FIG. 14. Italic positively cut by Claude Garamond 1545. From Thucydides, *L'histoire* . . . Pierre Gaultier, Paris, 1545.

duction of the curve. Notwithstanding this falling away in the roman, the cursive held consistently to the old form. It persists through the French italics of the period we have been discussing, and not until Grandjean de Fouchy, 1693, was there cut an italic *h* with a straight side parallel with the ascending stem. The *caractères de l'université* which attempt to include the roman and cursive as constituents of one fount retained the straight *h* and a curved *h* respectively. Thus it was that William Caslon did the same thing in his letters cut about 1720. Baskerville, on the other hand, was related to Grandjean, and therefore his letters are consistent in their inclusion of a straight h in both roman and italic.

These two points, the inclined capital and the modernized *h*, indicate the development of italic away from the chancery hand.

It would not appear, however, that the problem of italic has yet been solved. We need a pre-Grandjean letter which shall have the maximum consistency of character with its fellow and more often used roman; a character which shall not be a maze of conflicting angles as are several sizes of the *caractères de l'université*. We need a cursive which is open and easy to read. It is to be feared that the mischief which we have traced to Jenson has gone too far for us to hope with any success for a reversion to the more beautiful and the more practical curved *h*, but there can be no doubt, we think, that the chancery models of Arrighi offer a thoroughly practical starting point for the designing of an ideal cursive, free in design, open in line and harmonious with our classical old faces.

FIG. 15. Italic possibly cut by Claude Garamond or his pupils. From Valerius Maximus, *Dictorum factorumque memorabilium exempla*. François Gryphius, Paris, 1545.

APPENDIX

DEDICATORY EPISTLE ADDRESSED BY CLAUDE GARAMOND TO MATTHIEU DE LONGUEJOUE, BISHOP OF SOISSONS

That I, an unknown and private individual, should offer and dedicate the first fruits of my work as a publisher to you, Reverend Father, with whom I am unacquainted, may rightly be a matter of surprise to you and to anyone not fully cognisant of my purpose. I have been advised and persuaded to this course by Jean Gagny first almoner of the Most Christian king, a man who has deserved well of the literary world by the commentaries which he has issued on sacred literature and by promoting the publication of the labours of learned and pious men. I will say nothing further of him lest I should seem to praise him less for his own worth than for his services to me. Since he considered me capable of advancing the glory of the craft of printing by the art of engraving and letter-founding which I had studied from boyhood and with little profit to my private purse, with the goodwill which he manifests to all the industrious, he advised that I, who had been accustomed hitherto to engrave and cast types for the publishers, should enjoy my own labours and enter the publishing trade; for those, he said, who merely engrave types and go no further are only making honey for the publishers. When I raised the objection of the smallness of my means and asserted that such an undertaking would involve a large outlay, he promised to help me in that matter as far as his resources allowed and by procuring manuscripts of good books. He declared that the

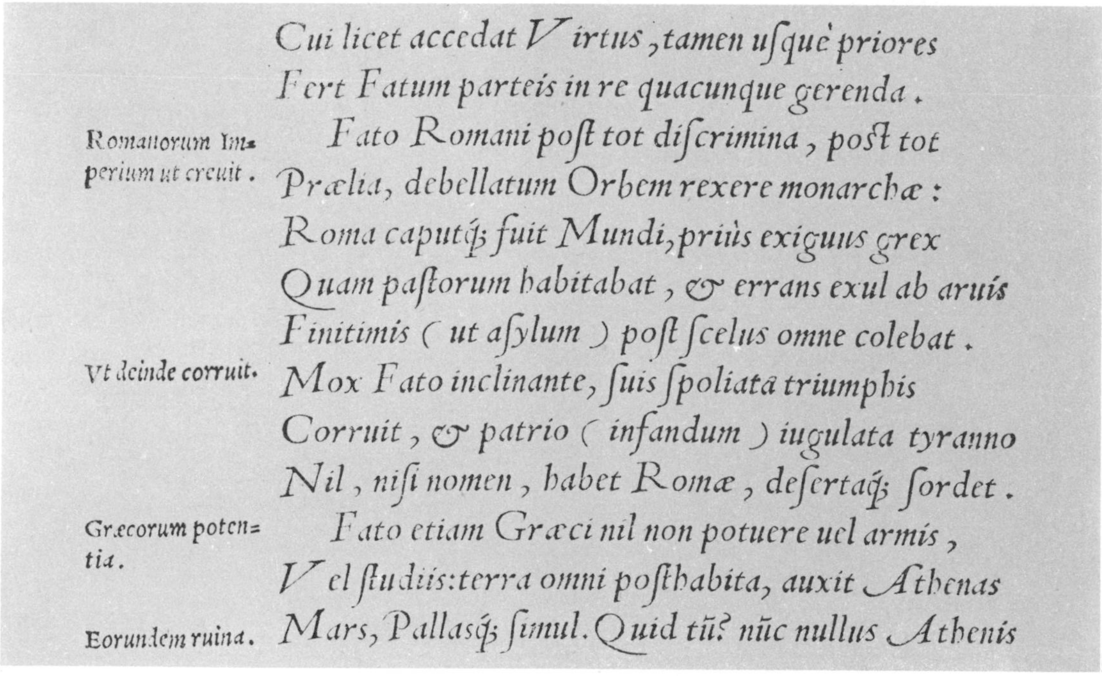
Cui licet accedat Virtus, tamen uſquè priores
Fert Fatum parteis in re quacunque gerenda.
Romanorum Imperium ut creuit. *Fato Romani poſt tot diſcrimina, poſt tot*
Prælia, debellatum Orbem rexere monarchæ:
Roma caputq; fuit Mundi, priùs exiguus grex
Quam paſtorum habitabat, & errans exul ab aruis
Finitimis (ut aſylum) poſt ſcelus omne colebat.
Vt deinde corruit. *Mox Fato inclinante, ſuis ſpoliata triumphis*
Corruit, & patrio (infandum) iugulata tyranno
Nil, niſi nomen, habet Romæ, deſertaq; ſordet.
Græcorum potentia. *Fato etiam Græci nil non potuere uel armis,*
Vel ſtudiis: terra omni poſthabita, auxit Athenas
Eorundem ruina. *Mars, Pallasq; ſimul. Quid tũ? nũc nullus Athenis*

FIG. 16. Earliest use of inclined capitals. From Etienne Dolet, *Carmina*. Sebastian Gryphius, Lyons, 1538.

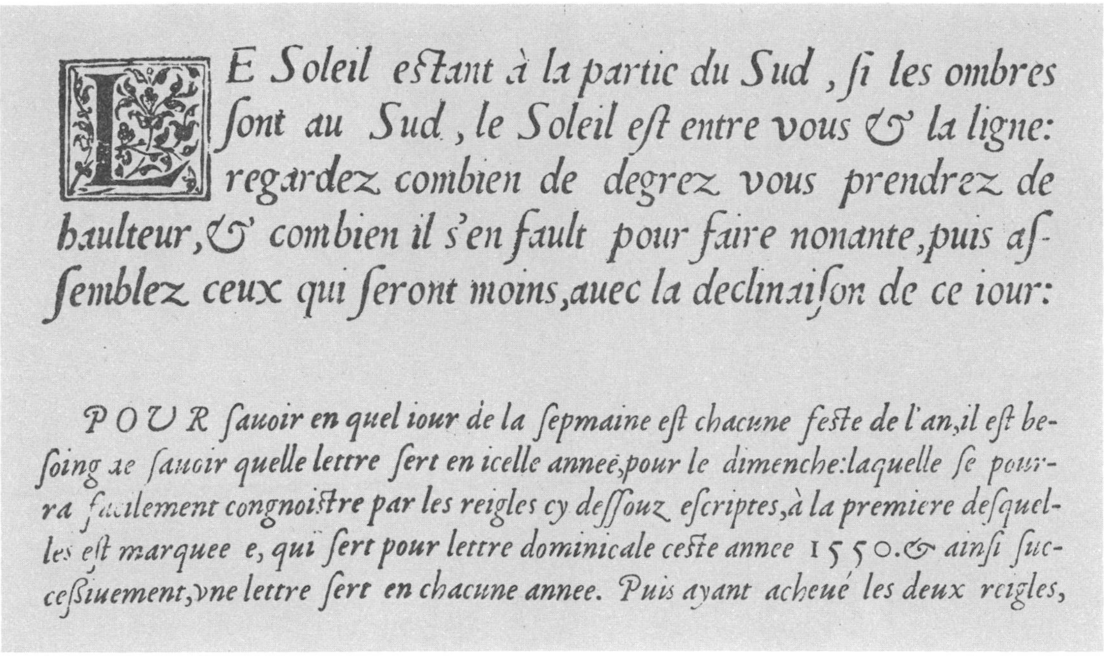

LE Soleil estant à la partie du Sud , si les ombres font au Sud , le Soleil est entre vous & la ligne: regardez combien de degrez vous prendrez de haulteur,& combien il s'en fault pour faire nonante, puis assemblez ceux qui seront moins, auec la declinaison de ce iour:

POUR sauoir en quel iour de la sepmaine est chacune feste de l'an, il est besoing ae sauoir quelle lettre sert en icelle annee, pour le dimenche: laquelle se pourra facilement congnoistre par les reigles cy dessouz escriptes, à la premiere desquelles est marquee e, qui sert pour lettre dominicale ceste annee 1550.& ainsi successiuement, vne lettre sert en chacune annee. Puis ayant acheué les deux reigles,

FIG. 17. Italics unrelated to Gryphius's. From Pedro de Medina, *L'art de naviger*. Guillaume Rouillé, Lyons, 1554.

best way of starting would be to cut as soon as possible new types after the italic letter of Aldus Manutius, adding in his liberality a considerable gift in order that I might be better able to advance the work. What then was there to delay me after the encouragement, advice, and help of such a generous friend? So I engraved italic types[1] after the model of the Aldine, with what success others will judge, though certainly they have satisfied the taste of Danés, of Vatable and of others. And not content with these I applied my mind to designing minute types of the same proportion and form (men of our trade call the fount 'glossa'). As these too seemed neat and elegant to Master Jean Gagny, he told me that he had received from you a learned and devout work of David Chambellan, formerly your father-in-law, who in earlier days had been the most distinguished of advocates and counsel in the Parlement, but after his wife's death a most devout deacon in the Church of Paris. Master Gagny thought this work worthy of being in the hands of all Christians, especially in this time of Lent. He added that he marvelled that the work had been completed in an age which produced few men of letters and by a man burdened with domestic affairs and the business of an advocate, at a time when he was immersed in pleading cases, nor could he cease to wonder how a man busily engaged in legal affairs and harassed by domestic troubles could find the

1. Omont, in the *Bulletin de la Société de l'Histoire de Paris*, 1888, p. 10, etc., has a footnote to the effect that Robert Estienne used the larger of these characters for the first time in the edition of Cicero's works of 1543-44 in 8°. What is the evidence for this statement? The type of the Cicero has upright capitals, more ligatures and other differences. The book from which figs. 15 and 16 are taken appears to have been unknown to Omont.

EPISTOLA.

Henricum III. Angliæ Regem fratrem patruelem in Britannia minori fusum vidit ; sed fortiori certè fuit ANNA *dum germanum audiit iteratis vicibus profligatum , & quas vt soror fraternæ gloriæ dispendio partas mærere potuit victorias, mox vt tua genitrix festiuo coluit apparatu. Tantas Hispani laudent dotes*

GALLICVS.   89

regnaret Regem constituit : cui etiam adduxit ab Aquitaniis partibus vxorem , quæ cernens videlicet iuuenem patre minùs fore industrium , vt erat ingenio callida , elegit agere diuortium , monuitque illum fictè , vt simul de qua aduenerat , redirent Prouinciam scilicet iure hereditario sibi subdituram. Ille quoque non intelligens mulieris astuciam , vt monitus fuerat ire parauit ; ad quam dum venissent , relinquens eum mulier suis adhæsit , cumque patri nunciatum fuisset, prosequens filium ad se reduxit , qui simul deinceps degentes post aliquot annos , absque vlla liberorum ope vterque obiit.

FIG. 18. Seventeenth-century French italics. From A. Dominicy, *Assertor Gallicus.* Imprimerie Royale, Paris, 1646.

leisure to acquire a knowledge of three languages, with which he alone in his age was familiar, combined with no ordinary knowledge of theology. As he said, you may find to-day several leading advocates with a knowledge of Latin, some few who have added Greek to Latin, but Matthieu alone, who has rivalled him by combining Hebrew with Greek and Latin, and none with his knowledge of theology in addition to the mastery of three languages. I have heard Gagny say that your Chambellan in sacred literature has such charm and facility that he may be compared with the learned men of by-gone days, and that in his writings his very soul inspired by the Holy Spirit seems to be speaking. Therefore in order that the devout and religious labours of such a man may not be lost to the men of our age and in order that those who are too entirely devoted to public affairs may learn by his example not to plead without intermission but to turn sometimes to God in the inner sanctuary of the soul, Gagny handed me the work to be printed in my new types. I at once thought that these first fruits should be dedicated to you alone, the author's son-in-law and one who boasts and thanks the gods who have given you children by the daughter of so learned and devout a man. Accept then this offering, which we have desired to go forth in your name in gratitude for the loan of the manuscript and for your generosity towards us. What manner of life was that of your father-in-law David Chambellan, I have desired to make clear to posterity from his epitaph, which has been added on the second page of the book. May God be with you. Paris, A. D. 1545, 18 Feb.

[1924]

ITALIAN SIXTEENTH-CENTURY BOOKS

The Presidential Address to the Bibliographical Society
19 March 1957

THE following notes are based on the Short-title Catalogue of Italian Books in the British Museum, 1465-1600. That Catalogue includes the incunables, but I am limiting myself to the sixteenth century. Dr. Scholderer has in two papers dealt with the fifteenth century in much the same way as it is here proposed to deal with the sixteenth. His first paper was the General Introduction to Part VII of the Museum's *Catalogue of Books printed in the XVth Century* (1935) and the second a paper read before the British Academy in 1949 entitled 'Printers and Readers in Italy in the Fifteenth Century'.[1] I shall begin with some statistics in order to show the importance of the Italian book-trade, in comparison with other leading European countries, and continue with some comments on the subjects of the books provided for Italian readers.

The British Museum collection of Italian sixteenth-century books numbers about 18,000. The first question it is desirable to answer is what proportion of the known number of published books this represents. We want to know whether the collection is large enough to be representative, that is to say, whether one can generalize from it. For example, if we find that in it the number of books printed at Rome is about three-quarters of those printed at Florence, may we assume that that is the general picture? The second reason for this inquiry is the wish to compare the Italian output during the century with the French, German, English, &c. I regret to say that no exact answer can be given to the question for want of the necessary catalogues, and one can only make assumptions for the time being in the hope that some day there may be a definite basis on which to work. When Italy, Germany, and France have produced catalogues parallel to the English *S.T.C.*, published by this Society, then the answer will be simple. Not only is there no Italian *S.T.C.*, but there is no catalogue of books printed in any one of the larger towns. Catalogues of well-known individual printers are of little use for this purpose, because a large library usually has a larger proportion of the books of a famous printer than of the less well known. For example, in this collection there are more than half the books printed by the Aldine family as recorded by Renouard (much more than half of those printed by the first Aldus). In the early days of book-collecting, when the classics came first, Aldines were much sought after, with the result that Aldus is well represented in most large libraries. Indeed, the Museum is seldom content with one copy of an Aldine. There are generally three or more, even seven copies. Again, of the printer Giolito the collection has about 480 books, about half of those recorded by Bongi,[2] and certainly well above the general average. Some figures can be given for three smaller printing-centres. For Padua the collection has 237

---

1. *Proceedings of the British Academy*, XXXV, 25-47. Reprinted in *Fifty Essays in Fifteenth- and Sixteenth-Century Bibliography* (Amsterdam 1966), pp. 202-215.
2. Salvatore Bongi, *Annali di Gabriel Giolito de' Ferrari* (2 vols., Roma, 1890-5).

books of the 572 recorded by Fantini,[1] i. e. about one-third. For Vicenza it has 63 books out of 260 recorded by Cristofari,[2] about a quarter. Some figures of Mantua have been provided for me by Mr. Dennis Rhodes, who has published a catalogue of Mantua books in *La Bibliofilia*. For Mantua the collection has 151 books out of the 310 noted by Mr. Rhodes (75 out of 268 for the sixteenth century), Hebrew not included. All this, for what it is worth, suggests that the collection includes about a quarter of the known books, and I am venturing to assume that this is a large enough proportion for purposes of generalization.

In the introduction to the Museum's *Short-title Catalogue of French Books* (1924) it was suggested that the catalogue included about one-fifth of the known books. That introduction was written more than thirty years ago and about 500 books have been added since. One may perhaps conclude that the French and Italian collections are more or less equally representative. I am going to assume that the British Museum has acquired sixteenth-century books of the chief European countries with more or less equal success and to suggest that the following table of the books produced by the leading European cities, based on the Museum's collection, is truly representative:

Venice	7,500	Wittenberg	1,400
Paris	6,400	Frankfurt	1,350
Lyons	2,500	Leipzig	1,000
Basle	2,380	Bologna	578
Antwerp	2,100	Milan[3]	527
Florence	1,890	Brescia	262
Rome	1,700	Ferrara	254
Augsburg	1,520	Naples	253
Strasbourg	1,500	Padua	237
Cologne	1,440	Siena	218
Nuremberg	1,400	Mantua	151

This table contains seven German towns as against eleven Italian, but Venice, Florence, and Rome are all higher in the list and their production exceeds that of the seven German towns. It so happens that none of the German towns printed steadily throughout the century. Wittenberg, Augsburg, and Nuremberg, for instance, were very busy during the Reformation period but much less so in the second half of the century, whereas Frankfurt's output was much greater in the second half. The total amount of printing in the German-speaking countries (that is, including the important city of Basle) is approximately equal to that of Italy, but is divided between a larger number of towns or places – more than 200. In Italy there were presses in the century in some eighty towns. Incidentally it may be noted that the great majority of these Italian

1. Bianca Saraceni Fantini, 'Prime indagini sulla stampa padovana del cinquecento' (*Miscellanea di scritti in memoria di Luigi Ferrari*, Firenze, 1952, pp. 415-85).
2. Maria Cristofari, 'La Tipografia vicentina nel secolo XVI' (ibid., pp. 191-214).
3. In the Museum's incunable catalogue Milan occupies about as many pages as Florence. The decline after 1500 is no doubt due to the French invasions and the continuous state of war for some thirty years. Whether Milan was captured by the French or liberated by the Spanish it was much the same to the citizens, who always paid the cost.

towns were in the northern half of the country. The volume of the incunable catalogue containing Dr. Scholderer's introduction includes a map, and Dr. Scholderer points out that the greater part of the presses fall to the north of a line drawn across the centre. This distribution holds good in the sixteenth century.

There is another point of interest that may be considered in connexion with this table. Where does London come in this order of cities? The difficulty of answering this question does not arise from lack of information. Thanks to the English *S.T.C.*, we have more exact figures to work with. There were about 12,000 books printed in London between 1501 and 1600, of which the Museum has about 6,800, well over half. How are we to compare this figure with the figures for continental cities? Naturally the national library has a far higher proportion of London printed books than of Venice or Paris printed books. If one supposes that the Museum had one-quarter of the 12,000 known books, that gives us 3,000; if a fifth, then we have about 2,400. It appears that London might come third on the list, or at least in the third place along with Lyons and Basle.

To return to Italy, the outstanding fact in these statistics is the importance of Venice as a printing-centre. Books were poured out steadily throughout the century and with little diminution at the end. There was no slump in the last quarter of the century as there was at Lyons and in the German Reformation centres. There was some decline in plague-years, especially in 1577. H. F. Brown says that in 1596 as a result of the introduction of the Clementine Index the number of presses fell from 125 to forty.[1] In this collection there is an average of seventy-five books a year in the decade 1581-90, dropping to fifty-five in the decade 1591-1600. The historians tell us that Venice was declining. She had been badly hit by the war of the League of Cambrai, she was losing her colonial possessions to the Turks – by 1600 only Crete was left – her trade with the East was falling off because of the opening of the route round the Cape of Good Hope, by the end of the Renaissance, roughly dated as about 1520 or 1527 (the date of the sack of Rome), scholarship had departed to the north of the Alps, and finally the French had taken the lead in the art of book-production. With all this one might expect to find a collapse of the book-trade. One can only suppose that the accumulated wealth of the city was so great that it took many decades to ruin the trade. All these books were not for the Italian market only. In the Frankfurt Fair catalogues one may find many books with Venetian imprints, mostly, of course, books in Latin, but some in Italian. As to the preponderance of Venice over other Italian cities this is much greater than might be expected from the population. That of Venice is given as about 150,000, of Florence about 100,000, and that of Rome fluctuating according to the policy of the Pope of the day from about 40,000 to 80,000.

Of individual Italian printers the most prolific was Gabriel Giolito (1541-78), represented in this collection by 480 books out of about 1,000 known books. The only printer of the century who much exceeded this output was Christophe Plantin at Antwerp. The whole of the Aldine family, three generations extending through a whole century, is represented here by nearly 600 books, and the whole house of Giunta at

---

1. *The Venetian Printing Press* (1891), p. 155.

Florence by about the same number. The Giunta were among the printers of official documents for the Dukes of Florence (from 1570 Grand Dukes of Tuscany), many of these being single sheets or pamphlets of two or four pages. It so happens that there is in the Museum a large collection – some 600 entries – of such state papers, whereas there is a very small collection of Venetian official publications. Such papers must no doubt exist, but they are poorly represented here. The result is that the Florence total is swollen by comparison with Venetian printers. Another official printer at Florence was Giorgio Marescotti (1563-1600), here represented by 585 entries. The figure for Florence as a whole (1,700) is boosted up. The chief sixteenth-century printer at Rome, Antonio Blado, was also an official printer, printer to the Camera Apostolica, and his total of 290 flatters him. Other printers who are represented by more than a hundred entries are the firm of Bindoni & Pasini (115), Comin da Trino (138), Angelo Gardano (163), the brothers Nicolini da Sabbio (140), Girolamo Scoto (176), Vincenzo Valgrisi (16), Giordano Ziletti (105), B. Sermatelli of Florence (113), and L. Torrentino of Florence (162). All save the last two are Venetian, and there are several other Venetians who approach the hundred mark.

After these figures I will turn to the subjects of the books provided for Italian readers. I begin with the classical authors of Greece and Rome. We have to remember that the task of getting the Greek authors into type began only at the end of the fifteenth century and that the majority of the *editiones principes* of the Greek authors appeared in the sixteenth century. There is a long list from Aeschines and Aeschylus through the alphabet down to Thucydides and Xenophon, all of whom were printed for the first time after 1500 in Italy. Just a few first editions were printed at Paris or at Basle. As to printers of Greek books, Aldus, of course, and his successors come first, followed by the Giunta at Florence. At Rome in 1542 Cardinal Cervini started a project for printing Greek manuscripts in the Vatican Library. A new type was cut and Antonio Blado was employed as printer. A folio edition of Homer in four volumes with the commentary of Eustathius opened the series. At Venice there appeared many editions of Greek liturgies for the Eastern Church. Venice was, in fact, engaged in printing liturgical works for many European countries besides Italy. But the three largest headings of Greek authors are in other fields, in philosophy, natural history, and medicine, namely, Aristotle, Galen, and Hippocrates. The heading of Aristotle is indeed remarkable. It covers more than thirteen pages and is the longest heading of an individual author in the Catalogue. The majority of the entries are Latin translations, not the original Greek. In particular at Venice folio editions of the philosophical and scientific works were published throughout the century, no doubt for the University of Padua. Typographically they are among the dullest of Venetian books. We think of Aristotle as the scholastic philosopher and we read that the scholars of the Renaissance were turning to Plato. Some of them certainly did, but the heading Plato has only eleven entries (nine after 1500). The students' textbooks continued to be Aristotle throughout the century. From this century, too, we date the beginnings of modern medicine with the anatomist Vesalius and men like Gabriello Falloppio. But progress was slow and the textbooks for the schools were Galen and Hippocrates. We find a parallel in the subject of astronomy. This was the century of Copernicus and Kepler, but our Catalogue is full of books of astrology, works beginning with the word *Prognosticatio*, forecasts of the future all founded on astrology.

Turning to the Latin classics we find that the order of popularity remains much the same as in the fifteenth century, as reported by Dr. Scholderer. Cicero was easily the most popular author, especially his Letters, and is followed by Ovid, Virgil, Terence, and Horace in that order. The entries at Cicero cover ten pages and those at Horace two and a half pages. The chief difference between the centuries is that after 1500 there is a higher proportion of versions in Italian. Perhaps the largest printer of Latin texts, and indeed one of the largest in Europe, was the second Aldus, Paolo Manuzio. Among his editions were not only schoolbooks but standard editions, as, for example, the folio edition of Livy edited by C. Sigonius which was published in 1555 and reprinted in 1566 and 1577.

Here seems to be the fitting place to refer to the Italian poets of the sixteenth century who preferred to write in Latin. Among them were men famous in their day, such as Antonio Beccadelli, Girolamo Fracastoro, Andrea Navagero, Jovianus Pontanus, Jacopo Sannazaro, and Hieronymus Vida. If these men had written in Italian they might be better known today – they might even be read.[1] At any rate their books are here recorded and preserved.

It has been said of the Italians of the Renaissance that they were no theologians. From this Catalogue one might conclude that this is true of the sixteenth, but hardly of the fifteenth century. The entries under the Fathers and the leading theologians of the Middle Ages are almost all incunables. Examples are Albertus Magnus, St. Ambrose, St. Augustine, St. Jerome, and St. Thomas Aquinas. In many cases, after a long gap, one meets with a large edition of the whole works of one of these theologians towards the end of the century, one of the results of the Counter-Reformation. For example, there is a folio edition of St. Ambrose in six volumes produced at Rome from 1579 to 1587, and another of St. Jerome in nine folio volumes printed at Rome by Manutius from 1564 to 1572. The same tendency is shown by the number of editions of the Latin Bible, twenty-five up to 1500 and twenty for the whole of the sixteenth century. Of Bibles in Italian there are eight editions up to 1500 and twelve between 1501 and 1600. After 1548 there is no edition of the New Testament in either Latin or Italian printed in Italy, a mark of the success of the Inquisition.

Books of controversial religion relating to the Reformation and the beginnings of Protestantism are not very numerous; they form no large section of the Catalogue. Girolamo Muzio wrote seven or eight anti-Protestant books, against Vergerio (1550), against Ochino (1551), against Bullinger (1562), and others. He is exceptional, as is also Bishop Lorenzo Politi. There are a few direct replies to Luther, and under Luther himself there are seven entries, only two of which are actually works by Luther. One is a translation of his well-known tract *An den christlichen Adel dey deutschen Nation* (and this translation was printed at Strasbourg), and the second a translation of his Catechism,

1. On the whole question of the Renaissance poets and the Latin language those interested may be referred to J. A. Symonds, *Renaissance in Italy*, vol. II, chap. 7.

printed at Tübingen. There are said to be other Italian translations, but they are not here represented. The whole question of Italian Protestant literature is full of interest not only to the ecclesiastical historian but also to the bibliographer, because of the rarity of the books and the obscurity of their origin. As this Catalogue includes all books in Italian wherever printed, one can follow the career of the Italian Protestants who went into exile from the time when the Inquisition was remodelled after the Spanish pattern in Rome in 1542, such men as Bernardino Ochino, P. P. Vergerio, Vermigli, and Curione. Their books were printed in Switzerland and southern Germany, for the most part without imprints. Down to about 1545 an Italian printer could venture on the publication of a book of a Protestant tendency, at any rate in the north. There is a work called in the English version *Of the Benefits of Christ crucified* which by its English printers is wrongly assigned to Antonio Paleario (della Paglia). There were a number of editions of the original Italian, some printed at Venice and some at Modena, but unfortunately none is in this collection. There is a copy of one edition in the library of St. John's College, Cambridge, which bears the imprint 'Venetiis, apud Bernardinum de Bindonis', 1543.[1] Here then is a Venetian printer boldly issuing a Lutheran work as late as 1543. But such books were few, and it seems fair to say that Italian readers took little interest in Luther and his works. Nor were they much interested in Erasmus, whose heading fills barely half a page.

Under the heading 'ROME, Church of' under the successive Popes are entered the bulls and other official publications. Here one will find a sort of summary of papal dealings with the other Italian states and foreign powers. For example, in April 1509 Pope Julius II issued a *Monitorium contra Venetos*; the beginning of the League of Cambrai. In July 1511 Julius issued a bull summoning the Lateran Council. In 1517 Leo X published an indulgence to those contributing to the cost of building St. Peter's. This was the indulgence which Tetzel was hawking round Saxony, to be followed by Luther's 'Theses' posted on the door of the church at Wittenberg. In June 1520 comes the *Bulla contra errores Martini Lutheri*. In October 1521 the Pope confers on Henry VIII the title of Defender of the Faith as a reward for his tract against Luther, the *Assertio septem sacramentorum*, lest he should feel he was not the equal of his Catholic Majesty and his Most Christian Majesty. We know how Henry defended the Faith and how Francis I showed his support for western Christianity. In November 1522 Pope Adrian VI fulminated again 'Adversus Lutherum'. On 4 May 1527 Clement VII issued a plenary indulgence to such Romans as should take up arms against Bourbon. It seems rather late, as Bourbon's army was already in Rome and the Pope besieged in the Castle of St. Angelo. On 7 March 1530 Clement pronounces in favour of Catharine of Aragon in the matter of the divorce and on 15 November 1532 there is a threat of excommunication against Henry VIII and Anne Boleyn. In 1538 under Paul III we meet a document of a different kind, called *Consilium delectorum Cardinalium de emendanda ecclesia*. This is the report drawn up by Cardinals Contarini, Caraffa (afterwards Pope Paul IV),

1. I have to thank Mr. H. M. Adams for this information. The book is by Benedetto Luchino. See D. Cantimori in *New Cambridge Modern History*, vol. 2, p. 262. He says (p. 254) there were at least 63 anti-Luchino treatises before 1536.

and others, presented to the Pope, on the reforms which ought to be carried out in the Church. It is a sort of blueprint of the Counter-Reformation, the basis of what was finally agreed on at the Council of Trent. In November 1544 Paul III summons the Council of Trent, but nearly twenty years were to pass before it completed its work. In February 1569 Pius V is again concerned with English affairs and issues a *Sententia declaratoria contra Elisabeth praetensam Angliae reginam.* In January 1572 the same Pope is still worried about the Turks and offers absolution to those fighting against the infidels. In September 1585 we find Henry of Navarre under papal censure. Pope Sixtus V issues a *Declaratio contra Henricum Borbonium assertum regem Navarrae.* In February 1592 Pope Clement VIII has an outburst against the Jews in a *Constitutio contra impia scripta Hebraeorum.*

There are three headings in the Catalogue which especially illustrate the history of the Counter-Reformation. They are the sub-heading 'Index Librorum Prohibitorum' under 'ROME, Church of', the heading 'TRENT, Council of', and the heading 'JESUITS'. The first Roman Index was printed by Blado at Rome in 1557. But this was not the first Index to appear in Italy, apart from those in other countries. Giovanni della Casa, the author of *Il Galateo* and an archbishop, printed an Index in Venice in 1549, when he was Papal Nuncio there. The original Venetian edition seems to have disappeared, but we know what was in it in a rather curious way. Della Casa had been in controversy with the Protestant P. P. Vergerio, now in exile. Vergerio printed this Index at Zürich in 1549, with his comments, the comments forming nine-tenths of the book. The number of editions of the Roman Index together with the editions issued by the Council of Trent, generally included with editions of the Council's Decrees, is thirty. Usually in the Index there is a list of printers who are banned wholesale, mostly printers at Basle and in Germany. The only Italian printer so treated is Francesco Brucioli, the Venetian, who had produced Bibles in the Italian version of his brother Antonio Brucioli.

Under the heading 'TRENT, Council of', there appear many editions of the Canons and Decrees agreed by the Council, often accompanied, as already said, by an *Index librorum prohibitorum.* There are also in the Catalogue a large number of speeches delivered by individual members of the Council, printed not at Trent, where there was no press at the time, but for the most part at Brescia.

Under the heading 'JESUITS' are entered first the Constitutions, Ordinances, Rules, &c. These are followed by a series of Letters from Missions, beginning in 1552. They are letters from India, China, and Japan, some translated from Spanish. They record an amazing story of the heroism and self-sacrifice of the Jesuits in the Far East, a story hardly to be surpassed in missionary history. The letters are also of value in the history of geography.

The Italians printed many more books in Hebrew than the rest of Europe put together. The various Italian rulers were comparatively – comparatively, I say – lenient to Jews, at any rate before the Popes of the Counter-Reformation. When the Inquisition was introduced, under conditions, into Venice in the 1540s, one of the conditions was that there was to be no interference with Jews, infidels, and Greeks. The merchants were profitable at Venice and in theory the Inquisitors were looking for Christian heretics. However, Venice had adopted the ghetto system. The Medici at Florence were also tolerant down to 1570, when Cosimo, desiring to carry favour with the Pope Pius V, concentrated all the Jews of Tuscany in a ghetto in Florence. The Renaissance Popes were tolerant, but in that age there were several anti-Semite priests, notably Giovanni da Capistrano and Bernardino da Feltro, who delivered vitriolic sermons against the Jews. At Rome Pope Julius III in 1553 declared the Talmud blasphemous, and great numbers of Hebrew books were burned in that year. Even Venice conformed, and there was a gap of ten years in Hebrew printing there. From 1556 to 1567 Cremona became the chief centre, and even there in 1559 it is said that more than 10,000 volumes were burned. Pope Paul IV (Caraffa) was an ardent anti-Semite and in 1555 renewed all the old, lapsed restrictions upon Jews. For the rest of the century the Popes were alternately tolerant and oppressive. Under Pius V the Jews were expelled in 1569 from the papal states, except Rome and Ancona. Sixtus V permitted their return, and Clement VIII turned them out again.

This outline explains why the printing of Hebrew was concentrated in the north-east, particularly in Venice. The houses producing these books, or the heads of them, were nearly always Christian, although they must have employed Jewish compositors. Daniel Bomberg (1516-1549), a Fleming, printed nearly 200 books in Hebrew, and Giustiniani nearly a hundred. Other Christian printers of Hebrew were Alvisio Bragadini, Domenico Farri, Giorgio de' Cavalli, Giovanni Griffio, and Giovanni di Gara. Outside Venice, Girolamo Soncino was printing in Hebrew early in the century at several towns including Pesaro, Fano, and Rimini. Other centres were Cremona, already mentioned, Ferrara, and Mantua. Where the reigning house, like the Este at Ferrara and the Gonzaga at Mantua, pursued an independent policy, there generally the Jews had a chance to express themselves. The Hebrew books were for the most part religious, Hebrew Bibles, service-books, and the Hebrew commentaries. But there was a little secular literature. According to Cecil Roth there was even a Hebrew translation of Petrarch. Of course, Jews also published books in Italian or Latin. David de Pomi had his defence of Jewish medical men published by Aldus in 1581. The Jews had a high reputation as medical advisers and almost every Pope, whether anti-Semite or not, had a Jewish doctor.

The total number of Hebrew books in this collection is about 600; of these 62 are incunabula. Roth gives the population of the Jews in Venice in the middle of the century as 1,500, which seems surprisingly small out of a population of 150,000, and considering their achievements.[1]

Vernacular literature is perhaps the most important section in the Catalogue. It may be said to be primarily useful to students of Italian literature, and it is not necessary to say much about it here. I shall therefore confine myself to a few minor points. The student will find here all the great names in Italian literature, from Dante and Petrarch through Ariosto down to Tasso. He will note that the largest heading is that of Petrarch (five pages) with eighty-six editions of the *Canzoniere* for the sixteenth century, while there

1. See C. Roth, *Venice* (Jewish Communities Series, Philadelphia, 1930), and *History of the Jews of Italy* (1946). For the bibliography, see D. W. Amram, *The Makers of Hebrew Books in Italy* (Philadelphia, 1909).

are but twenty-nine editions of Dante in the century. Ariosto occupies nearly four pages with seventy-eight editions of the *Orlando*, and Boccaccio four and a half pages (thirty-nine editions of the *Decameron*).

During the middle years of the century there was at work at Venice a group of hack-writers who take up considerable space in this Catalogue – they would take up even more if they were given entries for their editorial work, produced largely for the printer Giolito. Among them were Lodovico Dolce, Lodovico Domenichi, A. F. Doni, and Nicolo Franco. They were all at one time friends and at another time enemies of the unspeakable Pietro Aretino. Probably only historians of Italian literature read them today. J. A. Symonds calls Dolce and Domenichi scamps and at the same time finds them representative men of the age of Aretino. Domenichi printed at Florence in 1561 a play entitled *Progne* without mentioning the fact that it was a translation of a Latin play by Gregorio Coerer. Franco ended on the gallows in Rome in 1570, not as a result of his indecencies – they all vied with Aretino in that respect – but because of too daring remarks about the Popes. Some of them at any rate were hard workers and from the point of view of output seem to be as important as men like Trissino or Bernardo Tasso. They were perhaps the earliest group of writers working for the printers and living by their pens – the first Grub Street.

There is an interesting bibliographical point relating to the so-called *Rappresentazioni*, sacred dramas which are comparable to the Northern Miracle Plays. In origin they belong to the last years of the fifteenth century, a number of them being written by members of the Pulci family at Florence and some by Lorenzo de' Medici, but they were continually reprinted and many new ones were written throughout the sixteenth century and even in the seventeenth century at Florence and Siena. They were generally illustrated by one or more woodcuts and the original blocks continued in use for at least a century in some cases. Sixteenth-century editions seldom bear a printer's name or date, follow a traditional format, and are therefore extremely difficult to arrange in chronological order. In fact no one as yet has tackled the bibliography of the *Rappresentazioni*.

The Italians have no great reputation as dramatists. Even the best of the plays, such as those written by Ariosto and Machiavelli, are not very highly esteemed. On the other hand the number of plays appearing in this Catalogue is very large. J. A. Symonds says that the number known to students is computed at several thousands. But who now reads the plays of, for example, G. B. Giraldi? There are nine of them in this collection; the plot of one, the *Orbecche* (six editions here between 1543 and 1594), is described by Symonds. It is as full of crime and bloodshed as the plots of our minor Elizabethan and Jacobean playwrights. There are six plays by Luigi Groto (several editions of some of them), and three by Sforza degli Oddi, neither of whom is so much as mentioned by Symonds.

The number of books of music contained in this collection is about 750, a figure much higher than can be shown by any other country. The majority appeared in the second half of the century, and in the years before 1550 a number of the composers of the music here shown are not Italian but Flemish or French, e. g. Jacob Archadet, Josquin Després, and Andrew Willaert. With the coming of Pierluigi Palestrina (his earliest publication appeared at Rome in 1567) Italy took the lead in this as in all the other arts; sculpture, painting, and architecture. The majority of the books were printed at Venice, beginning with Ottaviano Petrucci, who worked also at Fossombrone. The two families of Scoto and Gardano were the most prolific printers in the second half of the century. There was also much music produced at Rome, beginning with the brothers Dorici.

On the aesthetic side, music books have at most periods been among the most attractive productions of their day, and this is certainly true of Italian music. There are to be found many pleasing title-pages at Venice, Rome, and other towns.

The news-letters, forerunners of newspapers, are of interest as revealing what historical events appeared to be important to Italian readers, or perhaps one should say of what events the authorities thought they should be informed. These pamphlets were usually small quartos of from four to six pages and may be printed in round text, roman, or italic. They are often accompanied by a woodcut illustration and are often quite attractive in appearance, especially those printed in italic. There are in this collection two volumes of news-letters and verses (thirty-four pieces in all) on contemporary events, acquired by the Museum in 1845, which once belonged to William Roscoe, author of the *Life of Pope Leo X*. Bound up with the tracts are slips with notes, written by Roscoe and giving references to his book. The tracts all relate to events during Leo's papacy (1513-21), and we can see what use Roscoe made of them and note that those in verse also (which are the more numerous) were found to be of interest to an historian. Incidentally, it may be noted that Italians were much inclined to occasional verse and the amount of such verse in this collection is very considerable. The first letter in the Roscoe volumes is entitled *Victoria sereniss. Henrici Octaui de Scotis reportata*, and relates to the Battle of Flodden and Henry's campaign in Flanders, noted for the Battle of Spurs, both in 1513. The letter is addressed to the Cardinal of England, Christopher Bainbridge, who was Henry's legate at the Papal Court. Bainbridge had been created Cardinal by Pope Julius II at Ravenna in 1511, along with several other ecclesiastics, for political reasons, in opposition to the French Cardinals. Bainbridge no doubt thought that this letter was good propaganda for his master Henry and gave it to a Roman printer, Beplin, to set up. Perhaps this was in general the manner in which these news-letters got into print, not through the enterprise of printers but because the recipients, usually men of some position, thought publication would serve their purpose. Another letter in the Roscoe volume was from Ramon de Cardona, the commander of the Spanish and Papal forces operating against Alviano, the Venetian commander. It is dated from Vicenza, October 1513, and is addressed to Matthaeus Lange, Bishop of Gurk, who was the Emperor Maximilian's representative at the Papal Court. It was no doubt Lange who had the letter printed at Rome, in this case by M. Silber. The tenth tract in the Roscoe series has the title *Nova victoria del Re de Portugallo in India*, also printed at Rome by Beplin. The discovery of the route to India round the Cape of Good Hope and the subsequent adventures of the Portuguese in India were important news, and unwelcome news to the Venetians. Roscoe's fourth tract, in verse and entitled *La Rotta de Scocesi*, again deals with the Battle of Flodden.

There are at least forty newsletters concerning the activities of the most important man in Europe in his generation, the Emperor Charles V. News about Charles was of interest to Italians as much as to Spaniards or Germans, since he largely decided their political fate for many years to come. We begin with an account of his election to the office of Holy Roman Emperor at Frankfort in 1519, printed by Silber at Rome. Next comes an account of his marriage at Seville in 1526 to Isabella of Portugal, printed by F. M. Calvo at Rome. In the same year are two accounts printed by Blado at Rome of the treaty between Charles and Francis I of France, made during the captivity of Francis following his defeat at the Battle of Pavia in 1525. As soon as Francis was free the terms of this treaty were thrown over. The printer of these two letters, Blado, produced many newsletters. As he was an official printer, printer to the Camera Apostolica, he presumably printed what he was given and it was the papal authorities who were the responsible publishers. The next important event in Charles's life was his coronation at Bologna in 1530 by the Pope Clement VII. There are two accounts, each in two editions, one account printed by Phaelli at Bologna. In the same year falls the Diet at Augsburg at which Charles in vain asked for help against the Turks and was presented with the Augsburg Confession. There is a letter about the agreement reached at Regensburg in 1532 as a result of which Charles himself took the field with an army largely German against Sultan Sulaiman. Both sides seem unwilling to risk a battle, but at least Charles saw the withdrawal of the Turks. In 1535 there are two letters about Charles's successful expedition to Tunis, where he achieved his sole success against the Turks and defeated Kairaldin, known as Barbarossa, the free-lance pirate, who was given command over the Turkish fleet. The benefit to the western Mediterranean was of short duration, and in 1541 Charles had to lead out another expedition and this time met with disaster at Algiers. After Tunis Charles made a sort of triumphal tour through Italy and there are letters giving an account of his entry into Messina, Naples, Rome, Siena, Florence, and Lucca, most of them printed by Blado at Rome in 1536. In 1539 and 1540 Charles passed through France, after careful negotiations, on his way to the Netherlands, and we have letters about his ceremonial entries into Poitiers and Paris. In the sixteenth century all countries alike shared this passion for ceremonies and processions, on which money was lavishly spent. Letters are numerous about the ceremonial tours of ruling princes, about their marriages, and finally about their funerals. There is another one about Charles in Brussels in 1544. More interesting, perhaps, is the account of Charles in the Smalkaldic War, when at Mühlberg in 1547 he gained his one real success in Germany and captured the Protestant leader, the Elector John of Saxony. Finally we end with four accounts of ceremonies following the death of Charles in 1559.

Many letters relate to the Turks. It was in this century that the Ottoman Empire became a deadly menace to Western Europe. The danger was most serious during the reign of Sulaiman called the Magnificent (1520-66), the most capable of all the Sultans. To the Italians the menace was very real as their coasts were frequently raided by the piratical Barbarossa and Italians carried off and sold as slaves. Sulaiman's army actually landed in the heel of Italy in 1537, but withdrew when the Sultan's ally, the Most Christian King Francis I, made a separate peace. At the beginning of his reign Sulaiman captured Belgrade in 1521, thus securing a bridgehead on the Danube and opening the way into Hungary. In 1522 he conquered the island of Rhodes after a fierce struggle with the Knights of St. John of Jerusalem. In 1526 came the Battle of Mohács, when the Hungarians, hitherto the chief spearhead against the Turks, were utterly defeated. Then in 1529 came the siege of Vienna. Many were the calls to the West to unite against this menace, calls from various Popes, the Emperor, and other princes. Charles V sincerely desired this unity, but all in vain. The Italians, including the Popes, had their own internal quarrels, Germany was completely divided, and his Most Christian Majesty of France was often in alliance with the Turk.

There is a newsletter written from Belgrade and dated 7 July 1532 by a Venetian. There were many Venetians in Constantinople, and Venice was well informed about happenings in the Near East. This particular letter describes the opening of the campaign already referred to, in which the Emperor Charles himself took the field. A letter from Constantinople dated November 1535 describes the recent success of the Shah of Persia against Sulaiman. It was fortunate for the West that Sulaiman had another enemy on his Eastern frontier and spent many summers campaigning near the Euphrates. In 1539 we have a letter about the capture of Castel Nuovo in Dalmatia by Barbarossa from the Venetians. It appears that Barbarossa had recovered from his defeat at Tunis. In 1565 we have a letter about the failure of the Turks in an attack on Malta. The Knights of St. John of Jerusalem, after their loss of Rhodes, had been settled in Malta, which they had turned into a strong fort. In 1570 and 1571 Venice lost Cyprus, almost the last of her colonies (only Crete was left), to the Turks. A letter from an escaped prisoner, Giovanni Posemeno, has a familiar sound; it is called *Perdita di Nicosia*. In October 1571 came the Battle of Lepanto, one of the so-called decisive battles, when the combined navies of Spain and Venice under Don John of Austria finally drove the Turkish fleet from the western Mediterranean. There are several contemporary letters and also a veritable flood of verse, much more than on any other occasion. Sulaiman was already dead; he died in 1566 still campaigning against the Austrians. His death and the Battle of Lepanto mark the end of the serious peril.

There are a number of letters relating to English affairs. We have already had the Battle of Flodden; and Henry VIII's divorce has turned up among the papal pronouncements. There is an anonymous letter from London about the death of Anne Boleyn in 1536, printed by Phaelli at Bologna. An historical event which seems to have aroused the greatest interest in Italy was the marriage of Philip of Spain and Queen Mary of England. The papal authorities hoped that this marriage would ensure the return of England to the Catholic Church. There are six letters in the collection, written by members of Philip's escort, and printed at Rome and Milan. In 1587 there are three different accounts of the execution of Mary Queen of Scots, one printed at Parma, one at Florence, and one at Cremona with another edition at Vicenza. It is often difficult to see why a newsletter was printed at a particular town because the name of the addressee of the letter is omitted in the printed version. The last letter relating to English affairs is edited by Bernardino Beccari and concerns the successes of the Catholics in Ireland in 1599. Beccari in this case is not writing from Ireland but compiled the news in Rome. He edited a number of similar newsletters for the Roman printer N. Muzio. Here we have either a printer or a journalist responsible for newsletters.

Of the various classes of books in this collection by no means all have been dealt with. Nothing, for example, has been said of Voyages and Travels, a subject which deserves a paper on its own. This was a century of great discoveries, in which man's knowledge of the world was greatly expanded. There are other smaller groups of great interest which must be passed over, such as 58 books in Spanish, writing-books, books on the duel, and books of the reform of the calendar. The new Gregorian calendar was introduced in 1582, but was not universally adopted, not because the astronomical facts were in dispute, but for reasons of religion.

I shall close with a note on the group of books on architecture. What the Italian architects were building in this century was to influence and control most European building for two centuries, one might almost say down to the Gothic revival. We must begin with Vitruvius, on whom the theory of Renaissance architecture was based. Then in alphabetical order may be cited the edition in Italian of Leon Battista Alberti (printed at Florence by Torrentino in 1550), Giacomo Barozzi, called Il Vignola (Rome, 1583), Pietro Cataneo (Aldus, Venice, 1554 and 1567), and the Roman architect Domenico Fontana on the Vatican obelisk (1590), though this book is in fact a work on engineering rather than on architecture. The raising of this obelisk roused the greatest interest, and besides Fontana's own book there are several other descriptions as well as the inevitable verse. Next we may cite Antonio Labacco (Rome, 1557), Andrea Palladio of Vicenza (Venice, 1570), and finally the five books of Sebastiano Serlio) Venice, 1537-51). Anyone who turns over these books will doubtless agree that the Italians were still capable of producing fine books at any time in the sixteenth century.

[1958]

BOOKS PRINTED AT LYONS IN THE SIXTEENTH CENTURY

THESE notes on printing at Lyons in the sixteenth century are based on an examination of the collection in the British Museum. As I shall draw some general conclusions on the assumption that the collection is representative, I must first give some reasons for that assumption. I know of no estimate of the total number of books printed at Lyons during the century. The chief work on the subject, Baudrier's *Bibliographie Lyonnaise*, is not yet completed, and so far offers no suggestion.[1] The only method of forming an estimate seems to be to take individual printers, and compare the totals as given by Baudrier with those in the Museum collection. Forty printers or publishers have been taken, chosen from various periods of the century, including both printers who would be sought after by collectors and printers likely to be neglected. The result arrived at is that the Museum has 1,356 books by these forty printers, and the number of entries in Baudrier for the same forty is 7,013, i. e. the Museum collection has between one-fifth and one-sixth of the books known to Baudrier. There are a small number of books in the Museum not included in Baudrier, and on the other hand Baudrier mentions many books of which he knows of no existing copy, quoted from various catalogues, some of them of some antiquity, e. g. Antoine Du Verdier's work of the sixteenth century itself. The existence of some of these books is not above suspicion, as Baudrier himself hints. In one case I have taken a printer not yet dealt with by Baudrier, Étienne Dolet. The Museum has 24 books by that printer, whereas according to R. C. Christie's bibliography, in his life of Dolet, Dolet published 84 books, i. e. 84 books actually seen by Christie or of whose existence he was satisfied. As would be expected, compared with Christie's more restricted list, the proportion of Dolet's books in the Museum works out as higher than the average for the forty printers, viz. more than one-fourth. The proportion of between one-fifth and one-sixth may be compared with figures taken from a bibliography of French Bibles. According to Van Eys's bibliography there were 112 Bibles and New Testaments in French printed at Lyons, of which the Museum has 19, just under one-sixth.

The whole collection amounts to 2,380 books. If then the proportion of one-fifth to one-sixth may be trusted the approximate number of books printed at Lyons in the sixteenth century would be 13,000. In working out this proportion I originally took twenty printers; after increasing the number to forty I found that there was practically no difference in the figure arrived at, so that in so far as Baudrier is a satisfactory guide the figure 13,000 seems to be fairly correct. I shall assume that between one-fifth and one-sixth of this number offers a representative collection, that is to say, representative of the typography of the presses and of the kinds of books produced. It must be remembered that in many cases a printer issued many editions of the same work during his

1. Baudrier's work was not completed; no volumes appeared after 1921.

career, and that of twenty editions differing in nothing but the setting up of the type three may be fairly considered representative. For instance, Sébastien Gryphius printed 20 editions of Terence, 12 of Valerius Maximus, and 9 of Catullus and Propertius, of which the Museum has 7, 3, and 2 respectively.

There would be little inducement for a collector to accumulate all these editions. In the case of Jean Pillehotte, who was printer for the Society of Jesuits, for the city of Lyons, and King's printer in the last twenty years of the century, the number of books in the Museum is much below the average, 26 out of 410. His books were for the most part official pamphlets of historical rather than of bibliographical interest, so that even the low proportion of one-sixteenth may in this case be considered to give a good idea of his production. On more general grounds I find that there are very few gaps in the Museum collection of the more notable Lyons books; that is to say, in searching for an individual book of any importance I have rarely found that there was no copy in the Museum. I shall therefore venture on some generalizations with the assumption that figures based on the Museum collection rest on a wide enough basis for generalization.

Of these forty printers Sébastien Gryphius heads the list for the largest number of books issued. Baudrier's catalogue contains 1,140 books from his press, of which the Museum has 264. Gryphius began his career at Lyons in 1523, not as a publisher, but as a printer for the 'Compagnie des Libraires', a combine of publishers engaged in the production of expensive law books. The earliest work bearing his name in the Museum is an edition of the works of Joannes de Imola in gothic type printed for that company in 1525. In 1528 he began to publish on his own account, having acquired fresh types, both roman and italic, and in particular began the production of his well-known octavo and sexto-decimo editions in italic type of the Latin classics. The extraordinary reputation which his name has enjoyed is due perhaps as much to his great services to scholarship as to his merits as a printer. His dealings with such scholars as the elder Scaliger, Étienne Dolet, Conrad Gesner, and Rabelais (he was the printer of Rabelais's scientific works) have added to his fame. He was a good printer, but not better than a number of other French printers of his day. To the modern collector there are several more interesting presses at Lyons, and Gryphius has long surrendered his position as the foremost Lyons printer of the century to Jean de Tournes. Perhaps Gryphius's most interesting books are his large folio editions in roman type, notably his Latin Bible of 1550, a fine book. He adds almost nothing to the history of book illustration and preferred even title-pages unadorned except by his mark. In some folios, for example his edition of Dolet's Commentaries, he used a decorated title-page which came from Basle and was used by Froben in his edition of Erasmus's *Adagia*, 1520, and by other Basle printers. The border of this title-page consists of cuts representing the chief Greek and Roman writers with the nine Muses at the bottom. The cut representing Aristotle bears the initials I. F., said to be the initials of Jacob Faber, and the initials I. F. appear also on some of the small woodcuts in Gryphius's New Testaments.

The printer second on the list is Benoît Rigaud, with 1,100 books in Baudrier and 106 in the Museum. The low proportion of this figure is readily understood when we consider

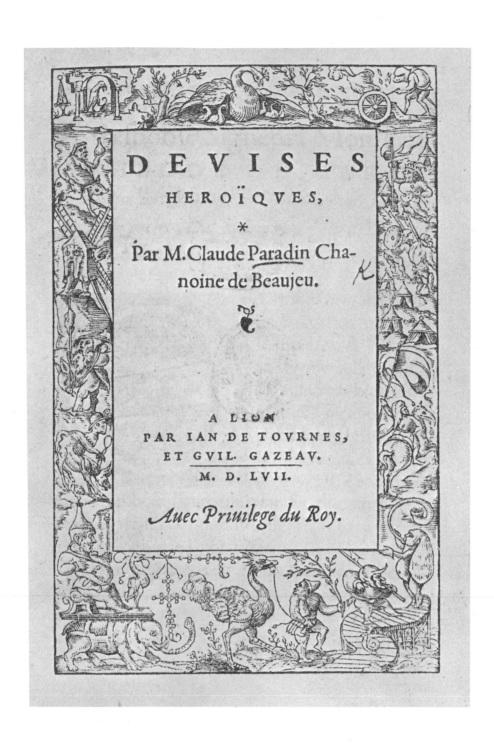

FIG. 1. A title-page of Jean de Tournes, 1557.

the nature of his publications. He was an official printer of the city and also King's printer, with the result that many of his books are mere tracts of little bibliographical interest. Also he was a printer of popular works in a cheap form less likely to survive the ravages of time. His reputation seems to rest on the rarity of his books and perhaps partly on the inferiority of his contemporaries rather than on any intrinsic merit.

The third on the list is Guillaume Rouillé (following Baudrier, I take that to be the spelling and pronunciation of his name, rather than Rouille or Roville, as the name became later) with 800 entries in Baudrier, well represented by 224 books in the Museum. Something will be said of him later in dealing with illustrated books. The large proportion of illustrated books published by him (he was probably not a printer) may account for the high proportion of his books in the Museum. If the figures for all the printers of the century were worked out, I have no reason to suppose that any other printer would compete with these three in amount of output.

I expect that the fourth place would be taken by the most interesting printer of the century, Jean de Tournes. Unfortunately he is not included in Baudrier. The Museum has 152 of his books, and for various reasons one would expect that to be a high proportion. His career was a short one, twenty-two years, compared with forty-five years for Rouillé, thirty-three for Gryphius, and forty-three for Rigaud. The excellence of his books, and the fact that so many of them were original French literature or translations of the classics, would tend to make him a favourite with collectors. I should estimate his output at not more than 600. Of him, too, more will be said in connexion with illustrated books.

Probably the fifth place would be taken by Simon Vincent; there are 61 books by him in the collection, so that his output would be about 350. The next highest figure is 554 (101 in the Museum) for the Giunta family, several generations extending from 1520 to the end of the century.

Three interesting printers of the first half of the century are rather scantily represented in the Museum collection: Olivier Arnoullet (21 out of 156 in Baudrier), Claude Nourry (18 out of 161), and his successor, Pierre de Ste. Lucie (9 out of 81). Books by these three printers, many of them French and Spanish romances, are very rare, and probably this comparatively low proportion is common to other libraries. Of Barthélemy Trot's 58 books the Museum has the high proportion of 25. He was the printer who shares with Balthazar de Gabiano the honour or dishonour of producing the excellent imitations of the Aldine italic classics.[1] Of another interesting smaller printer, Robert Granjon, who came from Paris and began to print at Lyons in 1557, the Museum has 9 books out of 19. Granjon was the originator of the types known as 'lettres de civilité', in which type are all these nine books printed at Lyons.

It is well known that the output of the French press during this century culminates about the middle of the century. An examination of the distribution of the books in the Museum collection shows that this was the case at Lyons. The output of the first ten years of the century averages 12·6 books per year. (Unless otherwise stated, all

1. In 1503 Aldus issued a complaint about these Lyons pirates and incidentally pointed out some errors in their imitations. Forthwith Gabiano started a fresh series of forgeries, making use of Aldus's own suggestions to improve them.

figures are based on the Museum collection.) There is a slow increase up to 1540; from 1541 to 1550 the average becomes 38·6, and between 1551 and 1560 reaches 49·4. In the next ten years there is a big drop to 24, and the output continues to decline, the average for the last ten years being 14. The falling-off corresponds exactly with the outbreak of the religious wars in France in 1562. The year 1563 is represented by only 15 books. The Lyons book trade was ruined. There was not merely a falling-off in numbers but a general deterioration; cheaper books printed on inferior paper become the rule, and for the collector interest disappears. The numbers in the last forty years of the century would be still lower but for the fact that the press had begun to be used for purposes of propaganda, taking the place of the modern newspaper. Proclamations and pamphlets relating to the war form a considerable proportion of the output of the presses, though in a provincial town like Lyons this is not so striking as in the case of Paris.

This decline was, as I have said, a result of the religious controversy in France, due partly to the persecution of the Protestants, but mainly to the economic consequences of the civil wars. Let us first deal with Protestants and the press. The first royal decree against printing in France was issued in January 1535, following on the affair of the Placards at Paris in November 1534. This decree actually forbade all printing; it might form an interesting subject for debate, whether, if that decree had been enforced, France would be a happier country today. But even in a modified form issued in February it was not registered by the *Parlement*. In 1543 the first list of condemned books was issued. This list contains, in addition to the works of Luther, Calvin, and the other professed Protestants, works by Marot, Dolet, and a number of Bibles issued by Robert Estienne. In June 1551 further decrees followed forbidding the printing of books on the condemned list or printing under an assumed name. But it was not so much the royal executive that was active in preventing the publication of works of a Protestant tendency as the Sorbonne and the Inquisition. The list of condemned books was issued by the Sorbonne. The Lyons printer, Étienne Dolet, burned at Paris in 1546, was the victim of Matthieu Ory, the Inquisitor, and of Lizet, President of the Paris *Parlement*.

At this time the central government of France was still comparatively weak, and Lyons enjoyed considerable independence. Many of the Lyons printers leant towards the new religion, but they do not appear to have suffered much for their religious opinions until after the outbreak of the war. As late as 1565 Claude Senneton printed an edition of Calvin's *Institution de la religion chrétienne*, while there were several editions of Marot's Psalms, a book on the condemned list, printed by Antoine Vincent in the sixties. Étienne Dolet was rather a free-thinker than a Protestant, and indeed the technical ground for his final condemnation was that, in translating Plato's supposititious dialogue, the *Axiochus*, he had wrongly made Plato declare that souls do not exist after death. Another printer, Balthazar Arnoullet, was arrested in 1553 for printing Michel Servetus's *Christianismi Restitutio*; but Servetus was equally obnoxious to both parties, and Arnoullet suffered for supporting a man of neither party in an age of intolerance. The risk of persecution was far less in Lyons than in the capital. The first Protestant martyr at Lyons, Claude Monnier, was burned in 1551, by which time scores

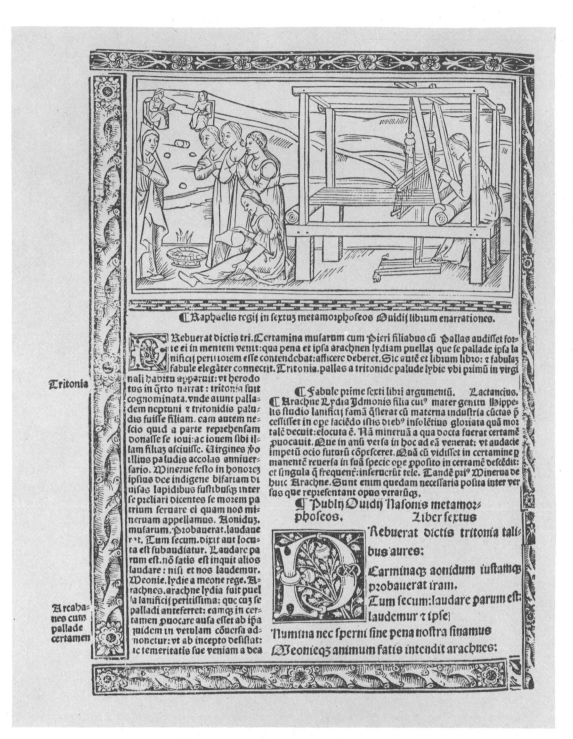

FIG. 2. Woodcut by Guillaume Leroy. From Ovid's *Metamorphoses*. Etienne Gueynard, Lyons, 1510. (Slightly reduced.)

had perished at Paris. It was in 1568 that the Protestant printers began to emigrate to Geneva and elsewhere. By that time the 'Ligue' had become powerful, and the city of Lyons had itself taken up the persecution under the influence of the 'Ligue'. In that year or soon afterwards several members of the house of Gabiano, Sibylle de la Porte, Claude Senneton, Antoine Vincent, and Sébastien Honorati emigrated to Geneva, and Jean Mareschal to Heidelberg. In August 1572 the massacre of St. Bartholomew at Paris was followed in Lyons by a massacre of Protestants, known as the *Vêpres*, from which the 'party of religion' never recovered in that city. Other Protestant printers continued to leave the city, Antoine Blanc (Candidus) about 1584, the younger Jean de Tournes, after many troubles, in 1585, and François Lefebure about 1590. During this period some of these printers adopted the practice of issuing their books with Lyons on the title-page, although they were printed at Geneva or elsewhere. Often in these cases there are found other copies of the books without Lyons on the title-page, and generally without any place of publication. It seems to have been bad business to put Geneva, the notorious home of heretics, on the title-page of a book. The Estienne family, after they had withdrawn to Geneva, issued their books with no place of imprint. Jean Mareschal at Heidelberg, Sébastien Honorati and Barthélemy Vincent at Geneva all followed this practice. There is a French Bible of Honorati's of 1570, of which there are copies with Lyons on the title-page, and other copies with Geneva. The confusion is increased by several publishers adopting the practice, who possibly were not printers at all, but agents for printers in towns outside France. René Postelier appears to have been a citizen of Lyons but probably not a printer, though there are a number of books bearing his name and Lyons as imprint, e. g. an edition of the *Rerum Britannicarum Scriptores* by Hieronymus Commelinus, dated 1587. There is another copy of the work with Heidelberg on the title-page. Pierre de Saint-André also appears to have had a similar connexion with Commelinus of Heidelberg and uses the same mark (cf. an edition of Pliny's *Natural History* of 1582). Guillaume Laemerius published, towards the end of the century, a number of folio editions of Cicero, Aristotle, and Plato, which appear to have been printed at Geneva, though published with Lyons as imprint. The career of Jean Lertout is also a mystery, which may be cleared up when Baudrier has published the documentary evidence relating to that printer, if he was a printer.[1] In addition to this several well-known printers, certainly working at Geneva, used the name of Lyons for business purposes when it suited them. There are a number of editions of classical authors by François Le Preux, an edition of Cassiodorus by Jacques Chouet, 1595, a Trogus Pompeius by Guillaume Cartier, and the works of François Hotman by the heirs of Eustace Vignon, 1599, all bearing Lyons. All these works are counted as Lyons books, and if left out would still further emphasize the decline in the output of books actually printed at Lyons.

But in the meantime the war itself had done far more to ruin the Lyons book trade than the persecution of the Protestants. In May 1562 the Huguenots, on the outbreak of the war, seized Lyons and remained in control for thirteen months. During those

---

1. Baudrier never gave any particulars on Jean Lertout.

months Lyons was more or less besieged, a fact which sufficiently accounts for the enormous drop in book production in 1563. The royalist troops re-entered the town in June 1563, but the state of war which continued for some thirty years was fatal to a recovery of the trade. Although many of the chief Lyons houses were Catholics, e. g. Rouillé, the Giunta, as well as the official printers, Jean Pillehotte, printer for the Society of Jesuits, Rigaud, and others, the economic condition of France down to the end of the century must have made business extremely difficult. It is a well-known fact that the whole of France was greatly impoverished by the wars, while this impoverishment was accompanied by a fall in the value of money which increased the difficulties of competition with towns such as Geneva. In the case of Rouillé, a Catholic whose books in any case were not connected with the religious question, for the years 1549 to 1562 the collection shows an average of 10 books published each year; in 1563 there is only one book from his house, and from that year until 1589 an average of 3 per year. These figures illustrate the fact that economic causes had more to do with the decline of the trade than persecution.

Illustrated Books

The history of book illustration at Lyons in the early part of the century belongs to a great extent to the history of book-illustration in the fifteenth century or to the history of German woodcutting. The cuts with which Olivier Arnoullet illustrated his romances had belonged to his father Jacques Arnoullet or to Guillaume Leroy. Claude Nourry, whose productions were similar to those of Arnoullet, also reproduced cuts of the previous century. Several Lyons printers, Johann Klein, Jacques Sacon, and Jean Marion, were employed by the Nuremberg publishers the Koburgers, and through this connexion a number of fine German woodcuts appear in Lyons books, especially the work of Hans Springinklee and Erhard Schön. Large woodcuts by Springinklee, bearing his mark, occur in the *Hortulus animae*, Klein, 1517, the Latin Bible printed by Sacon, 1521, and editions of the Letters of Jerome. The smaller series of cuts illustrating the Bible of 1521 and repeated in subsequent editions are attributed partly to Schön and a few to Springinklee. These series of small cuts continued to appear as late as 1561, when they are found in a Bible printed by Jacobus de Millis. Full details of the work of these German woodcutters will be found in Campbell Dodgson's *Catalogue of Early German Woodcuts in the Dept. of Prints*, vol. i. Another series of German cuts appears in several editions of Virgil, e. g. the edition of Sacon of 1517, and that of Crespin of 1529. This series was taken from the edition by Grüninger of Strasbourg printed in 1502.

In this early part of the century there is one native woodcutter whose work is found in many Lyons books, and that is the artist known as *Le maître au nombril*, who has been identified with Guillaume Leroy, the son of the fifteenth-century printer Guillaume Leroy. He worked especially for Étienne Gueynard and Simon Vincent. His series of small illustrations to the Bible, some of which were imitated from Venetian Bibles, appears frequently and is first to be seen in the Bible of 1516 by Gueynard. In the edition of Ovid's *Metamorphoses* issued by Gueynard in 1510 there are fifteen cuts attributed

Ioiada the Byshope, Athalia beyng kylled,
maketh Ioas kyng ouer Iſrahel, Mathan the
preſt of Baal is kylled befor the altare.

IIII.   R E G V M   XI.

Par Ioiada, Ioas conſtitué
Sur Iſrael fut en l'eſtat Royal:
Et Mathan presbtre idolatre tué,
Deuant l'autel de ſon faulx Dieu Baal.
                                    H

FIG. 3. Woodcut after Holbein. From *The images of the old testament
lately expressed, sed forthe in Ynglishe a. Frenche*. Jean Frellon,
Lyons, 1549.

GENESIS XXXVII.

Ruben telleth them that he willeth not defill
Handes, with the bloode of non of his bretherne:
But if it pleaſeth, that his clothes taket hei will,
And ſo caſt him into the olde ciſterne.

FIG. 4. Woodcut by Bernard Salomon. From *The true and lyuely*
historyke purtreatures of the woll bible. Jean de Tournes,
Lyons, 1553.

to Leroy (Fig. 2), which are perhaps his most striking work as an illustrator. They are of an archaic type and again show imitation of the Italians. If Baudrier's attributions are correct a great number of the Lyons title-pages, printers' marks, and initial capitals, as well as illustrations, are by this artist. I have not been able to trace the evidence on which Baudrier makes these attributions; possibly there is no other evidence than similarity of style. One of the title-pages used by Gueynard and attributed to Leroy has a long history. It is decorated with figures of salamanders and other quaint beasts, pieces of armour, &c. It was copied from the title-page used many times by Josse Bade and by other Paris printers. At Paris it first appeared on Bade's edition of Cicero in 1511, and was itself copied from Venice. An edition of Livy of 1493 seems to be its first appearance. At Lyons it continued to appear down to 1540, so that it has a history of about half a century.

In 1538 the brothers Guillaume and Melchior Trechsel printed for the Frellons two famous series of cuts after Holbein, the Dance of Death series and the Illustrations to the Old Testament (Fig. 3). The blocks for these two series were cut at Basle by Hans Lützelburger, so that Lyons has the honour only of printing them. During a period of about twelve years the Frellons brought out repeated editions of these two series, and the impressions of even the latest remain extraordinarily good. How far this is due to careful woodcutting and how far to the smallness of the editions I am not competent to say. The Illustrations to the Old Testament appeared both in editions of the Bible and separately with descriptive letter-press, in various languages, including English of a very quaint type and wonderful spelling.

A new period begins in 1546 with the work of Bernard Salomon, 'le Petit Bernard', for Jean de Tournes. Very little is known about the life of Salomon. According to Natalis Rondot, *Bernard Salomon*, Lyons, 1897, he worked exclusively for Tournes from 1546 to his death about 1560. To what extent he himself was a woodcutter is uncertain, though several plates bear his initials, e. g. the Nativity in the Illustrations to the New Testament. In Rondot will be found a full account of his work for Tournes. The two best-known series are the Illustrations of the Bible (Fig. 4) and the Illustrations of Ovid's *Metamorphoses*. The cuts for the Bible appeared separately with verses or short descriptions in at least six languages, again including English as curious as that of the Frellons, and in editions of the Bible. The impressions of the first editions of 1553 are much the best, the later impressions being markedly inferior when compared with the Frellon series. Many of the plates in the *Metamorphoses* series first appeared in an edition of Marot's works (Marot translated the *Metamorphoses*) in 1549, and the complete series in 1557. Tournes also brought out series of cuts to illustrate Aesop, the *Emblemata* of Alciatus, and a fine series of twelve cuts for his *Aeneid* of 1552 in the French translation of Desmasures (Fig. 5). Although the cuts bear a resemblance to the Italian and Parisian illustrators of the period (in fact, in nearly all his series he had been preceded by illustrators at Paris), there can be no doubt about the originality and freshness of this work of Bernard Salomon. How far he was responsible for the general decoration of Tournes's books, for his magnificent engraved capitals and title-pages, is doubtful. Rondot says he designed the architectural title-pages, such as appeared in the edition of Jean Le

Maire's *Illustrations de Gaule* of 1549. Tournes at any rate produced some magnificent books. His editions of Paradin's *Devises héroïques* (Fig. 1), of the works of Pontus de Tyard (Fig. 6), the poems of Louise de Labé (Fig. 7) and Pernette du Guillet, are beautiful books in every way.

Tournes's chief rival in the production of illustrated books was Guillaume Rouillé. He began in 1548 with his edition of the *Horae* and the *Emblemata* of Alciatus, both of which were issued many times (Baudrier gives more than thirty-five editions of the Alciatus). Many of the plates in the Alciatus closely resemble those of Tournes's edition which first appeared in 1547. His illustrations to the Bible, too, which first appeared in 1562, are in many cases close copies of the cuts by Salomon. He followed Tournes again in his illustrations to the *Metamorphoses*, a series often repeated and used also to illustrate verses by Barthélemy Aneau, called the *Picta Poesis*. Among the woodcutters employed by Rouillé was possibly Pierre Vase, or Eskrich as his name was in German. In Rouillé's edition of the *Horae* there are several cuts bearing the initials P. V., which have been assigned to Pierre Vase (see Rondot, *Graveurs sur bois à Lyon au 16ᵉ siècle*, 1897). There are several signed examples in Lyons books of the work of this artist under his German name, e. g. in the French Bible by Barthélemy Honorati, 1585, and the *Prosopographie* of Du Verdier, Honorati, 1589. Whether this identification of Pierre Vase and P. V. is sound is a matter for the expert, but certainly this P. V. was largely employed by Rouillé in his rivalry with Tournes and was an imitator of Bernard Salomon. Another artist employed by Rouillé was Georges Reverdi, a Piedmontese, whose work is not very clearly known. According to Baudrier, he designed several alphabets for Rouillé, including the well-known bird alphabet, and was one of the illustrators of Rouillé's own work, the *Promptuaire des Médailles*, which contains a number of portraits of contemporaries. In 1549 Rouillé published a fine illustrated book describing the entry of Henri II and Catherine de' Medici into Lyons, which possibly includes work by Salomon (Fig. 8). In 1550 he published Ariosto's *Orlando Furioso*, the first edition being in Spanish and the illustrations copied from those of Giolitti's well-known Venice editions. In 1555 he published Du Choul's works on Roman antiquities, Roman camps, baths, and religion, all well-illustrated books. His editions of Dioscorides are decorated with beautiful cuts of plants, though the illustrations of birds and animals in that work are less successful; this failure in the illustration of animal life seems to be general in the sixteenth century. One of Rouillé's most remarkable books appeared as late as 1567, the *Navigations et pérégrinations orientales* of Nicolas de Nicolay, with full-page illustrations of oriental costumes engraved on copper by Antoine Danet after Nicolay's drawings. This Nicolay was also the translator and illustrator of Rouillé's edition of Pedro di Medina's *Art de naviguer*, a beautiful book, first issued in 1554.

Rouillé's architectural title-pages are imitated from, and perhaps as fine as, those of Tournes. The one used on his octavos, e. g. Boccaccio's *Des dames de renom*, with a figure of Pan below, said to be by Pierre Vase, is particularly pleasing. If the artistic achievement of Rouillé is second to that of Tournes, his total output in the way of illustrated books is unrivalled by any other Lyons publisher.

Among the smaller printers who produced illustrated books we may mention Macé

495

LE X. LIVRE
DE L'ENEÏDE DE
VIRGILE.

ENDANT *ces cas le palais ample*
s'euvre
Du tout puissant Olympe, qui tout
keuvre.
Et lors le pere aux Dieux, qui en
ses mains
Tient le Royaume eternel des humains,
Ha le conseil des haults Dieux appellé,
Au luisant lieu de son siege estellé.
Ou, hault assis, la terre il voit d'illecques,
L'ost des Troyens, & des Latins avecques.
Tous se vont soir à l'hostel, qu'on trouva

Anditur interea
domus omnipoté-
tis Olympi:

Conciliúmque vo-
cat Diuûm pater, at-
que hominum rex

Sideream in se-
dem : terras vn-
de arduus omneis,

Castrâque Darda-
nidûm aspectat, po-
pulósque Latinos.

Considunt tectis bi-

Ouvert

FIG. 5. Woodcut by Bernard Salomon. From *L'Eneïde de Virgile*. Jean de Tournes, Lyons,
1560. (Slightly reduced.)

FIG. 6. Portrait of Pontus de Tyard. From Pontus de Tyard, *Solitaire second, ou prose de la musique*. Jean de Tournes, Lyons, 1555.

Bonhomme, who at first printed for Rouillé, but later published for himself; Sébastien Honorati, who published an Ariosto in 1556 with illustrations which copy those of Giolitti even more closely than Rouillé's edition; and Balthazar Arnoullet, son of Olivier, who brought out many editions of Leonhard Fuchs's botanical works with fine cuts. Arnoullet was also the printer of a work containing plans of cities, the *Epitome de la corographie de l'Europe*, issued in 1553.

The Giunta family were not great book illustrators, but there is an edition of Flavius Josephus issued by them in 1566 which contains several interesting series of cuts. One set of thirteen illustrations is an old series appearing in a Bible printed for the Giunta in 1546 by Thibaud Payen; a second series is by an unknown illustrator, one of the best artists whose work appears at Lyons, and who has been named the 'Maître à la Capeline' (Fig. 9). This artist also worked for Rouillé (Fig. 10). The third series consists of cuts by Pierre Woeiriot, ten of them signed (Fig. 11). Woeiriot also executed a series of engravings of funeral ceremonies for a book entitled the *Pinax Iconicus*, printed in 1556 by Clément Baudin (Fig. 12). Another famous example of engraved work is the Apocalypse by Jean Duvet, printed in 1561 by Jean de Tournes. This artist, who was so aloof from the spirit of his age that he was treated with contempt until modern times, has been compared to William Blake.[1] This work, as an example of book illustration, is one of the most remarkable of the century.

Most of this distinctively Lyons book illustration is confined to a period of some twenty years, from 1546 to 1566, and this period is also the most productive in the history of Lyons printing. Baudrier dates the decline of typography at Lyons from 1539, when there was a strike of journeymen printers. As a result of this strike some printers, e. g. Macé Bonhomme and Gaspard Trechsel, set up their presses in Vienne for a time. The workmen were beaten on this occasion, and there was a succession of strikes in the trade. Baudrier may be right as to the majority of printers, but 1539 seems too early when we remember that all the work of Tournes and Rouillé was later.

The Subjects of Lyonnese Books

An analysis of the subjects of the books published during the century, if revealing nothing new, illustrates what is known from other sources of the taste and culture of the age. In particular such an analysis emphasizes the reality of the revival of learning in the restricted sense of the revival of the study of Greek and Roman writers. Out of the 2,380 books published at Lyons there are 313 editions of ancient Latin authors, and a further 23 editions of the Latin Fathers. Of these Latin authors Cicero has the largest number of editions, 59, followed by Ovid with 26, Terence 22, and Virgil 21. The popularity of the Latin authors still remains much in the same order as in the Middle Ages. Thus, as against 22 editions of Terence there are only 8 of Plautus, 4 editions of Lucretius against 10 of Lucan, and only 3 editions of Tacitus.

Of Greek writers there are 126 editions, not including 80 editions of Greek medical

1. See A. E. Popham in *The Print Collector's Quarterly*, July 1921.

writers. Aristotle is the only Greek author (except the medical writers) well represented, with 27 editions. Practically all these Greek authors appear in Latin or French translations. Lyons seems to have made no attempt to compete with Paris in the publication of books in Greek. There are a number of books with fragments of Greek type, such as the *Aphorismi* of Hippocrates in Greek and Latin, and Aesop in Greek and Latin. Towards the end of the century there are editions of Aristotle and Plato in Greek, printed by G. Laemerius with 'Lyons' on the title-page, but really printed at Geneva. There is a very poor edition of Pindar by Pillehotte of 1598. Gryphius printed several books in Greek or partly in Greek; selections from the Bible in Hebrew, Greek, and Latin, 1528; a Psalter also in Hebrew, Greek, and Latin (these two are the only two specimens of Hebrew type at Lyons I have met); and Plutarch's *Symposion*, 1552. These books of Gryphius, together with a New Testament in Greek and Latin by Roussin of 1592, are the only tolerable specimens of Greek type in the whole collection, and even these are poor things compared with their Paris contemporaries.

The study of medicine at Lyons had been promoted early in the century by the Collège de Médecine, founded by Symphorien Champier, one of those remarkable many-sided men of the Renaissance, philosopher, historian, man of letters as well as physician, and a leading citizen of Lyons; but there were more famous schools of medicine in the south of France, notably at Montpellier. However, Lyons seems to have had the market for medical works, and that subject accounts for 320 entries, 80 of those being for Greek medical writers, 52 Galens, and 24 Hippocrates. Rouillé issued a great number of cheap Galens; in fact, most of these medical books are cheap and of no great interest bibliographically. There are none of the large anatomical works such as those printed at Paris, nothing by Ambroise Paré, and little by Conrad Gesner or Vesalius. Perhaps the finest medical work is the edition of the *Trésor des Pauvres* of Arnaldus de Villanova, printed by Claude Nourry in 1512.

The Lyons printers had also a large market for law books, although again other centres of learning were more famous for the teaching of that subject. Pantagruel in Rabelais went to Bourges to study law. The law books of that age were very expensive productions and at Lyons were generally published by trade associations, of which the most famous was known as the 'Compagnie des Libraires'. The device used by that company was a variation of the arms of Lyons, a lion rampant in a field of bees, and in bibliographical works this device has sometimes been attributed to individual printers working for the company. One can only admire the industry of the jurists of the age who could digest these huge folios. The number of law books in the collection is 244, not all of course of the size alluded to. Many of the books on Roman law are handy octavos or even smaller.

These three subjects together, Latin and Greek Classics, Medicine, and Law, account for one-half of the whole number of books, if we include with the Latin and Greek books books of classical antiquities and that numerous class of compilations from ancient authors so common during the Renaissance: Erasmus, Guillaume Budé, Cornelius Agrippa, Polydore Vergil, all wrote compilations of this kind. The enormous number of references to the Classics to be found in such writers as Rabelais are often

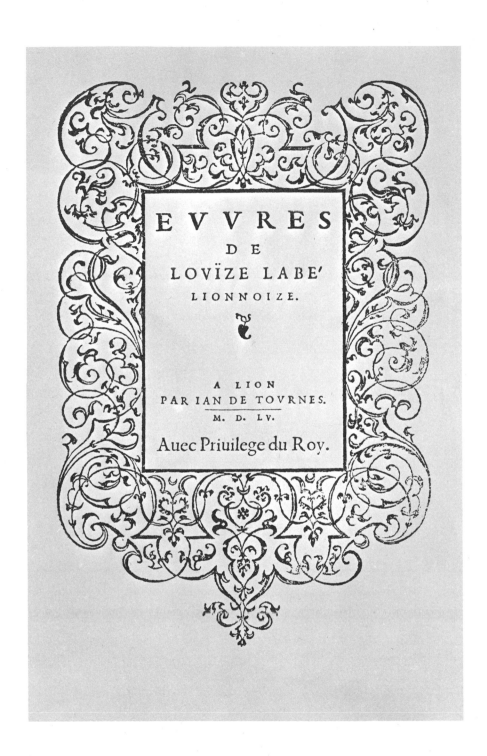

FIG. 7. A title-page of Jean de Tournes, 1555.

FIG. 8. From *La magnificence de la superbe entree de la cité de Lyon faicte au roy Henry deuxieme.*
Guillaume Rouillé, Lyons, 1549.

at second-hand, and taken from these compilations. Of Latin literature there still remain about 100 entries for Renaissance literature in Latin, poems, letters, &c., for the most part by Italian scholars, such as Cardinals Bembo and Sadoleto, Sannazaro, Pontanus, and Laurentius Valla.

Another large group is formed by the Christian writers, amounting to about 400 books. Included in this group are devotional works, with 9 editions of the *De Imitatione Christi*, theology, 8 editions of lives of the Saints, 45 liturgical works (but there is nothing at Lyons after 1500 to compare with the Paris *Horae*), and 143 Bibles or parts of Bibles. There are 65 Latin Bibles; the distribution of these 65 editions may be taken to illustrate the rise and fall of book production, only two of them belonging to the last thirty years of the century, and 49 of the 65 being issued in one-half of the century. Of 30 New Testaments, 25 are in one-half of the century.

Coming to the section of French literature, *i. e.* poems, essays, and fiction in French, we have the small number of about 160 books. In the case of a provincial town this figure has perhaps little value for purposes of comparison, as the capital would naturally produce the mass of this group; for instance, Ronsard, Montaigne, and Margaret of Navarre are represented by one entry each. Rabelais and Clément Marot, who both had some connexion with Lyons, have 15 and 8 entries respectively. The only member of the Pléiade who published at Lyons was Pontus de Tyard. Though not a native of Lyons his home was in Burgundy, not far distant. Tyard is a good example of the many-sided interests of the men of letters of the Renaissance. He began his career by

FIG. 9. Woodcut by the 'Maître à la Capeline'. From Flavius Josephus, *Antiquitatum Iudaicarum libri XX*. Giunta, Lyons, 1566.

FIG. 10. Portrait of Paolo Giovio, attributed to the 'Maître à la Capeline'. From Paolo Giovio, *Dialogue des devises et d'amours*. Guillaume Rouillé, Lyons, 1561.

publishing amorous poems with Jean de Tournes in 1555, and finished as a bishop, publishing books on music, astrology, astronomy, and mathematics.

With French literature is included a large number of popular poems known as 'farces'. There is in the Museum a remarkable collection of 64 of these 'farces' in the form known as 'agenda'. Perhaps they are not of much literary interest, but they have an historical interest and are excellent specimens of printing. Of these 64 short poems 36 were printed at Lyons in the forties by the successor of Barnabé Chaussard, Jean Cantarel, who had married Chaussard's widow. They are printed in fine heavy gothic type, the Lyons ones being decidedly superior to those printed at Paris contained in the same collection, and are decorated with charming little cuts in an archaic style.

In this section, too, there are 17 editions of the old romances. Together with the 41 translations of the Spanish romances, they point to the conservatism of the popular taste at a period which we think of as the beginning of modern French literature. Their popularity continued right down to the end of the century; there are 32 editions of the various books of Amadis de Gaule, all issued after 1570. Amidst the misfortunes of the civil wars the citizens of Lyons seem to have found some consolation in Amadis. These Spanish romances, issued by Benoît Rigaud, François Didier, and other printers, are cheap octavos, no rivals to the fine illustrated editions printed at Paris in the forties.

A group of History and Politics contains about 180 entries; but again that number may be misleading, as it includes those productions of the press, such as proclamations, edicts, &c., which would to-day hardly appear in book form. In the group are a number of good folio editions in roman type of Froissart (by Tournes), Comines, Olivier

FIG. 11. Woodcut signed with the initials of Pierre Woeiriot. From Flavius Josephus, *Antiquitatum Iudaicarum libri XX*. Giunta, Lyons, 1566.

FIG. 12. Two engravings by Pierre Woeiriot. From Lilius Gregorius Giraldus, *Pinax iconicus antiquorum in sepulturis rituum*. Clément Baudin, Lyons, 1556.

de La Marche, the works of Gabriel Simeoni and Paolo Giovio, all by Rouillé. Rouillé published many historical works, frequently illustrated. Some of these compilations included under History are hardly worthy of the name; for example, the works of Guillaume Paradin (there were three members of this family who worked for the Lyons publishers). In his *Angliae descriptionis compendium* he gives an account of some men at Stround on the Medway, who had tails ('caudati'), the reason being that they had cut off the tail of a horse belonging to Thomas, Archbishop of Canterbury.

The close connexion of Lyons with Italy is revealed by the publication of 75 books in Italian. Many of the Lyons printers were Italians, Barthélemy Trot or Trotti, the Gabiano, the Giunta, the Portonarii, the Honorati, Alessandro Marsili (of his 29 books mentioned by Baudrier, 7 are in Italian). Both Sébastien Gryphius and Guillaume Rouillé had learnt their trade in Italy in their youth, and Rouillé himself wrote in Italian. In fact, in the early part of the century there were very few Frenchmen printing at Lyons; when not Italians, they were Germans. There are Lyons editions of most of the Italian classics, including 6 editions of Dante and 7 of Petrarch's *Canzoniere*, most of them from the presses of Tournes and Rouillé.

In addition to the large groups of subjects already described, there remain about 220 books which fall into small groups, such as Geography and Travel, Astronomy, Astrology and Mathematics, Philosophy, Natural History and the Natural Sciences, &c. The contrast between the sixteenth and the twentieth century is illustrated by these groups, which form less than one-tenth of the whole, whereas from the English Catalogue for 1913 I find that they now form at least a quarter. In our collection there are 14 books on astronomy, all, I believe, accepting the Ptolemaic system. Some of them speak with respect of Copernicus as an astronomer, but regard his system as ridiculous. You will remember that Sir Francis Bacon rejected the Copernican system at an even later date. There are 16 books on astrology, chiromancy, and similar subjects. Among the books of Travel and Geography there are but 3 on America, which seems surprisingly few. Natural History and the Natural Sciences account for 42 entries (not including the Greek and Roman writers on agriculture and botany). Some of these have the genuine spirit of scientific research and observation, such as Rondeletius's work on Fishes, but others are rather of the nature of romances, e. g. the work known as *Les Merveilles du Monde*, printed by Olivier Arnoullet. There are about 30 books of a philosophical nature (again not including the classical writers); that is giving a wide interpretation to the word philosophy and including such works as Petrarch's *De remediis utriusque fortunae*.

This summary in general shows that the sixteenth century had still much in common with the Middle Ages. On the distribution of the groups we may compare some further figures taken from the English Catalogue for 1913; in that list religious works form about 7½ per cent. of the whole, in the Lyons collection about 17 per cent.; medicine 4 per cent. as against rather more than 13 per cent. at Lyons; law 3 per cent. against a little over 10 per cent. It is impossible to compare figures for the Latin and Greek Classics, as in the modern list they are lost in a group called Education.

[1922]

THE SUPPLY OF TYPES IN THE
SIXTEENTH CENTURY

In the early years of the history of printing every printer, we are told, had his own types, cut by himself or by one of his employees. A hundred years later we find that the leading printers in one city, and even to some extent throughout Europe, were using the same types, of which they bought matrices from men established as type-founders. We know that such is the practice in the printing trade today and that such was the practice in the time of William Caslon. It is not generally recognized or not adequately emphasized in the text-books dealing with the history of the printing-press that this dependence of printers on a few designers of types was already a fact in the middle of the sixteenth century. Even in the early decades of that century type-founding was already a trade, although the suppliers were not yet independent founders, but the great printing houses.

In the preface to his *Early Printed Books in the British Museum*, Part 2, Germany, 1501-1520, Robert Proctor writes, 'type-founding had become a regular industry, and the tendency for founts to follow a few stock models was constantly on the increase. It is amusing to see the way in which experiments such as Schöffer's archaistic or revived roman, the Lotter schwabacher, the Froben italic, the Schönsperger fraktur, were caught up and copied far and wide by enterprising founders.' From this passage, combined with the frequent occurrence of the word 'like' in the description of the types, we may infer that in Proctor's opinion the types not definitely said to be the same as other types were derived from different sets of punches, and that copies were numerous. This is not really consistent with the statement that type-founding had become a regular industry. A founder's method of business would be to sell matrices struck from one set of punches to a number of printers, and not to copy his original design. For example, of the type called by Proctor the Lotter Schwabacher, now generally known as the Wittenberg letter, there were two copies which were used by a large number of different printers. Some forty printers had matrices all struck from two sets of punches.

The extremely useful Type Register, occupying pp. 192 to 202 of Proctor's work, includes close on 900 types. Even when we deduct the cases in which Proctor states that types are identical, we are still left with something like 600 types, cut in one country over a period of twenty years, and used in about 2,200 books. It is on the face of it highly improbable that there can have been sufficient type-cutters in Germany to have produced such a large output, or that the printers could have afforded such a luxury. The number of craftsmen in any one generation able to carry out the extremely difficult task of engraving a set of punches was very small. In Great Britain in the middle of the eighteenth century, when this country had ceased to import types, five foundries supplied the wants of all the presses. The industrious William Caslon in his working life engraved about fifty sets of punches, including sets of roman capitals and counting the italics separately.

In order to test the suspicion that many of the types described by Proctor as 'like' were not copies, but derived from the same punches, I have examined most of the romans listed in the Type Register. First is an alphabet of roman capitals shown by Proctor at fig. 1, which was the design of Johann Froben of Basle. I show the results in tabular form, following the Register.

Large Capitals. 8 mm.

Printer and no. of type		Proctor's comment	My estimate
J. Schöffer, Mainz,	15	Like M. Schürer	The capitals of J. Froben, Basle
M. Schürer, Strasbourg,	13	Like Schöffer	Same
L. Schürer, Schlettstadt,	4	= M. Schürer	"
J. Pruess, jun., Strasbourg,	11	As M. Schürer	"
U. Morhard "	2	As M. Schürer	"
J. Landen, Cologne,	7	cf. Schöffer	"
E. Cervicorn, "	3	[no comment]	"
Elisabeth "	3	= Cervicorn	"
J. Soter "	5	Like Landen	"
Heinrich of Neuss	7	Very rough	A copy. Note E and M
Kaiser "	2	Rather rough	Same copy
			Total 2

The first series of body types are called by Proctor 'Text types'; they are about Gt. Primer in size, or from 110 to 100 mm. for twenty lines. Group 1 is illustrated at fig. 3 and is characterized by an M in which the central arms descend only about three quarters way to the base line. Quentell of Cologne had the type by 1499, and it is shown on pl. 284 of the facsimiles issued by the Gesellschaft für Typenkunde.

Text Size. German Style.

Printer and no. of type		Proctor's comment	My estimate
J. Schott, Strasbourg,	5	cf. Knoblouch	Quentell's roman
V. Schumann, Leipzig,	9	Very like Schott, Knoblouch, M. Schürer	Same
E. Öglin, Augsburg,	8	Very like Miller	"
J. Miller, Augsburg,	2	Like Öglin or Grim	"
M. Schürer, Strasbourg,	8	Like Knoblouch and Schott	"
L. Schürer, Schlettstadt,	1	= M. Schürer	" (but had new M of normal design)
J. Knoblouch, Strasbourg,	8	Like Schott	Same
J. Pruess, sen. "	18	Like Grüninger and Knoblouch	"
J. Grüninger, "	26	[no comment]	"
R. Beck "	12	cf. Pruess	"
J. Soter, Cologne,	2	Like Quentell	"
H. Quentell "	12	Like Pruess	"
T. Anshelm, Pforzheim,	3	Like M. Schürer, Knoblouch, and Schott	"
			Total 1

Grim 7 and Cervicorn 4 have the normal M; although this type may be substantially the same, I am counting it as different.

The next group is in the Italian style, lighter in weight and characterized by an A with a pointed apex.

Text Size. Italian Style.

Printer and no. of type			Proctor's comment	My estimate	
Press XXI, Nuremberg,		1	Resembling Hölzel	? an Italian type	
J. Weissenburger	"	1	= XXI	Same	
F. Peypus	"	3	= XXI	"	
H. Hölzel	"	8	= G. Stuchs	Group with broken T	
G. Stuchs	"	19	cf. Hölzel and J. Stuchs	"	"
J. Stuchs	"	5	= G. Stuchs	"	"
J. Rhau, Wittenberg,		6	[no comment]	"	"
J. Otmar, Augsburg,		19	= Öglin	Augsburg group, R differs	
E. Öglin	"	1	cf. J. Otmar	"	"
S. Otmar	"	1	= J. Otmar	"	"
				Total 3	

Text Size. Leipzig Style.

Printer and no. of type			Proctor's comment	My estimate
M. Lotter, sen., Leipzig,		12	Like Sertorius	Leipzig roman
J. Thanner	"	7	= Lotter	Same
V. Schumann	"	3	Exactly as Lotter	"
M. Landsberg	"	8	Practically identical with Lotter	"
				Total 1

Text Size. Erfurt Style.

Printer and no. of type			Proctor's comment	My estimate
H. Sertorius, Erfurt,		1	cf. Lotter	Erfurt roman
H. Knapp, Erfurt,		5	= Sertorius	Same
J. Rhau, Wittenberg,		1	= Sertorius	"
N. Marschalk, Rostock,		1	= Sertorius	"
				Total 1

In addition to these groups there are three romans of the text size each used by one printer only, N. Lamparter, Frankfurt a. d. O., 2, J. Schöffer, Mainz, 19, and the Abbey at Ottobeuren, 3, and a fourth used by two printers, N. Marschalk, Rostock, 3, and J. Dorn, Braunschweig, 6. The total of different romans of the Great Primer size comes to eleven.

The next series in the Register is called Middle Types, approximately English in size, varying from 92 to 86 mm. for twenty lines. The largest group is again characterized by an M with short central arms. It is illustrated at fig. 8 in Proctor, and also among the Strasbourg facsimiles of the British Museum Incunable Catalogue, and on three plates

(1258, 1277, and 1809) of the Gesellschaft für Typenkunde. M. Schott's type 4, 1495, is said in the Incunable Catalogue to be the same as Flach's type 7. J. Pruess's type 14 seems also to be identical, but J. Grüninger's type 22, 1496, may perhaps be different.

Middle Types. German Style.

Printer and no. of type		Proctor's comment	My estimate
M. Schürer, Strasbourg,	1	Of the usual sort	Strasbourg Middle roman
J. Grüninger "	22	Narrow	Different
J. Miller, Augsburg,	3	cf. Grim	Same as Schürer
V. Schumann, Leipzig,	5	Like Schöffer, Knoblouch, M. Schürer, &c.	" "
J. Schöffer, Mainz,	12	As Pruess, Hüpfüff, &c.	" "
J. Pruess, Strasbourg,	14	[no comment]	" "
J. Pruess, jun., Strasbourg,	2	= J. Pruess, sen.	" "
J. Knoblouch "	7	cf. Schott, Gran, &c.	" "
J. Köbel, Oppenheim,	5	[no comment]	" "
M. Flach, Strasbourg,	4	Like Knoblouch	" "
M. Hüpfüff "	10	Like Pruess	" "
T. Anshelm, Pforzheim,	7	[no comment]	" "
H. Gran, Hagenau,	16	Like Knoblouch	" "

Total 2

Group with normal M

Printer and no. of type		Proctor's comment	My estimate
U. Morhard, Strasbourg,	1	M is noticeable	Basle style
E. Cervicorn, Cologne,	1	[no comment]	Different
J. Soter "	3	Like Cervicorn	As Cervicorn
A. Lutz, Ingolstadt,	2	[no comment]	Doubtful
S. Grim, Augsburg,	5	Not normal	Different. Pointed A
J. Gymnicus, Cologne,	1	Like Cervicorn or Soter	As Cervicorn
Elisabeth "	1	= Cervicorn	"
Kaiser "	1	Very like Cervicorn	"

Total 4

Aldine Style.

Printer and no. of type		Proctor's comment	My estimate
J. Schöffer, Mainz,	18	Like Anshelm	? an Italian type
T. Anshelm, Tübingen,	11	Same style as Schürer	Same
M. Lotter, Leipzig,	16	Like Schürer	"
M. Lotter, jun., Wittenberg,	5	= Lotter sen.	"
M. Schürer, Strasbourg,	5	Very like, Schöffer, Anshelm	"
L. Schürer, Schlettstadt,	6	= M. Schürer	"
J. Gymnicus, Cologne,	2	Very like Lotter in face	Different

Total 2

Capcasa Style.

Printer and no. of type	*Proctor's comment*	*My estimate*
H. Hölzel, Nuremberg, 13	Broken T; like Öglin or Otmar	an Italian type
J. Stuchs " 6	= Hölzel	Same
J. Otmar, Augsburg, 26	= Öglin	"
E. Öglin " 2	cf. Otmar	"
S. Otmar " 2	= J. Otmar	"
Cornelis of Zieriksee, Cologne, 9	Qu differs	T also differs. Different

Total 2

Erfurt Style.

Printer and no. of type	*Proctor's comment*	*My estimate*
W. Schenck, Erfurt, 1	Unlike others	Erfurt style
M. Maler " 3	= Schenck	Same
Paul of Hachenburg, Erfurt, 4	Very like Schenck, but taller face	Different

Total 2

Sertorius Style.

Printer and no. of type	*Proctor's comment*	*My estimate*
H. Sertorius, Wittenberg, 2	cf. Lotter	Sertorius Style
N. Marschalk, Rostock, 2	= Sertorius	Same
J. Rhau, Wittenberg, 2	= Sertorius	"
M. Lotter, Leipzig, 13	Almost the same as Sertorius	"

Total 1

There is one more type of the middle size to be added, E. Ratdolt's 8, used also by J. Otmar (20). Total – 14.

Of the smaller romans I have examined only one group, Pica in approximate size, shown at Proctor's fig. 11. This type again appears twice in the Incunable Catalogue, where Quentell's type 13 (pl. 285 of the Gesellschaft für Typenkunde), it is stated, seems indistinguishable from J. Schott's type 4 (pl. 1545 of the Gesellschaft für Typenkunde). This was, in fact, a very popular design and was used in Germany until late in the sixteenth century. It was also exported and is found in Italy, at Paris, Lyons, Antwerp, and London. Fifteen German printers were using it by 1520.

Small Roman. German Style.

Printer and no. of type	*Proctor's comment*	*My estimate*
R. Beck, Baden, Strasbourg, 5	= Pruess	Small Strasbourg roman
J. Schott, Strasbourg, 4	cf. Knoblouch	Same
M. Schürer " 4	Like Knoblouch or Schott	"
L. Schürer, Schlettstadt, 2	= M. Schürer	"

Printer and no. of type		Proctor's comment	My estimate
J. Knoblouch, Strasbourg,	13	cf. Schott, Gran, &c.	Small Strasbourg roman
H. Gran, Hagenau,	14	cf. Knoblouch	„
H. Knoblochtzer,		Like Quentell	„
Heidelberg,	10		„
J. Pruess, Strasbourg,	16	Like Knoblouch	„
J. Pruess, jun. „	3	= Pruess, sen.	„
T. Anshelm, Pforzheim,	9	Like Schürer or Knoblouch	„
S. Grim, Augsburg,	6	cf. Miller	„
J. Rhau, Wittenberg,	7	Caps. like Quentell	„
J. Miller, Augsburg,	4	[no comment]	„
H. Quentell, Cologne,	13	Like Grüninger or Pruess	? Smaller
J. Schöffer, Mainz,	16	Like Grüninger, Pruess, Quentell, &c.	„
V. Schumann, Leipzig,	8	Very like Lotter, but M normal	Smaller face. Different
J. Grüninger, Strasbourg,	23	[no comment]	„ „
J. Soter, Cologne,	1	Like Quentell	Same as Quentell
			Total 3

Stated summarily my examination of all these romans suggests that there was in use in Germany during the period under review, one set of capitals, with one copy, and twenty-eight body types. They represent about 140 entries in the Register, or about one-fifth. If the same proportion may be presumed to hold good throughout the Register – and it is reasonable to think that it would, since there are equally long groups of Schwabachers, Rotundas, and Heading Types – we arrive at a result of about 180 types cut in about twenty-five years (some date from before 1501). Proctor's main purpose was to assign each book to a particular printer, and naturally therefore he pays especial attention to small points such as differences in commas, hyphens, and paragraph marks. It is possible that where there was not complete agreement of all sorts in any two types he regarded them as different, and that where he uses a term such as 'very like' he meant no more than this.

Proctor's Part 2 has been continued by Colonel F. Isaac in a volume dealing with Italy, Basle, &c., published in 1938. Isaac's descriptions of the relations between various types are rather more definite. He uses the term 'as' so and so, by which I take it he means he can detect no difference, and seldom describes a type as being 'like' another. There are many references to types used in the fifteenth century and these are not shown in the facsimiles. These facsimiles illustrate new types only, but they aim at illustrating every new type. For example, we find Stephanus Guileretus at Rome used seven types (not including Greek and Hebrew and a set of roman capitals); three are fifteenth-century and three came from other printers; and one type only out of the seven appears in the facsimiles. Similarly of the eight types used by Piero Pacini at Florence one only is illustrated. The facsimiles for Italy illustrate 156 types (excluding Greek), and the number of books catalogued is just over 2,000. The supply of new types then for this period, 1501-20, is not widely different from what I have estimated to be the supply in Germany during the same years.

The documentary evidence bearing on the subject is unfortunately very scanty so far. There is first of all one type specimen sheet, that of Johann Petri of Nuremberg, 1525, of which a reproduction was published by Conrad Burger in 1895. As we do not know whether this was a printer's specimen or a founder's specimen of types which Petri was prepared to sell, the sheet does not help us much. One point at least is worth noting. Three of the types shown were not of Petri's cutting, namely the roman capitals and one italic, which are Froben's, and the second roman, which is the same as Proctor's group of middle-sized romans with the normal M. One could hardly identify these three from the few lines displayed on the sheet, but a comparison with the types used in books printed by Petri gets over the difficulty. The second document consists of a letter from Luther to Georg Spalatin written in May 1519, in which Luther announces that Melchior Lotter the younger has arrived in Wittenberg and that he is well stocked with matrices from Froben. The elder Lotter was a type-cutter or had a type-cutter in his employ, who designed the Leipzig roman (Proctor's fig. 6) and the first Wittenberg letter, but even he depended in part, as we see, on purchased matrices. In the next year, 1520, there is a letter from Guillaume Budé[1] in Paris stating that Jodocus Badius had purchased Greek type from Germany; this was Froben's Greek, Basle being a German city to a Frenchman of that generation. From Thomas Platter's autobiography we learn that when he became a printer in Basle in 1536, he bought types from Peter Schöffer the younger, and he says that Schöffer was well equipped with all manner of punches. In all these cases we find that the suppliers of matrices or type were the larger printing houses, and not yet men trading only as type-founders.

Proctor says in his introduction that his reason for choosing the year 1520 for the limit of his work was the vast stream of pamphlets which was caused by the outbreak of the struggle for religious liberty, and which swamped the more literary output of the press. In spite of this vast stream it is a remarkable fact that in Germany in the next twenty years the supply of new types was very small. This can be illustrated by a summary of the types used at Wittenberg in this period.

For books in German the Wittenberg printers[2] used three Texturas and three Rotundas of a large size for headings and titles, five of them old types; for body types they had two small Rotundas, four sizes of Schwabacher, three so-called Wittenberg letters, Lotter's original design and two copies of that; of the new design, Fraktur, there were two heading and three body types, and there was one Upper-Rhine type. For books in Latin there were four sets of roman capitals (two of them copies), ten roman body types, and one italic. This makes a total of 36 types, of which twenty-one were already in use by 1520. Of the new types nine were possibly cut at Wittenberg, three of them by the firm of Cranach & Döring. Döring was a goldsmith and it may have been he who cut the Rotunda heading type used by the firm, the Wittenberg

---

1. See Renouard's *Bibliographie des impressions et des œuvres de Josse Badius*, i. 68.
2. This summary does not include Greek and Hebrew, which were very little used, and some large Rotunda headings found in a few words only. It is based on the collection in the British Museum and is no doubt incomplete. The omissions, however, are hardly likely to alter the picture as a whole. For the detailed list of these Wittenberg types see the Appendix.

Fraktur and the first copy of Lotter's Wittenberg letter. The only other new type of note was G. Rhau's small modelled roman capitals. This paucity of new types is representative of German presses in this period, with the exception of Nuremberg and Cologne. At Nuremberg appeared most of the new Frakturs, and at Cologne several new romans and one new italic.

The new Cologne italic, cut about 1525, illustrates the increasing interchange of types throughout Europe. It is an easily recognized design, larger than the usual Aldine or Froben italic. Besides its appearance in a number of German cities, it is found in books printed at Basle, Bologna, Rome, Louvain, Paris, and London. It is Thomas Berthelet's 95 italic shown at fig. 65a in Isaac's *English Printing Types*, vol. i, and it was the first italic used in Scotland (cf. Isaac, fig. 98).

I have been considering the state of the type-founding trade in the sixteenth century, but I ought not to pass over in silence the fifteenth century. This revolution in the methods of type production did not of course start abruptly in 1501, and there is ample evidence of the exchange of types among printers for many years before 1500. Dr. Konrad Haebler collected the references to the commerce in type in an article which appeared in the *Zentralblatt für Bibliothekswesen*, 1924, 'Schriftguss und Schriftenhandel in der Frühdruckzeit' (a translation appeared in the American periodical *Typographia*, vol. iii, July 1926). Haebler concludes that there is no evidence that type-founders were as yet a separate profession. Ernst Consentius in *Die Typen der Inkunabelzeit*, 1929, has collected further evidence bearing on the subject and contests Haebler's conclusion. In addition to the documentary evidence he quotes many cases in which incunabulists have recognized that a particular type was in the hands of more than one printer. He rightly emphasizes the fact that in the fifteenth century there was a very considerable number of printers who did not cut or even cast their own types. While Haebler's conclusion that the documents do not establish that type-founders formed a separate profession may be correct, nevertheless, towards the end of the century some printers seem to have been chiefly engaged in supplying type to other printers. There is the case of Nicholas Wolff at Lyons, and of Hendrik Lettersnijder of Antwerp, whose types, according to Kruitwagen, were used by 55 per cent. of the printers in the Netherlands between 1493 and 1540. Consentius uses these facts as a basis for an attack on the whole of the Proctor-Haebler method, the natural history method of studying the output of the printing-press. He maintains that the number of recorded instances of types changing hands is so large that, except in the earliest years, one can never be sure in the case of a book without imprint or date to whom the type used then belonged. But the conspectus of books assigned to a particular printer is seldom compiled from the occurrence of one type only, but from a combination of details, such as method of composition, initials and decorative material in general, and so on. Moreover, the same type is rarely identical in every detail, in measurement, extra sorts, &c., when in the hands of different printers.

In France, as in Germany, the Renaissance and the Reformation brought about a great increase in the number of printed books. In Paris some of the most important houses, for example Simon de Colines and Robert Estienne, had many new types cut for their exclusive use in the manner of the earliest printers. Colines's three new italics, for instance, and several of his romans are not to be found, at least in his lifetime, in the books of other printers. Nevertheless, Colines's working life was contemporary with that of the first independent French type-founder of whom we have any clear information, Claude Garamond. The story of his cutting the Royal Greek types for Francis I is well known. We have, too, the preface which he himself wrote for the edition of David Chambellan's *Pia et religiosa meditatio* printed in 1545, in which he tells us he had been cutting types for others all his life and had now cut the italic used in the Chambellan for his own use.[1] He did not, however, print the book himself, and, as far as we know he was never a printer. The beginnings of the Garamond roman and its connexion with the romans of Aldus Manutius have been traced by Beatrice Warde in an article in no. 5 of *The Fleuron*, 1926. There was an italic in use at Paris in Garamond's day, perhaps cut by him, which illustrates the economy of a type-founding age. It is well known from the books of Emblems printed by Denys Janot and is first found about 1540.[2] It was the only italic available to Paris printers who wanted something larger and more distinguished than the Froben or Aldine italics. At least ten Paris printers acquired it, besides three at Lyons, and two at Geneva. These printers did not copy one another's designs, but bought matrices or type from a common centre. One of these Lyons printers, who began work in 1542, was Jean de Tournes. His method of obtaining types was completely different from that of Colines and was the same as that of any average printer of the eighteenth or nineteenth century. From the prefaces of some of his books and from a study of his types we can deduce that Tournes neither cut types nor employed a type-cutter solely for his own use. All his types can be found in the books of other presses. There is a striking uniformity between his stock of types and those of two other contemporary European printers, namely Johannes Oporinus at Basle, and Lorenzo Torrentino at Florence. The connecting link in this case was the French type designer, Robert Granjon.

Granjon was occasionally a printer, but for the most part he was a designer and cutter of types, who worked in the same way as William Caslon, that is to say he supplied printers with matrices or type and kept the punches in his own hands. Moreover, his market was all Europe, not merely France. He himself worked at Paris, Lyons, Antwerp, Florence, and Rome, and there is hardly a printing centre throughout Europe in which at least his italic types are not to be found. I will take two examples of his work which show how international the trade in types had become. The first is a Double Pica roman,[3] which is first found at Jean de Tournes's press at Lyons in 1548, and shortly afterwards appears in the books of Oporinus at Basle and of Torrentino at Florence. In 1588 it may be seen in Rome printed books about the time when Granjon went to Rome to work for the newly established Vatican Press. The type is shown in the specimen book of the Vatican Press issued in 1628, under the name Parangone. Granjon's name is not mentioned, but from its history we may fairly conclude that he was the designer.

1. See also pp. 60, 99, 106-109.
2. For reproductions of this type see S. Morison's *Four Centuries of Fine Printing*, figs. 155, 161, 163, 270, and 280, and Updike's *Printing Types*, fig. 141.
3. For reproductions see Morison's *Four Centuries*, figs. 59 and 274.

The second example is a Cicero or Pica italic certainly cut by Granjon in 1565, a very well-known design of which matrices are still in existence to-day. We have now reached the career of Christophe Plantin of Antwerp (1555-89), a printer whose history is more fully documented than that of any other in the sixteenth century. From documents preserved in the Plantin Museum at Antwerp, from his specimen book of 1567, and his printed books we can see that his practice as to procuring types was exactly that of printers in general down to our day. There are documents extant relating to Plantin's purchase of the Cicero italic from Granjon in 1565, and it appears in the books of a number of other printers shortly afterwards, at Louvain, Antwerp, Frankfurt, Cologne, and Basle. It is shown in Plantin's *Index characterum*, 1567, and on the 1592 specimen sheet of the Egenolff-Berner foundry at Frankfort, where it is called 'Littera currens Ciceroniana, artifice Roberto Granjone prodita, vulgo Scolasticalis dicta'. It was widely used throughout the seventeenth century, especially in Germany and the Netherlands, among others by the Elzevirs. I have found it on six other specimen sheets, besides those of the Berner foundry, the house which apparently acquired the punches after Granjon's death. In England it was used by Roger Daniel about 1655 and by the Oxford University Press from about 1690. It was one of the so-called Fell types. The Oxford Press still possesses matrices and has used the type in our generation. Apart from this revival Granjon's Cicero italic was in continuous use for one hundred and fifty years. Such a life for a type is not at all unusual. English books of the early eighteenth century are full of types cut originally in the sixteenth century. Even if the punches had been lost, as long as sets of matrices survived the type could still be cast. As late as 1739 the Cambridge University Press was using a Pica roman which is found for the first time at Paris in 1549, a Cicero roman, again cut by Robert Granjon, as we know from Frankfurt specimen sheets of the seventeenth century.

In England in the sixteenth century we find a similar state of affairs, that is to say many printers using the same types, and also we find that our printers were very largely, one perhaps might say almost entirely, dependent on the continental printers or founders for their supplies. Col. Isaac's two volumes on *English and Scottish Printing Types 1501-1558*, published by the Bibliographical Society in 1930 and 1932, have a Type Index useful for our purpose. About forty romans are indexed, of which eighteen have been traced to continental sources. Of the others eleven are small sizes which I find too difficult to cope with; some are doubtful because found only in a few lines in poorly printed books, and five are classed as 'Garamonds'. Whether these are copies of the many romans based on Garamond's design, or, as I suspect, imported types, is a difficult question to answer. The Garamond design had by 1540 become the French standard roman, and to distinguish the many varieties would be a laborious, though perhaps not impossible task. Apart from this group of 'Garamonds' the romans traced include all the best-known types, those of Pynson, Worde, Treveris, Wolfe, Singleton, and Grafton. The three earliest came from Paris, four from Antwerp, four from Cologne, one from Strasbourg, two from Basle, one from Zwolle, and one from Ghent. Of the twenty italics in Isaac's Index, nine are doubtful as being too small or too little used to tackle. Of the eleven traced six are from Antwerp, three from Basle, one from Cologne, and one from Paris.

But of course during this period the usual English type was Textura or Black Letter, and the Index shows 240 of this family. How many actually different types these represent I do not know, but as an indication we may take Worde's 116 which appears nine times in the Index. This type, along with a number of others of the best Texturas, can be traced to Paris. The 116 (fig. 5 in Isaac) was used by Wolfgang Hopyl in Paris from 1506. Worde's 95 (Duff's type 8 – Isaac, fig. 3) is found with Trepperel and Le Noir, Paris, 1497, and is illustrated in Claudin's *Histoire de l'Imprimerie en France*, vol. ii, p. 161. Worde's 62 (Isaac, fig. 6) is found with Antoine Chappiel, Paris, 1497, and shown by Claudin, vol. ii, p. 353. Worde's 220 (Isaac's fig. 9) was used by Hopyl at Paris from 1515, and Worde's 70 (Isaac, fig. 10a) by Hopyl from 1504. Pynson's 130 (Isaac, fig. 20) was used by J. Maurand, Paris, in 1497 (cf. Claudin, ii. 215). J. Rastell's 93 (Isaac, fig. 36) was used by Hopyl in 1497 (cf. Claudin, ii. 72). Two varieties of Textura came from Antwerp. R. Jugge's 78 (Isaac, fig. 58 b and 59 a) is shown by Nijhoff in *L'Art typographique dans les Pays Bas* under the printer N. van Oldenborch of Antwerp. John Day's 77 (Isaac, fig. 87) is a Lettersnijder type, that is in the traditional Dutch style. Nijhoff shows it under F. Aertsen and W. Vorsterman, both of Antwerp.

Of other gothic types a few Rotundas were used in the early sixteenth century. Of these Worde's 53 (Isaac, fig. 8) is found at Paris with P. Pigouchet in 1499 (cf. Claudin, ii. 55) and Pynson's 64 (Isaac, fig. 18) was used by Hopyl from 1490 (cf. Claudin, ii. 68). One of the best of the Lettres Bâtardes, Peter Treveris's 81 (Isaac, fig. 64) came from Antwerp, where it was used from 1525 by Vorsterman.

The traditional English Black Letter, originally a French design, was regularly displayed by our founders, even in the eighteenth century, e. g. by William Caslon in his specimen of 1742. Some matrices of the sixteenth century have survived down to this day. In Palmer's *General History of Printing*, 1732, a Great Primer and a Two Line Great Black are shown. The author says that they were used by all printers in London and that he believed that they were struck from the punches of Wynkyn de Worde. Both sizes were in the Grover foundry and Rowe Mores, in his account of the James foundry, in which was incorporated the Grover foundry, says that he had discovered the punches. If the account I have given of the source of Worde's Texturas is correct he cannot have had the punches, but what Rowe Mores found may very well date back to the sixteenth century. Part of the stock of the James foundry descended through the Frys to the Fann Street Foundry, the firm of Sir Charles Reed, the father of T. B. Reed. In his book, *The Old English Letter Foundries*, T. B. Reed printed specimens from type cast from these early matrices (he says nothing of punches). From the Fann Street Foundry they were acquired by the Caslons and are now in the possession of Stephenson, Blake & Co. of Sheffield.

In arranging Texturas in his Type Index Col. Isaac found the lower-case letters s, w, and y useful. He makes three groups according to the absence or presence of serifs or terminals to the s. The many varieties of w are in part accounted for by the fact that the punches were cut in France and used for Latin texts; consequently there was no w and our printers had their own cut or used w's from other type families. For the purpose of distinguishing Texturas I have found some of the upper-case letters still more useful. These are larger and more easily remembered. There are two distinct kinds of A, one like the German Schwabacher, and the other more nearly resembling a roman A. There is a round and a square variety of both C and E. The M is nearly always the same, Haebler's M 32, although some of Pynson's types are distinguished by a different M. The most useful of all the capitals is the T, of which there is a square variety and three well-marked different round varieties. Any of these may be used as convenient spot letters.

As to documents relating to founders in England, there are a few references in Worman's *Alien Members of the Book-Trade*, all relating to the second part of the century. There is one Antonius d'Anvillier, 'fusor typorum' 1562, Hubert d'Anvillier 'caster of printing-letters' 1553-94, Amell de Groyter 'letter-maker for printers' 1583 (there was an Aimé de Gruyter who worked for Plantin), Gabriel Guyett 'letter-maker for printers' 1576-88 (perhaps a member of the family of the Netherlands founder François Guyot), Jerome Haultain 'letter caster for printers' 1574-85, Poll. Rotteforde 'founder of lettres for printers' 1571 (had then been in England for 14 years), and Charles Tressell 'a graver of letters for printers' and ' a carver to the printers', 1571-83. The earliest reference I have noted to an English founder is to Benjamin Sympson, 1597, in the Registers of the Stationers' Company. It is not clear that any of these men actually cut types, although one, Charles Tressell, is called a graver. Haultain, with whom we can connect some types used in the Marprelate tracts, is styled merely 'letter caster'. The first English founder whose types can be traced was Nicholas Niccols, who flourished two hundred years after the invention of printing.

APPENDIX

TYPES USED BY THE WITTENBERG PRINTERS, 1521-1540

JOHANN RHAU, called Grünenberg, – 1525

Proctor's types 1-3 and 5 are not found after 1520.

Type 4. Schwabacher 86, fig. 59 in Proctor. His usual type for texts in German. He sometimes used a different C (Proctor's C2) and E (Proctor's E4). All the Wittenberg printers, except Lotter, had this common Schwabacher, with variations in C and D and the looped ascending letters.

Type 6. Roman 110, as fig. 4. The Nuremberg roman in the Italian style described above. Used also by G. Thau and Weiss.

Type 7. Roman 77. The small Strasbourg roman described above. Used also by G. Rhau and Weiss.

Type 8. Textura 170, fig. 21 in Proctor.

Not before 1521

Type 9. Textura 164 with M 66. First used by M. Brandis, Magdeburg, 1497. See British Museum Incunable Cat., pl. LVIII, and pl. 398 of the Gesellschaft für Typenkunde. Used from 1521. Used also by Schirlentz and Weiss.

MELCHIOR LOTTER, – 1524

Proctor's types 2 and 4 not found after 1520.

Type 1. Textura 170 = J. Rhau 8, fig. 21 in Proctor.

Type 3. Wittenberg Letter 93, fig. 58 in Proctor. Used by no other Wittenberg printer, but by several Leipzig printers and by M. Sachse at Erfurt.

Type 5. Roman 88, fig. 9. Aldine style.

Type 6. Roman 66. Has normal M, *not* the M of fig. 11.

Type 7. Roman capitals, 12 mm.

Except type 7, all these were from M. Lotter, sen., Leipzig.

Not before 1521

Type 8. Roman 103, with normal M, = L. Schürer 1. From 1521 his usual types for books in Latin.

Type 9. Rotunda 140, as Ratdolt 9, fig. 32. A better display is on Ratdolt's Specimen sheet.

Type 10. Rotunda 67 = M. Lotter sen., 7, fig. 51. See *Das newe Testament*, edition in folio, 1524.

Type 11. Rotunda 58 = Hochfeder, Metz, 26. A Paris type. See *Das newe Testament*, edition in 8°, 1524.

Type 12. Schwabacher 67 = H. Lufft 1. See *Das newe Testament*, edition in 8°, 1524.

Type 13. Roman capitals 8 mm, as fig. 1. Froben's. Cf. Isaac's *Index*, Basle, pl. VII.

Type 14. Italic 85, as fig. 13. Froben's.

NICKEL SCHIRLENTZ, 1521-46

Type 1. Schwabacher 86 = J. Rhau 4. At first he used the round form of D, but later the normal. The chief text type until 1529, when it was superseded by type 8.

Type 2. Textura 164 = J. Rhau 9.

Type 3. Large Textura, as fig. 14 b.

Type 4. Rotunda 155, as fig. 31, with M 94.

Type 5. Italic 84, as fig. 13. Froben's. Used from 1527. See especially the Pentateuch in Latin, 1529.

Type 6. Roman capitals 8 mm. Copy of Froben's. Reproduced in Götze, *Die hochdeutschen Drucker der Reformationszeit*.

Type 7. Schwabacher 72 = H. Lufft 1. Used from 1527.

Type 8. Wittenberg Letter 93. Close copy of Cranach & Döring 6 = H. Lufft 9.

Type 9. Rotunda 140 = Lotter 9, as fig. 32. Used from 1529.

Type 10. Fraktur ('Gebetbuch') Heading = Lufft 8. Used from 1529.

Type 11. Fraktur 114. The Neudörfer-Andreä design, Nuremberg. Cf. Crous & Kirchner, *Die gotischen Schriftarten*, Abb. 87 and 126. Used from 1533.

Type 12. Roman 106, as fig. 3. Used from 1534.

HANS LUFFT, 1523-84

Type 1. Schwabacher 68. See *Das allte Testament*, 1523. This smaller size of the normal Schwabacher was possibly first cut for this edition, though M. Ramminger, Augsburg, had the type in the same year.

Type 2. Schwabacher 86 = J. Rhau 4.

Type 3. Textura 170, as fig. 21, = J. Rhau 8, Lotter 1.

Type 4. Roman 84. Found only in *Deuteronomios*, 1524. Very like a common Paris roman. Cf. *The Library*, June, 1936, p. 72. Already in use at Leipzig.

Type 5. Italic 84, as fig. 13. Froben's.

Type 6. Rotunda 140 = Lotter 9, Schirlentz 9, as fig. 32.

Type 7. Roman capitals 8 mm. Copy of Froben, fig. 1. Differs from Schirlentz 6.

Type 8. Fraktur ('Gebetbuch') Heading. Cf. Crous & Kirchner, *Die gotischen Schriftarten*, Abb. 81 and 119. Used from 1527. = Schirlentz 10.

Type 9. Wittenberg Letter 93. A close copy of Cranach & Döring 6. The D, E, G, M, and T differ = Schirlentz 8. This copy was used throughout Saxony and Thuringia. Cf. below under Cranach & Döring.

Type 10. Wittenberg Fraktur 75 = Cranach & Döring 7. Used for marginal notes from 1529.

Type 11. Schwabacher 53. See *Das newe Testament*, 1533. The normal design, not found earlier in this size.

Type 12. Roman 81. A Cologne type dating from 1527. For an account of this type, which still survives with the firm of Enschedé of Haarlem, their so-called 'Schöffer' roman, see the *Gutenberg Jahrbuch*, 1939, p. 197 (reproduction, p. 201). Used from 1534.

Type 13. Fraktur 90. The Neudörffer-Andreä design, Nuremberg. Cf. Crous & Kirchner, *Die gotischen Schriftarten*, Abb. 97. Used from 1535.

Type 14. Roman 106, as fig. 3. = Schirlentz 12. Used from 1537.

Type 15. Schwabacher 109, as fig. 52. First appearance at this press, 1541, of this common large Schwabacher.

L. CRANACH & C. DÖRING, 1523-4

The work of this anonymous press was described by Knaake, one of the editors of the Weimar edition of Luther's works, in an article in the *Centralblatt für Bibliothekswesen*, 1890, Bd. 7, pp. 196-207. But he gave no account of the types.

Type 1. Schwabacher 90 = J. Rhau 4.

Type 2. Rotunda 138. Some capitals, including M, M 18, are like those of fig. 23, as used by several other Wittenberg printers; others are like the Rotunda of fig. 14. The lower-case w is distinctive. Probably a new type. A full page may be seen in Luther's *Offinbarung des Endchrists*, 1524, no. 23 in Knaake's list.

Type 3. Upper-Rhine type 102, with some unusual capitals, *e. g.* A and E. It is shown by Götze among the types of W. Stöckel, Dresden, but that type belonged to H. Emser's printer at Dresden. Cf. Günther 'Der älteste Dresdener Buchdruck' in the *Zeitschrift für Bücherfreunde* 1916-17, p. 174, &c. Günther shows the type on p. 177, and suggests a Leipzig origin. In fact it appears on the title-page of the *Evangelium Matthei vñ Iohannis*, V. Schumann, Leipzig, 1522. For its use by Cranach & Döring see Luther's *Ein weyse Christlich Mess zuhalten*, 1524, Knaake 16, and also the second part of the original edition of Luther's translation of the Old Testament, which the Weimar edition assigns to Lotter.

Type 4. Roman 108, as fig. 3 in Proctor.

Type 5. Roman capitals 8 mm. Copy of Froben = Lufft 7.

Type 6. Wittenberg Letter 93. The upper case varies considerably from Lotter 3. Used also by H. Emser's printer at Dresden in the same year 1524. It is a curious fact that types 3 and 6 were used by this Wittenberg press and by a printer working for Luther's opponent, Emser. The other Wittenberg printers had a close copy of Cranach & Döring's design, and it was this copy which was so widely used in Saxony and Thuringia. I have found it in some forty different presses all within that central region of Germany, with off-shoots to Berlin to the north-east and Hannover to the north-west. Outside that circle it appears at Breslau in 1541, and in Copenhagen from 1559 (see Nielsen, *Dansk typografisk Atlas*, pls. XXX, XLI, XLVIII, and LXXIV).

Type 7. Wittenberg Fraktur 75. Crous & Kirchner assign this type to Cranach & Döring and reproduce two pages from Luther's translation of the *Psalter*, 1524, assigned by the Weimar edition to Lotter. The woodcut border on the title-page of the *Psalter* was afterwards used by J. Klug, who acquired most of the types of this press. The type was used also by J. Klug, S. Reinhart, H. Lufft, and G. Rhau. It is very like the small Fraktur of J. Petri, Nuremberg, which also dates from 1524.

JOSEPH KLUG, 1524-52

Originally with Cranach & Döring. He acquired at least five of their seven types.

Type 1. Wittenberg Letter 93 = Cranach & Döring 6.

Type 2. Rotunda 138 = Cranach & Döring 2.

Type 3. Schwabacher 90 = Cranach & Döring 1.
Type 4. Schwabacher 67 = Lufft 1. He mixes with it capitals from Lotter 11.
Type 5. Wittenberg Fraktur 75 = Cranach & Döring 7.
Type 6. Italic 84 = Froben's, as fig. 13.
Type 7. Roman capitals 8 mm = Cranach & Döring 5.
Type 8. Roman 108 = Cranach & Döring 4.
Type 9. Fraktur ('Gebetbuch') Heading = Lufft 8. Used from 1528.
Type 10. Roman 88, as fig. 8, = G. Rhau 9. Used from 1536.

Georg Rhau, 1525-48

Type 1. Schwabacher 86 = J. Rhau 4.
Type 2. Schwabacher 68 = Lufft 1.
Type 3. Rotunda 140, as fig. 32 in Proctor.
Type 4. Rotunda 144, as fig. 31.
Type 5. Wittenberg Letter 93 = Cranach & Döring 6. Rhau had both the original and the copy.
Type 6. Wittenberg Letter 93 = Lufft 9.
Type 7. Fraktur ('Gebetbuch') Heading = Lufft 8.
Type 8. Fraktur ('Teuerdank') Heading. Types 7 and 8 are on the title-page of Luther's *Auslegung der Evangelien*, 1528, printed by G. Rhau, according to Campbell Dodgson (*Catalogue of Early German and Flemish Woodcuts*, ii. 372 (129)); I have seen the title-page only. For the 'Teuerdank' type cf. Crous & Kirchner, Abb. 82.
Type 9. Roman 88, as fig. 8. Used from 1531.
Type 10. Small modelled roman capitals. Narrow M. A new type. From 1531.
Type 11. Italic 84 = Froben's, as fig. 13.
Type 12. Roman 78, as fig. 11.
Type 13. Copy of Froben caps. = Lufft 7.
Type 14. Fraktur 114. The Neudörffer-Andreä design, Nuremberg = Schirlentz 11. Used from 1537.
Type 15. Roman 110 = J. Rhau 6. Used from 1537.
Type 16. Roman 93. With normal M. = U. Morhard 1.
Type 17. Fraktur 75 = Cranach & Döring 7. Used in 1541.

Hans Weiss, 1525-40

Type 1. Schwabacher 86 = J. Rhau 4. He used two forms of C. and Proctor's E .
Type 2. Wittenberg Letter 93 = Lufft 9. He took this type to Berlin in 1540, where it remained in use until well after 1600. Cf. the reproductions in Crous, *Schrift und Satz im Berliner Buchdruck*.
Type 3. Rotunda 144, as fig. 31.
Type 4. Rotunda 140, as fig. 32.
Type 5. Textura 164 = J. Rhau 9.
Type 6. Schwabacher 112, as fig. 52. This size little used at Wittenberg. Cf. Lufft 15.
Type 7. Schwabacher 72 = Lufft 1.
Type 8. Italic 84 = Froben's, as fig. 13.
Type 9. Fraktur ('Gebetbuch') Heading = Lufft 8.
Type 10. Roman 108, as fig. 4, = J. Rhau 6. Used from 1537.
Type 11. Roman 78, as fig. 11, = G. Rhau 12. Used from 1537.
Type 12. Copy of Froben caps. = Schirlentz 6.

The minor printers, H. Barth, S. Reinhart, P. Seitz, and H. Frischmut, who printed only a handful of books, had no new types. The types of the seven chief printers are shown in A. Götze, *Die hochdeutschen Drucker der Reformationszeit*, 1905, Abb. 69-75. Götze does not go beyond 1530, and the reproductions are useful but far from reliable.

[1943]

SOME FRENCH BIBLE ILLUSTRATIONS
IN THE SIXTEENTH CENTURY

In the first quarter of the sixteenth century many illustrated Bibles were printed in Germany, Switzerland, the Netherlands, and even at Lyons, but as far as the Paris press is concerned there appears to have been a gap of about forty years between the illustrated Bibles published by Vérard and the next new series of Biblical illustrations. Cuts dating from the fifteenth century and cuts properly belonging to Books of Hours are found, as for example in the French Bible printed in 'lettres bâtardes' by A. Bonnemère in 1538. In this book, in addition to a number of woodcuts in the medieval style, we find some cuts from François Regnault's Books of Hours and the two cuts signed B. V. which had been originally drawn for Simon Vostre's Hours. The first Paris printer to illustrate a Bible in the Renaissance style was François Gryphius, a brother of the Lyons printer Sébastien. François is often said to have been a pupil of Geofroy Tory, but there is no evidence for this and in his Biblical illustrations he was certainly inspired by the artists of South Germany. In most of his books we find figure initials in the Basle style. In his Latin New Testament of 1537 there is a set of new cuts to the Acts of the Apostles and the Apocalypse. The Apocalypse cuts are copied from the Holbein designs, which had appeared at Basle in 1523 in a New Testament printed by Thomas Wolff. In the edition of 1539 the series covers the whole of the New Testament, and in the Latin Bibles of 1541 and 1542, there are cuts for the Old Testament also. These Old Testament cuts are copied from the series by Hans Sebald Beham,[1] printed at Frankfort by Christian Egenolff in various editions from 1534, some without the text of the Bible. Gryphius's title-page to the Bibles of 1541 and 1542 is a close copy of that by Beham. Beham's New Testament cuts are of later date. In the privilege to Gryphius's New Testament of 1537 (dated 16 Nov. 1537), the book is described as 'figuré par luy', and similarly in the privilege to the edition of 1539 'illustratum a Gryphius', from which it has been inferred that the illustrations were designed or cut by Gryphius himself. An edition of the New Testament appeared in 1552, without place of imprint. He appears to have left Paris in 1545, according to Renouard, but presumably returned.

In spite of the wording of the privileges it is difficult to believe that Gryphius was in reality the designer of this remarkable series of illustrations. Even those cuts which are not original are very cleverly adapted to the different and smaller size. If he were capable of producing such work surely something more would have been heard of him as an artist. One is bound to suspect that this is another case of the printer taking all the credit to himself.

The next series of Biblical illustrations is that which appears to have been planned by Pierre Regnault and is found in the *Biblia picturis illustrata*, P. Regnault, 1540, 8vo. The Old Testament cuts had already been issued separately in 1538, according to Nagler, in imitation of the Holbein cuts issued at Lyons. These cuts are oblong in

---

1. With the exception of the first few which are taken from Holbein's Dance of Death series.

shape, many are signed P. R., many I. F., and some bear both pairs of initials. The New Testament cuts are of a narrow shape, and one, the beheading of John the Baptist, is signed I. F. The Old Testament cuts were again issued separately by P. Regnault in 1544 with the title *Historiarum Veteris Testamenti Icones*, copying the title of the Lyons editions and even reprinting the prefatory matter containing Holbein's name.

The New Testament cuts for the Gospels appear also in *L'eternelle Generation de Christ*, a Harmony of the Gospels, printed by Conrad Néobar, 19 August 1540 (the best impression of these metal cuts), and in Erasmus's Commentaries on the New Testament issued by Galiot Du Pré in the same year. Those to the Apocalypse are found in Louis Chocquet's *Les demonstrances de l'Apocalypse*, Les Angeliers, 1541. The two series were used again in Regnault's Latin New Testament of 1542, and the complete set in Yolande Bonhomme's *Biblia* of 1551. The Biblia printed by Charlotte Guillard, 1552, has the New Testament cuts, but new illustrations to the Old Testament, much closer copies of the Holbein designs. In *La Bible translatee pour les simples gens*, P. Regnault, 1543, there are new cuts of the narrow shape also illustrating the Old Testament. In the French Bible of 1544-46, the set of oblong cuts is completed for the New Testament as well, whilst Regnault's mother, widow of F. Regnault, reissued the Old Testament cuts in the narrow form separately in 1551. These two series of cuts also appear to be by I. F., though unsigned.

Who were P. R. and I. F.? According to Papillon the initials represent P. Rochienne and I. Ferlato. One must assume that these men did exist and that Papillon had the authority of tradition for believing them to have been book illustrators. But without corroboration no trust is to be placed in his statement. As to Rochienne, in Audin and Vial's *Dictionnaire des artistes . . . Lyonnais*, there is the following entry. 'Né à Paris en 1520, à Lyon en 1549 et 1557. Passe, dit Rondot, pour avoir gravé les vignettes de la Légende dorée, imprimée à Lyon, par Jean Ruelle, en 1557.' On consulting the references given we find that the definite statement 'en 1520' should be 'vers 1520'. It appears also that these cuts of the *Légende dorée*[1] are the P. R. cuts printed originally at Paris, and finally that the only ultimate source of this circumstantial entry about P. Rochienne is Papillon. In Regnault's French Bible of 1544, in addition to the old series of P. R. cuts, there are two larger illustrations signed P. R. interlaced, with a cross above, the monogram of Pierre Regnault as it appears on one of his devices (Silvestre, No. 85). The two cuts are the Annunciation and the Nativity, of which the latter is found also in a Salisbury Missal, published by G. Merlin in 1556. If these two monograms do not refer to one and the same man, the coincidence is remarkable. It seems highly probable then that P. R. = Pierre Regnault the printer, who owned the blocks cut by I. F. in imitation of Holbein. Nagler identified P. R. and Pierre Regnualt but did not mention the two cuts referred to. One must believe in the existence of a Ferlato, but Papillon's guess that he was I. F. has not been corroborated. The researches of Hans Koegler (see Thieme-Becker under Faber, Jakob) and others have established the fact that Jacques Le Fèvre of Lorraine, who cut on metal many of Holbein's designs for the Basle printers from

1. Ruelle is only known to have printed at Paris, but at any rate the cuts were in Lyons by 1652, when they appeared in a French Bible printed by S. Honorati. Cf. Baudrier, vol. 4, pp. 183-5.

Iob.

262

CAP. XV.

¶ Eliphaz arguit Iob de sapientiæ &
munditiæ arrogantia. Describit impio-
rum maledictionem, quam falsò Iob in
nocenti tribuit.

A REspondens autem Eliphaz The-
manites, dixit.
Nunquid sapiens respõdebit qua
si inuentum loquens, & imple-
.i.sciētia bit ardore) stomachum suum?
mendaci Arguis verbis eũ qui nõ est æqualis tibi
=irutili- & loqueris quod tibi non expedit.
bus, Quantum in te est euacuasti timorem,
detraxi- & =tulisti preces coram)deo.
sti ipsi Docuit enim iniquitas tua os tuum, &
=versuto- imitaris linguam =blasphemantium).
rum Condemnabit te os tuum, & non ego:
=testabun & labia tua =respondebunt tibi).
tur con- Nunquid primus homo tu natus es, &
tra te. ante colles formatus?
=secretũ Nunquid=consilium) dei audisti:& inferior te erit eius sapientia?
B Quid nosti quod ignoremus? quid in-
telligis quod nesciamus?
Eccli.18 b ¶Et senes & antiqui sunt in nobis multo vetustiores, quàm patres tu i.
parui esti Nunquid grande est vt) consoletur
mas quòd te deus?sed=verba tua praua hoc pro-
= quidpiã hibent).
occultum Quid te eleuat cor tuum, & quasi ma-
est apud gna cogitans, attonitos habes oculos?
te. Quid tumet cõtra deum spiritus tuus,

vt proferas de ore tuo huiuscemodi
sermones?
Quid est homo, vt immaculatus sit, &
vt iustus appareat natus de muliere?
‖Ecce inter sanctos eius nemo =immu-   *Sup. 4.d.*
tabilis,)& cæli non sunt mundi in cõ   *=fidelis,*
spectu eius.
Quãto magis abominabilis & inutilis
hõ, qui bibit quasi aquas iniquitatem?
¶Ostendam tibi, audi me : quod vidi   **C**
narrabo tibi.
=Sapientes confitentur, & non abscon   *Quid sa-*
dunt patres suos!)   *pictes an*
Quibus solis data est terra,& non tranf *nuntia-*
iuit alienus per eos.   *rint,&sci*
Cunctis diebus suis impius superbit, &   *uerint pa*
numerus annorum incertus est ty-   *tres corũ*
rannidis eius.
Sonitus terroris semp in auribus illius:
& cum pax sit, ille insidias suspicatur.
Mon credit φ reuerti possit de tene-
bris,=circunspectans) vndiφ gladiũ.   *=expectãs*
Cum se mouerit ad quærendum panẽ,
nouit qnõd paratus sit in manu eius
tenebrarum dies.
Terrebit eũ tribulatio, & angustia val-
labit eum, sicut regem qui præpara-
tur ad prælium.
Tetendit enim aduersus deum manum
suam, & contra omnipotentem robo
ratus est.
Cucurrit aduersus eum erecto collo, & **D**

FIG. 1. Page from *Biblia Picturis illustrata*. P. Regnault, Paris, 1540.

FIG. 2. From *La grant Bible en Francoys Hystoriee et corrigee.*
Paris: Anthoyne Bonnemere. 1538. Folio.

1519 to 1526, was the same as I. F. from Paris. We find him in Paris in 1529; Coyecque (*Bulletin de la Société pour l'histoire de Paris*, 1894, p. 168) reproduces the following: 'Abandon par Jacques Le Fèvres, tailleur d'histoires, et Marie Bienaise, sa femme, au profit de Jean Petit le jeune, de leur part de toute l'imprimerie et cedulles de Jean Bienaise': dated 19 January 1529. Early in 1535 Le Fèvre's name is included in a list of men suspected of Protestant inclinations, but he appears to have come to no harm on that occasion. Koegler, who has studied his work in books printed at Basle and at Lyons, has no doubt that he is the I. F. of this Paris Biblical series, but, he says, after the master P. R. He is generally supposed to have cut on metal after the designs of other men only. But the New Testament illustrations done for Gryphius of Lyons appear to be actually designed by him, and similarly this Paris work may be his entirely, or at least that part of the series illustrating the New Testament. The initials P. R. are found on none of these latter cuts, and from the fact that they were used in the same year in the books of three different printers, one might infer that Regnault was not the owner of the blocks.

The example of these two series of illustrations led other printers to commission new decorations for their Bibles. In R. Estienne's edition of his Latin Bible of 1540 there are eighteen large illustrations, in Exodus and Kings, of the Tabernacle and the Temple of Solomon, the one on Fol. 35 being signed with the Lorraine cross. The series was copied by various printers and in addition to reprints by the Estiennes is found in folio Bibles issued by G. Merlin, 1565, N. Chesneau, 1566 (French), S. Nivelle, 1573, and J. Du Puys, 1587.

Another series on which the Lorraine cross is found was perhaps originally intended for the illustration of Hours; the first appearance of a few of these woodcuts is in Colines's octavo Hours of 1543, while others were issued in an Hours of 1552, G. Merlin, and a third of 1554, Magdeleine Boursette. The full series will be found in a Latin New Testament printed by S. Mesvière for the widow of F. Regnault in 1552. The simplicity of the designs and the absence of shading in these cuts are certainly after the Tory manner, but on the other hand the curiously squat figures could never have been drawn by that artist, apart altogether from the date. It is a remarkable fact that, except for these woodcuts of the Tory school and the plans in Estienne's Bibles, all the Paris Biblical illustrations, until we reach the work of Jean Cousin or the reputed Jean Cousin, were derived indirectly from Germany.

[1935]

GEOFROY TORY

THE second quarter of the sixteenth century was a critical period in the history of French printing, for in those years the humanistic types (roman and italic) superseded gothic as the normal founts for French printers, and the decoration of books followed the lighter, Italian model instead of the fashion set by Holbein and Urs Graf. That Geofroy Tory was one of the leaders who directed this revolution was established by Auguste Bernard in his biography of the scholar-artist published in 1857 (second edition 1865). Further claims which Bernard made for his hero are demonstrably extravagant in several directions, but in the absence of any independent investigation Tory is generally regarded by the uncritical as the prime mover not merely in book decoration but also in the development of French typography. In actual fact, as far as the evidence adduced in the course of this article goes, Tory had no direct influence on typography and even as an illustrator his influence has been exaggerated. The extent to which Bernard's hero-worship has misled us will be realized if it is pointed out that in the American version of Bernard's work printed by the Riverside Press in 1909 about half of the many reproductions of initials, borders, and illustrations are of doubtful origin. In Courboin's *Histoire illustrée de la gravure en France*, out of eleven reproductions of Tory's work, six are very questionably his. In No. 1 of *The Fleuron*, p. 87, there is a plate headed 'Geofroy Tory's initials adapted by the Pelican Press.' Of thirteen initials shown, only one can with any confidence be assigned to Tory; of the remainder six are doubtfully, and six certainly not his.

Since, however, Tory undoubtedly did play an important rôle in the history of book production, it is worth while to set out exactly where his work is to be seen, and to consider his career as a printer. While Bernard's book supplies the bibliographical details for this purpose, his account of Tory as a typographer is, as we hope to show, both meagre and inaccurate.

It was not until Tory had reached the age of about forty that he became a *libraire*. The books which he edited between 1508 and 1512 are interesting chiefly for their prefaces and dedications, since we learn from them details about his life; indeed his books, more especially the later *Champ fleury*, are almost the only biographical sources which we possess. His early work consists of Latin texts, beginning with Pomponius Mela edited for the Paris printers, and a Quintilian edited for the Lyons Press and printed in the plagiarized Aldine italic. We gather from these that during this period Tory was a schoolmaster or lecturer, that he had already studied in Italy and that some time between 1512 and 1522 he made another prolonged stay there; he speaks of visiting the Coliseum *mille fois*, so that evidently this was no brief visit. Bernard assumed that he was back in Paris by 1519, but this is an assumption made to fit his theories as to work to be attributed to Tory. Before 1522 there is no certain trace of his being in Paris, but it is certain that it was during this second visit that he became interested in the art of the period; he returned to France an artist whose taste had been formed by the study of Italian architecture and Venetian book illustration.

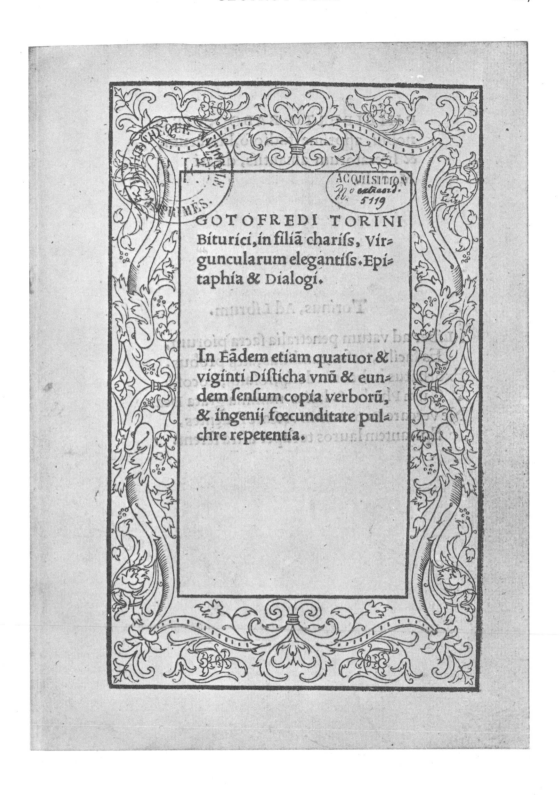

GOTOFREDI TORINI
Biturici, in filiā chariſſ, Vir=
guncularum elegantiſſ. Epi=
taphia & Dialogi.

In Eādem etiam quatuor &
viginti Diſticha vnū & eun=
dem ſenſum copia verborū,
& ingenij fœcunditate pul=
chre repetentia.

Fig. 1. The first Tory border, dating from 1524.

FIGS. 2 & 3. Pages from Tory's *Aediloquium*. Simon de Colines, Paris, 1530. (Reduced.)

On February 27, 1523, (new style) Tory rented a shop (an *ouvrière*) in the Rue St. Jacques from the widow of Wolfgang Hopyl; in the deed (see Coyecque's *Recueil d'actes notariés*) he is styled *libraire*. As far as we know this was Tory's first shop and this document is the earliest definite evidence of his return to Paris, though, as we shall see, there is some reason to suspect that he was at work in Paris in 1522. About a year later than our document, on February 15, 1523 (1524 new style), there was issued from the address of Simon de Colines (though without his name) a book entitled *Gotofredi Torini Biturici In filiā chariss. Virguncularum elegantiss. epitaphia & dialogi*. In this volume of uninspired Latin verse there are two points of interest for us. In the text there is direct reference to Tory's devotion to drawing, and on the title-page there is the well-known border used also on his first book of Hours and on several other books issued from his press in later years. With the *Epitaphia* (cf. Fig. 1) we can begin the study of Tory's authentic work as a book illustrator. In addition, the Tory canon consists of five books of Hours, the *Aediloquium*, *Champ fleury*, and a few other books printed by himself. These books from his own press, with the exception of two books by Guillaume Bochetel and the Hours of 1531, contain very little new decorative material. It is the Hours and *Champ fleury* which we must examine in order to gain an idea of his style and to form the canon with which other work attributed to him must be compared. In attributing the borders and illustrations of these volumes to Tory we are on sure ground, since in the first book of Hours we find his name, his mottoes and his device on the borders and on the illustrations, while as to *Champ fleury* he repeatedly refers to the illustrations as drawn by himself.

FIGS. 4 & 5. Pages from Tory's Cebes edition, 1529. (Reduced.)

This decorative material may be considered under three heads: (*a*) borders, (*b*) illustrations, and (*c*) initials.

(*a*) *Borders*. The Hours of 1525 is known in three issues, one with Colines's name and device on the title-page, a second with Tory's name and device, both dated XVII. Cal. Febr. 1525; the third has a title page in French bearing Tory's name and is dated 17 Janvier 1525. The first two issues have on the title-page the border of the *Epitaphia*. Each page (except the two pages of the privilege printed in gothic) is surrounded by a border of four pieces, the total number of different pieces being sixty-four. One is signed with Tory's name in full, others bear his various mottoes, such as, 'sic ut', 'non plus', 'mentibonae', 'deus occurrit', and others a version of his device of the *pot cassé*. The decoration is generally of a conventionalized floral style, but there are additional motives such as ribbons, trophies, fruits, and monograms relating to various members of the French royal family. These borders occur again in the Hours of 1531.[1] Some of them were lent to Colines, and are found in five books from his press (see Renouard's *Colines*). The Hours of 1527 in octavo printed by Colines has the title surrounded by rules. Each page of the text of this edition is surrounded by a four-piece border, there being 128 different pieces, while the cuts are placed within architectural borders, one of which is used on the title-page of the *Aediloquium*; both borders and cuts are again found in new editions by Oliver Mallard dated 1536 and 1538. In the

---

1. Also in the reprint by Oliver Mallard of 1542 and later editions by Thielman Kerver II, but by this time Tory's name and devices had been removed from most of the blocks.

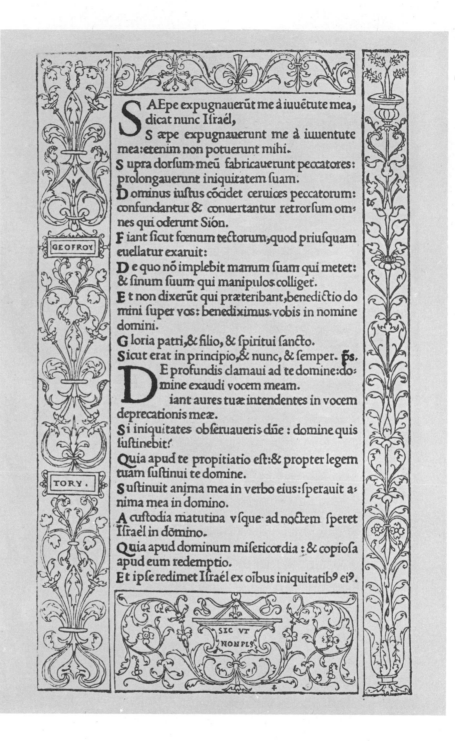

Fig. 6. Page from the first Tory Hours, 1525.

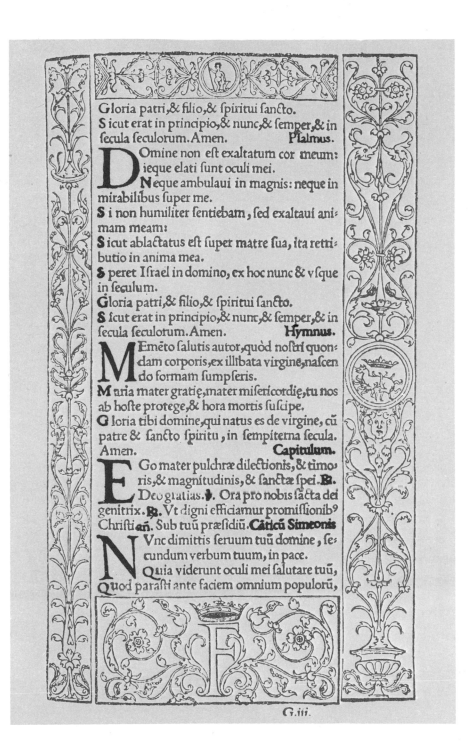

Gloria patri,& filio,& fpiritui fanfto.
Sicut erat in principio,& nunc,& femper,& in
fecula feculorum. Amen.   Pfalmus.

Omine non eft exaltatum cor meum:
ieque elati funt oculi mei.
Neque ambulaui in magnis: neque in
mirabilibus fuper me.
Si non humiliter fentiebam , fed exaltaui ani-
mam meam:
Sicut ablaftatus eft fuper matre fua, ita retri-
butio in anima mea.
Speret Ifrael in domino, ex hoc nunc & vfque
in feculum.
Gloria patri,& filio,& fpiritui fanfto.
Sicut erat in principio,& nunc,& femper,& in
fecula feculorum. Amen.   Hymnus.

Emeto falutis autor,quòd noftri quondam corporis,ex illibata virgine,nafcen
do formam fumpferis.
Maria mater gratie,mater mifericordie,tu nos
ab hofte protege,& hora mortis fufcipe.
Gloria tibi domine,qui natus es de virgine, cũ
patre & fanfto fpiritu , in fempiterna fecula.
Amen.   Capitulum.

Go mater pulchræ dileftionis,& timo-
ris,& magnitudinis,& fanftæ fpei.℞.
Deo gratias.℣. Ora pro nobis fafta dei
genitrix.℞. Vt digni efficiamur promiffionib⁹
Chriftiañ. Sub tuũ præfidiũ.Cãticũ Simeonis

Vnc dimittis feruum tuũ domine , fe-
cundum verbum tuum, in pace.
Quia viderunt oculi mei falutare tuũ,
Quod parafti ante faciem omnium populorũ,

G.iii.

FIG. 7. Page from the first Tory Hours, 1525.

Hours of 1529 (in 16mo) the pages containing the illustrations are surrounded by rules, but the other pages have new borders which are admirably adapted to the small size of the book. In the Hours of 1527 Tory's mottoes are found, though not in the edition of 1529, but the resemblance to the borders of the volume of 1525 is pronounced. We have omitted the Hours of 1527 in quarto printed by Simon du Bois; that is an exceptional volume and will be considered apart. The Hours of 1531, printed by Tory himself, has, in addition to the borders of the first Hours, five architectural borders, used also in the works by Guillaume Bochetel mentioned below. *Champ fleury* has the well-known border of the title-page, which was copied in London by Thomas Berthelet and is found in many English books, and the border of ribbon decoration with 'putti' surrounding the device on the last page, also copied in London. Finally the Cebes of 1529 (Figs. 4 and 5) has some new narrow borders which are little more than rules. The other books from his press, as far as known, show nothing new.[1]

All these borders are alike in being light designs on a white background in contrast with the traditional borders on a *criblé* background of the early Paris Hours. They contrast in colour and treatment. Tory's work is conventionalized and the motifs are inspired by Italian work, whereas the decoration of the early Hours is realistic and medieval in spirit.

(*b*) *Illustrations.* Tory designed three series of vignettes for Hours, intended for editions of three different sizes. The Hours of 1525 contains thirteen cuts, one bearing a Tory motto 'sic ut', 'non plus'; they measure 60 × 82 mm. The octavo Hours of 1527 has sixteen cuts measuring 42 × 65 mm. The Hours of 1529 in 16mo has 21 cuts measuring 36 × 62 mm. The Hours of 1531 has the cuts of the 1525 Hours and also two new cuts and two repeated from the editions of 1529. In *Champ fleury*, in addition to the diagrams of the Roman alphabet, 'l'homme scientifique', 'l'homme lettré', etc., there are two cuts, 'Hercules Gallicus' dated 1526, and 'Le Triumphe d'Apollo'. To these illustrations should be added his device in several varieties and a few small illustrations to the *Aediloquium*.

The cuts in the Tory Hours follow the traditional subjects of all Paris Hours, but the contrast in treatment is just as marked as in the case of the borders, Tory's drawings being made with few lines on a white ground and almost always without shading. They remind us irresistibly of Venetian book illustration, and especially of Francesco Colonna's *Hypnerotomachia Poliphili*. The fantastic style of this book would certainly appeal to the author of *Champ fleury*, and in the illustration on fol. 63 of the Aldine edition of 1499 we see the origin of the *pot cassé*. Not only did Tory follow methods the opposite of those used by the artists who decorated Pigouchet's Hours, but he also expressed in his illustrations a spirit which was strikingly different from all the earlier work. Instead of medieval naivety we find a self-consciousness which at times is almost sentimental; this is Tory's individual contribution, something which he did not bring from Italy. Finally we note that these cuts are essentially decorative; the crowded scene filled with detail was not attempted by Tory: an important point when we remember

1. Except the border of the Xenophon (Fig. 15).

that his was the age of the Holbeins, Urs Graf, Hans Weiditz and the other artists of South Germany whose mode of book decoration was threatening to establish itself in Paris.

We have so far omitted the Hours of 1527 in quarto printed by Simon du Bois. It is the only book in a gothic type with which Tory was connected and is otherwise unusual. It has the borders described in the privilege (quoted below) as *à la moderne*, which to a Frenchman of Tory's generation meant 'gothic', whilst renaissance work was described as *à l'antique*. The decorative scheme is realistic, showing birds, flowers, and animals, in this respect resembling the earlier borders. But the background is white and there is still a lightness of touch which would seem to be the natural result arrived at by the designer of the borders of the 1525 volume who was now trying his hand in the earlier style. The illustrations are thirteen in number and correspond in subject to those of Tory's first Hours. But if we compare, for example, the cut of the Flight into Egypt in the two books, it seems unlikely that both are by the same artist. Bernard, therefore, may be right in his opinion that these vignettes are not by Tory. In 1541 Oliver Mallard printed an Hours in octavo with borders *à la moderne*, closely resembling those of the 1527 edition, though on a smaller scale. There was another edition in 1542 with the cuts of the 1529 edition. These small borders appear again in an Hours for the use of Chartres printed in 1560 by Charles L'Angelier. Bernard assumed that they must have originally appeared in an edition printed by Tory, but no such edition has come to light and possibly never existed.

(c) *Initials*. In *Champ fleury*, besides the large roman initials, the construction of which is the main subject of the book, and the well-known L[1] in a square embodying the woodcutter's tools, there are at the end several plates of initials, including roman letters, *lettres tourneures* and *lettres fleuries*. Two of these sets form the decorative initials of the books from Tory's own press. The four-line roman initials will be found in the Eusebius of 1532 (their design will be referred to later) and the *lettres fleuries*[2] occur in a number of his books. The form of the large roman initials is exactly that of the large *criblé* initials used by Colines and Estienne. Estienne's set may be seen in his folio Latin Bibles of 1528 and 1532; and, as may be verified, the G bears the Lorraine cross, which led Bernard to assign the alphabet to Tory, an attribution very much strengthened by *Champ fleury* parallels.

This constitutes Tory's decorative work, the most important work which he did as far as book production is concerned. It is through these charming decorative designs that he influenced contemporary printers. If we examine the book of Denys Janot, one of the chief printers of illustrated books in the decade following Tory, we can trace the effect of his influence. It was not that Tory was directly copied but rather that he led the way to the study of Italian models and the style of the renaissance. While Tory was working in Paris the printers of Basle had suddenly acquired a European reputation: that their influence was considerable in Paris may be seen in the books of Pierre Vidoue, one of the busiest of the Paris printers. Yet at the very time when Paris books were showing copies of the work of Holbein and Urs Graf, Tory produced his decorative

1. This L and a similar A are found in the Bochetel books (cf. Fig. 10).
2. These were subsequently acquired by Denys Janot.

FIG. 8. Page from Tory's Hours, printed by Simon du Bois, 1527.

borders, etc., the 'colour' of which was more in harmony with the new romans and the italic founts then coming into fashion.

It is claimed for Tory that he not only designed the work which we have described but that in many cases he cut the blocks, and that indeed he made his livelihood mainly by the preparation of blocks for the Paris printers. Now there are two important passages in privileges granted to Tory which bear on this question. In the privilege printed in the Hours 1525, dated Avignon, September 23, 1524, we read: 'Nostre cher et bien ame maistre Geofroy Tory, libraire demourant a Paris, nous ha presentement faict dire et remonstrer que puis nagueres il ha faict et faict faire certaines histoires et vignettes a lantique, et pareillement unes autres a la moderne, pour icelles faire imprimer, et seruir a plusieurs usages d'heures, dont pour icelles il ha vacque certain long temps, et faict plusieurs grans fraitz, mises et despens'. In a second privilege printed in the Hours in quarto of 1527 and again in *Champ fleury*, dated 5 Sept. 1526, we read: 'ayāt regard et consideration aux peines, labeurs, fraiz & despens quil luy a cōuenu porter et soustenir, tāt a la cōposition dudit liure (*Champ fleury*), q̄ pour la taille desdites Histoires, Vignettes, Frises, Bordeures, Coronemēs et Entrelas, pour fair imprimer Heures . . .' Bernard was surely right in his contention that these passages refer to the preparation of blocks and not to the making of drawings. The reference in the first extract is to the material to be used in printing Hours. In the second extract the word *taille* certainly means the cutting of blocks; in the language of the day a woodcutter was a *tailleur d'images*. Therefore Tory himself cut some of these blocks; equally certainly his mark as a woodcutter was the Lorraine cross, as that mark is found many times in the Hours of 1525 and in *Champ fleury*. He is not known to have had any connexion with Lorraine, and why he should have adopted that signature remains a mystery. The fancied resemblance to the 'toret', the implement which has broken the vase in Tory's device, remains an unsatisfying explanation.

But if we accept the Lorraine cross as Tory's mark, are we to assume that all the blocks so marked which appear in French books between 1520 and 1535 were cut by him or at least under his supervision? It must be remembered that there appears to be no other claimant during those years, that the blocks in question all show the cross in the same form, and that the cross first appears about the time when we know from the document of 1523 that Tory was settled in Paris as a *libraire*. The earliest recorded appearance of the cross is on the title-page of a *Gradual* printed at Troyes by Jean Le Coq in 1521. This four-piece border with conventionalised decoration and winged 'putti' in white on a black ground is reminiscent of Italian work but cannot be claimed to be in Tory's individual manner, nor can it be established that Tory had direct dealings with this Troyes printer. Bernard mentions three devotional cuts marked with this cross in *Les hymnes communes de l'année*, translated by Nicolas Mauroy and printed by Le Coq's widow, undated,[1] but with a privilege dated 1527.

1. However, it is known that a number of blocks which originally belonged to Paris printers found their way to Troyes, and it is possible that these pieces were cut for the Paris press. The device of Le Coq (Sylvestre no. 875) was cut for the younger Le Coq and is not found before 1535. For the Lorraine cross in another form, see Blarrorivo, *Nanceidos opus*, 1518.

In 1522 we find blocks bearing the cross, in the form known from Tory's books, on title-borders in books printed by Colines, which may with some confidence be assigned to Tory. The *Commentarii initiarii in quatuor Euangelia* of Jacques Le Fèvre purporting to be printed at Meaux (Meldis), but certainly from the press of Colines, and dated June 1522, has a four-piece title-border signed with the cross. The book contains three large initials on a *criblé* ground, L, A, and I, which closely resemble the large alphabets of Estienne and Colines already referred to. In the same year Colines had another new border, described as *aux Lapins* (this was the sign of the first Estienne's shop and now Colines's address). This border, on a *criblé* ground, is found in a Melanchthon of July 1522, and frequently in later books of Colines. In 1523 we find a signed set of twelve cuts representing the twelve ages of man in a book of Hours printed by the widow of Thielman Kerver, dated May 20, 1523.[1] This set is an adaptation to a rather smaller scale of a set found in many editions of Kerver Hours, and the new designs are distinctly better than the originals. Of the same year is a cut of battle scenes in four compartments appearing on the title-page (and again in the text of the book) of the *Rozier Historial*, printed by François Regnault and dated February 10, 1522 (1523 new style). Under the year 1522, Bernard cites a title-border representing the medieval legend of Virgil, the story of Pyramus and Thisbe, and the judgment of Paris, done for Philippe Le Noir. I know it first in the *Histoire du Saint Graal* of Oct. 1523. This block also is a copy, a French version of a Basle woodcut after Urs Graf done for Conrad Resch who at this time was publishing at Paris. Here then we have four title-borders and thirteen illustrations all bearing the mark as it appears in Tory's books and appearing about the same time that he had rented a shop in Paris.

It has been objected that the number of blocks bearing this signature is too large to have been the work of one man or of one small establishment; but if we remember that Tory died in 1533 and we rule out all blocks which had not appeared by 1535 the number is not extraordinary. In addition to the above-described blocks there are three more title-borders (two for Colines and one for Gilles de Gourmont), twelve devices (several of them possibly done after Tory's death), and sixteen illustrations.[2] A full account of these blocks will be found in Bernard, who has, as far as I know, overlooked only two illustrations, that of Sacrobosco's *Textus de sphaera*, Colines, 1527 (this is a copy of the cut appearing in editions of Sacrobosco printed at Strasbourg), and a small cut of the Flight into Egypt in an oval frame, similar to the Ages of Man series, appearing in an Hours of G. Hardouin with a Calendar from 1528. It will be seen that for much of this work the preparation of blocks only is in question. Many of the devices are copies of earlier forms; one series of devotional cuts bears the initials L. R., those of the printer Louis Royer, who may also have been the designer. With the exception of the blocks made for Colines and Estienne, where something of the decorative quality and the grace of Tory's work can be traced, there is little here which adds to his reputation, and our conclusion is that this miscellaneous collection of woodcuts are

1. Bernard did not know this edition but refers to the cuts under the year 1528.
2. Of the cuts appearing in devotional books, representing about half of these illustrations, the exact number is uncertain.

FIG. 9. From Guillaume Bochetel, *Le sacre de la royne*, 1531.

FIG. 10. From Guillaume Bochetel, *Lentree de la royne*, 1531.

the designs of several artists of varying ability, but that all the blocks were prepared by Tory, or in his shop.[1]

For some twenty years after Tory's death new work continued to appear bearing this same signature of the Lorraine cross. Evidently this side of Tory's business was continued by some artist or artists unknown to us. As an instance of the excellent quality of some of the work from this *atelier* we may cite the cuts of the Dukes of Milan which appeared in a book by Paolo Giovio printed by Estienne in 1546. I say from the *atelier*, because it must be insisted that while cuts appearing some ten years or so after Tory's death may show his influence they cannot be attributed to him, unless evidence is produced which will explain why the blocks should have lain unused for such a period. Instances of this are naturally rare.[2] Another piece of work which is almost invariably ascribed to Tory is the set of initials and headpieces which accompany the *Grecs du Roi*.[3] When one considers how perfectly the decorative material harmonizes with the types one can hardly doubt that it was cut by an artist who had the types before him; and Tory died in 1533.

Other examples of inaccurate or doubtful attribution to Tory are the two books of Hours printed by Colines in 1543. Borders from the quarto edition are reproduced in Courboin, op. cit., as Geofroy Tory's work in spite of the fact that some of the borders bear dates 1536, 1537, and 1539. The detail in these cuts, including that of the illustrations, is rather over-elaborated, and decorative motifs of the late Renaissance appear such as are not elsewhere found in Tory. In both these Hours arabesque borders occur, perhaps the earliest appearance in France of such decoration apart from the pattern books.[4] Certainly Tory was familiar with the arabesque (cf. his bindings)[5] but whether he ever cut the arabesque as a motif for book decoration cannot be proved. One woodcut which contains no signature may be considered here. The Diodorus, translated by Antoine Macault and issued by Tory's widow in 1535, contains a fine woodcut of Macault presenting his book to King Francis I, copied from a miniature in Macault's original manuscript. This cut is also one of Courboin's reproductions. The reasons for assigning it to Tory are that the book was issued by his widow (the book was probably printed by Pierre Vidoue) and possibly had already been planned by Tory.

The illustration reminds one in its detail of the work of contemporary German artists and is quite unlike Tory's manner. The drawing is much superior to that of Tory's recognized designs; in fact our artist was never more than an amateur with the pencil. It is possible that Tory cut the block, but if so it is strange that he did not sign it. Our explanation of the cut being used in the Diodorus is that it belonged to the translator,

1. A systematic study of French woodcuts of the period, at present lacking, might extend our knowledge of the original designers.

2. Although cf. the Holbein Dance of Death and Old Testament cuts, first printed at Lyons in 1537, but cut at Basle some ten years earlier.

3. A document is extant relating to payment made to Garamond for the engraving of these types in 1541, and the first book printed in one of the new founts was a Eusebius of 1544.

4. One of the small arabesque borders was used on the title-page of a book by Oronce Fine, Colines, 1542. Arabesques are also found in a Cebes printed by Denys Janot in 1543.

5. Tory was not a practical binder, but had two or three blocks designed for covers, apparently in the last years of his life when he was a printer.

Figs. 11 & 12. Pages from Tory's Hours, printed by Oliver Mallard, 1542. (Reduced.)

Macault, who made use of it again in an edition of Cicero's *Philippicae*, also translated by him and printed by the De Marnefs at Poitiers in 1549.[1] In the preface to the Xenophon of 1531 there is mention of a Diodorus and a Thucydides to be sold at the *pot cassé*; these editions have not survived, that is if they were printed by Tory.

1. There are four other signatures, in addition to the Lorraine cross, found in French books and manuscripts which Bernard connected with Tory, two almost certainly wrongly and the other two questionably. (1) In a few editions of Hours published by Simon Vostre about 1515 are three cuts signed with a gothic G or a G and F. They are striking illustrations copied in part from Dürer. The style is not Tory's nor is there any evidence that he was cutting blocks by 1515; he was probably in Italy at that time. (2) Another G appears on some very fine miniatures in two manuscripts, *Les Commentaires de César* and *Les Triomphes de Pétrarque*, dating from 1519 and 1520. This is now held to be the work of Godofredus Batavus. Some of the miniatures are signed 'Godefroy'. (See the article under Batavus in Thieme and Becker's *Allgemeines Lexikon*.) These manuscripts were the basis of Bernard's reasons for supposing that Tory was a miniaturist and that he was back in Paris by 1519. A number of copies of Tory's Hours are extant which have been coloured. As the colouring is done in the same style it has been inferred that they were issued from Tory's shop so coloured. This is very possible and to that extent Tory may have been a miniaturist. (3) A few woodcuts signed G. T. appear in books printed at Troyes. I know these only in some very poor reproductions in Varlot's *L'illustration de l'ancienne imprimerie Troyenne*. The amateurish appearance of these cuts may be due in part to the reproductions. (4) About 1525 there appear in the books of Pierre Gringore several cuts bearing the monogram Gand and a small s with the Lorraine cross attached. Bernard interpreted this as 'Godofredus sculpsit'. In a book of Gringore's of 1521 there is an unsigned cut which is clearly one of the same set. This monogram, in a slightly different form, is found on a set of twelve plates representing the twelve labours of Hercules. Various interpretations of the monogram have been suggested (see Nagler's *Monogrammisten*) and the problem is still unsolved. As to the cuts in the Gringore books, anyone familiar with Tory's work will find it hard to credit that he had anything to do with such hideous and ill-executed blocks.

Eus in adiutoriũ
meum intende.
Dominę ad adiu
uãdũ me feſtina

Gloria pa. Sicut erat. Hyᵒ.
Emẽto ſalutis auctor,
cꝗ noſtri quondã cor-
poris: ex illibata virgĩe, na-

FIGS. 13 & 14. Pages from Tory's Hours, printed by Oliver Mallard, 1542. (Reduced.)

Tory tells us that he formed the idea of his *Champ fleury* in 1523 on the *jour de la fête aux rois*. Its original title was *L'art et science de la deue et vraie proportion des lettres Attiques*. We have seen that one of the cuts is dated 1526 and the book finally appeared on April 28, 1529. The contents are described as follows: Book I. 'L'exhortation a mettre et or-donner la langue françoise'; Book II. 'L'invention des lettres Attiques'; Book III. 'Sont deseignées toutes les dites lettres'. The work is extremely discursive and by no means follows the arrangement announced. There is much on the origin of letters in all the books, and passages relating to the French language are scattered through the work. By insisting that his countrymen should write in French, that the French language was as worthy of study as Latin or Greek and by the reforms which he proposed in French orthography, Tory holds a very important place in the history of French phi-lology. With the exception of one book of Hours all the books printed by Tory were in French, the majority of them being translations from classical texts made by himself. This fact marks him out as a man of original ideas among the humanists of his generation. In his affection for allegorical explanations and his pedantic display of learning he was a man of the Middle Ages. Like all the renaissance writers on the form of letters he discovers a relation between the proportions of the human body and the proportions of letters. Tory accepts the dictum derived from Vitruvius that the head is one-tenth of the body; to this he adds an allegorical connexion with Apollo and the nine Muses. All letters are derived from I and O; the mythological story of Io is brought in to account for this fundamental principle. When he comes, in the third book, to describe the method by which the roman letters are to be constructed, he does this very briefly and fills up

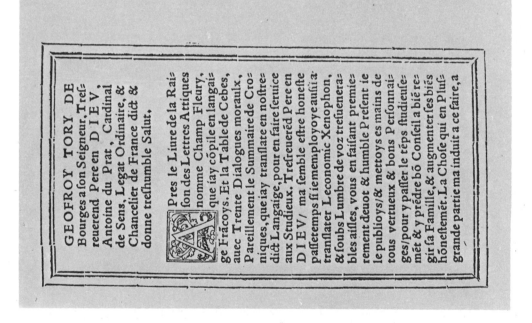

FIGS. 15 & 16. Pages from Xenophon, *Science pour senrichir honnestement*. Geofroy Tory, 1531. (Slightly reduced.)

his text by many quotations from ancient authors relating to pronunciation and other matters only remotely connected with his subject. The really relevant part of the book is very short. Tory refers to the work of Luca Pacioli, Sigismondo Fanti, Lodovico Vicentino and Dürer, condemning the Italians because they took nine to one as the relation of the head to the body. He accuses, probably wrongly, Pacioli of stealing his designs from Leonardo da Vinci and criticizes his letters in an arbitrary manner. His own method was to take a square, divide it into a hundred parts and to construct the letters with a rule and compass. The same means had been employed by his predecessors, but the actual design of his letters is his own, and in spite of its mathematical foundation is ultimately based on personal taste.

This was the first French attempt to put out a design of the roman alphabet and must have been of great interest to all the engravers of punches. Its indirect influence may have been important in interesting printers in the roman letter and confirming the already growing tendency against gothic, but of any more direct influence there is no evidence. Bernard quotes some commendatory verses by contemporaries, Antoine de Saix and an Englishman, Leonard Coxe. Apparently *Champ fleury* had a slow sale, for about the year 1536 Oliver Mallard, Tory's successor, brought out a re-issue of the original sheets, reprinting sig. A in a 'Garamond' roman. However, a new edition in octavo was ventured upon in 1549. In no case was the design followed by the men who engraved the new 'Garamond' romans in the years immediately following the appearance of *Champ fleury*. One has only to compare the capitals in the 'canon' size of Estienne's roman in the folio Bible of 1532 with the plate of roman letters at the end of Tory's book to realise that Garamond did not take *Champ fleury* as a model. Tory was committed to a square letter; the width of his M is actually greater than its height.

In considering Tory's career as a printer we are faced at the outset with the difficulty of deciding when he began to print. Bernard gives the Cebes of October 5, 1529, as his first book. There is no definite information in the book itself; from it we learn that the book is 'a vendre audict lieu (i. e. Tory's shop) par ledict translateur (Tory) et par Jean Petit'. The Hours in 16mo of February 8, 1529 (1530 N. S.), has in the colophon 'apud Gotofridum Torinum'. The Egnatius of April 13, 1529 (1530 N. S.), is described as being printed 'pour Maistre Geofroy Tory de Bourges'. The colophon of the next book, the *Procession de Soissons*, is ambiguous; the words are 'acheue dimprimer le XXIX iour Daoust M.D.XXX et est vendre par Maistre Geofroy Tory'; and so on until we come to the Xenophon of 1531, which is definitely described as being printed '*par* Maistre Geofroy Tory'. All the subsequent books with imprint have the *par* and not *pour*. If we interpret this strictly it should follow that Tory was only the publisher and not the printer of the earlier books. But in fact the Cebes and the Egnatius are in no way different from the later productions; all the material and method of lay-out are Tory's. The explanation may be that at first he owned no press and had his books printed in some other office. But, if so, he not only supplied the material but made himself responsible for every detail. For all practical purposes these books may be regarded as Tory's, including *Champ fleury*. Bernard states expressly that *Champ fleury* was printed by Gourmont, while the colophon says that it was printed 'pour Maistre

Geofroy Tory de Bourges et pour Giles Gourmont'. None of the material belonged to Gourmont, not even the Greek type. Of that type, Proctor said that it was like the early Greek used in Germany before Froben. I see no reason why we should not accept *Champ fleury*, which appeared on 28 April 1529, as the first book printed by Tory.

Tory owned a very small amount of typographical material. He had some rules (the pages of the Egnatius and the Xenophon are ruled), a set of *lettres fleuries*, sets of two-line and four-line initials after the design of the plate in *Champ fleury*, and two founts of roman type. The type of *Champ fleury*, an 11-point roman, is the type in which the great majority of his books are printed. It is akin to many other roman founts in use at Paris in the first quarter of the sixteenth century. We may compare it with the roman used by Guillaume Le Rouge twenty years before Tory began to print. An even closer parallel may be found in a type of Gilles de Gourmont; cf. a Guinterus of 1527. Many of the letters in the two founts are indistinguishable. The chief difference seems to be that Tory's is cast on a wider body. Tory felt the need of more light in his pages and obtained it in part by this method. His larger roman, a 17-point, used in the Euse-bius and the *Ordonnances du Roy* of 1532, is also cast on a wide body and is also of the family of the earlier Paris romans.

There are three books issued by Tory which show neither of these types, the Hours in 16mo of 1529 [1530 N. S.] and two little books by Guillaume Bochetel describing the coronation at Saint Denis of Queen Léonore and her entry into Paris early in 1531. These are among the finest Tory books, partly by reason of their decoration and partly because they are printed in types of a better design than those of Tory's own press. The type of the Hours in 16mo is a roman of about 9-point and appears to be identical with that of a little book of Hours printed by Pierre Vidoue for Germain Hardouin in 1526. Nor does Tory make any direct claim to have printed the book in question; its colophon reads '*apud* Gotofridum Torinum', whereas the Hours in 4to of the following year, actually printed by Tory, is described as being issued '*ex officina* Gotofredi Torini'.

In the two pamphlets by Bochetel – the *Coronnement* of 24 pages and the *Entrée* of 48 pages – we find three sizes of roman type. There are a few lines in a fount of about 10-point; the colophon of both books and various other passages are in an 11-point roman, which is the type of Tory's first Book of Hours printed by Colines and issued in January 1525. The main text of both books is printed in the Terentianus fount of Colines, the earliest 'Garamond' roman. The Terentianus appeared in November 1531, whilst a Galen of the same year has no month date. The colophons of the Tory books read 'acheue dimprimer le xvi iour de Mars MDXXX [1531 N. S.]. Et est a vendre a Paris par Maistre Geofroy Tory', for the *Coronnement*; and 'acheue dimprimer le Mardy Neufuiesme iour de May MDXXXI' for the *Entrée*. Since at any rate two of the types were Colines, the inference is that the books were printed by him. Although Tory was not yet the King's printer – he first describes himself as such in the Xenophon of July 1531 – he must have been commissioned by the Court to prepare these two

1. On p. 148 of No. 5 of *The Fleuron*, this fount is shown next to a pre-Garamond roman of Robert Estienne.

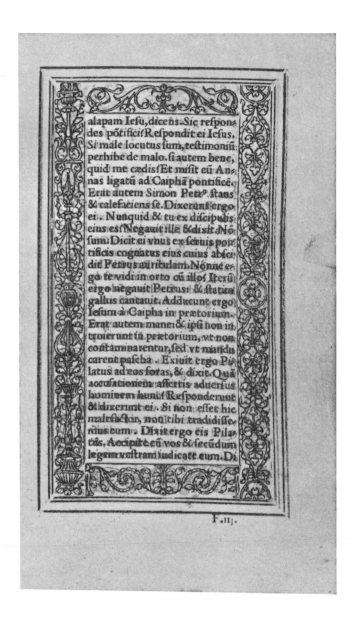

Fig. 17. Page from Tory's Hours, printed by
Simon de Colines, 1527.

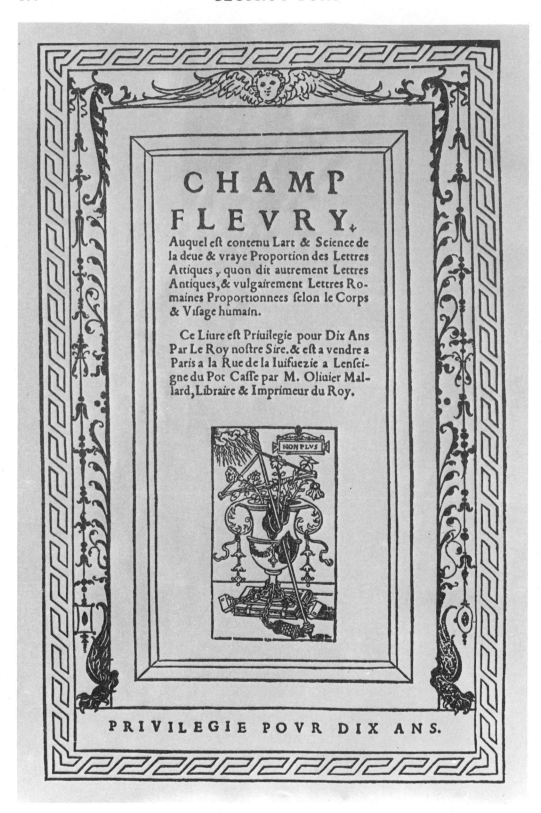

FIG. 18. Title-page from the re-issue of *Champ fleury*, 1536. (Slightly reduced.)

FIG. 19. The earliest known piece signed with the Lorraine cross. From
the Troyes Gradual, 1521. (Reduced.)

books. He very wisely entrusted the printing to the foremost Paris printer, and he was
fortunate enough to find ready, in the Terentianus fount, one of the best types of the
sixteenth century. In view of the colophons of the books, and Tory's other dealings with
Colines, this seems to us a more probable explanation of the procedure than the sup-
position that Tory borrowed the types and printed the books himself. In any case the
point of importance, in our endeavour to estimate Tory's influence on typography, is to
name the designer of these founts. The Terentianus fount, the immediate predecessor
of the true 'Garamond', is of great interest in the history of typography; the other
types found in the two books in question are hardly less so, since they are of the same
school.[1]

The type of the Hours of 1525 represents the first break from the traditional Paris
romans, a break which culminated in the work of Garamond. There is no direct evidence as to its designer. It is not unlikely to have been Colines himself. As far as
Tory is concerned, it can but be remarked that the evidence of the books which he
undoubtedly printed is against the claims which Bernard made on his behalf. For if
Tory designed either of these types it is inconceivable that he would have remained
content with his two old-fashioned romans. At the very time when the Paris printers
were taking up italics (there is no italic in any of Tory's books) and the new better designed romans, Tory followed a path of his own and remained outside the new movement. His books are original and the smaller ones are at least very pleasant volumes.
Of his most ambitious production, the folio Eusebius, little good can be said, so poor
is the presswork. Of direct Tory influence on French typography there is no trace.
His use of rules, his arrangement of a title-page with its small capital letters after the
design in *Champ fleury*, the resort to leading as in the *In Lodoicae mortem epitaphia*, were
all peculiar to himself. Fashion favoured the canon size of the 'Garamond' letter on
title-pages, the use of leading belonged to an earlier generation, and the appearance
of rules is very rare in French books of the period.

The claims which Bernard made for Tory as an engraver of types rest on the epitaph,
written a century and a half after Tory's death, by one Nicolaus Catharinus on informa-

1. The whole subject of French sixteenth-century founts and their origin was exhaustively treated by Paul
Beaujon (Beatrice Warde) in her lengthy study printed in No. 5 of *The Fleuron*, and it is only for the sake of
completeness that I am trespassing on this ground.

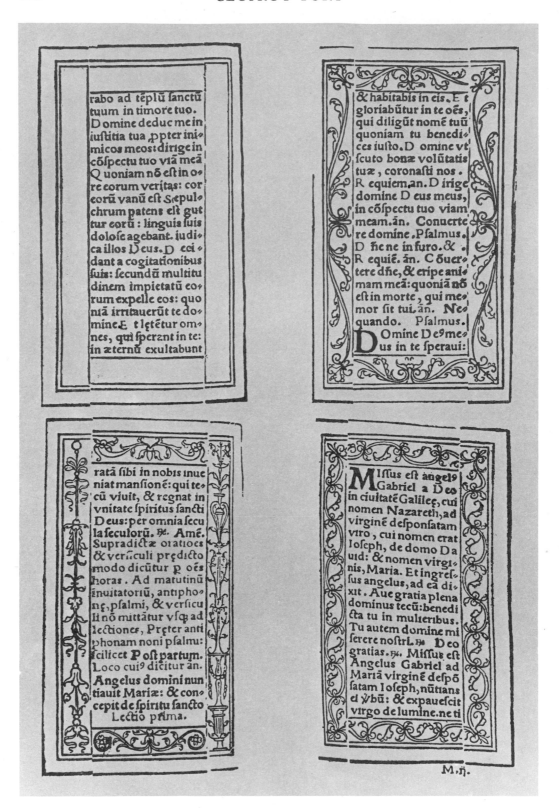

FIGS. 20–23. Pages from the Tory Hours, 1529 [1530].

tion supplied by a printer of Bourges, Jean Toubleau, who claimed descent from Tory. The epitaph in Latin verse is dated 1684, and gives a summary of Tory's career. It contains the lines: 'Primus omnium de re typographica sedulo disseruerit, Litterarum sive caracterum dimensiones ediderit, Et Garamundum calcographum principem edocuerit, Viri boni offcio, quoad devixit, Anno M.D.L. semper defunctus.' Toubeau's inaccurate information as to the date of Tory's death does not strengthen the value of the tradition relating to Garamond; but Bernard deduces from this document that, since Garamond was all his life engaged solely in the engraving of types, there is nothing in which Tory can have instructed him except type-cutting. Therefore Tory himself was an engraver of types and cut the new roman and italic letters of Colines and Estienne. But there is also a tradition, according to Lottin, that Garamond was at work by 1510. Perhaps we had better regard each tradition as equally valueless. We may suppose that Garamond was Tory's pupil in the sense that he was interested in the roman letter by the study of *Champ fleury*; but, as we have seen, his founts exhibit no trace whatever of acquaintance with Tory's models, and at the most Tory may have been responsible for urging Garamond to avoid gothic. It is at least possible that Tory did engrave types and there is a passage in *Champ fleury* which shows that he was familiar with the process; but it would be rash to credit him with more than the two romans in which the books from his press were printed – and even those cannot be proved to have come from his hands.

[1928]

ORONCE FINE AS AN ILLUSTRATOR
OF BOOKS

Oᴿᴼɴᴄᴇ Fɪɴᴇ, or Finé, is well known as a writer on mathematics, astronomy, and geography: but there is nowhere any connected account of his work as a decorator of books. In Nagler's *Monogrammisten* (ɪᴠ. 2916) under O. F. there is an incomplete account of the illustrations to the *Protomathesis*, and there are some valuable notes in the Fairfax Murray Catalogue of Early French Books. There is no entry under 'Fine' in Thieme and Becker's *Allgemeines Lexicon* and none of any moment in the earlier dictionaries of artists. L. Gallois, *De Orontio Finaeo*, Paris, 1890, gives us the biographical details relating to Fine, but is chiefly concerned with his importance as a geographer and with his three maps, two of the world and one of France. The decoration of the two maps of the world (there are reproductions in Gallois) are of interest from the point of view of this article, as there is a close similarity to some of the work here described.

Fine was born in 1494, the son of a doctor, at Briançon in the Dauphiné. He came to Paris to study and lived there most of his life as a teacher of mathematics. For twenty-five years, until his death in October 1555, he was Royal Professor of Mathematics. In the edition of his *De Rebus mathematicis*, printed by M. Vascosan in 1556, there is a Latin poem by his friend Antoine Mizauld, which is the ultimate source of most of the information as to his life. From statements of his son, Jean Fine, and of Mizauld, we know that Fine designed figures for his mathematical works. In the *De mundi sphaera*, Vascosan, 1555, Mizauld calls him 'Mathematicarum professor et illustrator', and in the preface to the *De rebus mathematicis*, 1556, he writes: 'librum una cum figuris, quas paulo ante quam abiret, ingeniosa manu ad unguem pinxerat, M. Vascosano . . . committere nihil sum cunctatus'. But that Fine did more than design mathematical and astronomical figures is established by his book *Protomathesis*.

This is a collected edition of his work up to that date and was printed in folio by Gerhard Morrhé for himself and Jean Pierre. On the title-page is an architectural border with a scene in the pediment depicting Hercules and the Hydra, below which is Fine's motto 'Virescit vulnere virtus'. At the foot on the left is a gothic L, presumably a wood-cutter's mark; the words 'Hanc Author proprio pingebat marte figuram' are printed on the border in italic type; on the verso of the title-page are the words 'Omnia decentibus figuris ab ipsomet authore depictis illustrata'. The crowned dolphin is found on the border as a decorative motive and, as we shall see, on much of Fine's other work, no doubt suggested by his birth place, the Dauphiné, and out of compliment to the Dauphin of France. The general style of the border is quite distinctive, and closely resembles the architectural border round Fine's second map of the world published about 1536 (see Gallois). In addition to mathematical figures the book contains the following decorative work. AA2 recto is surrounded by borders (the one at the top has the arms of the Dauphin, two syrens supporting a shield on which are the fleur de lys and dolphin), and the initials O. F. (the border is used several times in the book and in later works of Fine

ARITH. PRACT. LIB. IIII. FO. 41.

ad ultimam eiuſdem: aut ſi uelis, per mediorum ſubtractionem, extremorum
ratio eadem utrobique reperitur. Exempli gra
tia, ſint primi ordinis quãtitates A,B,C, ſecundi ue
rò D,E,F: ſintcp A,B & D,E ſeſqualtera,B C uerò et
E F,dupla,uel A B,& E F dupla, B C autẽ atcp D E
ſeſqualtera rationis habitudine proportionatæ.Si
igitur A ad B,ſicut D ad E,& B ad C,uelut E ad F,uel A ad B,ſicut E ad F,& ḃ ad C,
ueluti D ad E: ſubſumatur,ergo ſicut A ad C,ita D ad F. Prædictas ſex rationum
acceptiones,ſpeciesùe proportionum,demonſtrat Euclides quinto geometricorum
elementorũ:ad quem,ſi plura deſyderes,confugere poteris.Hæc enim ſunt princi
paliores,& noſtro ſuſcepto negocio ſatis utcuncp facientes, rationum atcp propor
tionum diffinitiones:quare de his in præſentiarum eſto ſatis.

De additione,atcp ſubtractione duarum quaruncuncp rationum aliunicẽ:
ſeu de productione rationis,ex duabus quibuſuis rationibus generatæ. Caput.II.

ON PARVVM VIDETVR ADFERRE IVVAMEN IIS,
qui circa magnam Ptholemæi conſtructionem (quam uocant Alma
geſtum) ſepiuſculè uerſantur,in promptu cognoſcere: quæ nam ratio
ex duabus quibuſuis oblatis,& inuicem adiunctis,mutuóue ſubtractis
quantitatum rationibus componatur.potiſſimum quum per regulam ſex propor
tionalium magnitudinum,ab eodem Ptholemæo ſubtiliter excogitam, & à nobis
in proximum clarius elucidandam,operæprecium ſit,eaſdem ſex quantitates inui
cem proportionales,ad quaternarium reducere numerum:& in uſum illius con
uertere regulæ,quæ tribus oblatis numeris,quartum docet inuenire proportiona
lem.quemadmodum proximo capite,ipſam quatuor proportionalium ex primen
do regulam,ſigillatim manifeſtum efficiemus.

IN PRIMIS ITAQVE, generatam ex duabus quibuſcuncp rationibus
inuicem adiunctis doceamus inuenire rationem:ſitcp hæc generalis & ſemper ob
ſeruanda regula.Propoſitis duabus quibuſuis quantitatum rationibus,in unam ra
tionem componendis,ducito primum terminum unius,in primum alterius termi
num:& productum facito primum terminum conſurgentis inde rationis. Deinde
multiplicato ſecũdum alterutrius terminum,per terminum ſecundũ reliquæ:pro
ductumcp ſtatuatur ſecũdus eiuſdem compoſitæ rationis terminus.Nã hoc modo
cõſurgẽtẽ ex duabus ‚ppoſitis rationẽ habebis:ab eo ſemper denominãdã numero,
q ex utriuſcp ‚ppoſitarȝ rationũ inter ſeſe multiplicatis denominatoribus cõponeƫ.

Sint primum in exemplum duæ rationes multiplices, A quidem ad B dupla, &
C ad D tripla:ex quarum compoſitione, reſultantem cogaris habere rationem.
Duc igitur A in C, aut è contra: & fiat B numerus,quem
ſubſcribito,pro primo ipſius producendæ rationis termi
no.Deinde multiplicato B in D, uel è diuerſo:& conſurgat
numerus F, pro ſecundo eiuſdem productæ rationis termino collocandus.Cõclu
das itacp,rationem A ad B, unà cum ratione C ad D: efficere rationem E ad F. At
qui ratio A ad B dupla, C autẽ ad D tripla ſuſcepta eſt:igitur ſi multiplicaueris 2,
ipſius duplæ rationis denominatorem,per 3 denominatorem ipſius triplæ , fient 6
denominator eiuſdem compoſitæ rationis.quapropter E ad F ſextuplã dicetur ha
bere rationem,ex additione duplæ cum tripla conſtitutam. Ex his facilè patet, ex
duabus rationibus duplis,generari quadruplam;ex duabus autem triplis,nocuplã;
ex binis uerò quadruplis,ſedecuplam.&ſc.

F I Dentur

FIG. 1. A Page from Oronce Fine's *Protomathesis*. Gérard Morrhé &
Johann Petri, Paris, 1532. (Reduced.)

FIG. 2. A page from Oronce Fine's *De mundi sphaera libri V*.
Simon de Colines, Paris, 1542.

printed by Simon de Colines). The borders at the sides are each in two parts; at the foot are two further strips upside down. On AA8 verso is a cut of a celestial globe with figures of Urania and the author below, on a criblé background. In the rings from which the globe is suspended are the initials O. F. The cut is repeated on f. 101 verso, with the name Orontius added in type on the scroll opposite the author, left empty on AA8 verso. The cut was used again in the *De mundi sphaera*, Simon de Colines, 1542, in folio (the connexion of this cut with one in Regiomontanus, *Epitome in Almagistum Ptolomei*, J. Haman, Venice, 1496, is pointed out by Fairfax Murray.) On f. 1 recto, and repeated several times in the book, there is a headpiece with mathematical instruments and the initials O. F. On f. 157 recto there are four border pieces at the sides, one being the same as on AA2 recto, and three new. The book is further decorated with three sets of initials; 1. a large set, measuring 56 × 56 mm, on a white background, of which there are here eleven letters (C.D.H.I.M.N.O.P.Q.R. and V.), the O bearing the initials O. F. and a portrait of Oronce Fine in the centre.[1] Dolphins are used as a decorative motive, while the conventionalized floral decoration is very similar to that of Fine's first map of the world, dated 1531, and printed in Grynaeus, A. Augereau for J. Petit and G. Du Pré, 1532. (See Gallois.) These initials are found also in another folio printed by Morrhé in this same year, the *Genialium dierum libri sex* of A. ab Alexandro; they passed into the hands of Vascosan who used them frequently down to 1554. 2. A smaller set of figure initials on a white background which also passed to Vascosan and were used by him as a Greek set, with the addition of the necessary letters. They are found also at Basle,[2] but whether they were originally derived from Basle (the printer Morrhé had other connexions with Basle, e. g. his Greek and italic types) or designed by Fine is doubtful. 3. A small figure initial A on a black background is used several times; this is in the Basle style but is not in Schneeli and Heitz.

The *Protomathesis* is the most important of the books illustrated by Fine, but not the earliest. On the verso of the title-page of Georgius Peurbachius, *Theorice nove planetarum*, J. Petit and R. Chaudière, 1515, is a cut of a celestial globe with figures of Astronomia and Ptolemy below; on the border at the foot is the monogram O. F. interlaced and a crowned dolphin. That this monogram is that of Fine is strengthened by its appearance in the same form on a globe in his *La Theorique des cielz*, J. Pierre, 1528. The cut was used again in various editions of Sacrobosco's *De sphaera*, printed by Colines, 1521, 1527, 1534, and 1538.[3] About this time Fine is found doing editorial work for the Paris printers, e. g. J. de Bassolis, *In tertium sententiarum opus*, F. Regnault and J. Frellon, 1517 (Fine's preface is dated 'Idibus Februarii, 1517'), and J. Martinez Siliceo, *Ars arithmetica*, H. Estienne, 1519. In N. le Huen, *Des sainctes peregrinations de Jherusalem*, F. Regnault, 1517, a work which is partly a translation from Breydenbach, there is a ballade containing the anagram Orontius Fine Physicus, printed on a folding woodcut of knights being blessed by the Pope. In Regnault's edition of Breydenbach of 1522, in addition to many old illustrations from various sources, there is one new cut of

1. See also Butsch, *Die Bücherornamentik der Renaissance*.
2. See Schneeli and Heitz, *Initialen von Hans Holbein*, 1900, No. 11.
3. See Renouard, *Simon de Colines*, p. 23.

CANON XVI.   61

partes ipfius primi numeri, uertuntur in partes 7, & minuta

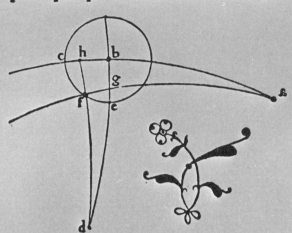

11,25,ferè. Tã
tus eft igitur
finus rectus
quæfitę ęqua
tionis *f g*: cu
ius arcus of-
fendetur ha-
bere gradº 6,
& min. 52,58.
Atqui totidē
partium, atq;
minutorũ ex
peritur effe,
quæ in tabu-
lis pafsim di-

uulgatis continetur æquatio, præfato 50 graduum refpondēs
argumento. Et quoniam manifeftum eft, arcum *b h*, maiorē
effe arcu *f g*: non eft igitur idem arcus *b h*, quæfita æquatio
ipfius octauæ fphæræ, fed præfatus arcus *f g*. Haud aliter pe-
riculum facere licebit, de cæterorum quorũcunque argumen
torum æquationibus. Hinc poterit ipfa æquationum octauę
fphæræ tabula, quæ in minutis fecundis fæpius peccare uide-
tur, recenti atque fidọ magis numerari calculo.

CANON XVI.

Q Vantum diftet uerum initium fignorum o-
ctauæ fphæræ, ab ipfo tabulari fignorũ exor-
dio, tandem fupputare.

   1   Hic fupponimus Alphonfinam, & omnium fequẽtium
pofitionem de motu octauæ fphæræ, ueram ac ftabilem effe,
donec meliorem obtinuerimus excogitationem. Neque in
præfentiarum intendimus ipfam edocere theoricam, utpo-
te, quæ pafsim diuulgata, & luculenter à quamplurimis tra-
dita eft: Sed ex ipfa fanè quàm intellecta motus octaui orbis
theorica, calculum Alphonfinum reuocare ad uernalẽ Ecli-

Fɪɢ. 3. A Page from the later edition of *De mundi sphaera libri V* (Michel Vascosan, Paris, 1555).
The flower ornament in the right-hand corner of the diagram is very
typical for Fine's style of illustration.

Jerusalem signed O. F. interlaced and the crowned dolphin. The second folio border of Josse Badius, used from 1529, was attributed to Oronce Fine by Butsch, and with good reason. Fine's edition of Euclid, printed by Colines in 1536, has a title-border on a criblé background, with four allegorical figures at the corners, Geometria, Astronomia, Arithmetica, and Musica. Although the border is not signed, the appearance of dolphins among the decoration, the fact that the border was used by Simon de Colines only for Fine's works (cf. the *Arithmetica*, 1542, and the *De mundi sphaera*, 1542, in folio), and the general style make the attribution most probable. The heraldic initial D in the Euclid bears the name Orontius; the initial itself is of the same design as the D in the set of large initials cut for Colines by Geofroy Tory, but the new decoration is presumably Fine's. Another folio title-border used by Colines for mathematical works, as in F. Sarzosus, *In aequatorem planetarum libri duo*, 1526, a border of knotted work with allegorical figures, is somewhat similar and has at the foot a shield with the Dauphin's arms. The head-pieces in this volume are also in the style of Oronce Fine. A third border of knotted work, without the allegorical figures, used on the title page of the *Quadratura circuli*, Colines, 1544, is practically the same design. The dealings between Fine and Colines seem to have been as numerous as between that printer and Geofroy Tory. The title-page of the octavo edition of the *De mundi sphaera*, Colines, 1542, has a four-piece border of pure arabesque work. This border forms one of a series used in a rare book, the small book of Hours issued by Colines in 1543. The borders are usually assigned to Tory, though he died ten years before this date. It is not impossible that the designer was Fine, who with his fondness for leaf-forms and 'petit fers' as decorations for his mathematical figures would be attracted by the arabesque. In a later book, *De duodecim caeli domiciliis*, Vascosan, 1553, there is a folding plate which is richly decorated with arabesques and the usual dolphins. It was perhaps because of the frequent occurrence of leaf-forms on Fine's figures that Weale suggested that he may have designed plates for bindings, although he attributed no particular design to Fine's hand.[1]

As a decorator of books Fine belongs entirely to the Renaissance and has nothing of the medieval manner of the previous generation at Paris. He took his dolphins, salamanders, and grotesques, and his architectural details from the art of the Italian renaissance, and yet the result is very different from that obtained by his contemporary Tory, who was inspired by the same source. Much of Fine's work has the appearance of being an imitation of metal work, and it is this fact which makes his decorative style so easily recognizable.

[1928]

---

1. In *Bookbindings at South Kensington Museum*, 1898, p. LXXVIII.

THE 'ANTWERP' ORNAMENTS

PRINTERS' flowers of the style illustrated in this article were in full bloom in the second half of the sixteenth century, and they were first cast about the year 1560. Joseph Moxon, typefounder, printer and publisher in London, and the first historian of the art of punch cutting, wrote that in his day, i. e. about 1680, they were considered old-fashioned and were not then much used. Type ornaments of a kind date back to the very early days of printing, but the building up of arabesque units into intricate borders, head- and tail-pieces belongs to the Elizabethan age in this country. There is contemporary evidence, contained in a rhyming chronicle by Marcus van Vaernewyck published at Ghent in 1568, that the French type-cutter Robert Granjon was the first to cast such units.

We may distinguish three stages in the development of arabesque flowers. First come the pattern books in which many artists of the sixteenth century presented their designs for the use of craftsmen in decoration. We may cite the book of the Nuremberg artist Peter Floetner, printed at Zürich in 1549, which includes some arabesque patterns cut on wood, and very similar in design to our particular flowers. The second stage is the application of these designs to the decoration of printed books in general. Another book printed at Zürich, in 1559, the *Romanorum imperatorum imagines*, is decorated with some of the actual woodcut patterns used in Floetner's book. Further examples of this second stage may be found in the books of Jean de Tournes of Lyons, many of which have arabesque borders round the title-pages and whose pages are lavishly decorated with arabesque head-pieces and fleurons. All this material was probably designed by Bernard Salomon, the artist whose chief work is to be found in the woodcut illustrations of Tournes's books. We reach the third stage when a typefounder analysed these arabesque models into their component parts and cast them as printing types. We have already stated that Robert Granjon has been credited with this innovation.

Turning now to the flower units reproduced here, we find that these units (there are five of them together with a short piece of rule) are among the flowers which were rarely used, though certainly second to none in their beauty of design and effectiveness in combination. They are not to be found in any contemporary type specimen book or sheet containing a display of the popular flowers as, for example, Plantin's *Index Characterum* (1567), or the 1592 sheet of the Egenolff-Berner foundry at Frankfurt-am-Main. In Stanley Morison's *Four Centuries of Fine Printing* (1924) there are four reproductions showing the use of these actual flowers, the earliest being a French version of Plutarch's *Lives* printed at Lausanne by François Lepreux in 1574. This Plutarch was an *édition de luxe* and the flowers are built-up round the medallion portraits of each of the biographies with great ingenuity and variety. Another reproduction in *Four Centuries of Fine Printing* is from a Lyons book, printed by G. Rouillé in 1577, where the title-page has a border made up of the same flower units. Lyons, according to Baudrier, was the place of origin of these particular units. In Baudrier's *Bibliographie Lyonnaise* (series 2,

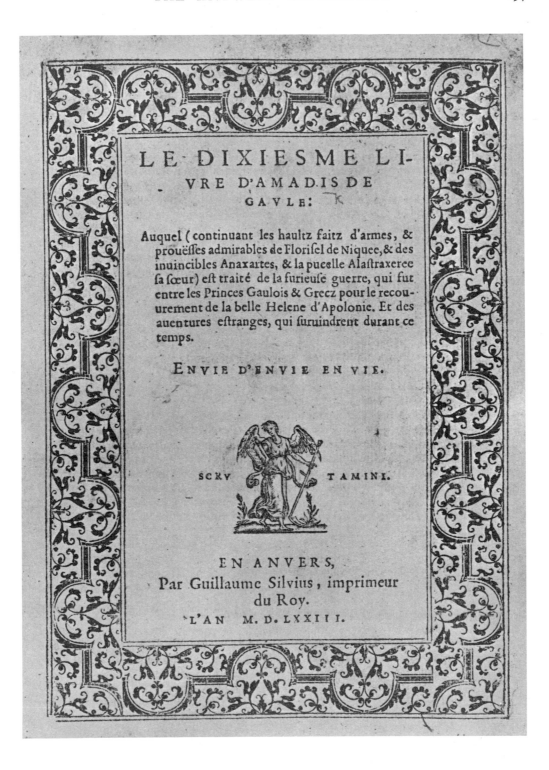

FIG. I. The first recorded use of the 'Antwerp' ornaments in an edition of Amadis de
Gaule. Guillaume Silvius, Antwerp, 1572.

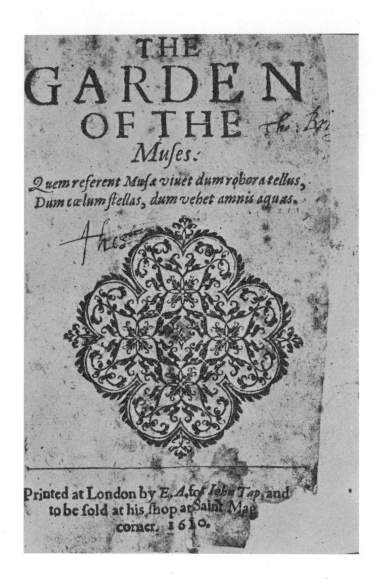

FIG. 2. A solid fleuron based on the Antwerp flowers,
as used by Edward Allde, London, 1610.

p. 275), there is a display of arabesque fleurons, some solid and some built-up, reproduced from the books of the Lyons printer, Jean Pillehotte. Six of these fleurons are
built up from our units. A similar page is shown in F. Meynell and S. Morison's article
'Printers' Flowers' in the first volume of *The Fleuron* (1923), which is by far the best
account we have of such decorations. According to Baudrier these fleurons were supplied
and presumably cast by the printer Pierre Roussin. Some of the books printed for
Pillehotte by Roussin have their imprint set in a cartouche of these flowers. As we may
gather from this and other passages in Baudrier's book Lyons, about this period, was a
centre for the trade in cast decorative pieces, headbands, initials and flower units.

Although Lepreux, the printer of the *Plutarch*, who was also a publisher at Lyons, may
have bought these flowers in that city, nevertheless it seems that they were not originally
designed there, but at Antwerp. Guillaume Silvius was using these units in built-up
borders on the title-pages of editions of the romance *Amadis de Gaule*, the earliest being
dated 1572 (Fig. 1) and several bear the year 1573. In fact, the printers of Antwerp
appear to have been the first to build up arabesque borders, and it is possible that it was
in Antwerp that Robert Granjon cut the necessary units. We know that Granjon was
living in that city in 1565-6, and we know, too, that Christophe Plantin in those years
bought from Granjon among many other things 'Poinçons de fleurons', i.e. flower units.
Plantin's earliest flower border (not the one under discussion) appeared in 1565 on the
title-page of an emblem book by Hadrianus Junius. Another border, formed of different units, surrounds the title of his *Index Characterum* (1567). Gilles Diest, also an
Antwerp printer, began building up borders in 1564, using flower units which were
later imported by the London printer, Henry Denham. From 1566 onwards the arabesque border was very popular with English printers at a time when such decorations
were still rare at Lyons.

Our particular units, as I have said, were rather rare, and, it appears, were never
used in England. However, the design was known and closely copied on *solid* title-
borders. In McKerrow and Ferguson's *Title-page Borders* (1932) there is shown (at
No. 200) a frame of four pieces, which is so exact a copy of these units as to be at first
glance deceptive. The border was first used by the London printer Henry Denham in
1583 and as late as 1627 by his successor Humphrey Lowndes. McKerrow and Ferguson
reproduce another frame among what they call 'fragments' used by John Wolf in an
addition of Castiglione's *The Courtier* (1598). Here the design is reminiscent, rather
than a copy of our units. Lastly, there is a solid fleuron, reproduced by Meynell and
Morison as the tail-piece to their article, which was in the stock of the London printer
Edward Allde (Fig. 2). This fleuron, though not built-up, closely resembles the fleurons
of Pierre Roussin. According to McKerrow, in an article which appeared in *The Library*
(September 1929), it was in use from 1610 to 1614. Many English song books of this
period have borders of flowers round their titles, but I have not found one made up
from our units. However, a contemporary at Heidelberg, Hieronymus Commelinus,
has a fine display of them on the title-page of a book of madrigals, printed in 1597
(Fig. 3).

There is one place where these units, or contemporary copies of them, have survived

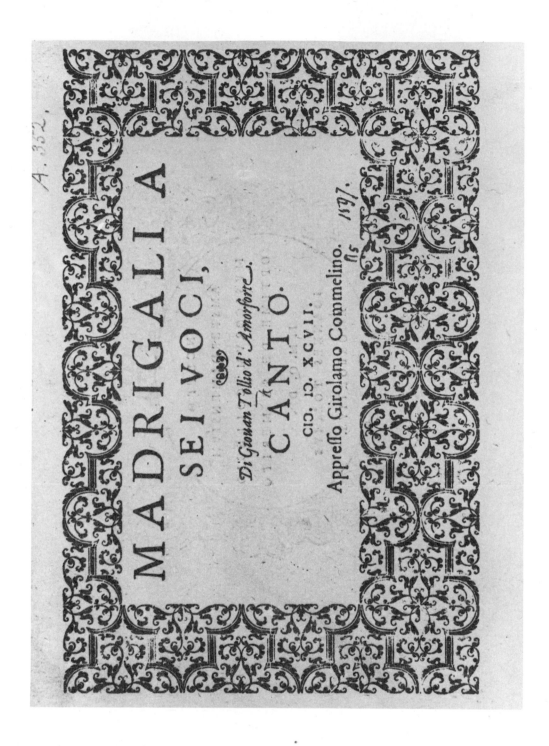

FIG. 3. The Antwerp ornaments as used in Germany, 1597. From Jan Tollius,
Madrigali a sei voce. Hieronymus Commelinus, Heidelberg, 1597.

down to the present day, and that is the Plantin Museum at Antwerp. Two of them are shown in the *Index Characterum* published by the Museum in 1905. At Amsterdam also they had a long life and appear on the specimen sheet of the Widow of J. Adamsz. and A. Ente, printed about 1700.

[1954]

The foregoing article was written for the house organ of a printer to point up his use of a range of printers' flowers by indicating their historical background. They were recut by the Monotype Corporation and the complete set consists of five flower matrices and one line in 24 points (Nos. 310-315)

with the optional addition an 18 point matrix (No. 219)

AN ALPHABET
BY PIETER COECKE VAN AELST

THE Renaissance artists, especially the Italian, were keenly interested in the Roman lettering found on inscriptions. Several of them designed alphabets modelled on the inscriptional letters and wrote treatises on the method of constructing the letters by geometrical means. Most of those which have survived have been reproduced and studied by writers of this and the preceding century. The earliest to which a date can be given, a manuscript of Felice Feliciano of Verona, 1463, preserved in the Vatican, was edited by R. Schoene in 1872 (in *Ephemeris Epigraphica*, i, p. 255, &c.), and further discussed by A. Khomentovskaia in *La Bibliofilia*, April, 1935, &c., p. 154, &c., with a reproduction. Another fifteenth-century Italian manuscript, copied by the German medical scholar Hartmann Schedel, is preserved at Munich and was described by Dehio in 'Zur Geschichte der Buchstabenreform in der Renaissance' (*Repertorium für Kunstwissenschaft*, iv, 1881, p. 269). The earliest printed treatise of the kind was produced at Parma about 1480 by Damianus Moyllus, a treatise which was reproduced by the Pegasus Press in 1927, with an introduction by Stanley Morison. The better-known work by Luca de Pacioli, entitled *De Divina proportione*, Venice, 1509, has also been reproduced by the Grolier Club, New York, 1933, again edited by Stanley Morison. The work of Albrecht Dürer on the same subject in his *Underweyssung der Messung*, and of Geofroy Tory in his *Champ fleury*, 1529, are both well known. Roman capitals are displayed in the books of many of the writing-masters from Ludovico Vicentino onwards. But there is one alphabet by a sixteenth-century artist which seems to have been overlooked. This is woodcut after the design of the Flemish artist Pieter Coecke van Aelst. The alphabet occupies two leaves in Coecke's translation of Book 4 of Sebastiano Serlio's book on architecture.

The fullest account of Pieter Coecke (1502-50) is given in Wurzbach's *Niederländisches Künstler-Lexikon*. He was painter, architect, and designer. He spent a year in Constantinople studying oriental carpets, and made drawings illustrating Turkish life, afterwards published as woodcuts. A list of his works, artistic and literary, is given in Wurzbach.

The various books of Serlio's work in the original Italian appeared separately, beginning with the fourth book, *Regole generali di Architetura sopra le cinque maniere de gli edifici*, printed at Venice by F. Marcolini in 1537. The bibliography of Coecke's translations of the first five books into Flemish and of books three and four into French is obscure. According to Kramm's *De levens en werken der Hollandsche en Vlaamsche Kunstschilders*, 1856-64, Book 4 appeared in 1539 at Antwerp, entitled *Generale Regelen der Architecture op de vyve manieren van edificien*. This edition does not appear in Nijhoff's *Nederlandsche Bibliographie*, where there is quoted only a translation from Vitruvius, also of 1539. But the assumption that Book 4 did appear in that year is borne out by the exact title given by Kramm and by the fact that there was an edition in

German (*Die gemaynen Reglen von der Architectur*) printed at Antwerp in 1542 and translated from the Flemish version of Coecke; there is a copy of this German translation in the Kunstgewerbe-Museum at Berlin. Book 3 was first published in 1546, as we can infer from the composite edition described below. The next edition of Book 4 appears to be that of 1549 (the date being within the woodcut title-border), of which there are copies in the British Museum and the Kunstgewerbe-Museum. The title reads: *Reglen van Metselrijen op die vijue manieren van edificien.* In 1553 appeared a composite edition of the first five books, Book 3 being dated 1546, Book 4 1549, and the three others 1553. There was a later edition at Amsterdam, 1606 (according to Brunet), 1626 (according to Wurzbach).

Coecke also translated Books 3 and 4 into French. Book 4 was published at Antwerp in 1545 (date within the woodcut title border), entitled *Reigles generales de l' Architecture, sur les cinq manieres d'edifices.* Brunet says this book appeared in 1542, but this is probably an error. The third book appeared in 1550.

The woodcut alphabet is at the end of Book 4, occupying fols. 71 verso and 72 recto in the French edition of 1545, and fols. lxxi verso and lxxii recto of the Flemish edition of 1549. In the French edition, at the foot of the alphabet are the words: 'Fin de le .IIIIe. liure d'architect. Sebastiē Serlii, translate & imprime en Anuers par Pierre vā Aelst.' In the letterpress of chapter xiii Coecke explains that Serlio at this point had dealt with coats of arms, and goes on to state his reasons for the change he has introduced. I give this account in the English translation of 1611:

But for that the workemen here in this country make no Armes after their owne pleasures, we wil let them pass, & in place thereof set downe a figure of Letters, the which the workeman hath occasion many times to cut, or place above Gates, Doores, in Freeses, and other table, therein to set names, titles, deuices, or other superscriptions, at the pleasure of the owners, or to know a Palace, or any other common places of office or otherwise. Neuerthelesse, for that here there are roofing workes set to all the place, I will set the figures of the Armes which he hath made after ye Letters, that the Booke may bee complete. The workeman hauing no knowledge of learning, should be much troubled, to seeke farre and near for one that should write them for him: and although that he hath them in writing, neuerthelesse for want of knowing the proportions, they may be spoyled in working, and so bring his worke in contempt, as also those that drew them for him. Therefore, although they are drawne by Lucas Patiolus, Geofry Tory, and Albertus Durer, who, neuerthelesse, agree not all together, therefore I will set these hereafter downe for a common rule, following our Author, who (letting pass all superstition) hath brought the Columnes & Pedastals into a due measure: by whose authoritie, I should almost say, that a man may make these letters greater or smaller according to the order of Columnes; but to write the Simetry, or not, that I may not digresse too far out of the way, I will follow Vitruuius, where hee sayth that a Ionica Columne is 9 parts high, and by shewing of divers Authors, this form of Letters is also found in Ionica, and so I leaue them of 9 parts: and whether a man would make them by Corinthia or Composita order of 10 parts, it would not be amisse, for as the Corinthia is most vsed for the slendernesse, so these Letters, for the most part, are made of 10 parts: by the Dorica and Thuscana they are made of eyght.

From this passage we see for whose instruction these models of lettering were intended, and that Coecke adopted the proportion of nine to one, that is to say the thickness of main strokes was to be one-ninth of the height. This was the ratio followed

Pieter Coecke van Aelst's alphabet as found at the end of book IV of his French edition
of Serlio, 1545.

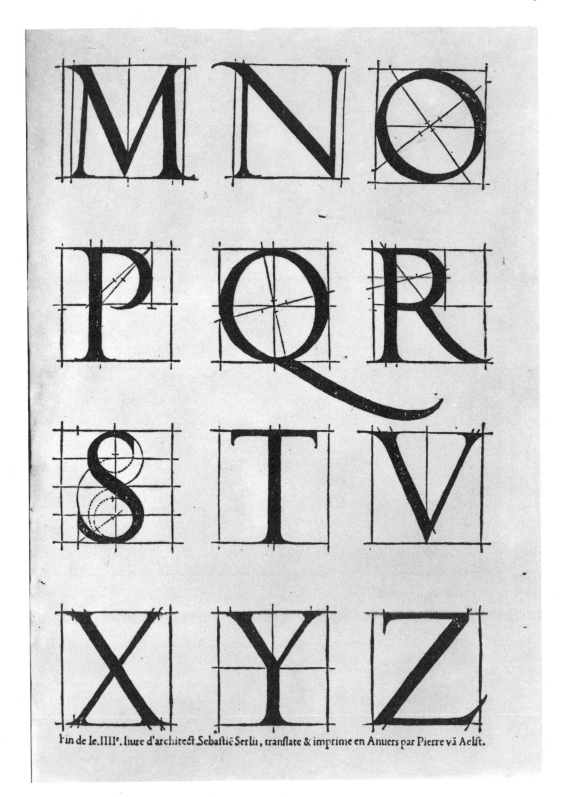

Fin de le.IIIIe. liure d'architect Sebastiē Serlii, translate & imprime en Anuers par Pierre vā Aelst.

by Pacioli. That Coecke took Pacioli as his model in the main is borne out by other details in his capitals, for example in the angle of stress in the O, which is very obtuse. Coecke, however, was not prepared to condemn those who preferred the proportion of ten to one, as had both Dürer and Tory.

The translation given above is taken from the English edition of the five books 'translated at the charges of Robert Peake from the Dutch', and printed in 1611 by Simon Stafford. The curious point about this English edition is that its illustrations are made from the same wood-blocks which were used in the Antwerp editions, including the roman alphabet and the woodcut title-borders. The three borders (Books 3 and 4 are repetitions) are nos. 253, 254, and 255 in McKerrow and Ferguson's *Titlepage Borders in England*. They were also used in a German edition printed at Basle in 1608, and probably also in the Flemish edition of 1606 (? 1626). Coecke's Roman capitals, then, were published in at least half a dozen editions, and yet attention has, it seems, never been drawn to them.

[1943]

SOME NOTES ON GERMAN RENAISSANCE TITLE-BORDERS

THE period of the Reformation was one of great activity for the printers of Germany and it was also the age of the woodcut title-border. These borders, of which many hundreds were designed in the generation from 1510 to 1540, are of great interest in the history of the woodcut and of the artists who designed this decorative work for the printers. Since in that time of controversy so many tracts were published without the name of the printer, the borders are often useful as a help to the identification of the place of printing. Although much has been written on the subject, much work remains to be done; a systematic catalogue of the whole of the borders of the period would be of great value. In the meantime even a few scattered notes may be of some use. The points here dealt with are, as far as I know, unrecorded. I put them forward with some diffidence, because of the difficulty of keeping abreast with all that has been published on the subject in German periodicals.

I

Augsburg. In the *Corpus Schwenkfeldianorum*, II, 27, the title-page of a Schwenkfeld tract dated 1524 is reproduced and the tract is there said to have been printed by Simprecht Sorg at Nikolsburg, since another by Balthasar Hubmaier of 1526 with the same title-border bears the name of that printer. The border (161 × 119 mm, opening 81 × 57) has at the top a bearded head, pillars at the sides, and at the foot five putti, one with a drum. The design was attributed by Röttinger in 1906 to the Master H. S. (see Hildegard Zimmermann in *Buch und Schrift*, 1927, note 157). There are at least two other books decorated with this border, a Luther tract of 1527, *Ob man vor dem Sterbn fliehen muge*, which the Weimar edition of Luther (Bd. 23) assigns to Simprecht Sorg, perhaps following the *Corp. Schwenk.*, and one by Urbanus Rhegius, *Ain Predig warumb Christus den Glauben ayn Werck Gotes genennt habe*, 1529. From the types used in these two tracts and the initials, an N in the Luther and a G in the Rhegius, they would appear to have been printed at Augsburg by Heinrich Steyner. The initials are part of a set designed by Hans Weiditz, some of which are shown in Butsch, *Bücher-ornamentik der Renaissance*, Taf. 31. The N occurs in Steyner's Old Testament in German of 1527-28, and both in his Bible of 1535. The typography of the Schwenkfeld of 1524 also agrees with that of Steyner. It is worth noting that from 1523, the year in which Steyner began to print, most of the recorded work of H. S. is found in the books of the Augsburg printer. I have not been able to see any books bearing the name of Simprecht Sorg and can only suggest that the border of the Hubmaier may turn out to be a copy.

II

Steyner's *Das new Testament*, 1529, in octavo, has an attractive border described in the Weimar edition of Luther, *Die Deutsche Bibel*, II, 456. At the top is a bearded head, and

FIG. 1. Border by Hans Sebald Beham. From Otto Brunfels,
Cathechesis puerorum. Christian Egenolff, Frankfurt [1535?].
Actual size.

at the foot, facing each other, are two bearded figures with bodies ending in foliage. Measurements 121 × 79 mm. In 1548 in Johann Agricola *Fünfhundert . . . Sprüchwörter*, without imprint, but apparently one of the last books printed by Steyner. If this is the work of H. S. it is one of his best, and in style it resembles a border attributed to him by Zimmermann *op. cit.* and reproduced in *Buch und Schrift* 1927, Abb. 16. That border, by the way, belonged to Hans von Erfurt (cf. the description by Schottenloher in the *Gutenberg Jahrbuch* 1927, Einfassung c). On the back of the title-page of Steyner's New Testament there is an undoubled H. S. cut, Christ with a lamb on his shoulders, which is not mentioned by Zimmermann.

III

Simprecht Ryff's *Der Psalter*, issued in August 1524 for Sigismund Grim, has a title-border which is in part a copy of a Holbein border. Ryff's border (171 × 115 mm, opening 98 × 75) has at the foot a scene depicting the story of Mucius Scaevola, the original of which was a metal-cut border by C. V. after Hans Holbein, reproduced by H. A. Schmid in *Jahrbuch der preuss. Kunstsammlungen*, 1920, p. 245. A closer copy of the border, used by Herwagen, is mentioned below. Ryff's border, after appearing in a number of his books, passed into the hands of Alexander Weissenhorn, cf. *Ayn kurtzer bericht so wir Georg . . . Hertzog zu Sachssen. etc.* 1529. Ryff had copies of several other Holbein borders, some of which have been recorded. The original of one, an octavo, is shown in Schmid, p. 240. Ryff's copy passed to Philip Ulhart and was described by Schottenloher (*Philip Ulhart*, 1521, Einfassung 11) together with another copy by Hans Lufft at Wittenberg. The border was perhaps more widely copied than any other Renaissance border. Schmid mentions several versions at Basle itself; there were at least three in use in the Netherlands (cf. Nijhoff, *L'Art typographique dans les Pays Bas*), and more than one at Venice. The original of a quarto border of Ryff's of Biblical scenes is shown in Heitz, *Basler Büchermarken*, 15, with the device of Thomas Wolf of Basle. Ryff's copy passed to Weissenhorn and was used by him at Ingolstadt as late as 1545, see J. Dobneck *Consyderatio de futuro concordiae in religione tractatu*. Another copy used by Andreas Lutz at Ingoldstadt was described by Schottenloher in the *Centralblatt für Bibliothekswesen* 32, 1915, p. 253, no. 4. Ryff had an octavo border (128 × 87 mm) depicting the death of Cleopatra for which Holbein's well-known and much copied border seems to have suggested the subject rather than to have been directly copied. See *Micheas propheta*, 1524.

IV

Frankfurt. The borders of Christian Egenolff have not been described in detail and probably a catalogue of his books would reveal some treasures. There is at any rate one excellent octavo border which must be the work of Hans Sebald Beham and which has not been recorded. It occurs in Brunfels's *Catechies puerorum*, undated, but perhaps one of Egenolff's first books printed at Frankfurt. At the top are four putti, one playing a stringed instrument, at either side a satyr blowing a horn and standing on a pillar, at the foot five mermen fighting. Measurements 122 × 81 mm, opening 68 × 47 (Fig. 1).

Another octavo border of irregular outline, height 135 mm, is found in 1534 in Wol-phius, *Rudimenta arithmetices*. At the top is Venus with sea-horses, at the sides pillars, at the foot five small biblical scenes. An interesting quarto border (173 × 120 mm, open-ing 74 × 58) depicts the story of David and Bathsheba. It is found in *Chronica von an vnd abgang aller Welt wesen*, 1534 and in 1535 in Hans Sachs *Der Kaiser Bildnussen und leben* (Fig. 2).

V

Hagenau. Johann Secer's edition of Lucian in Greek, 1526, has on the title-page an undescribed Weiditz border in the style of the borders round the pages of the *Devotis-simae Meditationes*, S. Grim, Augsburg, 1520. Secer's border, cut in four pieces, measures 133 × 92 mm, opening 91 × 58. The design consists of foliage with bird and a putto in the right-hand piece (Fig. 3).

VI

Ingolstadt. Schottenloher *op. cit.* no. 1, describes a border used by Andreas Lutz, a portal with a flat arch, decorated with arabesques, measuring 172 × 130 mm. This border was used by Johann Petri at Nuremberg in 1354 in the *Algorithmus demonstratus*, and again in a Luther tract of 1541, *Vermanunge zum Gepet wider der Türcken*, also printed by Petri, but without his name. (Cf. the Weimar edition of Luther, Bd. 51, p. 580. B.)

Fig. 2. Border from Hans Sachs, *Der Keiser Bildnussen und leben.* Christian Egenolff, Frankfurt, 1535. (Reduced.)

VII

Leipzig. Holbein's earliest border designed for Froben at Basle, a border with nine putti and bearing his name (there is a reproduction in Heitz, *Basler Büchermarken*, 27) was several times copied. The version used by Ramminger at Augsburg is assigned by Zimmermann, *op. cit.*, note 162, to H. S. and Zimmermann mentions also the copy by Weissenberger at Landshut (Proctor's A). Proctor records another version used by Ulrich Morhard at Strasbourg, and a reduced design in octavo of Johann Schöffer of Mainz is shown in Heitz, *Mainzer Druckerzeichen* V. 9. There is still another copy of which I have found no mention used by Nicolas Schmidt (Faber) of Leipzig in the *Acta Apostolorum* of Feb. 1522. It measures 162 × 119 mm, opening 85 × 66, is copied in reverse and has the initials N S on the shield at the foot.

VIII

Magdeburg. Hans Walther used a copy of a well-known Holbein border, reproduced in Heitz, *Basler Büchermarken*, 65. Under the arch at the top is a figure labelled Orpheus, at the sides scenes from the labours of Hercules, at the foot two angels supporting a shield bearing the monogram of Adam Petri. In Walther's copy the scenes at the sides are reversed and the shield bears the arms of Saxony. Measurements 163 × 124 mm, opening irregular. See Amsdorff, *Wahrhafftige Historia*, 1536.

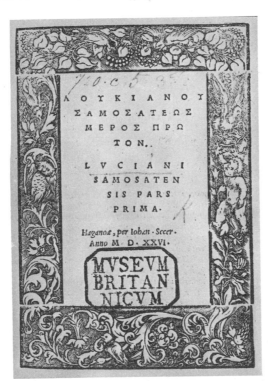

FIG. 3. Border by Hans Weiditz from the Lucian of Johann Secer,
Hagenau, 1526. (Reduced.)

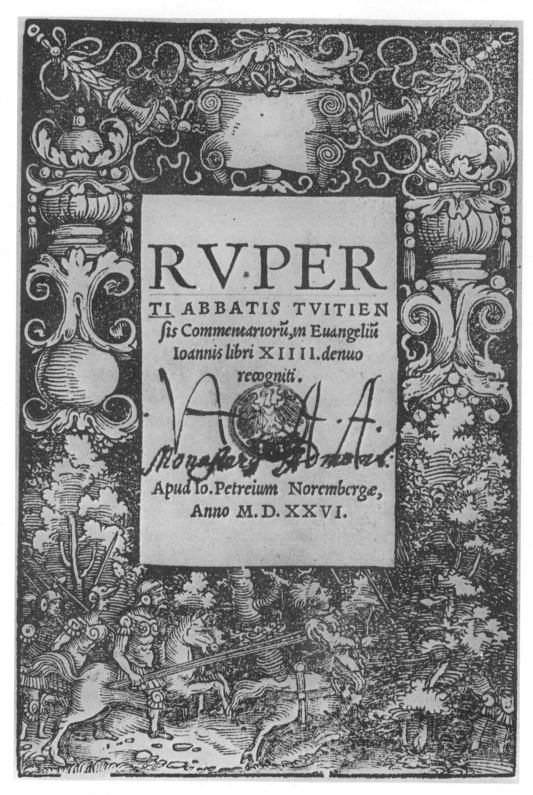

FIG. 4. Border by Hans Sebald Beham from *Ruperti abbatis monasterii Tuitiensis in Euange-lium Iohannis libri xiiii Commentarii denuo recogniti*. Johann Petrejus, Nuremberg, 1526.

IX

Nuremberg. In J. Luther's *Titeleinfassungen der Reformationszeit* a border used by Friedrich Peypus is shown, which is a copy in reverse of a metal cut after Holbein. The original is reproduced in Heitz, *Basler Büchermarken*, 71.

Another copy in reverse, taken from Peypus's version, is found in *Caroli Capellii . . . Sermones duo. Pragae per Joannem Colubrum MDXXXVII.* From Röttinger's *Erhard Schon* we gather that printers at Prague had dealings with Nuremberg artists.

In 1526 Johann Petri printed *Ruperti abbatis Tuitiensis commentarioru̅ in Evangeliu̅ Joannis libri XIIII*, with a good title-border, apparently an undescribed work of H. S. Beham. At the top is an empty scroll, at the sides pilasters, and at the foot two mounted knights, the one thrusting his lance into the back of the other; black ground. Measurements 141 × 92 mm, opening 69 × 47.

One of Petri's borders seems to be derived from Holbein's octavo border described above, under S. Ryff. It is not a close copy and is without the putti clasping the pillars, but the design cannot be independent. There are two books of 1523, without Petri's name, but printed in his italic and decorated with the border in question. One is Melanchthons's *Annotationes in Johannem*, and the other an edition of Erasmus, *De contemptu mundi*. In 1526 Joseph Klug at Wittenberg used a copy of Petri's border in Aurogallus, *De Hebraeis urbium . . . nominibus.*

X

Strasbourg. Under Ryff above we have described a border copied in part from a Holbein, depicting the story of Mucius Scaevola. A closer copy, but in reverse, measuring 128 × 82 mm, opening 71 × 49, was used by Johann Herwagen at Strasbourg in M. Bucer's *Enarrationes in Euangelia*, 1527, and later, in 1531, by Georg Ulricher in G. C. Tansteter, *Artificium de applicatione astrologie ad medicina̅.* Another unattributed Weiditz border appears in *Das Alte Testament*, J. Knoblouch, 1524. It is described in the Weimar edition, *Die Deutsche Bibel* II. 320. A portal with a battle of centaurs and men at the foot, a faun on the left side. Measurement 124 × 85 mm.

XI

The first border used by Wolfgang Köpfel in 1522 in Luther's *Eyn missiue allē den so von wegē des wort gottes*, etc. was derived from Matthias Hupfuff, a border on a black ground with widows at the foot holding a shield with Hupfuff's monogram, reproduced in Heitz, *Elsässische Büchermarken* VII, 2, and Butsch, Taf. 60. In Köpfel's tract the shield is empty; it was used again in 1524 by Johann Schwann in Keller's *Ein schon tracteclin vō der barmherzigkeit Gottes.* Köpfel's second border, found in at least four books of 1523 (cf. *Das siebēdt Capitel S. Pauli zu den Corinthern*) is a close copy of a Basle border, that of Nicolaus Lamparter reproduced in Heitz, *Basler Büchermarken* 24 b. At the top is an angel, at the foot two angels, between them a shield bearing Lamparter's initials. In Köpfel's copy (160 × 116 mm, opening 80 × 64) the shield is empty.

Johann Pruess also copied a Basle border, Holbein's Orpheus design already referred to under Magdeburg. Pruess's version is an adaptation rather than a copy; in place of the figure of Orpheus there is a woman's head, and at the sides scenes from the life of Samson in place of the labours of Hercules. On the shield at the foot are the initials F W H, which I cannot explain. Measurements 162 × 115 mm, opening 79 × 55; in four pieces. With the monogram it is found in the *Epistel Sancti Petri*, 1524, without the printer's name, but printed in Pruess's Upper-Rhine type. In Bugenhagen's *Was vñ weliches die sünd sey, etc.* of the same year, in the same type, the border is without the monogram on the shield, and similarly in Jacob Otter's *Die Epistel Sancti Pauli ad Titū*, 1524. Later in 1534 it is found in Schwenkfeld's *Von der erbavung des gewissens*. In *Corpus Schwenkfeld*. IV. 856, this tract is attributed to the press of Jacob Fröhlich, but the type is the same as Pruess's, who was still at work.

Another of Pruess's borders was a close copy of a design of irregular outline attributed by Campbell Dodgson (II, 152 [15]) to Weiditz and used by Grim at Augsburg. There is

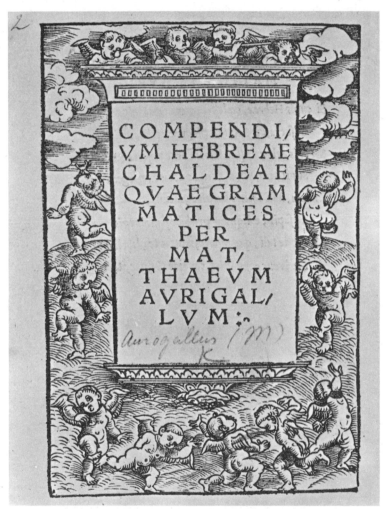

FIG. 5. Border, possibly by Lucas Cranach, from Matthaeus Aurogallus, *Compendium Hebreae Chaldeaequae* (sic) *grammatices*. Josef Klug, Wittenberg, 1525.

a bearded head and two birds at the top, and at the foot two masks, the opening being in the form of a sheet, 153 × 103 mm. I know of no book decorated with the copy which contains Pruess's name, but from the initials and the Upper-Rhine type (see Götze pl. 62 for some distinctive letters of the fount) the following books may be assigned to him: Luther's *Ein geschicht wie Gott eyner Erbarn kloster Junckfrawen ausgeholfen hat*, 1524 (Weimar edition Bd. 15, p. 82 E), Bugenhagen's *Etlich Christliche bedencken von der Mess*, 1525, and Oecolampadius's *Nūc dimittis*, 1530.

In an article by O. Clemen in the *Zeitschrift für Bücherfreunde*, 1921, mention is made of Pruess's copy of a border used by Thomas Anshelm at Tübingen from 1513; at the foot are six angels holding a seventh over a plate. Among the books said to contain Pruess's version is Bodenstein's *Sendtbrief . . . meldende seiner wirtschafft*, 1522. Freys und Barge in their bibliography of Bodenstein in the *Centralblatt für Bibliothekswesen*, 21, p. 225, no. 85, note that the piece at the foot is here in reverse. In fact the border, which is in four pieces, is an entirely different copy, and the type is not Preuss's. I am unable to say who the printer was.

In J. Luther's *Einfassungen* a copy of a border used by N. Schirlentz at Wittenberg,

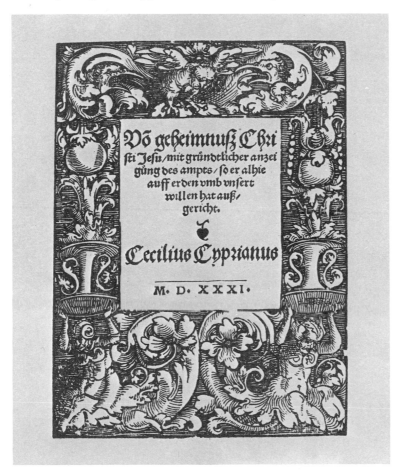

FIG. 6. Unidentified border from Cecilius Cyprianus. *Vom geheimnuss Christi Iesu*, sine loco, 1531.

22 d, is assigned to Knoblouch. I know of no book of Knoblouch's with the border in question, but I infer from the same Upper-Rhine type that Bugenhagen's *Eynfürung in den Passion*, 1524, decorated with the same copy, was printed by Pruess.

XII

Tübingen. Lazaras Schürer at Schlettstadt had a border (Proctor's A) in four pieces, with children riding grotesque animals, one resembling an elephant. The top piece bears the date 1519. This is a copy of a border by Cratander at Basle. The top and bottom pieces are described by Götze, no. 175, but with side pieces from another of Schürer's borders. There was also a copy at Antwerp (see Nijhoff, *op. cit.* Vorsterman, 44). An edition of Cato's *Disticha* of 1520 with Schürer's imprint has the border. But most of the books decorated with this piece were printed by Ulrich Morhard of Tübingen, formerly of Strasbourg. Morhard used it from 1524 and a list of the books will be found in Karl Steiff's *Der erste Buchdruck in Tübingen*. The border is no. 3 in Steiff's list and is called 'Die Wilde'.

XIII

Wittenberg. In Zimmermann, op. cit. note 78 b, there is a reference to Aurogallus's *Compendium Hebreae grammatices*, 1525, printed by Joseph Klug. The title-border is not the one inferred by Zimmermann, but a design, perhaps, by the elder Cranach. At the top are four angels, one blowing a flute, looking over a cornice, at each side two angels, at the foot five angels dancing. Measurements 125 × 82 mm, opening 70 × 48 (Fig. 5). The border was reproduced in the Fairfax Murray Catalogue I. 457, from a book by B. Gretzinger.

XIV

In the three following books the printers are unknown to me, but the borders may perhaps be familiar to some of our readers.

1. In C. Cyprianus, *Vō geheimnuss Christi Jesu*, 1531. At the top a bird in the centre, with a bird's head on either side, at either side a vase supported by a half figure; black ground horizontally shaded. 144 × 106 mm, opening 71 × 58 (Fig. 6).

2. In *Ein sprichwort Was ein Münch gedenckt Das darf er thun. c.* 1525. A portal, at the foot scene of monks burning books. 165 × 125 mm, opening irregular. The tract contains several crude cuts satirizing monks.

3. In Jan Hus, *Etliche Brieffe . . . an die Behemen geschriben*, 1537; at top battle of naked men, on left three female figures, on right woman with two children, at foot scene with many figures in a garden. 165 × 114 mm, opening 58 × 53; poorly cut.

[1929]

THE TITLE-BORDERS OF HANS HOLBEIN

Holbein's work for the Basle printers is described by H. A. Schmid in his article in the *Jahrbuch der preuss. Kunstsammlungen*, 1899, Bd. 20, supplemented by H. Koegler in Bd. 28, 1907, and also in Schmid's article on Holbein in Thieme and Becker's *Allgemeines Lexikon der bildenden Künstler*. It is very difficult to pick out the title-borders in the mass of references given by Schmid, and for that reason a separate list of this work may be of value. In the case of the many copies of Holbein's designs it has been possible to add some new information. Borders in four pieces, if designed as a whole, have been included, but not unconnected strips. For example, the pieces described by Woltmann, No. 231, including the well-known representation of peasants pursuing a fox, are excluded.

It may be mentioned that the editions of S. Münster's *Cosmographia*, in various languages, printed by Henricpetri at Basle in the second half of the sixteenth century, often contain excellent impressions of Holbein borders cut many years earlier.

Abbreviations

Butsch	A. F. Butsch, *Bücherornamentik der Renaissance.* 1878, 1881.
Heitz	P. Heitz, *Basler Büchermarken.* 1895.
Heitz, K. B. M.	P. Heitz, *Die Kölner Büchermarken,* 1898.
Heitz, E. B. M.	P. Heitz, *Elsässische Büchermarken.* 1892.
Heitz, M. B. M.	P. Heitz, *Frankfurter und Mainzer Druckerzeichen.* 1896.
Koegler	H. Koegler, Ergänzungen zum Holzschnittwerk des Hans und Ambrosius Holbein, in *Jahrbuch der preussischen Kunstsammlungen,* Bd. 28, Beiheft.
McKerrow & Ferguson:	R. B. McKerrow & J. Ferguson, *Title-page Borders used in England.* 1932.
Nijhoff	W. Nijhoff, *L'Art typographique dans les Pays-Bas, 1500-1540.* 1902-35.
Proctor	R Proctor, *An Index to the Early Printed Books in the British Museum.* Part II. Section I. Germany. 1903.
Schmid	H. A. Schmid, Holbeins Tätigkeit für die Baseler Verleger, in *Jarhbuch der preussischen Kunstsammlungen,* Bd. 20, p. 233 seq.
W.	A. F. G. A. Woltmann, *Holbein.* 1874.

BASLE

1. 181 × 118 mm. At foot, a scene from Livy, the story of Mucius Scaevola and Lars Porsenna; on left side, the initials H. H. = Hans Herbster the woodcutter; at top, group of putti. W. 223. Butsch 45. (Fig. 1.)

First used Oct. 1516, in Aeneas Gazaeus, *De immortalitate animae*, J. Froben. The book was edited by Beatus Rhenanus, Froben's press-corrector. Holbein is thought to have been advised by him in the details of his scenes from classical authors. (See S. Vögelin in *Repertorium f. Kunstwiss.*, Bd. x, p. 345, seq.)

Copies

A. Close copy by R. Pynson, London, 1518-1552. See McKerrow & Ferguson No. 8.

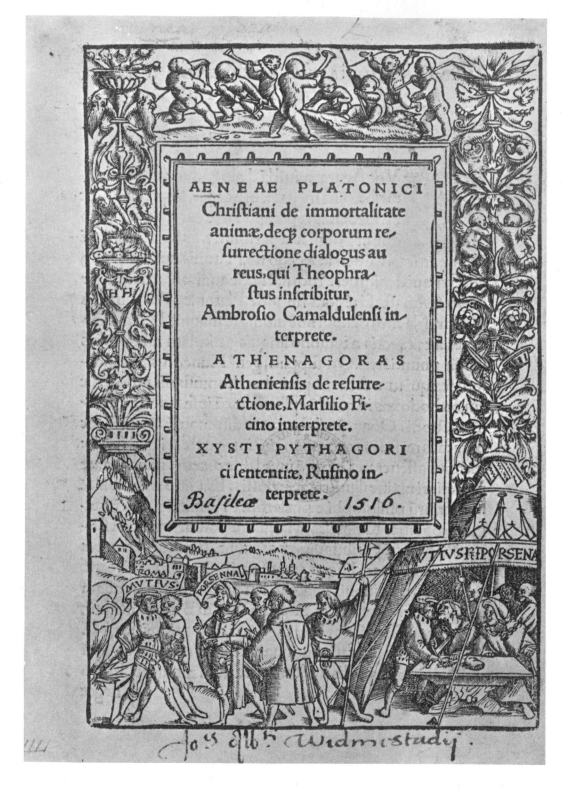

AENEAE PLATONICI
Chriſtiani de immortalitate
animæ, decʒ corporum re‑
ſurrectione dialogus au
reus, qui Theophra‑
ſtus inſcribitur,
Ambroſio Camaldulenſi in‑
terprete.
ATHENAGORAS
Athenienſis de reſurre‑
ctione, Marſilio Fi‑
cino interprete.
XYSTI PYTHAGORI
ci ſententiæ, Rufino in‑
terprete.
Baſileæ   1516.

FIG. 1. Border No. 1, from Aeneas Gazaeus, *De immortalitate animae* . . . Johann Froben, Basle, 1516. (Actual size.)

2. 181 × 119 mm. Nine cherubs on the arch; Froben's device on a shield at the foot; plates at the top bear the letters 'Hans' 'Holb.' W. 234. Butsch 41. Heitz 27. First used Nov. 1516, in T. Gaza, *Grammaticae institutio*. Schmid gives the date as Oct., but the copy in the British Museum is dated Nov. (Fig. 2.)

Copies

A. J. Weissenberger, Landshut, c. 1516.
    Proctor's A. With the arms of Bavaria and Landshut on two shields at the foot. Reproduced in Schottenloher's *Die Landshüter Buchdrucker*, Abb. 7.
B. M. Buchfürer, Erfurt, 1523. See M. von Hase, *Johann Michael genannt Buchfürer*. Einfassung 3. Close copy of A.
C. U. Morhard, Strasbourg, 1520, and Tübingen, Proctor's A. Steif, Der erste Buchdruck in T. No. 2. The shield is blank.
D. M. Lotter, Leipzig. Luther, *De bonis operibus* 1521. (See the Weimar edition of Luther, Bd. 6.) Indecipherable lettering on the plates, the shield blank.
E. M. Ramminger, Augsburg, 1522. Copy in reverse; at foot, two shields, one bearing double eagle, the other, lance and flag. Attributed to H. S. of Augsburg by H. Zimmermann in *Buch und Schrift* 1927, note 162.
F. Nicolas Schmidt, Leipzig, *Acta Apostolorum*, Feb. 1522. Copy in reverse, measuring 162 × 119 mm; initials N. S. on the shield.
G. J. Schöffer, Mainz, 1527. Reduced version, 127 × 88 mm. Reproduced Heitz, M. B. M. Taf. v (9).
H. M. Hillen van Hoochstraten, Antwerp. See Nijhoff No. 10. Initials M. H. on shield.
I. S. Corver, Zwolle. See Nijhoff No. 1. A Maltese cross on shield.

3. 180 × 120 mm. At foot, beheading of John the Baptist; Froben's device within wreath at the top. W. A. Holbein No. 1. Butsch 44. Heitz 30. First used March 1517.

Copies

A. Elizabeth van Werden, Cologne, 1518.
    Proctor's A. Used in 1519 by Heinrich van Neuss, and later by E. Cervicorn. A rabbit takes the place of Froben's device.
B. Philippe Lenoir, Paris, in *Les Cent Nouvelles Nouvelles*, s. a. and *Les Prophecies de Merlin*, 1528. A rose takes the place of Froben's device.

4. 181 × 125 mm. At foot, death of Lucretia; goat's head and beards either side; at top, two children hold handkerchief bearing the impression of Christ's face. W. A. Holbein No. 4. Butsch 43. First used April 1517, in Erasmus, *De duplici copia verborum*, Froben. Formerly attributed to Ambrosius Holbein, but Schmid in Thieme & Becker, art. H. Holbein, assigns it to Hans.

5. 184 × 125 mm. At foot, a frieze of tritons, etc.; over this, a small, empty shield supported by two cherubs; goat's head and mask either side; at top, three cherubs. First used May 1517, Froben. A close copy of a Venetian border (Butsch 7) first found in an Italian Bible of 1493. Koegler says the Holbein in copy is found in Oct. 1516 in Panzer 165, but Panzer's 165 is the T. Gaza referred to above as having border No. 2.

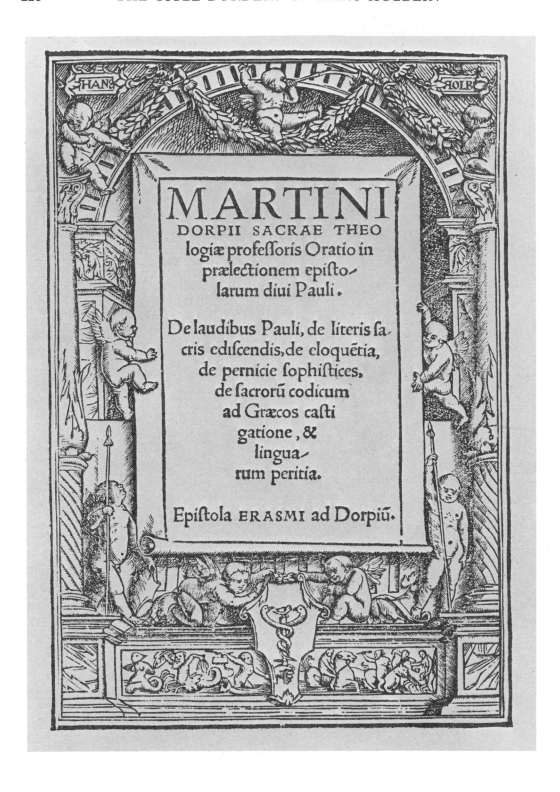

FIG. 2. Border No. 2, from Martinus Dorpius, *Oratio in praelectionem epistolarum divi Pauli.*
Johann Froben, Basle, 1520.

6. 181 × 118 mm. At foot, a triumphal procession of putti; putti round the sides; at top, two sphinxes and a medallion. W. A. Holbein No. 9. Found in Eramsus, *Querela pacis*, Froben, 1517.

Copy

A. T. Berthelet, London, 1530. See McKerrow & Fergusson No. 19.

7. 124 × 77 mm. At foot, two putti support a shield bearing Froben's device; musical instruments either side. W. A. Holbein No. 14. Heitz 45. March 1520, in Erasmus, *Paraphrases in Epistolas Pauli*.

8. 134 × 85 mm (irregular outline). At foot, two half figures support a shield bearing Cratander's device; left side, a goat (?); right side, a satyr; putto in either top corner. Heitz 93. Aug. 1520, in *Novum Testamentum*.

9. 174 × 120 mm. Left side, Lucretia; right side, daughter of Herodias holding head of John the Baptist; at foot, shield bearing Cratander's device supported by two putti; triangular arch. Heitz 95. First used Feb. 1521, in a Lactantius.

10. 152 × 92 mm (irregular outline). At foot, device of Cratander on a shield flanked by a mermaid (left) and a merman (right); a satyr either side; above them, five putti climbing in foliage.

Heitz 97.

First used Feb. 1521, in a Sallust.

11. 138 × 80 mm. At foot, a fountain, above which a plate bearing the initials I. F.; at sides, putti climbing palm trees; at top, a skull with an old man to left and an old woman to right; above the skull, a plate bearing the date MDXX.

July 1521, in Erasmus, *Paraphrases in Epistolas Pauli*, Froben. A metal cut by Jacob Faber (for whom see Thieme & Becker, art. Faber). In subject this border and Nos. 14 and 19 are connected with Holbein's Dance of Death series.

12. The 'Cebes' or 'Genius' border. An allegorical description of human life. At foot, a walled enclosure, at the gate of which is an old man 'Genius', and on the wall 'Fortuna'; at the top is the 'Arx Foelicitatis'; allegorical figures down the sides. For a full description and an account of the source of the story, see S. Vögelin in *Repertorium für Kunstwissenschaft*, 1882, p. 179, seq. The figure of 'Fortuna' may be compared with the devices designed by Holbein for Cratander at Basle, and for Pierre Vidoue at Paris. For an earlier device with a similar allegorical figure, see Kristeller, *Ital. Buchdruckzeichen*, Nos. 345 and 346.

Version A. 258 × 176 mm. In Tertullian, Froben, 1521. Four pieces, metal cut.

Version B. 274 × 182 mm. In N. Perottus, *Cornucopiae*, Cratander, 1521. Woodcut, bearing the cutter's signature 'Hermann' and 'HH'.

Version C. 252 × 169 mm. In St. Augustine, *De Civitate Dei*, Froben, 31 Aug. 1522. Four pieces, metal cut. The pieces are wider than those in A, and may be distinguished by the representation of the sun, moon and stars at the top.

Version D. 279 × 190 mm. In *Lexicon Graecum*, V. Curio, 1522. Woodcut. Distinguished by the fact that the gate, at which 'Genius' stands, is in the centre of the wall.

13. 264 × 177 mm (from reproduction in Heitz). At top, the Almighty; left side, Christ; right side, the Virgin Mary; at foot, device of T. Wolf. Four pieces.
Heitz 10.
In *Missale speciale*, 1521. The *Graduale*, Heitz 9, has a border made up of unconnected pieces.

14. 127 × 80 mm. At foot, Fortuna mounted on a horse; in right-hand corner, death as an archer; in left-hand corner, man hit by his arrow; at top, Superbia, Justicia and Avaricia; left-side, Prudencia; right, Spes. Signed I. F. (Jacob Faber). Metal cut. Used March 1522, in Erasmus, *Novum Testamentum*, Froben.
The three theological and the four cardinal virtues with their appropriate symbols frequently appear on title-borders. Holbein here has Hope with clasped hands, Justice with sword and scales, and Prudence holding a mirror. Ambrosius Holbein in the border cut for Froben depicting the victory of Arminius (Butsch 46) has Temperance, Justice, Charity and Fortitude, but Hans has not copied any of the details. Ambrosius's design is derived from a border in the well-known Como Vitruvius, 1503, where Faith, Hope and Charity, Justice, Temperance and Fortitude appear down the sides. (See reproduction in M. Gerlach, *Das alte Buch*, p. 105.)

Copies
A. H. Ruremond, Antwerp, 1525 (Nijhoff No. 8), used later, 1529, by J. Severinus and P. Silvius (Nijhoff No. 7) and in 1536 by F. Aertsen (Nijhoff No. 9) in four pieces.
B. A free copy by J. Gymnicus, Cologne. (Reproduction in McKerrow & Ferguson, Appendix No. 1.)
C. Copy of Gymnicus, J. Bydell, London, 1534-1538. McKerrow & Ferguson No. 29.

15. 244 × 165 mm. Left side, Peter, with key; right side, Paul with sword; symbols of the Evangelists in the four corners; at foot, device of Adam Petri.
W. 215. Heitz 64.
May 1522, in *Concordantiae maiores*. An 8° version (130 × 83) used from March 1523.
W. 216. Heitz 66.

Copy
A. H. Alopecius, Cologne, in Erasmus, *Enarrationes in Psalmos*, 1524. The Almighty in place of the shield at the top; Christ in place of Petri's device at foot.

16. 145 × 93 mm (irregular outline). At foot, Phyllis driving Aristotle; either side, a figure holding a standard – that on the right bears a head at the top.
July 1522, in Politianus, *Miscellaneorum centuria*, V. Curio.
Pamphilius Gengenbach had a border by A. Holbein, 1517, depicting the same scene, together with the medieval story about Virgil. (Heitz 26.) For the literature on the story of Phyllis and Aristotle, see Comparetti, *Virgilio nel Medio Evo*, vol. 1, chap. 8.

17. 188 × 122 mm. At foot, death of Marcus Crassus; device of V. Curio in pediment. Heitz 112.

Aug. 1522, in the *Rhetoricum libri* of George of Trebizond.

A copy with the shield blank, found in Ptolemy, *Geographia*, Henricpetri, 1540.

18. 132 × 84 mm (irregular outline).

Version A. At top, vase between two half figures, female left, male right; a putto clasps each column; on sill at foot, a head in medallion, facing left; a mask in each bottom corner. Metal cut by I. F.
W. 235. Schmid, p. 240.
First used Oct. 1522, by Adam Petri.

Version B. Copy in reverse with initials H. H. at foot.
Schmid, p. 241.
Froben, 1523.

Version C. Similar to B, but without the initials.
Used by J. Bebelius, 1523, in Διονυσίου οἰκουμένησ περιήγγησις Schmid mentions another copy used by V. Curio and two by Cratander. Is one of these the same as that used by Bebelius?

Copies elsewhere

A. H. Alopecius, Cologne, Aug. 1523, in Erasmus, *De conscribendis epistolis*. Copied from version B, but with rabbits in place of the masks.

B. Close copy of A. M. de Eguia, Alcalá, 1529, in *Musa Paulina* Alvari Gomez.

C. S. Ryff, Augsburg, May 1524, in F. Lambertus, *In Lucae Evangelium commentarii*. Afterwards used by P. Ulhart (see Schottenloher's *Ulhart*, Einfassung No. 11). Close copy of version C.

D. J. Soter, Cologne, 1525, in T. Gaza, *Introductionis grammaticae libri*. Like C, but with less white ground. Three pieces of this border are found in 1524, in John Fisher, *Assertionis Lutheranae confutatio*.

E. J. Petri, Nuremberg, 1523, in Erasmus, *De contemptu mundi* (not signed). A free copy, no putti at the foot of the columns.

Γ. J. Klug, Wittenberg, 1526, in M. Aurogallus, *De Hebraeis nominibus*. Copied from E.

G. H. Lufft, Wittenberg, 1526, in Luther, *Sermon von dem Sacrament des Leibs Christi*. A free copy. Lions appear on the panels at the foot of the columns in place of the masks.

H. J. Loersfelt, Erfurt and Marburg. Copy of G.
See Von Dommer, *Die ältesten Drucke aus Marburg*, No. 24.

I. M. Hillenius, Antwerp. (Nijhoff No. 12.) Plants on the panels in place of the masks.

K. T. de Borne, Deventer. (Nijhoff No. 36.) Copy of A. Alopecius, with rabbits.

L. A. Paffraet, Deventer. (Nijhoff No. 53.) Like K.

M. Bindoni & Pasini, Venice, 1530, in Bocaccio, *Il Philocopo*. (Also 1538). Close copy of version A, but without the masks.

N. P. di Nicolini, Venice, 1538, in G. Caviceo, *Il Peregrino*. Like M.

O. Comin da Trino, Venice, 1546, in D. Manzoni, *Libretto molto utile per imparare a legere*. A free copy.

19. 137 × 92 mm. At top, Superbia, Justicia and Avaricia; left side, Spes; right, Prudencia; at foot, death with his scythe. Metal cut.

W. A. Holbein No. 2.

Used in 1522, Latin Bible, T. Wolff.

The upper part is similar to No. 14.

20. 239 × 160 mm (irregular outline). At foot, the death of Cleopatra; right side, Dionysius Esculapius; left side, Dionysius taking the gold chains. (Fig. 3.)
     W. 226.

Copies

A. Metal cut by C. V. (174 × 123 mm). Proof only known. Koegler (in *Monatshefte f. Kunstw.* 1911, p. 392-3) considers this to be another version rather than a copy.
B. Copy in reverse signed C. V. interlaced and dated 1524 (168 × 117 mm). In *Sphaerae atque astrorum ratio*, Walder, 1536.
C. Another copy signed C. V. interlaced, in J. Brenz, *Syngramma claris. viror.*, 1526, according to Koegler.
D. E. Cervicorn, Cologne, 1523. Heitz, K. B. M. xxv. In top righthand corner the shield bears Cervicorn's monogram. Schmid apparently considers this to be the original block.
E. C. Wechel, Paris, 1529, in Celsus, *De medicina*. Close copy of Cervicorn.
F. 4° version. J. Prael, Cologne, 1534, and E. Cervicorn, Marburg, 1537. Heitz, K. B. M. xxvi, 84. Von Dommer, *Die aeltesten Drucke aus Marburg*, No. 36.
G. 8° version. E. Cervicorn, Cologne, Heitz, K. B. M. xxvi, 83.
H. 8° version. E. Cervicorn, Marburg. Close to G, but with flowers on the shield at the top in place of the three crowns of Cologne.
I. 8° version, in reverse; no shield. J. Schöffer, Mainz, 1527, in P. F. Andrelinus, *Epistolae proverbiales*.
K. S. Ryff's border in 8° in *Micheas propheta*, Augsburg, 1524, copies the scene at the foot only.

21. 278 × 186 mm. Four pieces. At foot, the crowning of Homer (signed I. F.); at top and sides, busts of classical authors, with Solomon in centre at top. Metal cut. March 1523, in Strabo, V. Curio. Later passed to S. Gryphius, Lyons.

22. 131 × 89 mm (from reproduction in Schmid, p. 245). At foot, story of Mucius Scaevola; at top, seated figure, representing Fame. Metal cut by C. V.

Copies

A. J. Herwagen, Strasbourg, 1527, in M. Bucer, *Enarrationes in Evangelia*. Copy in reverse. In 1531 used by Georg Ulricher at Strasbourg.
B. S. Ryff, Augsburg, 1524, in *Der Psalter*. Copies the lower part only (171 × 115).

23. 190 × 127 mm. At foot, story of Pelops being served up on a dish to the gods; device of V. Curio on a shield in pediment.
     W. 222. Heitz 106.
     Used 1523 in Luther, *Der zehen gebot ein nützliche erklarung*. Found later at Zürich.

Copy

A. A. Farckall, Colmar, 1524. Heitz, E.B.M. lxxv. Copy in reverse of the sides only.

24. 164 × 121 mm (irregular outline). Orpheus in pediment; either side, scene from the labours of Hercules; on shield at foot, monogram of A. Petri.
     W. 221. Heitz 65.
     Woodcut by Hans Lützelbürger, 1523.

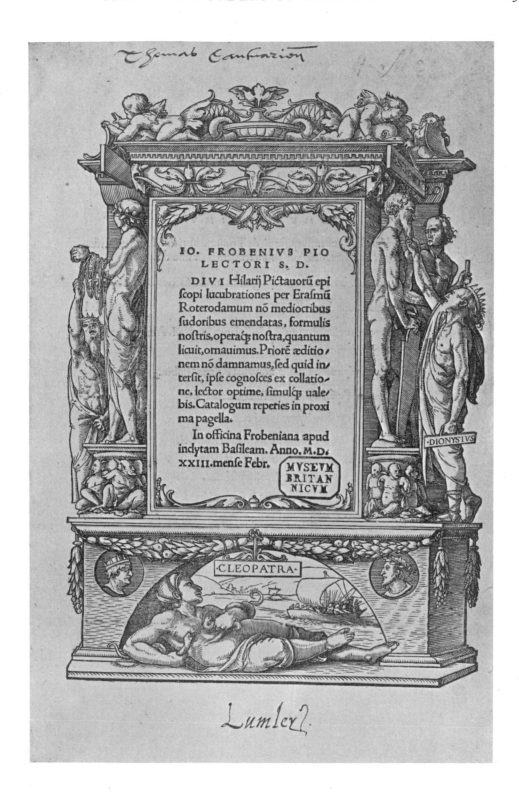

FIG. 3. Border No. 20, from Saint Hilary's *Lucubrationes*. Johann Froben, Basle, 1523.

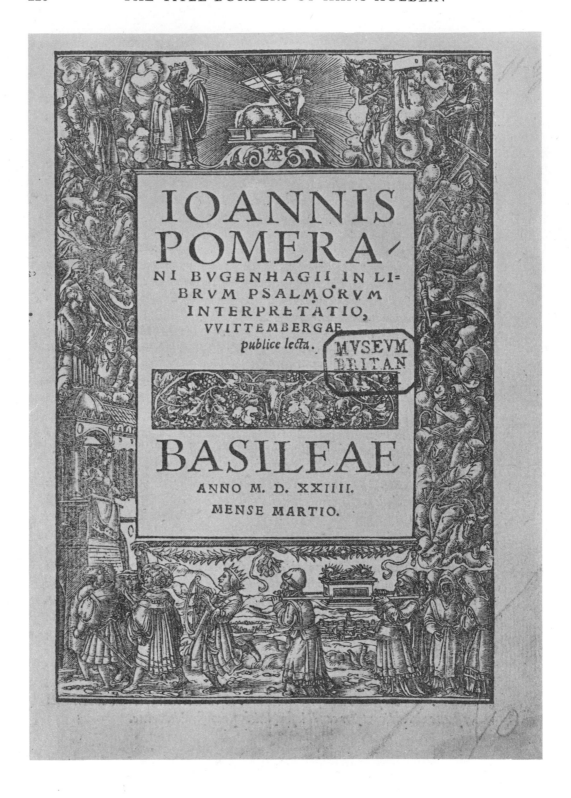

FIG. 4. Border No. 28, from Johann Bugenhagen, *In librum Psalmorum interpretatio.*
Adam Petri, Basle, 1524.

Copy

A. H. Walther, Magdeburg, 1536, in Amsdorff, *Wahrhafftige Historia.* The sides reversed, and the arms of Saxony on the shield.

25. 158 × 114 mm. At top, the baptism of Jesus Christ; round the sides and at foot, scenes from the life of St. Paul; at foot, in centre, a figure with scroll 'Digito compesce labellum', at his feet a shield bearing the monogram of T. Wolff; in left-hand bottom corner, initials of the woodcutter, Hans Lützelbürger. Four pieces.

W. 213. Heitz 15.

Used 1523, in *Das alte Testament.*

Copies

A. S. Ryff, Augsburg, 1524, with Ryff's device of a wild man on the shield. Later used by A. Weissenhorn at Ingolstadt. See J. Dobneck, *Consyderatio de futuro concordiae in religione*, 1545.
B. Andreas Lutz, Ingolstadt. See Schlottenloher in *Centralblatt f. Bibliothekswesen*, 32, 1915, p. 253, No. 4. In 1530 used by J. Stuchs at Nuremberg.

26. 129 × 87 mm. At foot, the story of Marcus Curtius; in background, a classical building. Metal cut by C. V.

W. 224. Butsch 55.

Used 1523, in Melanchton, *In Johannis Evangelium commentarii*, A. Petri.

27. (? size). At top, the story of Pyramus and Thisbe; at foot, the judgment of Paris. Reproduced in Schneeli, *Renaissance in der Schweiz*, Taf. XXIII. Metal cut by C. V. Proof only known.

28. 170 × 112 mm. At top, lamb and flag with David to left and crucifix to right, the monogram of A. Petri below the lamb; at foot, dance of David before the ark. (Fig. 4.) Metal cut.

W. 212. Heitz 71.

March 1524, in J. Bugenhagen. *In librum Psalmorum interpretatio.*

Copies

A. Close copy in reverse, without the monogram, in *Lexicon Graecum*, J. Walder, Basle, 1539.
B. J. Peypus, Nuremberg, 1528. In reverse; without the monogram. See J. Luther's *Titeleinfassungen*, Taf. 117.
C. J. Coluber, Prague, in C. Capellius, *Sermones duo*, 1537. Like B.

29. 232 × 172 mm. Four pieces. At top, the Trinity; symbols of the four Evangelists at the sides, the right side signed I. F.; at foot, dispersal of the Apostles.

Butsch 58.

Some pieces found in 1523, the four together first in 1524 by Cratander.

Copy of the piece at the foot at Ingolstadt, 1532, according to Koegler.

30. 126 × 86 mm. Monogram of A. Petri on shield at the top; in top left hand corner, creation of Eve; at foot, under arch, scenes from the life of Moses. Metal cut by C. V.

Heitz 67.

In *Das alte Testament*, 1524.

A free copy by C. Froschouer, Zürich. Distinguished by the pillars at the sides. In Zwingli, *Farrago annotationum in Genesim*, 1527.

31. 126 × 85 mm. At foot, Christ feeding the multitude; putti at the top and sides. Metal cut by C. V.

W. 214. Heitz 70.

In J. Bugenhagen, *In Regum libros annotationes*, A. Petri, 1525.

Copies

A. C. Froschouer, Zürich, 1526. See Oecolampadius, *De re Eucharistiae responsio*, 1526. Free copy. Triangular arch.
B. S. Ryff, Augsburg, 1526. See Luther, *Ayn Sermon aus dem III. capitel Matthei*. Like A, but with Holy Dove at top.

32. 120 × 82 mm. At foot, three peasant couples dancing; putti at the top and sides. Metal cut by C. V.

W. 233.

In Ovid, *Opera*, A. Petri, 1526.

33. 172 × 118 mm. Round arch cut off at top; in pediment four angels, two supporting a shield bearing the device of V. Curio; at foot, the crowning of Homer; date MDXXVI on stone at the foot on left.

Not found in any Basle book, but at Paris in 1528, in *Le Livre faisant mention des sept parolles de Jesus Christ*, S. Du Bois for C. Wechel. Reproduced by P. Renouard in *Byblis*, 1929, at p. 60.

34. 145 × 94 mm (irregular outline). At foot, death of Lucretia; triangular arch, at peak of which is the device of V. Curio.

Heitz 107.

Not known in any contemporary book. Occurs in Münster's *Cosmographia*, Henricpetri, 1578.

ZÜRICH

35. 128 × 86 mm. At foot, Christ and the 'heavy laden' – from the text in Matth. xi, 28; left side, armour; right side, musical instruments. Metal cut by C. V.

Used 1524, in Zwingli, *Der Hirt*, C. Froschouer. Zwingli frequently quoted the text illustrated. Reproduced by S. Vögelin in *Züricher Neujahrsblatt*, 1879-1882.

Copy in reverse, the Holy Dove at the top, by V. Curio, 1528, in J. Ringelbergius, *Institutiones astronomicae*. Later in a French New Testament, 1539.

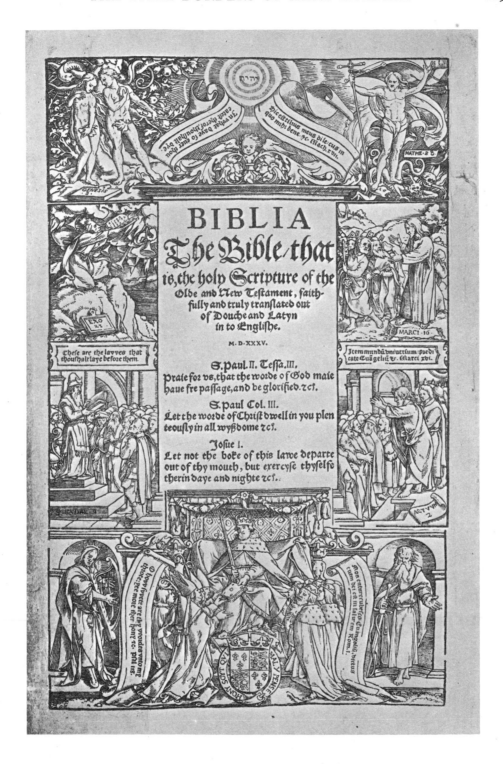

FIG. 5. Border No. 38 from *The Bible, that is the holy Scripture of the Olde and New Testament*... (Tr. Miles Coverdale.) Printed in Germany (Zürich? Cologne? Marburg?), 1535. (Reduced.)

PARIS

36. 144 × 95 mm. Four pieces. Round arch with urn in each top corner; square columns; at foot, frieze of putti with portrait within wreath in centre. Metal cut by I. F.

Used 1523 by P. Vidoue in Erasmus, *Ad Christophorum episcopum Basil.* See Koegler in *Monatshefte für Kunstwiss.* 1911, p. 301, note. Reproduced by Koegler in *Festschrift zur Eröffnung des Kunstmuseums*, Basle, 1936, p. 189. The frieze at the foot is derived from Burgkmair's woodcut of the planet Venus.

37. 127 × 80 mm. Arms of the Kings of France at top and sides; at foot, a shield bearing fleur de lys supported by two angels. Metal cut by I. F.

Used 1528 by P. Vidoue in the colophon of R. Gaguin, *De Francorum regum gestis.* Reproduced by Koegler, op. cit., p. 190.

The border of C. Wechel, attributed to Holbein by A. F. Didot in his *Essai typographique sur l'histoire de la gravure sur bois*, 1863, is probably not by Holbein, but by the 'Master of the Venus of 1531'. See H. Koegler, 'Wechselbeziehungen zwischen dem Basler und Pariser Buchschmuck', in *Festschrift zur Eröffnung des Kunstmuseums*, Basle, 1936, p. 206 and Abb. 63.

LONDON

38. 273 × 161 mm. Biblical scenes at the top and sides; at foot Henry VIII seated on throne. W. 237. McKerrow & Ferguson 31.

In the English Bible printed abroad in 1535, probably at Cologne (formerly said to be Zürich). (Fig. 5.)

McKerrow & Ferguson 45, used in the Great Bible of 1539, is wrongly attributed to Holbein.

39. A second English border is described by Woltmann (238) from a proof, without title. No English book containing this border has been recorded.

[1937]

BASLE ORNAMENTS IN PARIS BOOKS, 1519-36

THE school of Basle printers, who, under the leadership of Johann Froben, made Basle one of the leading cities in Europe in the book trade, left their influence in many towns of lower Germany, in the Netherlands, and at Lyons. The development of printing at Paris in the sixteenth century was not for the most part influenced by Germany, but yet even at Paris, at the very time when Simon de Colines, Geofroy Tory, and Robert Estienne were flourishing, the number of books printed reminiscent of Basle is rather remarkable. Tory's influence was mainly directed towards leading the book illustrators of Paris to the lighter and more purely decorative style of the Italians; he succeeded in this in spite of his marked inferiority as a draughtsman to the artists of South Germany. The innovations of Froben and the other Basle printers were not so much in typography as in the decoration of books, woodcut initials, and title-borders, which were for the most part cut after the designs of the two Holbeins and Urs Graf. In the following notes their work or copies of it is traced in books printed at Paris.

The man who introduced the Basle style into Paris was Conrad Resch, a citizen of Basle, who, according to Renouard, was working at Paris from 1516-26. Renouard says that he was also a publisher at Basle, but I know of only one book bearing his name which was printed at Basle, *Margarita philosophie*, edited by Oronce Fine, Petri, 1535. His address in Paris was in the Rue St. Jacques at the sign of the 'Écu de Basle'. This house had been known as the 'Corne de Cerf', and either Resch, or another Basle publisher, Watenschnee, changed the name to the 'Écu de Basle'. Resch appears at first to have had some sort of partnership with Josse Bade, and the earliest Paris book bearing his name and device of the scutcheon of Basle are typical of the books printed by Bade, e. g., the *Questiones et decisiones physicales*, edited by Georg Lokert, 1518. But in 1519 and 1520 there were published by Resch books with three different title-borders which are the work of Urs Graf.

The first one appeared on the *Anti-Morus* of G. Brixius of 1519. In the left-hand top corner is a naked boy holding a shield which bears the monogram of Urs Graf; at the right-hand top corner is a bearded man holding a plate on which is the date 1519. This title-border is not described by either His or Koegler in their account of the work of Urs Graf.[1] The same border may be seen on three other books undated, two without place or printer's name. The first (Fig. 1) is the *Probatissimorum ecclesiae doctorum sententie*, attributed to the press of Pierre Vidoue, a printer who did much work for Resch, and the second a Luther tract, *Quare pape ac discipulorum eius libri a M. Luthero combusti sint*, the German editions of which were printed at Wittenberg in 1520. According to the Weimar edition of Luther's works (1883, &c., Bd. 7, p. 152, seq.) there were two other Latin versions, but neither of them agrees with the edition here described. I have seen only the title-page of this book, but in view of the fact that this border is

---

1. His, *Beschreibendes Verzeichnis des Werks von Urs Graf*, in Zahn's 'Jahrbücher für Kunstwissenschaft.' (Jhrg. 6, p. 145, &c.) and H. Koegler in 'Anzeiger für Schweiz. Altertumskunde, 1908 (N. F. Bd. 9, p. 43, &c.).

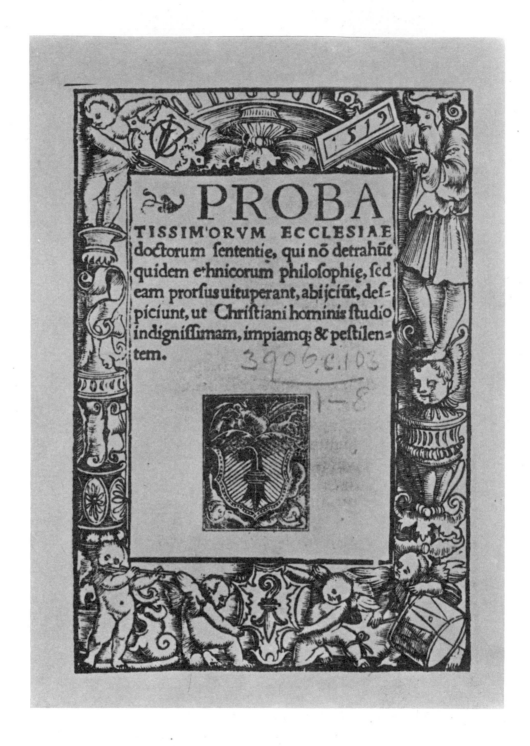

FIG. 1. Urs Graf border from *Probatissimorum Ecclesiae doctorum sententie*. Sine loco, 1519
(attributed to Pierre Vidoue).

printed from the same block as that of the Brixius and the other book mentioned, I conclude that the book was printed at Paris for Conrad Resch. The border makes a fourth appearance in a controversial tract by Edward Lee, Archbishop of York, against Erasmus, printed by Gilles de Gourmont and entitled *Apologia contra quorundam calumnias*.

The second title-border by Urs Graf appears in the *De aequinoctiorum solsticiorūque inuentione* of Albertus Pighius, no date, but presumably 1520, and no printer's name, but printed by Vidoue (Resch does not appear to have printed himself). In the right-hand top corner is Graf's mark with the dagger. This title-page is described by His, No. 319. As far as I know it appears only at Paris. Another book with the same border (Fig. 2) is the *Supplementum* by Gabriel Biel, Josse Bade, 1521.

The third title-border may be seen in Asconius Pedianus's *In orationes M. Tullii Ciceronis enarrationes* of 1520. This border (No. 318 in His) also is dated 1519 and is signed with Graf's, monogram at the foot. It depicts the story of Pyramus and Thisbe, the judgement of Paris, and the medieval legend of Virgil. Like much of Graf's work this legend is treated with great coarseness. Other examples of the use of the border are: the Greek Dictionary of Crastonus, Pierre Vidoue, 1 July, 1521 (at the end of this book is a device used by Resch which is not in Silvestre, three beasts being crushed in the folds of a serpent, cut on metal by I. F. after Holbein)[1] and the *De primatu Petri aduersus Ludderum* of Johann von Eck, Pierre Vidoue, 1521. In Etienne de L'Aigue's Commentary on Pliny, a book printed by Vidoue for Poncet Le Preux and Galiot Du Pré, it appears as late as 1530. This title-border has quite a long history at Paris, as it was copied for Philippe Le Noir, probably by Geofroy Tory, who signed it with the Lorraine cross. Le Noir used this copy on the title-pages of many books, especially French romances, e. g., *L'histoire du Sainct Graal*, dated 24 October 1523, and *Le proprietaire des choses*, translated by Jean Corbichon, 1525. Philippe Le Noir was the printer of another book, *L'experience et approbation Vlrich de Hutem touchant la medecine du boys dict Guaiacum*, which has a title-border copied from one of the best known of the borders designed by Hans Holbein for Froben, the John the Baptist border; the original may be seen in the Carteromachus of 1517. The French copy is found again in *Les Cent Nouvelles*, undated, and Merlin, 1528.

A number of other books published by Resch have woodcut borders in the Basle style, e. g., *Conuulsio calumniarum V. Veleni quibus Petrum nunquam Rome fuisse cauillatur per Ioannem Roffensem* [Fisher], undated. The original edition of this work was printed by Vorsterman at Antwerp in 1522. The book contains Fisher's reply together with the original 'calumnies' of Velenus. As further examples we may mention two works of Erasmus printed by Vidoue in italic type for Resch in 1523, the *De interdictu esu carnium* and the *Paraphrasis in Evangelium secundum Ioannem*, which have a title-border indirectly derived from Holbein.

All these books show the influence of the Basle borders only, but Pierre Vidoue himself, after the close of Resch's career at Paris in 1526, issued a number of editions

---

1. This is probably the earliest block after Holbein appearing at Paris. Cf. H. Koegler in 'Monatshefte für Kunstwissenschaft', 1911, p. 401 seq., the only account (a summary one) of Holbein's work for the Paris presses.

of Erasmus, which are exactly like Basle books in title-page, initials, and typography e. g., the *Vidua Christiana* and the *Responsio ad epistolam paraeneticam Alberti Pii*, both of 1529. The figure initials used in these books are not exact copies of any used at Basle, but a comparison with initials used by Adam Petri (No. xxxv in Schneeli and Heitz, *Initialen von Hans Holbein*) will show their origin. Good examples of these initials will be found in the *Tractatus noticiarum Gervasii Waim*, 1528, Vidoue for Jean Petit and Chrestien Wechel, and in Claude Seyssel's translation from Xenophon, *Histoire du voyage que fist Cyrus*, 1529, Vidoue for Galiot Du Pré. In 1531 Vidoue printed for Poncet Le Preux and Galiot Du Pré *Les Commentaires de Jules Cesar*, translated by Etienne de L'Aigue and R. Gaguin. In addition to the set of initials already referred to, this book contains six borders after Urs Graf, and three other initials (the A, C, and D) copied from a well-known set of German initials (they had been used already in 1527 by Vidoue in the *Cronique et Histoire* of Archbishop Turpin, printed for R. Chaudière). The borders are described in His (No. 327). The three initials are copied from a set cut by Hans Weiditz (? after Dürer) for Negker of Augsburg in 1521.[1] These were widely copied: e. g., by Cervicornus at Cologne, by Gryphius, Dolet, and François Fradin at press of Lyons, and at Antwerp.

In August 1526 Resch's shop was taken over by Chrestien Wechel, who had previously been Resch's agent. Wechel printed a large number of books at Paris from this date until his death in 1563, and nearly all of them show traces of Basle influence. For example the Galen, *De plenitudine*, 1528, has initials, the Theophrastus, *De historia et causis plantarum* of 1529 has a woodcut title-border (attributed to Holbein by Didot) and initials in the style of Basle. Many years later, in 1550 and 1551 Wechel issued various books by Louis Meigret, which, typographically, are excellent examples of French Renaissance work but still have the same German initials, a set which originally perhaps belonged to Simon Du Bois. Wechel also had two other Holbein title-borders, one a copy of the 'Cleopatra' border (see his *Cathena aurea super Psalmos*), the other a border depicting the crowning of Homer and entirely different from another Holbein cut of the same subject which passed to Gryphius at Lyons (see *Le liure faisant mention des sept parolles que Jésuchrist dit en larbre de la croix*, 1528). Another typical French printer, Michel Vascosan, also used Basle initials. In his edition of Cicero's Letters of 1534, and other books, will be found a curious set of figure initials on a white background, which are attributed to Basle by Schneeli and Heitz (No. LI). I do not know at what date they appear at Basle, but I believe that in this case they appeared first at Paris in 1530 at the Gérard Morrhé, and were possibly designed by Oronce Fine.

In typography proper the Basle printers influenced Paris in the printing of Greek and italic. We know that when Erasmus expressed his regret that Josse Bade had no Greek type, Bade made good his deficiencies from Basle. Proctor, in *Bibliographical Essays*, p. 97 seq., has shown that the printers of Greek at Paris up to 1540 can be divided into two schools; the one school following Italian models, and the other the Basle printers. Of this latter school were Bade, Vidoue, Wechel, and Gérard Morrhé. Much

---

1. See M. J. Friedländer, *Holzschnitte von Hans Weiditz*, 1922.

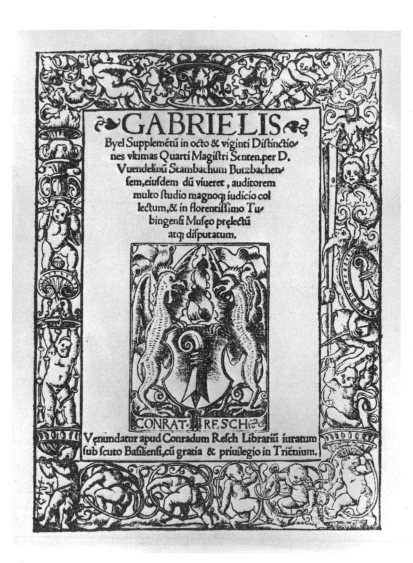

FIG. 2. Urs Graf border from Gabriel Biel, *Supplementum in octo & viginti distinctiones ul-timas Quarti Magistri senten. per D. Wendelinum Stambachum . . . collectum.* Jodocus Badius for Conrad Resch, Paris, 1521. (Reduced.)

FIG. 3. Border of German origin from Aristophanes, Κωμῳδίαι ἐννέα. Ed. J. Chéradame.
Pierre Vidoue for Gilles de Gourmont, Paris, 1527.

the same division might be made in the matter of italic types. Printers like Vidoue and Wechel, about the same year in which Colines introduced his new, non-Aldine italic, were using an Aldine italic derived from Froben.

I will conclude with two more examples of title-borders of South German or Basle style. In 1528 Vidoue printed for Gilles de Gourmont an edition of Aristophanes, of which each play has a woodcut title-border of German origin (Fig. 3), though the cut is signed with the Lorraine cross. The sides represent the adoration of the Magi, at the foot are extracts from the Psalms, on the left in Greek with the date (1527), on the right in Hebrew; at the top and bottom Gourmont's arms, with the letters E. G. There was also a Demosthenes, Λόγοι 'Ολυνθιακοί, with the same border issued in 1528, Plato's 'Απολογία in 1529, a Homer and Aristotle's *Organon* in 1530, a whole series of Greek texts.

The last title-border is from an edition of the Gospels with the commentary of S. Thomas Aquinas, printed by Didier Maheu in 1532. The title-page is surrounded by borders, which are close copies of borders by Urs Graf. They are described by His and numbered 325 b (here repeated on each side of the title-page), 325 d (at the foot), and 325 g (at the top). In the left-hand border at the centre is the letter D, and on the right-hand border an M., initials of the printer D. Maheu. The borders occur again on the title-page of Jean Bouchet's *Les triumphes de la noble dame*, Ambroise Girault, 1536. In this case the left-hand and right-hand borders are transposed, so that the initials read M. D.

[1927]

SOME COLOGNE AND BASLE TYPES 1525-52

By the second quarter of the sixteenth century printers had for the most part ceased to be their own type-cutters. The smaller houses bought their types from a few large firms or from the men who, like Claude Garamond and Robert Granjon in France, had established themselves as regular typefounders. As a result successful designs began to appear in many centres of printing and were by no means confined to their country of origin. In these notes I propose to describe a series of designs from two centres of typefounding, Cologne and Basle, by way of illustrating the fact that the trade was international. Of the fourteen types dealt with, four were cut at Cologne, or at least appeared first in Cologne printed books. That there was a punch-cutter at work in that city between the years 1525 and 1531, whose work was of sufficient merit to secure an international market, has not so far been noticed. The other ten types described appeared in books printed at Basle. Some were cut there and others were imported from France. The style of book production at Basle had by this time become somewhat monotonous both in decoration and in typography. At least this was true of the old-established houses, such as the Frobens and the Petris. However, some of the newer men, especially Michel Isingrin and Joannes Oporinus, introduced fresh types of considerable interest.

1. In 1525 there appeared at Cologne at the press of E. Cervicorn a new italic, St. Augustin or English in size, in a book dated 6 Nov. – *Elegantiæ vocabulorum ex L. Valla*, edited by J. Montanus. This new design is found at Strasbourg in 1527 at the press of W. Köpfel in a Psalterium, at Paris in 1530, used by G. Morrhé, at Louvain in 1537, used by R. Rescius. At Basle it appears in March 1536 in Calvin's *Christianæ religionis institutio*, printed by Winter, Platter, and Lasius. Cratander was using it by 1538 and it is frequently found in Basle books down to 1563 at least. It found its way also to Rome at the press of the Dorici Brothers; see *El Pedante* of F. Belo, 1538. In London it was acquired by Thomas Berthelet; it is his 95 italic (20 lines = 95 mm) illustrated in Col. Isaac's *English Printing Types, 1501-35*, fig. 65a. (Fig. 1.)

2. The second type is a roman, remarkable not for the extent of its use, but for the fact that it has survived down to our day in the possession of Messrs. Enschedé en Zonen, of Haarlem. That firm issued a specimen book displaying the type in 1926, *Een Romeinsch lettertype*. The Enschedés have attributed the cutting of this roman to Peter Schöffer the Elder of Mainz, for the reason that the type descended to them from Jacobus Scheffers, a member of the famous family, who was printing at Bois-le-Duc c. 1750. But this roman seems to have been acquired from Cologne, where it is first found in 1527 at the press of Peter Quentell, e. g. in John Fisher's *De veritate corporis Christi*, published in March, in Luther's *Epistola ad Henricum VIII*, published in April, and in a Latin Bible of the same year. (Fig. 2.)

3. Another new roman, rather smaller (20 line = 76 mm) appeared at Cologne in 1531, used by E. Cervicorn in Haymo's *Homiliarum sermones*, and by J. Prael in the

BEATISSIME PATER
ex articulis contentis in materijs alias da
tis. S. V. eliciuntur Conclusiones in-
frascripte coram. S. V. et suo Sa-
crosancto Senatu in amplissi-
mo Consistorio penulti-
ma Februarij propo-
site & dispu-
tate.

X MATERIIS nostris eli-   ɩ
citur etiam probabile & necessari
um impedimentum secundum com
munem opinionem.

 Ad allegandum notorium & iu-   ꝛ
stum impedimentum temporale citati admittitur
excusator sine mandato secundum com.

 Ad allegandum iustum impedimentum necessa-   3
rium temporale admittitur excusator sine mandato secundum com.

 Conclusio iustificabatur rationibus et auctori-   ɩ
tatibus infrascriptis.

 Qui abest causa reipublice is ex probali & ne-
cessario impedimento est absens glo. ordi. in. l.
si. de in integr. resti. et ibi Bar. post glo. ubi tractã
      B. 2. do de

FIG. 1. Type No. 1. From *Acta curiae Romanae in causa matrimoniali
cum Catharina regina*. Thomas Berthelet, London [1530?].

same year. Again it is found in London at Berthelet's press, his 73 roman (cf. Isaac, op. cit. fig. 64). At Basle I find it first in Luther's *Disputationes*, T. Platter, March 1538. In 1539 it was used by Isingrin.

4. A third roman appeared also in 1531 at the press of J. Soter, in Nicander's *Theriaca* issued in March. The type is found at Antwerp in 1540 at the press of J. Crinitus (cf. the reproduction in Nijhoff, *L'Art typographique dans les Pays Bas*. The M is different in the Antwerp fount). This roman also was acquired by Berthelet (cf. Isaac, op. cit. fig. 67) and was used by him first in 1533. Juan de Mey of Valencia used the roman in a Boiardo of 1555. This printer describes himself as 'Flandro', and we find that his fount is identical with the fount used by Crinitus at Antwerp, that is to say it has the second variety of M. The fact that Thomas Berthelet had three of these Cologne types seems to indicate that they may all have come from the same founder.

5. At Basle the first Garamond roman is found in 1539, in M. Bolzanius's *Institutionum in linguam græcam libri*, J. Walder, Sept. This roman, St. Augustin in size, is the same as the third size of Garamond used in Robert Estienne's Latin Bible of 1532, where it occurs in the preliminaries. After 1539 it is not uncommon at Basle.

6. The Canon size of Garamond, the heading type of Estienne's Bible, I have not found at Basle until 1545. From that year many good title-pages, decorated with this

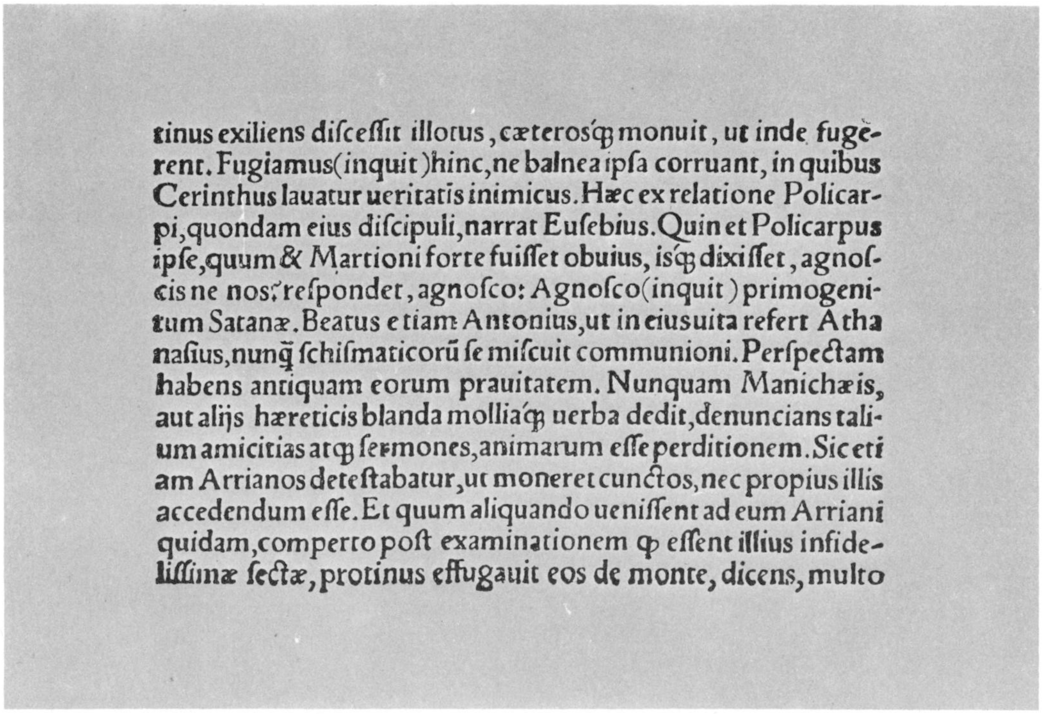

tinus exiliens diſceſſit illotus, cæterosq; monuit, ut inde fuge-
rent. Fugiamus(inquit)hinc, ne balnea ipſa corruant, in quibus
Cerinthus lauatur ueritatis inimicus. Hæc ex relatione Policar-
pi, quondam eius diſcipuli, narrat Euſebius. Quin et Policarpus
ipſe, quum & Martioni forte fuiſſet obuius, isq; dixiſſet, agnoſ-
cis ne nos? reſpondet, agnoſco: Agnoſco(inquit) primogeni-
tum Satanæ. Beatus etiam Antonius, ut in eius uita refert Atha
naſius, nunq̃ ſchiſmaticorũ ſe miſcuit communioni. Perſpectam
habens antiquam eorum prauitatem. Nunquam Manichæis,
aut alijs hæreticis blanda molliaq; uerba dedit, denuncians tali-
um amicitias atq; ſermones, animarum eſſe perditionem. Sic eti
am Arrianos deteſtabatur, ut moneret cunctos, nec propius illis
accedendum eſſe. Et quum aliquando ueniſſent ad eum Arriani
quidam, comperto poſt examinationem q̃ eſſent illius infide-
liſſimæ ſectæ, protinus effugauit eos de monte, dicens, multo

FIG. 2. Type No. 2. From John Fisher, *De veritate corporis et sanguinis Christi in eucharistia.* Peter Quentell for Franz Birckmann, Cologne, 1527.

Canon, appear in Basle books printed by Isingrin, Oporinus, H. Curio, and R. Winter. The Basle version has some small differences, notably the lower-case g, and may be a copy.

7. The large Basle italic, dating from 1534, used in the Galen of 1538, and by Sebastien Gryphius and Étienne Dolet at Lyons in 1537, is a well-known European type (cf. my *Type Designs*, pp. 146-8). There was a smaller size of the same design, first found at Basle in 1542, at the press of J. Oporinus; see Insulanus Menapius's *Encomium febris*. Westhemerus was using it in the following year. It was fairly common in Germany and also in London (Grafton's 71 italic in Isaac op. cit. fig. 33 b). It appears also on a specimen sheet, that of the Nuremberg printer, Valentin Geyssler (see a reproduction in *Ars Typographica*, vol. 2, no. 3, 1925). This is another of the types which found their way south of the Alps: see a Juvenal, G. Scotto, Venice, 1549, and the *Catalogus librorum haereticorum*, G. Giolito, Venice, 1554. The large Basle italic had been taken to Venice in 1541 by the younger Peter Schöffer. (Fig. 3.)

8. In 1549 we find the first appearence at Basle of an italic cut by Robert Granjon, in Fuchs's *De stirpium historia*, printed by Isingrin. This is the italic used from the same year, 1549, in several books printed at Paris by Granjon and Fezendat. It closely resembles the first Granjon St. Augustin italic dating from 1543 (cf. my *Type Designs*, p. 150).

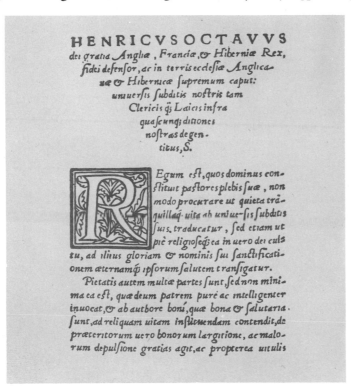

FIG. 3. Type No. 7. From *Orarium seu libellus precationum per regiam maiestatem & clerum latinè aeditus*. Richard Grafton, London, 1546.

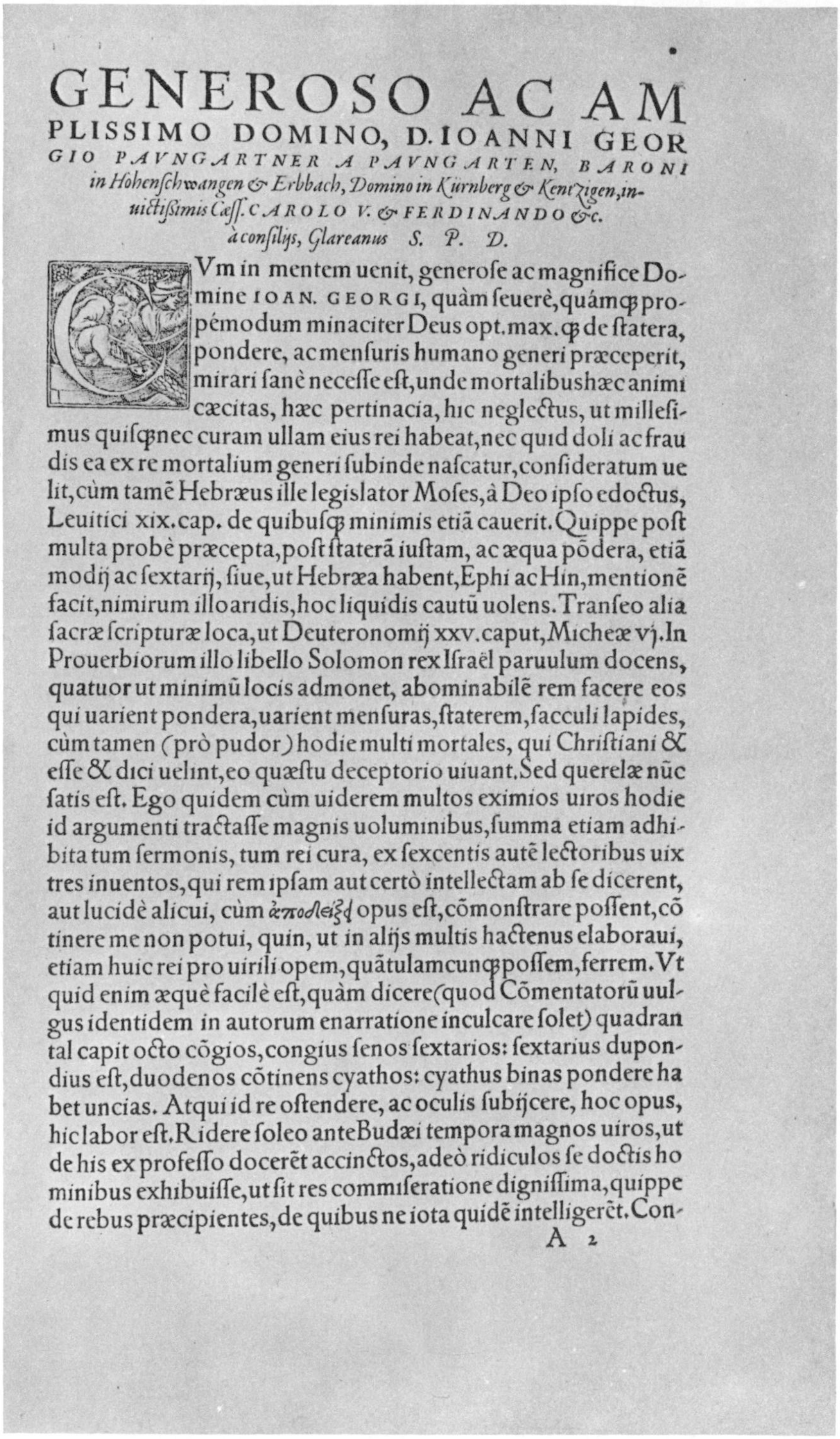

GENEROSO AC AM
PLISSIMO DOMINO, D.IOANNI GEOR
GIO PAVNGARTNER A PAVNGARTEN, BARONI
in Hohenſchwangen & Erbbach, Domino in Kürnberg & Kentzigen, in-
uictiſſimis Ceſſ. CAROLO V. & FERDINANDO &c.
à conſilijs, Glareanus S. P. D.

Vm in mentem uenit, generoſe ac magnifice Domine IOAN. GEORGI, quàm ſeuerè, quámꝗ pro-
pémodum minaciter Deus opt.max. ꝗ de ſtatera,
pondere, ac menſuris humano generi præceperit,
mirari ſanè neceſſe eſt, unde mortalibus hæc animi
cæcitas, hæc pertinacia, hic neglectus, ut milleſi-
mus quiſꝗnec curam ullam eius rei habeat, nec quid doli ac frau
dis ea ex re mortalium generi ſubinde naſcatur, conſideratum ue
lit, cùm tamē Hebræus ille legiſlator Moſes, à Deo ipſo edoctus,
Leuitici xix. cap. de quibuſꝗ minimis etiã cauerit. Quippe poſt
multa probè præcepta, poſt ſtaterã iuſtam, ac æqua põdera, etiã
modij ac ſextarij, ſiue, ut Hebræa habent, Ephi ac Hin, mentionē
facit, nimirum illo aridis, hoc liquidis cautū uolens. Tranſeo alia
ſacræ ſcripturæ loca, ut Deuteronomij xxv. caput, Micheæ vj. In
Prouerbiorum illo libello Solomon rex Iſraël paruulum docens,
quatuor ut minimū locis admonet, abominabilē rem facere eos
qui uarient pondera, uarient menſuras, ſtaterem, ſacculi lapides,
cùm tamen (prò pudor) hodie multi mortales, qui Chriſtiani &
eſſe & dici uelint, eo quæſtu deceptorio uiuant. Sed querelæ nūc
ſatis eſt. Ego quidem cùm uiderem multos eximios uiros hodie
id argumenti tractaſſe magnis uoluminibus, ſumma etiam adhi-
bita tum ſermonis, tum rei cura, ex ſexcentis autē lectoribus uix
tres inuentos, qui rem ipſam aut certò intellectam ab ſe dicerent,
aut lucidè alicui, cùm ἀποδείξϊ opus eſt, cõmonſtrare poſſent, cõ
tinere me non potui, quin, ut in alijs multis hactenus elaboraui,
etiam huic rei pro uirili opem, quãtulamcunꝗ poſſem, ferrem. Vt
quid enim æquè facilè eſt, quàm dicere (quod Cõmentatorū uul-
gus identidem in autorum enarratione inculcare ſolet) quadran
tal capit octo cõgios, congius ſenos ſextarios: ſextarius dupon-
dius eſt, duodenos cõtinens cyathos: cyathus binas pondere ha
bet uncias. Atqui id re oſtendere, ac oculis ſubijcere, hoc opus,
hic labor eſt. Ridere ſoleo ante Budæi tempora magnos uiros, ut
de his ex profeſſo docerēt accinctos, adeò ridiculos ſe doctis ho
minibus exhibuiſſe, ut ſit res commiſeratione digniſſima, quippe
de rebus præcipientes, de quibus ne iota quidē intelligerēt. Con-

A 2

FIG. 4. Type No. 9. From Henricus, *Liber de asse et partibus eius.*
Michael Isingrin, Basle, 1550. (Reduced.)

9. Also in 1549 is the first appearence of a remarkable new roman in the Basle style (20 lines = 120 mm), again at the press of Isingrin, on the title-page of J. Manardus's *Epistolarum medicinalium libri*, issued in March. The main text of this large book is in the Basle italic. More of the roman is to be seen in H. Loritus's *De asse*, 1550, and in a book with a Paris imprint, Fuchs's *Commentaires de l'Hystoire des plantes*, J. Gazeau, 1549, but actually printed by Isingrin. It is surprising that this good design was so little used; probably it came too late to compete with the new French romans. However, it turns up in a few odd places, at the press of P. Ulhart, Augsburg, 1557, V. Creutzer, Wittenberg, 1560, W. Eder, Ingolstadt, 1583, and also at Milan, at the press of F. Moschenius, 1563 (see the *Discorso di Mercurio Concorreggio*). (Fig. 4.)

10. *Le cento & dieci diuine considerationi* of Juan Valdes, Basle, 1550, without printer's name, shows some interesting types. The title is set in the 120 roman just described; the main text is in the Granjon italic, our no. 8. The 'Tavola' is printed in an italic of the school of the calligrapher and printer Lodovico degli Arrighi, an italic which was later in the possession of the Italian exile Pietro Perna. (For a reproduction see my *First Century of Printing at Basle*, pl. 50.) Perna is said to have been settled in Basle by 1542, and according to Thomas Platter purchased a printing plant in 1544 (cf. Manni's *Vita di Pietro Perna*, 1763). In Felix Platter's autobiography Perna's press is referred to in a

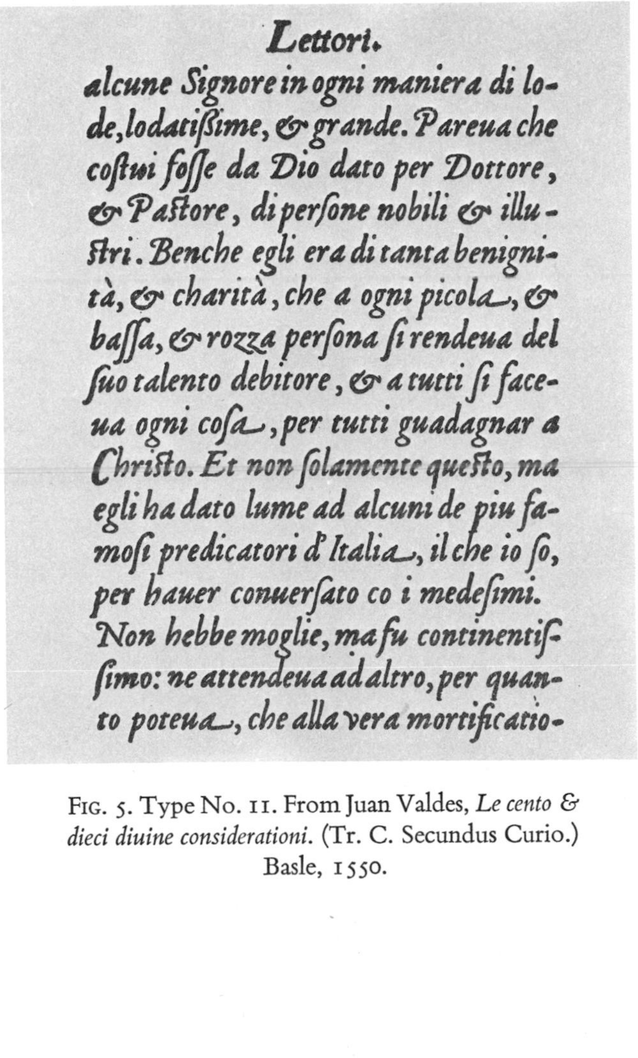
Lettori.
alcune Signore in ogni maniera di lode, lodatiſsime, & grande. Pareua che coſtui foſſe da Dio dato per Dottore, & Paſtore, di perſone nobili & illuſtri. Benche egli era di tanta benignità, & charità, che a ogni picola, & baſſa, & rozza perſona ſi rendeua del ſuo talento debitore, & a tutti ſi faceua ogni coſa, per tutti guadagnar a Chriſto. Et non ſolamente queſto, ma egli ha dato lume ad alcuni de piu famoſi predicatori d'Italia, il che io ſo, per hauer conuerſato co i medeſimi. Non hebbe moglie, ma fu continentiſſimo: ne attendeua ad altro, per quanto poteua, che alla vera mortificatio-

FIG. 5. Type No. 11. From Juan Valdes, *Le cento & dieci diuine considerationi*. (Tr. C. Secundus Curio.) Basle, 1550.

167

PETRVS VICTORIVS RE-
ginaldo Polo, Cardinali
Anglo.

NON eo consilio, uir optime & amplissi
me, calamū sumpsi, ut te consolarer, do-
loremq́ illum minuerem, quem cepisti ob interi
tum M. Antonij Flaminij, probi hominis, ac
summis ingenij dotibus præditi. Neq, enim tantum mihi tribuo, ut fortem uirum, usuq́ ac doctrina nostræ imbecillitatis peritum, audeam
monere: aut tibi eripio, quem scio nullo nego-
tio, quicquid remedij huic malo adhiberi potest, per seipsum inuenturum: sed ut tecum ali-
quantulum de graui hac plaga per literas lo-
querer, quæ cunctos optimarum artium studio-
sos merito perculsit. In quibus cum ipse inferio-
rem locum teneam, acumē tamen ingenij illius,
uitæ sanctitatem, præclaram eruditionem, morum elegantiam in primis dilexerim, uel suspe-
xerim potius: non potui mihi temperare, quin
ægritudinem párerem, ac de communi hoc da-
mno tecum quererer. Amisimus enim morte il
lius, florem poetarum, decusq́ ac splendorem hu
ius seculi, quod ille mirifice ornabat, ac plurimis, maximisq́ uirtutibus suis illustrabat. Hæc
autem de aliquo prolata, non me fallit, exupe-

m 4   rantiam

FIG. 6. Type No. 13. From Georgius Fabricius,
Odarum libri tres ad Deum omnipotentem. Johann
Oporinus, Basle, 1552.

letter of 15 Nov. 1556, but no book bearing his name is known before the year 1558. With the exception of this calligraphic italic all the types in the Valdes and one at least of the initials are to be found in Isingrin's books.

11. The address to the Christian Readers in this same book is set in a Gros Texte italic, a type used by Isingrin in an Aristotle of the same year and found in the books of Jean de Tournes at Lyons from 1549. The lower case of this Gros Texte closely resembles the Granjon italic of that size shown on the Egenolff-Berner specimen sheets of 1592 and 1622 and used by Plantin at Antwerp from 1564. It seems to have been Granjon's first version. The type was frequently used by Oporinus at Basle. (Fig. 5.)

12. The *Testamentum Novum* in the version of Sébastien Châteillon, J. Oporinus, Basle, 1551, is printed in an italic of which 20 lines measure 63 mm, a type used by Jean de Tournes at Lyons, for example in his Petrarch of 1544. As this design is exactly like Granjon's first St. Augustin italic, one can safely assign it to the same type cutter.

13. In 1552 the same printer Oporinus printed *Odarum libri tres* of G. Fabricius in a Cicero italic; which, if not cut by Granjon, is certainly of the French school. It closely resembles an italic used at Lyons by B. Arnoullet in J. Huttichius's *Imperatorum vitæ*, 1550, at Paris, by M. de La Porte in Ronsard's *Les Amours*, 1553, and at Venice by Giolito in an edition of Castiglione's *Il Cortegiano*, 1556. But there are differences, and both again differ from Granjon's Cicero italic as shown on the Egenolff-Berner specimen sheet of 1592, a type which can be traced back to 1554 at the press of M. Bonhomme, Lyons. The preface of Oporinus's book is in our italic here No. 11. (Fig. 6.)

14. In the preliminaries of an edition of Heliodorus, Oporinus, 1552, will be found a roman of Parangon size, of the same school but different from the 'Parangon de Garamond' of the Egenolff sheet. Note particularly the lower-case g. This roman was in common use at Lyons, perhaps first in G. Paradin's *Memoriæ nostræ libri*, J. de Tournes, 1548. It will be found also in a well-known book, Pedro de Medina's *L'Art de Naviguer*, G. Rouillé, Lyons, 1554. Oporinus printed the main text of his second edition of Vesalius, 1555, in this roman. The type is found also at Florence at the press of Torrentino, a printer who had a number of French designs.

[1939]

ENGLISH BOOKS PRINTED ABROAD

Iɴ Sayle's *Early English Printed Books in the University Library, Cambridge*, vol. iii, pp. 1410 f., under 'Zürich', a number of English books are connected together by the fact that they are printed in the same type, which was in the possession of Christopher Froschouer of Zürich. These attributions received some support from Robert Steele in his article 'Notes on English Books printed abroad' in *The Transactions of the Bibliographical Society*, vol. xi, 1912, and have been accepted, sometimes doubtfully, by the *Short-title Catalogue*. The type in question is a Schwabacher varying in size from 74 to 80 mm for 20 lines. The design goes back to 1500 (Fig. 1).[1] It became very popular and a large number of German, Swiss, and Netherlands printers had the type. As to how many of them were derived from the same original punches and how many were copies is fortunately not my concern. In some cases these Schwabachers in the hands of different printers can be distinguished by their measurements and by the appearance of extra sorts. Three ascending letters, *b*, *d*, and *h*, are found with loops in addition to the plain sorts. By the help of these differences and the occurrence of woodcut initials some attempt can be made to assign Sayle's Zürich books to the correct presses or at least towns. In the result it will appear that very few of the books in the *S.T.C.* assigned to Zürich are left undisturbed.

It will be as well to begin with the few books which in fact came from the press of Froschouer of Zürich. If Froschouer was not the printer of the first Coverdale Bible (*S.T.C.* 2063) he did print an English Bible in 1550 (*S.T.C.* 2080). The text of this edition is set in our Schwabacher. The type measures 76 mm, has looped *b* and *d*, not *h*, and an early form of ampersand. From the same press, also in 1550, came an English New Testament (*S.T.C.* 2860) printed in a 72 Fraktur. Both of these Biblical texts contain decorative material, including woodcut initials, known to belong to Froschouer. This material is illustrated in Leemann van Elck's *Die Offizin Froschauer*, 1940. Coverdale's *A Confutacion of that treatise which one J. Standish made*, [1541?], also is correctly assigned to Froschouer (*S.T.C.* 5888). The book is printed in the same Fraktur as the New Testament of 1550, with some use of an Upper-Rhine type to be found at Froschouer's press. There is also found one of the Zürich printer's initials. Edmond Allen's *A shorte catechisme*, 1550 (*S.T.C.* 361) completes the list of English books to be assigned to Froschouer. This book is set in his 76 Schwabacher with looped *b* and *d* and the antiquated ampersand. Mention should be made of another Zürich printer, Augustin Fries, who printed in roman type and signed two books by Bishop Hooper (*S.T.C.* 13741 and 13745). Fries and not Froschouer was the printer of another book by Hooper, *A declaration of the ten holy cōmaundementes*, [1548] (*S.T.C.* 13746). This book is set in a 77 Schwabacher of the same design as Froschouer's but with no looped

---

1. Shown on pl. 55 of the publications of the Gesellschaft für Typenkunde from the press of T. Anshelm, Tübingen. It is further reproduced at fig. 63 in Proctor's *Index to the Early Printed Books in the British Museum*, Part 2, Germany.

therto. If he will not redeme it/ then let it be
sold as it is worth.
¶ There shall no damned thynge be solde/nor
bought out/that any man damneth for the
Lorde/of all that is his good/ whether it be
men/catell/or lande. for euery damned thynge/
is moost holy vnto the Lorde. There shall
no damned thynge of man be bought out/
†but shall dye the death. All the tythes in the
lande/both of the sede of the lande/and of the
frutes of the trees/are the Lordes/ & shalbe
holy vnto the Lorde. But if any man will
redeme his tythes/he shall geue the fyfte parte
more therto. And all the tythes of oxen & the
shepe/and that goeth vnder ý rodde/ the same
is an holy tyth vnto the Lorde. It shall not
be oxed/whether it be good or bad / neyther
shall it be chaunged. But if any man chaunge
it/then both it/and ý it was chaunged withal/
shalbe holy/and not redemed. These are the
commaundementes/which the Lorde
gaue vnto Moses in charge vnto ý chyldren of Israel/vpon mount
Sinai.

The ende of the thyrde boke of Mo-
ses/called Leuiticus.

**The fourth bo-
ke of Moses called
Numerus.**

The first Chapter.

AND ý Lorde spake vnto
Moses in ý wildernesse of
Sinai/ in ý Tabernacle of
witnesse/the first daye of ý
secode moneth/in ý secode
yeare/whã they were gone
out of the lande of Egipte
and saydt: Take the summe of ý whole congregacion of ý chyldren of Israel/after theyr kyn-
redes/& theyr fathers houses / with ý numbre
of ý names/all that are males/heade by heade/
from xx. yeare and aboue/as many as are able
to go forth into ý warre in Israel. And ye shal

nubre them/accordinge to theyr armyes/thou
& Aaron/and of euery tribe ye shall take vnto
you one captayne ouer his fathers house.
These are the names of the captaynes/that
shall stande with you. Of Ruben: Elisur the
sonne of Sedeur. Of Simeon: Selumiel the
sonne of Zury Sadai. Of Juda: Nahasson ý
sonne of Amnadab. Of Isachar: Nathaneel
ý sonne of Zuar. Of Zabulon: Eliab ý sonne
of Helon. Amonge the chyldre of Joseph. Of
Ephraim: Elisama the sonne of Amihud. Of
Manasse: Gamaliel ý sonne of Pedazur. Of
Ben Iamin: Abidam the sonne of Gedeoni.
Of Dan: Ahieser the sonne of Ammi Sadai.
Of Asser: Pagiel the sonne of Ochram. Of
Gad: Eliasaph ý sonne of Deguel. Of Neph-
thali: Ahira the sonne of Enan.
These are the auncient men of the congre-
gacions/the captaynes amonge the trybes of
theyr fathers/which were heades and princes
in Israel.
And Moses & Aaron toke them/(lyke as
they are there named by name) and gathered
the whole congregacion together also/ý first
daye of ý seconde moneth/and rekened them
after theyr byrth/accordyng to theyr kynredes/
and fathers houses by theyr names/from xx.
yeare and aboue/head by head / as the Lord
commaunded Moses/and numbred them in
the wildernesse of Sinay.
The chyldre of Ruben/Israels fyrste sonne/
theyr kynredes & generacions / after theyr fathers houses/in the numbre of theyr names/
heade by heade / al that were males/from xx.
yeare and aboue/and were able to go forth to
the warre/were numbred to the trybe of Ru-
ben/xlvj. thousand/and v. hundreth.
The chyldre of Simeon/theyr kynredes &
generacions/after theyr fathers houses / in ý
numbre of the names heade by heade/all that
were males from xx. yeare and aboue/& were
able to go forth to the warre/ were numbred
to the trybe of Symeon/lix. thousand/and iij.
hundreth.
The chyldren of Gad/they: kynredes & generacions / after theyr fathers houses/in the
numbre of the names/from xx yeare & aboue/
all that were able to go forth to ý werre/were
numbred to the trybe of Gad/xlv. thousande/
vj. hundreth/and l.

B ij   The

FIG. 1. Page from *The whole byble, that is the holy scripture*. (Tr. Miles Coverdale.) Christoph Froschouer, Zürich, 1550. (Reduced.)

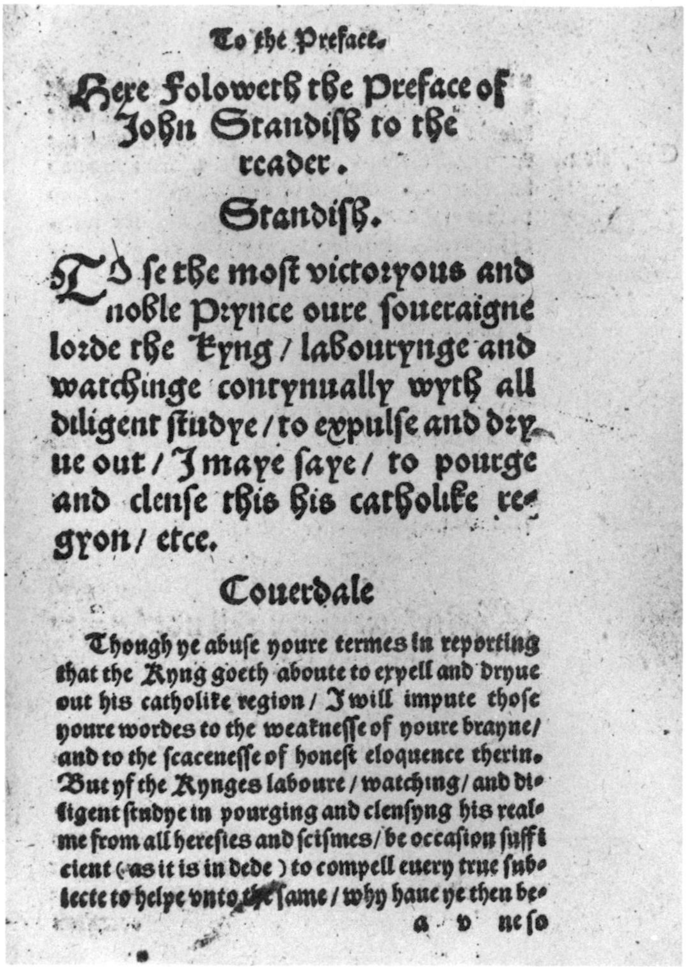

To the Preface.

Here Foloweth the Preface of John Standish to the reader.

Standish.

To se the most victoryous and noble Prynce oure soueraigne lorde the Kyng / labourynge and watchinge contynually wyth all diligent studye / to expulse and dryue out / I maye saye / to pourge and clense this his catholike regyon / etce.

Couerdale

Though ye abuse youre termes in reporting that the Kyng goeth aboute to expell and dryue out his catholike region / I will impute those youre wordes to the weaknesse of youre brayne/ and to the scacenesse of honest eloquence therin. But yf the Kynges laboure / watching / and diligent studye in pourging and clensyng his realme from all heresties and scismes / be occasion sufficient (as it is in dede) to compell euery true subiecte to helpe vnto the same / why haue ye then be-

a v ne so

FIG. 2. Page from Miles Coverdale, *A confutacion of that treatise, which one J. Standish made agaynst the protestacion of D. Barbes.* [Christoph Froschouer, Zürich, 1541?]

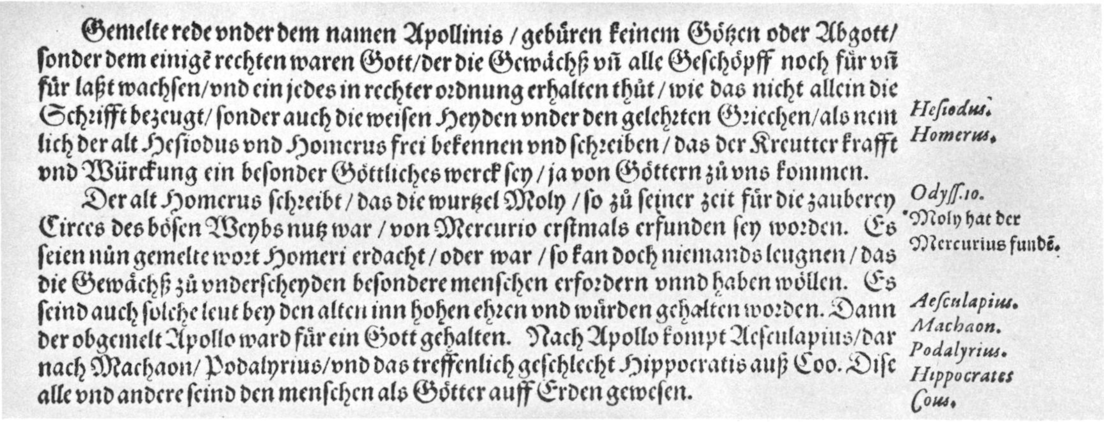

Gemelte rede vnder dem namen Apollinis / gebüren keinem Götzen oder Abgott/ sonder dem einigē rechten waren Gott/der die Gewächß vñ alle Geschöpff noch für vñ für laßt wachsen/vnd ein jedes in rechter ordnung erhalten thůt / wie das nicht allein die Schrifft bezeugt/ sonder auch die weisen Heyden vnder den gelehrten Griechen/als nemlich der alt Hesiodus vnd Homerus frei bekennen vnd schreiben / das der Kreutter krafft vnd Würckung ein besonder Göttliches werck sey / ja von Göttern zů vns kommen. *Hesiodus. Homerus.*

Der alt Homerus schreibt / das die wurtzel Moly / so zů seiner zeit für die zauberey Circes des bösen Weybs nutz war / von Mercurio erstmals erfunden sey worden. Es seien nün gemelte wort Homeri erdacht / oder war / so kan doch niemands leugnen / das die Gewächß zů vnderscheyden besondere menschen erfordern vnnd haben wöllen. Es seind auch solche leut bey den alten inn hohen ehren vnd würden gehalten worden. Dann der obgemelt Apollo ward für ein Gott gehalten. Nach Apollo kompt Aesculapius/dar nach Machaon/ Podalyrius/vnd das treffenlich geschlecht Hippocratis auß Coo. Dise alle vnd andere seind den menschen als Götter auff Erden gewesen.

Odyss.10. Moly hat der Mercurius fundē. *Aesculapius. Machaon. Podalyrius. Hippocrates Cous.*

FIG. 3. Type from Hieronymus Bock, *Kreuter Bůch.* Josias Rihel, Strasbourg, 1560.

ascenders. It is accepted as Fries by Leemann van Elck in his *Zürcher Drucker um die Mitte des 16. Jahrhunderts*, 1937.

Col. F. Isaac in his article on 'Egidius van der Erve' (*The Library*, 4th ser. xii. 336-52, 1932) has already assigned nine of these pseudo-Zürich books to Van der Erve's press at Emden. There are one or two additions to be made to Isaac's list. Among the 'Common Prayers used by Foreign Congregations in London' (*S.T.C.* 16571 to 16574) the edition in Dutch (*S.T.C.* 16571a) has the name C. Volckwinner in the imprint, a name suspected by Isaac to have been used by Van der Erve. The later edition, 1563, is also an Emden book. The Latin edition, translated by Joannes a Lasco, is assigned to Frankfurt in *S.T.C.* and also in G. Pascal's *Jean de Lasco*. This attribution is borne out by the typography and the initial E on p. 651 which belonged to Christian Egenoff of Frankfurt.[1] Finally *A warnyng for England*, 1555, (*S.T.C.* 10024) and Robert Watson's *Aetiologia*, 1556, (*S.T.C.* 25111) are also from the press of Van der Erve. All this is a parenthesis, as these books are not assigned to Zürich.

We come now to some groups of books which were printed at Strasbourg, several of them being set in the so-called 'Zürich' type. Henry Brinkelow's *The complaynt of Roderyck Mors*, [1550?] (*S.T.C.* 3762) has the imprint *Savoy, per Franciscum de Turona*. The book is set in a 96 italic and has several woodcut initials; both type and initials will be found at the press of Wolfgang Köpfel of Strasbourg, who printed many editions for the Reformers. The type is of Cologne origin and was used also by Berthelet in London. There is an illustration in Isaac's *English & Scottish Printing Types 1501-35* (1930), fig. 65a. The initials, an O on A3 verso, an H on C2 recto, and an A on E2 verso, will all be found in Köpfel's edition of Caspar Hedio's *Chronica*, 1545. The author describes himself in the preliminaries as 'a man banyshed my natyve contry'. He returned to London and died there in 1546. Several editions of the book were printed in London and are placed before this Strasbourg edition. Should not the order be reversed and the date 1550 be advanced?

Also from the press of Köpfel is a book by the Scottish Reformer Alexander Alesius. *Of the auctorite of the word of god*, [1537?] (*S.T.C.* 292). This work is set in Köpfel's Fraktur (Fig. 2). This type seems to have been used by Köpfel only. There is also the same initial A as in the Brinkelow. According to the list of the works of Alesius given in the *D.N.B.* there was a Latin edition of the book printed at Strasbourg in 1542. *S.T.C.* assigns the English book to Leipzig, where Alesius later settled as a Professor at the University, but not until 1543. There is one book in *S.T.C.*, edited by Alesius, which should be assigned to Leipzig, that is *Ordo distributionis sacramenti altaris*, (1548 *S.T.C.* 16459). It was printed by Valentin Papst, the best Leipzig printer of his generation and a printer with a distinctive style. The initials C on A2 and P on A4 will be found in his books, and also the unusual 4 mm roman capitals. *S.T.C.* describes the book, which has the imprint *Londini*, as 'printed in Germany'.

A second group of Strasbourg books came from the press of Wendelin Rihel and his

---

1. But the copy in the British Museum is made up from two editions. Sig. C-HH, pp. 1-548, are from the press of Van der Erve, Emden.

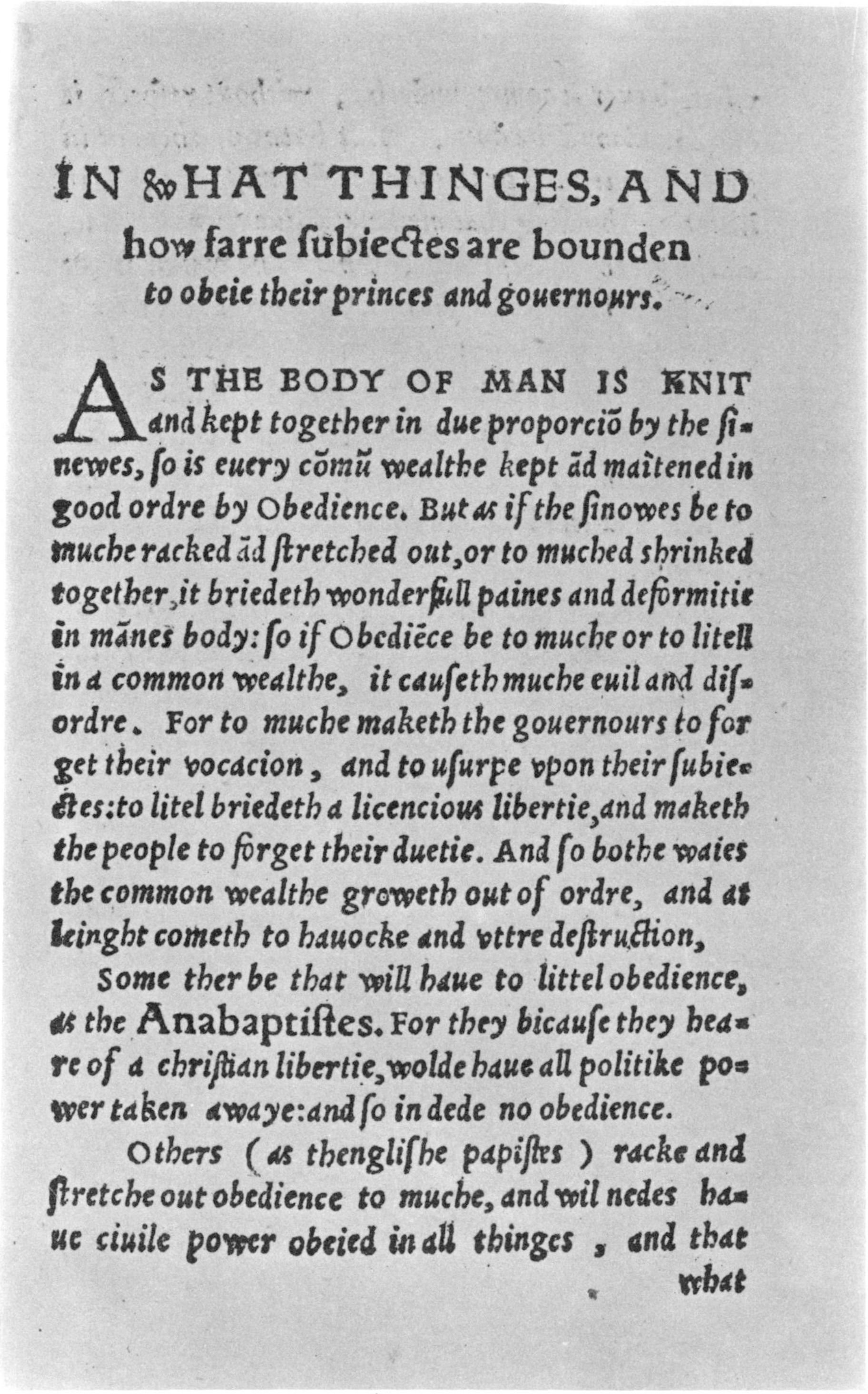

IN ẘHAT THINGS, AND
how farre fubiectes are bounden
to obeie their princes and gouernours.

S THE BODY OF MAN IS KNIT *and kept together in due proporciõ by the fi-newes, fo is euery cõmũ wealthe kept ãd maitened in good ordre by Obedience. But as if the finowes be to muche racked ãd ftretched out, or to muched shrinked together, it briedeth wonderfull paines and deformitie in mãnes body: fo if Obediēce be to muche or to litell in a common wealthe, it caufeth muche euil and dif-ordre. For to muche maketh the gouernours to for get their vocacion, and to ufurpe vpon their fubie-ctes: to litel briedeth a licencious libertie, and maketh the people to forget their duetie. And fo bothe waies the common wealthe groweth out of ordre, and at leinght cometh to hauocke and vttre deftruction,*

Some ther be that will haue to littel obedience, as the Anabaptiftes. *For they bicaufe they hea-re of a chriftian libertie, wolde haue all politike po-wer taken awaye: and fo in dede no obedience.*

Others (as thenglifhe papiftes) racke and ftretche out obedience to muche, and wil nedes ha-ue ciuile power obeied in all thinges, and that

what

FIG. 4. Page from John Ponet, *A shorte treatise of politike power . . .*
[Strasbourg?], 1556.

successors. *Certē godly, learned and comfortable conferences betwene D. N. Rydley and M. H. Latymer*, 1556 (*S.T.C.* 21048) is printed in 76 Schwabacher of the usual design, with looped ascenders. An Upper-Rhine type, different from Froschouer's but like that used by Fries, is found and in the margins the usual Strasbourg roman (fig. 3). The initial G on f2 recto is in the Euclid, Rihel, 1566, and the M on f. 36 verso is in I. S. Neanisci, 1565. The A on f5 recto I have not found, but it seems to belong to the alphabet of which some letters appear in the Dioscorides, 1565. The A turns up in a later Strasbourg book, the *Opera* of A. Turnebus, L. Zetzner, 1604. For the Schwabacher and Upper-Rhine type used in a signed Rihel book, see the *Kreuterbuch* of Hieronymus Bock, 1560. Another edition of the English book (*S.T.C.* 21049) is one of the Emden series. A book printed in the same Schwabacher and very similar in the layout of the title-page is Luther's *A faythfull admonycion*, Grenewych, C. Freeman, 1554 (*S.T.C.* 16980) and also *A treatise of the cohabitacyon of the faithfull*, 1555 (*S.T.C.* 24246). *A supplicacyō to the quenes maiestie*, 1555 [one issue 1550] (*S.T.C.* 17562), a book bearing the manifestly false imprint of J. Cawoode, is from the same press as the three preceding books i. e. Rihel. Another edition, in the Huntington Library, *S.T.C.* 17563, is perhaps a variant. Possibly also from the Rihels is *An answer to a certain godly mañes lettres*, [1557] (*S.T.C.* 658). The book is set in the same Upper-Rhine type with a few lines of Schwabacher. There is not enough of the Schwabacher to identify it and as this particular Upper-Rhine type was in the hands of several printers, the attribution is by no means certain. If any light could be thrown on the authorship of the tract in this case, as in a number of others, some confirmation of the town might be found. Much is now known of the whereabouts of the Marian exiles in the years in question.

A third Strasbourg group is connected with John Ponet, Bishop of Winchester, who some time after the accession of Mary betook himself to Strasbourg and died there in August 1556. His *A shorte treatise of politike power*, 1556 (*S.T.C.* 20178), one of the most famous of English books printed abroad in the sixteenth century, has long been attributed to Strasbourg. The book is printed in an italic of the usual Froben design but with a peculiar capital W. Whether this W was limited to a particular printer one cannot say, since it is only in English texts that a W would be needed. In the preliminaries is found an 80 Schwabacher with no looped ascenders. The text opens with a woodcut initial A which I have not found. The firm of Rihel had a closely similar A, but it seems unlikely that one printer would have two A's of almost the same design, and as the Schwabacher is not Rihel's one can perhaps rule out that press. The Schwabacher agrees with the type used by Köpfel. Wolfgang Köpfel died in 1554, but his heirs continued printing at Strasbourg until 1557, when they moved to Worms. A work in Latin attributed to Ponet, *Dialacticon viri boni et literati de veritate corporis Christi in Eucharistia*, 1557 (*S.T.C.* says 'Probably printed abroad'), was certainly from the Rihel press. It contains woodcut initials Q and D belonging to an alphabet much used by that firm from 1544 onwards. Ponet's *An apologie fully aunswering by scriptures . . . a blasphemose book gatherid by D. Steph. Gardiner and others*, 1555 (*S.T.C.* 20175) is from the same press as his *Shorte treatise*. This is printed in the 80 Schwabacher without looped ascenders, with some of the same italic in the preliminaries and a small Fraktur in the margins. Sayle connects with the *Shorte treatise* also *An anatomi* by A. Mainardi, 1556 (*S.T.C.* 17200) which is printed in the same italic.

There are two books by William Turner the botanist printed in a 74 Schwabacher of the usual design, with no looped ascenders, which come from a press different from any so far mentioned. Turner was a Cambridge protestant who about the year 1540 was imprisoned for preaching without a licence. After his release he went abroad and until the end of Henry VIII's reign pursued his scientific studies in Italy and Germany. According to *D.N.B.* he was in Basle in 1543, but the sole evidence for that visit is the imprint of *S.T.C.* 24353. Turner was certainly at Cologne in 1544 and had his book on birds printed there. His two controversial tracts, written under the pseudonym of William Wraghton (*S.T.C.* 24353 and 24355), were printed, not at Cologne, but at Bonn by Laurentius Mylius, the first printer in that city. In 1542 Hermann von Wied, Archbishop and Elector of Cologne, became a Lutheran and in 1543 he induced Bucer and Melanchthon to come to Bonn and assist in the preparation of his proposals for reform. The book, *Einfaltigs Bedencken*, was printed by Mylius at Bonn in 1543, and the Latin edition, *Simplex et pia deliberatio*, in 1545. A. Piel in his *Geschichte des ältesten Bonner Buchdrucks* (1924) gives a list of about thirty books from Mylius's press, including several works by Bucer and Melanchthon, but not these tracts in English. All the types of the two Turners may be found in the two editions of Hermann von Wied already mentioned. The calligraphic gothic A used in *The huntyng . . . of the Romishe fox* occurs several times in the *Einfaltigs Bedencken*, and the initial I on A 2 recto of *The rescuynge* appears thrice in the Latin edition. The books by Hermann von Wied are folios, and for a closer parallel in format one may compare the Bonn edition of Melanchthon's *Responsio ad scriptum quorundam delectorum*, especially the capitals of the title-page.

[1950]

BOOKS PRINTED AT HEIDELBERG
FOR THOMAS CARTWRIGHT

THERE is a group of books published by Thomas Cartwright the Puritan, while in exile in the years 1574 to 1577, which have been assigned to the wrong press or left unassigned. As a result of his unorthodox opinions and his share in heretical publications Cartwright was deprived of his chair at Cambridge in 1572, and an order for his arrest was issued bearing the date 11 December 1573. He escaped to the Continent and proceeded first to Heidelberg, where he lived for about three years. There is an excellent life of Cartwright written by A. F. Scott Pearson, Cambridge, 1925, to which the reader may be referred for biographical details and for the relation of the books to the Puritan controversies of the day.

Whilst at Heidelberg Cartwright saw through the press four books. They are all clearly from the same press; the printer was Michael Schirat. According to F. W. Roth, writing on Heidelberg sixteenth-century printing in the *Neues Archiv für die Geschichte der Stadt Heidelberg*, Bd. 4, 1901, p. 226 et seq., Schirat was at work from 1563 to 1577, but the books signed by him are very few. The book which is most helpful for the solution of our problem is the *Sanctae Inquisitionis Hispanicae artes aliquot detectae* by R. Gonsalvius, 1567. It is printed in an 86 roman with an italic of the Froben design for the preliminaries. An unusual fleuron, to be called Fleuron A, is found on leaf 2 and again on p. 209 and p. 233. On p. 228 is a larger fleuron, to be called Fleuron B, which is a well-known Lyonese design. There are nine initials, several of them used more than once, A, C, D, E, F, H, I, M, and T, open arabesque designs of about 35 × 35 mm, copied from Geneva. Another book by Schirat, an edition of the Heidelberg Catechism, *Catechesis Religionis Christianae*, 1563, is printed in the same roman and has three further initials of the same alphabet, O, P, and Q.[1]

The four books with which Cartwright was concerned are:

1. *Ecclesiasticae Disciplinae et Anglicanae Ecclesiae ab illa aberrationis ... explicatio*, Rupellae, excudebat Adamus de Monte, 1574. The work was probably written by Walter Travers and the preface, dated 'Quarto nonas Feb. 1574' is by Cartwright, the editor. The imprint has long been held to be fictitious and Weller in *Die falschen Druckorte* assigned the book to Basle. It is printed in Schirat's 86 roman and has on the title-page Fleuron A, with Fleuron B at the end of the preface. Initials N (a Z on its side?) and C are used, clearly belonging to Schirat's alphabet, although these two letters do not occur in the only two books signed by him which I have seen. There is another book with a false imprint which may also be assigned to Schirat – [Nicolas Barnaud] *Dialogus quo multa exponuntur quae Lutheranis acciderunt*, Oragniae, excudebat Adamus de Monte,

---

1. Another Heidelberg printer, Johann Mayer, shared in the publication of this book. On Mayer see W. Port, 'Johann Mayer, ein Reformierter Drucker des 16. Jahrhunderts' in the *Zentralblatt für Bibliothekswesen*, 1942, p. 140 et seq. Mayer does not appear to have printed any book in English.

1573. It is a closely similar volume to the book by Travers and has the initials A and I of the Schirat alphabet.

2. *A full and plaine declaration of ecclesiastical discipline*, 1574 (*S.T.C.* 24184), Cartwright's translation of Travers's book. The Epistle to the reader is set in the 86 roman and the main text in a 78 Schwabacher. An Upper-Rhine type and Fraktur headings are also used. An initial I of the Schirat alphabet occurs, with a T of another alphabet, not found. On the title-page is another fleuron, C, not found. I have unfortunately seen no book of Schirat's in German and therefore cannot check these types. They are all common designs, especially the Schwabacher. The *S.T.C.* assigns this book and the two following to Froschouer of Zürich, probably after Sayle and Robert Steele. Sayle, who found this Schwabacher in a number of earlier English books printed abroad and found it later used by Froschouer gave it the name of the Zürich type. This conclusion, ignoring the fact that many German printers had this design, has had the unfortunate result that a considerable number of English books are wrongly assigned to Zürich.

3. *A brieff discourse off the troubles begonne at Franckford*, 1574. Another issue is dated 1575 (*S.T.C.* 25442 and 25443). Attributed to William Whittingham. The typography is closely similar to that of No. 2. Initials A and S of the Schirat alphabet. Fleuron B on the last page. Assigned to Froschouer in *S.T.C.*, this time with a query.

4. *The second replie against Maister Whitgiftes second answer*, 1575 (*S.T.C.* 4714). By Cartwright. The Reply had been printed at a secret press near London before Cartwright left England. The typography is closely similar to that of Nos. 2 and 3. Initial F of the Schirat alphabet, and the T found in No. 2. Fleuron A on p. 666. *S.T.C.* assigns to Froschouer.

Towards the end of 1576 Cartwright left Heidelberg after the death of the Elector Frederick and proceeded to Basle. There he arranged for the printing of one more book.

5. *The Rest of the Second replie against Maister Vuhitgifts, second ansver* 1577 (*S.T.C.* 4715). This book, set in roman, was printed by a well-known Basle printer, Thomas Guarinus, successor of Isingrin. A comparison of the initials and typography of the book with those of Guarinus's Latin Bible, 1564, will provide ample evidence.

[1948]

SOME TYPES USED BY PAOLO MANUZIO

THE Accademia Veneziana, or Accademia della Fama, as it was called from its device of a figure of fame, was founded in 1556 by a wealthy Venetian, Federico Badoer. There were about one hundred members, among them Bernardo Tasso and Paolo Manuzio, son of Aldus, and there was an ambitious programme of publication. In 1562 the founder was involved in financial troubles, resulting in the closing of his Academy. Only a small part of the programme was carried out; between 1568 and 1572 some fifty-seven books were published 'dont aucune n'est volumineux', as Renouard says. Paolo Manuzio was the printer, and any interest which the Academy still arouses is mainly due to his typographical work.

In his *Annales de l'Imprimerie des Aldes*, third edition, 1834, p. 270, Renouard quotes a letter from Manuzio to the Academy, dated 28 July 1558, as follows:

Dovendosi dar principio allo stampare l'indice, mando prima a V. Excellentiss. tre mostre di caratteri, l'una per foglio, l'altra per quarto, la terza per ottavo ... Il carattere maggiore è quello che onorò molto le stampe di mio padre. Quell di ottavo ho fatto di intagliar io da un anno in qua. Il mezzano ho fatto venir di Franza, e sono tutti i piu excellenti nel suo genere.

Renouard's comment on this extract is not altogether satisfying. He says that the type for folios is that of the Bembo of 1495; that for quartos is a Garamond, ordered from France, Cicero in size; and that for octavos, cut a year previously, a Petit Romain as used in the edition of the grammar of Aldo Manuzio, 1558 (no. 5 in Renouard's list, p. 173).[1] The specimen of the three types submitted by Manuzio has not survived, and it becomes difficult to identify them. It is natural to assume that they will be found in the books actually printed for the Academy. With this assumption it appears that the folio type is certainly not that of the Bembo, never used by the younger Manuzio, at least in its original form, and unfortunately that it was not a type ever used by the elder Manuzio, in spite of the remark in the son's letter. The type of the *Somma delle opere*, 1558 (no. 1 in Renouard's list of the Academy publications), of the preface of the *Summa Librorum*, 1559 (Renouard's no. 2), and found in many other books printed by Manuzio, seems to be the only possible type in question. Its measurement is 114 mm for 20 lines, and it does not appear at Manuzio's press before 1554 although another Venetian printer, Valgrisi, was using it in 1549. The quarto type is really a St. Augustin, not a Cicero, and that it was cut by Garamond is a mere guess. The octavo type may be the Petit Romain, first used in 1558, but I prefer a Cicero, to be described later.

In Renouard's account of the Aldine types (pp. 407-9), he describes fourteen romans and italics. Types 1-5 are early romans not here in question. Types 6-8 and 12 are italics. Type 9, first found in Cicero's *Rhetorica*, 1546 (no. 7 in Renouard), a Cicero or Philosophie, is a French type, much used by Jean de Tournes at Lyons. A reproduction of this roman, as used by John Field in London, 1589, may be seen in Col. Isaac's 'Elizabethan Roman and Italic Types', *The Library*, June and September 1933, fig. 8. Type

---

1. In Renouard's list, the books of each year are separately numbered.

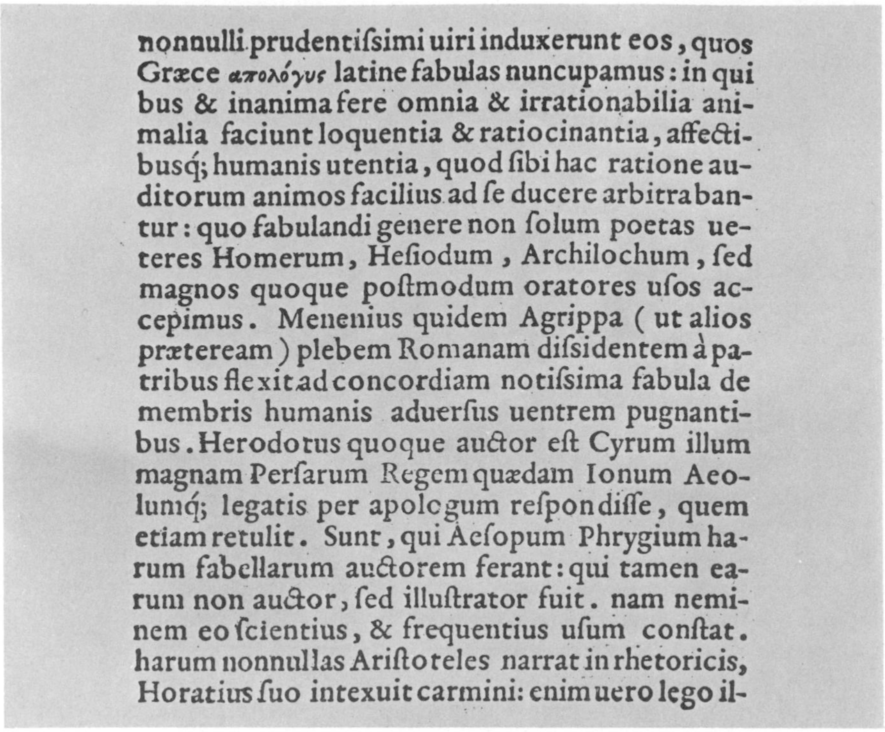

nonnulli.prudentifsimi uiri induxerunt eos, quos Græce απολόγυς latine fabulas nuncupamus : in qui bus & inanima fere omnia & irrationabilia ani malia faciunt loquentia & ratiocinantia, affecti busq́; humanis utentia, quod fibi hac ratione au ditorum animos facilius ad fe ducere arbitraban tur : quo fabulandi genere non folum poetas ue teres Homerum, Hefiodum , Archilochum , fed magnos quoque poftmodum oratores ufos ac cepimus . Menenius quidem Agrippa (ut alios præteream) plebem Romanam difsidentem à pa tribus flexit ad concordiam notifsima fabula de membris humanis aduerfus uentrem pugnanti bus . Herodotus quoque auctor eft Cyrum illum magnam Perfarum Regem quædam Ionum Aeo luniq́; legatis per apologum refpondiffe, quem etiam retulit . Sunt, qui Aefopum Phrygium ha rum fabellarum auctorem ferant: qui tamen ea runi non auctor, fed illuftrator fuit . nam nemi nem eo fcientius, & frequentius ufum conftat . harum nonnullas Ariftoteles narrat in rhetoricis, Horatius fuo intexuit carmini: enim uero lego il-

FIG. 1. Paolo Manuzio's new Cicero roman. From Marcus Antonius Natta, *De Dei locutione oratio*. Paolo Manuzio, Venice, 1558.

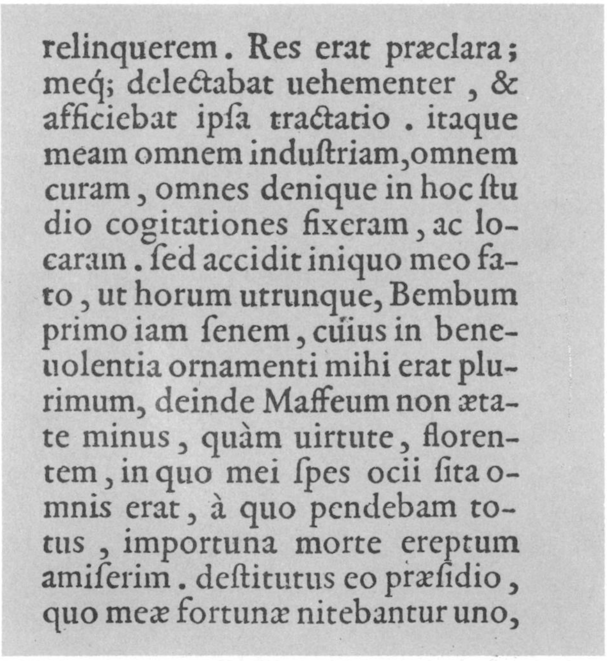

relinquerem . Res erat præclara; meq́; delectabat uehementer , & afficiebat ipfa tractatio . itaque meam omnem induftriam, omnem curam , omnes denique in hoc ftu dio cogitationes fixeram , ac lo caram . fed accidit iniquo meo fa to , ut horum utrunque, Bembum primo iam fenem , cuius in bene uolentia ornamenti mihi erat plu rimum, deinde Maffeum non æta te minus , quàm uirtute , floren tem , in quo mei fpes ocii fita o mnis erat, à quo pendebam to tus , importuna morte ereptum amiferim . deftitutus eo præfidio , quo meæ fortunæ nitebantur uno,

FIG. 2. Renouard's Type No. 13. From Paulus Manutius, *Antiquitatum Romanarum liber de legibus*. Aldus, Venice, 1559.

10 is a Petit Romain, in use from 1554 (Renouard's no. 4, p. 159). Type 11 is a Petit Text, used only for notes and the like. Type 13, described by Renouard as a Cicero, but really a St. Augustin (20 lines measure 92 mm), is the type which he regards as Manuzio's size for quartos. We find it in the *Summa Librorum* of 1559 (Renouard's no. 2 of the Academy books). However, another printer at Venice, Girolamo Scotto, had already used it in 1558 in an edition of Aristotle's *Physica*. Type 14 is a Petit Romain, first found in 1558, and different from type 10. According to Renouard this is the octavo type of Manuzio's letter, ordered a year previously, i. e. in 1557.

There are three romans used by Manuzio missing from this list of Renouard's. In the Sigonius of 1556 (no. 16 in Renouard, p. 169) there is a different Cicero roman, a Paris type. It will be found in the octavo edition of Geofroy Tory's *Champ fleury*, 1549. This type had an interesting history to which we shall return. Secondly, in the preface to the Latin Psalms of 1559 (no. 29 in Renouard), and in other books, we find a new Gros Texte (20 lines measure 114 mm), and thirdly in 1557 there is another Cicero, a new type (Fig. 1), used in a Sigonius (Renouard's no. 16, p. 172) and in many of the Academy books, e. g. nos. 6, 10, 11, 12, 13, and 19 of Renouard (p. 269, &c.). I suggest that this may be the type which Manuzio intended for octavos, which we are told was cut in 1557. As to the quarto type (Fig. 2), if the St. Augustin was this, ordered in France, it is strange that, although, as we shall see, it was widely used elsewhere, little of it is to be found in France, and that at a later date. The earliest appearance noted is in *La Camille de P. Boton*, J. Ruelle, 1573. Gabriel Buon printed an edition of *Les Oeuvres d'Ambroise Paré* in 1579 in this roman, and it was used by another Paris printer, Gilles Beys, Christophe Plantin's son-in-law, in 1582. At Bordeaux E. Vinet was using it from 1573, and S. Millanges from 1580 (cf. the first edition of Montaigne). Moreover, these three types, the Gros Texte, St. Augustin, and Cicero, all have a family resemblance, as though from the same hand. They all have a similar lower-case g and are much alike in weight. There we must leave the puzzle of Manuzio's letter.

The St. Augustin has several 'spot' letters which make it easy to recognize. The g has a long link and in design is quite unlike the Garamond g. The capital R is unusually narrow, and also the A and M to a less extent. Besides Scotto and Manuzio, a number of other Venetian printers soon acquired this roman, e. g. Valgrisi, Zaltieri, and Barbaro. Manuzio took it to Rome in 1562, when he moved there to help in establishing the Vatican Press, and in 1563 we find Antonio Blado using it. Percachino at Padua had it by 1562. The type was still in use in Italy in the seventeenth century (as may be seen from fig. 108 in Updike, from a book of 1623). One gets the impression that it was particularly an Italian type, until one finds that it was almost as common in several other countries. In 1560 we find it at Geneva at the presses of J. Crespin and of J. Bonnefoy, while Pietro Perna was using it at Basle by 1565. In 1561 at Antwerp Guillaume Silvius published a book, the *Tribonianus* of Jacobus Raevardus, which was printed for him by Plantin in a new fount of the St. Augustin. Plantin himself does not appear to have owned the type, but Silvius, who began to print on his own account in 1562, frequently used it. Other printers in the Netherlands also had it, e. g. P. Galle, Antwerp, 1572, and Hubert Goltzius at Bruges from 1564. The type was common in England from

1571, when John Day introduced it (see the reproduction of his 95 roman in Isaac, op. cit., fig. 5, and cf. fig. 286 in Updike). All the early folio editions of Burton's *Anatomy of Melancholy* were set in this roman, and many other English books throughout the seventeenth century.

In spite of the appearance of this St. Augustin in so many centres of printing, it is not to be found in a type specimen sheet before that of J. A. Schmid, produced at Antwerp about 1695, when the type had reached the end of its life. This Schmid was trained in the Luther foundry at Frankfurt. About 1670 he acquired the foundry of Reinhard Voskens, and while still at Frankfurt issued two specimens of Frakturs and Schwabachers and another of exotics (nos. 55, 56, and 58 in *Schriftproben deutscher Schriftgiessereien*, 1926, edited by G. Mori). By 1695 he was in Amsterdam, and in the Bagford collection in the British Museum there are some fragments of a specimen sheet published by him from an address in that city, 'op Rapenburg in de Foely dwaers-straat'. No heading has been preserved, if there ever was one. Two of the fragments contain Schmid's name, the Mediaen roman, and the Mediaen italic; on the italic we read 'Gesneden door Meester Jan Adolff Schmid, Lettergieter tot Amsterdam'. By the help of some manuscript notes on the fragments, relating to the prices, we can see that the sheet showed four romans, three italics, a Russian, four Hebrews, one Samaritan, and four sizes of non-ligatured Greek. The Russian, 'Text Ricisch', was at Oxford (it is the Sclavonian Great Primer, bought 1695 with punches). Some of the exotics were shown on the sheet published at Frankfurt in 1674. The non-ligatured Greeks were in the James Foundry; they were bought by Thomas James in 1710 from Johannes Rolu of Amsterdam. Rolu's specimen sheet (also in Bagford) displays other types from the Schmid foundry, including the St. Augustin roman.

Although the St. Augustin roman is shown by Schmid in a few lines only, all the useful 'spot' letters are there, and it seems to be the original type as used by Manuzio. When we find that the letter had been in more or less continual use since 1558 there seems to be nothing unlikely in this. On the other hand, the Mediaen shown by Schmid and bearing his name (although in this case the type is not, as the italic is, said to have been cut by him) bears a close resemblance to Manuzio's Cicero, but has certainly some different letters. This Mediaen then is probably a copy cut by Schmid.[1]

We have mentioned that Manuzio had a different Cicero roman, used from 1556 (cf. Fig. 3) not in Renouard's list, which we have found in Paris from 1549, in the octavo edition of Tory's *Champ fleury*, printed by V. Gaultherot. About the same time it will be found in some of the books printed by Robert Granjon at Paris, in partnership with M. Fezendat, and it was probably cut by Granjon. I have found it at Antwerp in 1558, at Frankfurt in 1574, and frequently in Dutch books of the seventeenth century. The italic usually found with it in Dutch books is the 'Cicero currens' of the Egenolff-Berner specimen sheet of 1592, which was certainly cut by Granjon. The roman is shown on several specimen sheets. It appears on the Frankfurt sheets of J. P. Fievet 1664

---

1. We now know that the St. Augustin roman here discussed was the work of Pierre Haultin of Paris. It is no. 39 in the 'Inventory of the Plantin-Moretus Museum Punches and Matrices', privately issued, 1960.

and J. D. Fievet 1682 as the 'Cicero Antiqua de Granjon'. (On the 1664 sheet the wrong roman is so described, and this is corrected on the 1682 sheet.) On the Van Dyck sheet of 1681 it is the Mediaen roman no. 2, one of the types which Ch. Enschedé had decided on other grounds, viz. that the Enschedé's had no punches, was not cut by Van Dyck. This roman has a few useful peculiarities, for example the E has the lower arm distinctly longer than the two upper arms, the M has no serif on the right-hand upright, and the P is small out of proportion. Dirk Voskens showed a very similar Mediaen roman, but with some different letters. However, Voskens kept the unusual P, from which we may infer that his type was an adaptation rather than a complete recutting.

The last specimen sheet on which this Cicero roman is shown is that of the Cambridge University Press, printed about 1735. It is the 'Old Pica' roman, which fortunately is used also for some of the headings, a fact which makes identification easier. Cambridge bought the type from Holland about the year 1698 (cf. S. C. Roberts's *History of the Cambridge University Press*, chap. v), and it was used for the notes of their edition of Horace published in 1699, and in a Virgil of similar format of 1701. The latest Cambridge printed book in which I have found it is of 1739, in the advertisements at the end of J. Chapman's *Eusebius*, almost two centuries after its first appearance at Paris.

[1938]

PANACES nonnullis Heracleum dicitur : ex quo opopanax colligi folet. Plurimum in Bœotia, & in Phocide Arcadiæ nafcitur: ibíque compendij, & quæftus, qui ex eo liquore faƈtitatur, gratia, ftudiosè colitur. Folijs eft afperis, in terra iacentibus, herbacei coloris, multùm ad ficulnea accedentibus, in ambitu quinquepartitò diuifis : caule, vt ferulæ, altifsimo, qui lanugine quadam incanefcit, folijs etiam minutioribus obfitus : mufcarijs, ceu anethi, in cacumine : flore luteo, & femine odorato, feruentéque. Radices habet multas ab origine vna, candidas, graueolentes, crafsi corticis, & fubamari guftus. Nafcitur in Cyrene Libyæ, & Macedonia. Excipitur fuccus incifa radice, recenti caulium pullulatu. Ea candidum fuccum emittit, qui ficcatus in fumma cute croceum colorem contrahit. Effluentem autem fuccum excipiunt, folijs excauato folo ftratis, quæ ficcata tolluntur. Simili modo caule mefsibus incifo, profluentem fuccum eximunt. Meliores ex radicibus, albæ, rigentes, diftentæque, ficcæ, quæ cariem non fentiant, aromaticæ, feruentes guftu. Fruƈtus ex media ferula cibo idoneus eft : fed ex agnatis ftolonibus, ab vfu cibario abhorret. Maxi-

FIG. 3. Paolo Manuzio's Granjon Cicero roman. From Pietro Andrea Matthioli, *Commentarii in libros sex Dioscoridis de medica materia.* Vincenzo Valgrisi, Venice, 1554.

THE ITALIC TYPES OF ROBERT GRANJON

THERE is, as yet, no general account of the work of Robert Granjon, one of the most prolific type-designers of the sixteenth century. For the few details known of his life the reader may be referred to P. Renouard's *Imprimeurs parisiens*, 1922-34, and for his work at Lyons to Baudrier's *Bibliographie lyonnaise*, vol. 2. The documents relating to the dealings between Christophe Plantin of Antwerp and Granjon are summarized (but not reproduced at length) in Max Rooses, *Le Musée Plantin-Moretus*, 1913, and in the *Index characterum* published by the Musée Plantin in 1905. He is perhaps best known for his Civilité types, and on this part of his work MM. Sabbe and Audin published a book in 1921.[1] In my article on 'Some Types of Paolo Manuzio',[2] I reproduced a Cicero roman cut by him. His other romans, his Greeks, and his oriental types, in the cutting of which he was engaged particularly in his later years in Italy, have received but a summary treatment. Probably his most distinguished work was done as a designer of italic types, and an attempt is here made to enumerate these in detail and to show at what period of his life they originated.

Granjon's italics fall into two groups, first those which may be attributed to him with the support of the De Molina document quoted by Baudrier, and secondly the group which is ascribed to him on the specimen sheets issued by the Egenolff-Berner-Luther foundry at Frankfurt, the earliest sheet being dated 1592. Baudrier, in his *Bibliographie lyonnaise*, vol. i, art. 'Molina', refers to a document of 24 August 1547, in which Gaspard de Molina, merchant of Lyons, ordered from Granjon types St. Augustin and Nonpareille like those supplied to De Tournes and Gryphius – 'ainsi que ledict Granjon les a baillées par cy devant à Jehan de Tournes et à Griffius.' Tournes had not been long established in 1547 and possessed only a small stock of types. By a process of elimination it can easily be established that the St. Augustin is the italic used in the *Recueil des œuvres* of Bonaventure des Periers, 1544, in *Marguerites de la Marguerite*, 1547, and in many other of his early books. Sebastien Gryphius had the same italic. As to Nonpareille, I can find no type so small in Tournes's early books.

The italics to be described, in chronological order of their first recorded appearance, number fourteen. The are among the best of the sixteenth century. If the attributions are accepted then Granjon was without a rival in that age as a designer of the cursive family of types. With one exception all these types have a decided inclination, much more pronounced than that of the italics of the school of Aldus or Arrighi. The exception is the 'Cicero Currens' of 1565, a remarkable design which is more upright and more condensed than any other size cut by Granjon. Again, they all have sloping capitals and for the most part capitals definitely shorter than the ascenders of the lower-case letters. A few earlier italics had inclined capitals, cut chiefly at Basle, but Granjon was the first to incline them

---

1. See also H.D.L. Vervliet, *Sixteenth-Century Printing Types of the Low Countries*, Amsterdam, 1968 and his introduction to *The Vatican Type Specimen*, Amsterdam, 1967. The same author deals with Granjon's stay in Rome in 'Robert Granjon à Rome', *Bulletin de l'Institut historique belge à Rome*, 38, 1967.
2. *The Library*, Sept. 1938, reprinted in this collection, pp. 255-259.

satisfactorily. The Cicero of the 1592 sheet is exceptional. Granjon appears to have cut capitals for the St. Augustin no greater in height than those of the Cicero, and we shall find that the contemporaries of Van Dyck in the next century regarded the upper case of the St. Augustin as a mistake. Lastly it may be said that the Granjon italic was the standard in European typography for two centuries, just as much as the Garamond roman.

LIST OF THE TYPES

1. St. Augustin (20 lines measure 98 mm). A type much used at Lyons by Jean de Tournes from 1544 and assigned to Granjon on the strength of the De Molina document mentioned above. It is found at Paris already in 1543 at the press of L. Grandin in Demosthenes *Oratio contra Philippi epistolam*, and in 1544 at the press of Denis Janot. At Lyons A. Constantin was using it in the same year as Tournes, and was followed by many other Lyons printers. The only type specimen in which I have found this St. Augustin is Plantin's *Index characterum*, 1567, where it is shown on C 3. For reproductions see A. Cartier's *Bibliographie des éditions des de Tournes*, vol. i, pp. 180, 182, 234, 235, 254, 255, 256, &c., and my *Type Designs*, fig. 46.

2. Garmond or Petit Romain (69 mm). In the preface to his edition of Petrarch, 1545, Tournes says that he has had the type in which the book is set specially cut, together with others suitable for the printing of verse. The Petrarch type, by its close resemblance in design to the St. Augustin, no. 1, may be assigned to Granjon. The only other printer I have found in possession of this size is Oporinus of Basle, who used it for the text of the *Testamentum Novum* in the version of Sébastien Châteillon,

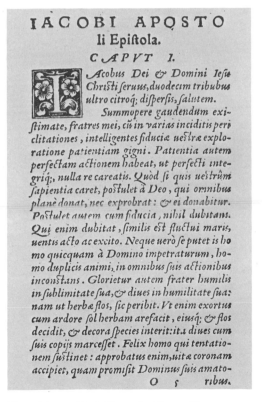

FIG. 1. Type No. 2: Petit Romain. From *Testamentum novum*.
Johann Oporinus, Basle, 1551.

1551. Operinus's fount measures only 63 mm and has a one-serif *M*; in this the fount is closer in design to the St. Augustin than the version used by Tournes.

3. St. Augustin (95 mm). A type which in the main seems to be the same as no. 1. The capitals *A* and Q differ, and especially the lower-case *v* used initially. Its earliest use was at Paris, by T. Richardus in Wildenbergius *Totius Naturalis Philosophiæ in Physicam Aristotelis epitome*, 1548; it was used in the same year at Florence by L. Torrentino in a number of books. This remarkable printer, who is said to have come from the Netherlands, was invited to Florence in 1547 by Cosimo I, Grand Duke of Tuscany. His stock consisted almost entirely of French types, including three Granjon italics. When Granjon himself formed a partnership in 1549 with Michel Fezandat we find the firm using this St. Augustin. It was used at Basle in 1549 by M. Isingrin, while the Giunta introduced it

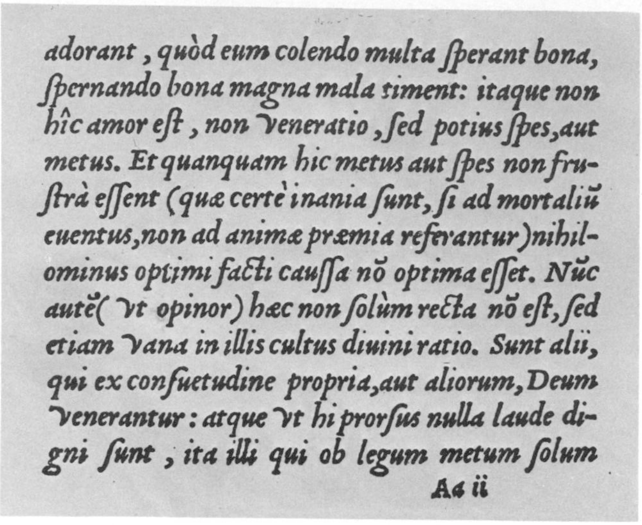

adorant, quòd eum colendo multa ſperant bona,
ſpernando bona magna mala timent: itaque non
hîc amor eſt, non veneratio, ſed potius ſpes, aut
metus. Et quanquam hic metus aut ſpes non fru-
ſtrà eſſent (quæ certè inania ſunt, ſi ad mortaliũ
euentus, non ad animæ præmia referantur) nihil-
ominus optimi facti cauſſa nõ optima eſſet. Nũc
autẽ (vt opinor) hæc non ſolùm recta nõ eſt, ſed
etiam vana in illis cultus diuini ratio. Sunt alii,
qui ex conſuetudine propria, aut aliorum, Deum
venerantur: atque vt hi prorſus nulla laude di-
gni ſunt, ita illi qui ob legum metum ſolum
A4 ii

FIG. 2. Type No. 3: Second Saint-Augustin. From Girolamo Cardano, *De subtilitate libri XXI*. Michel Fezendat & Robert Granjon, Paris, 1550.

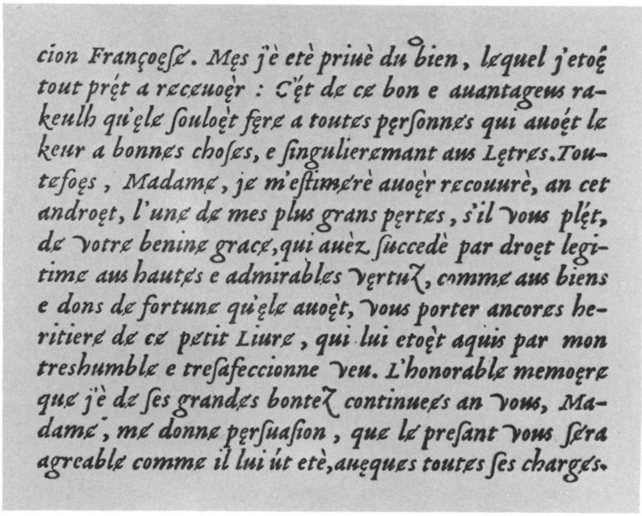

cion Françoęſɇ. Męs j'è etè priuè du bien, lɇquel j'etoę
tout pręt a rɇcɇuoęr : C'ęt dɇ cɇ bon e auantageus ra-
keulh qu'ęlɇ ſouloęt fęrɇ a toutɇs pęrſonnɇs qui auoęt lɇ
keur a bonnɇs choſɇs, e ſingulierɇmant aus Lętrɇs. Tou-
tɇfoęs, Madamɇ, jɇ m'eſtimɇrè auoęr rɇcouurè, an cet
androęt, l'unɇ dɇ mes plus grans pęrtɇs, s'il vous plęt,
dɇ votrɇ beninɇ gracɇ, qui auèz ſuccedè par droęt legi-
timɇ aus hautɇs e admirablɇs vęrtuz, commɇ aus biens
e dons dɇ fortunɇ qu'ęlɇ auoęt, vous porter ancorɇs he-
ritierɇ dɇ cɇ pɇtit Liurɇ, qui lui etoęt aquis par mon
treshumblɇ e treſafeccionne veu. L'honorablɇ memoęrɇ
quɇ j'è dɇ ſes grandɇs bontez continueɇs an vous, Ma-
damɇ, mɇ donnɇ pęrſuaſion, quɇ lɇ preſant vous ſɇra
agreablɇ commɇ il lui ût etè, auęquɇs toutɇs ſes chargɇs.

FIG. 3. Type No. 4: Cicero. From Jacques Peletier, *Dialogue de l'ortografe e prononciation françoęse*. Jean de Tournes, Lyons, 1555.

into Venice by 1552 (cf. an edition of Aretaeus in Latin, 1552, and the *De balneis*, Giunta, 1553). Lastly the well-known Venetian printer Francesco Marcolini in the last two years of his career, 1556 and 1557, made the second St. Augustin his principal text type. It is significant of the changing taste and of the increasing popularity of French designs that a printer such as Marcolini, who had so far followed the Arrighi model, made such a definite typographic change.

4. Cicero (82 mm), a type with strikingly small capitals and a sweeping initial *v* like that of the preceding type. I attribute it to Granjon because of its similitary of design to no. 3 and because it is found in the hands of the same printers. L. Torrentino of Florence had the type by 1548, though he seldom used the initial *v*. In Paris, M. Fezandat, about to become Granjon's partner, used it in 1549 for the text of François Habert's *Le Temple de chasteté*, and Tournes at Lyons had it in the same year. It is perhaps best known from its use in a number of books of verse printed by Tournes, e. g. the *œuvres*, of Louise Labé. Several printers seem to have discarded the florid *v*, e. g. B. Arnoullet at Lyons in an edition of Huttichius, 1550, the widow of M. de la Porte at Paris in Ronsard's *Les Amours*, 1553, and Giolito at Venice in his edition of Castiglione's *Il Cortegiano*, 1556. The type used by Oporinus at Basle in G. Fabricius's *Odarum libri tres*, 1552 (reproduced in the *Gutenberg-Jahrbuch*, 1939, p. 200, fig. 6), is possibly the same type, but with different capitals A and M.

5. Gros Texte (113 mm). This widely used type, dating from 1547 or 1548, is assigned to Granjon because the lower case is all but identical with that shown as Granjon's on the sheets of the Egenolff-Luther foundry. The earliest appearance traced is in J. Willich's *In Vergilii Bucolica commentaria*, T. Richardus, Paris, 1547 (1548 in the colophon). Torrentino used it in Aristotle's *De arte poetica*, 1548, Tournes in 1549, and Isingrin and Oporinus at Basle in 1550. For reproductions see Cartier, op. cit., pp. 333, 372, 374.

6. Gros Texte (second version). In 1552 in J. Girard's *Stichostratio epigrammaton*, M. Bonhomme, Lyons, we find a type which is identical in the lower case with the preceding Gros Texte, but has a different set of capitals, and these capitals agree with the 'Gros Texte de Granjon' as shown on the various sheets of the Egenolff-Luther foundry. The new version was in Venice by 1553 and is found in a book already mentioned, the *De balneis*, published by the Giunta. Gabriel Giolito had both versions; the earlier may be seen in Cornelio Musso's *Predica*, 1553, and the second in the following year in G. B. Giraldi's *Discorsi*. The second version was used by Giolito for the main text of Cavalcanti's *La Retorica*, 1559. Plantin at Antwerp had the type and there is a full display of it in his Galen of 1564. From that book we see that there were two forms of *v* and two ampersands. In the Egenolff-Berner specimen of 1592 the Gros Texte is imperfect and in that of 1622 is inadequately shown. In the specimen of 1664 and later ones we find a different lower-case *g* and a different ampersand. That the new *g* was in existence by 1592 can be shown from contemporary books, e. g. at the press of P. Landry, Lyons. The Elzevirs had the type in the new form beginning with Isaac Elzevir, grandson of Louis, the first printer of the famous house. Isaac acquired a press in 1617. The *g* appears in the specimen book of Johannes Elzevir of 1658 (cf. the reproduction in *Signature*, no. 10, November 1938).

7. Cicero (82 mm). The Granjon Cicero of the Egenolff-Berner specimen of 1592 and a number of later sheets. The earliest year traced of its use is 1554, in the preliminary matter of Rondeletius's *Libri de piscibus marinis*, M. Bonhomme, Lyons. Plantin at Antwerp had it (cf. the edition of Galen, 1564, already referred to) and it appears in his *Index characterum*, 1567, on C4. André Wechel was using it at Frankfurt by 1577 (cf. an edition of Horace). It was in very general use in the Netherlands in the seventeenth century and is shown in the specimens of the Voskens firm. The lower case is very close to the earlier Cicero, our no. 4.

8. Parangon (133 mm). This 'Cursiff Parangon de Granion' of the Egenolff-Berner sheet of 1592 was one of the most widely used types in Europe. The earliest use of it traced is at the press of Jean de Tournes of Lyons in 1555, in a tract *Ad principes Christianos cohortatio pacificatoria*. André Wechel

had it by 1560, and Plantin by 1563. This is one of the Granjon italics of which matrices have survived down to this generation. It is the Kleine Parangon shown in the 1905 *Index characterum* of the Plantin Museum at Antwerp.

9. The 'Curs. Petit Text de G.' (54 mm) of the Egenolff-Berner sheet of 1592. First found in the address 'Al Lettore' of *Il Nuovo Testamento*, Jean de Tournes, Lyons, 1556. It was used by Plantin, e. g. for a Catullus of 1560, and is shown on D 2 of his *Index characterum*, 1567. Like the preceding type, matrices of the Petit Text still survived in 1905, when the type was shown by the Plantin Museum under the description 'Petite Bible sur la Coronelle'.

10. Petit Romain or Gaillarde (66 mm). An italic of this size was used for the main text of *Il Nuovo Testamento*, 1556, and the *Metamorphose figurée*, 1557, both printed by Tournes. This type has already been attributed to Granjon, presumably on grounds of design, by D. B. Updike (cf. his *Printing Types*, fig. 146). I have not found the type on any specimen. In Paris there was a closely similar

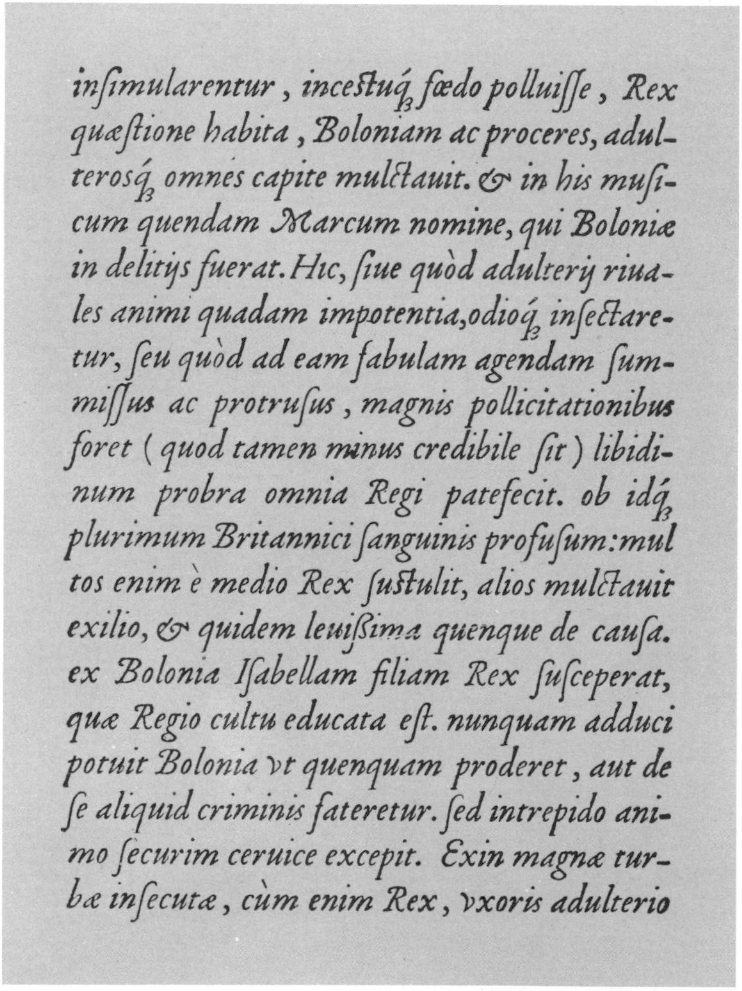
inſimularentur, inceſtuq́ꝫ fœdo polluiſſe, Rex quæſtione habita, Boloniam ac proceres, adulteroſq́ꝫ omnes capite mulctauit. & in his muſicum quendam Marcum nomine, qui Boloniæ in delitijs fuerat. Hic, ſiue quòd adulterij riuales animi quadam impotentia, odioq́ꝫ inſectaretur, ſeu quòd ad eam fabulam agendam ſummiſſus ac protruſus, magnis pollicitationibus foret (quod tamen minus credibile ſit) libidinum probra omnia Regi patefecit. ob idq́ꝫ plurimum Britannici ſanguinis profuſum: multos enim è medio Rex ſuſtulit, alios mulctauit exilio, & quidem leuiſſima quenque de cauſa. ex Bolonia Iſabellam filiam Rex ſuſceperat, quæ Regio cultu educata eſt. nunquam adduci potuit Bolonia vt quenquam proderet, aut de ſe aliquid criminis fateretur. ſed intrepido animo ſecurim ceruice excepit. Exin magnæ turbæ inſecutæ, cùm enim Rex, vxoris adulterio

FIG. 4. Type No. 5: Gros Texte, first version. From Guillaume Paradin, *Afflictae Britannicae religionis & rursus restitutae exegema.* Jean de Tournes, Lyons, 1555.

271

le figure del parlare, per lo modo che di sopra habbiam det
to. &) tra tutte le parti dell'oratione, quelle, che contengo-
no le sentenze, debbono essere &) pure, &) semplici, accio
che lo splendor delle parole non offuschi la luce delle senten-
ze, &) le faccia diuenir meno pregiate, &) meno efficaci di
quel, che debbono essere.

ORa poi che del decoro del parlare habbiam detto, co-
me ne ha chiamato il bisogno di questa introduttione, ri-
torneremo al diceuole, &) al decoro delle persone, per com-
pir quello che ci auanza di ragionare, quanto all'una, &)
all'altra fauola appertiene.

SErua M. Giulio, la Comedia una certa religione, che
mai giouane uergine, o polzella non uiene a ragionare in
Scena, &) pel contrario nelle Scene Tragiche ui s'introduco
no lodeuolmente. Et cio m'estimo io che sia, per che la
Scena Comica, per lo piu è lasciua, &) in essa interuengo-
no ruffiani, meritrici, parasiti, &) altre simili qualità di
persone di lasciua, &) di dishonesta uita: &) però non pa-
re, che conuenga al decoro di una giouane uergine uenire a
fauellare in tale Scena, &) tra queste persone. Et ancho-
ra che la Comedia fusse honestissima, come noi ueggiamo
essere i Captiui di Plauto, non ui s'introdurebbe anco
uergine alcuna; perche è gia cosi impressa ne gli animi de
gli huomini, che la Comedia porti con esso lei queste sorti
di genti, &) questi modi di fauellare, pieni di licenza; che
cio non sarebbe senza pregiudicio della polcella. Ma non
entrando nella Scena Tragica, se non persone grandi, Ma

FIG. 5. Type No. 6: Gros Texte, second version. From Giovanni Batista Giraldi, *Discorsi intorno al comporre de i romanzi, delle comedie, e delle tragedie.* Gabriele Giolito & Fratelli, Venice, 1554.

italic in use from 1548, e. g. in *Totius Naturalis Philosophiæ in Physicam Aristotelis Epitome*, T. Richardus. It is found also in a book printed by Fezandat and Granjon, *Le Tombeau de Marguerite de Valois*, 1551, by Lady Anne Seymour. It may be noted that at this period there was another italic of this size in general use at Paris, namely that cut by Claude Garamond and explicitly mentioned by him in the introduction to the *Pia et religiosa meditatio* of David Chambellan, P. Gaultier, 1545. (On this italic see *The Fleuron*, no. 5, pp. 134-9, with reproductions.) A number of other Paris printers besides Gaultier, who was directly associated with Garamond, acquired this type, e. g. O. Petit, G. Thibout, J. Ruelle, B. Prévost, and A. Wechel.

11. The italic of the size of the preceding shown on the Egenolff-Berner sheet, 1592, is called 'Curs. Garamond ou Immortel de Granjon'. This design, distinguished by a florid *v* and *&*, made its first appearance in books printed in Civilité by Granjon himself at Lyons, e. g. in L. Domenichi's

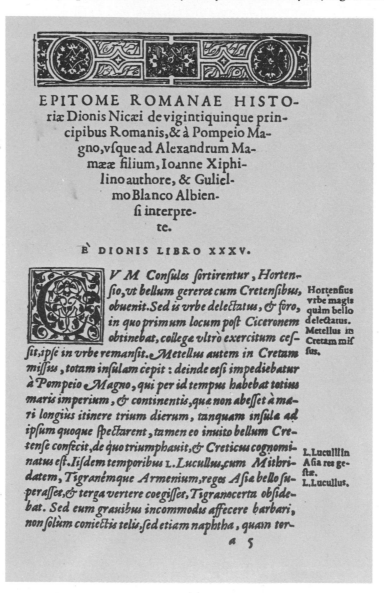

FIG. 6. Type No. 7: Cicero. From Dion Cassius, *Romanae historiae libri XXV*. Guillaume Rouillé, Lyons, 1559.

3

ORNATISSIMI CVIVSDAM
VIRI, DE REBVS GALLICIS,
Ad Staniſlaum Eluidium,
Epiſtola.

E Rebus, quæ in Gallia nuper
acciderunt, graues iſthîc rumo-
res, atque (vt tuis verbis vtar,
Eluidi amicorum meorum ma-
xime) atroces in Germania vo-
ces percrebruiſſe, non tam certè miror, pro tem-
porum iniuria, & ſtudiis partium, quàm nonnullis viris ſuccénſeo, optimis quidem illis, &
à nobis non alienis, ſed parùm herclè pruden-
tibus, qui dum in tuenda Regis Chriſtianiſſi-
mi aduerſus obtreƈtatores exiſtimatione, fidem
ſuam & officium probare, ſedulò nimis cu-
piunt, ab imperitis & leuibus, ne quid gra-
uius dicam, hominibus decepti, in rei ipſius, de
qua agitur, veritatem, non ſatis diligenter in-
quirunt : atque ita cupide cauſam defendunt,
vt quemadmodum, qui perditè amant, non næ-
uo aliquo, aut ſtruma in amicarum corporibus
A ij

FIG. 7. Type No. 8: Parangon. From Stanislaus Elvidius (= Joachinus Camerarius),
Orantissimi cuiusdam viri [Gui Du Faur] *de rebus Gallicis ad S. Elvidium epistola.*
Frédéric Morel, Paris, 1573.

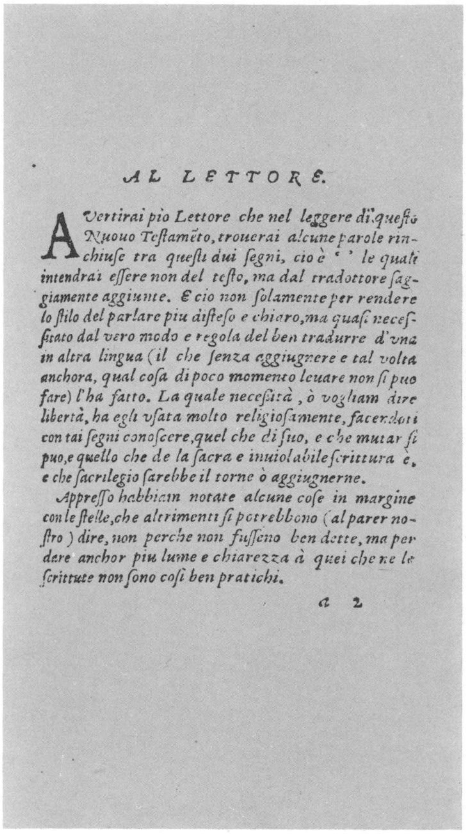

AL LETTORE.

AVertirai pio Lettore che nel leggere di queſto Nuouo Teſtamēto, trouerai alcune parole rinchiuſe tra queſti dui ſegni, cio è ' ' le quali intendrai eſſere non del teſto, ma dal tradottore ſaggiamente aggiunte. E cio non ſolamente per rendere lo ſtilo del parlare piu diſteſo e chiaro, ma quaſi neceſſitato dal vero modo e regola del ben tradurre d'vna in altra lingua (il che ſenza aggiugnere e tal volta anchora, qual coſa di poco momento leuare non ſi puo fare) l'ha fatto. La quale neceſſità, ò vogliam dire libertà, ha egli vſata molto religioſamente, facendoti con tai ſegni conoſcere, quel che di ſuo, e che mutar ſi puo, e quello che de la ſacra e inuiolabile ſcrittura è, e che ſacrilegio ſarebbe il torne ò aggiugnerne.

Appreſſo habbiam notate alcune coſe in margine con le ſtelle, che altrimenti ſi potrebbono (al parer noſtro) dire, non perche non fuſſeno ben dette, ma per dare anchor piu lume e chiarezza à quei che ne le ſcritture non ſono coſi ben pratichi.

a 2

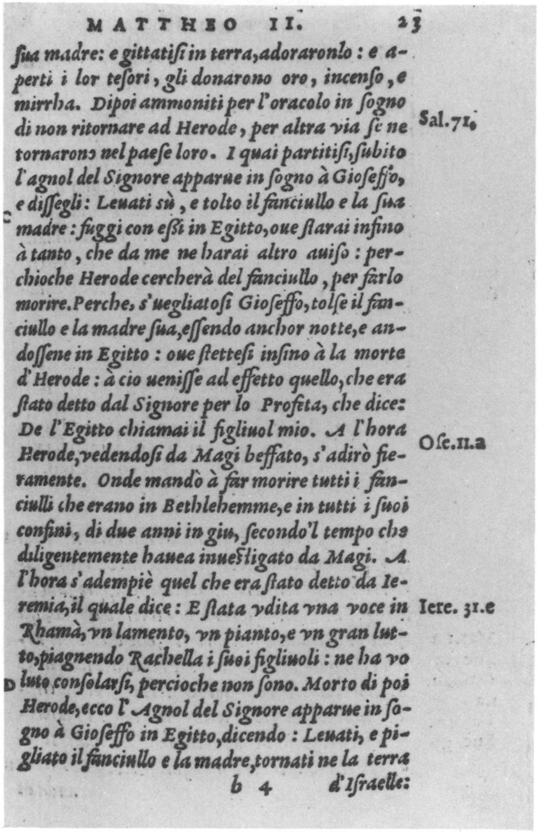

MATTHEO II. 23

ſua madre: e gittatiſi in terra, adoraronlo: e a-
perti i lor teſori, gli donarono oro, incenſo, e
mirrha. Dipoi ammoniti per l'oracolo in ſogno
di non ritornare ad Herode, per altra via ſe ne Sal.71.
tornarono nel paeſe loro. I quai partitiſi, ſubito
l'agnol del Signore apparue in ſogno à Gioſeffo,
e diſſegli: Leuati sù, e tolto il fanciullo e la ſua
C madre: fuggi con eſſi in Egitto, oue ſtarai infino
à tanto, che da me ne harai altro auiſo: per-
chioche Herode cercherà del fanciullo, per farlo
morire. Perche, s'uegliatoſi Gioſeffo, tolſe il fanciullo e la madre ſua, eſſendo anchor notte, e an-
doſſene in Egitto: oue ſtetteſi inſino à la morte
d'Herode: à cio ueniſſe ad effetto quello, che era
ſtato detto dal Signore per lo Profeta, che dice:
De l'Egitto chiamai il figliuol mio. A l'hora Oſe.11.a
Herode, vedendoſi da Magi beffato, s'adirò fie-
ramente. Onde mandò à far morire tutti i fan-
ciulli che erano in Bethlehemme, e in tutti i ſuoi
confini, di due anni in giu, ſecondo'l tempo che
diligentemente hauea inueſtigato da Magi. A
l'hora s'adempiè quel che era ſtato detto da Ie-
remia, il quale dice: E ſtata vdita vna voce in Iere. 31.e
Rhamà, vn lamento, vn pianto, e vn gran lut-
to, piagnendo Rachella i ſuoi figliuoli: ne ha vo
D luto conſolarſi, percioche non ſono. Morto di poi
Herode, ecco l'Agnol del Signore apparue in ſogno à Gioſeffo in Egitto, dicendo: Leuati, e pi-
gliato il fanciullo e la madre, tornati ne la terra
b 4 d'Iſraelle:

FIG. 8. Type No. 9: Petit Texte. From *Il nuovo Testamento*. Jean de Tournes, Lyons, 1556.

FIG. 9. Type No. 10: Petit Romain. From *Il nuovo Testamento*. Jean de Tournes, Lyons, 1556.

Facecies, 1559, a work in French and Italian, the French text being in Civilité and the Italian in the 'Immortel'. Sébastien Gryphius at Lyons also had it in the same year. It is mentioned in Plantin's Inventory of 1563, but I have not found it in any book printed by Plantin. John Day in London had it by 1568 and André Wechel used it in the notes of a Virgil *Bucolica* issued at Frankfort in 1582. Wechel, however, used a more normal ampersand.

12. The 'Cicero Currens', or Scholasticalis of the Egenolff-Berner sheet, 1592. Called 'Philosophie' by Plantin, who on 5 July 1565 made a contract with Granjon for the delivery of this and another, Garmond, italic. Matrices and punches were received between July and December 1565. Stanley Morison wrote some account of this type on a poster issued by the Oxford University Press on the occasion of their exhibition at Messrs. Bumpus in November 1930. See also my *Type Designs*, p. 158, for notes of its earliest appearances. Morison pointed out that the wrong capitals were shown with the type in the Oxford Specimen Book of 1693. This was no doubt deliberate. The seventeenth century thought that Granjon's upper case was often too small. As to the appearance of the type in England, it may be noted that the Oxford Press does not seem to have made any use of it until 1691, in the *Historia* of John of Antioch, and may not have bought it until about that year.[1] It is called a Fell type solely because it is shown in the first Oxford specimen book. There was one earlier English printer who used it, namely Roger Daniel. It will be found in several of his books published

1. Cf. Stanley Morison, *John Fell*, 1967, esp. pp. 128-131.

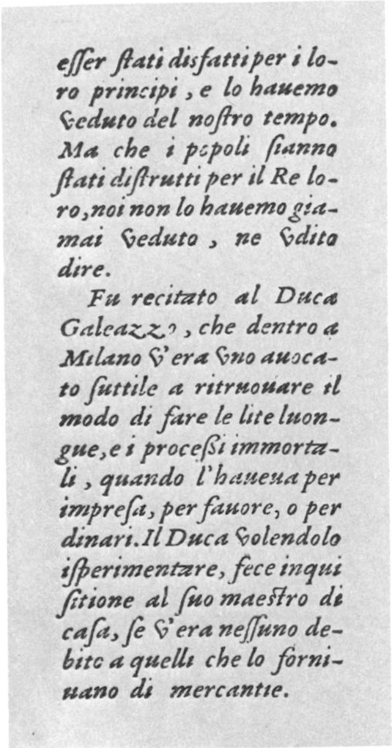

effer ftati disfatti per i loro principi, e lo hauemo ʋeduto del noftro tempo. Ma che i popoli fianno ftati diftrutti per il Re loro, noi non lo hauemo giamai ʋeduto, ne ʋdito dire.

Fu recitato al Duca Galeazʒo, che dentro a Milano ʋ'era ʋno auocato futtile a ritrouaare il modo di fare le lite luongue, e i proceʃʃi immortali, quando l'haueua per imprefa, per fauore, o per dinari. Il Duca ʋolendolo iʃperimentare, fece inqui fitione al fuo maeʃtro di cafa, fe ʋ'era neʃʃuno debito a quelli che lo forniuano di mercantie.

FABVLAE *fe ad Aefopum, fua in eum beneuolentia cōferunt, quod fat agat fui: fabula quippe & Homero & Hefiodo, nec non & Archilocho in Lycamben curæ fuit. fed ab Aefopo humana omnia ad fabellas redacta funt, fermone brutis non temerè impertito. nám & cupiditatem imminuit, & libidinem infectatur, & fraudem. Atque hæc ei leo quifpiam agit, & vulpes, & per Iouem equus, nec teftudo muta, ex quibus pueri difcunt, quæ in vita gerantur. Habitæ igitur in precio fabulæ, per Aefopum accedunt ad fapientis ianuam vittis eum deuincturæ, coronáꝗ, oleagina coronaturæ. hic, vt puto, fabulam aliquam texit. rifus enim faciei, & oculi in terram defixi id præ fe ferunt. pictorem, fabularum curas remiʃʃiore animo indigere, non latuit. Philofophatur. autem pictura & fabularum corpora. Bruta enim cum hominibus conferens, cœtum circa Aefopum ftatuit, ex illius fcena confictum. Chori dux vulpes depicta eft. vtitur enim ea Aefopus miniftra argumentorum plurium, ceu Dauo Comœdia.*

FIG. 10. Type No. 11: the 'Immortel'. From Lodovico Domenichi, *Facecies*. Robert Granjon, Lyons, 1559.

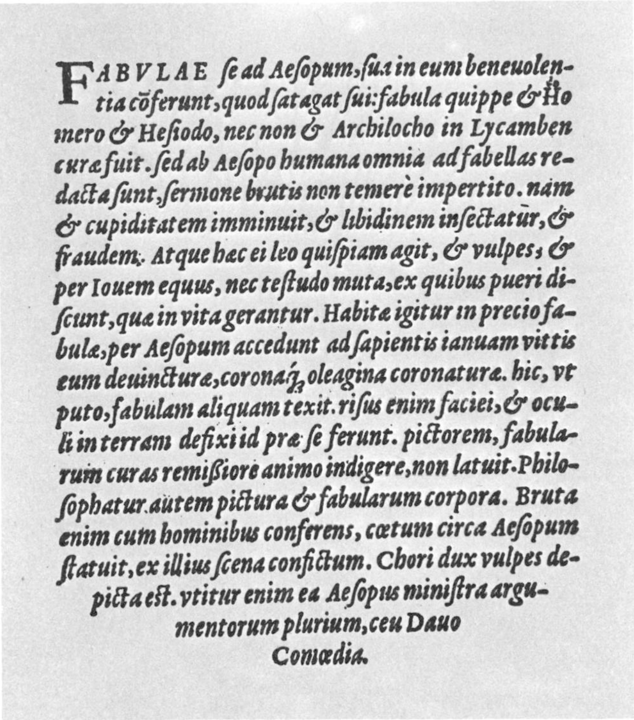

FIG. 11. Type No. 12: the 'Cicero currens'. From Aesop, *Fabulae*. Georg Corvinus, Sigmund Feyerabend & Successors to Vigandus Gallus, Frankfurt, 1566.

in London in the years 1655 to 1657, e. g. in John Clarke's *Phraseologia puerilis*, 1655. The type was very popular in Germany and the Netherlands in the seventeenth century, but I have not found it used in France or Italy. In specimens, in addition to those of the Luther firm, it appears on several other Frankfurt sheets, e. g. Fievet 1664 and 1682, Stubenvoll 1714, and Schippelius, 1755. It is in Plantin's *Index characterum*, 1567, in the specimen book of L. Fuhrmann, Nuremberg, 1616, and that of J. Elzevir, 1658.[1]

13. The St. Augustin (96 mm) of the Egenolff-Berner sheet, 1592. The earliest date to which this third Augustin has been traced is the year 1566 at the press of André Wechel, in Plutarch's *Septem sapientium convivium* in Greek and Latin, the Latin text being set in our type. Plantin received matrices of this size in April 1567, and at his press it is well displayed in Arias Montanus's *Humanæ salutis monumenta*, 1571, a book showing also Granjon's Gros Texte italic, 'Cicero Currens', and the Ascendonica to be described next. John Day in London had the type by 1569. In 1572 Day used it for the text of Archbishop Parker's *De antiquitate Britannicæ Ecclesiæ*, a book commended by T. B. Reed in his *Old English Letter Foundries*; Reed supposed the type to have been cut by Day. Charles Enschedé, in his article on the Elzevir Press,[2] says of this Augustin italic that the capitals are much too small, an opinion with which the Oxford Press appears to have agreed in the case of the Cicero Currens.

This size also found its way to Italy and a fine example of its use will be found in D. Barbaro's *La Pratica della Perspettiva*, C. and R. Borgominieri, Venice, 1569. It is shown in the specimen book issued at Rome by the Vatican Press in 1628 under the title 'Corsivo Barberino'.

1. See also 'Chistian Egenolff . . . and his Types', reprinted in this collection, pp. 272-280.
2. A translation was published in *Signature*, no. 10, Nov. 1938.

PLVTARCHI
CHÆRONEI SEPTEM
SAPIENTVM CONVIVIVM.

Interprete Guilielmo Plantio Cenomanno.

DIOCLES.

Dioclis extat epitome Medicinæ ad Antigonum
Regem Macedonum, adnexa fini libri primi
Pauli Æginetæ, inſtar epiſtolæ,

E NIMVERO *Nicarche, ſequens* ætas den-*
ſam rebus caliginem & obſcuritatem non
paruam allatura videtur, quãdo hodie de re-
bus tam recentibus, noſtrámque memoriam
minimè fugientibus falſò conſcripti libri,
vulgò fidem inueniunt. Nam nec ab illis ſe-
ptem Sapientibus ſolùm, vt accepiſtis, agita-
tum eſt conuiuium, ſed parte etiã altera longè pluribus, inter quos
& ipſe fui: quippè qui propter artem quam faſtito, & Periãdri fa-
miliaris & Thaletis hoſpes eram. Apud me enim diuerſabatur vir
ille, ita iubente Periandro: nec reſtè hiſtoriam retulit, quicunque is
fuit qui eam rem vobis narrauit: quem veriſimile eſt ex iis non
fuiſſe qui conuiuio interfuêre. Verùm quando otium abundè ſup-
peditat, & *ſeneſtus alioqui ipſa morti ſemper obuia dilationem
rei olim commemorandæ præſtare non poteſt, ſi diligenter atten-
deritis ab initio vt quæque geſta ſunt ordine omnia referam. Con-
uiuium inſtruxerat Periander non in vrbe, ſed in cœnaculo quodã
iuxta *Lachæum non longè à Veneris delubro, cui etiam tum à

A ij

Margin notes:
* Argumenti
occaſio.
Tẽpus non-
nulla obſcu-
rat, alia rete-
git.

* Senex non
ſatis locuplex
futuri ſpõſor.

* Lachæum
portus Corin-

FIG. 12. Type No. 13: Saint-Augustin. From Plutarch, *Septem sapientium convivium.*
André Wechel, Paris, 1566.

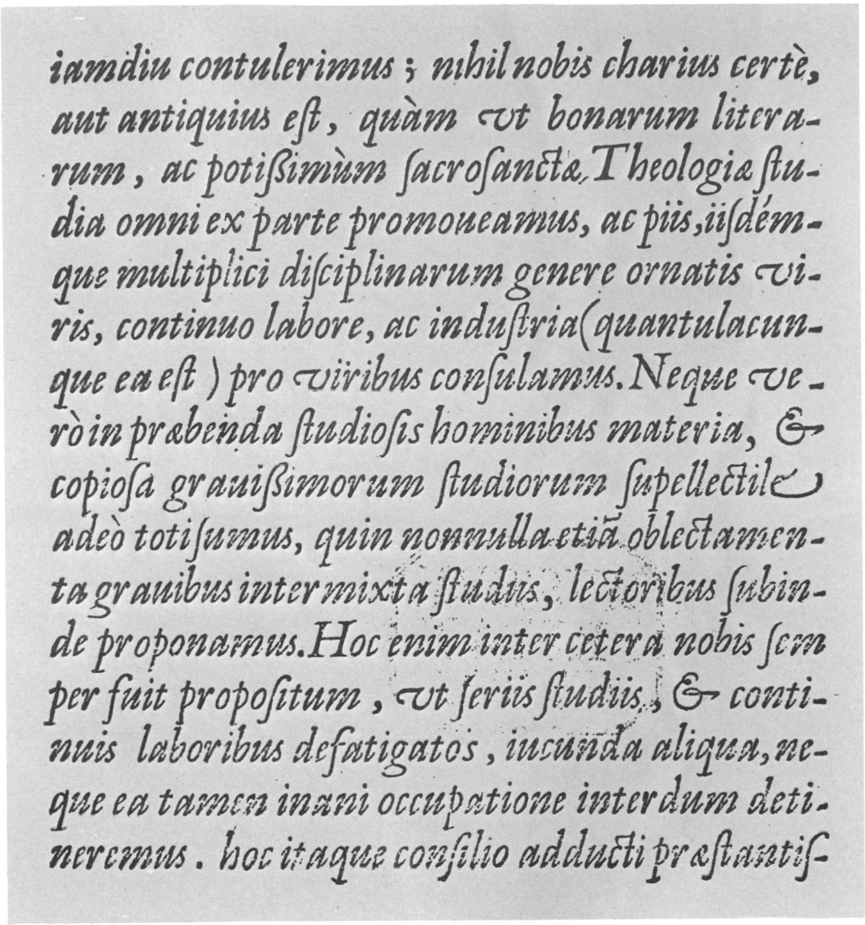
iamdiu contulerimus ; nihil nobis charius certè,
aut antiquius eſt, quàm vt bonarum literarum, ac potiſſimùm ſacroſanctæ Theologiæ ſtu-
dia omni ex parte promoueamus, ac piis, iiſdém-
que multiplici diſciplinarum genere ornatis viris, continuo labore, ac induſtria (quantulacun-
que ea eſt) pro viribus conſulamus. Neque verò in præbenda ſtudioſis hominibus materia, &
copioſa grauiſſimorum ſtudiorum ſupellectile
adeò totiſumus, quin nonnulla etiã oblectamen-
ta grauibus intermixta ſtudiis, lectoribus ſubinde proponamus. Hoc enim inter cætera nobis ſem
per fuit propoſitum, vt ſeriis ſtudiis, & conti-
nuis laboribus defatigatos, iucũda aliqua, neque ea tamen inani occupatione interdum deti-
neremus. hoc itaque conſilio adducti præſtantiſ-

FIG. 13. Type No. 14: Ascendonica. From Benedictus Arias Montanus, *Humanae salutis monumenta*. Christophe Plantin, Antwerp, 1571.

14. Ascendonica (142 mm). This size was not among the series in the possession of the Frankfurt firm and seems to have been the property of Plantin alone. In his last recorded dealing with Granjon Plantin ordered the punches of the Ascendonica in April 1570, and the type was used in the Polyglot Bible and in the Arias Montanus mentioned above. Matrices were still in existence in 1905 when the last *Index characterum* was issued by the Plantin Museum.

[1941]

[According to the 'Inventory of the Planting-Moretus Museum Punches and Matrices' (privately issued, 1960) there are at Antwerp five more Granjon italics than in the list here given, mostly small sizes. Moreover, Vervliet, in his introduction to the facsimile edition of *Indici di Caratteri nella Stampa Vaticana . . . 1628* (Amsterdam, 1967), ascribes four italics found there to Granjon, viz., No. 35 – Corsivo grosso (130 mm), No. 44 – Barberino (90 mm), No. 56 – Garamone (65 mm), and No. 57 – Corsivo Garamone (60 mm). Harry Carter, in his introduction to the facsimile edition of *Les caractères et les vignettes de la fonderie du Sieur Delacolonge 1773* (Amsterdam 1969), finds nine italics from Granjon's hand owned by the Lyons type-founder, some of them cast on several different sizes.]

CHRISTIAN EGENOLFF OF FRANKFURT
AND HIS TYPES

The Egenolff-Berner-Luther Type Foundry has attracted much attention in recent years, more especially since Gustav Mori discovered the first specimen sheet issued by the firm in 1592. The sheet has been reproduced several times and referred to many more times. Herr Mori himself has published a number of articles bearing on the history of the Foundry, and, further, a book entitled *Die Egenolff-Luthersche Schriftgiesserei in Frankfurt* (1926), which treats especially of the relations between the Luther house and printers in the United States.

But little has been published on the prehistory and beginnings of the foundry. How was the stock acquired? Can Christian Egenolff himself be said to have established the foundry? He has in fact been called the father of German typefounding. Was he a type cutter, and can any of the types known to have been in the foundry be assigned to him? These are some of the questions still unanswered.

We know that the foundry began its separate existence, apart from the printing establishment, in 1572 under Jacques Sabon, who had married Christian's daughter, Judith, in 1571. Sabon, originally of Lyons, first settled in Frankfurt shortly after Egenolff's death in 1555 – one may presume to help Christian's widow in the affairs of the foundry. As to Egenolff, we find that a contemporary, Jacob Micyllus, called him 'calcographus', but it is doubtful if that word means more than a caster of types, or if it might not be used loosely of any printer. According to Gustav Mori, Egenolff's first connexion with the trade was at Strasbourg as a founder for the well-known printer Wolfgang Köpfel. This certainly suggests that Egenolff was a technical expert engaged in the production of type, if not a designer himself.

A summary of the types used in Egenolff's own press and by his immediate successors may be of use towards answering some of the questions raised above. The summary here given is based on the collection in the British Museum, which for Egenolff himself contains about 150 of the 420 books which he is said to have printed. It must be unusual for a printer to acquire a type and then use it on one or two occasions only: therefore this summary is more likely to need correction in the dates given for the first appearance of a type than for its omissions. Egenolff's first press was established at Strasbourg in 1528 and in his three years in that city he used the following types.

1. AN UPPER-RHINE TYPE

Twenty lines measure 96 mm. The so-called Upper-Rhine type is a subdivision of Schwabacher with a particular M form, M44 in Konrad Haebler's index of M forms. Cf. my *Type Designs*, pp. 34-36. This design was used by Egenolff for the text of all his early books in the vernacular, and was very like a type used by his contemporary at Strasbourg, Johann Knoblouch; for instance, in the latter printer's edition of Melanchthon's *Die haupt artickel der gantzen heyligen Schrift* (1523). It is possible that Egenolff was the designer of his version, but in any case the type had gone out of favour many years before the establishment of the Foundry.

2. An italic, that of Johann Froben of Basle

This is the italic commonly found in Germany in the years 1520 to 1540 and even later. It was used by Egenolff for all his early Latin books. Froben's italic is illustrated at Fig. 81 of Updike's *Printing Types*.

3. A Schwabacher

(20 lines = 75 mm) I find this for the first time in 1530 in Paracelsus's *Wunderbarer vndd mercklicher Geschichten . . . Prognostication*. Several other Strasbourg printers, even before Egenolff's time, had this type; e. g., Johann Schott from 1504 (it is his Type 6 in Proctor's *Index to Early Printed Books in the British Museum*, Part, 2 Germany, reproduced at Fig. 63), Johann Knoblouch from 1506 (his Type 6), and Wolfgang Köpfel from 1528. The first printer to use it seems to have been Thomas Anshelm at Pforzheim in 1500. See the British Museum *Catalogue of Fifteenth-Century Books*, Part 3, Fig. LXV.

These three types are the only text types which I find Egenolff using while at Strasbourg. In addition he had three heading types (Nos. 4-6, *infra*).

4. Fraktur heading type, a copy of the early type called 'Theuerdank'

It was so called because first used in 1517 in the book of that name. A page from that work is shown in Updike at Fig. 74, and the type as used by other printers is illustrated in E. Crous's *Die gotischen Schriftarten* (1528), Abb. 82 and 120.

5. Fraktur heading type, still larger

It resembles the Gros Canon shown on the Luther specimen sheet of 1678, the earliest known specimen of the Foundry displaying their German or gothic types.

6. Alphabet of roman capitals

First used by Johann Froben at Basle in 1517. This alphabet may be said to be the first popular design of its kind, a design which spread to all the countries of Europe where printing was practiced. Until superseded by the Garamond Canon it was the favourite heading type for books set in roman or italic. Illustrations may be seen at figs. 80 and 82 in Updike, and on many of the plates of my *First Century of Printing at Basle*.

In 1530 Egenolff moved to Frankfurt, where his earliest fully dated book appeared in December.

7. The 'Gilgengartschrift'

One of the early Frakturs called after the book in which it first appeared at Nuremberg in 1517. It is illustrated in Crous's *Die gotischen Schriftarten*, Abb. 83, 84, and 121. Egenolff used it in a book dated May, 1531, J. Köbel's *Den Stab Iacob külich vnd gerecht zemachen vnd gebrauchen, damit an gebän zumessen*. Apart from heading type this was the only Fraktur used by Egenolff, and this unusual design survives in the books of his firm down to 1566 at least.

8. A roman

(20 lines = 90 mm) This again is a Basle type, the second size of the design which is characteristic of Basle printing during the most flourishing period of the press in that city. I refer to it again below

under the larger size. The present size I find first at Egenolff's press in an edition of Terentianus Maurus, dated February, 1532. Its earliest use at Basle known to me is in the *Historia naturalis* of the elder Pliny printed by Froben in 1525. The type is illustrated at fig. 80 in Updike from a Froben book of 1526, and also in Isaac's *English Printing Types, 1535-58*, fig. 3a, as used by Thomas Berthelet in London.

9. A SCHWABACHER

(20 lines = 90 mm) First found in 1532 in Sebastian Franck's *Zweintzig Glauben oder Secten*. This design I find also at the press of Wolfgang Köpfel at Strasbourg from 1524. Since Egenolff, as we have seen, was working for Köpfel from that year, it is possible that he cut the type, but if so it is rather strange that he did not use it himself in his early books. It is certainly superior to his Upper-Rhine type of the same size.

This Schwabacher is of particular interest because it has survived down to the present day, one of the oldest extant European types. It is identical with the Cicero No. 1531 of Messrs. Enschedé of Haarlem, a firm which possesses the finest collection of early types in the world. In their *Die hochdeutschen Schriften* (1919) Charles Enschedé assigned the type to the sixteenth century and pointed out that it is displayed in the Frankfurt foundry's specimen sheets of 1678 and 1718. But no details are given as to its early history either there or in Enschedé's *Fonderies de caractères dans les Pays Bas*. This gap is partially bridged in the *Catalogus van de typographische verzameling van J. Enschedé en Zonen* (1916), where E. Rösslin's *Kreuterbuch* (1535) is cited as being set in this Schwabacher. In fact, from 1533, and for many years, it was Egenolff's stock type for books in the vernacular.

10. Variation of UPPER-RHINE type

From 1537 Egenolff had another variety of Upper-Rhine type (similar to No. 1, above) but with different capitals H, S, and W, and some other letters. I find it first in J. Köbel's *Leyen Compas* (1537).

11. A ROMAN

(20 lines = 76 mm) In Reinhardus Lorichius's *De institutione principum*, the table of contents is set in a roman which was in common use at Strasbourg, and which was later popular in other German cities, in Antwerp, and in London. Fig. 11 in Proctor's *Index*, Part I, gives a reproduction and details of the various Strasbourg printers who had it. For its use by Whitchurch and Singleton in London see Isaac's *English Printing Types, 1535-58*, figs. 43b and 119b.

12. A ROMAN

(20 lines = 110 mm). On the title-page of the same book by Lorichius of 1538 are a few words in the larger size of the characteristic Basle roman. The earliest appearance of it noted is for the text of a well-known book, the *Defensor pacis* of Marsiglio of Padua, printed by Valentine Curio in 1522. Afterwards it was acquired by most of the other Basle printers and became popular in Germany. A number of London printers also had it; e. g., Reyner Wolfe, Richard Grafton, Edward Whitchurch, John Mayler, and Nicholas Hill, and reproductions from their presses may be seen in Isaac's *English Printing Types*. There is not much of it in Egenolff's books, as he had a roman of his own of the same size.

13. A ROMAN

(20 lines = 110 mm) This roman is not unlike the Basle 110 (No. 12, above), but may readily be distinguished by the sharp apex of the A and the somewhat unusual M. I have not found it elsewhere

In vogler nam mit jm sein vo
gelgarn/vnd gieng vß zuuog,
len/ Vnd als er sach ein bloch

Type No. 1

Johannes widman von Eger Meister Jun
den fryen künsten zů leyptzick enbiut Meister
Sigmůden von Smidmüle Beierscher natiō

Type No. 3

Obsecro autem uos fratres ,per nomen domini nostri Iesu
Christi, ut idem loquamini omnes, & non sint inter uos dissidia,
sed sitis integrum corpus eadem mente , & eadem sententia.

Type No. 2

Pat Jn darauf das Er all sach
Die nacht wolt han in guter acht

Type No. 4 (Theuerdanck)

Sprach noch rede dam

Type No. 5

IOANNEM FROBENIVM
NATO M·D·XVII·

Type No. 6

end / vnd vall darnach nyder
auff deine knye sprich also
Junckfraw Maria ich

Type No. 7 (Gilgengart)

and it was possibly cut by Egenolff. I find it first in 1540, used for the main text of Th. Dorstenius's *Botanicum*.

14. THE BASLE ITALIC

This is described in my *Type Designs* (pp. 146-49), and illustrated in Updike's *Printing Types* at fig. 104 (from an Italian book of 1552). It was in use by Egenolff from 1543. Gustav Mori says that Egenolff was one of the first printers to use italic; i. e., sloping capitals – presumably he is referring to this Basle type. Egenolff was certainly one of the first German printers to acquire it. It was another very popular type, spreading all over Europe, even south of the Alps. (Witness the illustration in Updike.)

15. A SCHWABACHER

(20 lines = 74 mm) This is another still extant type, Enschedé's Bourgis No. 1526, first found in Egenolff's books in 1550, in Cicero's *Von Gebüre vnd Billicheit* (a translation of the *De officiis*). The type was used by J. Faber Emmeus at Basle in 1528 in A. Marius's *Eyngelegte schrifft das opfer der Meß belangent*. It is found also in the German Bible printed by Peter Schöffer the younger, at Worms in 1529, and some of it is already in the folio edition of *Alle Propheten*, Worms (1527). It was also the type used for the first complete edition of William Tyndale's New Testament in English. When Francis Fry, in 1862, produced a facsimile of this edition (made from the only copy known), he assigned the book to the press of Schöffer at Worms. Fry's attribution has since been doubted and the suggestion made that the book was printed by Christopher Froschouer at Zürich. But Froschouer does not appear to have had this Schwabacher and there is little doubt that Fry was right. We know from Thomas Platter's autobiography that he acquired types from this Schöffer, who, he says, was well-stocked with punches – 'der hatt fast allerlei geschriften Punzen'. Probably Schöffer was a cutter of punches. The Enschedés in their *Catalogus* of 1916 mention an Apianus of 1564 as being set in their Bourgis No. 1526.

This brings us to the close of the first Egenolff's life in 1555. It will be seen that his roman and italic types came from Basle, with one exception, the 110 roman which may have been cut by him. He may also have cut the two Upper-Rhine types and the 90 Schwabacher. Of the fifteen types so far listed two Schwabachers were in the Foundry and are still extant. The following new types were used by his heirs.

16. A ROMAN

(20 lines = 83 mm) Another of the types which are still extant in the possession of the Enschedés, the so-called Schöffer roman. The Haarlem firm published a specimen of the type in 1926, in which they describe it as 'un caractère romain du quinzième siècle', and attribute the cutting to Peter Schöffer the elder, of Mainz. They bought the matrices in the late eighteenth century (1768) from a printer of Bois-le-Duc, Jacobus Scheffers, allegedly a descendant of the Schöffer family; hence the attribution. This roman was, in fact, cut at Cologne and the earliest date to which it has been traced is 1527, at the press of Peter Quentell of Cologne. Cf. 'Some Cologne and Basle Types', p. 238. The Egenolffs were using it from 1564 in the *De tuenda bona valetudine* of Helius Eobanus. Fig. 48 in Updike is printed from the actual type as it now exists.

17. AN ITALIC

(20 lines = 75 mm) This is an Antwerp type, much used by Christophe Plantin in his earliest books, and first found at the press of J. Steelsius of the same city in 1553. It may be seen in the Egenolff

nis,ac malorum,non intelligas,nisi facto periculo.
Dulcis inexpertis cultura potentis amici.
Expertus metuit.

Type No. 8

offs zier/mentel/ring/hůt/stab.Jh: schrifft ist Caldeisch/aber ihre Landtsprach
Arabisch.Sie seind etwa gewesen vnder

Type No. 9

O presbyteros.　O sacrilegos.
O castos.　　O priapos.
O papistas.　O Sodomitas.

Type No. 11

NÆ MIRANDVM,
Cum Gratia & Priuilegio Im-
periali nouo.

Type No. 12

species, Vna quę folijs est integris & crispis, caule
quadrato & uiridi, odore iucundo, & est satiua. AL-
tera etiam caulem habet quadratum & rubentem,

Type No. 13

prius dissoluet, ac dissipabit. FR A. Istud quidem,
quod tu dicis Timothee, proculdubio accideret, nisi
frigus montium, qui in Aethiopia maximi frigidissi

Type No. 14

teilē predi=cāten/schriftlich sind erschinen/Nä-
lich die/so sich in sonder nenen prediccāten des
Euangelij zů Basel des einen/mit jrn vnder

Type No. 15

books from 1566; e. g., in H. Knaust's *Lingua*, but with a different ampersand from that found at Antwerp. It was used also by John Day in London and is illustrated in Isaac's article on 'Elizabethan Types' in *The Library* (1933), fig. 18.

18. A ROMAN

(20 lines = 76 mm) I find this first in the same book by Knaust of 1566 in which the Antwerp italic was used. It appears to be the Brevier roman shown on the foundry's specimen sheet of 1622. It is not on the specimen sheet of 1592. Presumably the firm would know the origin of the type and did not consider the designer of sufficient importance to be mentioned.

19. A TERTIA (Great Primer) FRAKTUR

It is the one shown on the foundry's specimen sheet of 1678, the earliest sheet, as already mentioned, on which gothic types were displayed. It is found in J. Gobler's *Chronica der Kriegshandel des Keysers* (1566). The main text of this book is set in the 'Gilgengartschrift', a late survival of that unusual design. The Tertia Fraktur is the first type used by the Egenolffs which was in the traditional style; they were, in fact, very late in adopting Fraktur.

20. AN ITALIC

The 'Cicero Currens' of Robert Granjon, as shown on the specimen sheet of 1592. The type was cut in 1565, originally for Plantin at Antwerp,[1] but very soon afterwards it is to be found in books printed in Switzerland and Germany. In Frankfurt G. Corvinus had the type by 1566 and the Egenolffs by 1567, in H. Knaust's *Fortunæ mirandum regnum*. This is another surviving type, this time at the Oxford University Press, one of the so-called Fell types. Possibly it was not among the purchases made at the instance of Dr. Fell about the year 1672, since it does not appear in Oxford books printed before 1691. This is the first occasion on which we have found the Egenolffs using one of the types shown on the 1592 sheet. (See 'The Italic Types of Robert Granjon', fig. 11.)

21. A CICERO ROMAN

Found in the same book by Knaust of 1567. This roman was originally cut for Paolo Manuzio of Venice in 1557. In a letter of Manuzio's of 1558 addressed to the newly founded 'Accademia della Fama' at Venice, to which he had been appointed printer, he submitted three types for use in the books which the Academy proposed to publish.[1] The third size, intended for octavos, was probably the Cicero here in question – which he says he had ordered a year ago; i. e., in 1557. A reproduction of this Cicero, with some account of its history, was given in 'Some Types used by Paolo Manuzio'; see p. 256, fig. 1.

22. THE KLEINE CICERO FRAKTUR of the Enschedés

It is their No. 4225, first found in H. Schreiber's *Rechenbüchlin* (1572). The Enschedés identify their No. 4225 with the Cicero Fraktur shown on the 1678 specimen sheet of the Luther foundry; it had already appeared in another specimen, that of Johannes Elzevir, issued in Leyden in 1658. But some letters appear to differ; e. g., the g. However, as used by the Egenolffs the type agrees with that shown in 1678. In the *Catalogus* (1916), a book of 1574 is cited as being printed in J. Elzevir's Cicero Fraktur: but the type is not there identified with the Enschedé No. 4225.

1. See p. 255.

VS NERLIVS PETRO MEDICAE LAVRENTII
FILIO .S.
m doctissimorum hominum & horum grauissimorum fen-
ntia: grecas litteras non solum latinis plurimum ornamenti

Type No. 16

itaque mecum dubius deliberarem, quem huic
meæ Linguæ patronum ac Mecænatem potiſſi
mùm, è Germaniæ noſtræ Principibus, ordinis

Type No. 17

m Dei, ac precationem, de his ſi commune feceris fra
& aniles fabulas rejce temetipſum ad pietatem.corp
secutus ac futuræ Indubitatus ſermo, dignuſque qui

Type No. 18

und ſprichſt: kommet wider Menſchen kinder.
che. Du läſſeſt ſie dahin fahren wie ein Strom.

Type No. 19

Grimm? Lehre uns bedencken/ daß wir ſterben müſſen/
dich doch wieder zu uns/ unnd ſey deinen Knechten gnäd
ſo wollen wir rühmen unnd frölich ſeyn unſer Lebenlang.

Type No. 22

Und ſind wie ein Schlaf/ gleich wie ein Graß
frue bluet/ und bald welck wird/ und des Abends
Das machet dein Zorn/ daß wir ſo vergehen/ und

Type No. 23

23. MITTEL FRAKTUR

In the preface to the book by Schreiber of 1572 is the Mittel (English) Fraktur found on the Luther specimen of 1678. The Enschedés do not appear to have had this type, or at least it has not survived.

We have now traced the types used by the house of Egenolff down to a date when the foundry, under Sabon, was an independent establishment. We have traced three of the Enschedé 'Hochdeutsche Schriften' back to books printed by the Egenolffs in the sixteenth century. As to the Garamond romans and Granjon italics and Greeks of the 1592 sheet, we have found one only, Granjon's Cicero Currens italic, in their books down to 1572. The suggestion which has been made that Jacques Sabon was the medium through which these French types reached Frankfurt is not borne out by this evidence. It is possible that the three Frakturs (our Nos. 19, 22, and 23) were cut by Sabon, who had some reputation as a cutter of such types. But I suspect that if a search were made among German presses other than the Egenolffs' one or more of these Frakturs might be traced back to a date earlier than Sabon's arrival in Frankfurt. Occasional Garamond romans and Granjon italics appear in Frankfurt printed books after 1560, but at presses other than the Egenolffs'; e. g., a Latin Bible of 1566, printed by G. Corvinus. The real French influence begins with the arrival in 1574 of André Wechel from Paris. One of the first books printed by Wechel in Frankfurt, the *Dialexis de novæ stellæ apparitione* of Hagecius ab Hayck, is set entirely in Paris types. However, I know of no documentary evidence of dealings between this Paris printer and the Frankfurt foundry.

There is one other source from which these French types may have reached Frankfurt, namely, the house of Plantin at Antwerp. In the Plantin Museum at Antwerp there exists an inventory of a stock of punches and matrices belonging to Plantin, but deposited for some unexplained reason in the foundry at Frankfurt. Many of these types are certainly those shown on the 1592 specimen.

[1941]

ON RE-READING UPDIKE

DANIEL BERKELEY UPDIKE, of the Merrymount Press, Boston, died in December, 1941. Little notice was taken in this country of his death, owing to the state of war and to the fact that our typographical journals had in consequence ceased publication. This omission certainly did not mean that there was any falling off in our interest in Updike as a printer or in his chief published work, *Printing Types, their History, Forms and Use.* That book first appeared almost a quarter of a century ago. It is always worth a rereading and no excuse need be made for returning to it once more.

Printing Types has become an established classic among books on typographical history, one of the books which will not be superseded for generations, in the category of such works as T. B. Reed's *History of the Old English Letter Foundries* and Charles Enschedé's *Fonderies de caractères dans les Pays-Bas.* Among the reasons which have contributed to its success is perhaps first of all its comprehensiveness. The author deals with all periods in due proportion, and does not, as so many writers on the history of the printed book have done, leave the impression that printing of interest ceased with Christophe Plantin, to be revived again by William Morris. We may cite Updike's account of French printing in the eighteenth century, including the story of P. S. Fournier and the early Didots, his description of the Spanish book and of the book in England about 1800, of William Bulmer and his contemporaries and the study of type-specimen books and sheets. Better-known periods are not neglected; witness some seventy-five pages out of 505 devoted to Incunables. A second factor in establishing the reputation of his book is to be found in Updike's being not only an historian but a practising printer. The contemplation of a book suggests to him the problem facing the printer in laying out the material before him. For example, in vol. 1, p. 161, in describing a book printed by L. Torrentino at Florence in 1550, he notes the method of arranging the title-page and detects in the book a falling away from an earlier simplicity in the mixture of types used. Many books are examined in this manner in a refreshing style seldom attempted by his predecessors, who have been generally bibliographers or librarians. As the work of a printer *Printing Types* contains material more often found in manuals dealing with the technical side of the craft, such as the chapter on the evolution of the point system of type measurement, and that excellent chapter (chapter xxiii) towards the end of vol. 2 on the choice of types for a printing office. Finally a great contribution to the book's success is made by the illustrations, 367 in number, all excellent, with the exception of those which have had to be considerably reduced.

The comprehensive nature of the work has been stressed, but in this respect there is one omission to be noted, that is in the treatment of German printing, more particularly of the Reformation period. Considering the space given to Johann Froben of Basle, more should certainly have been said of his contemporaries in Germany. In the matter of book decoration and woodcut illustrations the period was one of the most remarkable in the history of the book, and one of considerable interest for its typography; it is true, however, that this typography is outside the main stream of the development of European types. Updike's book is based on lectures delivered, some of them during the war of 1914-18, which may account for this neglect and for one of the blunders in the book, the confusion between Johann Petri of Nuremberg, who issued a type specimen sheet in 1525, and the Basle printer of the same name, a mistake not corrected in the second edition of 1937. Incidentally it should be pointed out that, for technical reasons, in this second edition the corrections could not, for the most part, be made in the body of the text, but are added as notes, a necessity unfortunate for the student. For example, Beatrice Warde's rediscovery of the specimen book of Jean Jannon of Sedan, 1621, and the clearing up of the mystery of the origin of the so-called 'caractères de l'Université', is duly referred to in the notes, but the text remains the same, with the exception of the correction of Jannon's name for Garamond's on p. 238, and the alteration of fig. 168. The consequence is that a passage which was originally obscure still remains obscure in the main text of the book.

These notes, however, are not a belated review of *Printing Types*, but an attempt to suggest in what directions some future Updike might be expanded or modified as a result of recent studies. The publication of *Printing Types* was itself one of the causes which have promoted the interest in typographic studies. There is, for example, the question of the vocabulary to be used in describing types, and again the subject of the international exchange of types. When Updike wrote, the term Rotunda or Round Text for the Italian form of gothic had not come into vogue, at any rate among English writers. If it had been known to Updike its use would certainly have added brevity and clarity to a number of passages. For example, on p. 63 of vol. 1, of a Rotunda of Koberger's he writes 'a type less pointed than the first gothic types, reminding one a little of the early black-letter types of Italy and Spain'. Does not the term Rotunda convey all that in one word? Again, on p. 121 of vol. 1, of a common Rotunda used by Wynkyn De Worde, 'the smaller has a round quality which is a little like the Italian gothic type of the time'. Then there is the term *lettre de somme*; on p. 63 of vol. 1 it is used of a type since called *fere-humanistica* or *gotico-antiqua*, both terms which Updike would in any case have declined to adopt as being too precious. Elsewhere it is used of a Rotunda, e. g. on p. 60 of vol. 1. The term does not appear to have been known to the medieval writing masters, and should probably be abandoned. The useful group of Upper-Rhine types was unknown to Updike as a group, and consequently on fig. 77 he calls an Upper-Rhine type used by Froschouer at Zürich a Schwabacher.

The term *Old Style* is of very frequent occurrence in the pages of *Printing Types*. It is defined, or partially defined in a note on p. 18 of vol. 1, as the less modelled design in contrast with modern. To the American printer Old Style appears to mean a type like Caslon. Our printers prefer the term Old Face, as they are accustomed to the use of Old Style for a particular design, the revived old face of Miller & Richard, *c.* 1860. When describing types of the sixteenth century there seems to be some vagueness as to whether a particular type is to be called Old Style or not. For example, a book printed by Torrentino at Florence in 1550 (vol. 1, p. 162, fig. 103) is described as set in an 'old style font'. On p. 143 of vol. 1 the Vesalius of Oporinus of Basle is 'printed in a noble

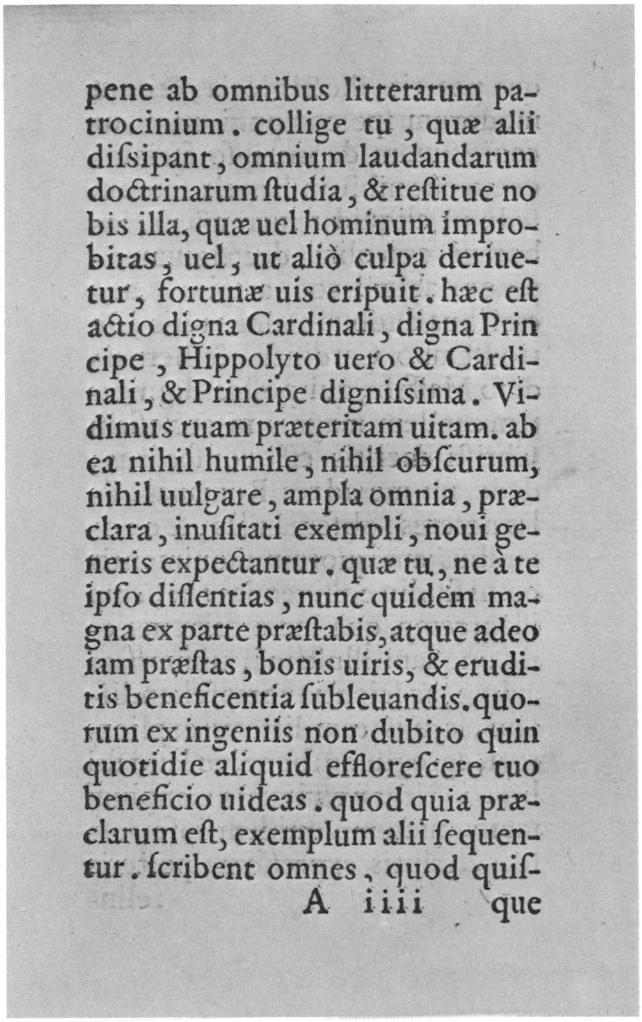

pene ab omnibus litterarum pa-
trocinium . collige tu , quæ alii
difsipant , omnium laudandarum
doctrinarum ftudia , & reftitue no
bis illa, quæ uel hominum impro-
bitas , uel , ut aliò culpa deriue-
tur , fortunæ uis eripuit . hæc eft
actio digna Cardinali , digna Prin
cipe , Hippolyto uero & Cardinali , & Principe dignifsima . Vidimus tuam præteritam uitam. ab
ea nihil humile , nihil obfcurum,
nihil uulgare , ampla omnia , præclara , inufitati exempli , noui ge-
neris expectantur . quæ tu , ne a te
ipfo diffentias , nunc quidem magna ex parte præftabis, atque adeo
iam præftas , bonis uiris, & erudi-
tis beneficentia fubleuandis. quorum ex ingeniis non dubito quin
quotidie aliquid efflorefcere tuo
beneficio uideas . quod quia præclarum eft, exemplum alii fequen-
tur . fcribent omnes , quod quif-
A iiii que

FIG. I. The roman (actual size) shown in Updike's
Printing Types (fig. 108) from Paulus Manutius,
Antiquitatum Romanarum liber de legibus. Aldus,
Venice, 1559.

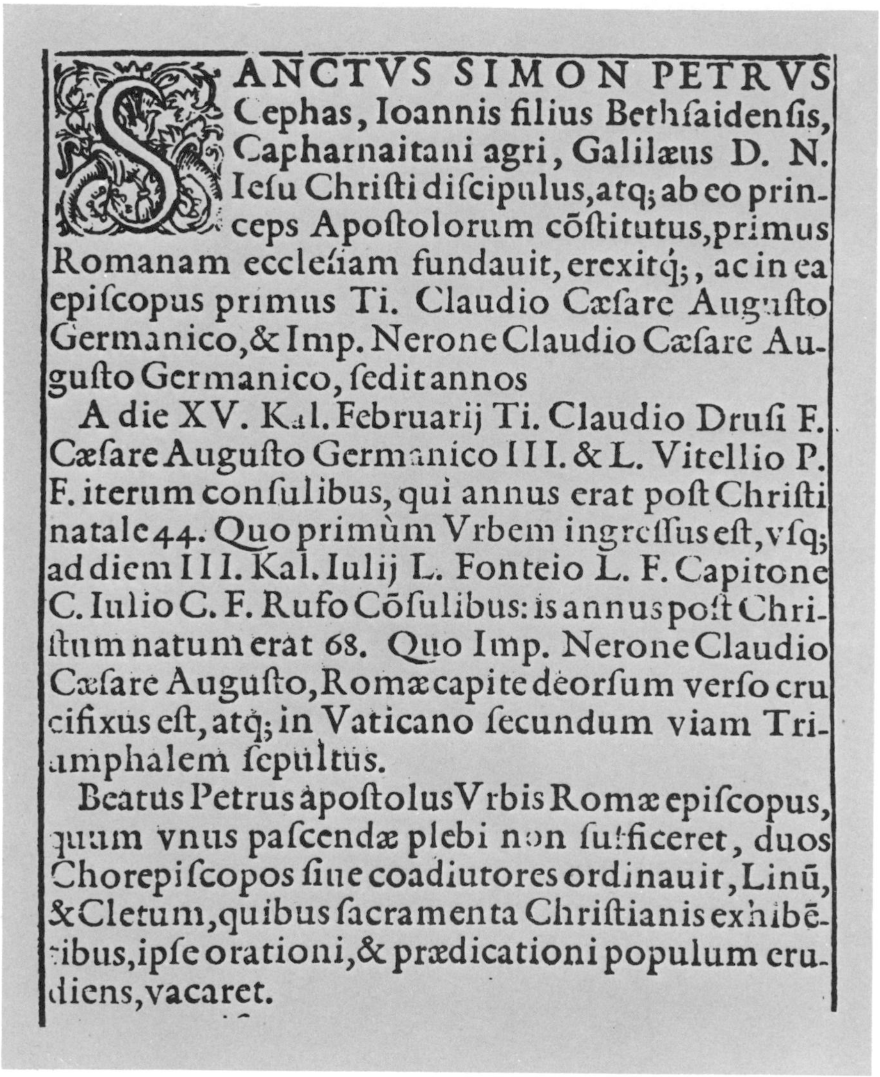

SANCTVS SIMON PETRVS
Cephas, Ioannis filius Bethſaidenſis,
Capharnaitani agri, Galilæus D. N.
Ieſu Chriſti diſcipulus, atq; ab eo prin-
ceps Apoſtolorum cõſtitutus, primus
Romanam eccleſiam fundauit, erexitq;, ac in ea
epiſcopus primus Ti. Claudio Cæſare Auguſto
Germanico, & Imp. Nerone Claudio Cæſare Au-
guſto Germanico, ſedit annos

A die XV. Kal. Februarij Ti. Claudio Druſi F.
Cæſare Auguſto Germanico III. & L. Vitellio P.
F. iterum conſulibus, qui annus erat poſt Chriſti
natale 44. Quo primùm Vrbem ingreſſus eſt, vſq;
ad diem III. Kal. Iulij L. Fonteio L. F. Capitone
C. Iulio C. F. Rufo Cõſulibus: is annus poſt Chri-
ſtum natum erat 68. Quo Imp. Nerone Claudio
Cæſare Auguſto, Romæ capite dèorſum verſo cru-
cifixus eſt, atq; in Vaticano ſecundum viam Tri-
amphalem ſcpultus.

Beatus Petrus apoſtolus Vrbis Romæ epiſcopus,
quum vnus paſcendæ plebi non ſufficeret, duos
Chorepiſcopos ſiue coadiutores ordinauit, Linũ,
& Cletum, quibus ſacramenta Chriſtianis exhibē-
tibus, ipſe orationi, & prædicationi populum eru-
diens, vacaret.

FIG. 2. The roman (actual size) shown in Updike's *Printing Types*
(fig. 158; from Saint Lambert's *Saisons*, Paris, 1775) and attributed
there to French sources. From Bartholomaeus Sacchi de Platina,
Historia de vitis pontificum. Maternus Cholinus, Cologne, 1574.

old style type'. A Josephus, Paris, 1557 (vol. 1, p. 200) is in a roman 'less classical and more old style than we have seen hitherto'. Apparently Updike finds the roman of the *Hypnerotomachia*, Paris, 1546, or Fine's *De rebus mathematicis*, Vascosan, Paris, 1556, more classical, i. e. more akin to Italian fifteenth-century romans. A little further on, a book by C. Paradin, De Tournes, Lyons, 1561 (vol. 1, p. 203), shows 'a robust old style roman'. But all these romans are either Garamonds or closely modelled on Garamond. If any or all of these romans are to be distinguished as a group from Caslon, is it because they are less modelled? In that case a name is needed under which they might be classified. Writing of the seventeenth century in France, Updike says 'French types became less Italian and more what we now call old style letter'. In the first half of the century at any rate the romans used were predominantly Garamonds, e. g. in the Delbene, 1609 (vol. 1, p. 106). On p. 226, vol. 1, Updike writes of a book set in one of the early romans of Firmin Didot 'the general conception of its type is still old style, but pared down to the last degree'. After that one can but feel that a fuller definition of this elusive term is sadly needed.

Much of this vagueness could be avoided if the designer of a particular type described could be named or its origin traced, and it is this direction that future historians of type design development may be expected to follow. When Updike wrote such knowledge was not available and he certainly had no such plan in view. Here are some examples of the kind of note that might be made. The Vesalius, printed by Oporinus at Basle, 1553 (or rather 1555), is set in a roman cut by the French designer Robert Granjon (it appears in the 1628 specimen book published by the Vatican Press at Rome), and the same type is shown in Updike's fig. 102 from a book printed by Torrentino at Florence, a printer who was well stocked with French types. His fig. 104 shows a page from a Venice book partly set in an italic to which the author refers several times, always in connexion with Italian books. This italic appeared first at Basle and was probably taken to Venice by Peter Schöffer the younger about 1540. Schöffer may have cut the type. At least we know from the autobiography of Thomas Platter that Schöffer was well stocked with all manner of punches. Also this italic was sold all over Europe and there is hardly one centre of printing in which it may not be found. Updike's fig. 108 is a page from a Venice book of 1623, set in a roman which dates back some sixty years. It was used by Paolo Manuzio in the books which he printed for the Accademia della Fama at Venice from 1558 to 1572, and became a common European type. His fig. 119 from a Florence book of 1691 is set in a roman described by Updike as of 'a distinctly modern note'. The same type appears again in his fig. 217 among Dutch types. In the second edition Updike has noted that this roman is the pseudo 'Janson', wrongly attributed to the Leipzig founder, Anton Janson, and still in use today; but the strange fact that one of the first printers to use it was working at Florence is not noted. In fig. 152 he shows an italic from the Delacolonge specimen book of 1773, which the author says 'appears to be of early date'. The same italic is shown on fig. 168, where it is described as 'Garamond's Caractères de l'Université'. This figure has been changed in the second edition, where it is recognized that the true, i. e. Jannon's, 'Caractères de l'Université' are shown on fig. 172. The italic of fig. 152 was used by Henri Estienne at Geneva from 1564. In

AV TRESILLVSTRE
PRINCE EMANVEL PHILIBERT,
DVC DE SAVOYE, PRINCE DE PIEMONT,
Conte d'Aft, &c. Gouuerneur dés
Païs-bas,& General de l'armee
de fa Majefté.

*IEN QVE DE LONG
tems, éprins par l'excel-
lente renommmee dés
vertuz trefilluftres de
votre ALTESSE, j'aye
defiré, auec mon perpetuel
feruice, luy offrir quelque
chofe de més labeurs :
Si eft ce que je n'euffe pas encore maintenãt ozé
entreprendre, luy dedier la traduction, & impreffion de l'œuure prefente (veu même qu'elle
eft ja de long tems fiene en fon naturel langage)
n'eût eté, que plufieurs Doctes & fauans per-
fonnages, qui ont fait l'experiëce de cés Secrets,
m'ont affermé, iceus eftre non feulement verita-*

*2   bles,

FIG. 3. The Double Pica italic (actual size) shown in Updike's *Printing Types* (fig. 257; from *Aelfredi regis regis res gestae*, John Day, London, 1574) and attributed there to John Day. From Alessio Piemontese (= Girolamo Ruscelli?), *Les secrets*. Christophe Plantin, Antwerp, 1557.

design it agrees with the series of Robert Granjon's italics which are shown on the specimen sheets of the Berner-Luther foundry of Frankfurt, but this size is not there. His fig. 158, from a Paris book of 1775, shows what Updike calls 'a very modelled old style font'. This design goes back to about 1570, when it is found at both Basle and Frankfurt. The specimen in Updike has some eighteenth-century features such as the capital J and may be a copy of the original design. It was in the foundry of Claude Lamesle, as may be seen in that founder's specimen book of 1742. Of fig. 229, from a book printed at Granada in 1545, the author says the page 'might have been taken bodily from one of Froben's editions'. The types are in fact of Basle origin, the capitals being Froben's and the body type the usual Basle roman exported to many countries. His Fig. 230, from a book printed at Alcalá in 1569, is described as being set 'in a pure and elegant roman type', a type which is surely the Garamond shown on the Luther foundry's sheet, and perhaps the same as that shown on fig. 239, from a book of 1774.

In the chapters on English books there are many reproductions which illustrate the dependence of our printers before Caslon on foreign type-cutters. In the text Updike here follows closely the account given by T. B. Reed in his *Old English Letter Foundries*, as, for instance, when he says of De Worde that he was his own type-cutter, and in the praise which he bestows on John Day for his typography. Day receives the credit for the excellent types which he imported from the Low Countries and from France, e. g. the Double Pica roman and italic of figs. 256 and 257, and the Double Pica italic of fig. 284. On p. 27 of vol. 2, the italic used in a book printed at Antwerp by Hubert Goltz in 1557 is said to resemble 'some used by John Day'. If Updike had not been under the impression that most large printers of the middle of the sixteenth century still cut their own types, he would surely have recognized that in this case it was not a matter of the resemblance of types, but of their identity. In the description on p. 127 of vol. 2 of two other books printed by Day, the Euclid of 1570 and Roger Ascham's *Scholemaster*, 1571, it should be added that the italics referred to are those of Robert Granjon. On pp. 135 and 136 of vol. 2 an edition of the *Theological Works* of Charles Leslie printed by William Bowyer in 1721 is described and the 'old style types' are said to be 'no doubt Dutch'. The italic used is that of Christoffel van Dyck, and the roman is probably also Dutch, at least it is found on the specimen sheet of an Amsterdam printer, Joannes Kannewet, issued *c.* 1710. It is even more interesting to find that the same roman and italic was used in John Selden's *Opera*, 1726 (fig. 290). Updike, misled by John Nichols and other authorities, assigned the Selden types to Caslon.

That a printer of Updike's experience should have failed to notice some of these parallels in the plates which he himself selected, is due to the fact that he was not expecting or looking for any such thing. He had not realized the implications of the statement that by 1540 type cutting and founding was an industry separate from that of printing, and that from that period one may expect to find any good type in the hands of many printers and even in several countries.

[1946]

TITLE-PAGES: THEIR FORMS AND DEVELOPMENT

I⸀ᴛ is a curious fact that the title-page was evolved at a comparatively late date in the history of the book, and is indeed almost unknown before the printed book. There are a few examples among early surviving manuscripts of a separate leaf being used for the title, but they are quite exceptional, and even these give the title on the back of this leaf. The usual practice of the calligrapher was to give any information considered desirable as to the author and the date and place of the making of the manuscript in the colophon. This practice was taken over by the printers, although in the first years of the new art they frequently said nothing as to place of printing, probably with the deliberate intention of concealing the fact that the book was produced by mechanical means. The title-page as we know it, giving the title, author's name and an imprint, being, in fact, a kind of advertisement of the book, was not well established until some years after 1500.

The title-page owes its origin, according to one theory, to the fact that printers found it necessary to protect the first leaf of the text. Whereas a manuscript would be bound as soon as the calligrapher had finished the text, most of the copies of a printed edition were delivered to a bookseller in sheets, and many might remain unbound for years. Hence arose the practice of beginning the book on the second leaf or on the back of the first leaf. The first page could then be used for the purpose of advertising the book, for the fully-developed title-page arose out of a commercial need. A few early examples of the addition of a brief title on the first page are known, the first being that of a Bull of Pope Pius II, printed by Fust and Schöffer at Mainz in 1463. The blank title-leaf is found for many years after that date, but by the end of the fifteenth century a title-leaf containing a brief description in a few words is common. As late as 1548 we find the brothers Dorici at Rome printing several volumes of the works of Cardinal Bembo with the title on the back of the first leaf. An edition of the Vulgate printed at Venice in 1487 by Georgius Arrivabene offers an example of the most rudimentary form of a title-page, with the single word *Biblia* on the first leaf.

The example of Ratdolt at Venice, who in 1476 printed a Calendar of Regiomontanus with woodcut borders and an imprint on the first leaf, was not followed by contemporary printers. Even this solitary case hardly presents a title-page in the form in which we know it, since the leaf, has a poem in praise of the book in place of a title. Of the fully developed title-page, giving title, author and full imprint, Dr. Konrad Haebler, the German authority on incunabula, knows of only one instance in the fifteenth century, a book by Johannes Glogoviensis printed by Wolfgang Stöckel at Leipzig in 1500; the title itself, however, is cut on wood.

The lettering of the simple fifteenth-century title-page was often that used in the text of the book, or sometimes a larger, heading type was used. Very frequently the words were cut on wood, and since for the printer it was as easy to print from a block con-

FIG. 1. Title-page from Nicolò Machiavelli, *Sopra la prima deca di Tito Livio*. Antonio Blado, Rome, 1531. The formal italic below the device, designed by Arrighi, was used in many of Blado's books.

FIG. 2. Title-page from Oronce Fine, *Quadrans astrolabicus*. Simon de Colines, Paris, 1534.
The border was probably designed by the author.

taining a design in addition to a brief title, the woodcut illustration on the first leaf soon followed. The examples of the John Lydgate, printed by Pynson, *c.* 1515, and of the *Deceyte of Women*, printed by Abraham Vele about 1550, are typical title-pages of popular books of the earlier printers. In Spain especially this combination of title and illustration, in that country often an heraldic cut, both cut on wood, became the fashion and persisted for many years in the next century. Scenes from school life often illustrated educational texts, while a school of woodcutters at Florence designed a famous series of illustrations which decorated the title-pages of devotional tracts by Savonarola and other works. The first printer's devices, the two shields of Fust and Schöffer and the double cross rising out of a circle at Venice, were added to the colophons, and it was only when the French printers began to use large devices surrounded by borders, for which there was no room on the last leaf, that the printer's name, or at least mark, began to appear on the title-page. Thus one further step was taken towards the title-page as we know it.

The sixteenth century is especially the age of the woodcut title-border (or metal-cut, for the material used for blocks was frequently metal). The practice of decorating the first leaf of the text with a woodcut border had been started by Ratdolt at Venice, and after 1490 was common among the printers of that city. In fact, several of the borders originally used for an opening were actually converted into title-borders after 1500. During the following century the variety of borders used in all the countries where printing was practised is remarkable. In Germany especially, during the years of the Reformation when the printing press was unusually active, a very large number of decorative borders were cut, many of them by artists of the first rank, including even Dürer and Holbein. The work of the Holbeins and Urs Graf at Basle is well known to all book collectors. Perhaps less familiar is the work of Hans Baldung Grien, Hans Weiditz and Daniel Hopfer at Strasbourg and Augsburg, and that extraordinary series of designs which appear on the Luther tracts printed at Wittenberg and on similar works produced in Saxony. Many of these borders are highly successful as decorative pieces. The fact that they are less familiar to us may be accounted for by two circumstances. In the first place the earlier book collectors were almost all collectors of the classics, and the first writers on the history of printing, except in the matter of the invention of printing, approached the subject from the point of view of the student of the Greek and Roman classical writers. In the second place the German printers cut themselves off from Western Europe by clinging to the gothic letter after Italy, France, and finally England had adopted roman and italic, even for books in the vernacular.

There is one point about the early woodcut borders which must seem strange to the printer of today, and that is the unsuitability of the decoration to the subject matter of the book. The sixteenth-century printer naturally found it economical to ignore the fact that a border originally intended for a Bible was not suitable for a medical work. He did not regard it as incongruous to use a border depicting scenes from Greek mythology in a French medieval romance. Even a printer of the class of Jean de Tournes uses the same piece on the title-page of a Xenophon and of a book of French verse. Nor was the average printer very particular about the state of a block. Especially in England, where the general standard was lower than on the Continent, a damaged block would be used as long as it held together.

In the second half of the century two rival fashions of decoration were developed which finally banished the woodcut border, first the method of decoration by type ornaments or printers' flowers, and secondly the engraved title-page. There is one example of type ornament known even in the fifteenth century, in an Aesop printed at Parma in 1483. After 1500, examples of borders made up of separate cast pieces are fairly frequent and are especially common in England in the books of Wynkyn de Worde and his contemporaries. But it is not until about 1560 that we find borders built up of type ornaments worked into arabesque patterns. It seems to have been Robert Granjon, the engraver of types at Paris and Lyons, who cut arabesque fleurons, divided them up and built up fresh patterns out of their component parts. The use of printers' flowers in borders is found at most centres of printing towards the end of the century and obtained its greatest popularity in the Netherlands and in England. Many fine examples are found in English books from about 1570 for the next fifty years. Joseph Moxon, who wrote on English letter-founding in 1683, tells us that they were considered old-fashioned in his day. They were revived again in the eighteenth century by P. S. Fournier at Paris, who cut many new designs which were copied all over Europe. Fournier's flowers could be built up to form all manner of ornaments and were more adaptable than the arabesques of the sixteenth century, when the original unit always resulted in the same pattern. Just as Granjon had devised a method of decorating without the use of the woodcut block, so Fournier designed his new flowers in order that printers might dispense with engraved vignettes. However, the vogue of the Fournier designs had a shorter life, and may be said to have been killed by the classical school of printing of the end of the century.

Engraving on copper was practised in the fifteenth century, but the engraved title-page originated about 1550. Curiously enough, the earliest known engraved border occurs in an English book, the *Anatomy* of Thomas Geminus, printed in London in 1545. In the following year we find a second example, cut by Corneille de La Haye for Balthazar Arnoullet at Lyons, where there was a remarkable group of engravers at work about this time. From 1548 the books of Enea Vico printed at Venice begin the fashion in Italy, where, after 1550, examples are fairly numerous. In the Netherlands also, beginning with the work of Hubert Goltzius at Bruges, they are met with almost as frequently as in Italy. It was, perhaps, Christophe Plantin at Antwerp who, more than any other printer, made the engraved title-border the fashion for all larger and more important publications. But it is especially with the seventeenth century that engraved borders are associated. The Elzevirs used them even on their pocket editions, while at the other extreme the massive volumes issued at Amsterdam and at Paris in the reign of Louis XIV are almost invariably introduced by an elaborate engraved frontispiece.

Perhaps the worst examples of these overloaded frontispieces are to be found in German books of the period. Often, also, the engraved border is only a bastard title, the proper

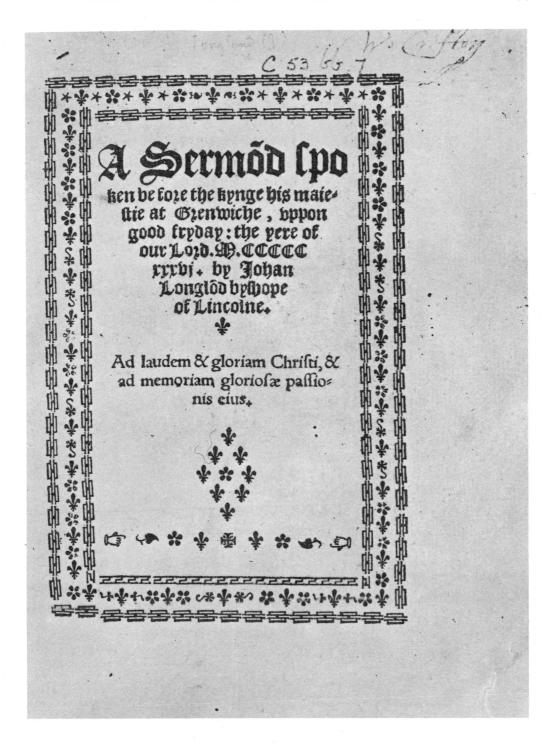

Fig. 3. Title-page from John Longlond, *A sermon spoken before the kynge* ... [T. Petyt?], London, 1536. Wynkyn de Worde and his contemporaries used cast pieces as ornaments, at least from 1504. Although the use of such ornaments was frequent, their arrangement on this title-page is uncommon.

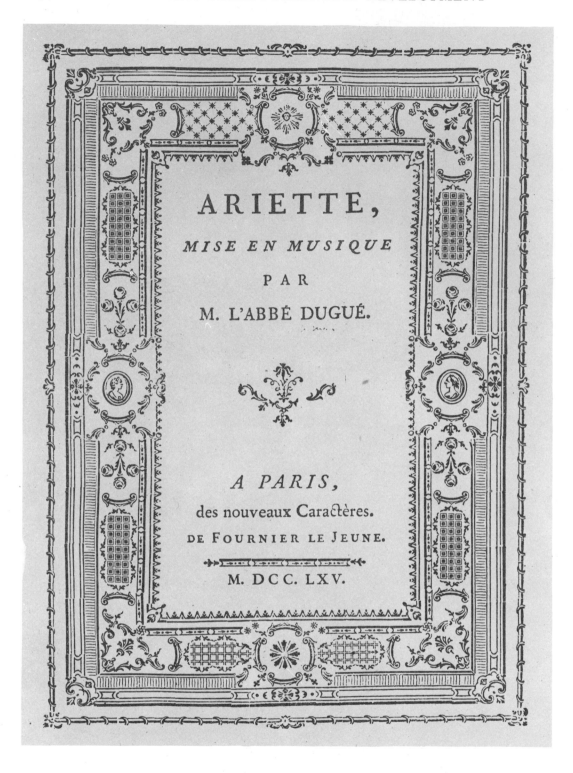

FIG. 4. Title-page from L'Abbé Dugué, *Ariette*. Pierre-Simon Fournier le jeune, Paris, 1765. This rather ornate border composed with Fournier's new ornaments is typical for the style of French typography in the late eighteenth century. (Reduced.)

title-page being set up in type. The earlier examples, dating from the sixteenth century, are in general the best, being simpler and not yet overburdened with a mass of detail. The good taste of the eighteenth century brought about a reform. But at Paris most books of this period had a typographic title-page and the work of the famous school of French engravers was lavished on the illustrations. However, the engraved vignettes of that age were often very effectively used. Even Baskerville did not always disdain the vignette, and it was the last form of decoration abandoned by Bodoni.

One other form of decoration may be mentioned, that of metal rules. Rules have been used occasionally at almost all periods, by Geofroy Tory, for example, among others. But as far as title-pages are concerned they are found most often in the seventeenth century.

The purely typographic title-page is naturally of greater interest to the modern producer of books. At all periods the title-page which was effected mainly by the arrangement of types has been common, and at most periods there have been printers who preferred to dispense with ornament of any kind. In the sixteenth century the books of the Paris printer, Michel de Vascosan, illustrate this severer manner, and the classical style of the great printers at the close of the eighteenth century was likewise independent of decoration. Some sort of arrangement of the letters displayed on the title-page suggested itself from the first, and very soon various shapes were tried. Perhaps the commonest arrangement was the conical one, or the so-called hour-glass shape, in which the lines of type begin by being long, to become short at the centre, lengthening again in the imprint at the foot. Others have preferred a natural arrangement, printing the matter exactly as if on a page of the text. Geofroy Tory, a book producer whose work was of great importance in the history of the book, seems to have been against the fashion of his day in his choice of the natural layout. It has certainly been the usual custom to aim at some sort of pattern in the division of the lines of type. In this respect the earlier printers had one advantage which was not enjoyed by their successors. They felt no difficulty about dividing a word in a title, even when the second part of the word was to be set in a different size or even a different kind of type. Frequently we find examples of such breaks in words as custom has made impossible for the modern printer. The simplification of the task for whoever was responsible for the layout is obvious. One rule which seems to have been almost universally observed is that the mass of the type must be in the top half of the page and not evenly distributed.

Equally important with the distribution of the matter is the question of the kind of type to be used, the sizes of type, upper- or lower-case, and the number of different founts. The simplest manner of using the letter exmployed in the text met with little favour and was soon displaced by the use of larger types and especially by the use of capitals. The heavy, square, roman capitals, like those of Froben at Basle, for the first line, with smaller capitals for succeeding lines, were more or less customary in Northern Europe in the first quarter of the sixteenth century. In some countries a mixture of a 'lettre de forme' and roman capitals was not unusual at the same period. With the introduction of the new Garamond romans at Paris about 1530 began the fashion of using the Canon and Double Canon sizes of the lower-case letters for titles. In the

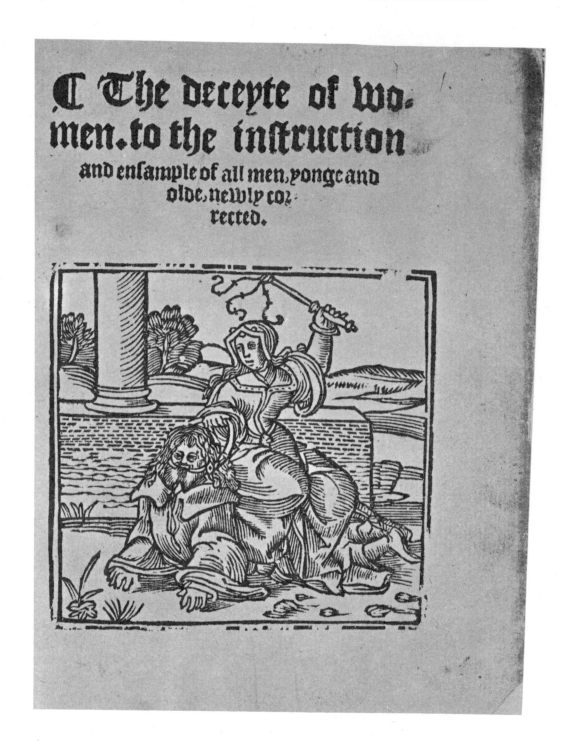

Fig. 5. Title-page from *The deceyte of women*. Abram Vele, London [1560?]. The combination of black-letter and a woodcut is usual in sixteenth-century English books. The book shown is undated and must have been printed after 1548. The woodcut is probably much older.

seventeenth century we find large and heavy roman capitals again in favour, often balanced by a woodcut ornament of a basket of flowers. This century, undoubtedly the worst in the history of typography, notwithstanding the Elzevirs, is especially remarkable for its crowded title-pages. It had become the custom to give as much information as possible about the contents of the book and the qualifications of author, editor, &c., and the printer took the opportunity of displaying as large a variety of his types as possible. No doubt the use of title-pages as posters for advertising is partly responsible for the custom. It has been established by documentary evidence that such methods of advertising books were usual in England and in Germany, and probably this was so in other countries also. Incidentally it may be pointed out that the posting up of title-pages accounts for some of the early collections, such as that of Bagford, now in the British Museum. Bagford has been attacked for his vandalism in mutilating books for the sake of his hobby, but it now appears that he may have been quite innocent of the charge. In any case the result on the title-page as a specimen of typographical arrangement was deplorable.

With the eighteenth century title-pages became simpler and letters became lighter, and the result is again work as good in its different style as that of the sixteenth century. The eighteenth century is certainly a great period in the history of book production, with its centre in Paris. In England the influence of Caslon and Baskerville at length raised our typography to a level with Continental work. For one innovation P. S. Fournier is mainly responsible, the introduction of outline and other decorative capitals which were so successfully used at Paris. At the end of the century we have the work of the Didots and Bodoni, the classical school, whose technical achievement has hardly been surpassed at any period. One may cavil at their conception of the ideal shape of letters, one may dislike their excessive use of hair lines and their flat serifs, but it must be admitted that as practical printers and type cutters their work was of first-rate quality. These classical printers were proud of their types and wished them to stand alone. Bodoni, who, at the beginning of his career, used ornaments copied from Fournier and engraved vignettes, in his later years more and more abandoned decoration and outline letters. The classical title-page is composed in roman capitals of varying size, but without the admixture of lower-case letters or italics and without the aid of decoration. Like Baskerville, these printers considered that type is itself sufficiently interesting to stand alone.

[1928]

ENGLISH TYPOGRAPHY
IN THE SEVENTEENTH CENTURY

TALBOT BAINES REED, in his *Old English Letter Foundries*, says that between 1700 and 1720 there was probably more Dutch type in England than English. How far does the popularity of Duch type extend back into the seventeenth century? There were, of course, a number of designs in general use derived from founders of the Low Countries, as well as of France, dating back to the sixteenth century. But as to Holland itself, it must be remembered the best designers of the century, the Voskens and Cristoffel van Dijck, began work there, the former in 1641 and the latter in 1647. We know that Joseph Moxon, whose specimen sheet is dated 1669, took the Dutch as his models, and in his *Mechanick Exercises* of 1685 he speaks highly of their work. But it is not unlikely that some types which Moxon regarded as Dutch, and of which the matrices may have been bought in Holland, were derived ultimately from Frankfurt. The typography of the leading Dutch printers, the Elzevirs, Blaeu, and Jan Jansson of Amsterdam, was, before 1650, predominantly French.

In these notes it is proposed to trace some of the Dutch types found in England, and to identify some English-cut types. The search is hampered by the scarcity of contemporary specimens and by the very low standard of press-work of the century, the worst in the history of English printing. The Sale Catalogue and Specimen of the James foundry of 1782, valuable as it is, is very disappointing in its diplay of roman and italic letters. The types are shown in very brief passages, and, unfortunately, that wretched extract from the Catiline Orations, beginning 'Quousque tandem', was chosen as a text, in imitation of Caslon; the result is that the most useful of all lower-case letters in roman, the g, never appears at all.

First a note on the Fell types.[1] We know from the letters of Thomas Marshall that negotiations for the purchase of these types were being carried on in 1672. But it appears that, for whatever reason, there was a long delay before they were in actual use at Oxford, ten years in fact. The first Oxford Bible in which a Fell type appears is that of 1682, in which there was used a little of the Double Pica italic. The address, 'Lectori', in the edition of Cyprian, 1682, edited by Dr. Fell, is set in the Double Pica roman, and the great folio Bible of 1685 has the main text in this roman. Of this type we know that Oxford has the punches, as well as the matrices, as is the case with many of the Fell types. Nevertheless, the type is shown on the specimen of the London printer, James Orme, c. 1698, contained in the Bagford Collection in the British Museum. Presumably Orme did not buy this type from Oxford, and we may infer that the Dutch founder either kept a set of matrices when he sold the punches to Oxford, or that he had sold the type before the date of that purchase, and that the punches were not cut especially for Oxford.

In the Oxford specimen of 1693, one type, a Great Primer roman and italic, which

---

1. Cf. Stanley Morison, *John Fell*, 1967.

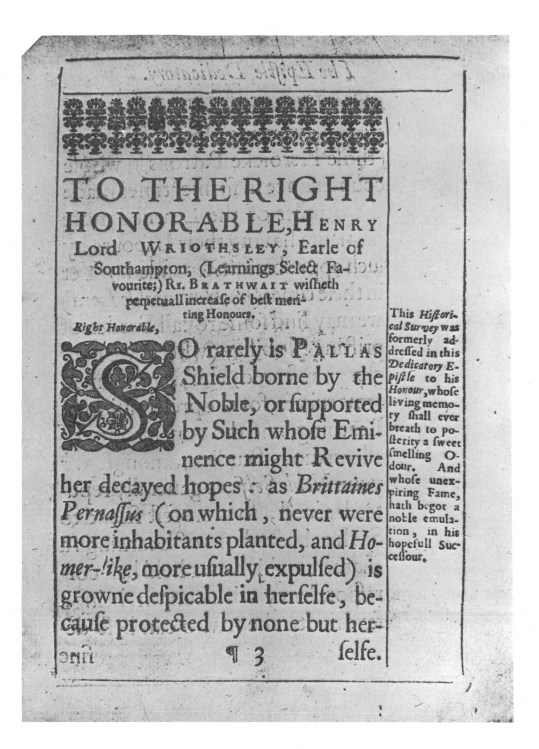

FIG. 1. Double Pica roman, probably cut in London. From Richard Brathwait, *A survey of history, or a nursery for gentry comprized in an intermixt discourse.* J. O(kes) for G. Norton, London, 1614.

I Am heartily glad to hear by your Lady you will be return'd to *London* to receive this, which, I pray, lose no
time to shew his H. I wrote you word before you went that
I thought I should soon be in *England*, for I am confident
they would have sent me, but your going into *Flanders* (of
which they had notice before you would have been crofs the
Sea, I cannot imagine, but sure I am they told me of it as
soon as I came to the Army) I suppose may have hin-
dred that, and retarded the propositions, which I have order to make his H. till now, for they have been much dif-
quieted about it, and I have had much a do to affure them,
that *I* was confident there was nothing defigned by it, to
their prejudice, for that *I* was sure the Duke was as much by
inclination as intereft difposed to prefer their Alliance and
Friendfhip to all others, and that they would take it for a
certain rule, that if they were not wanting to themfelves,
we should never be wanting to them. The King here is certainly difposed as much as can be for the intereft of his H.
but is wife and very cautious, however by thefe Propofiti-
ons, which *I* have order to make to his H. and which are
word for word as *I* took them from *Pere Ferriers* mouth, for
I writ them down prefently, and shewed it to him afterwards,
and keep it for my juftification, that *I* writ no more than *I*
was ordered, you will fee that it now depends only upon his
H. to confider of a way, that will beft fecure his interefts,
and

Fig. 2. Great Primer roman, cut by Nicholas Nicholls. From *A collection of letters relating to the Popish Plot*. For Samuel Heyrick, Thomas Dring, & John Wickins, London, 1681.

is not displayed, is referred to as 'cut by Mr. Nicholls not good'. In Horace Hart's book the type is shown in the appendix. This Great Primer of Nicholls was one of the favourite types of the Oxford Press from 1670 until the Fell types came into use. For example, R. Plot's *Natural History of Oxfordshire*, 1677, is set in Nicholls, as is also the later edition of 1686, in which volume the dedication ot James II is set in the Fell Canon. Nicholls's type is found also in London printed books. The earliest date at which I have found it is on Proclamations of the Lord Mayor of London printed by James Flesher in 1666. In view of this date we may assume that the designer was Nicholas Nicholls, who printed the tiny specimen of 1665, and who cut also a Hebrew type for the Oxford Press. Other types found in Oxford books before Fell are the Double Pica roman and italic used by John Day, originally cut for the Louvain Latin Bible of 1547. For examples see the preliminaries of William Beveridge's *Pandectæ Canonum Apostolorum*, the *Catalogus librorum Bibliothecæ Bodlejanæ*, 1674, and Anthony à Wood's *Historia Universitatis Oxoniensis*, 1674. Oxford had also the Elzevir Double Pica italic of which an account is given in my *Type Designs*, p. 160. It was used for the running titles in the folio Bible of 1680. The type is found also on the Lord Mayor Proclamations referred to above of 1659, and was already used by Flesher in 1657. This is the earliest use of a certainly Dutch type which I have found in England.

We will now consider two anonymous English specimen sheets, one from the Ames Collection in the British Museum, and the second from the Bagford Collection. The first was included in Berry and Johnson's *Catalogue of Specimens of Printing Types*, and is ascribed to the Grover foundry on the strength of a contemporary manuscript note. The second sheet, which contains many of the same types, is here reproduced. Whether the attribution to Grover is correct or not, it will appear that few, if any, of the types can have been cut by that foundry. The second sheet is surrounded by seventeenth-century flowers. At the top are acorns. The earliest appearance of this flower in England which I have noted is in Giovanni della Casa's *Galateo*, G. Webb, Oxford, 1628. In Plomer's *English Printers' Ornaments* there is a reference to an edition of the *Song of Solomon*, 1620, but I cannot trace the book. In any case the flower appears to be of Dutch origin and is found at Arnhem in 1619 and on several Dutch specimen sheets. On the Bagford sheet, at the sides, are harps, and at the foot vases, and a third decorative unit. The harp and vase appear in R. Montacutius's *Apparatus ad origines ecclesiasticas*, L. Lichfield, Oxford, 1635. The harp, at any rate, is English. Under a crown it represents Ireland. Similarly one finds the rose, leek, and thistle, each under a crown.

The type used for the descriptions is the Elzevir Double Pica italic already mentioned. The capitals of the Fat Cannon (1) appear in the early Oxford specimen books, but the origin of these has not been traced. The Lean Cannon (3) I have not identified. The French Cannon (2) is probably Moxon's – there is so little of it that one can hardly be confident. This is the first type shown on the 'Grover' sheet. The popularity of Moxon's Cannon is exemplified by its appearance in the early Oxford specimen books, in the book of the Edinburgh printer, James Watson, 1713,[1] often said to display Dutch

1. *History of the Art of Printing*.

types only, and on Benjamin Motte's sheet of 1713, where it is used for the heading. Types (4) and (5), Two-line English and Double Pica, are heavy faces of Dutch origin. They were used by the Elzevirs and appear to be identical with the Dubbelde Augustyn and Dubbelde Mediaan in Abraham Elzevir's *Proeve der Drukkerye*, 1713. In the specimen of Johannes Elzevir – father of Abraham – Leiden, 1658, these two sizes are called Cicerones Duplices and Ascendonica.[1] The larger size was used in J. F. Gronovius's *Allocutio ad Cosmum Etruriæ principem*, Leyden, 1668. In England the Double Pica appears in Hugo Grotius's *The Rights of War and Peace*, 1682. Type (6), Great Primer, was used by John Day. It is shown as fig. 3 in Col. Isaac's article on 'Elizabethan roman and italic Types'.[2] It was most probably an Antwerp type. For its appearance in a book of the generation of our sheet, see *The Works of King Charles I*, J. Flesher for R. Royston, 1662, where it is used for the main text. Type (7), English, appears to be substantially the same as the 95 roman used by John Day and shown as fig. 5 of Col. Isaac's article. Of the smaller types (8) Pica, (9) Long Primer, and (10) Brevier, I will only say that they may very well date back to the sixteenth century.[3]

Of frequent occurrence in English books of the mid-century are a Double Pica and a Great Primer roman and italic, with a distinctive lower-case g with a steeply descending loop, and two noteworthy capitals. The capitals are an E with a curled tail and a U of the same design as the lower-case u. Both are common in seventeenth-century types. The U is found as early as 1604 in Thomas Pie's *Usuries spright conjured*. The R with a curled tail, in typography, appears to begin in England, although no doubt taken over from the work of the engravers. The earliest use of this form which I have traced is in a heading type of 1635, on the title-pages of H. Goodcole's *The adultresses funerall day*, N. & J. Okes, and Sir George Buck's *The great Plantagenet*, N. & J. Okes.

The Double Pica and Great Primer romans, the text types in which these two forms first appear, can be traced back to 1636 and 1637, in books printed by Nathaniel Okes and by Richard Hodgkinson. The following numbers in the *Short Title Catalogue of Books printed in England to 1640* show one or both of the sizes: 3583[A], 15717, 18806, and 24660. These types, more especially the Great Primer, were in very common use in the middle years of the century. A smaller size of the same design, English, is also found. The Great Primer appears at a later date in the specimen of the London printer, James Orme, *c*. 1698. This size is found also in Dutch books, but not so early as in England. The Amsterdam printer, Jan Jansson, had the type from 1647, e. g. in H. Alting's *Exegesis logica Augustanæ confessionis*. It is found also in the *Hollantsche Mercurius*, Haarlem, 1650. In the Bagford Collection there is an undated specimen sheet of a Dutch printer, Johannes Kannewet,[4] of Amsterdam. The size is there given as *Text*, and as the

1. I have not seen this specimen, but I infer from Charles Enschedé's account of the two books that these types are the same in both.
2. In *Transactions of the Bibliographical Society*, Sept. 1933.
3. The lower part of the sheet is not reproduced here. The type area of the whole sheet measures 265 × 150 mm.
4. There was a publisher of this name at Amsterdam *c*. 1750. The sheet probably dates from the early years of the eighteenth century.

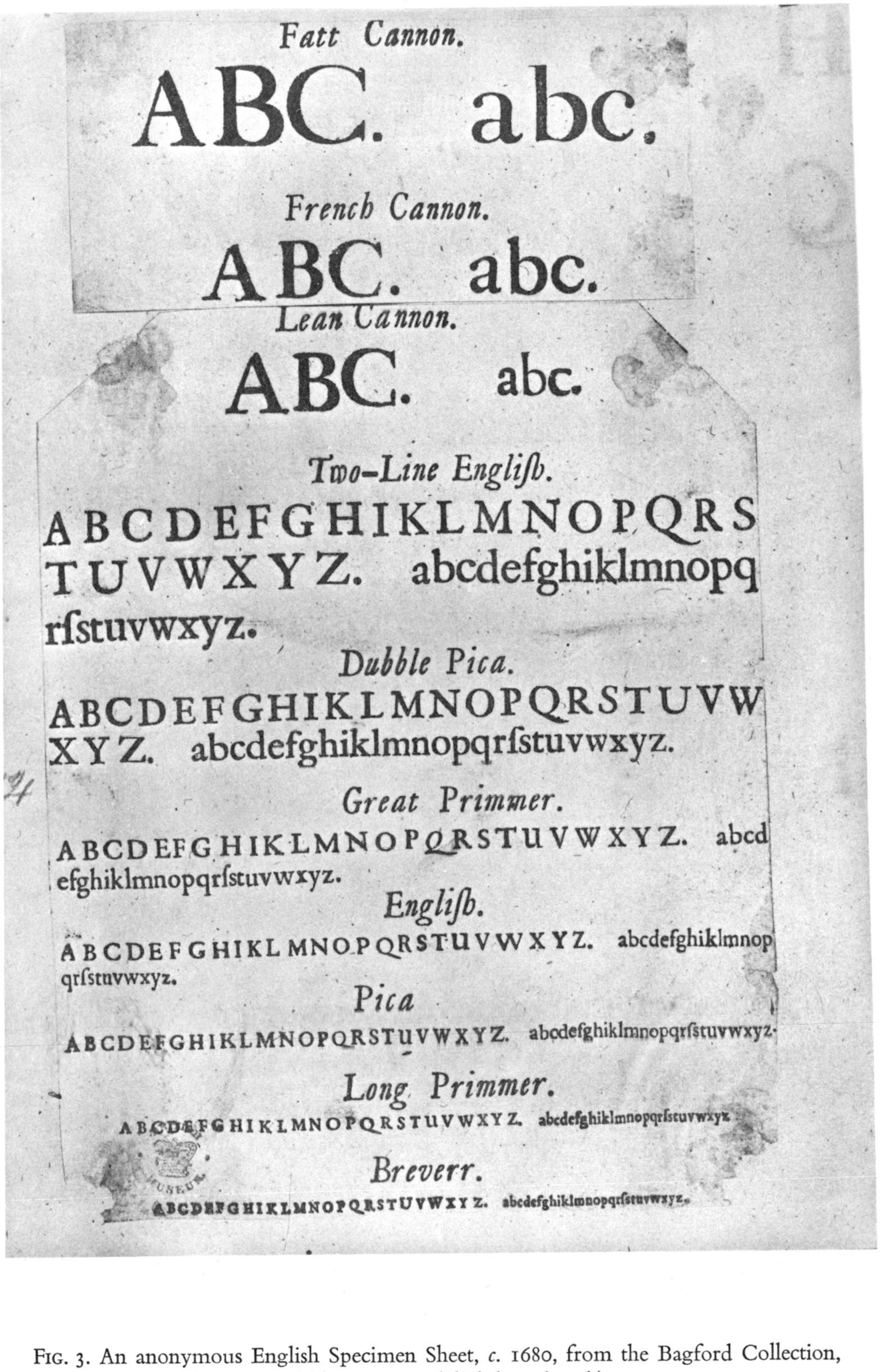

Fatt Cannon.

ABC. abc.

French Cannon.

ABC. abc.

Lean Cannon.

ABC. abc.

Two-Line Engliſh.

ABCDEFGHIKLMNOPQRS TUVWXYZ. abcdefghiklmnopq rſstuvwxyz.

Dubble Pica.

ABCDEFGHIKLMNOPQRSTUVW XYZ. abcdefghiklmnopqrſstuvwxyz.

Great Primmer.

ABCDEFGHIKLMNOPQRSTUVWXYZ. abcd efghiklmnopqrſstuvwxyz.

Engliſh.

ABCDEFGHIKLMNOPQRSTUVWXYZ. abcdefghiklmnop qrſstuvwxyz.

Pica

ABCDEFGHIKLMNOPQRSTUVWXYZ. abcdefghiklmnopqrſstuvwxyz.

Long Primmer.

ABCDEFGHIKLMNOPQRSTUVWXYZ. abcdefghiklmnopqrſstuvwxyz.

Breverr.

ABCDEFGHIKLMNOPQRSTUVWXYZ. abcdefghiklmnopqrſstuvwxyz.

FIG. 3. An anonymous English Specimen Sheet, *c.* 1680, from the Bagford Collection, British Museum. (Slightly reduced.)

type is used for the headings it is thoroughly displayed. Since the type is found first in England and was in common use there, it seems probable that in this case an English type was exported to Holland. It is known that Jacques Vallet, the Amsterdam founder who was invited to Oxford, in 1645 had punches cut by an Englishman, John Collet. It is also worth mentioning that Hodgkinson, one of the first printers to use the type in question, was in trouble in March 1637 for failure to pay for types received from the London founder, Arthur Nicholls, father of Nicholas Nicholls.[1] The younger Nicholls's type, discussed above, also had similar forms of the R and U. In fact, these two letters were so widely adopted in England that they were sometimes added to older designs in place of the original capitals, for instance in the case of the Double Pica roman of John Day, as used at the Oxford Press.

[1936]

1. See Domestic State Papers, Charles I, vol. 324, f. 307b.

NOTES ON SOME SEVENTEENTH-CENTURY
ENGLISH TYPES AND TYPE SPECIMENS

THESE miscellaneous notes on English type specimens and on types used by English printers in the seventeenth and early eighteenth centuries are intended as a contribution towards answering these questions: which were the types cut by English founders? and: what was the origin of the foreign types imported by our printers?

On the history of English types there are three classics to which frequent reference will be made. The first is Rowe Mores's *Dissertation upon English Typographical Founders*, published in a small edition in 1778 immediately after the death of the author. It was reprinted in 1924 by the Grolier Club, New York. Rowe Mores was the last owner of the James Foundry, in which foundry was incorporated a number of earlier, seventeenth-century foundries. I suppose almost every word of this *Dissertation* was reprinted in the second classic – T. B. Reed's *History of the Old English Foundries*, 1887. Where Reed deals with the history of printing in England, he has been superseded, but on his subject proper, the history of the foundries, his is still the best work we have.[1] The third classic is Updike's *Printing Types*, and on the importance of that book there is no need to dwell. Almost as important as these three for our subject is Charles Enschedé's great book on Dutch type-founders: *Fonderies de Caractères dans les Pays-Bas*, which will be referred to as Enschedé. I shall frequently refer also to the Bagford Collection in the British Museum. John Bagford began as a shoemaker, was himself a printer in a small way, and, with the intention of writing a history of printing, accumulated a vast collection of title-pages and fragments of various kinds. Bagford died in 1716. One of the latest fragments in the collection is a ticket dated 18 January, 1716, printed by John Bagford on the frozen Thames. The sixty-four volumes of his collection were bought by the Earl of Oxford and finally came to the British Museum. The importance of Bagford for us is that this collection included a number of type specimens, published and unpublished, most of them unique.

Research on the origins of English sixteenth-century types, so far as it has gone, leads one to suppose that there were hardly any type-cutters at work in this country in that period. Very many of the Texturas (Black Letters), the romans and the italics found in English books between 1500 and 1630 have been traced to continental sources, and, with the exception of John Day's founts of Anglo-Saxon, there is no evidence that any were cut in England. This was not the opinion held when Reed wrote, nor even at the time when Updike was published. Reed says: 'Day was among the first English printers who cut the roman and italic to range as one and the same fount.' We now know that in all probability every one of Day's romans and italics was imported from the continent, and also that no type-designer had at that date cut romans and italics to range. Day's Double Pica roman and italic are reproduced by both Reed and Updike, and are accepted as his types. Of the roman Reed says that it was worthy of Plantin. It was in

---

1. But cf. the new edition edited and enlarged by A. F. Johnson, 1952.

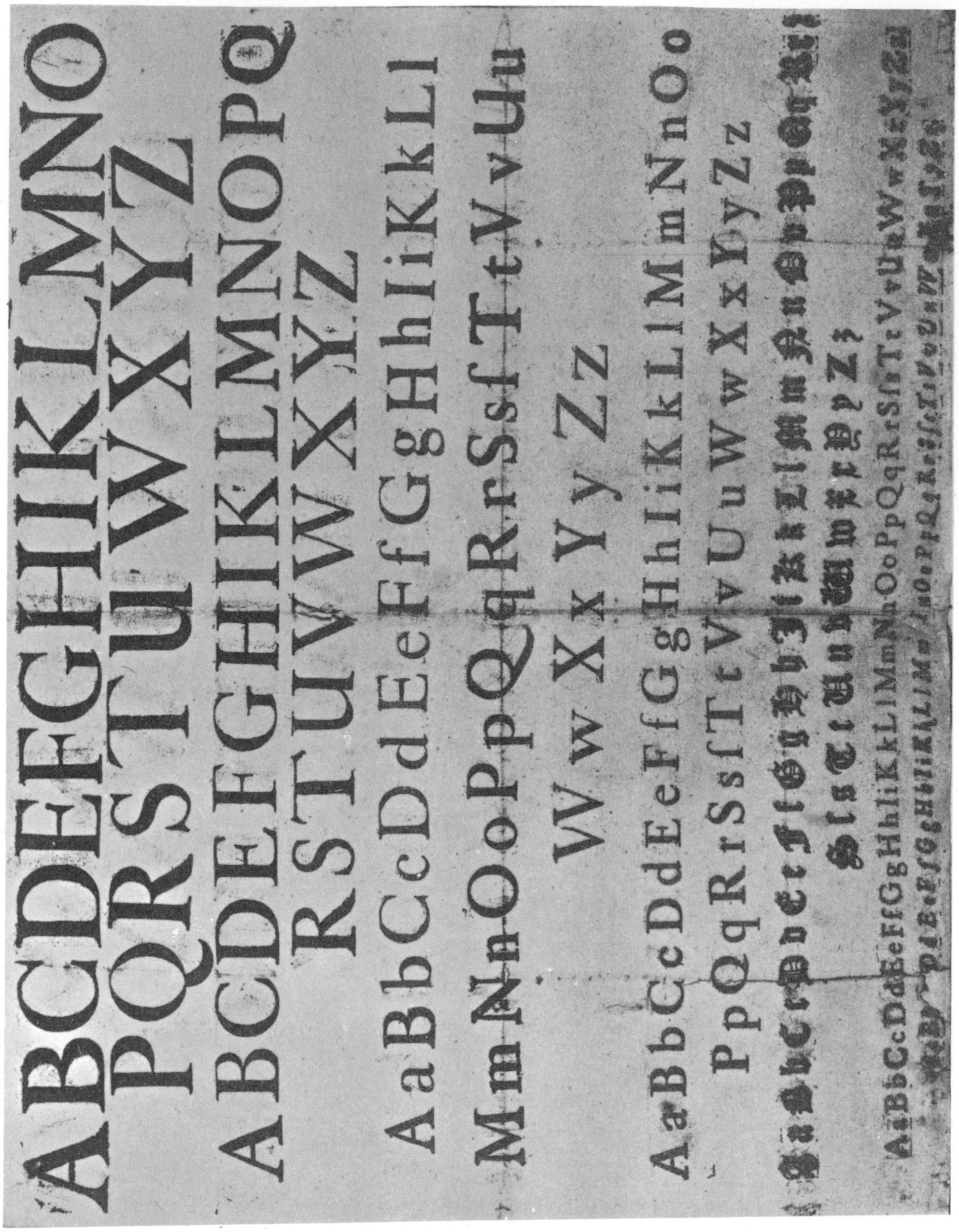

FIG. 1. An anonymous Specimen Sheet, c. 1700, from the Bagford Collection, British Museum. (Reduced.)

fact used by Plantin, but it was originally cut for the edition of the *Vulgate* printed at Louvain in 1547. The italic started life at Antwerp at about the same date. Reed praises the English italic in which Archbishop Parker's *De antiquitate Britannicae Ecclesiae*, 1572, was printed and presumes that it was cut by Day. This type is the Cursive St. Augustin of Robert Granjon shown on the Egenolff-Berner specimen sheet of 1592. Many of these types imported in the sixteenth century continued to be used throughout the seventeenth century and there is little doubt that in that century there were more pages set in these early types than in the new designs, whether foreign or English. Of romans and italics cut by English founders there seem to be none earlier than about 1635.

A reproduction of what I imagine to be one of the earliest romans cut in England was given in *Signature*, No. 3, July, 1936;[1] the type appears here on the specimen sheet of James Orme (Fig. 2). Note the lower-case g, and the capitals R and U. The R with curved tail is a form more familiar in the eighteenth century, for instance, in the designs of Fournier and Baskerville, but is fairly common in England in the seventeenth century. Typographically it seems to have begun in this country. It is found in the roman of Nicholas Nicholls, dating from about 1666, a roman which was at the Oxford University Press, and is described in the Oxford Specimen of 1693 as 'cut by Mr. Nicholls not good'. The U in the type of 1635 and in most contemporary English romans has the design of the lower-case.

There were at least three sizes of this design, Double Pica, Great Primer and English, and the Great Primer is found in Dutch books. It is even shown on a Dutch specimen, that of an Amsterdam printer, Joannes Kannewet, *c.* 1700. The earliest date I can find for it in Holland is 1647, and only the one size seems to have been used there. Since it was much more generally used in England, and is found in three sizes and at an earlier date than in Holland, I conclude that the type was really English.

The first English founder's specimen sheet showing a range of type was that of Joseph Moxon, 1669. The only known copy is in the Bagford collection.[2] The one successful type cut by Moxon was the Great Cannon, which became really popular as a heading type and has survived to this day in the copy made by William Caslon. Its earliest use in a book that I have noted is in Moxon's *Mechanic Dyalling*, 1668. The Double Pica roman is found on the title-page of Moxon's *Practical Perspective*, 1670, and in John Evelyn's *A Discourse of Medals*, 1697. The other romans I have not found. The two largest italics were not cut by Moxon. At this date a founder's specimen rarely consisted of his own types only. He was compelled to increase his stock by buying matrices from other founders. Moxon's English italic was a sixteenth-century type, widely used in the Netherlands from 1551. It is found also at Frankfurt, Cologne, Tübingen, and Zürich, in the second half of the sixteenth century. I have not seen it on any other type specimen or in any English books at all.

Moxon's Pica italic appears also in the Oxford specimen books. According to Hart

---

1. Reprinted in the present volume; see pp. 298–304.
2. The impression of this copy is unfortunately too poor for reproduction.

there were no punches or matrices at Oxford. It was one of the types presented by Francis Junius in 1677, not a Fell. It appears also on the specimen sheets of the successors of Van Dijck, as the Mediaen Cursijf. According to Enschedé the type was not cut by Van Dijck, since the punches were not acquired by Enschedé's firm when the stock of the Van Dijck types came into their hands. The earliest sheet of the Van Dijck types is that of 1681, and from the dates one might suppose that the type was cut by Moxon. But from the inferior casting of the types as shown by Moxon and for various other reasons one can feel confident that it did not start life in his foundry.

Among the specimens in the Bagford collection is an unpublished sheet of English types showing two alphabets of capitals, three romans, and one Textura or Black Letter, perhaps printed about 1700 (Fig. 1). The first alphabet of capitals is the same as the 5-line Pica capitals of the Oxford specimens. Four letters appear on the title-page of an edition of *Paradise Lost*, printed by Thomas Hodgkin for Jacob Tonson, in 1688. (There was another, edition in 1695.) They were not then exclusively Oxford's. Of the second alphabet of capitals I know only that they appeared in the headings of Proclamations, printed by the official printers, from 1659. Of the third alphabet the upper-case is common on the title-pages of English books. The earliest appearance noted on a title-page is of 1639 – *Relation of a Conference between William Laud and Mr. Fisher, the Jesuite*. They appear in the Oxford specimen books, on a Scotch printer's specimen of 1698, that of the Heirs of Andrew Anderson, Edinburgh, and in James Watson's book of 1713.[1] On another unpublished sheet in Bagford the type is called 'Fatt Cannon'. The lower-case is not easily found; on the title-page of the Milton of 1688, already mentioned, the words *Paradise Lost* are set in this type; the words *in twelve books*, on the same title, are in Moxon's Cannon, which is the fourth type on our sheet. The next is the 2-line Great Primer Black, which was one of the commonest heading types in England from 1530-1730. In Palmer's *General History of Printing*, 1732, this size and a Great Primer of similar design are shown; the author says that they were used by all printers in London and believes that they were struck from the punches of Wynkyn de Worde. Both sizes were in the Grover foundry, and Rowe Mores in his account of the stock of the James foundry, in which was incorporated the Grover foundry, says that he had discovered the punches. That the punches went back as far as Wynkyn de Worde seems very doubtful since de Worde got these types from Paris. The traditional English Black Letter was really French in origin. The 2-line Great Primer can be seen in almost any French printed Missal of the first half of the sixteenth century, where the Canon of the Mass was usually set in this size. In any case there seem to have been several versions of the type in existence. That shown, for instance, in the Oxford specimen book of 1706, bought in 1701, differs from that in the Grover foundry. William Caslon cut a copy, which appeared as a heading on his specimen sheet of 1742.

The last type on the sheet is found in English books from 1638 onwards. On this curious sheet all the types shown are probably English cut.

The specimen sheet of an English printer, James Orme, 1698 (Fig. 2) shows the capitals

---

1. *History of the Art of Printing*.

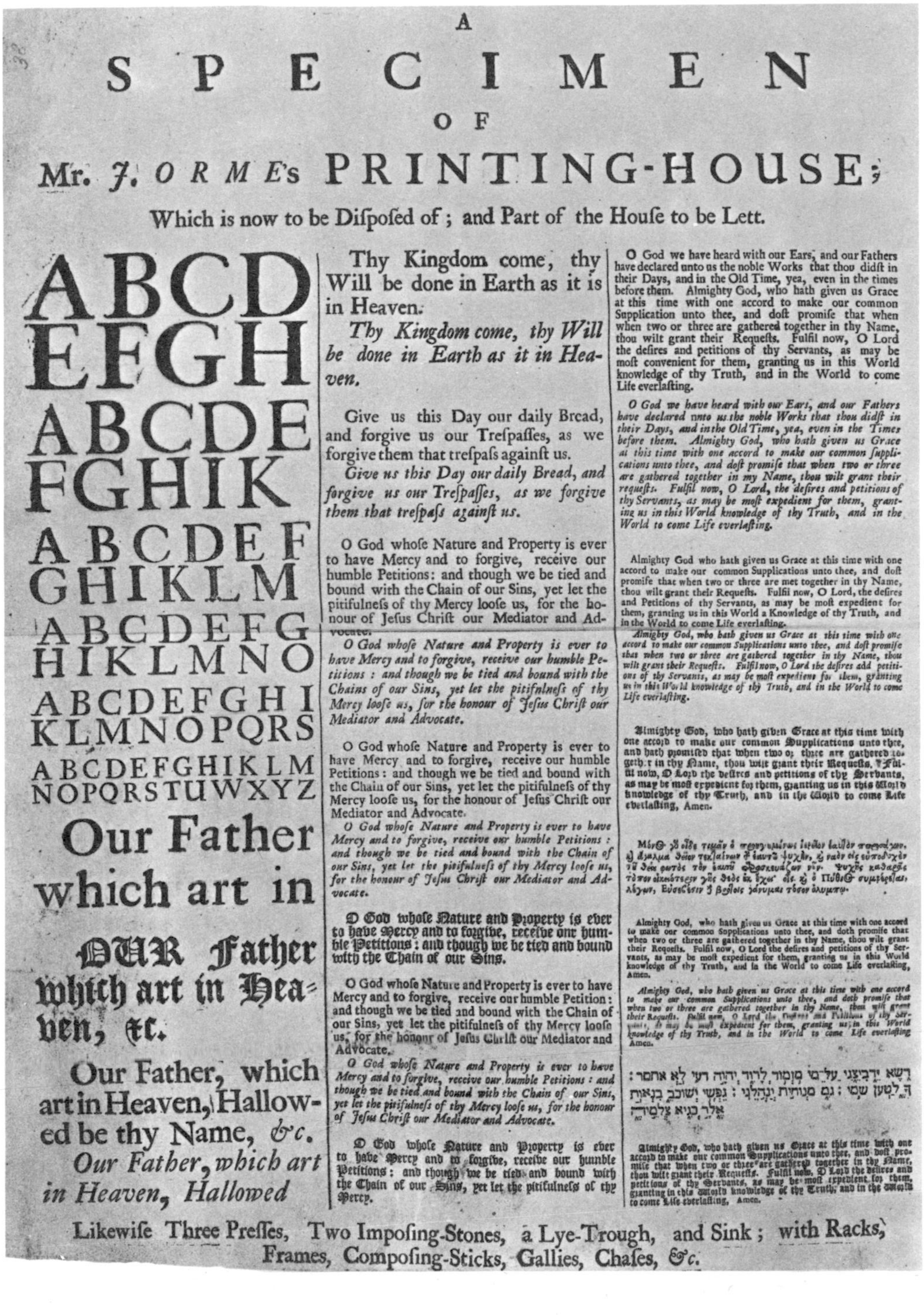

A

S P E C I M E N

O F

Mr. *J. O R M E*'s PRINTING-HOUSE;

Which is now to be Difpofed of; and Part of the Houfe to be Lett.

ABCD
EFGH
ABCDE
FGHIK
ABCDEF
GHIKLM
ABCDEFG
HIKLMNO
ABCDEFGHI
KLMNOPQRS
ABCDEFGHIKLM
NOPQRSTUWXYZ

Our Father which art in

OUR Father which art in Hea-ven, &c.

Our Father, which art in Heaven, Hallow-ed be thy Name, *&c.*

Our Father, which art in Heaven, Hallowed

Thy Kingdom come, thy Will be done in Earth as it is in Heaven.

Thy Kingdom come, thy Will be done in Earth as it in Hea-ven.

Give us this Day our daily Bread, and forgive us our Trefpaffes, as we forgive them that trefpafs againft us.

Give us this Day our daily Bread, and forgive us our Trefpaffes, as we forgive them that trefpafs againft us.

O God whofe Nature and Property is ever to have Mercy and to forgive, receive our humble Petitions: and though we be tied and bound with the Chain of our Sins, yet let the pitifulnefs of thy Mercy loofe us, for the ho-nour of Jefus Chrift our Mediator and Ad-vocate.

O God whofe Nature and Property is ever to have Mercy and to forgive, receive our humble Pe-titions: and though we be tied and bound with the Chains of our Sins, yet let the pitifulnefs of thy Mercy loofe us, for the honour of Jefus Chrift our Mediator and Advocate.

O God whofe Nature and Property is ever to have Mercy and to forgive, receive our humble Petitions: and though we be tied and bound with the Chain of our Sins, yet let the pitifulnefs of thy Mercy loofe us, for the honour of Jefus Chrift our Mediator and Advocate.

O God whofe Nature and Property is ever to have Mercy and to forgive, receive our humble Petitions: and though we be tied and bound with the Chain of our Sins, yet let the pitifulnefs of thy Mercy loofe us, for the honour of Jefus Chrift our Mediator and Ad-vocate.

O God whofe Nature and Property is ever to have Mercy and to forgive, receive our hum-ble Petitions: and though we be tied and bound with the Chain of our Sins.

O God whofe Nature and Property is ever to have Mercy and to forgive, receive our humble Petition: and though we be tied and bound with the Chain of our Sins, yet let the pitifulnefs of thy Mercy loofe us, for the honour of Jefus Chrift our Mediator and Advocate.

O God whofe Nature and Property is ever to have Mercy and to forgive, receive our humble Petitions: and though we be tied and bound with the Chain of our Sins, yet let the pitifulnefs of thy Mercy loofe us, for the honour of Jefus Chrift our Mediator and Advocate.

O God whofe Nature and Property is ever to have Mercy and to forgive, receive our humble Petitions: and though we be tied and bound with the Chain of our Sins, yet let the pitifulnefs of thy Mercy.

O God we have heard with our Ears, and our Fathers have declared unto us the noble Works that thou didft in their Days, and in the Old Time, yea, even in the times before them. Almighty God, who hath given us Grace at this time with one accord to make our common Supplication unto thee, and doft promife that when when two or three are gathered together in thy Name, thou wilt grant their Requefts. Fulfil now, O Lord the defires and petitions of thy Servants, as may be moft convenient for them, granting us in this World knowledge of thy Truth, and in the World to come Life everlafting.

O God we have heard with our Ears, and our Fathers have declared unto us the noble Works that thou didft in their Days, and in the Old Time, yea, even in the Times before them. Almighty God, who hath given us Grace at this time with one accord to make our common fuppli-cations unto thee, and doft promife that when two or three are gathered together in my Name, thou wilt grant their requefts. Fulfil now, O Lord, the defires and petitions of thy Servants, as may be moft expedient for them, grant-ing us in this World knowledge of thy Truth, and in the World to come Life everlafting.

Almighty God who hath given us Grace at this time with one accord to make our common Supplications unto thee, and doft promife that when two or three are met together in thy Name, thou wilt grant their Requefts. Fulfii now, O Lord, the defires and Petitions of thy Servants, as may be moft expedient for them, granting us in this World a Knowledge of thy Truth, and in the World to come Life everlafting.

Almighty God, who hath given us Grace at this time with one accord to make our common Supplications unto thee, and doft promife that when two or three are gathered together in thy Name, thou wilt grant their Requefts. Fulfil now, O Lord the defires add petiti-ons of thy Servants, as may be moft expedient for them, granting us in this World knowledge of thy Truth, and in the World to come Life everlafting.

Almighty God, who hath given Grace at this time with one accord to make our common Supplications unto thee, and hath promifed that when two or three are gathered to-gether in thy Name, thou wilt grant their Requefts. Ful-fil now, O Lord the defires and petitions of thy Servants, as may be moft expedient for them, granting us in this World knowledge of thy Truth, and in the World to come Life everlafting, Amen.

Almighty God, who hath given us Grace at this time with one accord to make our common Supplications unto thee, and doth promife that when two or three are gathered together in thy Name, thou wilt grant their Requefts. Fulfil now, O Lord the defires and petitions of thy Ser-vants, as may be moft expedient for them, granting us in this World knowledge of thy Truth, and in the World to come Life everlafting, Amen.

Almighty God, who hath given us Grace at this time with one accord to make our common Supplications unto thee, and doth promife that when two or three are gathered together in thy Name, thou wilt grant their Requefts. Fulfil now, O Lord the Defires and Petitions of thy Ser-vants, as may be moft expedient for them, granting us in this World knowledge of thy Truth, and in the World to come Life everlafting Amen.

Almighty God, who hath given us Grace at this time with one accord to make our common Supplications unto thee, and doft pro-mife that when two or three are gathered together in thy Name, thou wilt grant their Requefts. Fulfil now, O Lord the defires and petitions of thy Servants, as may be moft expedient for them, granting in this World knowledge of the Truth, and in the World to come Life everlafting, Amen.

Likewife Three Preffes, Two Impofing-Stones, a Lye-Trough, and Sink; with Racks, Frames, Compofing-Sticks, Gallies, Chafes, *&c.*

FIG. 2. J. Orme's Specimen Sheet, from the Bagford Collection, British Museum. (Reduced.)

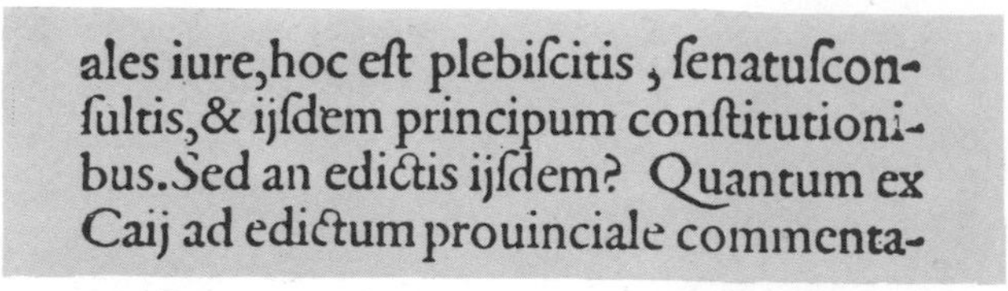

ales iure,hoc eft plebifcitis , fenatufcon-
fultis,& ijfdem principum conftitutioni-
bus.Sed an edictis ijfdem? Quantum ex
Caij ad edictum prouinciale commenta-

FIG. 3. The Saint-Augustin (or English) roman, first used in England by John Day in 1570. From Jacobus Raevardus, *Tribonianus,
sive de veris usucapionum differentiis adversus Tribonianum* . . .
Christophe Plantin for Guillaume Silvius, Antwerp, 1561.

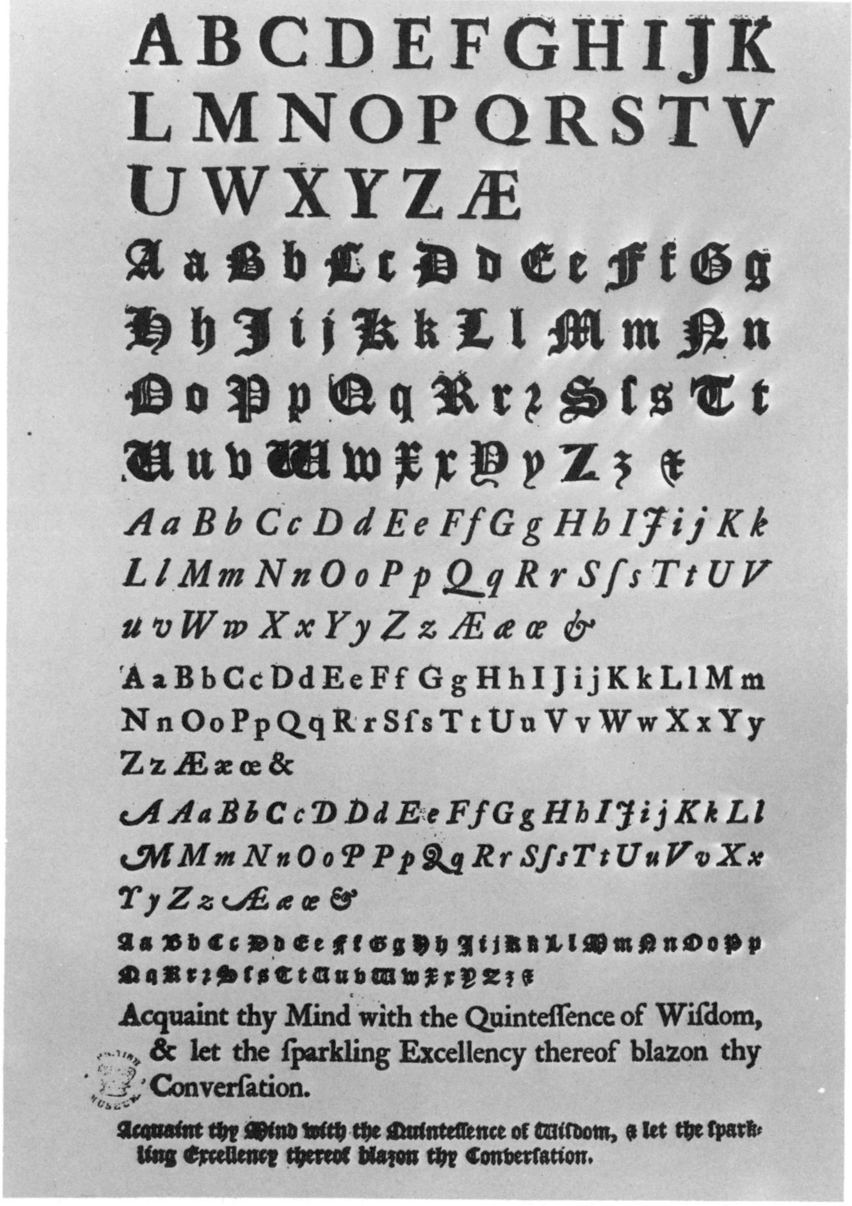

FIG. 4. Anonymous Specimen Sheet, *c.* 1700, from the Bagford Collection,
British Museum. (Reduced.)

which come second on the unpublished sheet just described, and the Oxford capitals found from 1639, but with no lower-case. The first type after the titlings is probably Moxon's, but with these few words, and over-inked at that, one cannot feel certain. Next is the 2-line Great Primer, of the Grover foundry possibly, but again over-inking makes identification difficult. Then there is the Fell Double Pica roman. The appearance of this type raises an interesting point. Did Oxford sell type, or are we to suppose that the Dutch founder who sold the punches to Oxford kept a set of strikes and continued to sell the type? The type is in fact not uncommon in London printed books. The matter at the foot of the sheet is set in this Fell roman. Next is the Great Primer of the type I have supposed to be one of the first English cut designs. The Pica Black, is of interest because it is the model closely followed by William Caslon in cutting his first Black Letter, shown on his specimen sheet in 1734. Orme's type is common; the earliest use noted is in a Common Prayer of 1660, but it may be much earlier.

The next reproduction (Fig. 3) is an example of a sixteenth-century type which was in common use in England throughout the seventeenth century. As far as I know it appeared first at Venice, at the press of Girolamo Scotto in 1558, and at that of Paolo Manuzio in 1559. The page shown is from a book printed at Antwerp by Christophe Plantin for Guillaume Silvius in 1561. The size is St. Augustin, or English to our printers. The letters to be noted are the narrow capitals M and R, and the long-linked lower-case g. It is soon found all over Europe and was brought to England by John Day in 1570 – there is a reproduction from a book printed by Day in Colonel Isaac's *English Printers' Types of the 16th Century* (pl. 67). As to the seventeenth century, it is the type used for all the early folio editions of *The Anatomy of Melancholy*. There are also two illustrations in Updike, which show the type: fig. 286 from the Elizabethan version of Tasso, 1600, and fig. 108, a fine example from a book printed at Venice in 1623. This St. Augustin appears on the specimen sheet of a Dutch founder, or of a German founder working at Amsterdam, Jan Adolf Schmid, issued about 1700, a hundred and forty years after the first appearance of the type. This Schmid was trained in the Luther foundry at Frankfurt and succeeded to the Frankfurt foundry of Reinier Voskens, uncle of Dirk Voskens. As to Schmid's dates, all we know so far is that he was still in Frankfurt in 1685, but was in Amsterdam by 1695. The specimen on which the St. Augustin roman is shown is in Bagford; it has been cut up and has no heading, but Schmid's name occurs on two of the fragments and the whole can be built up with the help of MS. notes on the fragments, which include the prices. There are other types on the sheet not cut by Schmid, two at any rate from the foundry of Reinier Voskens. There is shown also a fount of Russian, which was at Oxford, and some non-ligatured Greeks, which were in the James foundry.

As to the St. Augustin roman, can we feel any confidence that this was the old type dating from 1558 and not a copy made by Schmid? It may be that a type-cutter could produce a deceptive facsimile of an earlier type, but, from such evidence as we have, it does not appear that he did so. When a founder cut a new series of punches, he wanted to produce something that was his own, not something that might be taken for the work of another man. Perhaps one will have to allow an exception in the case of a type which had become standard, for instance Garamond roman. The Text (i. e., the Great Primer) size of Van Dijck's roman is for most people indistinguishable from the corresponding size of Garamond. At a later date, Caslon himself was faithfully copied.

Another unpublished and anonymous sheet from the Bagford collection (Fig. 4) begins with Moxon's Cannon and the 2-line Great Primer Black, the version found at Oxford. Then follows a 2-line English italic. This type appears to be of Dutch origin and is found on a Dutch specimen sheet of the Widow of Joannes Adamzoon and Abraham Ente. This sheet also is in Bagford; it was not described by Enschedé, and all I can discover as to the history of the firm is that Adamzoon was a founder and was associated with Dirk Voskens. The italic, together with the corresponding roman, appears in the Oxford Specimen of 1695; it is not in the 1693 book and there are no punches nor matrices at Oxford. The type is not uncommon in English books of the period. In Updike vol. 2, at the end of the chapter on Dutch types, there is a reproduction of a series of roman and italic types from the Ehrhardt foundry at Leipzig, taken from Gessner's *Buchdruckerkunst*, 1740. They are there described as Dutch. The italics and some of the romans are the same as those on the sheet of Adamzoon and Ente.

Our 2-line English is called Roman Cursiv in Gessner, and Klyne Cannon on the Dutch sheet. There is a mystery attached to this series. Printers will be familiar with a type known as Janson, sold by a German foundry and occasionally used in this country. Janson is the type shown in Gessner. If the German founders are right in attributing it to Anton Janson, a type-cutter at Leipzig, predecessor of Ehrhardt, how was it that contemporaries called the type Dutch? In any case we may be sure that English printers bought the type in Amsterdam.

Returning to our anonymous sheet, the next types are the Fell Double Pica roman and italic. Last of all is a Black Letter. But for this Black, one might have supposed that the sheet was printed at Oxford; all the other types were there, but this Black does not agree with any shown in the Oxford specimens.

These seventeenth-century English specimens illustrate two interesting points in typographical history; the first, that the trade in types was largely international, and the second, that type designs were very long-lived. It may be supposed that English printers of the generation of Moxon bought their foreign types in the Netherlands, but these types were by no means always cut by the founders who supplied them. The original punches may have been engraved in France or even in Italy, and, as likely as not, they may date from the middle years of the sixteenth century.

[1938]

AN UNRECORDED SPECIMEN SHEET OF A
SCOTTISH PRINTING HOUSE

THE National Library of Scotland has a copy of the earliest known specimen of types issued in Scotland, and one not recorded in Berry and Johnson's *Catalogue of Specimens of Printing Types*, Oxford University Press, 1935. The title reads: *A True Account of the Types of His Majesties Printing-House, belonging to the Heirs and Successors of Andrew Anderson, His Majesties Printer; Consisting of several Sorts. All added since the Year 1694.* The date in the colophon is 1698. The types shown are arranged in three columns, divided by rules. Col. 1 shows some large capitals and a French Canon; col. 2, Double English, New English and Pica, roman and italic; col. 3, Longprimar (2), Breviar and Pearl, roman and italic.

Of the large capitals I do not know the origin, but they appear also in the early specimen books of the Oxford University Press and in the well-known *Specimen of Types* of James Watson, Edinburgh, 1713. The French Canon is that of Joseph Moxon. This type was in general use in England, and was the only type of Moxon's which was successful. In col. 2 the Double English, roman and italic, are Dutch types. They appear on a specimen sheet preserved in the Bagford collection in the British Museum, that of 'De Weduwe van Johannis Adamsz. en Abraham Ente', Amsterdam, no date. This Adamsz. appears to have had business relations with Dirk Voskens,[1] but the type in question – called 'Klyne Canon' on the Dutch sheet – is not the same as Voskens's Canon. The heading of the Anderson sheet, after the first three words, is set in this Double English italic.

The 'New' English roman is, I believe, an English type dating back to about 1636. It has an R with a curved tail, a form which, in typography, appears to have been cut first in England. About 1636 two sizes of roman with this R were cut, of which the larger size, a Great Primer, is very conspicuous in English books of the seventeenth century. For examples, in some of which both sizes occur, see S.T.C. 15717, 18806 and 24660. The accompanying italic was perhaps not cut at the same time and may be older. The Pica roman is an even older type. It was used by the London printer Henry Denham in 1582. A reproduction of a page of this type is given at fig. 13 in Col. Isaac's article 'Elizabethan roman and italic Types.'[2] Note the shape of the g and the high-waisted R. The italic is no doubt of much the same age.

Of the small sizes shown in the third column, not too well printed, it is difficult to speak with any confidence. We may note that the 'Longprimar' no. 2 has the same R with a curved tail as the English. The 'Breviar' is evidently printed from new type, and, small as it is, can be seen very well.

This sheet of the Andersons contains no surprises. The selection of types shown is in

---

1. C. Enschedé, *Fonderies de Caractères dans les Pays-Bas*, p. 98.
2. *Trans. of the Bibl. Soc.*, 2nd ser., vol. XIV, 1933, p. 220.

A C C O

AT

Of the Types of His Majesties Printing-House, belon

His Majesties Printer ; Consisting of fe

HOPE IN GOD:

AND ALL SHAL GO WEL WITH THEE.

French Canon.

Doth not wisdom cry? and put forth her voice?

Double

For he flatter
own eyes, ur
found to be l

Double

The words of h
and deceit :
wise, and do g

New l

Fret not thy self because of
against the Workers of

New

Let them shout for joy, and
yea let them say continu
which hath pleasure in th

The fool hath said in his he
and have done abominabl

God looked down from heaven
any that did understand, Iha

UE

U N T

the Heirs and Succeſſors of Andrew Anderſon,
orts.　All added ſince the Year 1694.

nan.

mſelf in his

iniquity be

ick.

h are iniquity

left off to be

n.

either be thou envious

k.

avour my righteous cauſe;
LORD be magnified,
his ſervant.

God ; corrupt are they,
re is none that doth good.

f men, to ſee if there were

Longprimar Roman.

Let not them that are mine Enemies wrongfully rejoyce over me : *neither* let them wink with the eye, that hate me without a cauſe. For they ſpeak not peace, but they deviſe deceitful matters againſt them that are quiet in the Land.

Longprimar Italick.

I have been young, and now am old, yet have I not ſeen the righteous forſaken, nor his ſeed begging bread. He is ever merciful, and lendeth : and his ſeed is bleſſed. Depart from evil and do good : and dwell for evermore.

Longprimar Roman, No. 2.

He that reproveth a ſcorner, getteth to himſelf ſhame : and he that rebuketh a wicked man, getteth himſelf a blot.

Longprimar Italick, N°. 2.

Reprove not a ſcorner, leſt he hate thee : rebuke a wiſe man, and he will love thee.

Breviar Roman.

Be not thou afraid when one is made rich, when the glory of his houſe is increaſed. For when he dieth : he ſhall carry nothing away : his glory ſhall not deſcend after him.

Breviar Italick.

The fool hath ſaid in his heart there is no God ; corrupt they are, and have done abominable iniquity ; there is none that doth good. God looked down from heaven upon the children of men.

Pearl Roman.

Two things have I required of thee, deny me them not before I die. Remove far from me vanity and lies : feed me with food convenient for me : Leſt I be full, and deny thee, and ſay, Who is the LORD ? or leſt I be poor, and ſteal, and take the name of my God in vain.

Pearl Italick.

Be merciful unto me, O GOD, be merciful unto me, for my ſoul truſteth in thee : yea, in the ſhadow of thy wings will I make my refuge, until theſe calamities be overpaſt.

EDINBURGH,
Printed by the Heirs and Succeſſors of *Andrew Anderſon*, Printer
to the King's moſt Excellent Majeſty, City and Colledge,
Anno DOM. 1698.

general what one would expect to find at that date, some new Dutch types, some English and some types dating from the sixteenth century, probably of foreign origin. The collection, that is to say, well represents the state of our typography in the late seventeenth century.

[1936]

Overleaf: The specimen Sheet of the Heirs and Successors of Andrew Anderson, Edinburgh, 1698.

TYPE DESIGNS AND TYPE-FOUNDING
IN SCOTLAND

An examination of early Scottish books, or even of the reproductions in Dickson and Edmond's *Annals of Scottish Printing*, shows that Scottish typography in its beginnings was gothic. These gothic types all belong to one family, the most formal of all gothics, known as Textura or Text. Although first cut in France, such designs were so widely used and for so long in the British Isles, that they came to be regarded as characteristically English and under the name of Black Letter or Blacks have always been displayed in our founders' type specimen books. William Caslon's Blacks, cut in the second quarter of the eighteenth century, were of the same design as those of Wynkyn de Worde or of the early Scottish printers.

Andrew Myllar, who introduced printing into Scotland, is known to have worked in a Rouen printing house and on his return to Scotland took with him three sizes of Textura. Myllar's types were very like those being used in London, for example by De Worde, who also probably obtained some of his type in Rouen. The middle size of Myllar's types, called English by our printers, appears to have been cut especially for him, whereas the other two were in general use in France and in London (Fig. 1). No other style of gothic is known to have been used in Scotland. The edition of *A gest of Robin Hode* set in the Netherlands variety of Textura, known as Lettersnyder, was probably printed in the Netherlands.

With Thomas Davidson, *c.* 1530-1541, we enter a period in which Scottish printers obtained their types, with a few exceptions, from London and not directly from the Continent. This dependence on the London presses and founders lasted until towards the end of the seventeenth century, and even later to some extent. This statement is based not on documentary evidence, of which there is almost a complete lack, but on a comparison of the methods of lay-out and decoration, on the dates of the appearance of various types, and so on. Davidson's typography was predominantly gothic, but it was he who brought roman and italic letters to Scotland. His two romans and one italic were in the houses of several London printers, but all were of continental origin. Davidson's italic was brought to London by Thomas Berthelet and was cut in Cologne. If Davidson had bought matrices direct from continental founders at this date he would hardly have acquired designs which were already out of fashion. Further, there is some evidence of his direct dealings with London in the fact that he possessed a woodcut border and two woodcut illustrations formerly used by Peter Treveris in that city.

Two exceptions to this dependence on London may here be noticed. In 1571 Thomas Bassandyne printed at Edinburgh an edition of Robert Henryson's *The morall fabillis of Esope*, in which appears some of the Civilité cut by the French founder Robert Granjon, a form of gothic script not found in London, except in copies. It may have been acquired in Antwerp, where Granjon was at work in the years 1565 and 1566. The other example

is a Textura used by John Ross at Edinburgh from about 1574. This fount had some of
its capitals cut in the Netherlands style, known as Lettersnyder, and also was apparently
unknown in London. It is well displayed in *The Actis of the Parliament* (1575), an excellently printed book with a title-page surrounded by printers' flowers, a manner of
decoration common in London.

The first English Bible printed in Scotland, the New Testament by Thomas Bassandyne (1576) and the Old Testament by Alexander Arbuthnet dated 1579, was set in
roman types. Most English Bibles were still printed in Textura; even the Authorized
Version of 1611 was so set. But Arbuthnet's edition followed the English Bible printed
at Geneva, and thus he naturally adopted the continental usage. Three of the romans
used in the Edinburgh Bible are of interest, both because of their origin and because of
their future history. The main text is set in a roman, English in size, commonly used in
London, first by John Day in 1571. It was probably of French origin and is found in
many centres of printing (Fig. 2). It was a common type in English and Scottish printed books for at least a century. Compare, for example, George Buchanan's *Rerum
Scoticarum historia* (A. Arbuthnet, 1579) and various editions of William Drummond
of Hawthornden printed by Andro Hart at Edinburgh in the early years of the seventeenth century.

The running titles in Arbuthnet's Bible are set in a Double Pica roman, also used by
John Day and many other London and Edinburgh printers (Fig. 2). The type was cut
in the Netherlands about 1545, perhaps by François Guyot. The third type of the Edinburgh Bible was an alphabet of roman capitals used in display, which derives ultimately from Johann Froben of Basle, another common European design. The Edinburgh
Bible printed by Andro Hart in 1610 is in its main text a typographic repetition of
Arbuthnet's Bible, with some additions in the preliminaries; we find for instance one
of the italics cut by the French designer Robert Granjon and a fine series of roman capitals, which may be called Plantin capitals, after the press where they first appeared.

Towards the end of the sixteenth century two London printers, one, Thomas Vautrollier, a Frenchman, and the other, Robert Waldegrave, having connexions with La
Rochelle, printed for a time in Edinburgh and by their example hastened the tendency
to abandon the gothic for the renaissance letters, roman and italic. Waldegrave printed
the 'Basilikon Doron' of King James VI (1599) with the main text in a Double Pica italic,
one cut along with the Double Pica roman used in the 1579 Bible (Fig. 3). The edition
of James VI's *Daemonologie* printed by Waldegrave in 1597 is a similar volume typographically. But certain classes of books, especially liturgical works and editions of Scottish
verse, were still set in Textura, even down to the end of the seventeenth century.
Examples are Robert Young's edition of the *Common Prayer* (1637) and several editions
of the works of Sir David Lindsay printed by Andro Hart between the years 1614 and
1634. Most of the books of Hart, the best printer of his generation in Scotland, were in
roman. One may say that he printed in roman, except where he was bound by tradition.

In the preface to James Watson's *History of the Art of Printing* (1713), Watson, or
John Spotswood, who is said to have written this preface dealing with printing in
Scotland, states that until recently Scottish printers had imported Dutch composing

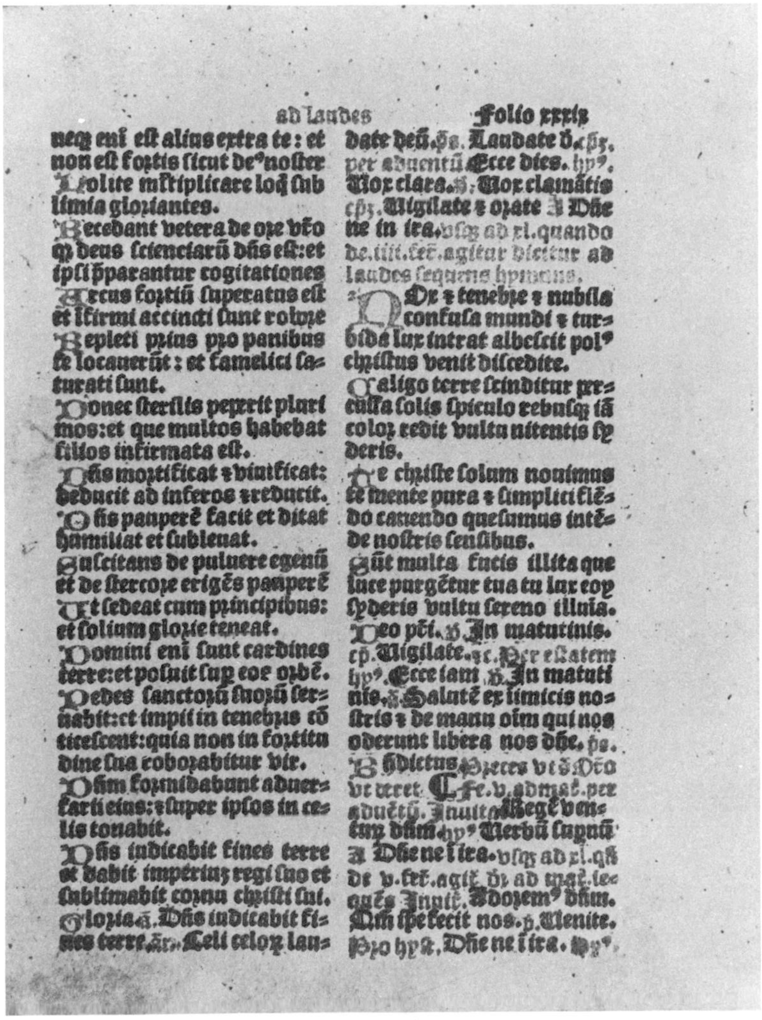

ad laudes Folio xxxix

neq enim est alius extra te: et
non est fortis sicut de⁹ noster
Nolite multiplicare loqui sub
limia gloriantes.
Recedant vetera de ore vestro
quia deus scienciarum dns est: et
ipsi preparantur cogitationes
Arcus fortium superatus est
et infirmi accincti sunt robore
Repleti prius pro panibus
se locauerunt: et famelici sa-
turati sunt.
Donec sterilis peperit plur-
imos: et que multos habebat
filios infirmata est.
Dns mortificat et viuificat:
deducit ad inferos et reducit.
Dns pauperem facit et ditat
humiliat et subleuat.
Suscitans de puluere egenum
et de stercore erigens pauperem
Ut sedeat cum principibus:
et solium glorie teneat.
Domini enim sunt cardines
terre: et posuit sup eos orbem.
Pedes sanctorum suorum ser-
uabit: et impii in tenebris con
ticescent: quia non in fortitu
dine sua roborabitur vir.
Dnm formidabunt aduer-
sarii eius: et super ipsos in ce-
lis tonabit.
Dns iudicabit fines terre
et dabit imperium regi suo et
sublimabit cornu christi sui.
Gloria. Aña. Dns iudicabit fines terre. Aña. Celi celorum laudate deum. Ps. Laudate d. Cap.
per aduentum. Ecce dies. hy⁹.
Vox clara. V. Vox clamantis
Cap. Vigilate et orate. A. Dne
ne in ira. vsq ad xl. quando
de. iiii. fer. agitur dicitur ad
laudes sequens hymnus.
Nox et tenebre et nubila
confusa mundi et tur-
bida lux intrat albescit pol⁹
christus venit discedite.
Caligo terre scinditur per-
cussa solis spiculo rebusq iam
color redit vultu nitentis sy
deris.
Te christe solum nouimus
te mente pura et simplici fle-
do canendo quesumus intende nostris sensibus.
Sunt multa fucis illita que
luce purgentur tua tu lux eoy
syderis vultu sereno illumia.
Deo patri. V. In matutinis.
cp. Vigilate. xc. Per estatem
hy⁹. Ecce iam. V. In matuti
nis. A. Salutem ex inimicis nostris et de manu oim qui nos
oderunt libera nos dne. Ps.
Benedictus. Preces vt s. Oro
vt tenet. Cf. Fe. v. ad mat. per
aductu. Inuit. Regem ven-
turum dnm. hy⁹ Verbum supnum
A. Dne ne i ira. vsq ad xl. qn
de v. fer. agit. dr ad mat. le-
gens Inuit. Adorem⁹ dnm.
Qui fecit nos. p. Venite.
Pro hymn. Dne ne i ira. hy⁹.

FIG. 1. A page from *Breviarium Aberdonense*. Chepman & Myllar, Edinburgh, 1509.

Offrings of the princes. Nombers. 67

at the dore of the Tabernacle of the Congregation.

11 Then the Priest shal prepare the one for a sin offring, and the other for a burnt offring, & shal make an atonement for him, because he sinned by ᵉ the dead: so shal he halowe his head the same day,

12 And he shal ᶠ consecrate vnto the Lord the daies of his separation, and shal bring a lambe of a yere olde for a trespasse offring, and the first daies shalbe voide: for his consecration was defiled.

13 ¶This then is the lawe of the Nazarite: When the time of his consecration is out, he shal come to the dore of the Tabernacle of the Congregation,

14 And he shal bring his offring vnto the Lord, an he lambe of a yere olde without blemish for a burnt offring, & a she lambe of a yere olde without blemish for a sin offring, and a ram without blemish for peace offrings,

15 And a basket of vnleauened bread, of *cakes of fine floure, mingled with oyle, & wafers of vnleauened bread anointed w̄ oyle, with their meat offring, and their drinke offrings:

16 The which the Priest shal bring before the Lord, and make his sin offring and his burnt offring.

17 He shal prepare also the ram for a peace offring vnto the Lord, with the basket of vnleauened bread, and the Priest shal make his meat offring, and his drinke offring.

18 And the Nazarite shal shaue the head ʰof his consecration at the dore of the Tabernacle of the Congregation, and shal take the heere of the head of his consecration, and ⁱ put it in the fire, which is vnder the peace offring.

19 Then the Priest shal take the soden shulder of the ram, and an vnleauened cake out of the basket, and a wafer vnleauened, & put them vpon the hands of the Nazarite, after he hath shauen his consecration.

20 And the Priest shal * shake them to and fro before the Lord: this is an holy thing for the Priest † besides the shaken breast, & besides the heaue shulder: so afterward the Nazarite may drinke wine.

21 This is the lawe of the Nazarite, which he hathe vowed, and of his offring vnto the Lord for his consecration, ᵏ besides that that he is able to bring: according to ᵬ vowe which he vowed, so shal he do after the lawe of his consecration.

22 ¶And ᵬ Lord spake vnto Moses, saying,

23 Speake vnto Aaron and to his sonnes, saying, Thus shal ye ˡ blesse the children of Israel, and say vnto them,

24 The Lord blesse thee, and kepe thee,

25 The Lord make his face shine vpō thee, and be merciful vnto thee,

26 The Lord lift vp his countenance vpon thee, and giue thee peace.

27 So they shal put my ᵐ Name vpon the children of Israel, and I wil blesse them.

CHAP. VII.

2 The heades or princes of Israel offre at the setting vp of the Tabernacle, 10 And at the dedication of the Altar. 89 God speaketh to Moses from the Merciseat.

1 NOw when Moses had finished the setting vp of the Tabernacle, and * anointed it, and sanctified it, and all the instruments thereof, and the altar with all the instruments thereof, and had anointed them and sanctified them,

2 Then † the princes of Israel, heades ouer the houses of their fathers (they were the princes of the tribes, who were ouer them that were nombred) offred,

3 And broght their offring before ᵬ Lord, six ᵃ couered charets, and twelue oxen: one charet for two princes, and for euerie one an oxe, and they offred them before the Tabernacle.

4 And the Lord spake vnto Moses, saying,

5 Take [these] of them, that they may be to do the ᵇ seruice of the Tabernacle of the Congregation, and thou shalt giue them vnto the Leuites, to euerie man according vnto his office.

6 So Moses toke the charets and the oxen, and gaue them vnto the Leuites:

7 Two charets and foure oxen he gaue to the sonnes of Gershon, according vnto their ᶜ office.

8 And foure charets and eight oxen he gaue to the sonnes of Merari, according vnto their office, vnder the hand of Ithamar the sonne of Aaron the Priest.

9 But to the sonnes of Kohath he gaue none, ᵈ because the charge of the Sanctuarie belonged to them, [which] they did beare vpon [their] shulders.

10 ¶The princes also offred in the ᵉ dedication for the altar in the day that it was anointed: then the princes offred their offring before the Altar.

11 And the Lord said vnto Moses, One prince one day, and another prince another day shal offer their offring, for the dedication of the altar.

12 ¶So then on the first day did Nahshon the sonne of Amminadab of the tribe of Iudah offer his offring.

13 And his offring [was] a siluer charger of an hundreth and thirty [shekels] weight, a siluer boule of seuenty shekels after the she-

m.j.

FIG. 2. Page from *The bible and holy scriptures*. Alexander Arbuthnet, Edinburgh, 1579.

cases and presses and that their manner of distributing type and of making ink was learnt from the Dutch. He mentions that Archibald Hyslop had been advised to get new material from Holland and that Robert Sanders and again John Cairns had brought workmen, and materials from Holland. Cairns died about 1680 and was succeeded by David Lindsay, who, with his partners, among them two Dutchmen, issued a single-sheet advertisement in 1681. This sheet is set in a Dutch roman, the St. Augustin roman (a size known to our printers as English) of Bartholomaeus Voskens of Amsterdam, as shown on his specimen sheet issued about 1670 when he was working at Hamburg. David Lindsay and his partners printed several books in the type, e. g. *The Laws and Acts of Parliament* (1681) and Robert Sibbald's *Scotia illustrata* (1684). The italic used by Lindsay to accompany this roman was not that of Voskens but that of his chief rival at Amsterdam, Christoffel van Dyck, an italic taken as a model by William Caslon. These were, I imagine, the first Dutch types used in Scotland. The Voskens roman is not known in English printed books, and the Van Dyck italic not until about 1697, when it was acquired by the Cambridge University Press. (Fig. 4.)

Watson's book of 1713 contains a specimen of his types, and in the same period we find two other type specimens issued by Edinburgh printers, the single sheet of the Heirs of Andrew Anderson (1698) and the book printed by John Moncur in 1709. The Anderson sheet[1] shows only one Dutch type, the 'Double English' roman and italic, unless possibly some of the smallest sizes were Dutch. The capitals displayed are to be found in English books from about 1640. The 'French Canon' is that of the London founder Joseph Moxon, and the 'New English' roman and italic were cut in London about 1636. The sheet states that all the types were added since the year 1694, but this English roman can be found in Edinburgh books many years before 1694, e. g. in Robert Young's edition of *The Acts of Parliament* (1641). John Moncur's book resembles Watson's in the types displayed, but again there are some English types such as Moxon's Canon, and the Canon shown on the title-page. James Watson's types are presumably for the most part Dutch, but they are not to be found on the specimen sheets of the best founders: there seems for instance to be nothing of the Voskens nor of Van Dyck. The use Watson made of his types may be seen in his editions of works of Robert Sibbald printed in 1706 and in 1710, and especially in *The Works of Sir George Mackenzie* (1716, 1722). In this last production we find that Watson, very wisely, was not entirely content with the types he showed in 1713 but printed Mackenzie in Van Dyck's roman and italic.

The success of the first great English type-founder, William Caslon, naturally was important for Scottish printers also, and many books produced by them in the eighteenth century show Caslon types; a good example may be seen in William Maitland's *History of Edinburgh* (Hamilton, Balfour and Neil, Edinburgh, 1753). It may be noted also that in John Reid's *Specimen of Printing Types* (Edinburgh, 1768), a book in which the printer adds the names of the founders from whom he acquired his types, Caslon's name is prominent.

---

1. Reproduced on pp. 314-315 of the present volume.

An even more important event in the history of Scottish typography was the establishment of the first Scottish type foundry, that of Alexander Wilson and John Baine, in 1742, and the close relations of this house with the brothers R. and A. Foulis of Glasgow. The earliest extant specimen book of Wilson's – Baine left the firm in 1749 – was not published until 1772, and it is difficult to work out a time-table of the dates of cutting of the various types shown. It is generally remarked that Wilson was influenced by John Baskerville of Birmingham. This is certainly true of the larger sizes, but some of the smaller sizes appear to have been cut before Baskerville issued his first prospectus, in 1754, of his Virgil. The Foulis Horace of 1744 contains some of Wilson's type, and the *Scots Magazine* was using his Long Primer italic from 1747. In these pre-Baskerville types Wilson already showed himself to be an eighteenth-century designer; he did not, like Caslon, take as his model the Dutch founders of the previous century.

Wilson's Great Primer no. 2, shown in the specimen book of 1772, I find for the first time in 1755 in F. Hutcheson's *System of Moral Philosophy*, printed by the Foulis. The English roman no. 1 – perhaps the best known of Wilson's designs and the one on which Messrs. Collins's 'Fontana' has been based in 1931 – was used in the Foulis Horace of 1760. The famous Double Pica Greek, a type which was shown in the subsequent specimen books of the firm down to 1834, was cut for the Foulis Homer of 1756-1758, and the Double Pica roman we know was cut for the edition of Thomas Gray's Poems of 1768.

The Foulis brothers of Glasgow were the leaders in Scotland of an improvement in typographic standards which was general in all countries of Europe in the eighteenth century. In Edinburgh we can compare the work of the Ruddimans in the middle of the century, and of William Smellie towards its close. The University of Edinburgh still observed the continental practice of expecting theses submitted for its approval to be written in Latin, a language notoriously favoured by typographers. The medical theses printed by the Ruddimans and later by the firm of Balfour and Smellie illustrate the higher level of workmanship demanded and the advantages of Latin.

The evolution of type designs from the tradition of Aldus, Garamond, and Caslon to what is called the modern-face reached its culmination in this country in the first years of the nineteenth century. What this change meant in Scottish typography can be followed in the early works of Sir Walter Scott, printed for the most part by James Ballantyne. Ballantyne was a good printer, and one who, as a book printer, was building up his stock at a time when fashions in letter design were rapidly changing. He was in a position to purchase the most admired specimens from the best founders. What was most admired in 1800 and in the few following years can readily be observed in the original editions of Scott's first books. His volume of translations from Burger, published in 1796, was printed by Mundell for Manners and Miller of Edinburgh and was a fair specimen of eighteenth-century work. The *Goetz of Berlichingen* (1799) was published and presumably also printed in London. With *The Eve of Saint John* (1800) the Ballantyne imprint appears. This work, *The Minstrelsy of the Scottish Border* (1802) and *Sir Tristrem* (1804) are all set in types of a transitional character which are not much short

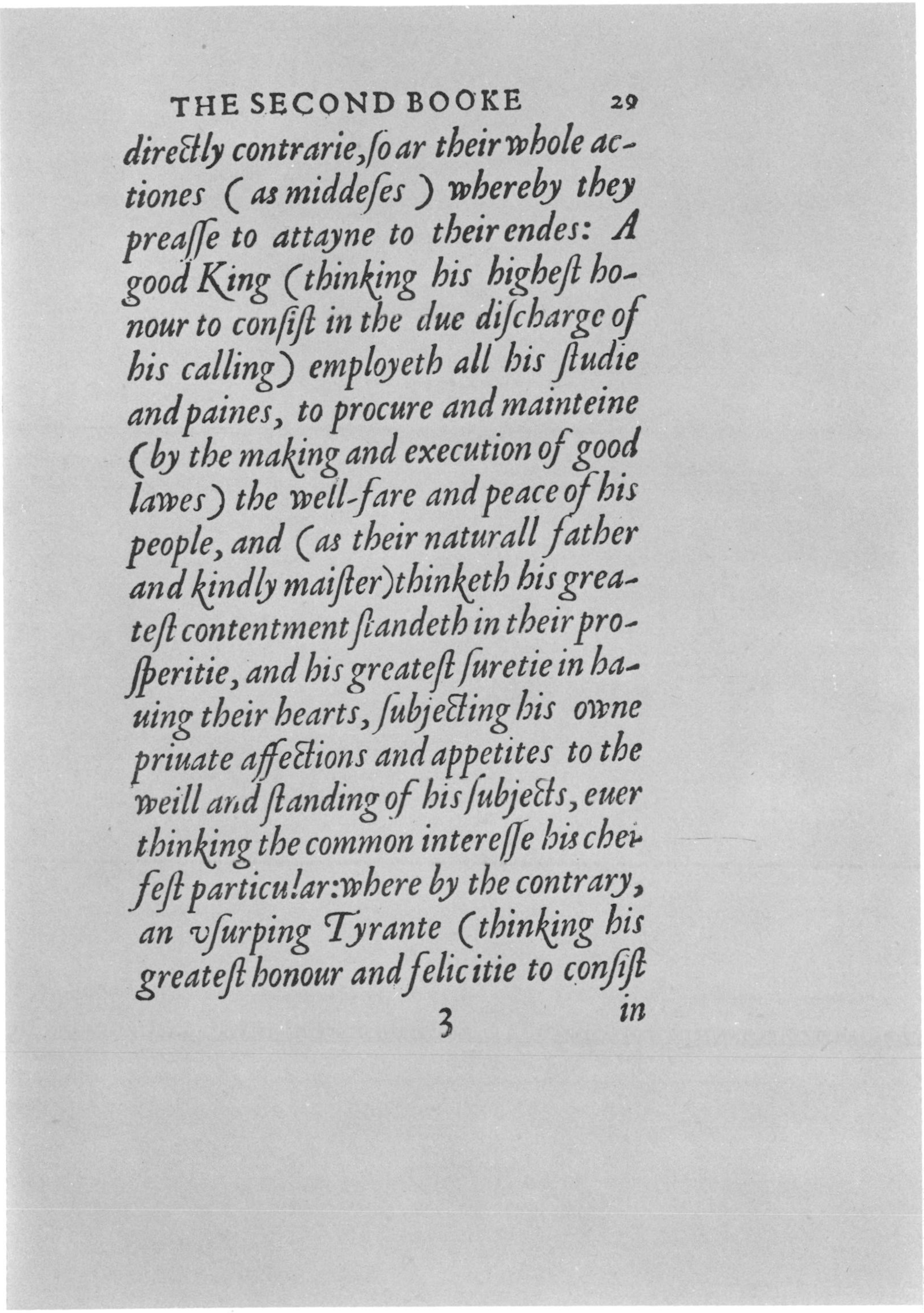

THE SECOND BOOKE 29

directly contrarie, so ar their whole actiones (as middeses) whereby they preasse to attayne to their endes: A good King (thinking his highest honour to consist in the due discharge of his calling) employeth all his studie and paines, to procure and mainteine (by the making and execution of good lawes) the well-fare and peace of his people, and (as their naturall father and kindly maister)thinketh his greatest contentment standeth in their prosperitie, and his greatest suretie in hauing their hearts, subjecting his owne priuate affections and appetites to the weill and standing of his subjects, euer thinking the common interesse his cheifest particular:where by the contrary, an vsurping Tyrante (thinking his greatest honour and felicitie to consist

3 *in*

FIG. 3. Page from King James VI, Βασιλικόν Δῶρον. Robert Waldegrave, Edinburgh, 1599.

SCOTIA ILLUSTRATA
SIVE
PRODROMUS
HISTORIÆ NATURALIS
IN QUO

Regionis natura, Incolarum Ingenia & Mores, Morbi iisque medendi Methodus, &
Medicina Indigena accurratè explicantur:

ET

Multiplices Naturæ Partus in triplice ejus Regno, Vegetabili scilicet, Animali & Minerali
per hancce Borealem Magnæ BRITANIÆ Partem, quæ Antiquissimum SCOTIÆ
Regnum constituit, undiquaque diffusi nunc primum in Lucem eruuntur, &
varii eorum Usus, Medici præsertim & Mechanici, quos ad Vitæ
cum necessitatem, tum commoditatem præstant, cunctis
perspicuè exponuntur:

CUM FIGURIS ÆNEIS.
Opus viginti Annorum
Sereniissimi Domini Regis CAROLI. II. Magnæ BRITANNIÆ, &c.
Monarchæ Jussu editum.

Auctore ROBERTO SIBBALDO M. D. Equite Aurato, Medico & Geographo
Regio, & Regii Medicorum Collegii apud EDINBURGUM Socio.

EDINBURGI,
Ex Officinâ Typographicâ JACOBI KNIBLO, JOSUÆ SOLINGENSI,
& JOHANNIS COLMARII, Sumptibus Auctoris.
Anno Domini M. D C. LXXXIV.

FIG. 4. Title-page from Robert Sibbald, *Scotia illustrata* . . . Edinburgh, 1684. (Reduced.)

of the modern face. With *The Lay of the Last Minstrel* (1805) the evolution is complete. The poem is set in a bold Great Primer roman having all the characteristics of the classical modern face. All those imposing quartos, *Marmion* (1808), *The Lady of the Lake* (1810), *The Vision of Don Roderick* (1811), *Rokeby* (1813) and *The Lord of the Isles* (1815), are set in this same Great Primer. We are told that Ballantyne, when he started his newspaper at Kelso, went to Glasgow to buy type, no doubt from the Wilson foundry. I know of no documentary evidence as to where he dealt subsequently when he started to print books, but from the evidence of contemporary type specimens it seems that the Great Primer roman, in which the six famous poems were printed, was acquired from the London firm of Caslon and Catherwood; perhaps also some of the earlier transitional types. In a specimen book issued by the firm in 1805 the Great Primer is dated 1802.

The Scottish founders were to become well known for their designs in the new fashion: but at the time when Ballantyne was looking round for the latest thing in typography the Wilson firm was not ready for him. Their first modern-face types were shown in 1812, and among them was no Great Primer like that used by Ballantyne. The second great Scottish foundry was set up in Edinburgh in 1807 by William Miller, once a foreman with the Wilson firm. Miller's earliest surviving specimen book is of 1815, and the modern faces shown are very like Wilson's.

The type which our printers know as Scotch roman is a variety of the English modern face, in which extreme hair lines and unbracketed serifs are avoided. Richard Austin, who, according to Hansard, cut modern faces for both the Wilson and the Miller firms, issued specimens of his types in 1819 and 1827. Austin wrote a preface to these publications in which he discusses the whole question of the new fashion in type design taken over from the French. He complains of the lack of durability of the new designs. What he himself aimed at in his Imperial Letter Foundry was what he had already done for Miller and Wilson. It seems probable then that the so-called Scotch face was Austin's design. His contemporaries in London were cutting types with extreme variations of thick and thin strokes, fat faces, or on the other hand anaemic types like the page from a Caslon specimen of 1844 shown by Updike on his fig. 338. The Scottish firms continued to sell their original modern faces, which in the course of time came to be known as Scotch. There were in fact many London books printed in similar types, and Richard Austin, a London founder, was their originator.

About the middle of the nineteenth century there began a gradual revival of interest in the old-face designs, beginning with William Pickering's experiments at the Chiswick Press with Caslon. To this revival the firm of Miller, now Miller and Richard, made a contribution with their type known as 'Old Style', cut by A. C. Phemister and first shown in 1860. This type, which was intended to meet the demand for old faces, whilst avoiding what the founders called their 'objectionable peculiarities,' was soon copied by the London founders and is still a popular design.[1] The original 'Old Style' may be seen in many books published at Edinburgh in the 1860s, and one of the finest examples of a book set in this type appeared at Glasgow, the edition of Sir Isaac Newton's *Principia* printed by Robert MacLehose in 1872.

1. The Monotype Corporation made it the model of their Series 2 and 151.

In our generation the Scottish printing houses are among the most important in the British Isles, and many books published in London bear the imprints of Edinburgh or Glasgow firms. Their stock of types has been subjected to two sweeping changes, first the complete reversal of fashion in type designs and secondly the coming of the type-casting machines, the Linotype and the Monotype. Typographers have relegated the modern faces of the nineteenth century to use in technical books and are setting their books in Caslon or in types based on pre-Caslon models. The obvious advantages of type-casting machines, coupled with the enterprise of their manufacturers in supplying types of good design and in a sound tradition, have had revolutionary results. Scottish printers of books generally use the types of the Monotype Corporation. In a *Catalogue of an Exhibition of Contemporary Book Typography*, held at the Heriot-Watt College, Edinburgh (1933), there is included a section of books printed in Scotland. The names of the types used are given, and they are almost all Monotype designs. We are back once more in a period when the types used by Scottish printers are acquired in London.

[1944]

THE EXILED ENGLISH CHURCH AT
AMSTERDAM AND ITS PRESS

THE Barrowist or Separatist Church at Amsterdam dates from about 1593. Shortly after the execution of Barrowe, Greenwood, and Penry in 1593 most of their followers, who had been imprisoned in March of that year, were released and according to the terms of a recent Act had the choice of conforming or of 'abjuring the Realm of England'. They proceeded to Holland, settling finally in Amsterdam. In the autumn of 1597 they were joined by their pastor Francis Johnson and his brother George, who, earlier in the year, after four years of imprisonment, had been shipped off to Canada. The expedition which they accompanied failed and returned to England, and the brothers went on to Amsterdam. A house was acquired in that city and the Church organized with elders and deacons and as teacher the well-known Henry Ainsworth.[1] Already in 1596 there had appeared *A true confession of the faith*, a work which the *S.T.C.* (237) assigns to Ainsworth, but which, according to Burrage,[2] was probably written by Johnson while still a prisoner. The book is generally assigned to Amsterdam, but it is not impossible that it was printed in London, as the Black Letter used is not the Dutch Lettersnijder.[3]

Before the Church in Amsterdam set up its own press, several books were printed there by members, in addition to the *Confession*. Three of them at least were the product of the same, unidentified, press. They are: F. Johnson's *An answer to Maister H. Iacob*, 1600, (*S.T.C. 14658*; *S.T.C.* says Middelburg?); *Certayne letters, translated*, 1602, (*S.T.C. 7298*; this book contains the *Confession*); and George Johnson's *A discourse of some troubles in the banished English church*, 1603, (*S.T.C. 14664*) a book important for the details the author supplies about the inner history of the Church.

Before many years a press was set up under the management of Giles Thorp, who between 1604 and 1622 printed about forty books, of which eight only are signed. Thorp was a deacon in the Church by 1612 and an elder by 1618. That he died about the year 1622, not long after Henry Ainsworth, is inferred from the fact that the name of Henry May is cited as elder instead of Thorp from 1623. The earliest book bearing Thorp's imprint is of 1607, but internal evidence seems to show that he was at work from 1604. Thorp was not a commercial printer. He produced books written by members of his Church or by men who were closely associated with them.

---

1. See H. Dexter's *Congregationalism*, 1880, Lectures V and VI.
2. *The Early English Dissenters*, 1912, i. 152-4.
3. The bibliographical references to the various editions of this *Confession* are misleading. Dexter, 223, cites a Latin edition of 1598 and refers to a copy in the Bodleian, but I am assured that there is no such edition at Oxford. Dexter, 224, cites an English edition of the same year, with copies in the British Museum and in York Minster Library. This is not a separate edition of the *Confession* but is part of Ainsworth and Johnson's *Apologie or defence*, 1604 (*S.T.C. 238*). Nevertheless there may have been editions of 1598, since the editions of 1607, both Latin and English, have a preface dated 1598. The English edition of 1602 (*S.T.C. 18434*) is another ghost, being a part of *S.T.C. 7298, Certayne letters translated*, 1602.

Although Thorp signed so few of his books, yet by tabulating his types and ornamental material, especially the woodcut initials, it is possible to attribute with some confidence the unsigned books. Especially useful is his alphabet of open arabesque initials, unlike those of any other printer. His types are those in common use, but they are limited in number, while some of the roman capitals used in headings can be of great help. Apart from initials the only ornaments used are printers' flowers, made up into head- or tail-pieces and, with a few exceptions, not used as continuous borders.

Types

Black-letter

Text 220.   Text 92.

Lettersnijder 70. Schilders at Middelburg had this. See Fig. 68 in Prof. Dover Wilson's article, *The Library*, 1911.

Lettersnijder 40 (Psalms, 1620 only).

Roman

Rom. *118*. A Frankfurt type, dating from 1566. Not found in England until many years later. For an illustration see *The Library*, Sept. 1937, p. 204. (Reprinted in *The Type Specimens of Claude Lamesle*, Amsterdam, 1965.)

Rom. *92*. Used also by Schilders, cf. Wilson, Fig. 72. For an account of the type see 'Some Types used by Paolo Manuzio', pp. 256-257 in the present volume. (See Figs. 1, 2, 4, and 5.)

Rom. *83*. A Garamond.

Rom. *80*. Used also by Schilders, cf. Wilson, Fig. 73. See p. 256 in the present volume.

Rom. *70*.

Rom. *70b*. Used from 1619, a better design, probably Garamond.

Italic

Italic *92*. R. Granjon's Augustin. Used by Schilders, cf. Wilson, Fig. 80. See also 'The Italic Types of Robert Granjon' in the present volume p. 264 and Fig. 12. (See Figs. 1, 2, 4, and 5.)

Italic *80*. R. Granjon's Cicero. Used by Schilders, cf. Wilson, Fig. 82. See also 'The Italic Types of Robert Granjon', p. 263 and Fig. 6. From 1622 measures 83 mm to suit the new roman.

Italic *80*. This is the 'Curs. Garamond ou Immortel de Granjon' which has two *V*'s and two ampersands. Thorp seems to have used the plain ampersand only.

Used also by Schilders, cf. Wilson, Fig. 84. See also 'The Italic Types of Robert Granjon', p. 264 and Fig. 10. (See Fig. 3.)

Italic *70*. Used with the new roman from 1619. This type was in the stock of Brewster's 'Pilgrim Press' at Leiden. It is no. 6 A in Harris and Jones, *The Pilgrim Press*, 1922, p. 70 and Fig. 23.

Italic *66*. Brewster's type 1 . (See Fig. 11.)

Roman capitals

11 mm. With wide M. Used also by Schilders. (See Fig. 4.)

7 mm. In common use. Perhaps originally cut for Plantin. See *The Library*, June 1936, p. 78. (See Fig. 4.)

5 mm.

Greek and Hebrew, occasional words.

Initials

White letters on an open arabesque ground in two sizes:

1. *c.* 20 × 17 mm, used in the early years. I have found only A, D, F, L. M, P, T, V, and W. Not used after 1620. (See Figs. 2 and 3.)

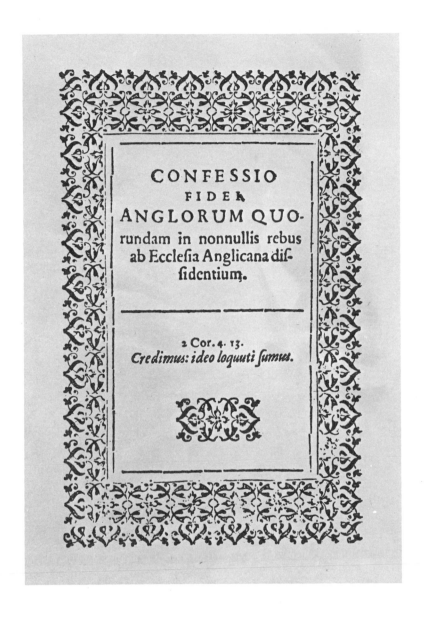

FIG. 1. Roman and italic 92 mm. From *Confessio Fidei*, 1607.

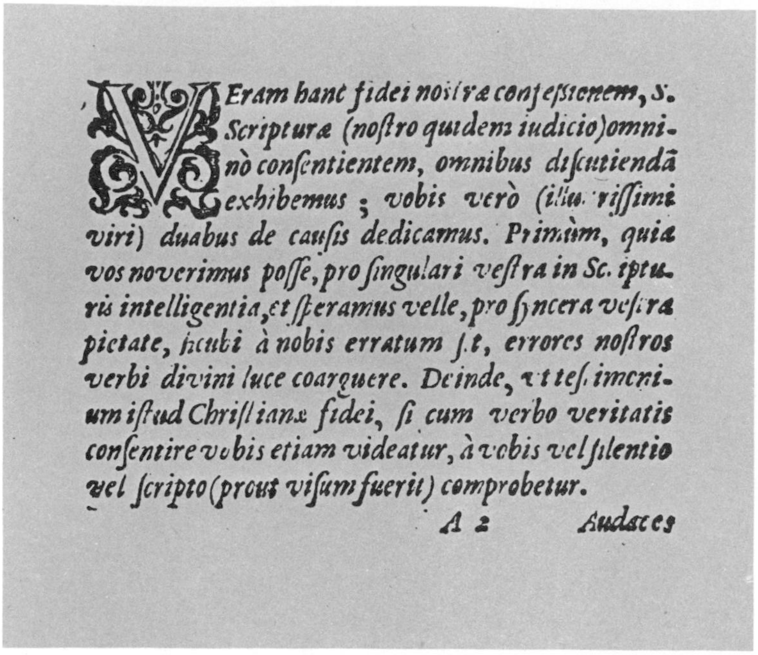

VEram hanc fidei noſtræ confeſſionem, S. Scripturæ (noſtro quidem iudicio) omninò conſentientem, omnibus diſcutiendã exhibemus; vobis verò (illuſtriſſimi viri) duabus de cauſis dedicamus. Primùm, quia vos noverimus poſſe, pro ſingulari veſtra in Scripturis intelligentia, et ſperamus velle, pro ſyncera veſtra pietate, ſicubi à nobis erratum ſit, errores noſtros verbi divini luce coarguere. Deinde, ut teſtimonium iſtud Chriſtianæ fidei, ſi cum verbo veritatis conſentire vobis etiam videatur, à vobis vel ſilentio vel ſcripto (prout viſum fuerit) comprobetur.

A 2 Audaces

FIG. 2. Italic 92 mm and initial V of the smaller set.
From *Confessio Fidei*, 1607.

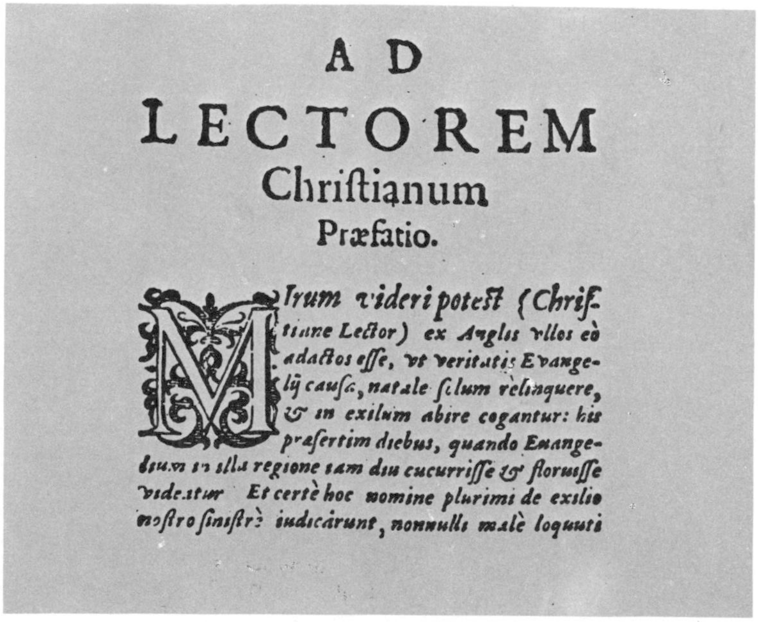

AD
LECTOREM
Chriſtianum
Præfatio.

MIrum videri poteſt (Chriſtiane Lector) ex Anglis vllos eò adactos eſſe, vt veritatis Evangelij cauſa, natale ſolum relinquere, & in exilium abire cogantur: his præſertim diebus, quando Evangelium in illa regione tam diu cucurriſſe & floruiſſe videatur. Et certè hoc nomine plurimi de exilio noſtro ſiniſtrè iudicârunt, nonnulli malè loquuti

FIG. 3. Italic 70 mm and initial M of the smaller set.
From *Confessio Fidei*, 1607.

2. 23 mm in height, of which are found eleven letters in Thorp's lifetime. Used from 1609. (See Figs. 5, 7, and 9.)

One fleuron, a common arabesque design, is found in the Niclas of 1608 and in Ainsworth's *La Communion des Saincts*, 1617. The only other ornaments are a few flower units, found in most of the books, generally built up as head- or tail-pieces.

List of Books printed by Thorp, 1604–22

The type used for the main text of the book is given first. The occurrence of two or three words of a type is not recorded, unless it has not appeared before. Where the types are not given, I have not seen the book but am relying on photostats. Imprints, when they occur, are given.

1604 AINSWORTH (H.) and Johnson (F.). An apologie or defence of such true christians as are commonly called Brownists. 1604. *S.T.C.* 238.
  – rom. 70 and lettersnijder 70; rom. and ital. 92; rom. 118; caps. 7 mm. Initial F of smaller alphabet.
  The Confession of Faith is included. *S.T.C.* 239 is from a different press, probably also Amsterdam.

1605 BROUGHTON (H.). Certayne questions ... [handled] between H. Broughton and H. Ainsworth. 1605. *S.T.C.* 3848.
  rom. and ital. 70; rom. and ital. 92; rom. 118. Border of flowers round title.
  Edited by F. B. This is Francis Blackwell, a member of the Church. Cf. Scheffer's *History of the Freechurchmen called the Brownists*, 1922, p. 81.

1606 JOHNSON (F.). An inquirie and answer of T. White. 1606. *S.T.C.* 14662.
  – rom. and ital. 70; rom. and ital. 92; rom. 118; caps. 5 and 7 mm. Initial T of smaller alphabet.

1607 AINSWORTH (H.). The Communion of Saincs. Giles Thorp, 1607. *S.T.C.* 228. *S.T.C.* gives the imprint in a bracket, but a copy of the title-page in Joseph Ames's *Title-pages* (in the British Museum) bears Thorp's name, its first appearance. I have not been able to see this book.
  The Confession of faith of certayn English people, living in exile in the Low Countreys. 1607. *S.T.C.* 18435.
  – rom. and ital. 92; rom. and ital. 70; rom. 118; caps. 5 mm. Initial T (p. 67) of smaller alphabet.
  Confessio fidei Anglorum quorundam in nonnullis rebus ab Ecclesia Anglicana dissidentium. s. n.
  – rom. and ital. 70; rom. and ital. 92; rom. 118; caps. 5 and 7 mm. Initials V, M, and D of smaller alphabet. Border of flowers round title. A translation of the preceding.
  The copy in the British Museum has a second title-page, once pasted over, reading: 'Confessio fidei Anglorum quorundam in Inferiori Germania exulantium ... Anno 1607', presumably a cancelled title. Cf. Dexter 322.

1608 AINSWORTH (H.). Counterpoyson. 1608. *S.T.C.* 234.
  – rom. and ital. 92; rom. and ital. 70; rom. 118; lettersn. 70; text 92; caps. 7 mm. Initials A, T, M, and W of smaller alphabet. Flowers.
  JOHNSON (F.). Certayne reasons a. arguments proving that it is not lawfull to heare the present ministerie of the Church of England. 1608. *S.T.C.* 14660.
  – rom. and ital. 92; rom. and ital. 70; rom. 118; caps. 7 and 5 mm. Initials T and A of the smaller alphabet. Flowers.

NICLAS (H.). An epistle sent unto two daughters of Warwick. Giles Thorp. 1608. *S.T.C.*
18553. Ed. H. Ainsworth.

– rom. and ital. 70; lettersn. 70; rom. and ital. 92; rom. 118; text 92; caps. 7 and 5 mm.
Initials A and T of smaller alphabet. Fleuron on p. 5.

1609 AINSWORTH (H.). A defence of the holy scriptures . . . against M. Smyth. G. Thorp. 1609.
S.T.C. 235.

– rom. and ital. 80; rom. and ital. 92; caps. 7 and 11 mm. Initials T and I of larger alphabet.
Flowers.

M. Smyth was John Smyth the Se-Baptist who reached Amsterdam in 1608. See Burrage,
i. 226 ff.

JOHNSON (F.). A brief treatise conteyning some grounds and reasons, against two errours
of the Anabaptists. 1609. *S.T.C.* 14659.

– rom. and ital. 80; rom. and ital. 92. Contains no initials.

As Johnson was still Pastor of the Church the probability is that Thorp was the printer,
though complete proof is lacking.

RAINOLDS (J.). An answere to a sermon preached the 17 of April, 1608 by G. Downame.
1609. *S.T.C.* 20605.

Pt. 1 – the Answer to the preface; not from Thorp's press.

Pt. 2 – the Answer.

– rom. and ital. 80; rom. and ital. 92. Initial T. Small ornament at end. The book cannot be
by Rainolds (as in *S.T.C.*) who died in 1607.

Halkett and Laing assign the book to one Sheerwood.

1610 BROUGHTON (H.). Job. 1610. *S.T.C.* 3868.

– rom. and ital. 92; caps. 11 and 7 mm. Initials T and I. Flowers.

Broughton at this time was Minister of the English Church at Middelburg and not a
separatist. He had been in controversy with Ainsworth (see above in 1605), but nevertheless
Thorp printed three of his books.

BROUGHTON (H.). A revelation of the holy apocalyps. 1610. *S.T.C.* 3883.

– rom. and ital. 92; caps. 7 mm. Initials M, I and T. Flowers.

CARPENTER (John). Quaestio de precibus et leiturgijs duabus epistolis tractata, quarum altera
scripta erat per J. Carpenterum, altera per F. Johnsonum. Prostat apud viduam Levini
Hulsij, Francofurti, 1610.

– rom. and ital. 92; rom. and ital. 80; caps. 7 mm. Initials I, M, and A.

Carpenter describes himself as 'Anglus, nuper Ecclesiae Romanae nunc Anglicanae, Presby-
ter'. He can hardly have been the John Carpenter of *D.N.B.*

CLYFTON (R.). The plea for infants . . . G. Thorp, 1610. *S.T.C.* 5450.

– rom. and ital. 92; rom. and ital. 80; caps. 7 and 11 mm.

Clyfton was one of the group of Puritans from Scrooby, who, with their pastor John Robinson, reached Amsterdam in 1608. On the split between Ainsworth and Johnson which
took place at the end of this year, Clyfton remained with Johnson and became Teacher under
him.

ROBINSON (J.). A justification of separation from the Church of England. 1610. *S.T.C.* 21109.

– rom. and ital. 80; rom. and ital. 92; caps. 7 mm. Initial T. Flowers.

Robinson had at first, in 1608, joined the Church at Amsterdam, but in 1609 moved to
Leyden, where he was to be Pastor until his death in 1625. The Church at Leyden had as
yet no press.

1611 AINSWORTH (H.). An arrow against idolatrie. 1611. *S.T.C.* 221.

– rom. and ital. 92; caps. 7 mm. Initial T. Flowers.

BROUGHTON (H.). A petition to the King for authority to expound the Apocalyps. 1611. *S.T.C.*
3876.

– rom. and ital. 92; caps. 11 mm. Initial S. Flowers.

A
DEFENCE
OF THE HOLY SCRIP-
TURES, WORSHIP, AND MINISTERIE,

ufed in the Chriftian Churches feparated
from Antichrift:

Againft the challenges, cavils and contradiction
of *M. Smyth :* in his book intituled
*The differences of the Churches
of the Separation.*

Hereunto are annexed a few obfervations
upon fome of *M. Smythes* Cenfures;
in his anfwer made to
M. Bernard.

By *Henry Ainfworth,* teacher of the
Englifh exiled Church
in AMSTERDAM.

Imprinted at Amfterdam by Giles Thorp
in the yere 1609.

FIG. 4. Capitals 11 and 7 mm; roman and italic 92 mm. From Henry Ainsworth,
A defence of the holy scriptures, worship, and ministerie . . . Giles Thorp, Amsterdam, 1609.

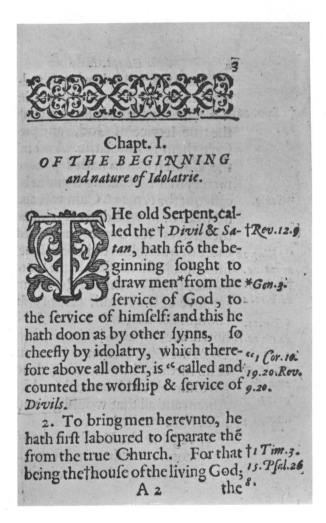

Fig. 5. Roman 92 mm and initial T of the larger set. From Henry Ainsworth, *An arrow against idolatrie*. [Amsterdam], 1611.

SANFORD (Hugh). De descensu domini nostri Jesu Christi. Amstelodami. In aedibus Ægidii Thorpii, 1611.

– rom. and ital. 80; rom. and ital. 92; caps. 7 and 11 mm. Initials Q, C, I, and D.

The author died about 1607 and the book was completed by Robert Parker, then in Amsterdam. See *D.N.B.*

1612 AINSWORTH (H.). The book of psalms. Giles Thorp, 1612. *S.T.C.* 2407.

– rom. and ital. 80; rom. 70; lettersn. 70; rom. and ital. 92; caps. 7 and 11 mm. Initials I and O. Flowers. Musical notes.

LECLUSE (JEAN DE). An Advertisement . . . of Mr. Thomas Brightman his book, namely, A Revelation of the Apocalyps. 1612. (Not in *S.T.C.*)

– rom. and ital. 83; ital. 93; caps. 7 mm. Initials G and F.

In the copy in the Congregational Library the author's name is added in manuscript.

Lecluse, formerly a printer at Rouen, was an Elder of the Church. See Burrage, op. cit.

1613 AINSWORTH (H.). An animadversion to Mr. Clyfton's advertisement. G. Thorp, 1613. *S.T.C.* 209.

– rom. and ital. 80; rom. and ital. 92; rom. 70; lettersn. 70; caps. 7 mm. Initials A and D. Flowers.

BATE (R.). *S.T.C.* 1580. See below, 1624.

RAINOLDS (J.). A replye answering a Defence of the Sermon preached . . . by G. Downame. 1613-14. *S.T.C.* 20620.

– rom. and ital. 80; rom. and ital. 92; caps. 7 and 11 mm. Initials I and T. Flowers.

Wrongly entered under Rainolds in *S.T.C.* See above, under 1609.

Author not known.

1615 AINSWORTH (H.). The Communion of Saincts. 1615. *S.T.C.* 229.

– rom. and ital. 92; rom. 70; lettersn. 70; caps. 7 and 11 mm. Initial F. Flowers.

AINSWORTH (J.). The trying out of the truth in letters between J. and H. Aynsworth. [Published by E. P.] 1615. *S.T.C.* 240.

– rom. 70; lettersn. 70; rom. and ital. 92; caps. 7 and 11 mm. Initials A and I. Flowers.

John Ainsworth was a Roman Catholic and apparently not related to Henry. Cf. *D.N.B.*

ROBINSON (J.). A manumission to a manuduction. 1615. *S.T.C.* 21111.

– rom. and ital. 80; rom. and ital. 92; caps. 7 and 11 mm. Initials A and I. Flowers.

Brewster's press at Leyden, where Robinson was Pastor, was not started till 1617.

1616 AINSWORTH (H.). Annotations upon Genesis. 1616. *S.T.C.* 210.

– rom. and ital. 70, double coll.; rom. and ital. 80; caps. 7 and 11 mm. Initials M and I. Flowers.

A collection of sundry matters. 1616. *S.T.C.* 5556.

– rom. and ital. 92; caps. 7 mm. Initial T.

Attributed to Henry Jacob, for whom see the next entry.

JACOB (H.). A confession and protestation of the faith of certaine christians in England. 1616. *S.T.C.* 14330.

– rom. and ital. 92; rom. and ital. 80; caps. 7 mm. Initials W and M.

Jacob had been Minister of the English merchants at Middelburg. In this year, 1616, he had returned to London and founded what is generally considered the first Congregational church. See *D.N.B.* and Burrage, op. cit.

1617 AINSWORTH (H.). Annotations upon Exodus. 1617. *S.T.C.* 212.

Typography as Genesis, 1616. Initial N.

AINSWORTH (H.). Annotations upon the book of Psalms. 1617. *S.T.C.* 225.

Typography as Genesis, 1616. Initials D and O.

AINSWORTH (H.). La Communion des Saincts. Amsterdam, par Giles Thorp [1617]. Translated by Jean de Lecluse.

– rom. and ital. 92; rom. and ital. 70; rom. 118; caps. 5 mm. Small initials M, L, and P. Fleuron as in Niclas, 1608. Border of flowers on title-page.

The date is taken from the Catalogue of the Congregational Library. For Lecluse see above, under 1612.

1618 AINSWORTH (H.). Annotations upon Leviticus. 1618. *S.T.C.* 214.
Typography as Genesis, 1616. Initial A.
AINSWORTH (H.). The Communion of Saints. 1618. See below, 1628.

1619 AINSWORTH (H.). Annotations upon Numbers, 1619. *S.T.C.* 215.
Typography as Genesis, 1616. Initial A.
AINSWORTH (H.). Annotations upon Deuteronomie. 1619. *S.T.C.* 216.
Typography as Genesis, 1616. Initial T.
HARRISON (JOHN). The Messiah already come. G. Thorp, 1619. *S.T.C.* 12858.
– rom. and ital. 80; rom. and ital. 92; caps. 7 and 11 mm. Initial F. In addition, the preliminaries (? from another press) include several types, an initial F, and two factotums not found in Thorp's books. The author says the first edition was printed in the Low Countries seven years ago. It is an unusual book for Thorp to print, being intended for Jews. The author was in 1619 in the suite of Frederick of Bohemia. See *D.N.B.*
STARESMORE (S.). The unlawfulness of reading in prayer. 1619. *S.T.C.* 23235.
– rom. and ital. 70ᵇ (new); rom. and ital. 92; caps. 7 mm. Initials A and W. Flowers.
Staresmore at this time was still in London, a member of the Independent Church of Henry Jacob. See Burrage, vol. i, p. 317. Later he went to Amsterdam and wished to join the Ainsworth Church.
WILKINSON (J.). An exposition of the thirteenth chapter of the Revelation. 1619. *S.T.C.* 25647.
– rom. and ital. 70; ital. 92; caps. 7 mm. Initials I (on verso of title-page) and T. Flowers.
The author was a Barrowist of Colchester. See Burrage, i. 192-4 and 370-5, where the tract is reprinted, but the facsimile of the initial I has only a distant resemblance to the original.

1620 AINSWORTH (H.). A reply to a pretended Christian plea. 1620. *S.T.C.* 236.
– rom. and ital. 80; rom. and ital. 92; caps. 7 and 11 mm. Initials T and W. Flowers.
All the psalmes. 1620. *S.T.C.* 2731. *Tr.* H. Dod.
– rom. and ital. 70; lettersn. 40; rom. 83, 92, and 114; lettersn. 70 and ? 83; caps. 7 mm. Initials M, I, and F of smaller alphabet. On p. 308 small tail-piece, on R 12 recto a tail-piece (repeated on S 6 recto) and on S 3 verso a head-piece, not found elsewhere. For Dod see *D.N.B.*
As there is some material not found elsewhere, the attribution to Thorp is doubtful.
CALDERWOOD (D.). The speach of the Kirk of Scotland to her beloved children. 1620. *S.T.C.* 4365 and 22040.
– rom. and ital. 92; caps. 7 mm. Initial A.
Calderwood, the Scottish divine and historian, went into exile in Holland in August 1619 and remained there until the end of James's reign (see *D.N.B.*). During this period most of his books were printed by Thorp or his successors.
CALDERWOOD (D.). A defence of our arguments against kneeling. 1620. *S.T.C.* 4354.
– rom. and ital. 70; ital. 80; rom. and ital. 92; caps. 7 mm. Border of flowers round title.
CALDERWOOD (D.). A dialogue betwixt Cosmophilus and Theophilus. 1620. *S.T.C.* 4355.
– rom. and ital. 80; ital. 92; caps. 7 mm.

1621 AINSWORTH (H.). Annotations upon Genesis. 1621. *S.T.C.* 211. A reissue of *S.T.C.* 210.
BAYNES (P.). The diocesans tryall. 1621. *S.T.C.* 1640.
– rom. and ital. 70; rom. and ital. 80; caps. 11 and 7 mm. On the author, d. 1617, see *D.N.B.*
CALDERWOOD (D.). The altar of Damascus. 1621. *S.T.C.* 4352.
– rom. and ital. 70ᵇ; rom. 80; ital. 92; caps. 7 and 11 mm. Flowers.
PROCTOR (T.). The right of kings. 1621. *S.T.C.* 20410.

   – rom. and ital. 92; caps. 7 mm. Initials W and I. Flowers.

   I can find nothing about Proctor. It seems a strange book for Thorp to print.

PROCTOR (T.). The righteous mans way. 1621. *S.T.C.* 20411.

   – rom. and ital. 92; rom. and ital. 70 . Initials M and W. Flowers.

SCOTLAND, CHURCH OF. The first a. second Booke of Discipline. 1621. *S.T.C.* 22015.

   – rom. and ital. 70[b]; rom. and ital. 92; caps. 7 mm. Flowers. ? Edited by Calderwood.

1622 AMES (W.). A reply to Dr. Mortons general defence. 1622. *S.T.C.* 559.

   – rom. and ital. 70[b]; ital. 83; caps. 7 and 11 mm. Flowers.

   This work is attributed also to Calderwood (*D.B.N.*). That attribution is strengthened by the connection with Thorp.

CALDERWOOD (D.). Scoti του τυχοντος Paraclesis. 1622.

   – rom. and ital. 70[b]; rom. and ital. 92; Greek; caps. 7 and 11 mm. Initial S. Flowers. The page of Errata is set in italic 66, for which see below. Attributed in *D.N.B.* to James Sempill.

SCOT (WILLIAM). The course of conformitie. 1622. *S.T.C.* 21874.

   – rom. and ital. 70; rom. and ital. 83; rom. and ital. 66; caps. 7 mm. One line D. Pica rom. Flowers.

   According to Halkett and Laing, where the date is misprinted 1602, seen through the press by Calderwood. Sometimes attributed to Calderwood. On Scot see Hew Scott's *Fasti Eccl. Scot.* v. 142.

Thorp's Successors

The exact date of Thorp's death is not known and it is possible that he was responsible for a few of the books listed below. It is convenient to make the break at the beginning of 1623, since from that year we find considerable changes in the typography and decoration of the books. The material from this date consists of a mixture of types and initials used by Thorp and the types and initials of William Brewster's press at Leyden, the 'Pilgrim Press'. Brewster's stock had been seized in 1619 by the University of Leyden under pressure from the Ambassador of James I. In *The Pilgrim Press* of J. Rendel Harris and S. K. Jones, Cambridge, 1922, it is suggested (pp. 56–9) that the material may have been released and have reached Amsterdam, but the story was not followed up. For the proof that Thorp's successors or Thorp himself acquired the actual material used by Brewster we rely on the appearance of certain breaks, *e.g.* in the small bear ornament (1*b* in Harris and Jones) and in an initial I (No. 10 in Harris and Jones) (see Figs. 6 and 8). The set of 4 mm caps. has also proved very useful, since they were not in common use.

   As to the name of Thorp's successor, one book of 1625 has the imprint 'Amsterdam, printed by R. P.', another of 1626 the imprint 'Amsterdam, printed by Richard Plater', and one tract in Dutch of 1627 is signed by Plater. I have found no further information about Richard Plater. According to John Paget's *Defence of Church Government*, 1641, p. 160 [152], John Canne, who became Pastor of the Church about 1630, also had charge of a 'Printer's work-house'. *Man's Mortallitie*, a tract published in January 1644 with the imprint of John Canne, Amsterdam, was in fact printed in London. There is also a vague reference to Canne's press in the 1640 edition of William Bradshaw's *Unreasonableness of the Separation*. The most important reference to Canne as a printer was supplied by B. Evans in his *Early English Baptists*, vol. 2, p. 108.[1] From a document in Dutch of 1638 it appears that Canne was called before one of the city tribunals and fined £ 300 for printing books likely to promote disorder against His Royal Majesty of Great Britain. Canne stated that he 'had let a work be printed', entitled *A Necessity of Separation from the Church of England*, that he had reprinted a work entitled *A Brief Relation of Certain special and most natural passages*, that he also printed the *Covenant named . . . Van Scotland*, and even a part of the book named *A Dispute against the English Popish Ceremonies*. Of these books Canne's *Necessity of Separation* was printed by the Thorp press in 1634 and Canne states that he 'had let it be printed'. *A Brief Relation* concerns the affairs of Bastwick, Burton, and Prynne, and one edition (*S.T.C.* 1570) came from the so-called 'Richt Right' press in 1638 (cf. Sayle, pp. 1433-5). What the next title means I cannot say, unless it conceals an edition of *The Confession of Faith of the Kirk of Scotland*, which also was reprinted by the 'Richt Right' press (*S.T.C.* 22026). Of *A Dispute*, which was written by George Gillespie, the only edition in *S.T.C.* (11896) is from a different press, also at Amsterdam. From all this one may infer that the printing-house which Canne controlled was the 'Richt Right' press, which, as far as traced, was at work from 1637 to 1642, and which was in some way the successor of the Thorp press. Canne's book *A Stay against Straying*, 1639, was printed at the 'Richt by Right' press, and also *Syon's Prerogative royal*, 1641, which is attributed to Canne John Paget. The material used is:

Roman types

Two-line English. Not enough to measure. First in 1628.
93 mm. Frankfurt type. Cf. *The Library*, Sept. 1937, p. 203.[2] Brewster's type 8, see Harris and Jones, Fig. 32. (See Figs. 8 and 9.)
92 mm. Same as Thorp. Sometimes mixed with the 93.
83 mm. A Garamond. As Thorp. (See Fig. 10).
70 mm. Same as Thorp. 68 mm. from 1631.
68 mm. Used from 1631.
66 mm. Brewster's type 7. Used in 1628.
52 mm. In the margins of Ames, 1633, only.

Italics

118 mm. Brewster's type 3 (Harris and Jones). (See Fig. 8.)
93 mm. Same design as Thorp's 92.
83 mm. Same design as Thorp's 80, cast to suit the new rom. 83.
70[b] mm. Same as Thorp.
66 mm. Brewster's type 1[b]. Used already by Thorp in 1622. (See Fig. 11.)

Roman capitals

11 mm. Same as Thorp.
10 mm. Used by Brewster. See Harris and Jones, Fig. 6. (See Fig. 6.)
8 mm. Used by Brewster. See Harris and Jones, Figs. 6, 13, and 18. (See Fig. 9.)
7 mm. Same as Thorp.

1. I have to thank Mr. P. Zagorin of Harvard for this reference.
2. Reprinted in *The Type Specimens of Claude Lamesle*, Amsterdam, 1965.

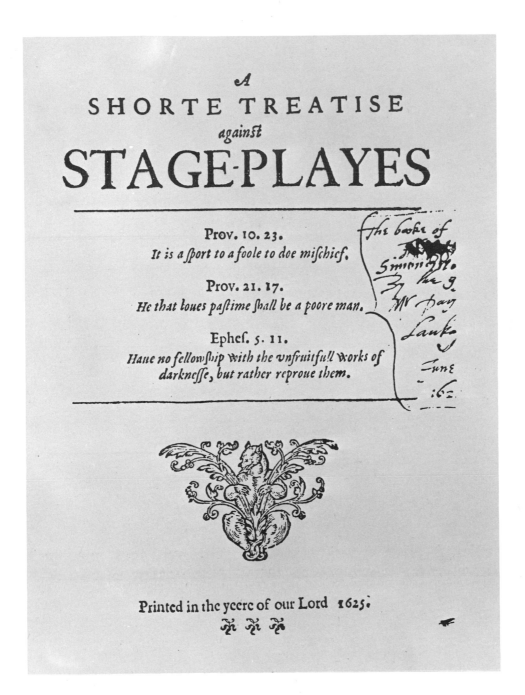

FIG. 6. Capitals 4 and 10 mm; bear ornament. From [Alexander Leighton],
A shorte treatise against stage-playes. [Amsterdam], 1625.

(3)

AN HVMBLE
SVPPLICATION
TENDRED
to the High and Honourable Houſe
OF
PARLIAMENT,
Aſſembled May xviij.
1625.

Hereas Stage-playes are repugnant to the written Word and Will of Almightie God, the onely wiſe Gouernour & righteous Judge of the whole world; dangerous to the eternall ſaluation both of the actours and ſpectatours; breede many inconueniences wherefoeuer they come; procure the judgments of God to the whole kingdome, for ſinne tollerated pourchaſeth Gods wrath to the whole nation, as appeareth Joſhu. 22. 18. and Salomon ſayth Prov. 14.34. Sinne is a reproach to any people; and haue beene juſtly cenſured and

A 2   *worthily*

Fig. 7. Headpiece, Brewster No. 4; initial W of the larger set; italic 118 mm. From [Alexander Leighton], *A shorte treatise against stage-playes.* [Amsterdam], 1625.

4 mm. Used by Brewster. A distinctive alphabet, note the M and R. Many illustrations in Harris and Jones. Used by Jansson and J. F. Stam of Amsterdam. (See Fig. 6.)

Ornaments

Two *Bear tail-pieces* of the Brewster press, no. 1 in Harris and Jones. Note the break in the smaller ornament, as in Fig. 9. (See Fig. 6.)

Head-piece, no. 3[b] of Brewster. See Fig. 22 in Harris and Jones.

Head-piece, arabesque, Brewster's no. 4 in Harris and Jones. See Figs. 23 and 24. (See Fig. 7.)

Initials

The Thorp alphabet, with several new letters in the Robinson of 1625.

The Brewster alphabet, see Harris and Jones. Fig. 33. These initials are cast; they are found at several Dutch presses and with Edward Raban in Scotland. Sayle (6634) gives the year 1607 as their earliest appearance, as far as he has noted. This set used at Hanau was perhaps the model after which the Dutch set was copied. They are not from the same blocks. I have found none earlier than those in Hugh Broughton's *An Exposition upon the Lord's Prayer*, not dated but printed after Broughton's death in 1612. Some of these initials seem to have had flaws in the original punches and show the same imperfections at all presses, notably the O and T. Fortunately the Brewster initials had some flaws of their own (cf. the description in Harris and Jones, p. 68), and the most useful is the break in the I (See Fig. 8.) These Brewster initials and ornaments I have not found at the Thorp press before 1624, but some of the Brewster types appear from 1622.

List of Books printed by Thorp's Successors, 1623-35

1623 AINSWORTH (H.). A censure upon a dialogue of the Anabaptists. 1623. *S.T.C.* 226.
No copy of this book recorded in this country. From the description kindly sent by the Union Theological Seminary, New York, and considering the author, I conclude it to be one of the Thorp books. There are no initials.
AINSWORTH (H.). Solomons Song of Songs. 1623. *S.T.C.* 2775.
– rom. and ital. 70; rom. and ital. 83; rom. and ital. 93; caps. 7 mm. Initials C and L. Flowers.
AMES (W.). A reply to Dr. Morton's particular defence. 1623. *S.T.C.* 560.
– rom. and ital. 70; rom. and ital. 83; rom. 93; caps. 7 and 11 mm. Flowers.
Attributed also to D. Calderwood.
CALDERWOOD (D.). Altare Damascenum. 1623. *S.T.C.* 4353.
– rom. and ital. 70; rom. and ital. 92; rom. 93; caps. 7 and 8 mm. Initial Q. Flowers.

1624 This is the first year in which I have found the ornamental material and the 4-mm caps. from the Brewster press. According to this evidence the two following undated books cannot be put earlier than this year.
BATE (R.). Certain observations of M. Randal Bate whilst he was prisoner. *S.T.C.* 1580 (there dated 1613?).
– rom. and ital. 83; caps. 4 and 7 mm. Initial I. No title-page. Begins with Sig. B.
Included also in *S.T.C.* 227. See Burrage, i. 176, and cf. below, 1630. A poem about Bate or Bates was published in 1641, from which we learn that he died in 1613, a prisoner in the Gatehouse.
ENGLAND, CHURCH OF. Certaine advertisements for the good of the church. *S.T.C.* 10404 (there dated 1621).
– rom. and ital. 83; rom. and ital. 93; caps. 4, 7, 10, and 11 mm. Brewster initial R.
This was written in 1621 and refers to a speech of James I to Parliament delivered on 26 March of that year. On the title of the copy in the B. M. there is a note 'printed about 1623'.
AINSWORTH (H.). An arrow against idolatrie. 1624. *S.T.C.* 222.
– rom. and ital. 83; rom. and ital. 93; caps. 4 and 8 mm. Brewster initial T.

CALDERWOOD (D.). A dispute upon communicating. 1624. *S.T.C.* 4356.
– rom. and ital. 70; ital. 83; caps. 4, 7, and 8 mm.

CALDERWOOD (D.). An epistle of a christian brother. 1624. *S.T.C.* 4357.
ital. and rom. 83; ital. 66; caps. 7 and 10 mm.

CALDERWOOD (D.). An exhortation of the particular kirks in Scotland. 1624. *S.T.C.* 4358.
– rom. and ital. 83; caps. 4, 7, and 10 mm. Initial W.

LEIGHTON (A.). Speculum belli sacri. 1624. *S.T.C.* 15432.
– rom. and ital. 93; ital. 118; ital. 70; caps. 4 and 7 mm. Initials T, W, and A.
Leighton had studied medicine at Leyden but seems to have been in London in this year.
He returned to Holland in 1628 to print his book *Sion's Plea*, which brought such trouble
upon him. The first edition of that book was printed at the Thorp press; see below.

LEIGHTON (A.). A friendly trial of some passages in the Treatise of faith by E. Culverwel.
1624. *S.T.C.* 15431.
– caps. 4 mm. No initials.

An oration or speech appropriated unto the Princes of Christendom. 1624. *S.T.C.* 18837.
– rom. and ital. 83; rom. 93; caps. 4, 7, 10, and 11 mm. Initial G. Brewster head-piece no. 3.
An edition of the Dutch version appeared in 1608. The author was Jacobus Verheiden and
the original Latin title was *De iure belli Belgici*. Cf. Knuttel's *Pamfletten*, n. 954.

ROBINSON (JOHN). A defence of the doctrine propounded by the Synode at Dort. 1624.
S.T.C. 21107[a].
– rom. and ital. 83; rom. 93; caps. 4, 7, and 11 mm. Initial W, and Brewster initial T.
Flowers.

Robinson's Appeal, *S.T.C.* 21107, forms part of *S.T.C.* 23605.

1625 BACHILER (S.). Miles christianus. Amsterdam, printed by R. P., 1625. *S.T.C.* 1106.
– rom. and ital. 93; rom. and ital. 83; ital. 118; caps. 4, 7, and 10 mm. Initials B and R,
Brewster initial T.
There was a reissue in 1629. The author was not a Separatist, but preacher to one of the
English regiments in Holland.

JAMES I, King. An humble petition to the king's most excellent maiestie *S.T.C.* 14425.
– rom. and ital. 93; caps. 4, 7, and 10 mm. Initial M.
In this book the author, writing in England, refers to another tract he had written, addressed
to Parliament, and which he calls *Supplicatorie Advertisements*. This is probably *Certaine advertisements* (*S.T.C.* 10404) (see above, 1624). He mentions also a work in Latin addressed to
the Bishops, which is probably the tract signed Θεοφιλος Φιλαδελφος (*S.T.C.* 19829)
(see below). All three tracts are similar in style and are strongly anti-papal.

LEIGHTON (A.). A shorte treatise against stage-playes. 1625. *S.T.C.* 24232.
– rom. and ital. 93; ital. 118 and 66; caps. 4, 7, 10, and 11 mm. Initial W, Brewster initial I,
Brewster head-piece no. 4, and Bear tail-piece no. 1 .
The attribution to Leighton is based on a passage in his *Speculum belli sacri*, p. 269.

PHILADELPHOS (T.). Ad reverendissimos patres Ecclesiarum Anglicarum Episcopos. 1625.
S.T.C. 19829.
– rom. and ital. 93; caps. 4, 7, and 11 mm. Initial R.

ROBINSON (J.). A just and necessarie apologie of certain Christians called Brownists. 1625.
S.T.C. 21108.
– rom. and ital. 83; ital. 66 and 118; caps. 4, 7, and 11 mm. Initial T. Flowers.

ROBINSON (J.). Observations divine and morall. 1625. *S.T.C.* 21112.
– rom. and ital. 93; ital. 118; caps. 4, 7, and 10 mm. Initials T, G, I, E, W, O, A, F, S, D,
C, M, L, H, N, and Z. Brewster initials T, S, M, and I. Brewster head-piece no. 3 and tail-
piece no. 1 b.
A reissue in 1628 has the title *New Essayes or observations*. Title-page by a different (? London)
press. Cf. Sayle 6986. A further reissue, 1629. *S.C.T.* 21112[a], 21113.

(5)

A SHORT

TREATISE

O F

STAGE-PLAYES.

The Preface.

IN all ages the Prophets haue applied their preachings to the prefent occafions: and the generall concurffe of many baptifed Chriftians to Stageplayes, euery where in thefe times, haue occafioned the Lords remembrancers, which ftand continually on their watchtowres, both more diligently to examine the nature of Stage-playes, which haue had much countenance, and fome defenfe; to trie whether they be warrantable by the word of God or no; and alfo

FIG. 8. Capitals 11 and 4 mm; roman and italic 93 mm (mixed with 92 mm); Brewster initial I. From [Alexander Leighton], *A shorte treatise against stage-playes.* [Amsterdam], 1625.

S. (G.). Sacrae Heptades, or seaven problems concerning Anti-christ. 1625. *S.T.C.* 21492.
   – rom. and ital. 93; rom. and ital. 83; ital. 66 and 118; caps. 4 and 7 mm. Initials A and T. Brewster head-piece no. 3.
   Doubtfully attributed to George Sandys.

1626 FORBES (J.). A fruitfull sermon at Delft. Amsterdam, printed by Richard Plater, 1626. *S.T.C.* 11130.
   – rom. and ital. 93; caps. 7 mm. Brewster initial I on A2 recto.
   Presumably Richard Plater is the R. P. of the Bachiler, 1625.
   Forbes was Pastor of the English merchants at Delft.

1627 Een generael en waerachtigh verhael van al 't gheene datter o 't Eylandt de Ree, 1627 . . . Ghedruckt by Richard Plater.
   Lettersn. Initial D. See Knuttel, no. 3732.

1628 AINSWORTH (H.). The Communion of Saincts. 1628. *S.T.C.* 231.
   – rom. and ital. 83; rom. and ital. 66; ital. 118; rom. 93; caps. 4 mm. Initial F. Brewster tail-piece no. 1 . Border of flowers round title.
   S.T.C. 230 is dated 1618. It is another copy with the date misprinted.

LEIGHTON (A.). An appeal to the Parliament, or Sion's Plea against the Prelacie. s. n. *S.T.C.* 15430.
   – rom. and ital. 93; ital. 66 and 118; caps. 4, 8, and 11 mm. Initials S, W, and R. Brewster head-pieces no. 3. Two engravings.
   Leighton returned to Holland to print this book and his misfortunes on his return to London are notorious in the history of persecution. There were two editions of the book. *S.T.C.* 15429 follows the Thorp edition closely, copying the engravings, initials, and head-piece. The typography is not so close; it is in fact superior. It was probably printed by J. F. Stam of Amsterdam (cf. R. Boye, 1635, *S.T.C.* 3450, for the copy of the W). The engravings are described in the Catalogue of Prints in the British Museum, *Political and Personal Satires*, i. 64-6, but from the copy. The order in *S.T.C.* should be reversed.[1]
   The fullest account of Leighton is in D. Butler's *Life of Robert Leighton*, chaps. 2 and 4.

R. (I.). The spy. Strasburgh, 1628. *S.T.C.* 20577.
   – rom. and ital. 93; ital. 66 and 118; 2 line Eng. rom.; caps. 8 mm. Initial M (new and larger design after the Thorp model). Brewster initial A (newly cast) and N. Brewster head-piece no. 3. With a folding engraved plate.
   This poem is attributed by Hazlitt to John Rhodes, but the attribution seems unlikely in view of the date and character of Rhodes's known works. Another attribution to John Robinson is not accepted by Burrage.

1630 AINSWORTH (H.). Certain notes of Mr. Henry Aynsworth, his last sermon. 1630. *S.T.C.* 227.
   – rom. and ital. 83; rom. and ital. 93; caps. 4 mm. Initials B, T, and I. Brewster W.
   This was published by Sabine Staresmore. On Staresmore and his efforts to be admitted to the Church at Amsterdam, see Burrage, i. 171-7. The book includes a letter to the Church at Amsterdam from Robinson dated 18 Sept. 1624 (sig. C) which appears in *S.T.C.* 21107 as a separate piece. Bound up with it in the Bodleian copy is the tract by Randal Bate, described above, 1624.
   The Thorp press had printed a book for Staresmore in 1619 and here we find the press again producing another tract of his compiling, although his candidature was rejected by the Church.

AR. (A.). The practise of Princes. 1630. *S.T.C.* 722.
   – rom. and ital. 83; caps. 11 mm. Initial W. Brewster tail-piece no. 1 on title-page.
   I can find no information about this book.

CASAUBON (I.). The originall of popish idolatrie. 1630. *S.T.C.* 4748.

---

1. But cf. p. 348.

A

DECADE OF

GRIEVANCES;

*Presented and proved to the right Honourable
and High Court of*

PARLIAMENT;

Againſt

*The Hierarchye, or Goverment of the Lord Biſhopps
and their dependent Offices, by a multitude of such as
are senſible of the ruine of religion, the sinking of the
ſtate, and of the plotts and inſultations of enemies
againſt both.*

RIght Honourable and High Senators,
you are not unacquainted, howe the aff-
righting and turmoyling troubles of the
heart ſpeake in the faces of all true hear-
ted ſubiects, expreſſed often by their
ſighes and groanes, and alſo vented by
their patheticall complaints; the *moving cauſe* whereof Deut. 32.
B   is   35.

FIG. 9. Capitals 8 and 4 mm; initial R of the larger set; roman and italic 93 mm.
From Alexander Leighton, *An appeal to the Parliament; or Sion's Plea against the
Prelacie.* [Amsterdam], 1628.

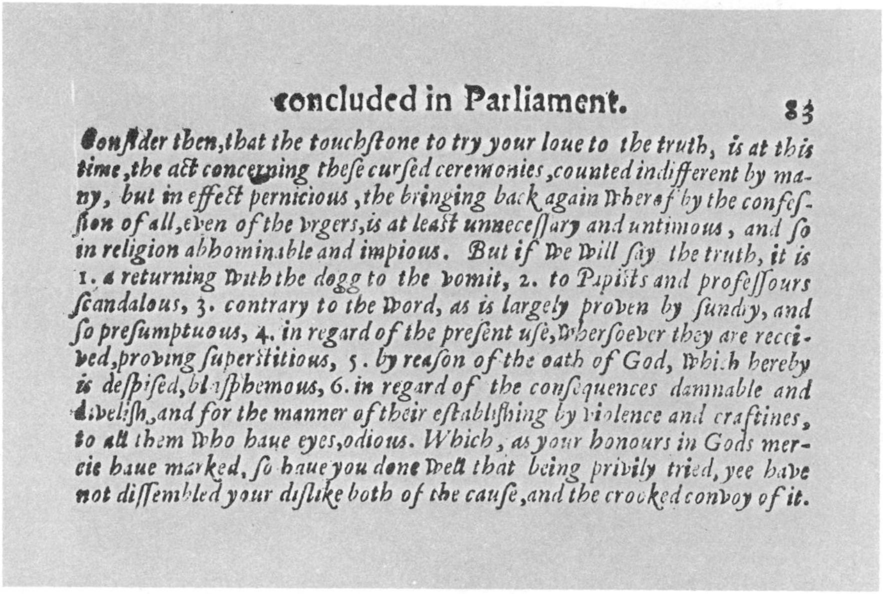

concluded in Parliament.   83

Confider then, that the touchstone to try your loue to the truth, is at this time, the act concerning these cursed ceremonies, counted indifferent by many, but in effect pernicious, the bringing back again whereof by the confeffion of all, even of the vrgers, is at least unnecessary and untimous, and so in religion abbominable and impious. But if we will say the truth, it is 1. a returning with the dogg to the vomit, 2. to Papists and professours scandalous, 3. contrary to the word, as is largely proven by sundry, and so presumptuous, 4. in regard of the present use, whersoever they are received, proving superstitious, 5. by reason of the oath of God, which hereby is despised, blasphemous, 6. in regard of the consequences damnable and divelish, and for the manner of their establishing by violence and craftines, to all them who haue eyes, odious. Which, as your honours in Gods mercie haue marked, so haue you done well that being privily tried, yee haue not diffembled your dislike both of the cause, and the crooked convoy of it.

FIG. 10. Roman 83 mm. From William Scot, *The course of conformitie.*
[Amsterdam], 1622.

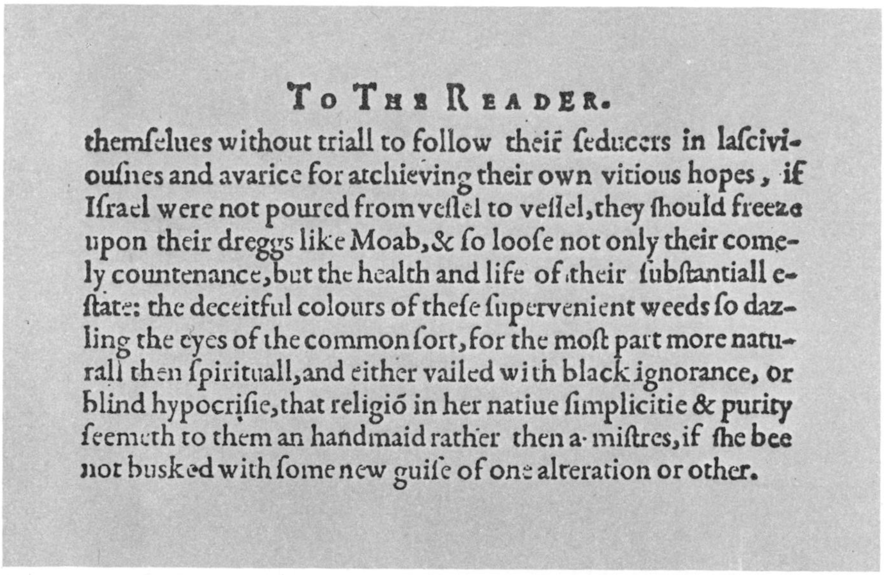

TO THE READER.

themfelues without triall to follow their feducers in lafcivioufnes and avarice for atchieving their own vitious hopes, if Ifrael were not poured from veffel to veffel, they fhould freeze upon their dreggs like Moab, & fo loofe not only their comely countenance, but the health and life of their fubftantiall eftate: the deceitful colours of thefe fupervenient weeds fo dazling the eyes of the common fort, for the moft part more naturall then fpirituall, and either vailed with black ignorance, or blind hypocrifie, that religiõ in her natiue fimplicitie & purity feemeth to them an handmaid rather then a· miftres, if fhe bee not busked with fome new guife of one alteration or other.

FIG. 11. Italic 66 mm. From William Scot, *The course of conformitie.*
[Amsterdam], 1622.

    – rom. and ital. 83; ital. 118; rom. 2-line English; caps. 7, 8, and 10 mm. Initial C. Brewster
initial I and tail-piece no. 1 b.

    Wrongly assigned to Casaubon by the translator A. Darcie in the London edition of 1624.
This Amsterdam edition is 'published by S. O.' as are two of the following books. ? S. O. =
Stephen Ofwood. But in a letter of June 1633 he is reported as having long since fallen from
the Church. Cf. Burrage, ii. 273.

1631 T. (A.). A christian reprofe against contention. 1631. *S.T.C.* 23605.

    – rom. and ital. 83; rom. 68; ital. D. Pica; caps. 4 and 7 mm. Brewster initials M and T.
Two small initials C and W not found in the other books. Brewster tail-piece no. 1 .

    The D. Pica ital., 68 rom. and two initials have not appeared before. The book is the answer
of the Amsterdam Church to the claims of Staresmore. Burrage suggests (i. 176) that A. T.
may be Anthony Thatcher.

    TWISSE (W.). A discovery of D. Jacksons Vanite. 1631. *S.T.C.* 24402.

    – rom. and ital. 83; rom. and ital. 93; rom. 1-line English; caps. 4, 8, 10, and 11 mm. Initials
T and I. Brewster tail-piece no. 1 b. Flowers.

    Twisse was a Puritan but not a separatist. At this time he was Rector of Newbury.

    TWISSE (W.). The doctrine of the synod of Dort. s. n. *S.T.C.* 24403.

    – rom. and ital. 83; ital. 93; caps. 8 mm. Initials S, L, and B.

    The British Museum Catalogue gives the date as *c.* 1650. From the typography I conclude
that it can be little later than the preceding entry. Not in Thomason.

1632 The Booke of Psalmes in English Metre. [By H. Ainsworth.] 1632. Not in *S.T.C.*

    – rom. 66. Brewster initial O. Border of flowers round title-page and device bearing the
words 'Right Right', as used later by the 'Richt Right' press, with the alteration in the lettering.
Attribution to the Amsterdam press is doubtful.

1633 AMES (W.). A fresh suit against human ceremonics. 1633. *S.T.C.* 555. 'Published by S. O.'

    – rom. and ital. 93; rom. and ital. 52 (in margins); ital. 118; caps. 4, 7, and 11 mm. Initials
A, V, and M. Brewster initials T and M. Brewster head-pieces nos. 3 and 4. Brewster tail-
pieces nos. 1ª and 1ᵇ.

    Ames died in November 1633, when he was Minister of the English Church at Rotterdam.
The types and initials of the preliminaries, including the long preface by Thomas Hooker,
have not been included; they must be from another press. Cf. Sayle 7015. Sir William Boswell in a letter from The Hague of 20 September 1633 says that the book was printed by
Staresmore.

1634 CANNE (J.). A necessitie of separation. 1634. *S.T.C.* 4574.

    – rom. and ital. 93; ital. 118; caps. 7 mm. Initial H. Brewster initial T.

    Canne became Pastor at Amsterdam about 1630. Cf. Burrage, i. 178 ff. We have already
noted that he is reported to have had charge of a 'printer's work-house'.

    EMANUEL, PRINCE OF PORTUGAL. A declaration of the reasons moveing Don Emanuel to for-
sake the Romish religion. 1634. *S.T.C.* 7678.

    – rom. and ital. 93; rom. 68; ital. 118; caps. 7 and 8 mm. Initial A.

1635 FORBES (JOHN). Four sermons. 1635. *S.T.C.* 11129 (date misprinted 1625). 'Published by S. O.'

    – rom. and ital. 83; and ital. 93; ital. 118; caps. 7 mm. Initial C and H. Brewster tail-piece
no. 1 b.

    Forbes, Minister at Delft, had died in 1634.

    This is the last publication of the press, as far as I have been able to trace the history.
Some of the material passed into the hands of the so-called 'Richt Right' press, as already mentioned.

[1951]

J. F. STAM, AMSTERDAM, AND ENGLISH BIBLES

JAN FREDERICKSZ STAM was a commercial printer at Amsterdam from 1628 to 1657, who was also responsible for several books written by English Puritans and a number of English Bibles. Many of these books in English are unsigned and all the Bibles, with the exception of one edition of 1633, which bears his name on the title-page of the the New Testament (*S. T.C.* 2309). The following notes include a list of Stam's English books, signed and unsigned, and an attempt to show which editions of the English Bible are to be assigned to his press.

Stam's name first appears in the records in 1628, when, at the age of twenty-six, he married the widow of Joris Veseler and took over the printing of the *Courante uyt Italien*, published by Jan van Hilten. The earliest number which bears Stam's name is that for 18 November 1628. The last book known to have been printed by him appeared in 1657 and he died in 1667.[1] His predecessor, Veseler, already had some connexion with English booksellers, since he was the printer of the English editions of several Corantos of 1620 and 1621.[2] He printed at least two books by English Puritans. John Paget's *An Arrow against the Separation of the Brownists*, 1618, and Thomas Proctor's *Religions Crowne*, 1621; both bear his imprint. Paget was for thirty years Minister of the English Presbyterian Church in Amsterdam. Calderwood's *A Solution of Dr. Resolutus*, 1619, can also be assigned to Veseler on the strength of the initials which we shall find later in the possession of Stam. Two other tracts in English bearing Veseler's name, *S.T.C.* 16839 and 22131, are news-pamphlets.

The list of Stam's books in English, apart from Bibles, is as follows:

1. LEIGHTON (A.), An appeal to the Parliament; or, Sion's Plea against the Prelacie [1628]. *S.T.C.* 15429. Not signed. The original edition (*S.T.C.* 15430) is from the press of the Separatist Church at Amsterdam. (Cf. p. 344). The order in *S.T.C.* is wrong. Three of the initials in the original edition, S, W, and R, are copied, as well as the engraved illustrations. Stam's edition may, of course, be later than 1628.
2. The book of prayses, called the psalmes. Opened by Alexander Top, 1629. *S.T.C.* 2415. Signed. second part, 'The Arguments', is from a different press (? English).
3. PREMPART (J.), A historicall relation of the famour siege of . . . Busse, 1630. *S.T.C.* 20202. Signed. There was also an edition in Dutch printed by Stam in the same year.

For the years 1631 to 1634 I find nothing printed by Stam in English (except Bibles). Possibly he was the printer of the series of news-books in English published by Jan van Hilten in 1633 (Dahl, *Bibliography*, nos. 402-4).

4. BEST (W.), The churches plea for her right. 1635. *S.T.C.* 1974. Signed.
5. PAGET (JOHN), An answer to W. Best. 1635. *S.T.C.* 19097. Signed. On this controversy between Best and Paget see Burrage, *Early English Dissenters*, i. 309.

1. See M. M. Kleerkooper, *De Boekhandel te Amsterdam* ('s-Gravenhage, 1914).
2. See F. Dahl, *A Bibliography of English Corantos and Periodical Newsbooks, 1620-1642* (Bibliog. Soc., 1952), *Dutch Corantos, 1618-50* (1946), and 'Amsterdam – Cradle of English Newspapers' (*The Library*, 5th series iv. 166-78); also L. Hanson, 'English Newsbooks' (*The Library*, 4th series, xviii. 355-84).

6. BOYE (R.), The importunate begger for things necessary, 1635. *S.T.C.* 3450. Not signed. The author, a silenced minister, was concerned in the distribution of Prynne's tracts.[1]

7. ODELL (T.), A brief and short treatise, called the Christians Pilgrimage, 1635. *S.T.C.* 18780. Signed.

8. ODELL (T.), Isaacks pilgrimage, 1635. *S.T.C.* 18781. Signed.

These two pieces are in verse and the first has a dedication to Queen Elizabeth. Odell was in 1603 a member of the Separatist Church of Francis Johnson at Amsterdam, as appears from George Johnson's *Discourse*, 1603. In 1615 he joined the Dutch Mennonites. Cf. Burrage, op. cit., i. 250.

9. BURTON (HENRY), An apology of an appeale, 1636. *S.T.C.* 4134. Not signed.

10. BURTON (HENRY), For God, and the king, 1636. *S.T.C.* 4142. Not signed.

There is a London edition of each of these tracts by Burton, *S.T.C.* 4135 and 4141, from the the same press as the edition of Prynne's *Divine Tragedy* mentioned below (but the author was probably Burton).

11. PRYNNE (W.), Certaine quæries propounded to the bowers at the name of Jesus, 1636. *S.T.C.* 20456. Not signed.

12. PRYNNE (W.), A divine tragedie, 1636. *S.T.C.* 20459. Not signed. There is another edition in which the large initial C and the initial T are copied from Stam, no doubt printed in London, as also is Sayle 6363, a piece not separately entered in *S.T.C.* Cf. also the curious story about the letter C in *Domestic State Papers*, 1637, pp. 174, 175. But the passage relates to the printing of the 'Brief Instructions to Churchwardens', which has no initials. An edition of the *Divine Tragedy* of 1641 has the name of Henry Burton on the title-page.

13. PRYNNE (W.), The Lords day the Sabbath day, 1636. *S.T.C.* 20468. Not signed.

14. PRYNNE (W.), The unbishoping of Timothy and Titus, 1636. *S.T.C.* 20476. Not signed.

15. BASTWICK (J.), A briefe relation of certain passages in the Starre-Chamber, 1637. *S.T.C.* 1569. Not signed.

16. MORTON (T.), New English Canaan, 1637. *S.T.C.* 18202. Signed. On this tract about New England and its author, see *D.N.B.*

17. PRYNNE (W.), A breviate of the prelates, 1637. *S.T.C.* 20454. Not signed.

18. PRYNNE (W.), XVI New quæres, 1637. *S.T.C.* 20475. Not signed.

19. A catechisme of Christian religion, 1639. *S.T.C.* 5185. Signed. There is a device on the title-page which formerly belonged to J. de Meester of Alkmaar. It is reproduced in *Bibliotheca Belgica*, series 2, tom. XVIII. This is an edition of the Palatine Catechism used for a time in the Church of Scotland. Cf. *S.T.C.* 16592, where it is printed with the Psalms. The widow of J. Veseler had already printed an edition at Amsterdam in 1626 and Stam produced another in 1652, the latest English book from his press which I have found.[2]

It is proposed to make use of some of the types and decorative material found in these books for identifying the Bibles printed by Stam. The material is as follows:

The two principal body types found in these books are an English and a Pica roman and are larger than the text type of the Bibles, which measures only 52 mm.

Types

Two-line English roman.

142[a] roman. The Pilgrim Press of W. Brewster at Leyden made much use of the capitals of this type, but Stam had the lower case also. (Fig. 2.)

142[b] roman. A different type.

11 mm. roman capitals. (Fig. 1.)

13 mm. roman capitals.

1. See [Thomas Birch] *Court of Charles I* (1848), ii. 273-4.
2. *S.T.C.* 26125-7, *A guide unto Sion*, are wrongly assigned to Stam.

Ornaments

1. Tail-piece, with two cherubs, irregular outline, 50 mm wide. Copied from an ornament found in Barker's London Bibles as early as 1603.
2. Triangular tail-piece, irregular outline, 38 × 64 mm.
3. Head-piece, winged female figure, no outline, 23 × 75 mm. Found in Psalms, 1629.
4. Head-piece, head flanked by two female half-figures, no outline, 40 × 97 mm. Copied from an ornament found in Barker's Bibles, at least from 1599. (Fig. 2.)

Initials

Ser. 1. Large figure initials, 43 × 49 mm C, H (in Odell, 1635), and G (in Stam's Dutch Bible, 1644).

Ser. 2. White letters on arabesque ground, no outline, 34 × 34 mm D, H, O, T. The T (Fig. 3) was used by Veseler in 1619, with no crack.

Ser. 3. Conventional decoration, no outline, 25 × 25 mm A, B, C, G, I, M, O, P, T, V, and W. The I has human figures, the M fruits, and the T grotesque animals. This is the commonest series used by Stam.

Ser. 4. Cast initials, as used by Brewster's press at Leyden and other Dutch printers. See fig. 33 in Harris and Jones, *The Pilgrim Press*. Stam had the E, F, H, I, and O.

Ser. 5. Similar to ser. 3, no outline, *c.* 17 × 16 mm I and T. The I is reproduced in Lea Wilson's *Bibles in English*, pp. 91, 92.

Ser. Cast initials, arabesque ground, no outline, 17 × 17 mm. Used formerly by Veseler's widow on the news-sheets printed for Jan van Hilten. B, I, and T.

Stam also used various odd small initials. I have filled up some gaps among the initials from Stam's Dutch Bible of 1644. His other books in Dutch, so far as I have seen them, being in Black Letter, are of little help.

It has long been known that several editions of the English Bible bearing the imprint of the Deputies of Christopher Barker and the date 1599 were in fact printed abroad at later dates. A petition of Robert Barker of June 1601 to the Council is preserved, in which he complains that Andrew Hart and John Norton impugn his privilege by printing Bibles at Dort.[1] It appears then that the printing of Bibles in Holland began at the very opening of the century, but whether the edition printed at Dort has survived is uncertain. The editions with which we are concerned are *S.T.C.* 2174-80 and 2309. In the *Historical Catalogue of the Bible Society* they are nos. 188-94 and 364.[2] *S.T.C.* 2309 has on the title-page of the New Testament the imprint 'Imprinted at Amsterdam, for Thomas Crafoorth. By John Fredericksz Stam, dwelling by the South-Church, at the signe of the Hope. 1633.' Sir William Boswell, English ambassador in Holland, refers to this edition in a letter of 20 September 1633 (*Domestic State Papers*). All editions, except *S.T.C.* 2180, have a woodcut title-border, repeated in the New Testament, copied from Barker's border (no. 230 in McKerrow and Ferguson's *Title-page Borders*). There are two varieties, reproduced as nos. 6 and 7 in the Appendix to McKerrow and Ferguson. Stam's border is no. 6. All the editions are in quarto, have the same pagination and signatures, and must have been set up the one from the other.

---

1. Historical MSS. Commission, *Calendar of MSS. at Hatfield House*, Pt. xiv, p. 179.
2. These references are to the original edition of 1903. In the new edition they are nos. 248-255 and 473; but see footnotes p. 353.

THE
BIBLE,
THAT IS,
The holy Scriptures conteined
in the Olde and Newe Teſtament,

TRANSLATED ACCORDING
to the Ebrew and Greeke, and conferred with the
beſt tranſlations in diuers languages.

With moſt profitable Annotations vpon all the hard
places, and other things of great importance.

FEARE YE NOT STAND STILL, AND
behold the ſaluation of the Lord , which hee will
ſhew to you this day , Exod.14.13.

But the Lord deſiuereth him

THE LORD SHALL FIGHT FOR YOU,
therefore hold you your peace. Exod.14.14.

IMPRINTED AT LONDON
by the Deputies of Chriſtopher Barker, Printer to
the Queenes moſt excellent Maieſtie.

1599.
Cum priuilegio.

Fɪɢ. 1. Title-page from *The Bible, that is, The holy Scriptures conteined in the Olde and Newe Testament* . . . Deputies of Christopher Barker, London, 1599.

THIS SECOND
PART OF THE BIBLE,
CONTEINETH THESE
BOOKES.

Pfalmes.	Ioel.
Prouerbes.	Amos.
Ecclefiaftes.	Obadiah.
The fong of	Ionah.
Salomon.	Micah.
Ifaiah.	Nahum.
Ieremiah.	Habakkuk.
Lamentations.	Zephaniah.
Ezekiel.	Haggai.
Daniel.	Zechariah.
Hofea.	Malachi.

FIG. 2. Page Aa 1 of the 1599 Bible.

In Lea Wilson's *Bibles in English*, 1845, and in several later catalogues these editions are distinguished by variations in the first verses of the book *Esther*. I propose to distinguish them here by changes in the typography and ornaments, and thus in addition to present the evidence that they were printed by Stam. Pages particularly to be noted are the two title-pages, woodcut and type-set [Fig. 1], a leaf at the opening of the second part, which begins with *Psalms* (Aa1) [Fig. 2] – the leaf contains a list of the books in this part – and the page preceding *Revelation*, on Ooo5 verso [Fig. 3].[1] These two last leaves seem to be peculiar to Dutch printed editions.

S.T.C. 2174, no. 188, or A,[2] in the *Historical Catalogue of the Bible Society*. The woodcut title-page is the same in all Stam's editions. Type-set title-page has the 13 mm caps. and two-line English roman. Also a woodcut illustrating the crossing of the Red Sea, which is found in *The Catechism of Christian Religion*, 1639 and 1652. This woodcut is found on all the type-set title-pages. 'To the Christian Reader' opens with an initial B of ser. 6. Opening of *Genesis*, initial I; opening of *Numbers*, initial T of ser. 5.

Sig. Aa1 recto (opening of part 2, the *Psalms*, &c.), a head-piece, no. 4, as in Stam's Dutch Bible of 1644. Titles of books set in 142[b] roman.

Opening of *Matthew*, heraldic T.

Sig. Ooo6 verso (opening of *Revelation*), initial T of ser. 2.

Sig. Oqq1 recto, tail-piece no. 1. This is in all editions.

Because of the number of errors it has been suggested that this edition is the earliest.

S.T.C. 2175. Bible Society no. 189, or B.[3]

The two title-pages are as in *S.T.C.* 2174. 'To the Christian Reader', initial B different from *S.T.C.* 2174. Sig. Aa1 agrees with *S.T.C.* 2174.

Sig. Aaa2 recto has an initial D (a squirrel, 26 × 26 mm) which is in Stam's Dutch Bible of 1644.

Sig. Ooo6 verso as in *S.T.C.* 2174.

S.T.C. 2176. Bible Society no. 190, or C.[4]

On type-set title-page, 13 mm caps. The words 'Cum privilegio' are set in a new italic (first found with the Elzevirs in 1631).

Sig. Aa1 recto, the 142[b] roman.

Sig. Aaa2 recto, a different initial D (decoration of a bird, also in the Dutch Bible, 1644).

Sig. Ooo6 verso, initial T of ser. 3. Band of flowers as in *S.T.C.* 2174.

S.T.C. 2177. Bible Society no. 191, or D.[5]

On type-set title-page, 11 mm caps.

Sig. Aa1 recto, the 142[a] roman.

Sig. Aaa2 recto, a different initial D (21 × 24 mm, plant in centre).

Sig. Ooo6 verso, different flowers at the top of the page. Opening of *Revelation*, initial T of ser. 6.

S.T.C. 2309 is the same as this edition with the addition of Stam's imprint as already given.

S.T.C. 2178. Bible Society no. 193, or F.[6]

Easily distinguished by the rules round every page. On the type-set title-page, 13 mm caps. and the words 'Cum privilegio' in the new italic as in *S.T.C.* 2176. 'To the Christian Reader' has the initial B of *S.T.C.* 2175.

Sig. Aa1 recto as in *S.T.C.* 2174 and 2175.

Sig. Aaa2 recto has a different initial D (18 × 18 mm).

Sig. Ooo6 verso has ornament no. 3 in place of flowers.

S.T.C. 2179. Bible Society no. 192, or E.[7]

On type-set title-page, 11 mm caps.

1. The three illustrations are reproduced from *S.T.C.* 2179.   2. Now no. 248.   3. Now no. 249.
4. Now no. 251.   5. Now no. 252.   6. Now no. 254.   7. Now no. 253.

Sig. Aa1 recto, the 142ª roman.
Sig. Aaa2 recto, a different initial D (23 × 23 mm, flower in centre).
Sig. Ooo6 verso as in *S.T.C.* 2174.

The notes here given about these six editions are sufficient evidence that they are all from the same press and that the press was that of Stam. Only a small part of Stam's material has been found at the press of his predecessor Veseler or Veseler's widow. As to the order of printing, one might infer from the typography that the editions with the 13 mm caps. and the new italic on the title-pages are later than those having the 11 mm caps. and the old italic. In books signed by Stam the 142ª roman precedes the 142ᵇ roman. This order does not agree with the order inferred from the correctness or otherwise of the text. If these six editions are all printed by Stam, then from what we know of Stam's life we can conclude that none of them was printed before 1628. They are editions of the Geneva version, with notes, and all are without the Apocrypha. Thus it appears that they were intended for a Puritan market. In 1615 Archbishop Abbot had prohibited the issue of the Bible without the Apocrypha, while Archbishop Laud had forbidden the importation of Geneva Bibles by a decree of Star Chamber dated 1 July 1637.[1] When Laud took such a step one can be sure that such Bibles were being imported at that time.

There is another quarto Bible, *S.T.C.* 2180, Bible Society no. 194, or G,[2] which has some relation to Stam's editions. This edition has a similar woodcut border (no. 7 in the Appendix to McKerrow and Ferguson). Some of the ornaments are very similar to those in Stam's quarto Bibles. The layout, pagination, and signatures are also similar. It is evident that the printer of this Bible copied Stam or that Stam copied him. Lea Wilson suggested that this edition was printed at Dort; perhaps he knew of Barker's appeal to the Council referred to above. It is also known as the Goose Bible, because of the device of a goose found on the title-page of the Metrical Psalms which accompany the edition. Bound up with most of these quarto Bibles is generally found an edition of Sternhold and Hopkins's Metrical Psalms. *S.T.C.* 2499 distinguishes four editions; the three with an ornament of two cherubs flanking a rose are from Stam's press.

After printing a Dutch Bible in 1644 Stam produced in 1645 another English Bible, in quarto unsigned. It is described as being 'according to the copie printed by Roger Daniel... of Cambridge' and is no. 453[3] in the Bible Society's *Catalogue*. It has an initial G of ser. 1, initials G, I, and T of ser. 3, and the triangular tail-piece. He also printed Bibles in octavo and duodecimo. From his press is the edition in 8°, *S.T.C.* 2274, Bible Society no. 307.[4] It is dated 1625 and has on the title-page a woodcut copy of McKerrow and Ferguson's border no. 233. The copy is no. 5 in the Appendix to McKerrow and Ferguson. The opening of Genesis has the same initial I found in most of Stam's quarto Bibles, the one reproduced in Lea Wilson. The opening of Psalms has head-piece no. 3. At the end of the Apocrypha (here included) and again at the end of Revelation is tail-piece no. 1. If this Bible was really printed in 1625 then the first ap-

1. See Prynne's *Canterburies Doom*, 1646, p. 513.
2. Now no. 255.   3. Now no. 584.   4. Now no. 399.

THE ORDER OF TIME,

wherevnto the Contents of this
booke are to be referred.

The yeere of Chrift.

1.&c.

34.

67.

70.

97.

1073.

1217.

1295.

1300.
1301.
1305.

THE dragon watcheth the Church of the Iewes, which was ready to trauaile : She bringeth forth, fleeth, and hideth her felfe, whileft Chrift was yet vpon the earth.

The dragon perfecuted Chrift afcending into heauen, hee fighteth and is throwen down : and after perfecuteth the Church of the Iewes.

The Church of the Iewes is receiued into the wildernefle, for three yeeres and an halfe.

When the Church of the Iewes was ouerthrowen, the dragon inuaded the Catholike Church, all this in the 12. chap.

The dragon is bound for a 1000 yeeres, chap.20.

The dragon raifeth vp the beaft with feuen heads, and the beaft with two heads, which make hauocke of the Church Catholike, and her Prophets for 1260 yeeres after the Paffion of Chrift, chap. 13.and 11.

The feuen Churches are admonifhed of things prefent, fomewhat before the end of Domitian his reigne, & are forewarned of the perfecution to come vnder Traiane for ten yeeres, chap.2. and 3.

God by word and fignes prouoketh the world, and fealeth the godly, chap.6 and 7.

He fheweth foorth examples of his wrath vpon all creatures, mankinde excepted, chap.8.

The dragon is let loofe after 1000. yeeres, and Gregory the vij. being Pope, rageth againft Henrie the third then Emperour, chap.20.

The dragon vexeth the world 150. yeeres, vnto Gregory the ix. who writ the Decretals, and moft cruelly perfecuted the Emperour Frederick the fecond.

The dragon by both the beafts perfecuteth the Church, and putteth the godly to death, chap 9.

The dragon killeth the Prophets after 1260. yeeres, when Boniface the viij. was Pope, who was the author of the fixt booke of the Decretals : hee excommunicated Philip the French King.

Boniface celebrateth the Iubile.

About this time was a great earthquake, which ouerthrew many houfes in Rome.

Prophecie ceafeth for threes yeeres and an halfe, vntill Benedict the fecond fucceeded after Boniface the viij. Prophecie is reuiued, chap.11.

The dragon and the two beafts, oppugne Prophecie, chap.13.

Chrift defendeth his Church in word and deed, chap.14. With threats and armes, chap. 15. with fingular iudgements, chap.16.

Chrift giueth his Church victorie ouer the harlot, chap. 17. and. 18. Ouer the two beafts, chap 19. Ouer the dragon and death, chap.20.

The Church is fully glorified in heauen with eternall glory, in Chrift Iefus, chap.21. and 22.

THE

FIG. 3. Page Ooo 5 verso of the 1599 Bible.

pearance of these two ornaments is earlier than found in signed books and the edition must have been printed by Veseler's widow.

As to editions in duodecimo, *S.T.C.* 2330, Bible Society no. 409,[1] is a 12° dated 1638. It has on the title-page a woodcut border which is no. 8 in the Appendix to McKerrow and Ferguson. It is probably from Stam's press. There is an initial P at the opening of Thessalonians which is in his quarto Bibles at the opening of Ephesians. This Bible was imported in 1656 according to W. Kilburne's *Dangerous Errors*, 1659, as quoted in the Bible Society's *Catalogue*. Kilburne accuses Kiffin and Henry Hills of being responsible for this edition. Probably in all cases an English bookseller was the moving spirit. The Bible Society quotes also a passage from Robert Baillie, 1668, referring to the same edition.

In Kleerkooper's *De Boekhandel te Amsterdam* there is reproduced an agreement, dated 29 March 1644, between Hugo Fitz, merchant of Amsterdam, and J. F. Stam and Thomas Craffurt about the delivery and payment for 6,000 Bibles in 12°. It is suggested in the Bible Society's *Catalogue* that their no. 448[2] may be a copy of the edition referred to.

In 1645 Jan van Hilten himself took over the printing of his news-sheet and Stam's business seems to have declined. From Charles Enschedé's *Fonderies de caractères dans les Pays-Bas*, p. 97, we learn that in 1650 the whole of his workshop was bought for 5,000 guilders by the type-founder Jacques Vallet. This may mean that Stam had a foundry attached to his printing business and that this foundry was sold. Stam still printed an occasional book, the latest being of 1657, *Het eerste deel der Napelsche Beroerte*.

[1954]

---

1. Now no. 529, to which is attached a long, relevant note.
2. Now no. 578.

TYPOGRAPHY AT THE CAMBRIDGE
UNIVERSITY PRESS, *c.* 1700

MUCH has been written about the Fell types and the reform in printing at the Oxford University Press towards the end of the seventeenth century, but little about the contemporary revival at Cambridge. No type foundry was established at Cambridge, but with the help of new types purchased from Holland in 1697 and the few following years, a number of books were produced well worthy to be compared with Oxford books printed with the Fell types.

For details of the measures taken by the University from 1696 towards the improvement of their press, the reader may be referred to S. C. Roberts's *History of the Cambridge University Press*, chapter v. We learn that on July 10, 1696, the famous Dr. Richard Bentley, who to some extent played the part of Dr. John Fell at Oxford, was given authority to buy types. In January 1698 we hear that a large consignment of Dutch types (fifty-two alphabets) had reached Harwich on its way to Cambridge. Again, on August 23 of the same year, the inspector of the press, Cornelius Crownfield, has 'leave to send to Rotterdam for 300 l. weight of the double Pica letter in order to the printing of Virgil, Horace, &c.' On May 3, 1699, it was ordered that 400 lb. weight of Paragon Greek Letter be sent for to the Widow Voskens (i. e., the widow of the founder, Dirk Voskens) in Holland. We see that Cambridge bought types, not matrices, and bought them in Holland. From a comparison of books printed at Cambridge from 1697 onwards with the specimen sheets of contemporary Dutch founders many of the new founts can be identified, and it appears that most of the dealings were with the Van Dijck firm. Nowhere in England was there such a fine display of Van Dijck's romans and italics as at Cambridge in the early years of the eighteenth century.

Christoffel van Dijck was the most distinguished type-cutter in Holland in the seventeenth century. He was born in 1601, and worked in Amsterdam at first as a goldsmith. In 1648 he was established as a type-founder, and between that year and his death in 1671 or 1672 he cut many types – romans and italics, Greeks, Hebrews, and Black Letters. His stock ultimately came into the hands of the firm of Enschedé of Haarlem, and to this day that house still possesses a few of his types: one Greek, one Hebrew, three Blacks, but no romans, and only one size of italic, Text, i. e., great primer. No specimen sheet issued by Van Dijck himself is known, but we have several issued by his successors. Van Dijck's son Abraham died shortly after his father, and the foundry was purchased by Daniel Elzevir, whose widow printed a specimen sheet of the stock in 1681. This sheet – the earliest we know – is reproduced in Willems's *Les Elzevir*, 1880, and there is also a reduced reproduction in Updike's *Printing Types*: Fig. 207. Charles Enschedé, in his *Fonderies de caractères dans les Pays-Bas*, gives specimens of the surviving types of Van Dijck, and also a table showing which of the types on the sheet of 1681 were cut by Van Dijck and which were from other foundries. From the records of his firm Enschedé knew that in some cases his ancestor had acquired the actual

275

QUINTI

HORATII FLACCI

SATYRARUM

LIBER II.

SATYRA I.

Sunt quibus in fatyra videar nimis acer, & ultra
Legem tendere opus: fine nervis altera, quidquid
Compofui, pars effe putat, fimilefque meorum
Mille die verfus deduci poffe. Trebati,
Quid faciam, præfcribe. Quiefcas. Ne faciam, inquis, 5
Omnino verfus? Aio. Peream male, fi non

Mm 2   Opti-

FIG. 1. Double Pica roman (Christoffel van Dijck's Ascendonica) from Horace, *Opera.*
Cambridge, 1699. (Reduced.)

punches, and these types he judged to have been cut by Van Dijck. Of the rest we know, in any event, that some were older than Van Dijck; some, for instance, were sixteenth-century types acquired from the Luther foundry at Frankfurt.

I propose now to trace some of the Van Dijck types in Cambridge printed books.

Although the first document relating to the arrival of Dutch types at Cambridge is of 1698, yet it appears from existing printed books that the Press had some Van Dijck types already in 1697. A collection of poems entitled *Gratulatio Academiae Cantabrigiensis de reditu Gulielmi III*, is set in Van Dijck's Text (great primer), roman and italic; this size of the italic is the one which has survived to this day. The verses in Greek and Hebrew at the end are grouped separately because, as we are told, the new types had not arrived '*quod typi novi Academici nondum ad nos pervenerint*'. In 1698 the Press was using the Augustijn (English) roman and italic of Van Dijck, e. g., in a sermon of Francis Hutchinson. In the edition of Horace published by Jacob Tonson for the Press in 1699 we meet a whole series of Dutch types, most of them Van Dijck's. The main text is set in a double pica roman, Van Dijck's Ascendonica. The dedication is in his Kleine Kanon, with a little of the italic. The address 'Lectori' before the notes is in the Text size, which the Press had by 1697. Finally, the notes are set in a pica roman and italic, among the most interesting of the types acquired at this time, which we will describe more fully. We may add that the editions of Virgil, 1701, and of Catullus, Propertius, and Tibullus, 1702, are exactly similar volumes typographically.

The pica roman used for the notes is also shown on the Van Dijck specimen sheets. It is the Mediaen romeyn, No. 2. Charles Enschedé says that this type was not cut by Van Dijck, for he found that no punches were acquired by his firm. His conclusion in this case is borne out by the fact that the type was in existence long before Van Dijck's day. This roman has several spot letters which make it easily recognizable. In the upper-case the E has the lower arm distinctly longer than the upper and middle arms, the M has no serif on the right-hand upright, and the P is an oddly small letter. In the lower-case, the g has a long link, and is quite different in design from the Garamond g. This type is a Paris design of the sixteenth century; the earliest book in which I have found it is in the octavo edition of Geofroy Tory's *Champ fleury*, V. Gaultherot, 1549. About that time the well-known French type-designer, Robert Granjon, printed a few books in Paris in partnership with Michel Fezendat. Our pica roman appears in those books, so that it is not impossible that it was cut by Granjon. The type had a fairly wide sale in Europe; we have noted its use in Venice by Paolo Manuzio, and by Girolamo Scotto in 1557, at Antwerp in 1558, and in Frankfurt in 1574. On the specimen sheets of the Voskens firm there is a Mediaen roman, which is either the same type with some altered letters, or a deliberate copy. The italic which the Cambridge Press used with this pica is not on the Van Dijck sheets. Except for the swash J, this italic agrees with the Cicero italic shown by Voskens, which is a sixteenth-century type cut by Robert Granjon, and shown on most of the specimens of the Luther foundry at Frankfurt.

There is in existence at the Press 'A Specimen of the Letters belonging to the University of Cambridge', a unique sheet which displays romans and italics from two-line English to minion, and also a few exotics. Unfortunately, so little of each size is shown

432.

LECTORI S.

Cum non fuerit hujus inftituti aliquid Commentarii Horatio apponere; quod quidem nobis tot doctiffimorum Interpretum, & fupra omnes, *Lambini, Torrentii,* & *Dacieri* felix in hac parte induftria fupervacaneum fecerat: id præcipuè laborandum duximus, ut quantum lucis Poetæ optimo ex Scholiis in hac Editione omiffis defiderari videatur, tantum etiam ei ex Textu fummâ fide & diligentiâ accurato accederet. Undique igitur conquifitis, atque inter fe collatis optimæ notæ Exemplaribus, quæ poft artem Typographicam inventam in lucem prodiêre; cùm in fingulis fere fingulorum paginis aliquid à cæteris diverfum occurreret, quod non Typographorum incuriæ, fed nimiæ plerumque Editorum diligentiæ deberi conftitit; dum eorum alii unius atque alterius apud fe Membranæ téftimonio, alii ingenio fuo plus æquo tribuentes, Conjecturis fuis & Caftigationibus plagam fubinde Horatio infligerent: placuit in tanto omnium diffenfu, liberum exercere judicium, & præclarum illud Poetæ noftri præceptum in eo edendo fequi; nempe in nullius verba addictum jurare, fed ad fontes potiùs remotos, quantum per damnofæ ætatis injuriam licuit, accedere; unde aquas magis aliquando jucundas, aut faltem minùs turbatas haurire contingeret. Quocirca, præter magnum illum MSS. numerum, quibus *Muretus, Lambinus, Fabricius, Cruquius, Pulmannus* & *Torrentius* ufi funt, alios etiam ex utriufque apud nos Academiæ Archivis, & Reverendi Doctiffimique Viri *Thomæ Gale* Ecclefiæ *Eboracenfis* Decani Mufæo fuppeditatos, in hujus Operis adornandi confilium adhibuimus. Oxonienfes quidem Codices ad *Tan. Fabri* Exemplar, operâ Ornatiffimorum VV. M^{ti} *Creech* Collegii *Omnium Animarum*, & M^{ti} *Dennifon* Collegii *Univerfitatis* Soc. accuratiffimè collatos præftitit, & ad nos tranfmifit Cl. *Arthurus Charlet* S. T. P. ejus Collegii Præfectus digniffimus. E Cantabrigienfibus, pulcherrimum Cardinalis *Bembi* Codicem, *Henrici Wottoni* Equitis apud Venetos quondam Legati munus, quâ folet benevolentiâ, ex Collegii *Regalis* Bibliothecâ ultro obtulit Eruditiffimus *Carolus Roderick* S. T. P. ejufdem Collegii Præpofitus. His adjuti fubfidiis, quorum Notas inferiùs adhibitas fubjecta Tabula indicabit, noftram hanc Editionem ad optimorum Exemplarium

Fig. 2. Text size of Christoffel van Dijck's roman, from Horace, *Opera.* Cambridge, 1699. (Reduced.)

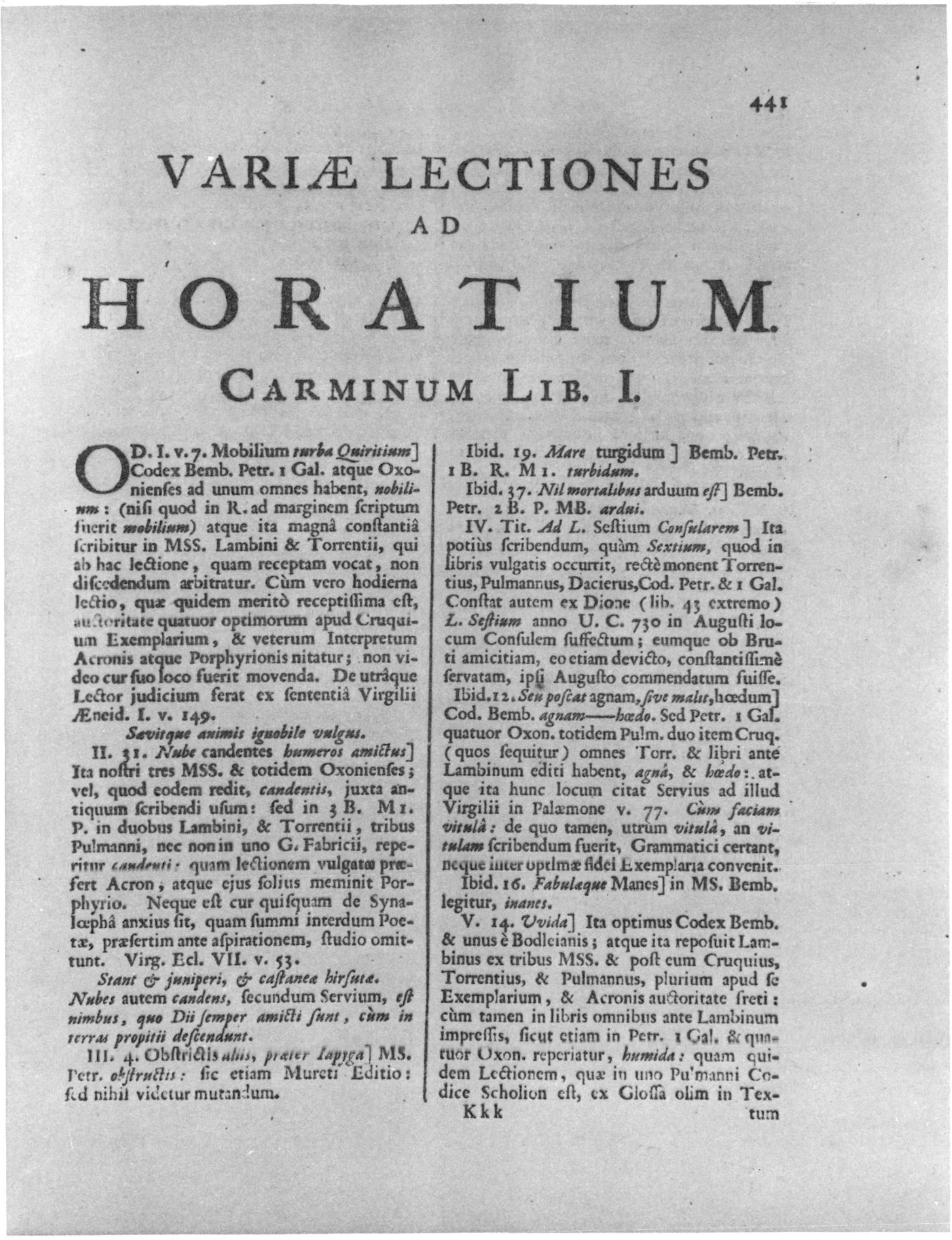

441

VARIÆ LECTIONES
AD
HORATIUM.
CARMINUM LIB. I.

OD. I. v. 7. Mobilium *turba Quiritium*] Codex Bemb. Petr. 1 Gal. atque Oxonienses ad unum omnes habent, *nobilium* : (nisi quod in R. ad marginem scriptum fuerit *mobilium*) atque ita magnâ constantiâ scribitur in MSS. Lambini & Torrentii, qui ab hac lectione, quam receptam vocat, non discedendum arbitratur. Cùm vero hodierna lectio, quæ quidem meritò receptissima est, auctoritate quatuor optimorum apud Cruquium Exemplarium, & veterum Interpretum Acronis atque Porphyrionis nitatur; non video cur suo loco fuerit movenda. De utrâque Lector judicium ferat ex sententiâ Virgilii Æneid. I. v. 149.

Sævitque animis ignobile vulgus.

II. 31. *Nube* candentes *humeros amictus*] Ita nostri tres MSS. & totidem Oxonienses; vel, quod eodem redit, *candentis*, juxta antiquum scribendi usum: sed in 3 B. M 1. P. in duobus Lambini, & Torrentii, tribus Pulmanni, nec non in uno G. Fabricii, reperitur *candenti*: quam lectionem vulgatæ præfert Acron, atque ejus solius meminit Porphyrio. Neque est cur quisquam de Synaloephâ anxius sit, quam summi interdum Poetæ, præsertim ante aspirationem, studio omittunt. Virg. Ecl. VII. v. 53.

Stant & juniperi, & castanea hirsuta.

Nubes autem *candens*, secundum Servium, est *nimbus*, *quo Dii semper amicti sunt, cùm in terras propitii descendunt.*

III. 4. Obstrictis *aliis, præter Iapyga*] MS. Petr. *obstructis*: sic etiam Mureti Editio: sed nihil videtur mutandum.

Ibid. 19. *Mare* turgidum] Bemb. Petr. 1 B. R. M 1. *turbidum.*

Ibid. 37. *Nil mortalibus* arduum *est*] Bemb. Petr. 2 B. P. MB. *ardui.*

IV. Tit. *Ad L.* Sestium *Consularem*] Ita potiùs scribendum, quàm *Sextium*, quod in libris vulgatis occurrit, rectè monent Torrentius, Pulmannus, Dacierus, Cod. Petr. & 1 Gal. Constat autem ex Dione (lib. 43 extremo) *L. Sestium* anno U. C. 730 in Augusti locum Consulem suffectum; eumque ob Bruti amicitiam, eo etiam devicto, constantissimè servatam, ipsi Augusto commendatum fuisse.

Ibid. 12. *Seu poscat* agnam, *sive malis*, hoedum] Cod. Bemb. *agnam——hoedo.* Sed Petr. 1 Gal. quatuor Oxon. totidem Pulm. duo item Cruq. (quos sequitur) omnes Torr. & libri antè Lambinum editi habent, *agnâ*, & *hoedo*: atque ita hunc locum citat Servius ad illud Virgilii in Palæmone v. 77. *Cùm faciam vitulâ:* de quo tamen, utrùm *vitulâ*, an *vitulam* scribendum fuerit, Grammatici certant, neque inter optimæ fidei Exemplaria convenit.

Ibid. 16. *Fabulæque* Manes] in MS. Bemb. legitur, *inanes.*

V. 14. *Uvida*] Ita optimus Codex Bemb. & unus è Bodleianis; atque ita reposuit Lambinus ex tribus MSS. & post eum Cruquius, Torrentius, & Pulmannus, plurium apud se Exemplarium, & Acronis auctoritate freti : cùm tamen in libris omnibus ante Lambinum impressis, sicut etiam in Petr. 1 Gal. & quatuor Oxon. reperiatur, *humida*: quam quidem Lectionem, quæ in uno Pulmanni Codice Scholion est, ex Glossâ olim in Textum

K k k tum

FIG. 3. Mediaen romeyn No. 2 from Van Dijck's Specimen sheet, but cut before 1549 at Paris, possibly by Robert Granjon. From Horace, *Opera*. Cambridge, 1699. (Reduced.)

that identification is difficult. In the case of the pica roman, however, we are helped by the fact that this size is used for the headings. We can confidently identify the 'old pica' as the roman used for the notes of the Horace of 1699 and in the edition of Tory of 1549. We can also identify the 'old great primer' and 'oldest great primer' as Van Dijck's Text, roman and italic, and the 'new great primer' as Caslon's. The sheet is not dated, but on two of the specimens the dates 1730 and 1721 occur, apparently with no special significance. Since Caslon's great primer is shown, the sheet can hardly have been printed before 1732.

There are still two other Dutch types, or types purchased in Holland, found in Cambridge books of this period. The edition of Sir Thomas Browne's *Christian Morals*, 1716, is set in a roman, English in size, which appears on the specimen sheet of an Amsterdam printer, Johannes Kannewet, *c.* 1710. The italic shown with it is Van Dijck's Augustijn, and this italic also accompanied it in Cambridge- and London-printed books. I have not found the roman on a specimen of a Dutch founder, but we may presume that it was Dutch. This type was used for the main text of the edition of John Selden's works printed at London in two large volumes in 1726, and it is so like Caslon that it has been mistaken for his.[1] Part of the second volume of the Selden is set in a different roman, still with the same Van Dijck italic, a type which also was at Cambridge and which is shown on the Van Dijck sheets. It is his Augustijn No. 2, which, according to Enschedé, was not cut by Van Dijck, but came from the Luther foundry at Frankfurt. It does not appear on the earliest Frankfurt sheets, but on a sheet of 1664. This roman has a lower-case g in which the loop is rather wider than the bowl, and, if we may trust to this one letter, it appears to be the 'Old English No. 2' of the Cambridge specimen sheet. As to its use in Cambridge-printed books, it will be found in several volumes of the octavo edition of the works of Cicero. This edition, known as the edition '*cum notis variorum*', began to appear in 1725, and its publication extended over a number of years. The *Academica*, 1725, edited by John Davies, is set in the Augustijn No. 2 of the Van Dijck sheet, and with it is used the italic also shown by Van Dijck. This second Augustijn italic of the Dutch founder is a mixed affair, the upper-case only, according to Enschedé, being cut by Van Dijck, while the lower-case is Granjon, dating from about 1566. The succeeding volumes of the Cambridge Cicero remained the same in format and in typography, until we come to the *De Oratore*, 1732, in the edition of Zachary Pearce. This volume is in the same format, but the type used is Caslon's English roman and italic. This size of Caslon had been used already at Cambridge in Cicero's *De Divinatione*, 1730, but only in the address to the reader. Caslon's great primer, which, as already mentioned, appears on the Cambridge specimen sheet, I have first found at Cambridge in 1733, in *Remarks on Christianity as Old as Creation* by M. Tindall.

We have enumerated seven romans and five italics used at Cambridge which were Dutch, or at least purchased in Holland, and this list could, no doubt, be extended. There were probably some Dutch titlings, and almost certainly some of the sizes below pica were similarly acquired. As to these smaller sizes, it is more difficult to identify

1. See *The Monotype Recorder*, vol. xxxv, No. 4, 1936–7, on Caslon's imitations of Dutch types, with reproductions; reprinted, in sightly different form, in Reed, *Old English Letter Foundries*, 1952.

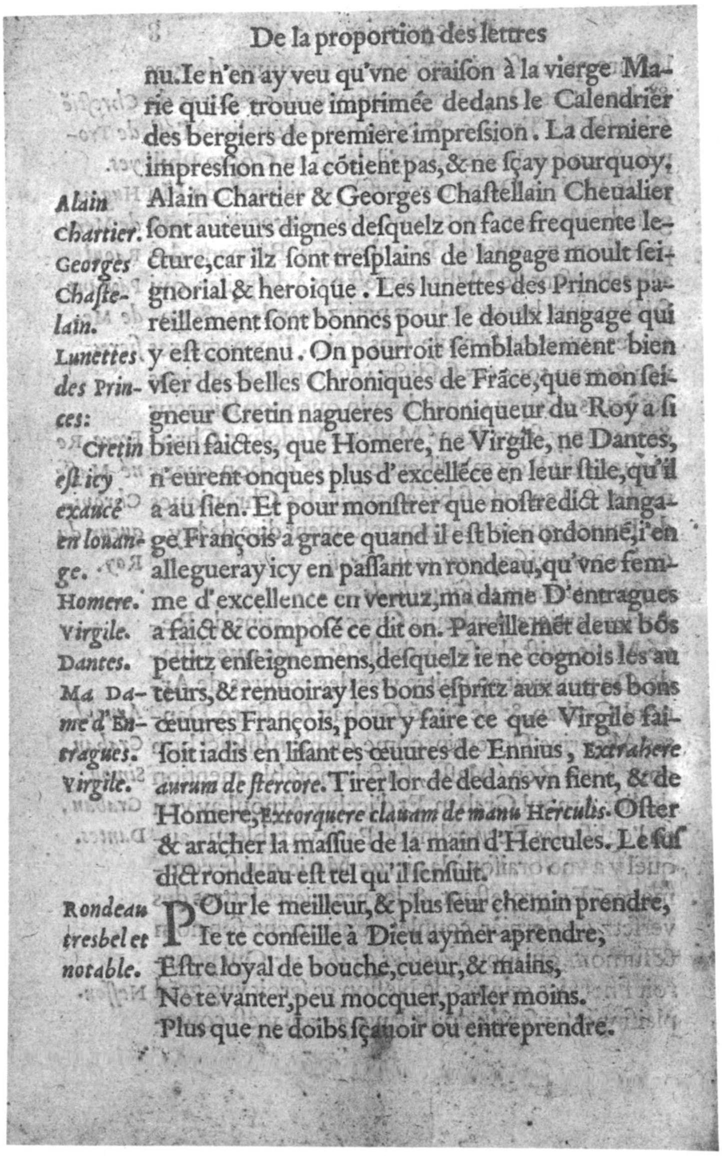

De la proportion des lettres

nu. Ie n'en ay veu qu'vne oraifon à la vierge Marie qui fe trouue imprimée dedans le Calendrier des bergiers de premiere impreffion. La derniere impreffion ne la côtient pas, & ne fçay pourquoy.

Alain Alain Chartier & Georges Chaftellain Cheualier
Chartier. font auteurs dignes defquelz on face frequente le-
Georges cture, car ilz font trefplains de langage moult fei-
Chafte- gnorial & heroïque. Les lunettes des Princes pa-
lain. reillement font bonnes pour le doulx langage qui
Lunettes y eft contenu. On pourroit femblablement bien
des Prin- vfer des belles Chroniques de Frâce, que monfei-
ces: gneur Cretin nagueres Chroniqueur du Roy a fi
Cretin bien faictes, que Homere, ne Virgile, ne Dantes,
eft icy n'eurent onques plus d'excelléce en leur ftile, qu'il
exaucé a au fien. Et pour monftrer que noftredict langa-
en loüan- ge François a grace quand il eft bien ordonné, i'en
ge. allegueray icy en paffant vn rondeau, qu'vne fem-
Homere. me d'excellence en vertuz, ma dame D'entragues
Virgile. a faict & compofé ce dit on. Pareillemēt deux bōs
Dantes. petitz enfeignemens, defquelz ie ne cognois lés au
Ma Da- teurs, & renuoiray les bons efpritz aux autres bons
me d'En- œuures François, pour y faire ce que Virgile fai-
tragues. foit iadis en lifant es œuures de Ennius, *Extrahere*
Virgile. *aurum de ftercore.* Tirer lor de dedans vn fient, & de
Homere, *Extorquere clauam de manu Herculis.* Ofter
& aracher la maffue de la main d'Hercules. Le fuf
dict rondeau eft tel qu'il fenfuit.

Rondeau POur le meilleur, & plus feur chemin prendre,
tresbel et Ie te confeille à Dieu aymer aprendre,
notable. Eftre loyal de bouche, cueur, & mains,
Ne te vanter, peu mocquer, parler moins.
Plus que ne doibs fçauoir ou entreprendre.

FIG. 4. The Pica roman from the Cambridge Horace, as used in Geofroy Tory, *Champ fleury*. Vivant Gaultherot, Paris, 1549.

designs with confidence. Reed, in his *Old English Letter Foundries*, says that between 1700 and 1720 there was probably more Dutch type used in England than English. This was certainly true of Cambridge printing, with the proviso that some of the types bought in Holland did not start life there. All the main body types used at Cambridge in this period were of Dutch origin, and these new types were chiefly responsible for the decided improvement in the University printing.

[1938]

THE 'GOÛT HOLLANDOIS'

IN THE first half of the eighteenth century books printed in Germany in roman types, that is to say books written in Latin, of which there were still a large number, present an unusual appearance, very different from the corresponding publications of France and Italy. This strangeness is due to the fact that the pages are set solidly in types which are of comparatively heavy weight, somewhat condensed, and which have a large x-height, that is to say have short ascenders and descenders. The types are in what the French designer, P. S. Fournier, called the 'goût hollandois', although he should more correctly have written the 'goût allemand'. They represent a break with the Garamond tradition, under the influence of the Black Letters, Fraktur and Schwabacher, which, in common with all Black Letters, have a large x-height. Attention has been directed to the history of such types by Stanley Morison in an article entitled 'Leipzig as a centre of type-founding', which appeared in *Signature*, no. 11, 1939.

Morison's article is concerned in particular with a series of romans and italics called 'Janson', perhaps the best design in the style and apparently the only one surviving to-day. He discusses the possible connexion of the series with Anton Janson, type-founder at Leipzig, their early appearance in Holland, and their contact with Black Letter. He stresses their importance in the history of type forms, since they are in some ways the forerunners of the modern faces. In the present article I propose to trace the beginnings of the style back into the seventeenth century by a comparison of types shown on some founders' specimens and those found in printed books. I shall begin with a few notes on the use of the pseudo-Janson series in the last decade of the seventeenth century; these notes, however, do not clear up, but rather increase the mystery of the origin of this design.

One of the few things which can be definitely asserted about the history of the 'Janson' series is that it did not originate with Anton Janson, type-founder at Leipzig. A further argument, in addition to those advanced by Morison against the attribution to Janson, can be drawn from the specimen sheet of his successor, J. C. Edling, published at Leipzig in 1689. This sheet displays none of the pseudo-Janson romans or italics. It seems likely that they were originally cut either at Amsterdam or at Leipzig, or possibly some sizes at the one city and some at the other. And yet they do not appear in books printed at either city before about 1700, as far as I have been able to discover. One size only of the italic found its way to England and appears in three English specimen books or sheets, that of Oxford, 1695, of the Heirs of Anderson, Edinburgh, 1698, and of James Orme, 1698. In English printed books it can be traced back to 1692, e. g. on the title-page of John Shower's *Mourner's Companion*, London. Thomas Rymer's *Fœdera*, the first volume of which appeared in 1704, has a fine display of this italic in the preliminaries. The size is the Kleine Canon of the German and Dutch specimens. It is worth noting that on the Amsterdam specimen of Adamzoon and Ente dating from *c.* 1710-15, only two romans are shown, Groote Paragon and Groote Text, and nine sizes of italic, whereas ultimately the complete series included fourteen sizes of each.

It appears from fig. 119 in Updike's *Printing Types* that a printer at Florence, G. P. Cecchi, used the type as early as any one so far recorded, in the third edition of the *Saggi di naturali esperienze* of the Accademia del Cimento. Cecchi had at least five sizes, Ascendonica, Paragon, Tertia, Mittel, and Corpus, and all his books that I have seen after 1691 show one or more of them. The types continued in use at Florence at least as late as 1784. A few of the best books printed by Cecchi and his successors are: L. Adimari, *Poesie sacre*, 1696, *Ricettario Fiorentino*, 1696, both Cecchi, F. Redi's *Sonetti*, 1702, and A. M. Salvini's *Sonetti*, 1728.

The only printer I have found of the seventeenth century whose use of pseudo-Janson can be compared with that of Cecchi in extent is Ulrich Liebpert, typographer of the Electors Frederick William and Frederick III of Brandenburg, at Berlin. Of dated books showing the type I know of nothing earlier than 1696, e. g. various works of the numismatist Laurentius Beger. There is in the British Museum a collection of elegiac poems and the like relating to the death of the Elector Frederick William, an event which took place in 1688. None of these pieces bears a dated imprint and, although doubtless in manuscript by 1688, it is probable that their printing dates from a few years later. Other works by L. Beger, e. g. *Spicilegium antiquitatis* of 1692, suggest that Liebpert had no pseudo-Jansons by that year. Liebpert had the Tertia and Mittel sizes, and other examples of his use of the type may be seen in an edition of Bidpai in Greek and Latin, 1697, and in a *Specimen versionis Coranicæ*, 1698. That the two printers before 1700 who most favoured this design were working respectively at Florence and at Berlin does not help us to trace the home of the founder.

To return to the general history of types of a large x-height, as pointed out by Morison, no part was at first taken in the development by the old-established Luther foundry at Frankfurt. That house was well stocked with French types characterized by long ascenders and descenders, and it was not until the eighteenth century that the Luther firm was forced by the trend of fashion to imitate the Leipzig and Nuremberg typecutters. An examination of the specimen sheets issued by Anton Janson at Leipzig and by the house of Baumann at Nuremberg will throw some light on the origin of the new style.

Anton Janson issued two dated broadsides of roman and italic types, the first in 1678, reproduced as fig. 3 (reduced) by Morison, op. cit., and the second of large sizes only in 1683. Both sheets open with ten lines of 'modern' titlings (not all are 'modern' on the earlier sheet). Morison has reproduced a sheet [fig. 4] of similar roman capitals issued by the Luther firm in 1716, called by them 'Fette Versalien'. Such capitals, with a sharp differentiation of thin and thick strokes and a uniform narrowness, are already foreshadowed in Janson's titlings, most of which are shown also in Paulus Pater's *Dissertatio*, 1710. The condensation has not yet been thoroughly carried out, but the intention is already there. Similar 'fette' capitals were shown by Conrad Baumann at Nuremberg in 1669, and in books they may be found at least as early as 1652, e. g. on the title-page of A. Vimina's *La Gara*, Vienna.

Following the titlings are three very large sizes of romans (the first only on the 1678 sheet), Missal, Kleine Missal, and Grobe Canon. These three sizes, presumably

*excellere in hoc genere cupiat: in quo propter ignoran-
tiam plerorumque parvum quoque laborem magnæ eruditionis fama sequi solet? De isto vero libro Arabes
idem, quod de Homero suo Græci contendunt: eum esse,
in quo neque, quem imitaretur, Muhammed habuerit, neque spem reliquerit cuiquam, qui vellet eundem imitari.
Tantamque illi in omni genere laudem, tantam simplici-
tatem styli, tantam sermonis puritatem, elegantiamque
huic uni libro tribuunt: Quam neque capere, nec inter-
pretari quisquam, nisi multum diuque exercitatus possit.
Itaque etiam ex illa gente maxima esse dicitur multitu-
do eorum, qui in explicandis unius hujus libri sensibus
fuerunt occupati. Quorum aliquos non contemnendos,*

FIG. 1. The pseudo-Janson italic. From *Specimen versionis Coranicae.*
Ulrich Liebpert, Berlin, 1698.

LECTORI S.

Pistolas scribe-
re vulgare qui-
dem & omni-
bus in proclivi; benè
scribere id vero ardu-
um & difficile. Excel-
luerunt hac in re apud
seculum prius viri ma-
gni & nõ nisi cũ hono-

FIG. 2. Two-line Pica roman shown by Bartholomaeus
Voskens and Anton Janson. From Joannes Wowerius,
Epistolarum centuriae II. Hamburg, 1608.

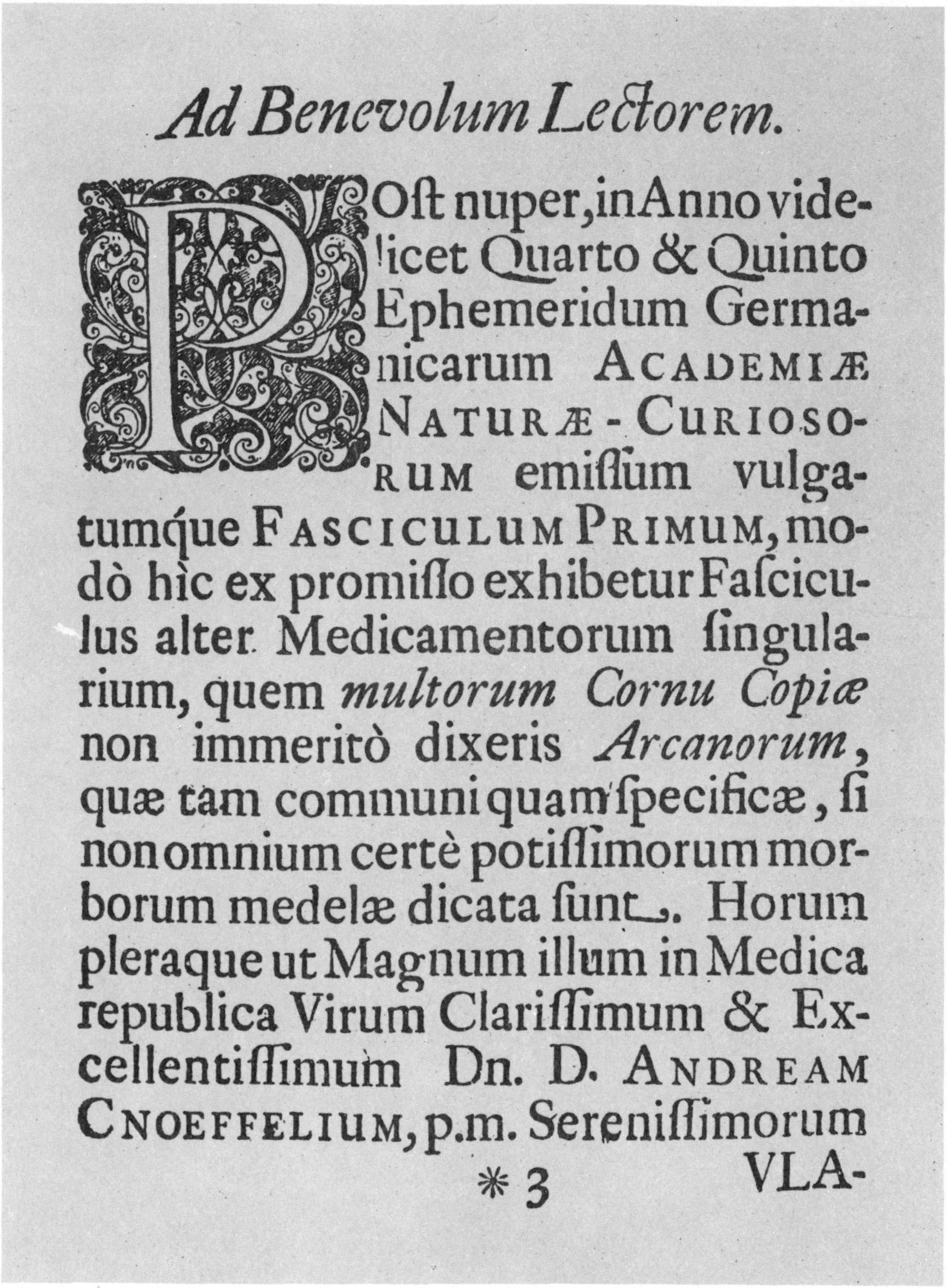

Ad Benevolum Lectorem.

Post nuper, in Anno vide-
licet Quarto & Quinto
Ephemeridum Germa-
nicarum ACADEMIÆ
NATURÆ - CURIOSO-
rum emiſſum vulga-
tumque FASCICULUM PRIMUM, mo-
dò hìc ex promiſſo exhibetur Faſcicu-
lus alter. Medicamentorum ſingula-
rium, quem *multorum Cornu Copiæ*
non immeritò dixeris *Arcanorum*,
quæ tam communi quam ſpecificæ, ſi
non omnium certè potiſſimorum mor-
borum medelæ dicata ſunt. Horum
pleraque ut Magnum illum in Medica
republica Virum Clariſſimum & Ex-
cellentiſſimum Dn. D. ANDREAM
CNOEFFELIUM, p.m. Sereniſſimorum

* 3   VLA-

FIG. 3. Anton Janson's Text roman with Reinhard Voskens's italic. From
Miscellanea curiosa Academiae Naturae Curiosorum. Leipzig, 1677.

cut by Janson, belong to the new style by virtue of their weight and x-height, although very little condensed. I have not seen the Missal in any book, but as far as one can judge from the two lines shown on the sheet one must allow that this type in serif formation also is a 'modern face'. Next follows Kleine Canon, roman and italic. From a note of Herr Gustav Mori I understand that this roman was cut by Pancratz Lobinger, type-cutter at Nuremberg. I have found the type in books printed in Austria, e. g. in J. L. Schönleben's *Dissertatio de prima origine domus Habspurgo-Austriacæ*, J. B. Mayr, Labaci, 1680. Mayr used the type also at Salzburg in the *Corona gratulatoria seu gratulationes quas magnis principibus accinuit Universitas Salisburgensis*, 1681. A good display of both the roman and the italic may be seen in C. Zeigener's *Oratio in laudem illustris Academiae*, Brunswick, 1687.

The next size, Roman (2-line Pica in English), is again not Janson's and belongs to an earlier generation. It is found on the sheet issued by Bartholomaeus Voskens at Hamburg about 1665,[1] and that founder probably acquired it in that city, for it occurs in books printed there from 1602. A few words appear in the imprint of an edition of the Psalms in Hebrew printed by Philip de Orr for Froben and several pages in the preliminaries of the Old Testament in Hebrew issued by the same firm in 1603, and again in Rodericus a Castro's *De universa mulierum medicina*, 1603. It was in use at Wittenberg by 1606, Frankfurt an der Oder by 1609, and Jena by 1610, and is in G. L. Fuhrmann's specimen book, Nuremberg, 1616, where the size is described as Petit Canon and the design wrongly attributed to Garamond. It was in common use throughout Germany in the seventeenth and early eighteenth century. It is shown in Ernesti's *Die wol-eingerichtete Buchdruckerey*, 1721 and 1733 (Type no. VI). The accompanying italic was, we may confidently assume, cut by Reinier Voskens of Amsterdam, who worked for a time in Frankfurt and issued a specimen sheet there about 1665.[2] On this sheet Voskens describes the types as 'mit eigener Handt geschnittenen Schrifften'. The sheet displays four romans, three italics, four Frakturs, and one Script, so that the achievement is quite possible. A specimen of the Luther foundry of 1664 also shows this italic, and again Ernesti's book (Type no. XXIV) and Pater's *Dissertatio*.

With the next size, Text (Double Pica), we return to the new style. The earliest use of this size, a very popular type for preliminaries which I have come across in books, is in 1666 in J. G. Trumphius's *Scrutinium chimicum vitrioli*, S. Krebs, Jena. The italic shown with it by Janson is again a design of R. Voskens, his Parangon Cursiiff. This may be seen in a Leipzig book, J. Brunnemann's *Commentarius in duodecim libros codicis Justinianei*, 1679. Both the roman and italic appear in Ernesti (nos. VII and XXV) and in Pater.

Of Janson's Parangon roman the variety of letters shown is not sufficient to allow of identification. The design does not mark it off as definitely one of the new group, although its x-height is rather greater than that of a Garamond. If this is the Parangon Antiqua in Ernesti (no. VII), then it dates back to a period before Janson. I find this

1. Reproduced in G. Mori's *Die Schriftgiesser B. Voskens in Hamburg und R. Voskens in Frankfurt*, 1923.
2. Idem.

roman at Hamburg in 1650 at the press of J. Rebenlinus and at Salzburg in 1663, used by J. B. Mayr. This is the smallest size shown on the sheet of 1683. The Tertia on the sheet of 1679 is also inadequately displayed, although I suspect that in this case we have a sixteenth-century type. The same italic appears to accompany both the Parangon and the Tertia, and may very well be another sixteenth-century design.

Janson issued another, smaller sheet, which is reproduced to size by Morison at his fig. 1. This is the most interesting of all Janson's specimens, because it contains direct evidence that the types shown were actually cut by Janson. The Mittel roman is dated 1673, the Cicero roman 1672, a Cicero Arabic 1673, and a Cicero Samaritan 1674. All four are signed with the initials A. I. The two romans are the earliest body types in the new style and were widely used in the next generation. The Mittel appears in W. Schickhardus's *Jus regium Hebraeorum*, Leipzig, 1674. It is shown by Pater in 1710, on p. 39, where it is described as 'Grobe', a word which seems to have the same meaning as the French term 'gros œil', that is large-faced. Whether it also conveys the meaning of heavy, which is a usual characteristic of the family, is not clear. The Mittel was still being shown in 1727, for example on the sheet of J. B. Kirchner, Brunswick.[1] The 'Neue grobe Cicero' shown by Pater and reproduced by Morison bears a close resemblance in design to Janson's Cicero. Some of the capitals are different and Pater's type appears to be the heavier, but whoever cut the later design clearly modelled himself on Janson. Pater's type was already in use at Leipzig by 1686, as may be seen in the Leipzig edition of the *Catalogus universalis* for that year. Obviously, one would say, a German type, but for the surprising fact that Pater calls it 'Amstelodamensis'. The type occurs in no Amsterdam specimen known to me and I have failed to find it in any Amsterdam printed book. In the passage in Pater describing the size Cicero, which Morison has translated,[2] Pater refers to the types in the Ehrhardt foundry at Leipzig acquired through the heirs of Edling from Janson. F. C. Lesser in his *Typographia jubilans*, 1740, causes confusion by adding the words 'bought in Holland', a statement which might apply to the series of pseudo-Janson types, which were also in the Ehrhardt foundry, but is surely not correct of the true Janson material. Pater has diplayed, as we have seen, several sizes of romans and italics which descended from the Janson foundry, and one would expect him to show the Cicero along with the Mittel from the same foundry. If Janson himself, as stated by some modern writers, with what authority is unknown to me, was of Dutch origin, this might be the explanation of the confusion.

On Janson's sheet of 1678 a second Mittel roman is shown, a type which was in existence by 1672, as may be seen in J. M. Schwimmer's *Tractatus politicus de academicis professoribus*, J. Bielcke, Jena. Whether or not this roman was cut by Janson, neither of the italics of this size displayed on the sheet were of his design. The first is the 'Neue grobe Mittel Cursiv' of Reinhard Voskens, *c.* 1665, and the second is a sixteenth-century type. This latter italic was common at Frankfort from about 1570, but appears to have been cut at Antwerp, where it will be found from 1551 (e. g. in C. Stummelius's *Stu-*

---

1. Reproduced by E. Crous in *Die Schriftgiessereien in Königsberg*, 1926.
2. Op. cit., p. 11.

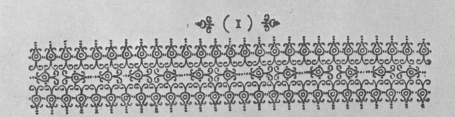

Prooemium.

elix certè Pharisaismus, qvô Paulus,
qvi antea qvidem qvàm Christo no-
men dederat, Pharisæus sed nomine
saltem impiè pius & indoctè doctus
errabat, postea verè Pharisæi dignus
cognomine à Servatore ipso selectus
segregatusq; ad obeundum præclarissi-
mum illud prædicationis Evangelii munus fuit, ita ut
qvi antea Pharisaicæ factionis propugnator fuit, postea
dogmatum ejusdem refutator factus sit, qvi olim rapa-
cissimus lupus, postea diligentissimus ovium Pastor, qvi
primùm infensissimus Ecclesiæ persecutor, demum ob-
servantissimus ejusdem Curator evaserit. Ejus autem
rei fundamentum si velis urgere, certam adeò firmam-
q; eandem sacræ reddiderunt paginæ, ut nulla ulterius
dubitatio de eadem oriri qveat. At verò si nomina ipsius
placuerit ad trutinam revocare, nihil freqventius Inter-
pretibus, nihil qvoq; magis tritum est, qvàm eum è
Saulo factum esse Paulum, hoc est è turbulento pacifi-
cum, ut loqvi amat Erasmus, vel è superbo humilem,
qvod placuit Augustino; Qvomodo verò hæc duo ipsi
tribuantur nomina, an binominis fuerit, an vero in Ju-
          A   daismo

FIG. 4. Janson's Mittel roman. From F. Blomgreen, *Onomatologia Pauli*. Copenhagen, 1701.

☙(3.)❧

I. N. S. S. T. A.

PRÆFATIO.

Ot inter nobiliffimas & fplendidiffimas dotes, quibus fuperbit homo, non poftremum fibi vendicat locum memoria, ut ideò à venerandâ antiquitate non immeritò tam honorificis nobilitata fuerit denominationibus. Dicta fiquidem legitur artium & difciplinarum cella penaria; quod ficuti cellæ affervant cibaria, ut ex his quoties opus fuerit, ea poffint depromi, fic memoria pari modô recondat & affervet artes & fcientias, induftriâ noftrâ antehac nobis acquifitas, ut quoties neceffum fuerit, eas reddere queamus. Porrò vocatur fcientiarum cuftos, eorum, quæ difcimus, reconditorium, Mufarum mater, divinitatis argumentum, eruditionis ταμεῖον, id eft promtuarium ac thefaurus, cum hujus beneficio omnia noftra cum illo Philofopho nobifcum portare poffimus. Hâc mediante uti nobis licet iis, quæ à pueritiâ vidimus, audivimus, legimus & addidicimus. Hâc inftructus effe debet, literis qui feliciter operam eft daturus, & contra eâdem deftitutus, perpetuis infcitiæ cimmeriis damnatus à Jove tenebris, nunquam folidæ divæ Reginæ fapientiæ folium adfcendere poterit, eam quippe non abs re Poëtæ filiam memoriæ finxere, de quâ alias recte fcriptum exftat, ufus me genuit, mater me peperit memoria. Quò nobilior autem memoriæ eft thefaurus, eò magis is expofitus eft periculis & injuriis. Hoftis enim hominum ἄπωνδος, Sathanas, hanc iis invidet felicitatem, illosq; aftu ea privare conatur, ut vi-

A 2   deli-

FIG. 5. Conrad Baumann's italic. From G.W. Gilg, *Dissertatio medica de memoriae laesione.* H. Mayer, Altdorf, 1691.

dentes, J. Latius). It is shown on several Frankfurt sheets of the seventeenth century, and on one of them, that of J. P. Fievet, 1664, it is described as 'uffrecht'. It is also the English italic on Joseph Moxon's sheet of 1669 and was used in his *Practical Perspective*, 1670. Of the two Cicero italics of Janson, the first is of contemporary design (? cut by Janson) and the second of the sixteenth century, possibly Robert Granjon's.

The evidence of these sheets shows that Janson was one of the first designers of romans in the new style. His Mittel Antiqua in particular was about 1700 the most widely used body type of the kind in Germany. It appears also that the earliest designs to be cut were large sizes intended for use in preliminaries, a fact which suggests that economy of space was not the controlling motive. German printers preferred the new style because they thought in terms of Fraktur.

Conrad Baumann of Nuremberg was contemporary with Janson and a cutter of somewhat similar romans, and also of italics, which, although of poor design, are interesting. The specimen sheet of his successor, J. G. Baumann, issued in 1699 and showing a full range of the firm's romans and italics, was reproduced by Gustav Mori in *Das Schriftgiessergewerbe in Süddeutschland*, 1924, pl. xiv. Conrad Baumann had already published in 1669 a sheet on which are shown types of all families, including the most interesting ones of the later specimen of 1699. In particular it appears that the five italics, Roman, Text, Tertia, Mittel, and Cicero, had been cut before 1670. The three smaller sizes are definitely 'grobe' faces, suitable for use with the heavy roman designs. The Mittel Cursiv was in fact often used with the Mittel Antiqua of Janson, who had provided no italic which properly agreed in colour with his romans. Imitations of Baumann's italics will be seen on the Frankfurt sheets of the eighteenth century, and the designs of Christian Zinck of Wittenberg were of the same school. (cf. below, p. 376). Baumann became a citizen of Nuremberg in 1663 and some of his types were already in use by that year; the Roman (2-line Pica) and Text (Double Pica) Antiqua and Cursiv are to be found in Eggerer's *Fragmen panis Corvi Proto-Eremitici*, M. Cosmorovius, Vienna, 1663. There is a reproduction from this book in Anton Mayer's *Wiens Buckdrucker Geschichte*, 1883, vol. i, p. 351, showing the Text Antiqua which appears on the sheet of 1669 (there is a different Text Antiqua on the sheet of 1699), a roman similar in weight and x-height to Janson's Text. The Mittel Antiqua on the earlier sheet is also different from that shown in 1699. This design was clearly cut with Baumann's Mittel Cursiv and harmonizes with it better than the later Mittel. The books of Heinrich Meyer, printer at Altdorf, in which many of the Baumann types appear, indicate that the second Mittel superseded the first about the year 1690, the italic remaining the same. I find the Baumann Cicero italic in the books of Heinrich Meyer from 1675 and the Mittel from 1681. We have mentioned that several of Janson's types are shown in Ernesti's *Wol-eingerichtete Buchdruckerey*. This book was printed at Nuremberg and, as might be expected, displays also several Baumann types. These are the Tertia, Mittel, and Cicero italics (nos. xxviii, xxx, and xxxiii).

Baron Pufendorff's *Histoire du règne de Charles Gustav*, Nuremberg, 1697, is a large folio of a high standard of production compared with the average German book of the period and shows Baumann types at their best. The main text is set in the second

Q. D. B. V.

PROOEMIUM.

Ulla forte externarum, quibus corpus noftrum animale affici folet, læfionum, tot & tantis implicita fuiffe dubiis, & tam multas inter eos, qui rerum harum periti funt, lites excitaffe videtur, quam theoria & curatio fiftulæ lacrymalis, morbi non adeo infrequentis & valde molefti, & qui fæpe refractariæ admodum naturæ effe folet. Ortum vero fine dubio traxerunt hæ, quibus laborat, difficultates, præcipue a minus fufficienti cognitione partium anatomica, harumque ftructuræ, & ufus, cui in œconomia animali inferviunt; ad quæ acceffit, quod varia denominatio morbis natura fua multum inter fe

A   difcre-

Fig. 6. Christian Zinck's italic. From H. G. Heyland, *De fistula lacrymali.* I. Titius, Leipzig, 1724.

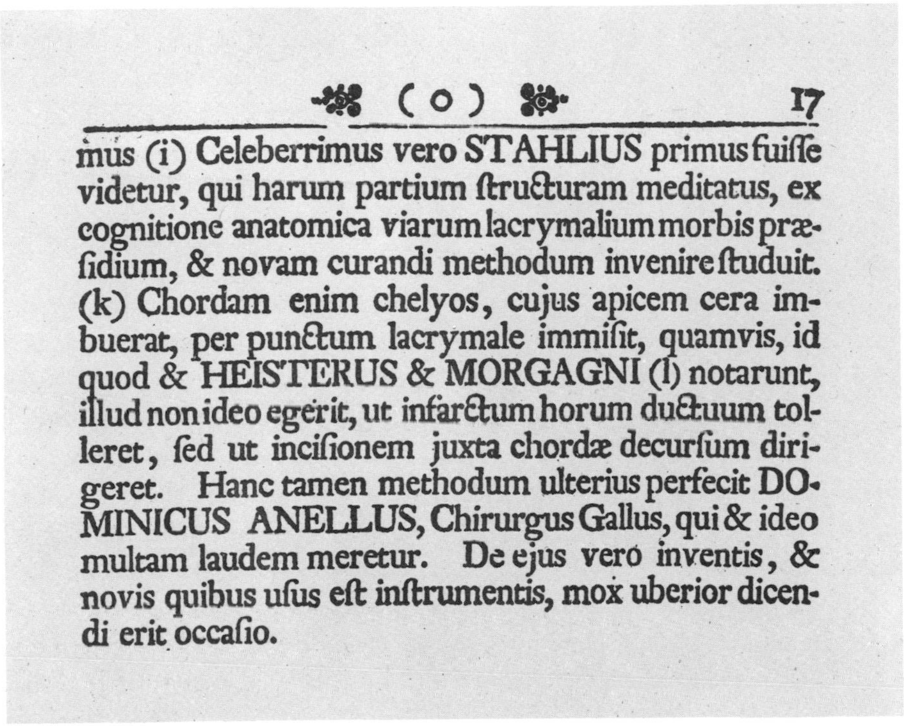

❀ (O) ❀   17

mus (i) Celeberrimus vero STAHLIUS primus fuiſſe
videtur, qui harum partium ſtructuram meditatus, ex
cognitione anatomica viarum lacrymalium morbis præ-
ſidium, & novam curandi methodum invenire ſtuduit.
(k) Chordam enim chelyos, cujus apicem cera im-
buerat, per punctum lacrymale immiſit, quamvis, id
quod & HEISTERUS & MORGAGNI (l) notarunt,
illud non ideo egerit, ut infarctum horum ductuum tol-
leret, ſed ut inciſionem juxta chordæ decurſum diri-
geret. Hanc tamen methodum ulterius perfecit DO-
MINICUS ANELLUS, Chirurgus Gallus, qui & ideo
multam laudem meretur. De ejus vero inventis, &
novis quibus uſus eſt inſtrumentis, mox uberior dicen-
di erit occaſio.

FIG. 7. Christian Zinck's roman. From H. G. Heyland, *De fistula
lacrymali*. I. Titius, Leipzig, 1724.

Mittel Antiqua with the original italic, and in the preliminaries appear the Text Antiqua and Cursiv of the 1669 sheet.

That Fournier was mistaken in supposing that the 'goût hollandois' originated in Holland is further borne out by the designs of Christian Zinck, type founder of Wittenberg (*b.* 1698). Zinck appears to have been trained at Leipzig and it is in Leipzig-printed books that his types are to be found. The favourite roman types at Wittenberg in the twenties were the pseudo-Janson series. No specimen sheet issued by Zinck is known earlier than 1746, but many of his types are shown in the specimen of Bernhard Christoph Breitkopf, Leipzig, 1739, which is included in Gessner's *Buchdruckerkunst*. Breitkopf, the founder of the well-known house of Breitkopf and Härtel, was born in 1695, came to Leipzig in 1714, and in 1719 married the widow of Johann Caspar Müller, thereby acquiring a foundry. His specimen of 1739 shows, besides types by Zinck, titlings by J. P. Artopaeus and some sixteen types by Müller, mostly smaller sizes. The romans and italics of Müller (1675-1717) are not of great significance; perhaps the most interesting is his Mittel Cursiv, found, along with its roman, in Leipzig books from 1715. See L. H. Mylius, *Dissertatio de anatomia*, Immanuel Titius.

Among Zinck's romans and italics, all of the new school, shown by Breitkopf in 1739, the most striking is the italic in three sizes, Doppelmittel, Text, and Tertia. In these German italics there was a tendency to flatten the tops of the x-height letters, and in Zinck's design the idea is carried to the extreme and combined with a rigid regularity in the angle of inclination. That Zinck's italic won popularity is shown by the copies found on Frankfurt sheets, e. g. J. F. Halle, 1740, and J. H. Schippelius, 1755 and 1768. The first size cut by Zinck appears to have been the Tertia. A little of this size is found in a medical dissertation by P. G. Schacher printed by I. Titius and dated 21 December 1722. The main text of the tract is set in Müller's Mittel roman. The reproduction (Fig. 6) is taken from another book printed by Titius in 1724, of which the main text is set in a different Mittel roman, which I take to be also by Zinck. It is impossible to base any identification on the miserable three-line specimen of Zinck's Grobe Mittel Antiqua given by Breitkopf, but I infer that the type of the tract by Heyland is by Zinck from the similarity in the design of the capitals of this roman and Zinck's italic, principally the G and R. The italic accompanying it is Müller's. This Mittel roman of Zinck's is very similar to the Augustijn roman of Fleischman, which was cut in 1732. Charles Enschedé says that this latter roman had an 'énorme attraction' in the eighteenth century, and it is probably the type which Fournier had in mind when he wrote of the 'goût hollandois'. But Fleischman was only continuing the fashion of the school in which he was trained.

One of the earliest general reviews published in Germany was the *Acta Eruditorum*, founded at Leipzig in 1682 by Otto Mencke. In scope it corresponds to the English *Philosophical Transactions* and it was continued for a century. As it was written in Latin its typography is of interest for our subject and many of the types we have described will be found in its pages. A publication of that nature is naturally conservative as to its main text, and it is for the most part in preliminaries and head-lines that these designs are to be seen. In the early volumes there occur occasional lines of the Roman Antiqua which we have found from 1602, of Janson's Text Antiqua, and the Text italic cut by Reinhard Voskens. J. C. Müller became the printer from 1711 and he introduced the Mittel italic of the pseudo-Janson series for headings. In 1715 he changed the typography of the main text and for the next forty years this was set in Müller's Kleine Cicero. This was a type of small x-height, similar to that used in previous volumes, but showing some modern tendencies in the capitals and the lower-case g. In 1719 Breitkopf became the printer and in 1721 introduced Müller's Mittel italic, and finally Christian Zinck's Tertia italic in 1727.

[1939]

[The mystery of the so-called Janson type has now been cleared up. Harry Carter and G. Buday have shown that they were cut by Niklas Kis, a Hungarian who was working at Amsterdam, *c.* 1690. They published their account of Kis in the *Linotype Matrix*, 1954, and again in the *Gutenberg Jahrbuch*, 1957.]

JOHN BAGFORD, ANTIQUARY, 1650-1716

JOHN BAGFORD, 'shoemaker and antiquary', is chiefly remembered for his collection of ballads and a miscellaneous accumulation of pieces bearing on the history of printing, both of which collections came to the British Museum with the Harleian Manuscripts. For most of his life Bagford was a book agent, searching out and purchasing books, printed and manuscript, for the leading collectors of his day. The chief contemporary sources for what we know of his life are the letters and remains of Thomas Hearne, the Oxford diarist, of James Sotheby, and Humfrey Wanley, the librarian of Edward Harley, Earl of Oxford. Very little is known of Bagford's early life and that little comes from two letters of James Sotheby to Thomas Hearne, written on the occasion of Bagford's death on 5th May, 1716. These letters were reprinted in *Letters written by Eminent Persons in the Seventeenth and Eighteenth Centuries*, London, 1813. According to Sotheby Bagford was born, probably in Fetter Lane, in 1650 or 1651 – he told Sotheby shortly before his death that he was not sure whether he was sixty-five or sixty-six. At first he was a shoemaker in Turnstile, and afterwards was a bookseller at the same address. Sotheby was a Cambridge man and also of Gray's Inn. The letters are written from Hatton Garden. According to Hearne by 1725 he had grown 'an idle, useless sot'. We are not told whether Bagford's shop was in Great or Little Turnstile. Just off Little Turnstile is Gate Street, where is The Ship Tavern, a modern inn built on the site of an old tavern dating back to the sixteenth century. Outside the Ship is an inscription which states that among the distinguished frequenters of the house was Bayford (sic) 'shoemaker and antiquary'. The others mentioned are Richard Penderel, one of the brothers who aided Charles II in his escape after the Battle of Worcester, the Chevalier d'Eon and John Smeaton, the engineer. At the time of his death Bagford was living in Islington, and was buried in the Charterhouse, of which institution he was a pensioner, by the nomination of John Moore, Bishop of Ely, one of the book collectors for whom Bagford worked.

Bagford married at an early age, as we learn from a note in the Collections in his own hand. This is a memorandum of the baptism, dated 31st October, 1685, of John, son of John and Elizabeth Bagford, at St. Anne's, Blackfriars, (Harl. 5997). There is also preserved a power of attorney, dated 6th April 1713, in which this son John, a seaman, authorizes his father to draw his wages in case of his death. In Thomas Hearne's *Remarks and Collections*, Oxford, 11 vol., 1885-1921, there are many references to Bagford, most of them relating to his proposed *History of Printing*. The first we hear of this history is in a letter to Sir Hans Sloane, another of Bagford's patrons, dated 24th July 1704. Hearne and his correspondents expressed their doubts as to Bagford's competency to carry out the plan. He had acquired an immense knowledge of early books, but, they feared, lacked the necessary education and judgement. A sheet of proposals was issued, together with a specimen of the *Life of William Caxton*; of these there are several copies among the Collections (cf. Harl. 5906. b). If one may judge by the style and contents of these specimens, we have lost nothing by Bagford's failure to produce the book. Some use of the Collections was made both by Samuel Palmer in his *General History of Printing*, 1732, and by Joseph Ames in his *Typographical Antiquities*, 1749.

There are tributes to Bagford in two of Hearne's published works; the first is in the preface to his edition of Roper's *Vita D. Thomae Mori*, 1716, and the second in the appendix to his edition of the *Chartularium* of Hemingus Wigorniensis, Oxford, 1723. The latter is quoted in full in Dibdin's *Bibliomania*, 1811, and by W. Y. Fletcher in the paper referred to below. Hearne writes in the highest terms of Bagford's knowledge and enthusiasm and expresses the greatest respect for his moral character. In general his contemporaries admired him as a man and commonly referred to him as 'honest John Bagford'. He appears to have served his clients well and had little interest in money. In consequence he died a poor man and a pensioner.

Four of Bagford's papers have appeared in print. In 1707 he contributed a paper to the Philosophical Transactions of the Royal Society, entitled *An Essay on the Invention of Printing*. This is partly an account of the author's visits to Holland and his search for relics of Coster. It is accompanied by a description of Bagford's Collections written by Humfrey Wanley. The *Monthly Miscellany* for April and May 1708 contains articles by Bagford on the antiquities of London, and the number for June of the same year a very interesting contribution on the libraries of London, in part by Bagford and continued by William Oldys. Finally in Hearne's edition of John Leland's *De rebus Britannicis Collectanea*, 1715, vol. 1, is a letter by Bagford on the antiquities of London.

Of those who have written about Bagford in later times John Nichols's remarks in his *Literary Anecdotes*, vol. 2, are based on the notes contributed by the Rev. John Calder to the 1786 edition of *The Tatler*. Calder added nothing new and made several mistakes, which have been repeated. For example he supposes that it was Bagford himself who was baptized in 1785. The next authority to be noted is T. F. Dibdin, who reprints in his *Bibliomania* the passages on Bagford to be found in Hearne's works. Dibdin was the first to accuse Bagford of being a mutilator of books. He imagines that the Collections were amassed by tearing out the title-pages and other pages of interest from books. Other writers of the nineteenth century continued this attack, for instance William Blades in his *Enemies of Books*, and J. W. Ebsworth who edited the Bagford Ballads in 1878. In 1898 the Bibliographical Society came to the defence of Bagford. In the Transactions of the Society for that year (vol. 4) W. Y. Fletcher wrote the fullest account of Bagford we have and pointed out the absurdity of supposing that a poor bookseller would destroy the value of books which he might sell. Bagford himself has left a note which throws some light on the matter. He says that he was allowed to take what he wanted from the waste books of Christopher Bateman, who was the leading second-hand bookseller of the day (Harl. 5910, pt. 3).

One more publication which must be mentioned is again in the Transactions of the Bibliographical Society, vol. 7, 1904. In that volume appeared a paper by Cyril Davenport on *Bagford's Notes on Bookbinding*, followed by *A Rough List of the Contents of the Bagford Collection*. This list is a much fuller description of the contents than that given by Wanley in 1707 or by Fletcher in 1898. It is in fact an adequate and indispensable guide to students of the collection.

If Bagford can be exonerated from the charge of being what Blades called a Biblio-clast, there is another transaction in which he took the leading part and where he is not free from blame, at least judged by modern standards of scholarship. There is in the British Museum a series of drawings by William Faithorne the younger, made for Sir Hans Sloane about the year 1700, which purport to be portraits of early English printers. Two of the portraits, those of John Day and John Wight, are genuine. The other six are fakes, being copies of woodcut portraits of other men. Four of them were exposed and the originals traced by Dibdin in his edition of Ames's *Typographical Antiquities*. A fifth, that of Grafton, appears to be a portrait of Thomas Hill, a writer on gardening in Elizabeth's reign. The sixth, that of Reyner Wolfe, is also highly suspect, although the original has not yet been traced. It should be added that there are only six of the original drawings extant, Pynson and Jones being missing. In the list written by Bag-ford which accompanied the drawings the portrait of Jones is included, but Pynson is again missing. However there can be little doubt that the reputed portrait of Pynson was from the same source. Woodcuts were made from the drawings, which were used by Ames in his *Typographical Antiquities*. Ames (p. 54) says that they were 'collected, I imagine, by Mr. Bagford'. John Lewis adapted the bearded portrait of Caxton for his *Life of Master Wyllyam Caxton*, 1737, and added at the foot the lettering 'inv. Bagford'. In the headpiece of Bagford's specimen sheet for the *Life of Caxton* a version of the same portrait is introduced. Altogether there seems no doubt that Bagford was responsible for the hoax and in some cases at least he must have known who the originals were. He probably did not regard the proceeding as reprehensible. Such false attri-butions are likely to persist and in spite of Dibdin's exposure we find that as late as 1873 they were accepted by H. Curwen in his *History of the Booksellers*.

Bagford was not a printer, or only to the extent that he printed cards on the frozen Thames in 1716. There is a specimen in his Collections (Harl. 5936). Accompanying it is another curious sheet issued by Bagford on 2 January 1716, on which he calls him-self 'Patron of Printing'. This sheet was 'printed at his Majesties Printing-office in Black-Fryers'.

[1950]

THE KING'S PRINTERS, 1660-1742

I N *The Library*, 1901, H. R. Plomer wrote on 'The King's Printers under the Stuarts' and explained the confusion caused by the frequent changes of imprint. In the introduction to the *Bibliotheca Lindesiana. A Catalogue of Royal Proclamations*, 1910, Robert Steele gave an account of the various patents. The following notes deal with the period from the Restoration to the death of John Baskett, in 1742, and are based partly on imprints and partly on papers in the Public Record Office.

After the Restoration Major John Bill and Christopher Barker III were reinstated as King's Printers at Hunsdon House, Blackfriars. From the Domestic State Papers we find that Roger Norton, in May 1660 and again in August 1661, petitioned to be restored to his share in the privilege inherited from his father Bonham Norton. He asserted that the office was 'now held by gentlemen who do not understand printing'. There seems to have been some doubt about Norton's claim and no grant was made, but some recompense was made to his son in September 1667 (Roger I died in 1662), when a grant was made to the younger Roger for forty years, on the surrender of his former patent of the office of printer, typographer, and bookseller, in Latin, Greek, and Hebrew, with the sole privilege of printing the Bible in Latin, and all grammars in Greek and Latin. It also appears that at the time of the Great Fire, 1666, when Hunsdon House was burnt down, Norton was living there. After the fire he moved to Clerkenwell and subsequently to Little Britain. He was never accepted as the King's Printer and his name is not found in the imprints of Bibles, Prayer Books, or Proclamations. Between 1660 and 1676 the only names in the imprints are those of John Bill and Christopher Barker or their assigns. Barker seems to have farmed out his share at once to George Sawbridge, Henry Hills, and others. John Bill, if not himself a printer, took a direct interest in the affairs of the printing office when it was removed after the Fire to the Savoy, and it was Bill who resisted the attempts of the assigns of Christopher Barker to remove it again to Little Britain (*Domestic State Papers* 18 Aug. 1671). On 4 November of the same year Christopher Wren recorded his approval of the plans for the rebuilding of the King's Printing House in Blackfriars 'set out by the said Mr. Bill'.[1] Robert Hooke also in his Diary, under date 10 October 1674, notes 'At St. Paules with Sir Ch. Wren and Major Bill at Printing House'.

During this period the actual printer and manager was Thomas Newcombe. From the *Calendars of Treasury Books* on 13 May 1668 we find a record of payment to Thomas Newcombe as King's Printer, and similar records in November 1676 and in January 1680. By this time he had become more than the manager, for in 1675 he and Henry Hills received a patent for thirty years to date from the termination of the Barker patent (*Rot. Pat.* 27 Chas. II). On 11 May 1677 we learn that Newcombe and Hills were sworn in as King's Printers. It is stated that, as the assign of John Bill, Newcombe had managed the office since the Restoration 'having some time ago purchased a right in

---

1. See Wren's *Court Orders*, Wren Soc., vol. 18, 1941, p. 32.

certain letters patent granted by the late king to Charles and Matthew Barker for 30 years, and having been granted in his own name letters patent of the King's Printing Office for 30 years after the expiration of the said grant'. The patent granted to the younger sons of Robert Barker, Charles and Matthew, was made in 1635 (*Rot. Pat.* 11 Chas. I) and was to run from January 1679-80, the year in which the first Barker patent, now held by John Bill and the assigns of Christopher Barker, expired. All this is reflected in the imprints. In 1677 we find the names of John Bill, Christopher Barker, Thomas Newcombe, and Henry Hills. After 1679 Barker's name dropped out, his patent having expired. Under what arrangement Bill still continued is obscure. Evidently he and his heirs had some share in the patent for the next thirty years. According to an 'Abstract of the several Patents of King and Queen's Printers', made in 1709, the grant to Charles and Matthew Barker was vested in Charles Bill and Thomas Newcombe. By 10 November 1682 the imprint had become, 'The Assigns of John Bill deceased,[1] Newcombe, and H. Hills'. Bill must have died between November 1681 and November 1682; Newcombe died on 26 December 1681. There is an account of his funeral procession on 2 January 1682 in the *Impartial Protestant Mercury*. He was buried at Dunchurch in Warwickshire. His son, also Thomas, was sworn in as King's Printer on 1 February 1682. The name of the younger Newcombe does not appear in Plomer's *Dictionary*. In 1685 the imprint became, 'Charles Bill, Henry Hills, and T. Newcombe'.

There were further changes after the withdrawal of James II. Henry Hills had become a Roman Catholic, with the result that on 12 December 1688 an anti-papal mob attacked the printing house in Blackfriars. Hills escaped to St. Omer and died shortly afterwards (cf. Plomer's *Dictionary*). He disinherited his eldest son Henry, and left his interests in the patent in charge of his second son Gillham Hills. On 13 August 1691 Henry Hills petitioned against this arrangement on the ground that money out of the profits of the printing house was being sent to recusants. There was a further petition on 9 June 1698, but all apparently in vain. Thomas Newcombe the younger appears to have died in April 1691, and from that date until January 1710 the imprint, 'Charles Bill and the Executrix of Thomas Newcombe', remained unchanged. The name of Charles Bill dropped out with the expiration of the Barker patent and the imprint became 'Assigns of Thomas Newcombe and Henry Hills, deceased'.

The public records for this period reveal several new names. In December 1692 in the *Calendar of Treasury Books* there are several references to the settlement of the bills of the King's Printers, amounting, since 1688, to nearly £ 12,000. A money warrant was be made out for Edward Brewster and Dorothy Newcombe (presumably the widow of Thomas Newcombe). The amount was to be made up partly by loans, and among the lenders were Brewster and Newcombe themselves and also John Baskett for £ 1,109. On 14 December 1693 payment was made to Brewster, Gillham Hills, and Dorothy Newcombe. On 8 March 1694 in connexion with the petition of Henry Hills we hear that the managers of the printing office, Edward Brewster and John Williams, were to be called. On 2 November 1694 payment was made to Brewster, G. Hills, and Richard

---

1. *Calendar of Treasury Papers*, 1709 (22).

Hutchenson. Of this Hutchenson I can find nothing more. In February 1696 payment was to Brewster and G. Hills, and to the same down to 1706. On 16 December 1706 payment was made to Brewster and John Williams. In connexion with the settlement in 1702 Williams is mentioned as 'agent to the said printers for near twenty years'. On 25 September 1710 payment was to Williams alone and also in 1712, 1713, and 3 February 1714, and he was styled 'agent to Her Majesty's printers'.

Edward Brewster is presumably the bookseller who was Master of the Stationers' Company in 1689-92. Plomer's *Dictionary* has no record of him later than 1699 and no evidence that he was a printer. John Williams, who seems to have been the important man at the printing office after the death of the Newcombes until the end of Queen Anne's reign, is not mentioned in Plomer. There are two curious fragments in the Bagford Collection[1] relating to Williams. The first is headed: 'Books printed at the King's Printing-House in Blackfryers, and there sold and delivered by John Williams, at the Rates under-mentioned. 1686. viz.' (There follows a list of Bibles, Prayer Books, &c., with prices.) The second consists of a half-page showing the Royal Arms, Arms of the City of London and of the Stationers' Company, heads of Luther and Calvin, and an imprint which reads 'Mr John and Mrs Elizabeth Williams. Printed at Her Majesty's Printing Office in Black-Fryers, Novemb. 22. 1707'. Another note of Bagford's states that Williams lived in a house which was on the site of Roger Norton's house, burnt 1666.[2] In 1712 Williams was a partner with John Baskett and Samuel Ashhurst in purchasing the privilege of printing at Oxford, but not when the agreement was renewed in 1734.[3] Thomas Hearne described the three as 'men of little probity, as 'tis feared', probably quite without justification.

We come now to John Baskett, of whom we have already had a record in 1692. He was a stationer, in the modern sense of the word, for many years before he became a printer. There are several references to him in the public records as supplying stationery ware to the government. Presumably the Mr. Baskett mentioned in the *Calendar of Treasury Books* for 1695 (x. 1115) is the same man. The next reference I find is of 25 June 1703, where he is called stationer, as he is in further entries down to January 1717 (date of this last doubtful).[4]

When did Baskett become King's Printer? The date is given as 1709 in the usual works of reference, e. g. Nichols's *Literary Anecdotes*, D.N.B., and Plomer's *Dictionary*. This seems to be an inference from the fact that January 1709-10 was the last month of the Barker patent. Baskett's name first appeared in the imprints in March 1711 in the form 'John Baskett and the assigns of Thomas Newcombe and Henry Hills deceased', which remained the style down to 1723. From the imprints one could infer that he bought a share in the Newcombe and Hills patent, but I have found no document confirming this and no account of his being sworn in as King's Printer. On 13 October 1713 a reversionary patent was granted to Benjamin Tooke and John Barker for thirty

1. Harl. 5936 (1 and 18).
2. Harl. 5910. iv (168).
3. *The First Minute Book of the Delegates of the Oxford University Press*, 1943.
4. See *Calendar of Treasury Papers*, clxxi, 20.

years from the end of Hill and Newcombe's patent in 1739-40 (*Rot. Pat.* 12 Anne). This reversion was bought up by Baskett, according to Steele, but again I have failed to find the relevant document. On 15 December 1715 Baskett acquired a further reversion for thirty years to run from 1769-70 (*Rot. Pat.* 2 Geo. 1). It was this reversion which was sold to Charles Eyre's father in 1724 for £ 10,000.[1] In 1723 the name of Newcombe dropped out of the imprints, and in the years 1725-7 we find the addition of Thomas Norris, assignee of George Hills. This Norris was no doubt the bookseller of London Bridge, died 1732. Plomer does not record his connexion with Baskett. From September 1727 until his death in 1742 the name of Baskett appears alone on the imprints.

Baskett, not content with being King's Printer in England and with his lease of the Oxford privilege, tried to establish himself in Scotland also. The patent held by the Anderson family as King's Printer in Scotland expired in 1712 and a new patent, dated 11 August 1711, was granted to Robert Freebairn for forty-one years. Baskett and James Watson each purchased a third share in this privilege, as appears from subsequent litigation. Freebairn, by taking part in the Rebellion in 1715, forfeited his rights and a fresh patent was granted on 6 July 1716 to Baskett and Agnes Campbell, Anderson's widow. Watson retained his third share and continued to print Bibles in Edinburgh, said to be more correct than the London- or Oxford-printed Bibles.[2] Baskett brought an action against him and against his agent in London, Henry Parson. He appears to have been successful in part only, and stopped Watson from selling his Bibles in England. He himself seems to have made little use of his Scotch privilege and only three Bibles are recorded bearing an Edinburgh imprint and Baskett's name.

On 14 January 1738 the King's Printing House in Blackfriars, which had been built by Major John Bill after the Great Fire of 1666, was again burnt down, with a loss to Baskett of £ 20,000, it is said. On this occasion the younger William Bowyer, remembering the help given by Baskett to the elder Bowyer in 1712 when his printing house in Dogwell Court was burnt down, presented Baskett with a press and the iron-work of another. John Rich, manager of the theatre in Portugal Row, Lincoln's Inn Fields, offered Baskett the temporary use of the theatre. It is not recorded whether Baskett made use of the offer, but before long, as appears from his will,[3] he had rebuilt his dwelling-house and printing-shop. These were the buildings which were finally sold to John Walter and which still survive, at least in part, among the premises of *The Times*. But by that time Printing House Square had ceased to be the home of the King's Printer.

NOTE ON HUNSDON HOUSE

The first King's Printer who established himself at this address was Bonham Norton, by 1629. Previously Robert Barker's address was Northumberland House, St. Martin's St., Aldersgate. The name Hunsdon was derived from George Carey, 2nd Baron Hunsdon, who by 1585 had acquired a

1. See Austen Leigh, *William Strahan and his Ledgers*, 1923. If there is no mistake about the date, the price paid seems extraordinary.
2. See John Lee, *Memorial for the Bible Societies in Scotland*, 1824, and an article on Watson by W. Couper in the *Scottish Historical Review*, 1910.
3. There is a summary of the will in Plomer's *Dictionary*.

lease of some buildings forming part of the old Dominican monastery.[1] Carey died in 1603 and subsequently the house was occupied by the French Ambassador and it was in a gallery attached to the house that there occurred in October 1623 the terrible accident known as the Fatal Vespers. Some 300 Catholics had assembled to hear a sermon from the Jesuit Robert Drury, when the floor collapsed and nearly 100 people, including Drury, lost their lives.[2]

Hunsdon House was destroyed in the Great Fire of 1666, and for a few years official publications bore the imprint 'In the Savoy'. Major John Bill undertook the rebuilding and from a note by Sir Christopher Wren, dated 4 November 1671, we learn that Wren as His Majesty's Surveyor approved the site, which was 'at or near the place used formerly for His Majesty's Printing House'. We have already noted that Bill's house was burnt down in January 1738. Of this building I have found no illustration. In Bigmore and Wyman's *Bibliography of Printing*, art. 'King's Printers', there is a view of a building which they label the King's Printing House, but which is, in fact, a view of Apothecaries' Hall in Water Lane close by, a building erected after the Great Fire and still surviving.

CHRONOLOGICAL SUMMARY

1660–Jan. 1680. Last years of the original Barker Patent, held by John Bill II and Christopher Barker III. Barker sold his share to Henry Hills and others. From 1677 Thomas Newcombe, the manager during this period, and Hills recognized as King's Printers.

1680–Jan. 1710. Patent of Charles and Matthew Barker, held by John Bill, Newcombe, and Hills. Bill, d. 1682, succeeded by Charles Bill. Newcombe, d. 1681, succeeded by Thomas Newcombe II, who died 1691 and was succeeded by Dorothy Newcombe. John Williams the manager from 1691. Edward Brewster held a share from 1692.

1710–Jan. 1740. Patent of Newcombe and Hills, both deceased. From 1711 John Baskett held a share. The assign of Newcombe drops out in 1723, and the assign of Hills in 1727 or 1728. Baskett from 1728 the sole King's Printer.

1740–Jan. 1770. Patent of Tooke and Barber, which had been bought by Baskett.

[1948]

---

1. See Chambers, *Elizabethan Stage*, ii, 475, &c.
2. See *Domestic State Papers*, and contemporary tracts.

ENGLISH TYPE SPECIMEN BOOKS

THE importance of type specimens for the study of typographical history is self-evident. A type may, of course, have been in use several years before it appeared in a specimen book, but in general we can compile a fairly accurate history of the first appearances of types and of their relations to one another from these books. This source is almost entirely lacking for the early days of printing. Even when the type-founders were well established as a separate trade and had formed the habit of issuing sheets or books displaying their types, such specimens have often not survived down to our day. They were regarded as of temporary use and not as historical documents. It is only in comparatively recent years that attempts have been made to gather these documents together. In England the pioneers were William Blades and T. B. Reed, whose collections have made the library of the St. Bride Institute the richest in the country in this branch of bibliography.

Apart from their historical importance and their rarity, these specimens have a further attraction for collectors: they are handsomely produced books, at least in the eighteenth century. The type-founder naturally took pains to have his advertisements well printed, and they often bear the address of a leading printer of the day. The title-pages are generally successful, in spite of the fact that there was a temptation to show as many different styles of letter as possible on that page. The display of printers' flowers and ornaments lends further variety to their pages. In England, the best may be said to begin with Caslon and to last for three-quarters of a century. The earlier sheets are as poor as most seventeenth-century English printing, while those of the nineteenth century are technically well produced but in other ways unattractive.

The series of specimens in England begins later than in other countries, and begins at a low level. The earliest known is a miserable little sheet, preserved in the Record Office, of Nicholas Nicholls (1665), showing a few types of a very small size, namely Pearl. The next is the sheet of Joseph Moxon (1669), showing his romans and italics cut after Dutch models. The types are poor in themselves and the only surviving copy, in the British Museum, is a poor impression.

A better display of English types is given by a printer's specimen issued by James Orme, when about to dispose of his stock in 1698. No specimens have survived, if any were issued, of the chief founders of this early period, neither from the Grover foundry nor from that of Andrews. The gap between Moxon and Caslon is filled by a few printers' specimens, often of foreign types, and by the books issued by the Oxford University Press. Among these printers' specimens are two from Edinburgh, John Moncur (1709) and James Watson (1713), which display avowedly Dutch types. From London we have sheets by John Humphreys and H. Meere (of about 1710), B. Motte (1713), one from the Cambridge University Press (c. 1740), Hart and Strahan (c. 1740), and one from M. Mechell (1748). Although the last three are of later date than the first Caslon sheets, the types shown are of an earlier period. It may be added that only one copy has so far been recorded of any of these sheets.

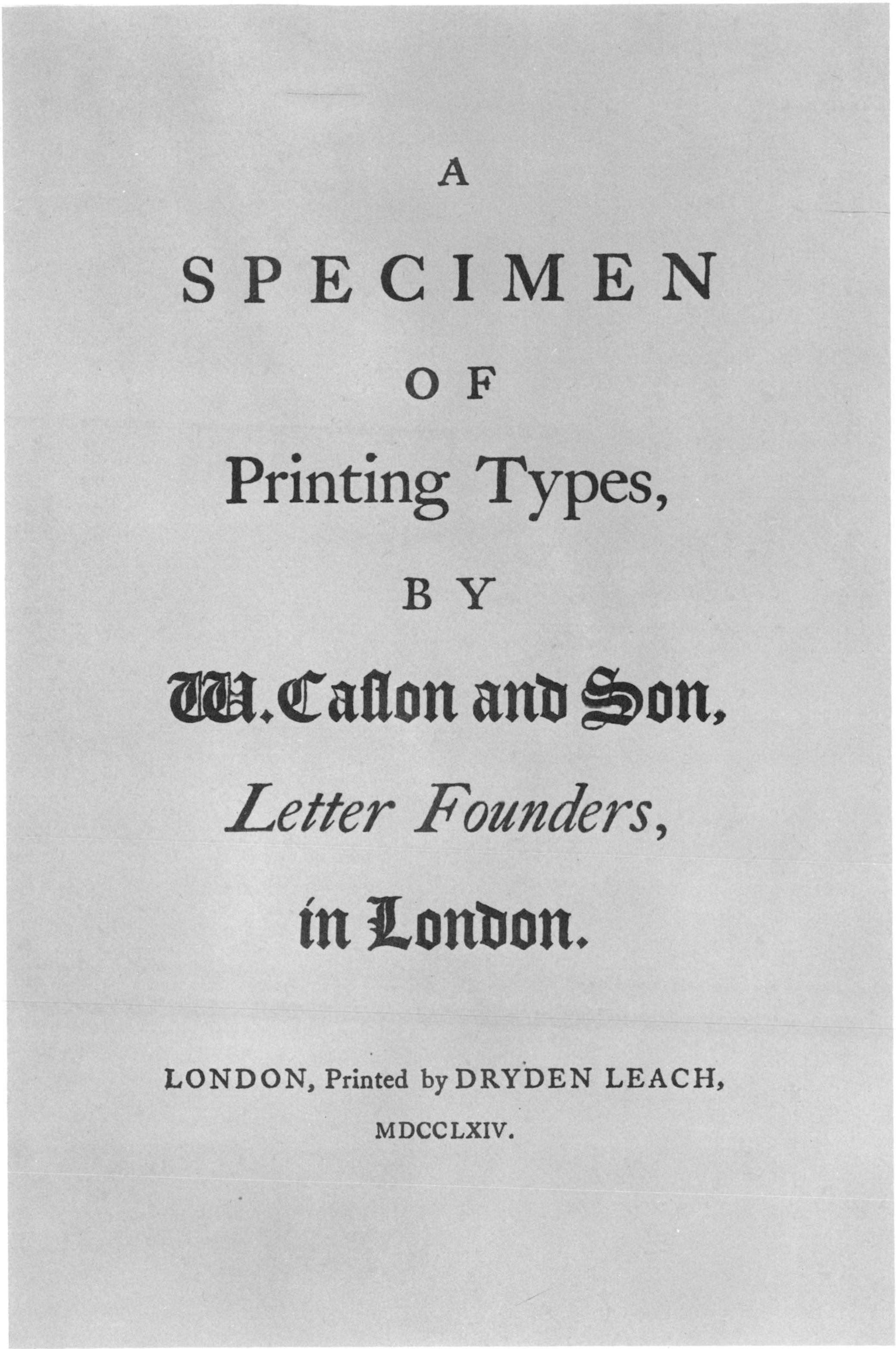

A
SPECIMEN
OF
Printing Types,
BY
W. Caſlon and Son,
Letter Founders,
in London.

LONDON, Printed by DRYDEN LEACH,

MDCCLXIV.

FIG. 1. Title-page from Caslon's Specimen Book, 1744.

Before passing to the Oxford Press there is one book to be considered, of much later date, but the most important document we have as a record of earlier English type, namely the Sale Catalogue of the James Foundry of 1782. The foundry was started by Thomas James in 1710. He purchased many matrices in Holland, but also gradually acquired most of the material of the earlier English foundries, that of the Grovers and of Andrews among others. By the time of the sale the stock had become of anti-quarian interest rather than of practical value. It included some Blacks which may have come down from Wynkyn de Worde, Caxton's successor; at least they closely resemble types used by that printer. Some romans and italics descended from John Day, and a Gothic script type used by Sir Walter Raleigh in 1583, Greeks and Orientals used in the London Polyglot Bible of 1657, and the Alexandrian Greek dating from about 1643, were some of the interesting survivals. The catalogue showed also the Cursorials or Latin scripts of the Grover foundry dating from about 1700, two sizes of which were used by, and perhaps originally cut for, Ichabod Dawks in his News-Letter. A specimen printed from type cast from the original matrices is given in Stanley Morison's book on Dawks.

Punches and matrices have sometimes had an amazingly long life, and not a few of these early English matrices still survived when T. B. Reed wrote his *History of the Old English Letter Foundries* in 1887. These relics were bought at the James sale by Edmund Fry, whose stock was purchased in 1828 by William Thorowgood of the Fann Street Foundry. Messrs. Stephenson, Blake & Co., of Sheffield, later acquired the stock of the Reeds. As to the sale catalogue itself we have to confess that the only known copy is in America, the British Museum having only a photographic facsimile.

The earliest specimen *book* issued in England is that of the Oxford University Press of 1693. Although a few of the types shown are English, the great majority are of foreign origin. When Bishop John Fell about the year 1672 decided to bring the Oxford Foundry up to date, he was aware that the matrices needed could not be procured in England. We know of the dealings of his agent in Holland, and also that types were purchased from Germany and France. Some of the specimens shown in the book of the body types, roman, italic, and Greek, were of French origin. It is now known that the matrices were acquired, possibly indirectly through Dutch founders, from the Luther foundry at Frankfort. In the seventeenth century this was the most important foundry in North Germany, and the best of their material came from French punch-cutters of the sixteenth century. Their romans were derived from the punches of Claude Gara-mond, and the italics and Greeks from the punches of Robert Granjon, two of the most important engravers of types in the history of the trade. Thus the Oxford Press can boast to day of the possession of original Garamond and Granjon types.

We come now to the work of William Caslon, who started his foundry about 1720 and issued his first specimen sheet in 1734. It is unnecessary to day to praise Caslon's types, but we may remark that this sheet of 1734 is a display of English types, and that as a piece of printing it is far superior to anything of the kind which preceded it in this country. There are many copies known bearing the date 1734, but only two actually of the first edition, bearing the address Ironmonger Row: one in the British

FIG. 2. Title-page from Thorowgood's Specimen Book, 1839.

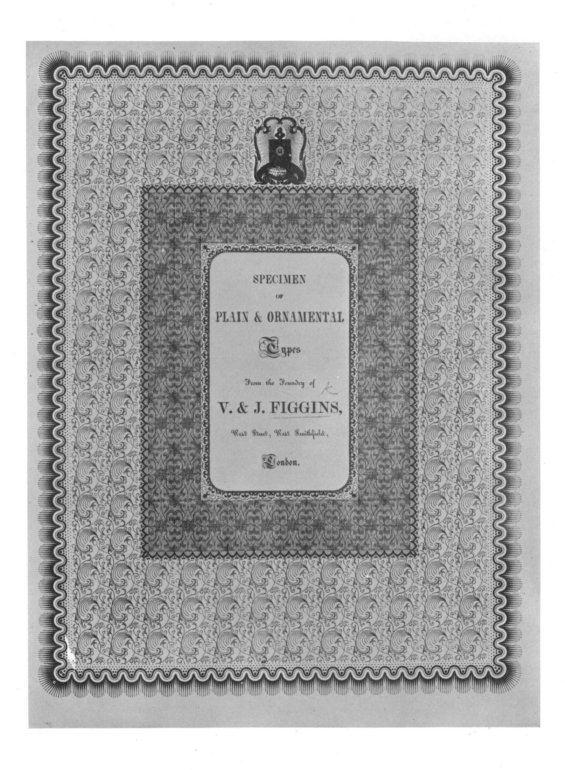

FIG. 3. Title-page from Figgins's Specimen Book, 1850.

Museum and one in the library of the American Typefounders. The other editions, all dated 1734, bearing the address Chiswell Street, appeared in Chambers's *Cyclopædia* of 1738 and subsequent editions. Meanwhile Caslon himself had published other sheets, one in 1742, on which William Caslon II's name occurs for the first time, another in 1748, and a third in 1749. The increasing interest in the collecting of specimens is illustrated by the recent history of these sheets of 1742 and 1748. Reed, writing in 1887, referred to them as lost sheets. D. B. Updike sent a communication to *The Fleuron* No. 1 describing a newly discovered copy of the 1748 sheet. It now appears that there is also a copy of this 'lost' specimen in the Bodleian, and of the 1742 sheet there are copies in the possession of the Bodleian, the Bibliothèque Nationale, Messrs. Enschedé, the Haarlem founders, also G. W. Jones used to possess one.

In 1763 Caslon published his first specimen book, and from that date the Chiswell Street books have appeared at fairly regular intervals. In them we can trace the history of English typography in some detail. In 1785 we find William Caslon III's first modern script (an earlier variety was cut by Thomas Cottrell), new developments of flowers copied from P. S. Fournier, and again of cast ornaments. Towards the end of the century we find the Baskerville imitations and in 1805 the earliest modern faces of the Caslon firm, some sizes bearing the date 1802. A little later we meet the new advertising types, fat-faces, Egyptians or antiques, and finally sans-serifs. The Caslon firm did not originate any of these new styles of letter, although one of the less popular letters did make its first appearance in a Caslon book, the type called Italian, a reversed Egyptian, shown in 1821.

William Caslon was not the only English type-cutter of his generation. To-day John Baskerville's letter is rated equally highly. His specimen sheets, five in number, form an interesting and handsome group. The earliest, issued in 1754, is really a prospectus of his first book, the *Virgil*; the second of 1757 shows four sizes of his roman and italic, the third and fourth still more sizes, and the fifth, issued about the time of Baskerville's death in 1775, is a complete display of his work. Of this there is another issue bearing the date 1777, and further there are at least two French specimens of his types, published after the main part of his stock had been sold to Beaumarchais. All these sheets are rare and I suppose no one library or collector has a complete set.

After 1765 the number of founders and specimens began to increase and many of them show the influence of Baskerville in their typography; for instance, those of Alexander Wilson, whose earliest specimen appeared in 1772, and the rare and attractive broadsides of Isaac Moore (Bristol, 1766, London 1768 and 1770). Another contemporary, Thomas Cottrell, an old apprentice of William Caslon, produced several original founts. His script was earlier than that of Caslon mentioned above, and was the first of its kind in this country. He was the first founder to cast large poster letters, up to twelve lines pica, and the broadsides on which they are displayed are another rarity, only one copy of each, preserved at Stockholm, being known. He also engraved the last English Gothic script, the law-hand called Engrossing. This fount appears in his specimen book, but the original broadside on which it was diplayed by William Richardson seems to have perished entirely.

The next original specimens are those of the British Letter Foundry, John Bell and his successors. The two first of 1788 and 1789, issued by Bell, are known from a single copy only in the Bibliothèque Nationale. Those of S. & C. Stephenson, 1789 and 1796, are somewhat less rare and show more of the work of the punch-cutter, Richard Austin. The Bell type is likely to become more familiar to us, since it has been produced by the Monotype Corporation. Austin had a foundry of his own at a later period, the Imperial Letter Foundry in Worship Street, and issued two specimens, in 1819 (one copy only known) and in 1827. In these one can see how Austin treated the modern face, and further modern types from the same hand are displayed in the specimens of Alexander Wilson & Sons from 1812, and of William Miller, of Edinburgh, 1813, 1814, &c.

The revival of printing is reflected in printers' rather than in founders' specimens. In general it is the printers who in this generation have produced books fit to rank with eighteenth-century work. Thus we have had in recent years excellent specimen books from the Pelican Press, Messrs. Lund Humphries, Messrs. Balding and Mansell, The Kynoch Press, and especially from The Curwen Press. The Monotype, the Linotype, and the Ludlow Companies have produced handsome specimens displaying one particular type, and have even taken the revolutionary step of giving us some information about the origin of the type in question.

[1933]

THE HOMES OF THE LONDON TYPEFOUNDERS*

THE printers and booksellers of London in the past, as is well known, gathered together in small areas of the City. At different periods in the history of printing there has been a Fleet Street group, another around St. Paul's, and a third in and near Little Britain. One would expect the typefounders to establish themselves near their customers and we do, in fact, find them in the period with which we are concerned working not far from one another. In the history of typefounding in London, for two centuries the area over which the founders were spread is only about two miles in breadth and rather less than a mile in depth, and most of them are to be found towards the centre of that area. It is a district which suffered severely in the bombing raids on London of 1940 and 1941. Even before the war of 1939-45 few of the actual houses occupied by the old founders had survived, and to-day the last survivors have gone. When devastated London has been rebuilt some of the streets where those foundries were will probably disappear. It will therefore perhaps be of some interest to plot these sites on a map and to make a tour of the streets where the foundries were situated.

We are dividing the area into two parts, the first being west of Ludgate Circus, and the second and more important one to the east of that point.

We start at *Dorset Street*, Salisbury Square, south of Fleet Street. JOSEPH JACKSON, an apprentice of William Caslon, had set up for himself in Cock Lane in 1763, and about 1770 moved to Dorset Street. In the Directories his address is variously given as 107 Salisbury Court, 107 Salisbury Square, and Dorset Street, all presumably the same premises (1).[1] He made a reputation as a cutter of exotic types, among which were a Domesday fount, an uncial Greek, and the first Sanskrit cut by an English founder. After his death in 1792 his foundry was bought by WILLIAM CASLON III, who had recently parted from the Chiswell Street foundry. After two years in Finsbury Square, Caslon brought the foundry back to Dorset Street, and the firm continued there until 1819, when it was taken over by Blake, Garnett & Co, afterwards Stephenson, Blake & Co. of Sheffield.

We continue our tour westwards up Fleet Street and turn north into Fetter Lane. On the left we pass *Bream's Buildings*, a street which to day runs through to Chancery Lane. In 1791, when SIMON STEPHENSON, once the partner of John Bell, established the BRITISH LETTER FOUNDRY here (2), we could not have approached it from Chancery Lane. Bell had given up his part in the concern at the end of 1789, and the foundry was finally sold by auction in 1797. Further up Fetter Lane in an area now completely devastated and rebuilt differently we reach on the right *Nevil's Court*. Here was the foundry of THOMAS COTTRELL (3), another apprentice of William Caslon, from 1758 to 1785. We may note that in this court there were some houses surviving until late into the

---

* Jointly with W. Turner Berry.
1. Numbers between brackets refer to the map on p. 398.

1930s from the seventeenth century.[1] One of them was still there in 1940. Cottrell was at No. 9, next door to the houses described by the Commission.

Further north on the same side in *Dean Street* (or Dean Lane), and on the corner of this street was (and is again) the London Office of the Monotype Corporation. At No. 23 was the foundry of HUGH HUGHES (4) from 1824 to *c.* 1840. At one time Hughes had been with Robert Thorne at the Fann Street Foundry. He was well known as an engraver of music types.

From the top of Fetter Lane we might continue further north up Leather Lane or Hatton Garden into Clerkenwell, but the district has been so transformed by the building of new streets, ending with Clerkenwell Road in 1878, that we should not find the sites of the foundries formerly situated in that district. Off Farringdon Road, a little to the north of the junction of Clerkenwell Road and Farringdon, on the left side, is all that is left of *Ray Street*, the last address of the FIGGINS FOUNDRY from 1865 (not on our map). This area was formerly called Hockley-in-the-Hole and was notorious in the early eighteenth century for cock-fighting, bear-baiting, and other rough sports. Clerkenwell, in general, was not the drab district it has since become. At the time when the waters were taken at the various wells there were many pleasure resorts in what was still a semi-rural suburb.

In *Farringdon Road* from 1867 to 1872 was the AUSTIN LETTER FOUNDRY of J. & R. M. WOOD (not on our map), formerly of West Smithfield, and best known as the publishers of the *Typographic Advertiser*, the earliest periodical in this country issued by a foundry.

Further east, along Clerkenwell Road, on the south side, was *Red Lion Street* (now Britton Street, presumably named after John Britton, the antiquary, who began his London life in these parts), where, in 1830, at No. 54 (not on our map) lived ANTHONY BESSEMER, father of the famous inventor, Sir Henry Bessemer. The father had been a punch-cutter in Paris up till the Revolution and later had set up a foundry at Hitchin.

To return to the top of Fetter Lane, we will proceed westward up Holborn, and at Gray's Inn Road we shall pass the site of *Middle Row*, one of those curious blocks of houses which stood out in the roadway to the obstruction of traffic in more than one London street. C. HANCOCK, who had bought Hugh Hughes's music matrices about 1840, lived in Middle Row, and later at 32 Gloucester Street, a road leading from Theobald's Road to Queen Square.

Further up Holborn we come to Kingsway, where was formerly *Little Queen Street*, leading south into Great Queen Street. The building of Kingsway and Aldwych is one of a number of reconstructions of London streets in the nineteenth century which have blotted out many old landmarks. Other instances are Shaftesbury Avenue, Charing Cross Road, Queen Victoria Street, and Holborn Viaduct.

In Little Queen Street lived LOUIS POUCHÉE (5) from 1823 to 1830, when his foundry was sold by auction. Pouchée was the first man to introduce a type-casting machine,

---

1. They are described in the series published by the Royal Commission on Historical Monuments, London, vol. 4.

the invention of Henri Didot, of Paris. He carried on a competitive war against the old-established foundries and lost. His machine was finally bought by a group of founders and destroyed. For the rest of the century the treatment of Pouchée by the combined founders was a ground of reproach continually brought up against them by their critics.

We turn right into *Great Queen Street*. Here, in Queen's Head Yard, was the small foundry of WILLIAM HOWARD (6), an ex-sailor, who cut some types for the Chiswick Press. Among these were the Basle roman, last used by William Morris, just before he started the Kelmscott Press, and the Chiswick Press reproduction of a Caxton type.

At the end of Great Queen Street, leading south-east, is *Great Wild Street* (now Wild Street), and it was in this street that Pouché started his 'New Foundry' (7) about 1815. Leading out of Wild Street is *Wild Court*, where Benjamin Franklin worked at the press of John Watts in 1725, after leaving Samuel Palmer in Bartholomew Close.

We will return to the corner of Great Queen Street and turn south down *Drury Lane*. Here at No. 43 lived ISAAC MOORE (8), who had been punch-cutter to the Fry firm in Bristol and in Worship Street, Moorfields, and from whom he had separated about 1776. He still styled himself 'letter founder and printer'.

Leading west out of Drury Lane is *Russell Street*, in which street JOSEPH MOXON (9) took refuge after the Great Fire, when his house on Ludgate Hill, at the sign of the Atlas, had been burnt down. He was in Russell Street, at the same sign of the Atlas, in 1669, 1670, and 1671, and it was from this address that his type specimen sheet appeared in 1669. He had started founding ten years before, when his shop was in Cornhill, at the opposite edge of the area we are to traverse.

From the foot of Drury Lane we make our way into the Strand, although, of course, there was no Aldwych in the eighteenth century. On the north side of the Strand between the modern Wellington Street and Burley Street was *Exeter Change*, and at the 'Corner of Exeer Change' was the British Library of JOHN BELL (10); here, in 1788, Bell started his British Letter Foundry with Richard Austin as punch-cutter, an important event in the history of English type design. With Austin's new roman of 1788 we reach the first modern face, which was to prove the prevailing fashion throughout the next century. Bell and Stephenson's specimen book of 1789 has the address, 'In the Savoy', which must mean on the south side of the Strand. The firm seems to have required additional premises for the foundry.

We will now turn east along the Strand as far as the Law Courts, on part of which site was formerly *Crown Court*. Here was the press of an interesting printer and type-cutter, RICHARD WATTS (11). Watts was Cambridge University Printer from 1802 to 1809, then was printing at Broxbourne, Herts., and finally settled in Crown Court. He printed for the British and Foreign Bible Society and cut a large number of oriental and other exotic types for their Biblical translations. This wonderful collection was enlarged by his son, W. M. Watts, and is still preserved in the hands of Messrs. Clowes & Sons.

For the second part of our tour, to the east and north-east, we will start at *Printing House Square*, the home of the King's Printer before 1770 and now of *The Times*. There was never a regular foundry here, but JOHN WALTER bought the Printing House (12) in 1784 as a home for his logographic press, and for a few years it was a foundry to that extent.

We pass on to *Ludgate Hill*, where JOSEPH MOXON, the author of *Mechanick Exercises* and Member of the Royal Society, lived at the sign of the Atlas (13), near Fleet Bridge. Moxon was a typefounder from 1659, when he was in Cornhill near St. Michael's Church, to *c.* 1683, but always at the sign of the Atlas. He dealt also in maps, globes, and mathematical instruments, hence his sign. Samuel Pepys bought a globe there in 1664. Moxon appears to have been on Ludgate Hill at the time of the Great Fire in 1666, and was back there again in 1672 and there he published the first part of his *Mechanick Exercises* in 1677. In the meantime he had been in Russell Street, Westminster, as we have already seen.

If we continue up Ludgate Hill we pass Old Bailey, where on the west side in *Prujean's Court* (or Prujean's Square) was SAMUEL JALLESON (14), one of the minor founders, working about 1727 to 1729.

Turning north into Ave Maria Lane, we come to Paternoster Row, having a good view of Stationers' Hall on the way. We turn right up Paternoster Row and come to *Paul's Alley* on the right and *Ivy Lane* on the left, both now completely devastated. The earliest typefounder whose address we know was JOHN GRISMOND, who lived first at Little North Door, St. Paul's, then in Paul's Alley (perhaps the same address) (15) and then in Ivy Lane (16). Grismond was one of the four authorized founders under the Star Chamber Decree of 1637. Of the other three, Thomas Wright, Arthur Nicholls, and Alexander Fifield, we have no addresses.

We pass on up Ivy Lane, turn west in Newgate Street, and then north up Giltspur Street. We have now passed outside the old City Wall and shall remain on the outside for the rest of the tour.

On the left side of Giltspur Street we pass *Cock Lane*, notorious for its ghost, but also the home of JOSEPH JACKSON (17), who learned his trade with William Caslon and was founding in Cock Lane on his own account from 1763 to *c.* 1770. We know already that he earned repute for his cutting of exotic types and we have seen that his second address was in Salisbury Square.

Further up Giltspur Street we come to *West Smithfield*, where at No. 85 was the Austin Letter Foundry, under J. & R. M. WOOD (18), from 1856; as we have seen they moved to Farringdon Road in 1867. It was at this Smithfield address that they published *The Typographic Advertiser* (1862–68).

Leading out of West Smithfield was formerly *West Street* (or Chick Lane), where at Nos. 17 and 18 was the FIGGINS FOUNDRY (19) from 1801 to 1865. In 1865 it moved to Ray Street, as we have seen. Vincent Figgins was apprenticed to Joseph Jackson, and in 1792 established his first foundry in *Swan Yard*, Holborn, a little to the south of West Street (off our map). Both these sites disappeared at the time when the Holborn Viaduct and the modern Charterhouse Street were built.

At the north-east corner of West Smithfield begins Long Lane, and the second street running north was the original *Charterhouse Street* (now Hayne Street), where was the

Inside: Sketch map of the same part of the City of London: present situation.

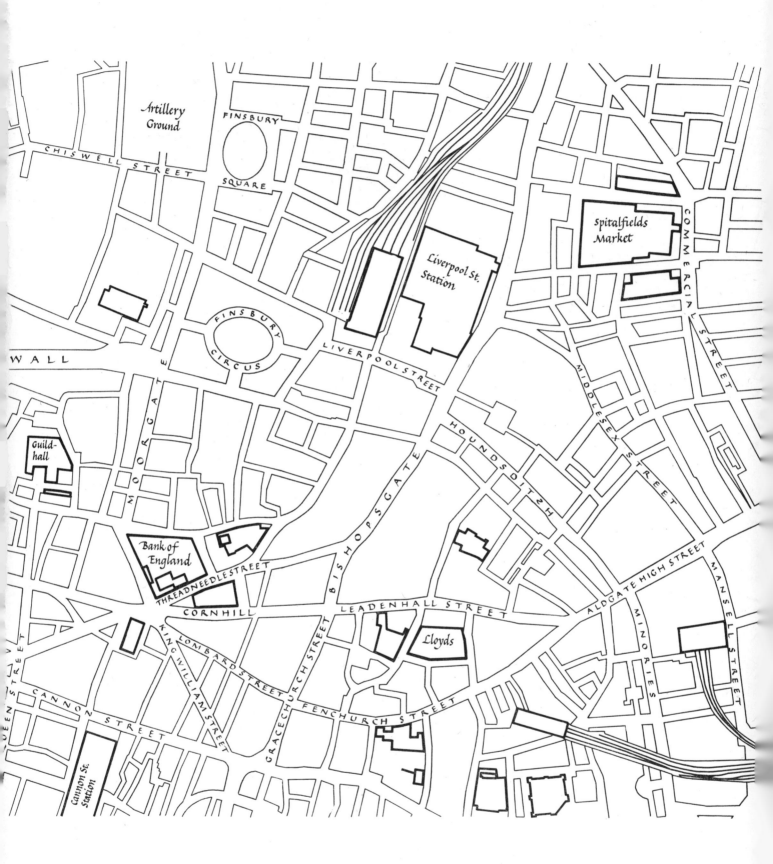

Artillery
Ground

FINSBURY
SQUARE

CHISWELL STREET

FINSBURY
CIRCUS

WALL

Liverpool St.
Station

spitalfields
Market

COMMERCIAL STREET

LIVERPOOL STREET

Guild-
hall

MOORGATE

BISHOPSGATE

HOUNDSDITCH

MIDDLESEX STREET

ALDGATE HIGH STREET

MANSELL STREET

Bank of
England

THREADNEEDLE STREET

CORNHILL

LEADENHALL STREET

GRACECHURCH STREET

MINORIES

Lloyds

FENCHURCH STREET

QUEEN STREET

CANNON STREET

KING WILLIAM STREET

LOMBARD STREET

Cannon St.
Station

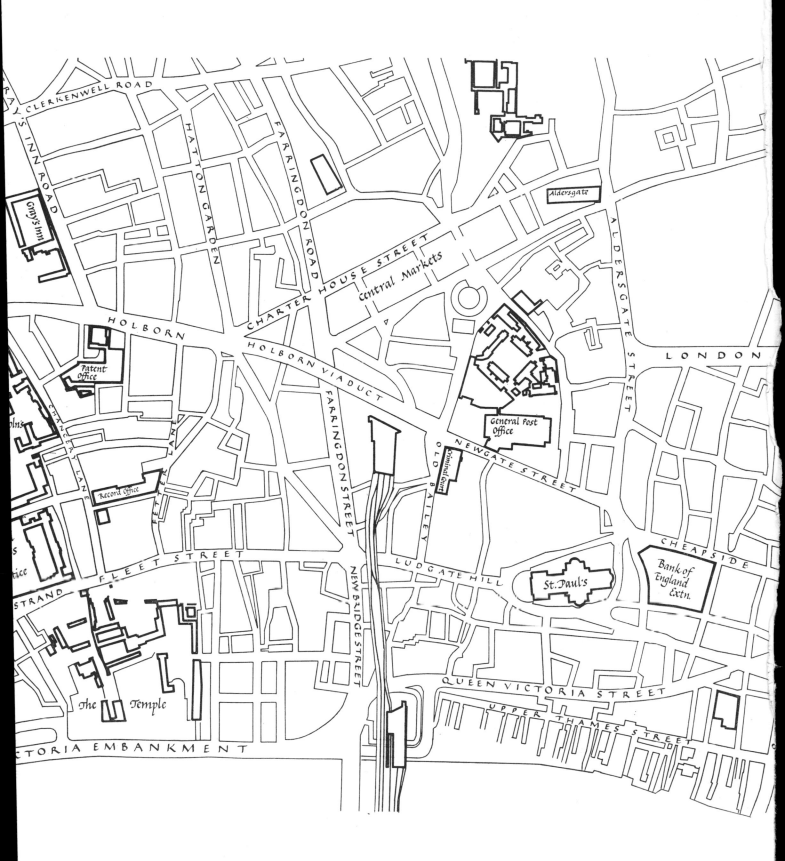

little further up Aldersgate (then Goswell Street, still on the same side, but now utterly destroyed) (32). The Fann Street Foundry, successively under Thorne, William Thorowgood, Robert Besley, and lastly the Reeds, was continued throughout the nineteenth century. Thorowgood, at the sale of the Type Street or Polyglot Foundry (the Frys), acquired, besides Fry's own designs, the types surviving from the Grover and James Foundries. To the fact that the Fann Street Foundry was in possession of these matrices we owe T. B. Reed's *History of the Old English Letter Foundries*.

Before leaving Aldersgate there is one more address to note, No. 120, on the west side, opposite Hare Court, where lived from 1833 to 1856 WOOD & SHARWOOD (33), successors to Richard Austin of the Imperial Letter Foundry. This house is shown in Tallis's *London Street Views*, 1839.

We will leave Aldersgate via Barbican and continue eastwards through Beech Street into Chiswell Street, through the devastated area. The origin of the name Chiswell is unknown but it is found as early as the thirteenth century. In Chiswell Street on the south side is *Moor Lane*. In 1788, when EDMUND FRY (34) moved his foundry to this area, the north end of Moor Lane was still undeveloped and the name which he gave it, *Type Street*, was apparently accepted and it is called Type Street in Horwood's map, though now Moor Lane.

Continuing Moor Lane, south of London Wall, is *Basinghall Street*, where at the time of the Plague in 1665 lived the founder JOSEPH LEIGH (35), near the Nag's Head Tavern.

Further along *Chiswell Street* was, at Nos. 22 and 23, the CASLON FOUNDRY (36), the most famous of the London foundries. William Caslon settled there in 1734 and the business was continued in the same premises for just over one hundred and seventy years. When the street was first numbered, about the year 1766, Caslon's was No. 62. In 1824 the street was renumbered, and the house then became Nos. 22 & 23. In 1909 the firm moved to the opposite side of the street, the south side (37), and became Nos. 82 & 83. About the year 1790 Richard Austin, whose foundry we shall reach shortly, was living at No. 7, and his trade card as an engraver, bearing this address, has survived.

Chiswell Street ends in *Finsbury Square*. When WILLIAM CASLON III (38), in 1792, bought Jackson's Foundry and moved it to this quarter, the square had only recently been built. The directories do not give Caslon's number, but if, as stated by T. B. Reed, the house was afterwards occupied by James Lackington, it was situated at the south-west corner of the Square. Lackington, who had previously been in Chiswell Street, called his new shop the Temple of the Muses and made it one of the sights of London. The main front appears to have been in Finsbury Place, now Finsbury Pavement. It is said that a coach and six could be driven into the shop. It was destroyed by fire in 1841.

Continuing north into City Road, we come on the east side to *Worship Street*, which probably in the eighteenth century was a much pleasanter street than it has now become. Here at different times were two foundries, the FRYS (39) at No. 15, from *c.* 1685 to 1788, and RICHARD AUSTIN (40) at No. 10, the Imperial Letter Foundry, from *c.* 1815 to 1833. Austin was an important man in the story of English typography, since he cut the John Bell types and the modern faces of the Scotch foundries, Alexander Wilson, of Glasgow, and William Miller, of Edinburgh. Austin's foundry in Worship Street was continued by his son George and then by R. M. Wood and was later removed to Aldersgate. The Fry Foundry before coming to Worship Street had been at 8 *Queen Street*, a short street running south out of Worship Street, now apparently without a name (41). Isaac Moore, the manager and first punchcutter for the Frys, issued a specimen from this address in 1768.

We return to City Road and continue north to Old Street, turn west and pass along until we reach St. Luke's Church on the north side, which was consecrated in 1733. On the west side of the church is *Helmet Row* (42), where Caslon first turned to letter-cutting about the year 1720. On the east side is *Ironmonger Row*; it was from this address (43) that Caslon published the first issue of his specimen sheet bearing the date 1734.

In the churchyard of St. Luke's is the Caslon family tomb, where are buried William Caslon and several members of his family. We will end our tour at Caslon Street, the present fitting name of the former New Street, lying immediately east of Ironmonger Row.

[1946]

THE MODERN-FACE TYPE IN ENGLAND

In the vocabulary applied to our printing types there are many cases of ill-chosen names, like the absurd 'gothic' or 'grotesque' for the sans serifs. Another unfortunate example is the term 'modern-face', universally used of a family of types which has ceased to be modern. Our book typography is for the most part old-face. The modern face is limited, with rare exceptions, to technical books and newspapers, and even in these branches is only continued by the force of a convention which is likely to be broken before long. This name for the roman, which was in favour throughout the nineteenth century, can hardly be rejected at this date without introducing confusion. It stands for a well-marked family of types. We propose here to define the characteristics of this family and to give some account of its development in this country.

Whether a letter is drawn by the pen of a calligrapher or is reproduced from metal type the ultimate design is affected by two matters in particular, the shape of the serif and the relation of the thick and thin strokes. Serifs can be thin or heavy, horizontal or inclined, bracketed or unsupported. The thick strokes may taper gradually to slightly thinner strokes, or they may descend abruptly to hair-lines. The curved strokes may have the thickest part in the centre; in the o the two thickest parts may be horizontally opposite, a form produced by a pen held at right angles to the paper. Or again the thickest curves may be below the centre, or, in the o, diagonally opposite. In the one case we speak of the vertical shading or stress in the design, in the other we call the shading or colour diagonal. It is according to these characteristics that our roman types are classified. The romans of the early printers and of all the printers of the old-face period down to 1700, or to 1750 in England, had inclined and bracketed serifs, gradual shading and diagonal stress. The nineteenth-century type had flat, unsupported serifs, abrupt shading, and vertical stress. In between the two, that is in the eighteenth century, we find a number of types which are in design between these extremes; they have broken from the old tradition, but are still short of the final development.

We will now examine a fount of modern-face roman with these main characteristics in mind. The serifs on the upper case will be seen to be flat, thin, and unsupported. Flat serifs have always been normal to the roman inscriptional capitals, but in the old-face letters these serifs were always supported by a triangular piece or a curved arc on the under side, nor did they end in sharp points. In the lower case the same flat, thin serifs are found on the tops of ascending letters, such as h and l, and on the m, n, r, and u; the foot serifs also on the d and u have become horizontal, while in some modern-faces there is a similar foot serif to the b and a top serif on the right of the q. All these points are unknown in the old-face romans. The abrupt shading and vertical colour may be considered together, and are evident in all the curved strokes of both upper- and lower-case. The contrast between thick and thin strokes, with the thickest part in the mathematical centre, is well illustrated by the capital C and the lower-case e. The general result is a rigidly vertical design of great regularity. Mathematical exactness and regularity appear to have been qualities admired by the designers of the modern-

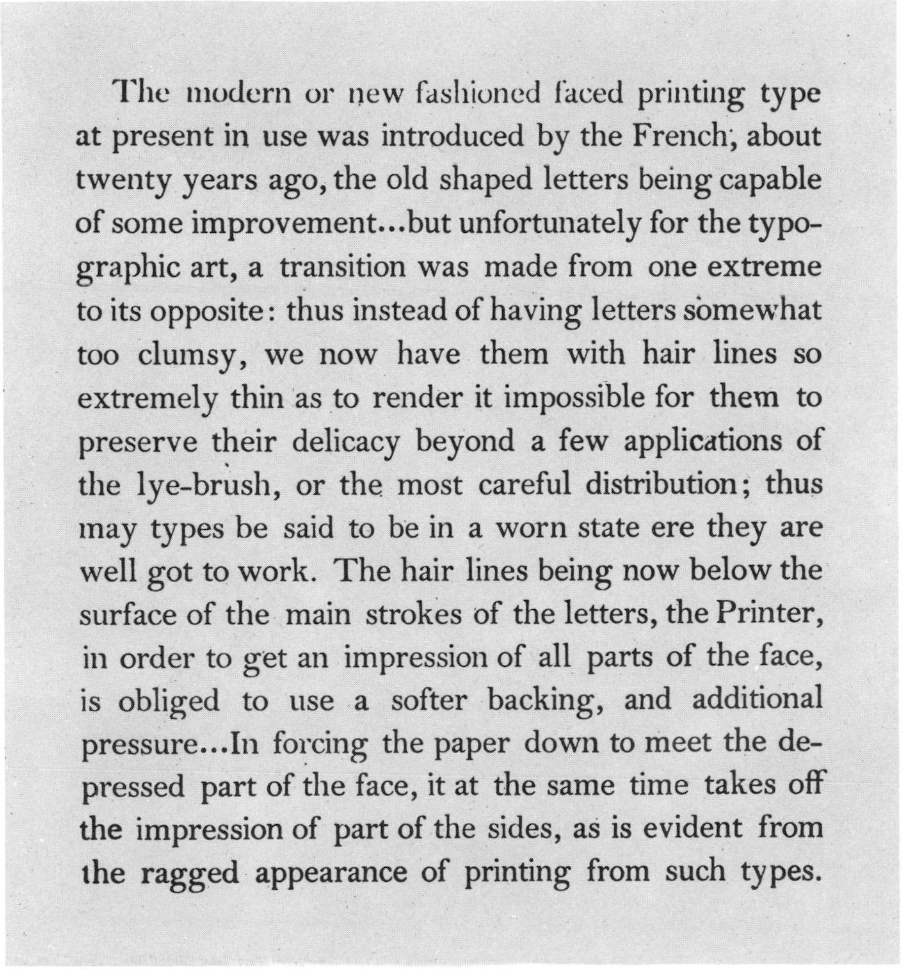

The modern or new fashioned faced printing type at present in use was introduced by the French, about twenty years ago, the old shaped letters being capable of some improvement...but unfortunately for the typographic art, a transition was made from one extreme to its opposite: thus instead of having letters somewhat too clumsy, we now have them with hair lines so extremely thin as to render it impossible for them to preserve their delicacy beyond a few applications of the lye-brush, or the most careful distribution; thus may types be said to be in a worn state ere they are well got to work. The hair lines being now below the surface of the main strokes of the letters, the Printer, in order to get an impression of all parts of the face, is obliged to use a softer backing, and additional pressure...In forcing the paper down to meet the depressed part of the face, it at the same time takes off the impression of part of the sides, as is evident from the ragged appearance of printing from such types.

Fig. 1. John Bell's type as presented in a specimen book of the Imperial Letter Foundry. The text was written by Richard Austin in 1825.

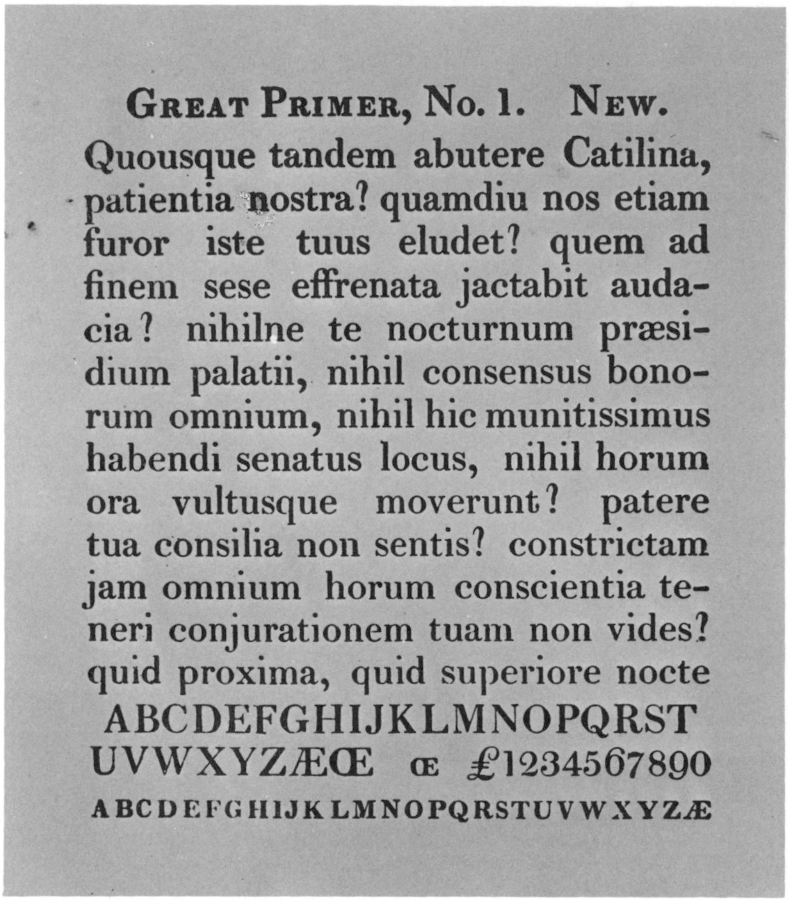

GREAT PRIMER, No. 1.   NEW.
Quousque tandem abutere Catilina,
patientia nostra? quamdiu nos etiam
furor iste tuus eludet? quem ad
finem sese effrenata jactabit audacia? nihilne te nocturnum præsi-
dium palatii, nihil consensus bonorum omnium, nihil hic munitissimus
habendi senatus locus, nihil horum
ora vultusque moverunt? patere
tua consilia non sentis? constrictam
jam omnium horum conscientia teneri conjurationem tuam non vides?
quid proxima, quid superiore nocte
ABCDEFGHIJKLMNOPQRST
UVWXYZÆŒ œ £1234567890
ABCDEFGHIJKLMNOPQRSTUVWXYZÆ

FIG. 2. Robert Thorne's type as presented in his 1803 specimen
book. It shows all the characteristics of a 'modern' face.

face. Their desire for regularity is shown by what we may call the fourth characteristic, the uniform width of the capitals. Instead of that pleasing variation between the wide round letters and the H and M, and on the other hand the narrow E, F, and L, a variation which is found in a famous model of roman lettering, that on the Trajan columns, and which has often been copied by twentieth-century designers, in the modern face we find monotonous uniformity. Individual letters which may be noted as differing from the old-face are the short ranging J (along with short-ranging figures) and the R with a curved, yet vertical tail; in the lower case the bowl of the a is larger, and the upper storey is almost closed by the curve of the top arc; the eye of the e is large, the g has a curly ear instead of the early, straight remnant of a connecting stroke; the t, lastly, is a taller letter and often has an unbracketed cross-stroke.

This design, like many others in our typographical history, had its origin in France. The story of its development in the hands of the French type-cutters may here be briefly summarized. In the last decade of the seventeenth century the Royal Printing House in Paris decided that the time had come to bring their typography up to date. The final design produced by their engraver, Philippe Grandjean, was known as the 'romain du roi', and this roman, although not a modern face in every detail, had taken a long step in that direction and is always accepted as the father of the family. Although the design was something new in typography it was not an original creation, but simply the adaptation to type of the fashionable lettering of the engravers. The writing-masters were by this time working on copper plate, and it was the use of this medium which had led to the popular thin serifs, hair-lines, and vertical stress. Owing to the fact that it was forbidden to copy the 'romain du roi' it was many years before the next step was taken. It was not until 1784 that Firmin Didot carried the design to its logical conclusion and produced the first fully-developed modern-face roman. Didot was not satisfied with his first attempt, which to us appears perhaps the best of the modern faces, but went on to design founts of more exaggerated shading such as became popular throughout Europe about 1800. He was imitated by all the French founders, and especially by the distinguished Italian type-cutter, Giambattista Bodoni, who might be called the master of the modern face. His well-known specimen book, the *Manuale Tipografico* of 1816, contains the finest display of the classical modern face ever issued. In the preface to that book Bodoni discusses the principles of type design, for the most part in rather vague terms. On two points, however, he is clear: on the importance of regularity and of sharpness of cut.

The first indications of the movement in the same direction in England are found in the types of John Baskerville, who began work at his press in Birmingham in 1750. William Caslon, who was then at the height of his popularity, was entirely devoted to the old face and might never have heard of the 'romain du roi'. It is a significant fact that Baskerville, who followed many careers, had at one period been a writing-master. He had doubtless seen books printed at the Imprimerie Royale, but nevertheless he could have found all the forms which he transferred into type in contemporary English writing-books. To us today Baskerville roman appears to belong to the old-face school, but when compared with the true old-face Caslon the innovations of the design are evident. The serifs are still inclined, but less so than in Caslon; the shading is not vertical but is more nearly so, as may be seen by comparing Caslon's e with Baskerville's e. Of individual letters, the Q with its elaborate tail and the eighteenth-century R may be noted. The R has a curled tail but is without that ugly verticality found in the full modern-face. There are two 'spot' letters, useful for purposes of recognition, a g with the tail not quite closed, and W w, upper and lower case, with no middle serif. The w is particularly useful in English texts, where that letter occurs so frequently. The modernity of the Baskerville italic is much more evident than is the case with the roman. The angle of the slope is more uniform than in earlier English italics. The design of certain letters has been altered with the purpose of regularizing the inclination, the *a*, for example, and the *m* and *n* have been squared up, as it were. The swash capitals are, perhaps, inconsistent, but add a pleasant flavour to an italic which, in comparison with its roman, has received less than its due share of praise.

Baskerville in his own day did not meet with all the success he hoped for. There is evidence of some professional jealousy and of a pretence that his work was that of an inexperienced amateur. Rowe Mores, the purchaser of the James Foundry, in his *Dissertation upon English Foundries*, had the impertinence to declare that Baskerville could 'hardly claim a place amongst letter-founders'. The regular founders never mention his name in their specimens, but nevertheless there is ample evidence that they copied his types. One of these imitations is displayed today by Messrs. Stephenson, Blake and Co., and is now known as 'Fry's Baskerville'. It was presumably cut by Isaac Moore, the first type-designer of the Fry firm. It bears a close resemblance to Baskerville in the modernity of the cut, and also in its openness and roundness. Distinguishing letters are the Q with a tail starting inside the counter of the letter, the straight-tailed R, the a with a more open upper storey, and the g; this last letter has the tail unclosed but finished with a little curl not found in Baskerville.

Towards the end of the century we meet several romans which are on the very verge of the modern-face, and yet do definitely stop short. Of these, two in particular call for notice: the type of William Martin and that of John Bell. Martin was a brother of Robert Martin, who had worked with Baskerville. About 1795 William produced his types for the Shakespeare Press, of which William Bulmer was the moving spirit. The American type-founders have recently reproduced the Martin type and have given it the name of 'Bulmer', not unfittingly. The roman is less open and round than Baskerville; the serifs are almost, but not quite, flat; the variation between thick and thin strokes it more pronounced, and the shading more vertical; yet there is not that mathematical verticality found in the contemporary Didot and Bodoni. The e in particular is old-face in the distribution of weight. The g is a narrow letter with the appearance of leaning backwards. The top of the t appears to fall forwards.

The John Bell type, cut by Richard Austin, is a little earlier in date than Martin's – the first specimen appeared in 1788 – but we mention it here because it has been called the first English modern-face. Stanley Morison, who discovered the specimens of Bell's British Foundry and who has traced the history of the design, calls it our first independent letter and classes it as a modern face. He notices in particular the cutting of the serifs, which are bracketed in a curved arc and end in sharp points. Finely cut serifs may be characteristic of modern work; the early methods of printing would merely have obscured anything so delicate. But if 'modern-face' is accepted as the name of the classical types of Didot and Bodoni, and for the normal nineteenth-century type, then John Bell's is not a modern face. It lacks that precise regularity given by mathematical verticality of shading and abrupt stress. The serifs are flat but bracketed, the distribution of weight in, for instance, the e, is not quite vertical, and the shading is by no means abrupt. The fount has short-ranging figures, a short-ranging J, and a second, modern t with an unbracketed cross-stroke.

The contrast between this beautiful type and what we regard as our first modern face is striking. In 1803 Robert Thorne issued a specimen book containing some 'new' letters, one of them dated 1800 and another 1802. Here we have an undoubted modern face with all the mathematical regularity of the family and all the characteristics we have already described. Note the monotonous uniformity of the capitals and the sharp contrast of thick and thin strokes. Thorne's design was popular – though it is difficult to understand why – and was immediately copied by the other founders. Fry showed the new style in the same year and was soon followed by Caslon and Figgins. It is a curious fact that most of the founders protested against the innovation and yet were unable to hold out against the popular demand. Dr. Edmund Fry complained that his firm had been obliged to melt down all their old types, and declared that in his experience the types on the new system were not so serviceable nor so agreeable to the reader as, what he calls, the 'Caslon-shaped Elzevir types'. The text of our example of the John Bell letter is taken from the preface of a specimen of the Imperial Letter Foundry and was written by Richard Austin shortly before his death in 1825. It will be seen that Austin, too, objected to the new letters on technical grounds, and preferred those of thirty years before.

In spite of the taste of the leading type-founders the modern face was to be the standard of the nineteenth century. It was not only the normal book-type, but it had an unfortunate influence on many of the display types of that century. The monotony of the upper case of the early sans serifs is derived from the traditional modern-face capitals, and it is because the designers of to-day have thrown over that influence that they have succeeded in reforming the sans serif. Similarly, we may contrast the uninteresting early Egyptians with twentieth-century versions of that letter, like Memphis and Beton, both German designs. What is known as the Latin face and the notorious Cheltenham, both have the uniform capitals, the vertical shading and the horizontal serifs of the modern-face.

The so-called classical types of Didot and Bodoni had no exact parallel in England. Thorne's design was already inferior, and what was to follow was even worse. Apart from the general characteristics described above, the nineteenth-century letter in this country had a number of ugly individual forms which are not found in Bodoni, or even in Thorne, in some cases. In the upper case the C and G are much less open than in Bodoni, the M is unpleasantly narrow and the R finishes with an ugly little turn up. In the lower case the nearly closed upper storey of the a and the very large eye to

There are a few more striking
Fashions can change and each
There are few more striking

FIG. 3. A comparison between the types of William Caslon, John Baskerville,
and a truly 'modern' face (as recut by the Monotype Corporation).

the e are bad forms; the unkerned f, the button-hook tails of the j and y, and the top-heavy t are no better. The italic, too, has quite as many poor letters. One of our modern faces forms an exception, namely, the face known as Scotch Roman. It has better designed serifs, resembling those of the John Bell type, and avoids a number, though not all, of the unpleasant features described. This design may be due to Richard Austin, who is known to have cut modern-face types for the two Scotch foundries, the Wilson firm, of Glasgow, and the house of William Miller, of Edinburgh.

[1932]

FAT FACES: THEIR HISTORY, FORMS, AND USE

Of the nineteenth-century Jobbing Types, that is, types cut with the intention of serving the advertising world, the earliest were what we know as the Fat Faces. There were some jobbing types in the eighteenth century apart altogether from the early *Union Pearl* and the *Outline* capitals of the end of the century, meant for title-pages. Thomas Cottrell, a pupil of the first William Caslon, had cut large poster letters, up to 12-line pica, called by Rowe Mores 'letters of proscription', before 1770. Mrs. Nicolette Gray, in her *Nineteenth century ornamented types*,[1] traces the evolution of the Fat Faces from these letters of proscription. Mrs. Gray gives an example from the Fry Foundry, dated 1808, a letter which is still old-face in design, but has the extreme contrast between thick and thin strokes, which is one of the characteristics of Fat Faces. From Mr. Ruari McLean[2] we learn that James Callingham in 1871 had seen the origin of Egyptians in these eighteenth-century poster letters, in this case those of William Caslon III, 1785. Incidentally it may be recalled that there were three methods of producing placard types. In the eighteenth century they appear to have been cast in sand after a primitive process similar to that supposed to have been used by Coster or whoever it was who produced the earliest Dutch types. The Caslon firm in Salisbury Square, the foundry acquired by William Caslon III after his break with the original firm, invented a process of their own, to which they gave the name, *Sanspareil*. This consisted in casting the face of the letter in the usual way and then mounting the letter on wood, thereby saving metal. The other founders in the nineteenth century took to cutting large letters in wood, and several small firms were established which specialized in wood letters.

The characteristics of the Fat Faces are for the most part the same as those of the classical modern face: thin, flat serifs, vertical stress and abrupt contrast of thick and thin strokes. To these characteristics we must add exaggeration of the contrast between thick and thin. The thickness of the main strokes as compared with their height is in the proportion of 1 to 2½. At what particular point a type ceases to be a Bold Face and becomes a Fat Face is hard to decide. The letter of Fry's shown in Stower's *Printer's Grammar*, 1808, is a Bold Face while the somewhat stouter letter in the example here shown from Savage's book[3] is certainly a Fat Face.

The founder, Robert Thorne, who had learnt his trade with Thomas Cottrell, is generally credited with being the first designer of Fat Faces. William Savage, in 1822, says that Thorne 'has been principally instrumental in the revolution that has taken place in Posting Bills, by the introduction of fat types', and T. C. Hansard in his *Typographia*, 1825, says that 'the extremely bold and fat letter, now prevalent in job printing, owes its introduction principally to Mr. Thorne'.

These two critics may have included Egyptians and other designs among fat letters

1. *Nineteenth-century ornamented Types and Title-pages.* 1938.
2. 'An Examination of Egyptians.' *Alphabet and Image.* No 1, 1946.
3. *Practical Hints on Decorative printing.* William Savage. 1822.

and may not have had in mind in particular what we call Fat Faces. At any rate Hansard
shows as 'typographical monstrosities' a Black Letter of corrupt design, an Antique,
i. e. Egyptian and an Italian, but no Fat Face. The contemporary specimen books lend
no support to the claim for Thorne, since no specimen from that founder is known after
1803. His jobbing types were first shown by his successor Thorowgood in 1820. Of the
other founders the first to show a Fat Face appears to have been the new Sheffield firm
of Bower and Bacon, or Bower, Bacon and Bower, as it was styled in 1810. They
were followed by Figgins, by Fry, by W. Caslon IV, all in 1816, and by L. Pouchée
in 1819. The fact that all the founders copied the original design is a proof that there
was a demand for the type, and that it preceded the Egyptians and Sans Serifs can readily
be shown by a search through contemporary documents. According to Savage the
founders, in their own defence, asserted that these novelties were not intended for use in
books, so that the search should be directed to posters and leaflets. Fat Faces will be
found on theatre bills and lottery advertisements at latest from 1810. Mrs. Gray finds
no example before 1812 which she can accept as a fully developed Fat Face, but certain
display types in the two specimens here shown, a title-page from a collected edition of
voyages and travels by Seume and others, published by Phillips of Blackfriars, and a

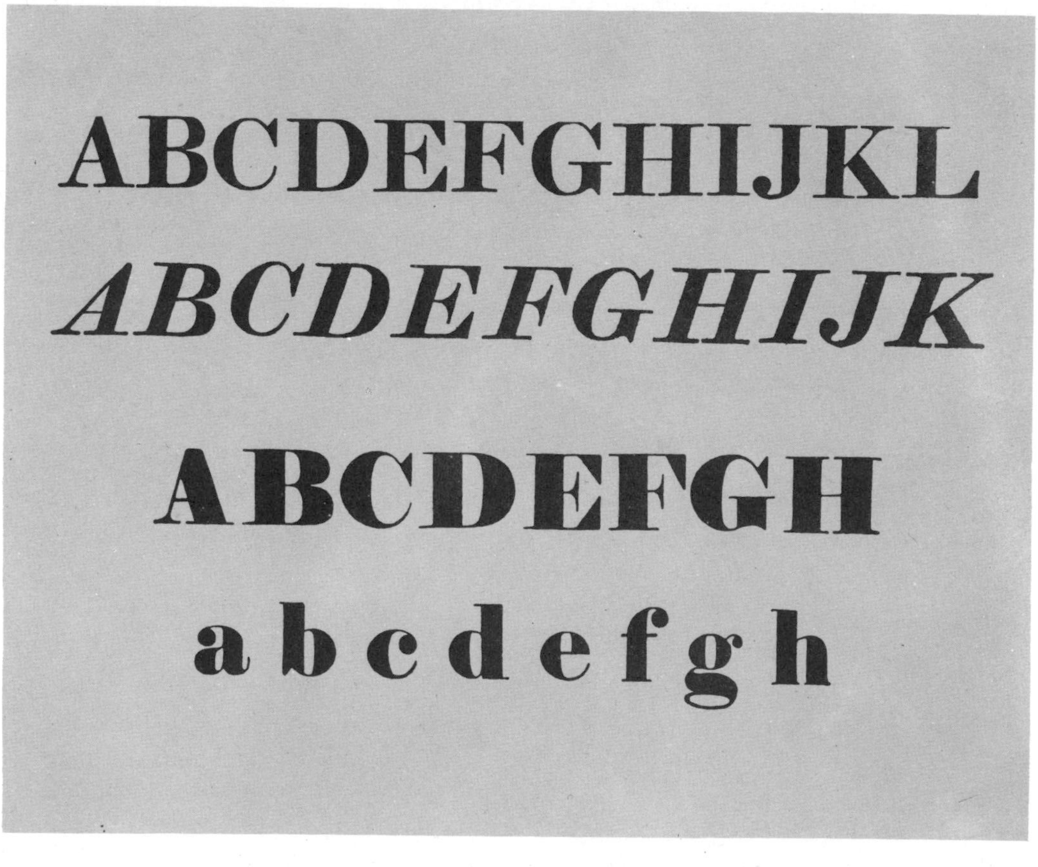

FIG. 1. The transition from Bold Face to Fat Face. Above: the 'French Canon' from
Stower's *Printer's Grammar*, 1808; below: the 'Canon, Modern' from Savage's *Pratical
Hints*, 1822. (Slightly reduced.)

notice of a lottery by T. Bish, 1810, are surely more than Bold Faces. Bish's handbills and those of the other farmers of lotteries, illustrate the development of the design from the Bold Faces and suggest that these Bold Faces rather than the placard types of Cottrell were the begetters of the Fat Faces. It does not appear that printers like Hansard looked with disapproval on the new Bold Faces, as he shows a *Canon* roman of heavy weight in his *Typographia* as the normal style, and they were in fact freely used by many of the leading printers of the day, for example by John Johnson, the typographer of Sir Samuel Egerton Brydges's Lee Priory Press.

To return to the lottery bills, these lotteries were Government concerns and were farmed out to men like T. Bish, of 4 Cornhill and 9 Charing Cross, and others. The Government raised many millions by this method, occasionally for particular purposes, such as the founding of the British Museum in 1753. The managers who had the

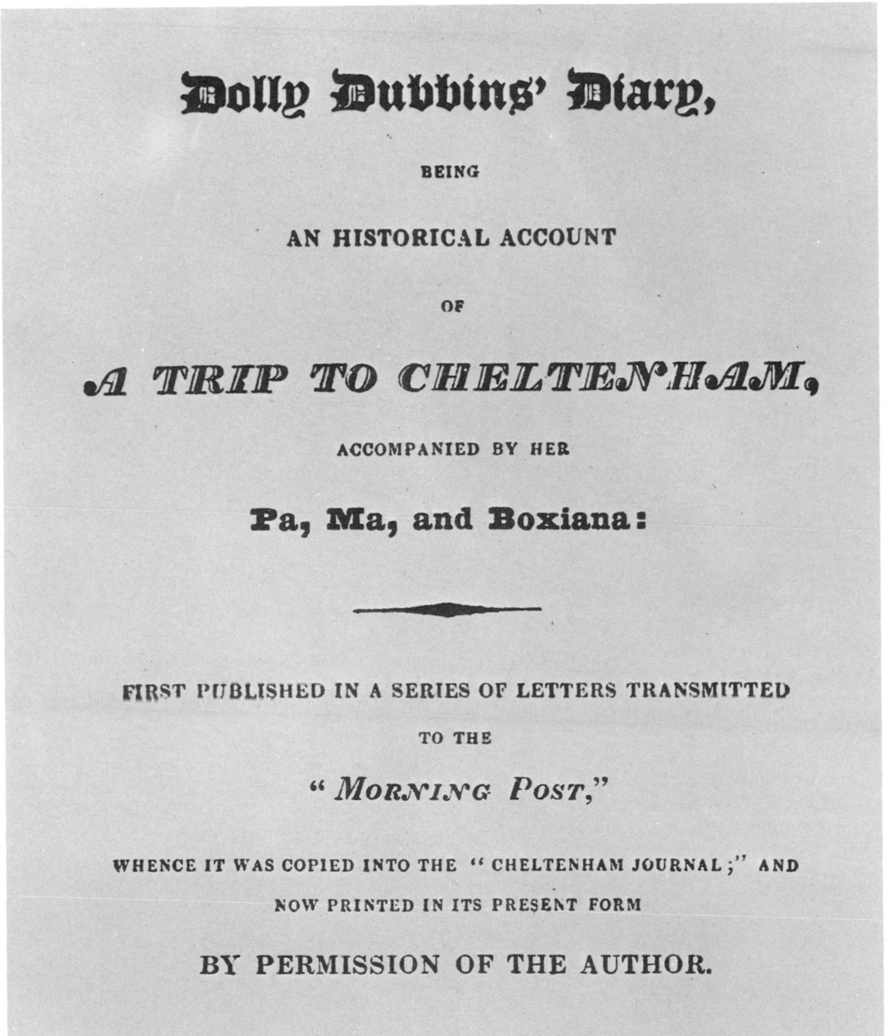

Dolly Dubbins' Diary,

BEING

AN HISTORICAL ACCOUNT

OF

A TRIP TO CHELTENHAM,

ACCOMPANIED BY HER

Pa, Ma, and Boxiana:

FIRST PUBLISHED IN A SERIES OF LETTERS TRANSMITTED

TO THE

"MORNING POST,"

WHENCE IT WAS COPIED INTO THE "CHELTENHAM JOURNAL;" AND

NOW PRINTED IN ITS PRESENT FORM

BY PERMISSION OF THE AUTHOR.

FIG. 2. A comparatively modest use of fat faces in the title-page of a popular pamphlet issued during the reign of George IV (1829).

bills printed showed little taste in display but as they seem to have been anxious to use the latest types, they are useful for our purpose. One can see the coming in of the Egyptians and the more ornamental letters. Unfortunately many of the bills bear no date and they come to an end in 1824, in which year the Government decided that the social evils arising out of the encouraging of gambling outweighed the advantages of this means of raising money. It is an odd coincidence that William Thorowgood in 1820 is said to have bought Thorne's foundry out of the proceeds of a successful lottery ticket.

If the Fat Faces, as distinct from the Bold Faces, were not widely used in books and were not intended by the founders for such use, they are often found on the title-pages of popular pamphlets, sometimes penny issues of the classics, and in guide-books, but usually they were used for the display lines in broadsides, ballads and news pamphlets, especially those relating to sensational happenings, murders, deaths by fire and all the horrors which seem to have found so ready a sale during the Regency and the reign of George IV. The last dying words of some murderer bearing a Seven Dials imprint generally had a heading set in a Fat Face. The headings of Sunday newspapers are another source, beginning with *The Sunday Monitor* in 1814 and *The Weekly Dispatch* in 1815.

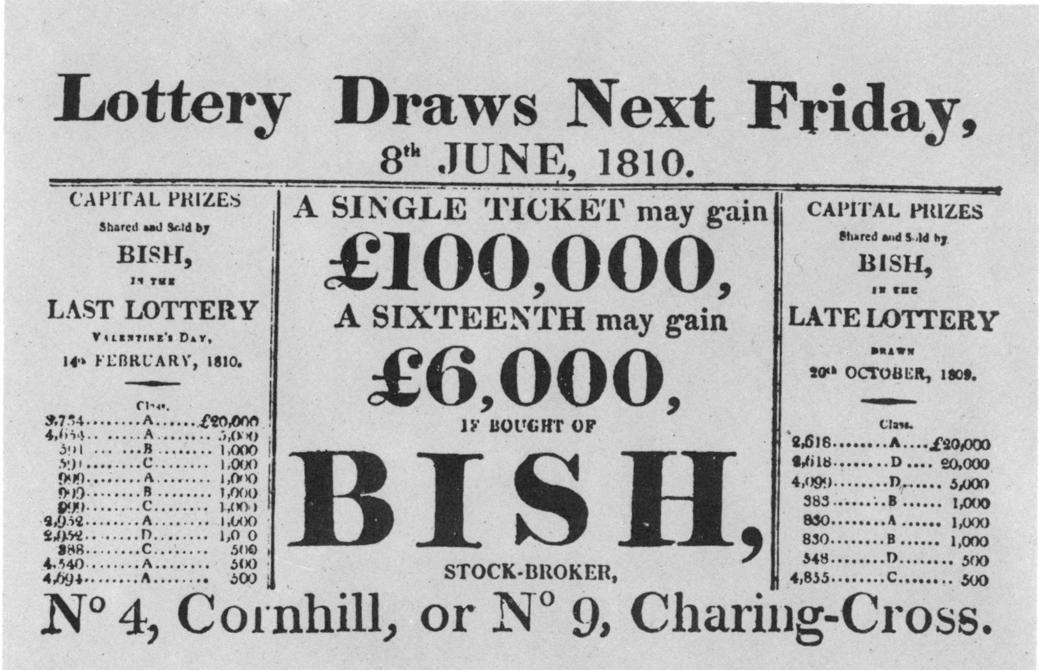

Lottery Draws Next Friday,

8th JUNE, 1810.

CAPITAL PRIZES
Shared and Sold by
BISH,
IN THE
LAST LOTTERY
VALENTINE'S DAY,
14th FEBRUARY, 1810.

Class.		
3,754	A	£20,000
4,654	A	5,000
591	B	1,000
591	C	1,000
990	A	1,000
990	B	1,000
990	C	1,000
2,952	A	1,000
2,052	D	1,0 0
388	C	500
4,540	A	500
4,694	A	500

A SINGLE TICKET may gain
£100,000,
A SIXTEENTH may gain
£6,000,
IF BOUGHT OF
BISH,
STOCK-BROKER,

CAPITAL PRIZES
Shared and Sold by
BISH,
IN THE
LATE LOTTERY
DRAWN
20th OCTOBER, 1809.

Class.		
2,616	A	£20,000
2,618	D	20,000
4,099	D	5,000
383	B	1,000
830	A	1,000
830	B	1,000
548	D	500
4,855	C	500

N° 4, Cornhill, or N° 9, Charing-Cross.

FIG. 3. An example of the very early use of Fat Face display types in a lottery notice issued in 1810. (The poorly printed original considerably reduced.)

As to how the founders imagined the types might be used it is significant that Thorowgood in his specimen book of 1839 shows a full range down to *Nonpareil*. The smaller sizes would hardly be legible on posters. This range of Thorowgood's has no particular name – each specimen is known by the size only – nor did any of the other founders invent a name for the family. We have to remember that 'Fat Face' is a twentieth-century title and that fat types, as already said, included various families. It is not until the 1850s that we find the Caslon foundry using the name *Albion* for a Fat Face and the Figgins calling their variety *Elephant*, a very apt descriptive title and one revived in recent years.

In the later years of the nineteenth century Fat Faces ceased to be shown in the specimen books, crowded out perhaps by the new German and American importations. But they never altogether ceased to be used, for example by the Queen's Printers, Eyre & Spottiswoode, on Proclamations. The official printers were naturally conservative in their typography and were slow to adopt any innovating letters. However, when once they had discovered that the Fat Faces were in their right place on a Proclamation they never abandoned them.

When the revival of these early jobbing types took place in the nineteen-twenties most of the old founders had passed out of business, and, with a few exceptions, the original

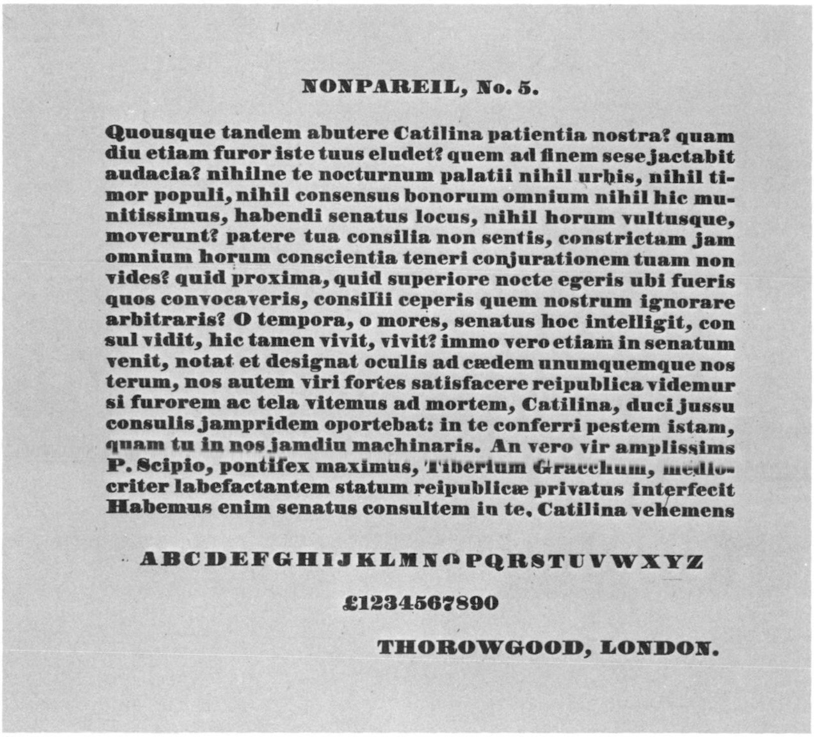
NONPAREIL, No. 5.

Quousque tandem abutere Catilina patientia nostra? quam diu etiam furor iste tuus eludet? quem ad finem sese jactabit audacia? nihilne te nocturnum palatii nihil urbis, nihil timor populi, nihil consensus bonorum omnium nihil hic munitissimus, habendi senatus locus, nihil horum vultusque, moverunt? patere tua consilia non sentis, constrictam jam omnium horum conscientia teneri conjurationem tuam non vides? quid proxima, quid superiore nocte egeris ubi fueris quos convocaveris, consilii ceperis quem nostrum ignorare arbitraris? O tempora, o mores, senatus hoc intelligit, con sul vidit, hic tamen vivit, vivit? immo vero etiam in senatum venit, notat et designat oculis ad cædem unumquemque nos terum, nos autem viri fortes satisfacere reipublica videmur si furorem ac tela vitemus ad mortem, Catilina, duci jussu consulis jampridem oportebat: in te conferri pestem istam, quam tu in nos jamdiu machinaris. An vero vir amplissims P. Scipio, pontifex maximus, Tiberium Gracchum, mediocriter labefactantem statum reipublicæ privatus interfecit Habemus enim senatus consultem in te, Catilina vehemens

ABCDEFGHIJKLMNOPQRSTUVWXYZ

£1234567890

THOROWGOOD, LONDON.

FIG. 4. By the 1850s the wide demand for Fat Face types had encouraged founders to produce even very small sizes. In Thorowgood's 1839 Specimen Book a Nonpareil may be found, here leaded with 2 points.

MARGATE

BRIGHTON

MAMA

GREAT BRITAIN

CHESTERFIELD

THE MANCHESTER and STOCKPORT COMPANIES.

COMMEMORATUS 1834.

◄NOTTINGHAMSHIRE►

FIG. 5. A fairly representative, but by no means exhaustive, range of mid-nineteenth-century Fat Face variants, most impressive in number and in *bizarrerie*, taken from various early nineteenth-century type specimens. Slight differences in design and weight were adequate reasons for typefounders to introduce additions. Thus the words 'Margate' and 'Brighton' were shown on the same page of one specimen book, and the word 'Mama' shows the vigorous contrasts offered to the printer with different versions of the same characters in one fount.

matrices of the Fat Faces seem to have disappeared. Consequently the types had to be imported or new punches cut. The exceptions were three sizes of Fat Face, 36-pt, 48-pt, 60-pt shown by the Kynoch Press in 1934. These were different designs. Each was vigorous and, as the Press claimed, 'much pleasanter' than the twentieth-century *Bodoni* extra-bold. The Curwen Press also acquired the 48-pt variant from Stephenson, Blake of Sheffield, and this type is here shown with the others previously mentioned. This particular survivor is not a complete Fat Face, as compared for instance with the earliest specimens of Blake, Garnett & Co, but is what the Germans call *Halbfette*.

However, it was not in England that the revival really began, but in the United States and Germany. The American Typefounders showed their *Ultra Bodoni* in 1928, well named, for that is exactly what a Fat Face is, an exaggerated design after the true classical modern face of *Bodoni*. Intertype also had a *Bodoni Modern* of similar design, while some of the German founders brought out their original early nineteenth-century types. Schelter & Giesecke of Leipzig, for example, displayed a *Moderne Fette Antiqua*, which they date 1830; cut, therefore, in the early days of that foundry from versions produced in England. In contemporary advertising, Fat Faces (or at least the upper cases) are still popular. In pre-war days one had only to look at publishers' announcements of new books in the Sunday Press to see them in abundance, and very restrained and respectable they look today when they are used in advertisements or dust-wrappers, whatever was thought of them in 1810.

[1947]

TYPOGRAPHIA,
OR THE PRINTER'S INSTRUCTOR

Typographia, *or the Printer's Instructor*, by John Johnson, printer in Brook Street, Holborn, 1824, is a book well known in the annals of English printing. It has, in turn, been roughly handled and over-praised. In fact, the book is of no great importance, but, on the other hand, the career of Johnson himself as a printer is full of interest, and is connected with a backwater in the history of our press which is well worth a glance. If Thomas Bensley and William Bulmer, with their unadorned and straightforward style of book production, may be accepted as the leading printers of their generation and the men whose influence was to prevail in English printing for many years, then Johnson was outside the main stream. No mention of him will be found in Updike's *Printing Types*, and one cannot complain of the omission.

Before examining *Typographia* we should consider the press where Johnson learned or evolved his style – the Lee Priory Press. Lee Priory, near Canterbury, had been Gothicized in 1785 by the well-known architect James Wyatt, his first venture in this style. At that time the owner of the house was Thomas Barrett, a friend of Horace Walpole. Barrett left the house to his great-nephew, the eldest son, still a minor, of Sir Samuel Egerton Brydges. In 1813, when the private press was started, Egerton Brydges was living there with his son and one must suppose that he was the moving spirit. In his *Autobiography* Brydges rather disclaims responsibility; he says that a compositor (Johnson) and a pressman (John Warwick) persuaded him to allow them to set up a press. Brydges was to supply the copy and the printers were to take the financial risk. He declares that they might have done very well if they had not quarelled in 1817, since the limited editions produced were fetching high prices. The books printed were the works of Egerton Brydges and his friends, together with reprints of rare specimens of English literature.

From our point of view the importance of the press is in the style of production evolved, whether by Brydges or Johnson. In any case it was a style which Johnson continued for the rest of his career. The text types used were the latest modern face romans, with perhaps a more abundant use of italic than was the custom among contemporary printers. All pages were surrounded by rules or simple flowers, and the books were decorated with wood-engraved illustrations, head- and tail-pieces, and initials. A collection of the cuts may be seen in Edward Quillinan's *Woodcuts and Verses*, 1820, the cuts bearing the signatures of well-known wood-engravers, such as Kent, Nesbit, and Branston. The heraldic initials and views of gothic ruins, together with the plentiful use of black letter, point to the influence of the antiquarian Brydges and seem appropriate to the home of the press, Wyatt's Gothicized mansion. Although Brydges reprinted a number of early English works he produced no type facsimiles, unlike a contemporary private press, that of Sir Alexander Boswell at Auchinleck. Nor did Lee Priory show any inclination towards 'period' printing; wood engraving after the manner of Thomas

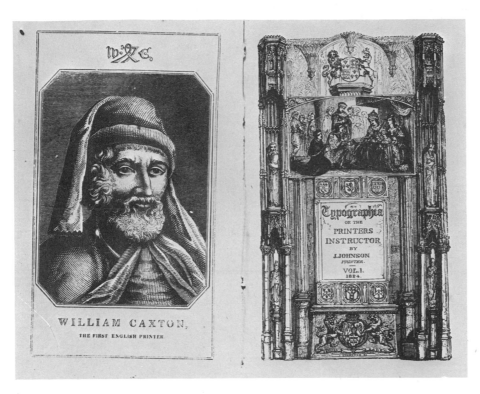

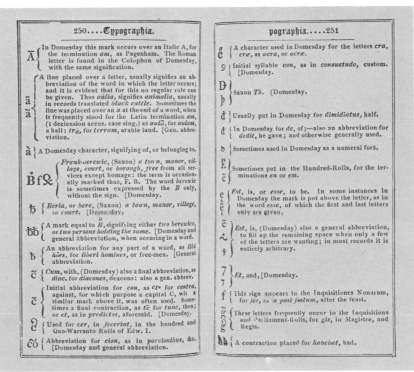

FIG. 1. The smaller edition of Johnson's *Typographia* (page size 5″ × 3″).
Top: engraved title-page and frontispiece; bottom: two text pages.
(All from Vol. 1; reduced.)

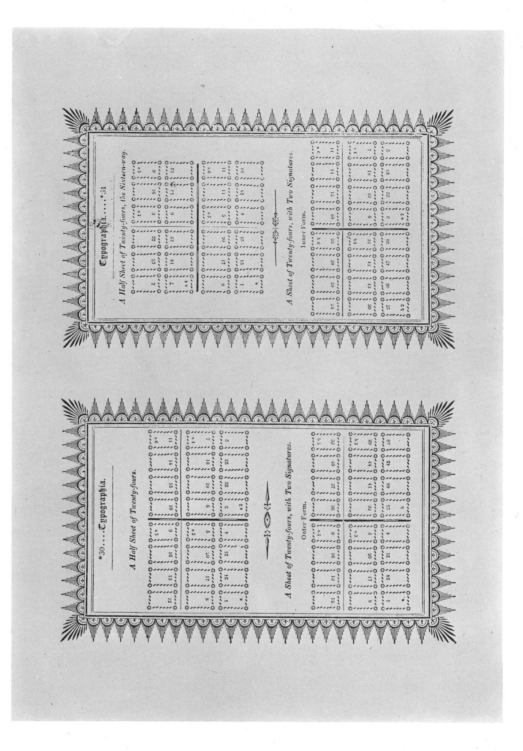

FIG. 2. The larger edition of Johnson's *Typographia* (page size 7½" × 4½");
two pages from Vol. II. (Reduced.)

Bewick was, of course, very up to date, and the gothic details in decoration also arose out of a movement of the day. Finally we may add that the press-work and the technical side of the press were of first-rate quality.

Johnson left Lee Priory in 1817 after a quarrel. According to Brydges the quarrel was with Warwick, but if so it is rather strange that after the press had closed in 1822 Warwick became Johnson's neighbour in Brook Street. In the introduction to *Typographia* Johnson declares that he had undertaken the task of writing the book 'from mental affliction, brought on by the cruel and unjust treatment which he had experienced from those connected with the private press at Lee Priory'. In the year in which he left Lee Priory, Johnson produced his first independent venture, an edition of *The Club* by James Puckle, issued from St. James Street, Clerkenwell. This book bears a close resemblance to the Lee Priory style, with its wood-engraved illustrations and initials, and the rules round every page. The designs were by Thurston, and various engravers were employed. By the following year, when he issued the first prospectus of *Typographia*, Johnson had moved to Brook Street, where he lived for the next thirty years at the Sign of the Apollo Press.

Typographia did not appear until 1824. The author tells us that the work had been held up by lack of means, and that he had at last received 'pecuniary assistance' from Edward Walmsley, another antiquarian amateur. The book was published by Longmans, in two volumes, and was issued on four different sizes of paper at prices rising from thirty shillings to four guineas. Even the largest size was only a demy octavo. The text is set in Brevier, a small enough size for most eyes, but the very extensive quotations are set in an even smaller size, and the footnotes in smaller still. All the pages are surrounded by borders built up from flowers – modern flowers like those displayed on the title-pages of contemporary type specimen books. These borders are omitted in the thirty-shilling edition; there was no room for them.

The running titles are in black letter, followed by the page number on the same line. There are no signatures. The book is dedicated to Earl Spencer, the President, and to the Members of the Roxburghe Club, the distinguished body of book collectors, the Black Letter school, who by this time had already published a number of their reprints of rare texts. Vol. 1 has a wood-engraved frontispiece, a portrait of Caxton, and two title-pages, the first a symbolical picture in honour of the art of printing against a background of a Gothic chapel. The title-page proper is an elaborate construction of printers' flowers, the sort of game in which Johnson indulged on other occasions as we shall see. Among the preliminaries there is a pedigree of the Spencer family, introduced as a specimen of composition in a very small size of type, in this case Diamond, the smallest size supplied by our founders at the time. It probably never occurred to the author that the matter was irrelevant. The subject of the first volume is historical. The author, or rather compiler, deals with the invention and then with the history of English printing down to 1600. The reason for these limits is because that is what he found in his principal source book, namely Dibdin's edition of Ames's *Typographical Antiquities*. Johnson acknowledges his obligation to Dibdin, but even so the extent of his borrowing must have been something of a shock. Johnson's Vol. 1 adds nothing whatever to our knowledge. Even his wood-engravings are recuttings of portraits and devices of printers already to be found in one or more of the editions of Ames. He copied the series of portraits of Caxton (the frontispiece), De Worde, Pynson, and others, which he knows to be fakes devised by John Bagford and exposed by Dibdin.

Vol. 2 is made up in much the same way, opening with a wood-engraved portrait, this time of the author himself, but not a success. The two title-pages both differ from those in the first volume but are of similar design, the one engraved on wood and the other built up from flowers. The author allows himself a page to advertise his 'Memorial of William Caxton', a sheet which was to contain over 60,000 movable pieces of metal and about 150 patterns of flowers. Another irrelevancy occurs in the middle of the book where there is inserted a genealogy of Joseph Ames, author of *Typographical Antiquities*. The contents of this second volume embrace the usual subjects which a compositor, a pressman, or student of printing may be expected to know. Again Johnson owes much to his predecessors, the *Printer's Grammar* of John Smith and the more recent book by Stower. The author makes due acknowledgment, as also to Dr. Edmund Fry for borrowings from Fry's *Pantographia* relating to the history of alphabets.

But in this volume the author has something of his own to add. He writes as a practical printer, and much of what he has to say is based on his own experience. For us, what is chiefly interesting is the information he supplies about the contemporary press, its customs and tendencies. For example he writes about the new advertising types and their de-signers: 'They have not taken the whole range of fancy, in bringing forward ornamented letters, together with a new character which they term Egyptian; this latter is all the rage at present, particularly in placards, jobs, &c.' Johnson certainly used ornamented capitals, but I have not come across any use of Egyptian in his books. There is an interesting chapter called 'Fine Printing', in which the author gives his opinion on the standards of English printing at the time when he was writing. He holds that there had been a deterioration in the past twenty years and he gives three reasons for that deterioration. The first is the increase in the number of outdoor apprentices employed in the trade; an increase due to the masters' efforts to keep down the cost of wages. The other reasons are the application of the stereotype process and the invention of steam-driven presses. The author has something to say in praise of Lord Stanhope's many inventions, with the exception of his alleged improvement in the making of stereos. As to steam presses we must remember that Johnson ran a very small business, perhaps almost a one-man show. He was not interested in newspaper printing or in mass production, and could afford to air his prejudices.

We have already referred to Johnson's fondness for playing with flowers, a harmless amusement which in its extravagant form probably began in this country with the sheet printed, and no doubt contrived by Samuel Hazard of Bath, for the Type Street Foundry of Edmund Fry about the year 1790. We have seen that Johnson built up the two title-pages of his *Typographia* from flowers, and took the opportunity of announcing his elaborate specimen in honour of Caxton. At the Caxton celebration of 1877 this 'Memorial of William Caxton', containing over 60,000 pieces of metal, was shown along with two other sheets printed by Johnson. The first was 'The Printers' Address to

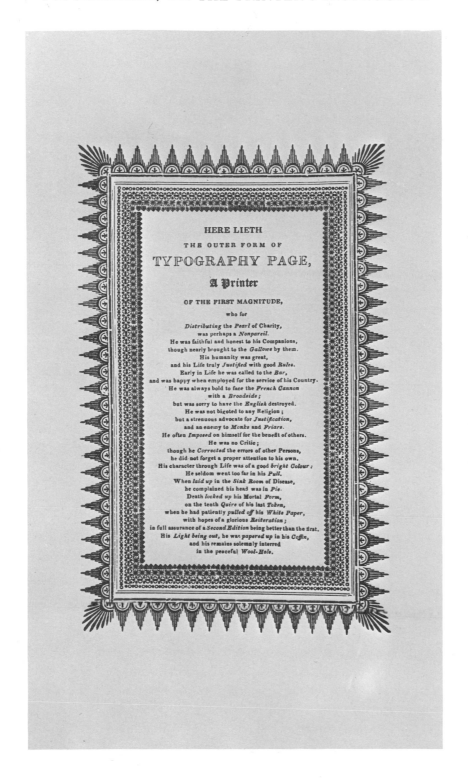

FIG. 3. A page from the larger edition of Johnson's *Typographia* showing decorative border. (Actual size.)

the Queen (Caroline)', 1820, and the second 'The Address of Congratulation from the letterpress printers of London to Queen Caroline', 1821.

It is not easy to find other books printed by Johnson. Of such as are known all but one bear obvious marks of their origin and are worth recording. The exception is an edition of the first two books of the *Pentateuch* in Irish, printed by Johnson in 1819 for the Bible Society, in the Irish type of Dr. Edmund Fry. We have already mentioned the James Puckle printed in the year in which he left Lee Priory. The next work we have found appeared in 1820. This was the *Book of Life* by Richard Thomson, a poem of four pages produced as a specimen of printing for the Roxburghe Club. The use of Black Letter on the title-page and the flowers surrounding each page are in the familiar style. To print anything for the Roxburghe Club was a distinction. The author of the poem, Richard Thomson, was later librarian of the London Institution. He is said to have helped Johnson in the compilation of *Typographia*, and later we shall find the two again in association. In 1822 there was published another work well known in the history of English printing, William Savage's *Practical Hints on Decorative Printing*, of which Johnson printed most of the letterpress. In 1823 we have another specimen of wood engraving, Hugh Hughes's *The Beauties of Cambria; Sixty Views*, in which the pages of letterpress are surrounded by rules. Engraving, but this time on copper, is the *raison d'être* of the next publication, which appeared in 1824, *Physiognomical Portraits*, with letterpress in French and English by Edward Walmsley, the man who assisted Johnson financially in the publication of *Typographia*.

The last book with which we have found Johnson connected appeared in 1829 and was, after *Typographia*, the most substantial work which he printed. The book is Richard Thomson's *Historical Essay on the Magna Charta*, a work of over 600 pages and, as a specimen of book production, an outstanding example of the work of the gothic revivalists. Every page not only has its rules, but has a headpiece thought to be suitable to a book devoted to the age of chivalry, in which heraldry and medieval architecture form the background. There are also some wood-engraved initials, and among the engravers employed were H. White, G. W. Bonner, W. Hughes, A. J. Mason, and several others. The book is certainly outside the main stream of English printing, but it is related to a movement in English architecture, that of Pugin and his followers, which is of never-failing interest. Johnson might well be satisfied with his share in the work, as the printer.

We have found no further book bearing Johnson's imprint, although his death did not take place until 17 February, 1848, at the age of seventy-one. One can only guess as to the source of his income from the time when he left Lee Priory. Obviously, the few books we have found can have been little more than a side line. That he was a man of no importance in the industry as a master printer is illustrated by the absence of his name from the various lists of printers given in Ellic Howe's *The London Compositor*, 1947. He was a minor printer who followed his own road, but one who stamped his individuality on every book he produced.

[1949]

OLD-FACE TYPES IN THE VICTORIAN AGE

THE story of the slow revolution in our book typography from the modern faces of the nineteenth century back to the old faces has not been recorded in much detail. One receives the impression that this originated with the Chiswick Press and that the next event of importance in English typography was the founding of the Kelmscott Press. William Morris and his pupils certainly did much to raise the general level of printing, but they have nothing to do with the story of the development of the book types used by the ordinary publishers. In 1840 our typography was without exception modern-face. After that year the old faces crept in slowly, and their use gradually increased, year by year, until the picture is now reversed. This change-over would have taken place if Morris had never printed, and was in fact ensured before his first type was cut. The following notes are an attempt to fill some of the gaps in that story.

An account of the actual revival of Caslon Old Face by the younger Charles Whittingham of the Chiswick Press may be read in the text books such as Reed's *Old English Letter Foundries* and Updike's *Printing Types*. The reader may, however, be reminded that the story as there given is not quite complete. The printing, for Longmans, of *Lady Willoughby's Diary* in 1844, was not Whittingham's first experiment with the type. He at the time several books in hand to be set in Caslon for William Pickering, and had already, from 1840, used Caslon capitals on title-pages for that enterprising publisher. The details are given in Geoffrey Keynes's *Bibliography of William Pickering*. From 1844 the Chiswick Press frequently used the type. Of many successful volumes it is pleasant to recall that gayest of all school books, the Euclid of 1847, with its illustrations in colour.

At the Great Exhibition of 1851 Whittingham was one of the jurors for printing, and in his report, issued in 1852, he writes: 'Mr. Whittingham at the suggestion of Mr. Pickering first reintroduced the old letters of Garamond and Jenson, and many of the London printers have since followed.' The remark about the 'many' London printers is somewhat surprising at that date, for it is only rarely that one comes across a book of the forties or early fifties set in an old face unless from the Chiswick Press. Whittingham's chief follower was Joseph Masters, a publisher and printer of religious books of the Anglo-Catholic school. In 1847 Masters had a book, *A Short Account of Organs*, printed in Caslon at the Chiswick Press. In 1848 he himself printed two books in the same style and type, a *Book of Common Prayer*, and J. E. Millard's *Historical Notice of the Office of Choristers*. The *Common Prayer* he describes as being printed in the 'Old Elzevir type'. A third volume followed in 1849, *The Devout Chorister*, by T. S. Smith. Amongst a large number of books in modern face Masters continued to produce an occasional volume in Caslon, all charming little books not unworthy of Whittingham. In the sixties the devotional books which he printed for the Rev. Orby Shipley are among his best work. By 1860 Caslon had become a favourite type for books of that class; for example the *Pietas Privata*, 1859, was printed by J. Unwin for Ward & Co. in Caslon. A Catholic printer, John Philp, was yet another old-face enthusiast. A page from his

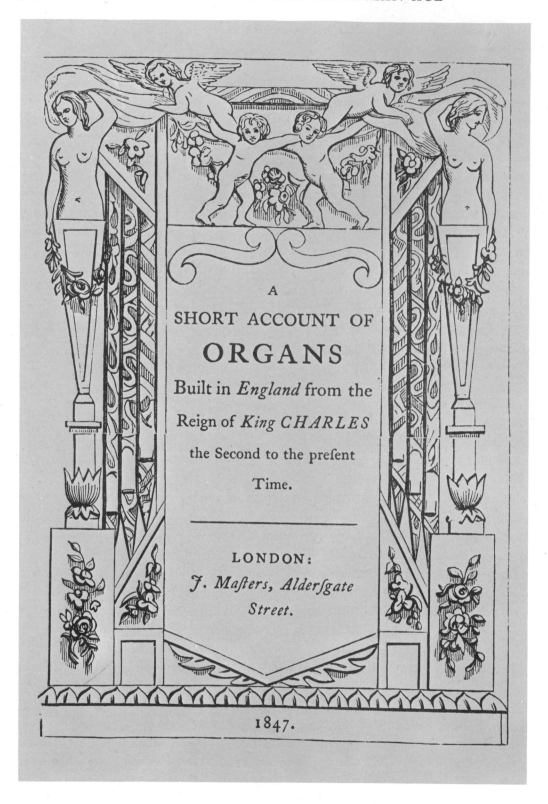

FIG. I. Caslon as used in 1847 by the Chiswick Press for Joseph Masters.

edition of the *Garden of the Soul*, 1860, is shown in Stanley Morison's *Four Centuries of Fine Printing*. Another of Philp's publications, also of 1860, was a music book, a *Cantata on the Passion of Jesus Christ*, of Saint Alphonsus Maria de Liguora, in which the title-page and preliminaries are handsomely set in Caslon, and a third was a *Life of St. Catherine of Siena*, 1867.

Among early examples of Caslon-set books of a more general nature are R. A. Willmot's *Pleasures of Literature*, published by T. Bosworth in 1852, and an edition of Tupper's *Proverbial Philosophy*, printed in 1854 by Vizetelly for T. Hatchard. The Tupper belongs to a group of book, in old faces produced for Christmas and described in the advertisements as 'Elegant Presentation Books'. In 1855 Clay printed for Sampson, Low & Co. editions of Keats's *Eve of St. Agnes*, Thomas Campbell's *Pleasures of Hope*, and Goldsmith's *Vicar of Wakefield*, all in old-face types. Similar volumes followed each year and a particular style of binding is associated with these books. They are all in embossed cloth covers, gaudily decorated. The advertisements in *The Publisher's Circular* become of interest on this point. This periodical was issued by Sampson, Low & Co., who no doubt were responsible for the new illustrated display pages, chiefly of Christmas books, set in Caslon capitals. The first occurrence of this new style was in 1854, although the books so advertised in that year were themselves printed in modern face. In 1855 there are half a dozen of these Caslon-set advertisements, three in 1856, none in 1857 and fifteen in 1858, most of the books being printed in old faces.

The original Caslon was not the only eighteenth-century type to be revived. The example of the Chiswick Press had led other founders to look over their old stock, and we find, for example, Vincent Figgins, in a specimen book of the fifties, showing a page of the original romans of the first Vincent Figgins, dated 1795. Another transitional type of the end of the eighteenth century was used by the Brothers Dalziel, the wood engravers, who started their own 'Camden Press' in 1857. This type, possibly a Caslon of the 1790s, may be seen in Doyle and Planche's *The Old Fairy Tale*, 1865. The roman can be distinguished from the original Caslon by the A, with a pointed apex, the Q with the tail starting inside the counter of the letter and the curly-tailed R. The italic has some unusual letters, the *b* and *p* for instance, and is not really an old face at all.

The ordinary publishers as yet certainly did not believe that the old faces were more legible. They were all right for books which might or might not be read, but they were not going to use them for sensible reading matter. We may note in passing that Caslon was reintroduced into the United States in 1858, by L. Johnson & Co. of Philadelphia. The English founders were in no hurry to copy, and the next experiment was made by Whittingham himself.

This was the type known as *Basle Roman*, which was cut for the Chiswick Press by William Howard of Great Queen Street. Updike, referring to its use by William Morris in 1889, says that it was cut about fifty years before that date. I have found no example of its use earlier than 1854, but possibly Whittingham's report of 1852, with its reference to the letters of Jenson, is an indication that it was in existence by that date. In 1854 it was used for the text of the Rev. William Calvert's volume of religious verse entitled *The Wife's Manual*. There were later editions in 1856 and in 1861, both set in the same

HISTORICAL NOTICES

of

The Office of

CHORISTERS.

By the

REV. JAMES ELWIN MILLARD, B.A.

Head Mafter of Magdalen College School,
Oxford.

Imprinted by JOSEPH MASTERS, at his Dwelling
Houfe in *Alderfgate,* within the City of
London : fold alfo at his Shop, 78,
New Bond Street, in the
City of Weftminfter.

m d ccc xlviii.

FIG. 2. In 1848 Joseph Masters on his own press made an even more 'orthodox'
use of Caslon than Charles Wittingham.

type. The title-page was set in Caslon, as there appears to have been only one size of the Basle roman, 10-11 point, and no italic. William Howard was an ex-sailor, and from the account given of him in A. Warren's book on *The Charles Whittinghams*, 1896, seems to have been something of a character. He had a small foundry in Great Queen Street from 1842 to 1859 (he died in 1864), and was much employed by Whittingham. He had a hand in the cutting of the Chiswick replica of one of Caxton's types.

Apart from experiments to reproduce Caxton's books in type-facsimile the Basle roman was unique in this country as an attempt to copy an early design. The type is based on the kind of roman used in the early part of the sixteenth century by Johann Froben of Basle. It is a pre-Garamond roman, what we should call a Venetian rather than an old face, such as was in use at Basle and at Lyons, down to about 1550. It is a heavy face, with an oblique stroke to the eye of the e, and other characteristics which ally it with fifteenth-century types. The stress is definitely diagonal, so much so that the o has an angular appearance. The old-fashioned long ſ was used with the fount and the squarish terminals of this letter are conspicuous. The short s has a noticeably steep spine. An oblique stroke is used for the dot over the i, which is another fifteenth-century characteristic.

This type was much too exotic to appeal to printers in general, but its antique flavour attracted William Morris. In 1889 he had his prose romance, *A Tale of the House of the Wolfings*, set in Basle roman. He dropped the long ſ but on the other hand he had his pages set solid – the pages of *The Wife's Manual* were leaded – which emphasized the blackness of the face. The title is in Caslon capitals and the table of contents in an italic, which is presumably the Aldine italic of the Chiswick Press, another of their experiments in the reproduction of earlier designs. In another romance, *The Roots of the Mountains*, 1890 (the book actually appeared in 1889), Morris used the type again, but had a different e cut, one with the bar nearly, but not quite, horizontal. The only other books which I know of set in Basle roman, are three volumes of religious verses by the Rev. Orby Shipley, *Lyra Eucharistica*, 1863; *Lyra Messianica*, 1864; and *Lyra Mystica*, 1865.

Many years after Whittingham had shown an interest in Caslon Old Face, in 1857, it made its first reappearance in a specimen book of the Caslon firm. In 1860 there appeared the first specimen of Miller & Richard's *Old Style*, a modernized old face. This was cut by their employee in Edinburgh, Alexander C. Phemister. In the specimen of 1860 eight sizes are shown, from Great Primer to Pearl. The founders state that it was intended to meet the growing demand for old faces and explain that 'they have endeavoured to avoid the obejctionable peculiarities, whilst retaining the distinctive characteristics of the mediæval in this connection', it is but one more example of the odd vocabulary used by founders. Old faces are certainly nearer in time to the Middle Ages than the modern faces, but to call the roman of the Italian renaissance medieval is to make hay of typographic history.

An examination of the type will reveal what the founders understood by the 'objectionable peculiarities' of the earlier letters. It has two of the chief characteristics of the old faces, the bracketed and inclined serifs and the gradual stress.[1]

1. This is not so in all versions of Old Style; for example in Miller & Richard's No. 4 Old Style.

On the other hand the stress is vertical and there is a regularity and a certain sharpness of cut which are modern. The upper case is not unlike Caslon, but there is a uniformity of width about the letters which is a relic of the modern face. For example, the H, M, and W are narrower, and the bowls of the P and R wider than in Caslon. The A has a flat top (in Caslon it is oblique). The curves of the C and G are more open, and the C has no lower serif, while the top serif is more spur-shaped. In the lower case the bowl of the a, and the eye of the e are larger, and the t is taller than in Caslon. These are no doubt the letters which appeared peculiar to type designers trained in the modern-face school. Perhaps the letter which differs most from Caslon is the g. The tail or loop begins with a steep inclination, a form which is possibly a reminiscence of the French Old Style or Elzevir, a type which just preceded Miller & Richard's design. However that may be, this g is a most useful 'spot' letter. The italic is steeply but more regularly inclined than Caslon. Note especially among the capitals the A, V, and W. In the lower case there is one peculiarity that is easily remembered. The thin up-strokes take off from the very foot of the thick down-strokes. The main stem of the p is conspicuously tall.

This excellent face succeeded in certain quarters and found imitators before long. At least one may perhaps say 'before long' in relation to the slow moving history of typography. Phemister, cutter of the original design, went to the U.S.A. in 1861, and by 1863 had produced for the Dickinson Foundry of Boston another version known as *Franklin Old Style*. He died in the United States in 1894, after a busy career as a designer of types. Genzsch & Heyse, of Hamburg, in 1868, showed their *English Mediæval*, for which they said they had procured matrices from a leading firm of English founders, presumably Miller & Richard. In the meantime in the *Printers' Register* for 1866 four interesting advertisements are to be seen side by side. Miller & Richard announce the completion of their series of Old Style types, while the Caslon firm assert that their Old Face is 'invariably selected by the *Literati* as the only genuine Old Face Type'. In September 1866, Stephenson, Blake & Co. of Sheffield, display their 'New Series of Old Style Types', which differ in some small points from the original Old Style. The A has a pointed apex, the S a steeper spine, and the T spurs to its serifs. The angle of inclination of the italic is not so great. In October 1866, Reed & Fox, the Fann Street Foundry, show their 'New Series of Mediæval Founts', a close imitation of Miller & Richard; as to the name, if the original founders could refer to the old faces as medieval, there is some excuse for Reed & Fox. In 1868 yet a third firm, the Patent Typefounding Company (afterwards Shanks), produced an Old Style.

It is evident then that by this time Old Style had been accepted and the fact can be illustrated from the printed books of the period. For example, John Payne Collier, one of the 'Literati' of the day, a well-known Shakespearian scholar, published privately many reprints of tracts from early English literature. From 1862 onwards these are generally printed in Old Style. W. P. Nimmo, an Edinburgh firm – it will be remembered that Miller & Richard's foundry was in Edinburgh – used the new letter from the early sixties. John Philp, from about 1867, seems to have preferred Old Style to Caslon, for instance, in his edition of Joannes Lanspergius's *An Epistle of Jesus Christ to the Faithful*

AN

EPISTLE OF JESUS CHRIST

TO THE

FAITHFUL SOUL,

that is devoutly affected towards Him :

Wherein are contained certain divine infpirations
teaching a man to know himfelf, and inftruct-
ing him in the perfection of true Piety.

Written in *Latin* by the devout fervant of Chrift,
JOANNES LANSPERGIUS, *a Charter-Houfe Monk;*

and Tranflated into *Englifh* by
LORD PHILIP, XIXTH EARL OF ARUNDEL.

(*Reprinted from the Edition of* 1610.)

Dedicated, by Permiffion, to
HIS GRACE THE DUKE OF NORFOLK,
Earl Marfhal of England, &c., &c.

Second  *Thoufand.*

LONDON :
JOHN PHILP, 7, *Orchard Street, Portman Square.*
1867.

FIG. 3. A typical title-page as set by John Philp in the 1860s.

Bartolozzi
And his Works
By Andrew W. Tuer

A BIOGRAPHICAL AND DESCRIPTIVE ACCOUNT OF

The Life and Career of FRANCESCO BARTOLOZZI, R.A.

(ILLUSTRATED)

WITH SOME OBSERVATIONS ON

The present Demand for and Value of his Prints; the way to detect Modern Impressions from Worn-out Plates
and to recognise Falsely-tinted Impressions ; Deceptions attempted with Prints ;
Print Collecting, Judging, Handling, &c. ; together with a
List of upwards of 2,000—the most extensive record yet compiled—of the
Great Engraver's Works.

" Sous leurs heureuses mains le cuivre devient or."

VOL. II.

London: Field & Tuer, yᵉ Leadenhalle Preffe. Hamilton, Adams & Co., Paternoster Row.
New York : Scribner & Welford, 743 & 745, Broadway.

[COPYRIGHT.]

Fig. 4. The title-page of Vol. II of Andrew Tuer's book on Bartolozzi, showing both the merits and idiosyncrasies of Tuer's typographic style. The book appeared in 1882.

Soul, 1867, and many of his later books. He was however no longer his own printer, but generally employed J. Ogden. About the same time, before 1870, Hodder & Stoughton also were issuing books of a religious nature in Old Style. Again the advertisements in the *Publishers' Circular* show that from 1864 Old Style began to rival Caslon in display.

Herbert Horne's *Hobby Horse* of 1888 has often been quoted as the classical example of the use of Old Style and as a pioneer volume in the abandonment of the modern face. A trial number of the *Hobby Horse* had been printed in 1884, in Caslon, but the first regular issues from 1886 were set in a small size of Old Style. The larger size, used from 1888, certainly displayed the good qualities of the type, but by that date it had been used for more than twenty years and often effectively used. One printer in particular had not waited for the *Hobby Horse* to show the reading public what could be done with Old Style. This was Andrew White Tuer of the Leadenhall Press, a versatile printer and publisher whose work deserves to be better known.

Tuer (1838-1900) was born in Sunderland, educated at Newcastle-on-Tyne and York, and came to London as a medical student at Guy's Hospital. He never completed his course there, and in 1862 we find him established as a wholesale stationer at 136 The Minories. In the following year he was joined by Robert Field, the firm being known as Field & Tuer. About 1868 they moved to 50 Leadenhall Street, where they printed and published *The Paper and Printing Trades Journal*, the first number of which is dated December, 1872. This journal, one of the earliest of its kind, was published by Field & Tuer for nearly twenty years, being continued later by John Southward. From the first it was printed in Old Style with a display title, in the early numbers, in Old Style italic; after a few issues this titling was dropped and a block substituted. Some woodcut initials, generally reproductions from the sixteenth-century examples, were used as decoration. There is little or nothing of lasting interest in the matter of the periodical, and the advertisements are not above the average of the day, that is to say they are very poor. Even Field & Tuer's own advertisements of their Japanese papers and their 'Stickphast' are no exception.

In 1880 Tuer started another venture, which he called *The Printers' International Specimen Exchange*, consisting of examples of lay-outs, mostly of advertisements, contributed by compositors. The preliminaries were set in Caslon and the title in Lyons capitals. This upper case, originally cut in 1848 by the Lyons printer Louis Perrin, represents the first step in France in that revival of earlier forms of lettering which we are tracing in England. Perrin's design had been used for some years by the Chiswick Press and was shown in a specimen of their types issued in 1867. Tuer frequently employed it for titles. As to the specimens, they are but one more example of the general low level of the taste of the printing trade of that age. Amongst the few tolerable pages are those designed by men of the Leadenhall Press. The whole series looks like an attempt by Tuer to teach his competitors how to do their job, and an unsuccessful attempt, if one may judge by the later volumes. Tuer published an annual volume down to 1887, and from 1888 the publication was taken over by *The British Printer*.

The most interesting part of Tuer's career begins in 1879 when his firm began to publish books, including a number of which Tuer himself was the author or compiler.

His first book was an odd publication called *Luxurious Bathing*, in which a treatise on baths from a hygienic point of view was combined with twelve landscape etchings by Sutton Sharpe. The typography of the book was Caslon Old Face. Several other editions appeared with etchings from other hands, equally disconnected from the subject of Tuer's essay. The firm continued to publish down to Tuer's death in 1900, at first as Field & Tuer; in the course of the year 1890 Field's name dropped out and the imprint became The Leadenhall Press. Field, who died in 1891, appears to have been merely a sleeping partner or financial backer. The publishing house could boast of a fairly extensive and somewhat unusual list. A number of their books dealt with the fashions and manners of bygone days, many were reprints of earlier books illustrated by contemporary blocks, and others reprints of early children's books. Among the authors on their list were Max Orell (Paul Blouet) and Jerome K. Jerome. A few of the books were printed in Caslon and a few in an old face which is not Caslon, but the great majority in Old Style. Only rarely did the Leadenhall Press think it desirable to use a modern face; one example is a lecture by Sir William Flinders Petrie printed in 1884. A few of the firm's earlier efforts might be described as 'arty', but Tuer's taste seemed to improve rapidly and the failures were few. The books were well printed, on good paper, with interesting title-pages, and decorated often with a daring quite exceptional at the time.

The most important of Tuer's own works was his life of the engraver Bartolozzi, which appeared in two large volumes in 1882. There was a smaller edition without the plates in 1885. Although it has nothing to do with our subject, a digression apropos of Ruskin and this book, illustrative of the manners of the great, may be permitted. Although Tuer's own tastes inclined to the eighteenth century and the Regency, he was a great admirer of John Ruskin and was continually quoting him. A copy of the Bartolozzi was sent to the great man, who after a considerable delay replied on the 16th December, 1884, in these terms: 'The Bartolozzi has reached me safely, but I have no time to acknowledge books sent to me out of my line. I see it is rising in price, and when I come to it, with your good leave will return it, as it is of no use to me.'

To return to the typography of the book itself, the text is in Old Style, the title in a bold italic of the old-face school and the running title in Old Style italic within rules. The title-page is well arranged and very full. Tuer never shrank from saying all that he wanted to say on the title-page and would not have approved of the anaemic fashion of the present day. The imprint is set in swash capitals, one of Tuer's failings; he was altogether too fond of these letters and his more usual imprint in lower-case Old Style italic is much to be preferred. The Bartolozzi is a large quarto, the size of the page being controlled by the plates, and Tuer is very successful, with the help of ruled pages, in coping with the difficulties of a large page. Another volume on an ambitious scale is Hoppner's *Bygone Beauties*, ten portraits engraved by Charles Wilkins about 1803 and printed from the original plates. The title-page shows a daring mixture of types; one line is in a large lower-case Old Face, one in Lyons Capitals, one in Outline capitals, and others in italic. The text pages are decorated with head- and tail-pieces and woodcut initials.

Tuer's best volume is perhaps *The Follies and Fashions of our Grandfathers*, published

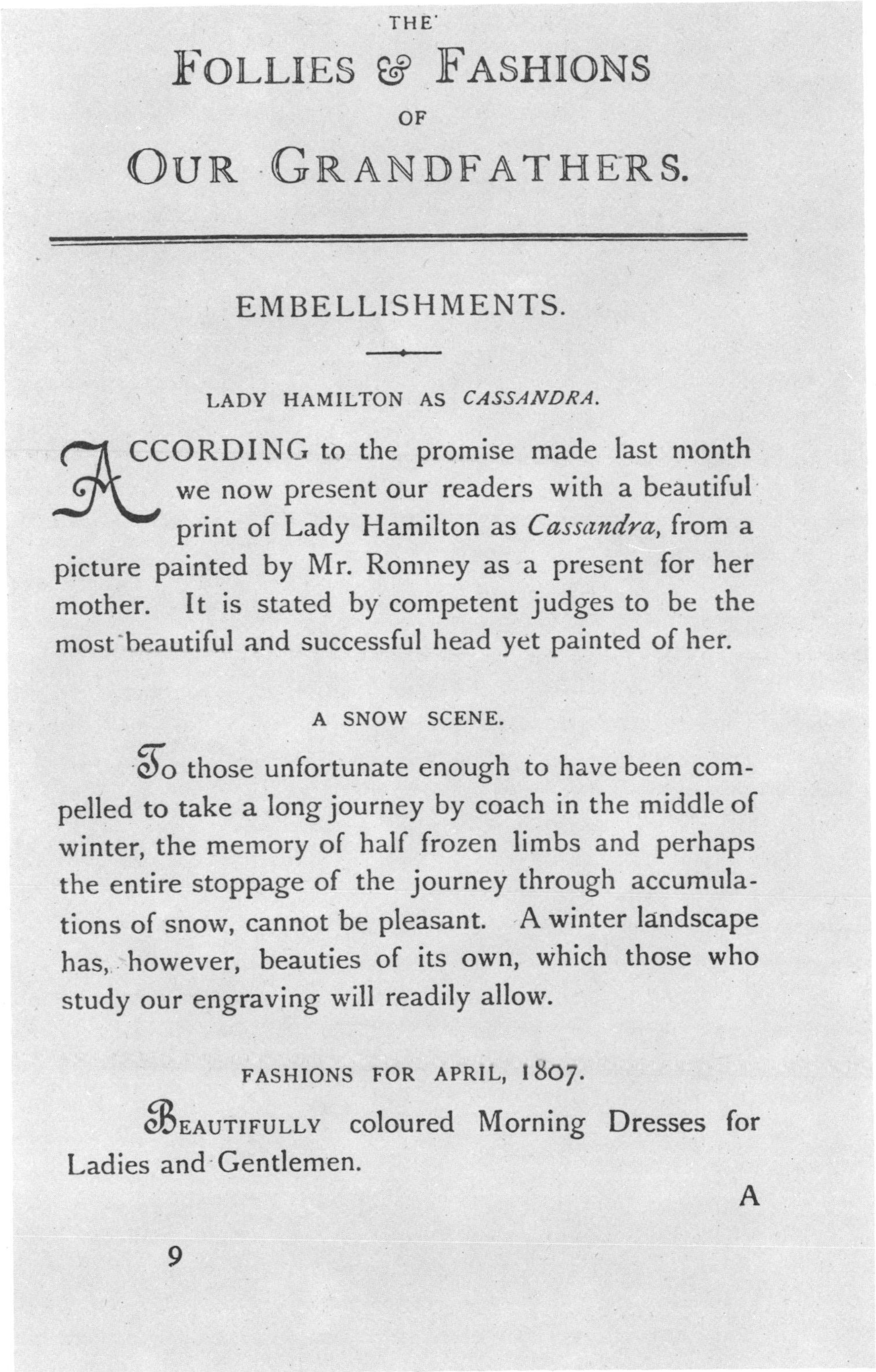

THE

FOLLIES & FASHIONS

OF

OUR GRANDFATHERS.

EMBELLISHMENTS.

LADY HAMILTON AS *CASSANDRA*.

ACCORDING to the promise made last month we now present our readers with a beautiful print of Lady Hamilton as *Cassandra*, from a picture painted by Mr. Romney as a present for her mother. It is stated by competent judges to be the most beautiful and successful head yet painted of her.

A SNOW SCENE.

To those unfortunate enough to have been compelled to take a long journey by coach in the middle of winter, the memory of half frozen limbs and perhaps the entire stoppage of the journey through accumulations of snow, cannot be pleasant. A winter landscape has, however, beauties of its own, which those who study our engraving will readily allow.

FASHIONS FOR APRIL, 1807.

BEAUTIFULLY coloured Morning Dresses for Ladies and Gentlemen.

A

9

Fig. 5. A page from *The Follies & Fashions of our Grandfathers* (1886-87), probably Tuer's best volume, showing an attractive use of Caslon's outline series.

in 1886. The title is set in an Outline italic, the chapter headings in Outline roman capitals, and the text in Old Style. Some unusual small script initials are used at paragraph openings. The text consists of extracts from fashion and other journals of the year 1807, bearing on social life, with illustrations, many of them printed from contemporary plates. Tuer contrived to get hold of an extraordinary number of old copper-plates and made very good use of them. In an article in No. VI of *The Fleuron* Stanley Morison noted Tuer's use of Outline letters, and said that he was the only printer between Thorne and our own generation who used such letters. The roman capitals are possibly the Caslon Outline capitals dating from about 1790; the italic Outline letters may have been prepared at the Leadenhall Press by cutting away the centre of the strokes. Tuer was of an ingenious turn of mind and the use of the script initials we have mentioned was another of his tricks. The smaller ones are simply the capitals of a fount of English Ronde, and the larger the capitals of one of the fancy types of the age, resembling the Caslon *Gutenberg* series. As detached thus by Tuer from their proper founts they are not unsatisfactory.

Of Tuer's other books two are similar in content to the *Follies of our Grandfathers*, and again have illustrations from original plates; they are *London Cries*, 1882, and *The First Year of a Silken Reign*, 1887, written with C. F. Egan and dealing with the year 1837. Three later volumes form a notable contribution to the history of children's books: *The History of the Horn Book*, 1896, *Pages from Forgotten Children's Books*, 1898, and, his last book, *Stories from Old-Fashioned Children's Books*, 1900. Another compilation, entitled *1,000 Quaint Cuts from Books of Other Days*, 1886, displays the initials, factotums, head- and tail-pieces and devices cut for the Leadenhall Press, together with woodcuts from old chapbooks, cuts of the school of Bewick, and some modern cuts by Joseph Crawhall.

Besides Tuer's own books his Press published many other books of interest from the typographical side as well as from their subject matter. In particular we may single out a little series of four numbers called *The Leadenhall Press Sixteenpenny Series, Illustrated Gleanings from the Classics*, 1886-88, The 'Gleanings' were from Samuel Richardson, Sterne's *Tristam Shandy*, Thomson's *Seasons* and Solomon Gessner. They were illustrated from original copper-plates of dates from 1778 to 1820, and decorated with the Outline capitals, tail-pieces and natural flower forms. The price of these charming little books is unusual. The natural flower forms had appeared in and were presumably cut for F. G. Heath's *Tree Gossip*, 1885 (1884), one of the most pleasing of the small books issued by the Press.

Before Tuer's career came to an end Caslon Old Face and Old Style had ceased to be exceptional in our typography. Yet so conservative are English printers that there was no demand for any further experiments either in the reproduction of early designs or in types of any originality. In the United States Franklin Old Style was soon followed by Ronaldson and a number of types of the same school. It is a striking fact that in this country, apart from the privately owned faces of the Kelmscott, Doves and other private presses, the first acceptable book type to be cut after the Old Style of 1860 was the 'Monotype' Imprint of 1913.

In view of this conservatism it is perhaps not so surprising to find that today more books are actually set in Old Style than in any other type. But these are no longer the choicest books. Old Style has become the poor relation in typographical society. It is seldom given a chance to show its best qualities. It has had its day, and in its day has played a role of some importance.

[1931]

NINETEENTH-CENTURY TYPEFOUNDERS
AND MECHANICAL INVENTIONS*

TALBOT B. REED's history of the *Old English Letter Foundries* carries the story of British type-founding down to the year 1830. The author gives a list of the patents concerning founding taken out up to that year, but none of these inventions had brought about any considerable change in the method of producing types as practised since the fifteenth century. The only invention which disturbed the trade was that introduced by Pouchée in 1823, a machine for accelerating the casting of type, and we shall see what became of that attempt. Between the time of Pouchée and the end of the century there were to be great changes, resulting in a complete transformation of the methods of type manufacture and in the driving out of business of many of the old letter founders.

A full list of British and American patents relating to printing is given in Legros and Grant's *Typographic Printing Surfaces*, 1916. Those relating to typefounding alone are far too numerous to be repeated here. We shall mention only those which were of some importance in the history of British typefounding. For descriptions of the machines the reader may be referred to Legros and Grant.

There are three inventions which are of particular significance for founders; the application of a pump to the old hand-casting mould, type-casting machines, and composing machines. Composing machines were designed primarily for the printers, but ultimately, in combination with casting machines, they were to transform the methods of type production. First came the pump, by means of which molten metal was forced into the matrix, so that the strange convolutions of the hand-caster became unnecessary. The first patents in this country for such a pump were taken out by A. F. Berte in 1806 and 1807. The same idea was embodied in the casting machine of the famous engineer, M. I. Brunel, in 1820. The first pump with a spring-propelled piston was the American patent of Mann and Sturdevant, 1831, forestalling the inventions of Sir Henry Bessemer and of the American David Bruce, both of 1838. Bessemer's machine is described in his *Autobiography*, published in 1905, where the author states that he sold his invention to Alexander Wilson of Edinburgh, who allowed it to fall into oblivion. In the *Reports by the Juries*, Class XVII, of the Great Exibition of 1851 (the reporters for this section were A. F. Didot, Charles Whittingham of the Chiswick Press, and Thomas de la Rue), complaint is made that England was behind America and the Continental countries in the use of casting machinery. None but hand moulds were shown at the Exhibition. The jurors gave an account of the destruction of the Pouchée machine at the instigation of the founders; and in a footnote on p. 409 it is stated of some unnamed American invention that 'Messrs. Figgins, who purchased it, have abstained from putting it in practice, probably in deference to the journeymen type-founders'. J. R. Johnson, of the Patent Typefounding Company, who also invented a casting machine, at a later date repeated these accusations against the regular founders (see below), and it certainly

---

* This paper formed the basis of Chap. 22 of A. F. Johnson's new edition of Reed, 1952.

Fig. 1. The Pouchée type-casting machine. It was 'calculated to cast from one hundred and fifty to two hundred types at one operation. It consists of a mould formed by a combination of steel bars with grooves and matrices, which are secured by a frame and brace of iron, upon a strong wooden bench; and a lever carrying a heavy rammer is intended to fall down into the middle of the mould, for the purpose of driving a portion of fluid metal through small apertures into the grooves and matrices, where the body and face of the letter is cast. When the operation is completed and the mould and cast within it removed and opened, the types are found standing out on each side of the cast, like the teeth of a comb. The types are broken off and dressed by hand.' (Description and engraving taken from the *London Journal of Arts and Sciences*, Vol. 7, 1824.)

appears that there was some reluctance among the old founders to encourage the spread of new inventions.

John Louis Pouchée started a foundry in Great Wild Street (now Wild Street) about 1815 and we gather from the prefaces of his specimen books, issued in 1819 and in 1827, that it was his intention to break down the monopoly of the old founders. In 1827 he claimed that he had reduced the cost of type by twelve per cent. The invention which he sought to exploit was a system of Henri Didot's, called 'polymatype', which consisted of a machine casting some 200 types in one operation. The matrix was a long bar of 200 matrices and, after casting, the types were seen adhering to the bar like teeth on a comb. Although the machine was used for many years in France, Pouchée appears to have had no success with it in this country, and finally, according to the jurors at the Great Exhibition, it was purchased by the other founders through the agency of Reed, a printer of King Street, Covent Garden, and destroyed on the premises of the Caslons. In 1873 James Figgins, in defending the old founders against the attacks of J. R. Johnson, declared that Pouchée himself admitted that the machine was a failure and had had it destroyed on his own premises. Pouchée's son, in a letter to the *Printing Times* of the same year, stated that the machine was carried out to sea and thrown overboard.

However, from about the middle of the century, most type casting, at any rate in the larger houses and in newspaper offices, seems to have been done by machinery. The firm of Clowes, who printed the Exhibition catalogues in 1851, were at that time casting by machinery. Even in 1843 we find from G. Dodd's *Days at the Factory* (p. 329) that Clowes were casting their own types, though with hand moulds. It would be interesting to know from which founder they obtained their matrices. The model generally adopted first was the machine of David Bruce, or some modification of it, patented in America in 1838. Miller & Richard were using this machine from 1849. Bigmore and Wyman state that in 1862 the Marr Typefounding Company had an unrivalled plant for casting by machinery, partly the invention of their employee James Henry.

The record for speed was attained by the Rotary Casting Machine of Frederick Wicks of *The Times* (1840-1910), first patented in 1881. After improvements had been made this machine could cast 60,000 types an hour. This meant that a newspaper could go to press every day with new type and dispense with the labour of distribution. On the other side it should be noted that in February 1863 J. & R. M. Wood inserted a curious notice in Wood's *Typographic Advertiser* to the effect that for the last fifteen years they had given up casting by machinery, because the types so produced were porous and liable to break under pressure.

The earliest composing machine in this country was that of an American, William Church, patented in 1822. A similar machine, at least in the composing part, was designed by Sir Henry Bessemer in 1840, though apparently Bessemer had not heard of his predecessor; both used the key board or so-called guide plate system, by which on the striking of keys types were released and poured down into the composing bed. The patent for Bessemer's design was taken out by Young and Delcambre and was known under their name. A description of the machine and an illustration will be found in Bessemer's *Autobiography*. No English composing machines were shown at the Great Exhibition of 1851.

The Hattersley machine, invented by Robert Hattersley in 1853 and patented in 1857 and 1859, marked an advance, because the types were composed in a short line accessible to the compositor for justifying. The machine was described in the *Printers' Register* for September, 1870, with a further article in October 1874, and again in 1877 at the time when it was exhibited at the Caxton Celebration of that year. It was then accompanied by the Hattersley justifying machine. The *Printers' Register*, edited by the energetic J. M. Powell, was most encouraging to inventors, unlike some of the trade journals, and devoted many pages to descriptions of new machines.

The use of a continuous paper strip for automatic setting was first suggested by D. Mackenzie in 1848 and the idea was utilized by Alexander Machie in 1867 (described in the *Printers' Register* for September 1870, and again in December 1874, and by Ellic Howe in the *Monotype Recorder*, Spring, 1937). The machine invented by Karl Kastenbein in 1869 was taken up by *The Times* and used in their office for many years. It is described in the *Printers' Register* for March 1876, and again in 1877 in connexion with the Caxton Celebration. Other machines described in the *Register* are the Hooker in December 1873 (shown by Messrs Clowes at the Caxton Celebration), the machine of Alexander Fraser of the firm of Neill & Co., Edinburgh (patented 1872), in January, 1878, and the Wicks Logotype Composing Machine (cf. pl. xxix in Legros and Grant) in March 1880. Nevertheless in the numbers for November and December, 1878, we find that the question whether composing machines pay is still being debated.

The Thorne type-setting and distributing machine, worked on the rotary system, was patented by J. Thorne in the United States in 1887 and in Great Britain in 1888. It is described in Legros and Grant, chap. xxvi. J. Southward in his *Type-Composing Machines*, 1891, speaks very highly of this machine, although he holds that composing machines on the whole had proved a failure. The increased speed of composing was not sufficiently great as compared with hand-setting, when the initial cost, the wear on types and the frequent breakdowns of the intricate mechanisms were taken into consideration. It was the overcoming of these difficulties which explains why composing machines were so slow in attaining final victory. Any composing machine could beat the hand compositors in speed, but the advantage might easily be lost from a variety of causes. With the Thorne 10,000 types an hour could be set, the keyboard was less fatiguing to work and the wear on types slight. Southward prophesied that machines on the rotary principle would supersede all others including the Linotype. In fact before many years the Thorne patents were bought up by Linotype.

If the founders were at first nervous about casting machines, the Trade in general was naturally more outspokenly opposed to the introduction of composing machines. The *Compositor's Chronicle* from 1841 to 1843 contains several satirical articles about the Young-Delcambre machine and its use in printing the *Family Herald*.[1] The *Journal of the Typographic Arts* for January 2nd, 1860, has an unfavourable criticism of the Hatters-

---

1. See *The trade*, Ellic Howe, 1943, chap. 11.

FIG. 2. The Young-Delcambre composing machine. This machine, invented by Sir Henry Bessemer, was marketed in Europe by the patentees, an Englishman and a Belgian, under their own names. The machine was similar to one invented in 1822 by William Church, an American.

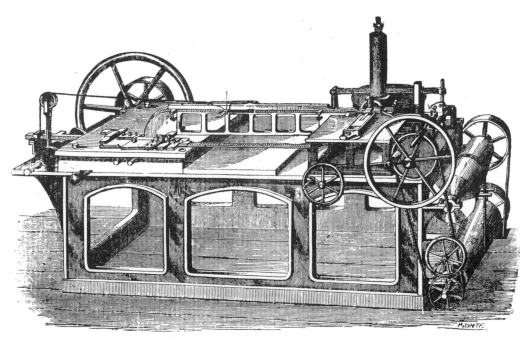

FIG. 3. Johnson & Atkinson's type caster. It was invented by J. R. Johnson with the help of Josiah King, a typefounder. This version was marketed in the 1860s.

ley machine, and the *Printers' Journal* for June 5th 1865, has a leader declaring such machines to be a failure. However, in the number for June 22nd 1865, this paper admits that the Alden machine (patented in 1857 by Timothy Alden in America) was an improvement. This machine had already in 1863 received favourable notices in Wood's *Typographic Advertiser*.

No English machine had been shown in 1851 at the Great Exhibition, although there were shown three German machines and one Danish. The Danish machine was that of Sørenson, of which there is a description in G. Dodd's *Curiosities of Industry*, 1852, where it is called a birdcage-looking apparatus. The total number of inventions subsequently patented concerning composing, justifying and distribution of types was very large. When, finally, in the Linotype the operations of casting and composing were successfully combined in one machine the death-knell of the old English Letter Foundries had sounded.

The severest critic of the old founders was John Robert Johnson, a chemist who became interested in typefounding at the time of the Great Exhibition of 1851. Johnson read a very interesting paper to the Royal Society of Arts in March, 1873 (printed in the Society's Journal for March 21st, 1873), in which he gave an account of the origin of his foundry, described his inventions and entered on some outspoken criticisms of the state of typefounding in England. His paper starts with a short history of the application of machinery to English typefounding and he quotes the official reports of the jurors for the Great Exhibition as to the backwardness of our founders compared with those of other countries. No English moulds, other than the old hand-casting moulds, had been exhibited and no composing machines, although there had been shown three such machines from Germany and one from Denmark. Johnson describes the fate of Pouchée's machine and again quotes the jurors of the Great Exhibition as the authority for the story of its being bought by the other founders and destroyed in the Caslon foundry. In general he accuses the founders of pursuing a narrow policy injurious to human progress.[1]

The first invention described by Johnson, for which he took out patents in 1852 and 1854, was an alloy for producing hard metal. His claim to have effected a revolution in this respect seems extravagant. The passage in which he appears to accuse the founders of pirating his invention is somewhat obscure. The founders in general were being forced to harden their types so that they might stand up to the pressure of power-driven machinery. Richard Austin claimed to have discovered an alloy which produced

1. Johnson's criticisms were direct and unequivocal: they also have implications which have been ceaselessly topical during the Machine Age. He wrote: 'It would appear, therefore, that if typefounding machinery was not used in England at the date of the Exhibition of 1851, it was not on account of its imperfections, or want of efficiency, but because English Trade Unionism deemed the introduction of machinery hostile to its interests. Hence the condition of typefounding in 1851, at which time the Union was flourishing in the full vigour of triumphant success. And here we have an instructive lesson in political economy. It would appear that Trade Unionism, when based upon a narrow, exclusive spirit, is as injurious to human progress, when intelligent educated men are the constituents of that Union, as when the imperfectly educated working classes are its originators; for here it was not the combination of the workmen, but of the masters, who perpetrated the wilful act of destruction referred to, and the argument which no doubt influenced them was that powerful one with which inventors are familiar, "Let well alone".'

harder metal and Antony Bessemer, according to his son, had his own secret method. In January 1860, the Patent Typefounding Co. against John Walter of *The Times*, asked for an order to inspect the type used by *The Times*. This demand was at first refused but in March of the same year permission was granted. As a result in February 1861 an action was brought against Richard (Miller & Richard of Edinburgh) who had supplied the type which Johnson claimed infringed his patent. The defence was that there was no novelty in the alloy, and Johnson was non-suited. In his paper of 1873 Johnson refers to a patent taken out in 1855 by R. Besley of the Fann Street Foundry and jeers at its complicated process.

Next came his casting machine, produced with the help of a founder, Josiah King. It was generally stated that the early casting machines were a failure because they produced 'big bodies'. This defect Johnson remedied by making his mould with a fixed opening. Subsequently he found that Sir Henry Bessemer had had the same idea, although in other respects the machines were different. Johnson's machine was bought by the Oxford University Press, adopted by the Imprimerie Impériale in Paris in 1855 and shown at the International Exhibition of 1862. An illustration of the machine was included in the Journal of the Royal Society of Arts for 1872, vol. xx, p. 909, and also in A. C. J. Powell's *A Short History of the Art of Printing in England*, 1877.

In 1855 Johnson formed a partnership with John Huffam King at 33A Liquor-pond Street, Gray's Inn Lane. J. H. King was apparently a son of Josiah King, mentioned above, and presumably related to Thomas King, who appears as a founder first in Pigot's Directory for 1826-27. The firm of T. & J. H. King received an honourable mention of their music type at the Great Exhibition, 1851, and in the London Directory for 1854 the firm is entered as Thomas and John H. King, their address being 4 Bartlett's Buildings, Holborn. Johnson found their stock of types inconsiderable and proceeded to supply the deficiency by the electrotype process. He found that under the Registry of Designs Act, 1839, full property in any new character could be secured for four years, but no copyright was recognized for merely modified forms of letters. He blandly admits that he had made use of this loophole and asserts that the other founders had been mad enough to copy each others' punches, but considered it immoral to make use of the electrotype process. The electrotype process of reproducing metal objects by means of a galvanic battery was invented in 1839 by M. H. von Jacobi of St. Petersburg and Thomas Spencer of Liverpool independently (see the *Athenaeum*, 1839, p. 334).[1] As to who was the first to apply the process to the production of matrices from cast type we find that T. W. Starr took out a patent in the United States in 1845 for preparing matrices for type by the electrotyping process. According to DeVinne,[2] Edwin Starr of Philadelphia first made such matrices for the James Connor Foundry, New York. By the time of the Great Exhibition of 1851 the process was in use in the United States and there is already mention of its misuse. In the display of the Austrian Imperial Printing Office at the Exhibition their electrotype matrices were commended. From

1. See also W. Savage, *A Dictionary of the Art of Printing*, London, 1841, art. Galvanism.
2. *Plain Printing Types*, p. 18.

1862 onwards to the end of the century the older foundries were continually complaining of the unfairness of this practice. The firm of J. H. King & Co. further attempted to introduce a system of point measurements for types following P. S. Fournier and the Didots. In 1857 J. S. Atkinson formed a company to purchase J. H. King & Co.'s business and patents, and the new company was removed to 31 Red Lion Square under the name of the Patent Typefounding Company. Johnson, together with Atkinson, perfected one more invention, a machine for dressing the types after casting, patented in 1859, with improvements patented in 1862.

Johnson's paper was followed by an animated discussion. James Figgins defended the founders against the accusations brought by Johnson. He declared that Pouchée himself had found that his machine was unsatisfactory and had had the machine destroyed on his own premises. He denied that the founders had united to oppose the introduction of machinery; they had in fact bought the patents of Stewart and Duncan and of Kronheim and Newton, shared the expenses of the machines and offered them to all founders and printers, and there were at least three hundred of these machines in use in England and Scotland. R. H. Gill, of Miller & Richard, stated that machinery for casting had been used by his firm from 1849. (According to A. C. J. Powell this was the machine of the American, David Bruce, previously mentioned in connexion with the invention of the pump with spring-propelled piston.)

The Patent Typefounding Company issued their first specimen in 1859, at which time the two managers were Joseph M. Powell and Peter Martin Shanks. J. M. Powell (1822-74) was an energetic type-broker and among his many interests was the well-known monthly journal, the *Printers' Register*, of which he was the editor and proprietor. An obituary notice of Powell appeared in the October issue for 1874. In a supplement to the August issue for 1868 there appeared an article, 'Progress of Typography', which is concerned with hard metal and the casting machine of the Patent Typefounding Company; the article is in fact a forerunner of Johnson's paper read to the Royal Society of Arts. Powell appears to have shared Johnson's opinions about the Associated Typefounders, and it is perhaps significant that about this time the old founders, who had been lavishly advertising their various Old Style types, ceased to use the pages of the *Printers' Register*. In October 1872, there is more about Johnson's hard metal and in April 1873, a long summary of Johnson's paper.

For further criticism of the old founders reference may be made to an article in the *British and Colonial Printer* for April 28th, 1892, entitled 'The "Associated Founders". An unsatisfactory retrospect.' Three main charges are made, first that they opposed the introduction of typefounding machinery, next that they obstructed the assimilation of type bodies and thirdly that they resisted the introduction of an improved alloy for type metal. After commending the fertility of invention of the Americans the writer follows much the same line as Johnson's paper, telling the story of Pouchée's machine. He accuses the Caslons of attempting to introduce a point system favourable to their own foundry, a charge firmly contradicted in *Caslon's Circular*. Another remarkable accusation is made to the effect that owing to the competition of the Wilson foundry the Associated Founders in London combined to lower the height to paper of the types they cast. It is stated that this device was practised until early in the nine-teenth century and that the old height became known as Scotch height. I have found no other reference to this state of war among the founders. If there is any truth in it, one would have expected to hear of many complaints from the printers.

As to the assimilation of type bodies, that is the introduction of a point system of measurement, probably the conservatism of the printers was chiefly to blame for the long deferment of this reform in Great Britain. Before the final adoption of such a system there had been four attempts in this direction, one of them put forward by one of the old foundries. The first proposal was made by a printer, James Fergusson, about 1824. His system was based on the size Nonpareil. In 1841 Bower Brothers of Sheffield published *Proposals for Establishing a Graduated Scale of Sizes for the Bodies of Printing Types . . . Based upon Pica as the Common Standard*, but appears to have met with no success. Next came the system of J. H. King & Co., afterwards the Patent Typefounding Co., which the firm introduced about 1855, but which had no influence on the other founders. P. M. Shanks wrote an article on this scheme in Rust and Straker's *Printing and its Accessories*, 1860. It was also based on Pica, which was divided into twenty points. The fourth system was the proposal of T. W. Smith, the director of Caslon's, put for-ward in 1886. *Caslon's Circular* had already printed articles by Theodore L. DeVinne on the point system and that journal continued to press for the introduction of the system. It was not until 1888 that the English founders came to an agreement to adopt the American system, and even then some years elapsed before the new measurements can be said to have been in general use. J. Southward in his *Modern Printing* gives the year 1905 as the date of the completion of the reform. In 1904 Sir Henry K. Stephenson, of Stephenson, Blake & Co., gave a lecture on *Type-founders and the Point System* which was largely a defence of the old founders against the accusation that they were to blame in this matter.

With the exception of T. W. Smith, representing the Caslon firm, the old letter foundries cannot be said to have been in the van of reform in a mechanical age. The criticisms of the jurors at the Great Exhibition in 1851, of J. R. Johnson in 1873 and of others at later dates seem to be justified, when we compare the advances that had been made at those dates both on the continent of Europe and in the United States of America.

[1946]

REFERENCES
BIBLIOGRAPHICAL NOTE
INDEX

REFERENCES

A Short History of Printing in the Sixteenth Century (pp. 41-82)

ITALY

BROWN, H. R. F.: The Venetian printing press. London, 1891.

FUMAGALLI, G.: Lexicon typographicum Italiae. Florence, 1905.

RENOUARD, A. A.: Annales de l'imprimerie des Alde. Paris, 1834.

SORBELLI, A.: Storia della stampa in Bologna. Bologna, 1929.

GERMANY

DAVIES, H. W.: Catalogue of a collection of early German books in the library of C. Fairfax Murray. London, 1913. 2 vols.

GÖTZE, A.: Die hochdeutschen Drucker der Reformationszeit. Strassburg, 1905.

HASE, O.: Die Koberger. Leipzig, 1885.

PROCTOR, R.: An index to the early printed books in the British Museum. Germany, 1501-20. London, 1903.

STOCKMEYER, I., and REBER, B.: Beiträge zur basler Buchdruckergeschichte. Basle, 1840.

FRANCE

BAUDRIER, H. L.: Bibliographie lyonnaise. Lyons, 1895-1921. 12 vols.

British Museum: Short-title catalogue of books printed in France, 1470-1600. London, 1924.

DAVIES, H. W.: Catalogue of a collection of early French books in the library of C. Fairfax Nurray. London, 1919. 2 vols.

MELLOTTÉE, P.: Histoire économique de l'imprimerie. Paris, 1905.

PICOT, E.: Catalogue des livres composant la bibliothèque de feu M. le baron J. de Rothschild. Paris, 1884-1920. 5 vols.

RENOUARD, A. A.: Annales de l'imprimerie des Estienne. Paris, 1843.

RENOUARD, P.: Imprimeurs parisiens. Revised edition appeared serially in *La Revue des bibliothèques*, 1922-34.

THE NETHERLANDS

NIJHOFF, W.: L'Art typographique dans les Pays-Bas, 1500-1540. The Hague, 1902-35.

– and KRONENBERG, M. E.: Nederlandsche bibliographie van 1500 tot 1540. 's- Gravenhage, 1919-23.

ROOSES, M.: Le musée Plantin-Moretus. Antwerp, 1914.

SPAIN

British Museum: Short-title catalogue of books printed in Spain before 1601. London, 1921.

BURGER, K.: Die Drucker und Verleger in Spanien und Portugal von 1501-1536. Leipzig, 1913.

THOMAS, H.: Spanish sixteenth-century printing. London, 1926.

ENGLAND

DUFF, E. G.: A century of the English book trade. Bibliographical Society, London, 1905.

– The English provincial printers to 1557. Cambridge, 1912.

– The Printers of Westminster and London from 1476 to 1535. Cambridge, 1906.

ISAAC, F. S.: English and Scottish printing types, 1503-58. Bibliographical Society, London, 1930, 1932. 2 vols.

McKERROW, R. B.: A dictionary of printers and booksellers in England, Scotland and Ireland, 1557-1640. Bibliographical Society, London, 1910.

POLLARD, A. W., and REDGRAVE, G. R.: A short-title catalogue of books printed in England, Scotland & Ireland, 1475-1640. Bibliographical Society, London, 1926.

SCANDINAVIA

MOLLER, B.: Svensk bokhistoria. Stockholm, 1931.

NIELSEN, L.: Dansk typografisk Atlas, 1482–1600. Copenhagen, 1934.

POLAND

LAM, S.: Le livre polonais au XVe et XVIe siècle. Warsaw, 1923.

Type Designs and Typefounding in Scotland (pp. 317–326)

DICKSON, Robert, and EDMOND, J. P. *Annals of Scottish Printing.* 1890.

ISAAC, F. S. *English & Scottish Printing Types, 1501–57.* 2 vols. 1930–32.

UPDIKE, D. B. *Printing Types,* 2nd edition. 2 vols. 1937.

McKERROW, R. B. *A Dictionary of Printers and Booksellers . . . 1557–1640.* 1910.

PLOMER, H. R. *A Dictionary of . . . Booksellers and Printers . . . 1641 to 1667.* 1907.

PLOMER, H. R. *A Dictionary of . . . Printers and Booksellers . . . 1668 to 1725.* 1922.

BUSHMELL, G. H. *Scottish Printers, Booksellers and Bookbinders, 1726–1775.* In *A Dictionary of . . . Printers and Booksellers . . .* by H. R. Plomer, etc. 1932.

WATSON, James. *The History of the Art of Printing.* 1713.

BERRY, W. T., and JOHNSON, A. F. *Catalogue of Specimens of Printing Types by English and Scottish Printers and Founders.* 1935.

MacLEHOSE, James. *The Glasgow University Press.* 1931.

MURRAY, David. *Robert & Andrew Foulis and the Glasgow Press.* 1913. (Records of the Glasgow Bibliographical Society, vol. II.)

RUFF, William. *A Bibliography of the Poetical Works of Sir Walter Scott.* 1937. (Edinburgh Bibliographical Society Transactions, vol. I.)

BIBLIOGRAPHICAL NOTE

Works in book form by A. F. Johnson include:

The First Century of Printing at Basle. London 1926, Ernest Benn Ltd. 4to. 27 pp. + 50 illustrations.

The Italian Sixteenth Century. London 1926, Ernest Benn Ltd. 4to. 34 pp + 50 illustrations.

French Sixteenth-Century Printing. London 1928, Ernest Benn Ltd. 4to. 32 pp. + 50 illustrations.

One Hundred Title-Pages, 1500-1800. Selected and arranged with an introduction and notes. London 1928, John Lane The Bodley Head Ltd. 4to. XXIV pp. + 100 plates.

German Renaissance Title-Borders. Facsimiles and Illustrations No 1 (of series). London 1929, The Bibliographical Society. 4to. VII + 20 pp. + 86 plates.

Decorative Initial Letters. Collected and arranged with an Introduction. London 1931, The Cresset Press. Folio. XXIII + 248 pp. Illustrated.

A Catalogue of Engraved and Etched English Title-Pages. Down to the Death of William Faithorne, 1691. Facsimiles and Illustrations No 4 (of series). London 1934, The Bibliographical Society. 4to. XI + 109 pp. Illustrated.

Type Designs: their History and Development. London 1934, Grafton & Co. 8vo. VIII+ 232 pp. Illustrated. (Several times reprinted.)

Catalogue of Specimens of Printing Types by English and Scottish Printers and Founders, 1665-1830. Compiled by W. Turner Berry and A. F. Johnson. Introduction by Stanley Morison. London 1935, Oxford University Press. 4to. LIII + 98 pp. and 24 plates.

A Catalogue of Italian Engraved Title-Pages in the Sixteenth Century. Supplement to The Bibliographical Society's Transactions, No 11, 1936. 4to. XI + 27 pp. and 8 plates.

A History of the Old English Letter Foundries. With Notes Historical and Bibliographical on the Rise and Progress of English Typography by TALBOT BAINES REED. A new edition revised and enlarged by A. F. Johnson. London 1952, Faber & Faber Ltd. 4to. XIV + 400 pp. Illustrated.

An Encyclopedia of Type Faces. London 1953. With W. Turner Berry and W. P. Jaspert (Several times reprinted).

The Type-Specimens of Claude Lamesle. A Facsimile of the first edition printed at Paris in 1742. With an Introduction by A. F. Johnson. Amsterdam 1965, Menno Hertzberger & Co. 8vo. 11 + CLXXXII pp.

He published articles and papers in:

The Library (1922, 1927, 1929, 1930, 1936, 1937, 1938, 1939, 1940, 1942, 1943, 1948, 1950, 1951, 1954, 1955, 1958, 1965).

The Fleuron (1924, 1928, 1930).

Gutenberg-Jahrbuch (1928, 1931, 1935, 1937, 1939, 1950).

Zeitschrift für Bücherfreunde (1929).

The Woodcut (1930).

The Monotype Recorder (1931, 1937).

The Book Collector's Quarterly (1932, 1933).

Paper & Print (1932, 1933, 1934, 1946).

Penrose's Annual (1932, 1933, 1934, 1935).

The Penrose Annual (1937, 1938, 1940, 1949).

The Colophon (1933).

Curwen Press News Letter (1934).

Signature (1936, 1950).

Edinburgh Bibliographical Society Transactions (1936, 1944).

Typography (1938).

The Dolphin (1938).

Print (1941).

Message (1942).

Alphabet & Image (1946, 1947, 1948).

The New Mechanick Exercises (1954).

He contributed a chapter to *Bibliographie des Editions des de Tournes, Imprimeurs Lyonnnais* (Paris 1937) on the type faces of Jean I de Tournes (translated into French), and an article to *Festschrift Joseph Benzing* (Wiesbaden 1964).

INDEX